Contents

THE POLITICAL ECONOMY OF MERCHANT EMPIRES

JAMES D. TRACY

Editor

CAMBRIDGE
UNIVERSITY PRESS

CAMBRIDGE UNIVERSITY PRESS
Cambridge, New York, Melbourne, Madrid, Cape Town, Singapore, São Paulo

Cambridge University Press
The Edinburgh Building, Cambridge CB2 2RU, UK

Published in the United States of America by Cambridge University Press, New York

www.cambridge.org
Information on this title: www.cambridge.org/9780521410465

First published 1991
First paperback edition 1997

A catalogue record for this publication is available from the British Library

Library of Congress Cataloguing in Publication data
The Political economy of merchant empires / James D. Tracy, editor.
p.   cm.
Essays originally prepared for a conference on the rise of
merchant empires, organized by the Center for Early Modern History,
Oct. 1987.
Includes bibliographical references.
ISBN 0-521-41046-0 (hardback)
1. International trade – History – Congresses.   2. Shipping –
History – Congresses.   3. Merchants – History – Congresses.
4. Europe – Commerce – History – Congresses.   I. Tracy, James D.
II. University of Minnesota. Center for Early Modern History.
HF1379.P653   1991
382'.09–dc20   91-7444
                                          CIP

ISBN-13 978-0-521-41046-5 hardback
ISBN-10 0-521-41046-0 hardback

ISBN-13 978-0-521-57464-8 paperback
ISBN-10 0-521-57464-1 paperback

Transferred to digital printing 2007

Acknowledgments

L<small>IKE</small> the essays that appeared in *The Rise of Merchant Empires*, most of those in this volume were originally prepared for a conference on "The Rise of Merchant Empires," organized by the Center for Early Modern History in October 1987. The conference, and hence the two volumes, was made possible by the generous support of the National Endowment for the Humanities, the Bigelow Foundation of St. Paul, and the University of Minnesota College of Liberal Arts. The smooth functioning of the conference owed much to the skillful-yet-cheerful management of Lucy Simler, associate director of the center. I also want to express my thanks for special help from some of the authors represented here: Douglass North and Michael Pearson took part in the discussions from the time of the center's original planning session (October 1984), and pushed us to make the conference a more ambitious undertaking than it would otherwise have been. After the conference, the thoughtful criticism and suggestions of Geoffrey Parker and Thomas Brady were most useful in sorting out the papers into two separate volumes: one dealing with changes that the new European ventures effected in traditional patterns of trade; the other with possible reasons for the eventual triumph of the Europeans over rival trading concerns. I am much indebted to Kurt Stadtwald for the Bibliography, and to John Jenson for the Index. Finally, if readers of this volume learn half as much and have half the pleasure I have had in working with all of those responsible for it, it may be accounted a success.

Introduction

JAMES D. TRACY

"From experience, your lordships ought to know very well that in India trade is driven and maintained under the protection and favor of your own weapons, just as the weapons are furnished from the profits of trade, in such wise that trade cannot be maintained without war, nor war without trade."
Jan Pieterszoon Coen to the Heren XVII (Board of Directors of the United East India Company), Bantam, 27 December 1614.[1]

The Rise of Merchant Empires dealt with changes in the growth and composition of long-distance trade between roughly 1450 and 1750. This volume, *The Political Economy of Merchant Empires*, focuses on why European concerns eventually achieved a dominant position in global trade, at the expense (especially in Asia) of well-organized and well-financed rivals. In responding to this question, one can argue that Europeans had better means of transportation, or better business methods, including more sophisticated forms of credit. Alternatively, one can contend that Asian business methods were in no way inferior, and that Europeans owed their triumphs solely to the use of superior armaments for commercial aims. Finally, one may conclude, as Professor Steensgaard does in an important essay, that Europeans succeeded because they created forms of organization in which "the use of violence was subordinated to the rational pursuit of profit."[2] Which-

I am grateful to Professors Michael Pearson (University of New South Wales) and Anthony Reid (Australian National University) for their helpful criticisms of an earlier version of this essay.
[1] H. T. Colenbrander, *Jan Pieterszoon Coen: Bescheiden omtrent zijn bedrijf in Indië* (7 vols., The Hague, 1919–53), I, 97–98. Volume VI, separately titled *Jan Pieterszoon Coen: Levensbeschrijving*, is in effect a summary of Coen's correspondence. See also the comment on this citation in Professor Parker's chapter, note 42.
[2] Niels Steensgaard, "The Dutch East Indian Company As an Institutional Innovation," in Maurice Aymard, *Dutch Capitalism and World Capitalism* (London, 1982), 255. For the view that Europeans owed their triumphs to military superiority, see Irfan Habib, "Merchant Communities in Precolonial India," in James D. Tracy, ed., *The Rise of Merchant Empires* (Cambridge and New York, 1990), 398–9; and the chapter by Geoffrey Parker in this volume.

1

ever approach one may favor, the issue involves careful attention to the principal feature that differentiates European enterprises from indigenous trade nerworks in various parts of the globe – that is, the fact that they organized their major commercial ventures either as an extension of the state, like Portugal's *Estado da India*, or as autonomous trading companies like the English East India Company (EIC) and the Dutch United East India Company (*Vereenigde Oost-Indische Compagnie*, or VOC), which were endowed with many of the characteristics of a state, including the capacity to wage war in furtherance of their interests.

In the Eastern seas, no European enterprise was more willing to resort to war to gain its objectives than the VOC, and the Heren XVII were nowhere quicker to employ force than in the Spice Islands or northern Maluku (the Moluccas). Northern Maluku was at one time the only source of cloves, but clove trees were planted farther south during the sixteenth century, especially on Amboina, and on Hua-moal, a peninsula forming the southwestern tip of the large island of Seram. The Banda Islands, southeast of Amboina, remained the only source of nutmeg and mace. Having devoted their acreage to cash crops, island cultivators were wholly dependent on rice brought in great junks from the ports of north Java, which called either in to the Moluccas or at the island of Great Banda, where Bandanese traders offered not only the homegrown nutmeg and mace, but also cloves they brought from the Moluccas in junks or outriggers (proas).[3] When the Portuguese took Melaka (1511), they began sending ships to north-ern Maluku, but with orders to avoid the use of force. A Portuguese fortress was built on the island of Ternate (1522), as part of an agree-ment with the sultan, but only after the remnants of Magellan's fleet, passing through the archipelago, had built a Spanish fort in the rival island kingdom of Tidore. The *Estado da India* initially attempted to make the purchase and transport of cloves Crown monopolies, but by 1540 the trade was left open to all comers. In struggles with the ruling family of Ternate, the Portuguese were eventually driven from their fortress on the island (1575), but they had in the meantime built a fortress on Amboina, where Jesuit missionaries (starting with St. Francis Xavier) had notable success in converting the not-yet Islam-icized population of the southern portion of the island. Yet the prin-cipal markets for fine spices were still in northern Maluku and, to the south, and on the island of Great Banda; and both regions were still

---

[3] M. A. P. Meilink-Roelofsz, *Asian Trade and European Influence in the Indonesian Archi-pelago between 1500 and about 1630* (The Hague, 1962), 93–9.

frequented by Asian merchants of many nations. Thus, a century of Portuguese presence in Southeast Asia had not radically altered the structure of a traditional system of trade that was to be smashed to pieces in the early seventeenth century by the Dutch.[4]

Appropriately enough, the monopolistic aims of the merchant oligarchs of Amsterdam met their stiffest resistance in this region from the Islamicized merchant oligarchs of the Banda Islands.[5] When the VOC was formed (1602) by initiative of the States General, the first four fleets to the Indian Ocean were sent out with the patriotic objective of conquering Portuguese possessions in the east, which since 1580 had been part of the Spanish Crown. These expeditions met with little success, save for the conquest of the Portuguese fort on Amboina (1605), and the prospect of a cessation of hostilities with Spain made the Heren XVII concentrate their attention on what was most important. Early in 1609 a specially dispatched *jacht* caught up with Pieter Willemszoon Verhoeff, admiral of the fourth fleet, and delivered news of a twelve years' truce that was to take effect on September 1, together with orders to gain control of the Banda Islands and northern Maluku before that date because these groups of islands "are the principal target we are shooting for." In northern Maluku, Dutch traders had for some years been formally allied with the Sultan of Ternate against a combined Spanish-Portuguese garrison on Tidore, but the sultan was less than punctilious in observing contracts for exclusive delivery of cloves to the VOC because prices were being driven up steeply by competitive bidding among English, Portuguese, Javanese, and Malay merchants. In the Banda group, the enforcement of similar contracts for the delivery of nutmeg and mace was even more difficult because the company had to deal with the *orang kaya* (literally, rich men)[6] who ruled each island, and who collectively had a proud seafaring tradition. Thus, when Verhoeff anchored in the roadstead of Banda Neira with an imposing fleet (April 1609), the *orang kaya* first granted him

[4] Vitorino Magalhaes Godinho, *Os Descobrimentos e a Economia Mondial* (4 vols., Lisbon, 1981–4), III, 135–58; John Villiers, "Trade and Society in the Banda Islands in the Sixteenth Century," *Modern Asian Studies* 15 (1981): 743–9.
[5] Villiers, "Trade and Society in the Banda Islands," describes the Bandanese *orang kaya* as "a kind of mercantile aristocracy." In the Netherlands, the close connections between the ruling oligarchy of the leading cities and the directors of the VOC (especially the Amsterdam chamber) were well known; one may compare the town *regenten* listed in J. E. Elias, *De Vroedschap van Amsterdam* (reprint, 2 vols., Amsterdam, 1964) with the lists of large investors in J. G. van Dillen, *Het Oudste Aandeelhouderregister van de Kamer Amsterdam der Vereenigde Oost-Indische Compagnie* (The Hague, 1958), 61, 81.
[6] Villiers, "Trade and Society in the Banda Islands," 730; Meilink-Roelofsz, *Asian Trade and European Influence*, 93–9.

the desired permission to build a fortress, but then summoned him to a council in a remote corner of the island, where, having agreed to send away their escort, the Dutch admiral and his advisers were massacred. There followed a period of intermittent warfare in which neither side could gain a decisive edge. By Dutch estimates there were only about 15,000 Bandanese, yet they could not be dislodged from the mountain citadels to which they retreated when under attack.[7] Bandanese war proas (*kora-koras*) could not give battle to a fleet of East Indiamen, but they could outrun any European vessel, and Dutch mariners could not learn to maneuver them as deftly as native seamen did.[8]

By 1615 the Heren XVII were urging their servants in the east to seize and burn Bandanese *kora-koras*, or even to "exterminate or chase out the leaders, and repopulate the country with pagans,"[9] considered more tractable than the Muslim Bandanese. Jan Pieterszoon Coen, who was president of the factory at Bantam in 1617, was named governor-general by an order of the Heren XVII dated October 1617. Four years later, Coen led a major assault on Great Banda and several smaller islands, in which, by Coen's estimate, 2,500 Bandanese died by hunger or by the sword, and some 3,000 more were transported into exile, leaving their burned villages to be repopulated by docile cultivators from elsewhere in the archipelago. On receiving Coen's report of the episode, the Heren XVII rapped him on the knuckles: "We would have wished for matters to be taken care of with more moderate measures." But it is clear, as M. A. Meilink-Roelofsz concludes, that the governor-general had merely been carrying out his masters' instructions.[10]

The Heren XVII of course recognized that there were many local

---

[7] Villiers, "Trade and Society in the Banda Islands," 727; Armando Cortesao, ed. and tr., *The Suma Oriental of Tome Pires and the Book of Francisco Rodrigues* (2 vols. = *Hakluyt Society*, 2d ser., vols. 44, 49, London, 1944), I, 211.

[8] Coen to the Heren XVII, 7 October 1619, *J. P. Coen, Bescheiden omtrent zijn Bedrijf in Indie*, I, 501–2; for a recent edition of a manuscript of what has every appearance of being Galvao's lost "Historia das Molucas," see Hubert Th. M. Jacobs, *A Treatise on the Moluccas* (Rome and St. Louis, 1971), 155.

[9] Instructions from the Heren XVII, dated 30 April 1615, in *J. P. Coen, Bescheiden omtrent zijn Bedrijf in Indie*, IV, 307: "dat men nu deselve onse force en schepen mochte gebruycken omme yets groots tot affbreuck van den vyande uut te mogen rechten ende de Bandanesen te vermeesteren, de principale uut te doen roeyen ende verjagen, ende 't land liever met heydenen wederom te doen peupleren." Cf. Coen to the Heren XVII, 22 August 1617, ibid., I, 259–60.

[10] The fullest treatment remains that by J. A. van der Chijs, *De Vestiging van het Nederlandsche Gezag over de Banda-Eilanden* (Batavia, 1886); Coen to the Heren XVII, 6 May 1621, in *Bescheiden omtrent zijn Bedrijf in Indie*, I, 625–33; Meilink-Roelofsz, *Asian Trade and European Influence*, 197–203, 207.

markets in which it made better economic sense simply to join in as traders, rather than to deploy the force that would be necessary to achieve a dominant position.[11] Yet Coen's deliberate destruction of an indigenous trading society in the Banda Islands shows how far the builders of Europe's merchant empires were prepared to go, especially when presented with the opportunity to gain control of the supply of particularly valuable commodities that were uniquely localized. By way of an introduction to this volume, it may be useful to reflect on the mentality that supported such campaigns, as well as many less dramatic applications of force in furtherance of trade. Rather than attempting a survey of the globe, or of the vast Indian Ocean, the discussion that follows will concentrate on Southeast Asia,[12] a rich trading region where three European nations each found the use of force necessary to some degree. The discussion that follows will first review differing strategic aims for which force was employed, and then consider how modern students of this region have reinterpreted Southeast Asian trade in the era of early European contacts, suggesting that things were not quite as they seemed to the builders of Europe's merchant empires.

I

From an early date, the Portuguese clearly had a grand strategy for controlling the trade of the Indian Ocean by controlling the major entrepôts.[13] Albuquerque's decision to make for Melaka in 1511 seems to have been an afterthought, but when his fleet was drawn up in front of the great harbor's fortifications the governor had no doubt of his purpose: "We shall perform [a great service] to our Lord in casting the Moors out of this country, and quenching the fire of this sect of Mafamede [*sic*]," for if Melaka were taken "the Moors" would

---

[11] Colenbrander *J. P. Coen: Levensbeschrijving*, 45–6, 59, 83, and Governor General Gerard Reynst to the Heren XVII, 26 October 1615, in W. Ph. Coolhaas, ed., *Generale Missiven van Gouverneurs-General en Raden aan Heren XVII der VOC*, I, 1610–38 (*Rijksgeschiedkundige Publicatiën, Grote Serie*, vol. 104, The Hague, 1960), 47: the VOC seized a Portuguese fort on Solor, but then abandoned it because it could not be used to control the sandalwood trade from nearby Timor.

[12] For a superb overview, see Anthony Reid, *South East Asia in the Age of Commerce*, vol. I, *The Lands below the Winds* (New York, 1988); Prof. Reid will deal with trade in the second volume.

[13] In a very useful review essay on Meilink-Roelofsz's *Asian Trade and European Influence*, D. K. Bassett, "European Influence in Southeast Asia, c. 1500–1630," *Journal of Southeast Asian History* 4 (1963), 186–7, believes that the author gives too much credit for Portugal's grand strategy to Afonso de Albuquerque, the conqueror of Goa and Melaka.

be deprived of the "spices and drugs" that nourished a network of trading communities stretching from the Red Sea to the Indonesian archipelago.[14] The strategic thinking of the Portuguese conquerors seems to have been based on a vivid if somewhat simplistic perception of the importance of seaports, which shines through with particular clarity in the *Suma Oriental* of Tomé Pires, the apothecary who, in Portuguese Melaka, became a diplomat. As Pires guides his reader along the Asian coastline, it is evident that some cities are much more important than others. Thus, Aden is "the key not only of Arabia but the strait," Hormuz is the "key of Persia," and Goa is "the key of first and second India," that is, Gujarat and the Deccan. For just as "doors are the defense of houses, so are seaports the help, defense, and main protection of provinces and kingdoms." Melaka is not called the key to anything, but Pires thinks of it in the same terms. For example, he expects that "the kings of Pase and Pidie," the chief ports of northern Sumatra, "will be tributaries and vassals to him who now owns Melaka" because otherwise in a year's time there will be no Pase and Pidie, and those who realize it are "making themselves vassals [to the Portuguese] before they have to." Elsewhere, Pires allows himself a lapidary comment on what the recent capture of Melaka will mean for Portugal's chief rival among Christian states: "Whoever is lord of Melaka has his hand on the throat of Venice."[15]

Nearly a hundred years later, when Dutch ships arrived in the East, the entrepôt strategy had clearly failed to meet the high expectations of the Portuguese, but it was nonetheless not without its charms for the newcomers. After all, the VOC in effect began as an enterprise for the conquest of Portuguese-held emporia, prompting investors familiar with the trading practices of the private companies that preceded the VOC to protest this unwonted use of trading capital for military aims.[16] But, beginning with the appointment of the first governor-general in 1609, the VOC shifted to a single-minded focus on controlling the supply of key commodities, starting with fine spices. One could attempt to control supply by buying up whatever came on the market in an entrepôt like Bantam, where the VOC and the EIC both had factories, but this strategy had little chance of success at a time when, owing to the continuing accessibility of the Banda

---

[14] Walter de Gray Birch, tr., *The Commentaries of the Great Affonso Dalbuquerque* [by his natural son, Bras de Albuquerque] (4 vols. = *Hakluyt Society*, 1st ser., vols. 53, 55, 62, 69, London, 1875–84), III, 116–18.

[15] *The Suma Oriental of Tomé Pires*, 15, 19, 56, 144–5, 287.

[16] Steensgaard, "The Dutch East India Company As an Institutional Innovation," 245–7.

Islands to traders of many nations, nutmeg and mace fetched higher prices there than at Bantam.[17] The logical alternative was the policy, worked out in correspondence between the Heren XVII and their servants in the East, of keeping all "foreign" traders out of the Bandas and northern Maluku – that is, not just the troublesome English, but also Javanese, Malays, and Klings (from India's Coromandel coast).[18] Modern scholars have shown a certain understandable partiality for Dutch critics of this policy, including Dr. Laurens Reael, Coen's predecessor as governor-general. Reael pointed out, correctly, that cultivators of the spice plants were being impoverished by the company's policy of buying spices cheap while selling rice dear, and that Dutch shipping was not satisfying local demand, not just for the preferred varieties of rice and cotton cloth, but even more for countless other articles in which only small-scale traders would take an interest. Reael also believed that schemes for repopulating the Banda Islands were not workable, as was suggested by the fact that colonists brought in to settle Banda Neira after the Dutch had expelled the natives soon returned whence they had come: "One has great trouble forgetting the sweetness of the land where one is born and reared." But even a man of Reael's temper was bound by the logic of his position, as the representative of a commercial power that claimed the attributes of a state. For example, when the men of an important village on Great Banda seized the president of the local VOC factory in retaliation for an unwarranted Dutch attack on local shipping, Reael knew what had to be done: "Although we for our part are not wholly free of blame, still, such things must not be allowed to pass unavenged."[19]

Coen's refusal to shrink from any measures necessary to gain control of the supply of nutmeg and mace marked out the future direction of company policy. In order to control the supply of cloves, the com-

---

[17] For the focus on the Spice Islands, see paragraph 22 of the Heren XVII's instructions to Pieter Both, dated 9 November 1609, in Pieter van Dam, *Beschrijving van de Oost-Indische Compagnie*, vol. III, ed. F. W. Stapel (*Rijksgeschiedkundige Publicatiën. Grote Serie*, vol. 87, The Hague, 1943), 524; Meilink-Roelofsz, *Asian Trade and European Influence*, 243.

[18] Coen to the Heren XVII, 10 November 1614, and the Heren XVII to Coen, 30 April and 30 November 1615, in *Bescheiden omtrent zijn Bedrijf in Indie*, I, 82–3, IV, 306, 331–2.

[19] Reael to the Heren XVII, 10 May, 2 July, 127 December 1617, 7 May, 20 August 1618, in *Generale Missiven van Gouverneurs-General aan Heren XVII*, I, 71–4, 77–9, 82–4, 87–94 (the settlers whom Reael describes as leaving of their own volition are said by Coen to have been chased away by the Bandanese: Colenbrander, *J. P. Coen, Levensbeschrijving*, 83–4.) Meilink-Roelofsz *Asian Trade and European Influence*, 196–202; S. Arasaratnam, "Monopoly and Free Trade in Dutch-Asian Commercial Policy: Debate and Controversy within the VOC," *Journal of Southeast Asian Studies* 4 (1973): 1–16.

pany subsequently undertook protracted campaigns against the Muslims of northern Amboina (1634–7), and against their confreres on Huamoal, who received assistance from the Sultanate of Ternate (which claimed lordship of this region) and from the burgeoning Muslim port of Makassar (1652–7). In the end, a victorious VOC caused the trees on all the clove plantations of northern Maluku and Huamoal to be uprooted, while *hongis* manned by the now Protestant Christians of southern Amboina patrolled the archipelago to guard against unauthorized planting.[20] Because the Dutch could not wholly curtail "foreign" shipping in the islands, they eventually resorted to seizing the major entrepôts where goods from the Spice Islands still got through: Melaka (1641), Makassar (1667), and Bantam (1682).[21] It was only in the eighteenth century, as the advantages of a less tightly regulated trade gradually became apparent, that the VOC lost ground to its rivals.

The EIC's aims for trade in Southeast Asia are less transparent, partly because the weight of documentation for the English company's early history falls more on India.[22] It is clear, however, that Dutch commercial aggression in the archipelago offered the English a golden opportunity. A succession of EIC agents reported that the people of northern Maluku would starve if the English did not bring the foodstuffs they had promised, and that the Bandanese would sacrifice their lives rather than submit to domination by the Hollanders.[23] To be sure, voices within the EIC warned against imitating the Dutch by investing so heavily in fortified bases. But John Jourdain, who was president of the EIC factory of Bantam when Coen held the same post for the VOC, urged his superiors in London to send out a force that would test the real intentions behind the bellicose words of the Dutch, and, if need be, provide a shield behind which the English might offer islanders the free trade they so ardently desired. The fleet of five well-armed vessels that arrived in the Banda Islands in 1616

[20] H. de Graaf, *De Geschiedenis van Ambon en de Zuid Molukken* (Franeker, 1977), 82–7, 108–30; G. J. Knaap, *Kruidnagelen en Christenen: de VOC en de Bevolking van Ambon, 1656–1696* (Dordrecht, 1983), 17–28.

[21] The best overviews are C. R. Boxer, *The Dutch Seaborne Empire, 1600–1800* (New York, 1988, reprint of 1973 edition), 103–16; Holden Furber, *Rival Empires of Trade in the East* (Minneapolis, 1976), 31–38, 50–64; and F. S. Gaastra, *Geschiedenis van de VOC* (Haarlem, 1982), 37–42.

[22] K. N. Chaudhuri, *The English East India Company* (London, 1965), 12–15. It also seems that the EIC's Court of Directors was less willing than the Heren XVII to commit to paper matters of grand strategy – that is, if one may judge from Court minutes and other documents summarized in Noel Sainsbury, ed., *Calendar of State Papers, Colonial Series, the East Indies, China, and Japan, 1513–1629* (6 vols., London, 1862–84).

[23] *Calendar of State Papers, Colonial Series,* I, nos. 783, 1004, 1006, 1071; II, nos. 99, 245.

seems to have been a response to Jourdain's arguments; these ships made it possible for the EIC to maintain fortresses for short periods of time on first one and then another of the smaller islands of the Banda chain. But such provocations led the Dutch to make good their threats of force against the English despite the formal alliance between the two nations that had been dictated by conditions back home, where both were united by hostility to Spain. The Heren XVII simply would not allow anyone else to share in the fruits of their considerable military investment in the Spice Islands trade.[24] The famous "massacre" of English traders and their Japanese allies on Amboina (1623)[25] was a further blow to EIC ambitions in this region, and the company subsequently had to be content to join forces with other European and Asian merchants who aimed at circumventing the Dutch spice monopoly, rather than attempting to contest it directly.[26]

One adopts a strategy because one hopes to achieve something, but also because one fears what may happen in the absence of a coherent plan. The fears of Europeans stationed in Asia were structured not merely by national rivalries back home, but also by the fact that, despite their differences, they all had in common what one may call the psychology of an interloper.[27] Twentieth-century historians can agree that it was usually the Europeans who broke violently into Asian trading systems that had been relatively peaceful before their arrival. But the men who first came to Asia from the far west almost invariably saw themselves as beset by greedy Asian foes whose conniving ways revealed a skullduggery that decent folk in Europe had not yet imagined. Many of these Asian enemies were adherents of a creed that made them sworn enemies of all Christians. Recent scholars have been skeptical of the importance of crusading zeal as a stimulus

---

[24] On the aversion to military expenditures within the EIC, see *Calendar of State Papers,* I, nos. 371, 522, and Meilink-Roelofsz, *Asian Trade and European Influence,* 196; for Jourdain's views, see *Calendar of State Papers,* I, nos. 783, 888, and II, no. 143. Bassett, "European Influence in Southeast Asia," 206, suggests that Jourdain's activities in the archipelago undermined whatever credibility Reael's views may have had with his superiors in the Netherlands.

[25] D. K. Bassett, "The 'Amboinese Massacre,' " *Journal of Southeast Asian History,* 1 (1960): 1–5; De Graaf, *Geschiedenis van Ambon,* 73–7. English and Dutch writers are still not agreed on whether the executions should be seen as an excess of zeal on the part of officials not trained in the law, or as a thinly veiled effort to expel the English from the spice trade.

[26] Bassett, "The 'Amboinese Massacre,' " 6–29: EIC imports from Southeast Asia increased rather than decreased after 1623, with cloves being obtained mainly at Makassar.

[27] What seems crucial here is Robert Lopez's distinction between "inner" and "outer" zones of long-range trade, touched on in this volume in the chapters by Russell Menard and Anne Pérotin-Dumon.

for Portuguese expansion,[28] and one may also doubt whether Asia's many communities of Muslim traders manifested any greater religious solidarity among themselves than Europe's Christian nations did. Yet the Portuguese did not always imagine things when they saw "the Moors" behind the problems they encountered in India, and, even if they did, imaginary fears are no less important to those who think them real. Thus, before the conquest of Goa, Albuquerque blamed the sufferings of his countrymen in India on the fact that they lacked "a stronghold wherein they might be safe from the vexations which the Moors of every land every day inflicted on them." Roughly a hundred years later, Coen was no doubt equally earnest in thinking that the Dutch had to have a fortress on Java, "cost what it may," among other reasons "so that we no longer stand at the mercy of faithless Moors."[29] Indeed it was a Christian cliché that all "Moors" were "faithless" because they had been taught that promises made to infidels are not binding.[30]

If the Protestant Dutch did not have the same crusading heritage as their Iberian rivals, the fervor of a protracted war for independence from Catholic Spain made up for this lack, inspiring in them too the conviction of fighting in a righteous cause, against the forces of manifest iniquity. Expressions of confidence in the special favor of God are less frequent in Coen's correspondence than in (for example) the *Commentaries* of Bras de Albuquerque, but, one must assume, not less deeply felt.[31] Whatever damage the English might do to Dutch interests, Spain was always "the enemy" in VOC correspondence, and Dutchmen overseas had an understandable tendency to project onto the Asian scene the emotions of a war for national survival back home. Thus, VOC officials in the Spice Islands feared an attack from the northeast, even though Spanish forces in Manila did less and less as time went on to exploit their toehold in northern Maluku. Coen assumed that Asians had a European, specifically Dutch, understanding of the great conflict: once the VOC established a fortified base on Java, traders of all nations would flock to it because "the good old

---

[28] Godinho, *Os Descrobrimentos*, I, 45–62. But see also the chapter in this volume by Professors Subrahmanyam and Thomaz, note 6.

[29] *Commentaries of Afonso Dalbuquerque*, I, 1–5; Coen to the Heren XVII, 1 January 1614, in *Bescheiden omtrent zijn Bedrijf in Indie*, I, 7.

[30] Colenbrander, *J. P. Coen, Levensbeschrijving*, 51, 135–6.

[31] *Commentaries of Afonso Dalbuquerque*, I, 129–31; Coen to the Heren XVII, 29 September 1618, in *Bescheiden omtrent zijn Bedrijf in Indie*, I, 399. On the Dutch sense of the righteousness of their cause, see S. Arasaratnam, "The Use of Dutch Material for Southeast Asian History," *Journal of Southeast Asian History* 3 (1962): 95–05.

free manner of our nation is highly praised," while "the proud severity of the Spaniard is hated throughout the world."[32]

In more general terms, European traders of every nation saw themselves as beset by enemies, European or Asian, who watched for any opportunity to deprive them of the fruits of their honest labor, whether by force or by treachery. Pires is again especially instructive for the Portuguese outlook in Southeast Asia. Except for the great entrepôt of Melaka, whose peaceful trading conventions are discussed in detail, his survey of littoral states reads like a census of naval armaments, with cities and principalities listed one after another in terms of the number of "lancharas"[33] they have, and their tradition of raiding their neighbors; by the time he gets to the adjacent islands of Bali, Lombok, and Sumbawa, the language is formulaic: "They are robbers; they have lancharas; they go plundering." If Muslim sea princes are sometimes described as "chivalrous knights," it may be that Pires saw them as gentleman adventurers, just like the Portuguese, and just as dangerous.[34] Ternate was the one maritime principality with which the Portuguese concluded a formal alliance, but to judge from the account of Antonio Galvao, who commanded the garrison there from 1537 to 1540, proximity did not inspire confidence. Galvao had a good grasp of the islanders' seafaring tradition, and in fact used a Moluccan *hongi* to establish a Portuguese presence on Amboina. But he did not admire the warlike ways of the Ternateans: "They are always waging war, they enjoy it; they live and support themselves from it." Worse, "they are intriguers, treacherous, malicious, untruthful, and ungrateful." Galvao even had a theory according to which the dregs of humanity were shipped by stages across Asia, so that "murderers come to India," and "monstrous cases" are transplanted to the Moluccas. (In defense of the stern and upright Galvao, it might be noted that he was not much kinder in speaking of his compatriots, erstwhile fighting men whose greed could not be kept within bounds "once they had gotten the smell of the clove.")[35]

---

[32] Colenbrander, *Levensbeschrijving*, 79, 81; *Bescheiden omtrent zijn Bedrijf in Indie*, I, 215–16.

[33] According to Bassett, "European Influence in Southeast Asia," 189, the lanchara had a single square-rigged sail and two steering oars in the stern.

[34] *The Suma Oriental of Tomé Pires*, 139, 144–7, 167, 194, 207. By ascribing hostile intent to the maritime states of Asia, Pires was, of course, providing a justification for Portuguese aggression. Nonetheless, his account generally receives high marks from modern students of Southeast Asia.

[35] *A Treatise on the Moluccas*, 72–5, 161, 167, 169; De Graaf, *Geschiedenis van Ambon*, 29–30.

More than half a century later, the Dutch complained of their Ternatean "allies" in much they same way. The sultan was sunk in debauchery, his people were "tyrannical, greedy, and murderous"; from time immemorial they had been murdering and enslaving the "good-natured" people of two smaller islands, who now complained of their sufferings to Pieter Both, the first governor-general of the VOC.[36] On Java's northwest coast, where the Dutch were almost desparate to establish a "rendezvous" or fortified headquarters – it was again Coen who solved the problem by seizing Jacatra in 1619 – there had been continuous recrimination between the VOC and the Pangeran of Bantam, who governed the city in the name of the kingdom's boy ruler. The English, who had less of a stake here, had no difficulty with measures taken by the pangeran to prevent the Dutch from controlling the pepper trade, but the Dutch naturally found his behavior extortionate. When Chinese traders attempted to corner the pepper market, apparently with the pangeran's approval, Coen, in righteous indignation, seized pepper already laden in Chinese junks, and "bought" it at low prices previously agreed to.[37] Finally, it need hardly be added that the "murderous Bandanese" were a stable fixture in the ring of treachery that surrounded the honest traders of the VOC.[38]

The only area in this region where the EIC may have had a greater stake than the VOC was in Sumatra, especially in Aceh, where Sultan Iskandar Muda (1607–36) established strict control over many of the ports that served as outlets for the inland pepper-growing districts. In the port city of Aceh, and in the west-coast port of Tiku, EIC men found precise equivalents of the perfidious Ternateans and the murderous Bandanese. The Gujaratis, with whom the EIC had such difficulty in Cambay, were "Judas villains" whose continuing presence in Aceh was the main obstacle to English interest. The corrupt *orang kaya* of the port cities, who now submitted to the sultan's will and collected his customs, demanded bribes above and beyond what had already been given them. Worst of all was Iskandar Muda himself, who sought with growing success to exercise a right of preemption, and make foreign merchants buy their pepper from his agents. To William Nicolls, for some years EIC resident at Aceh, the sultan was "almost a madman" in 1617, and in 1619 "so tyrannical I fear for my

[36] Both to the Heren XVII, 26 July 1612, *General Missiven van Gouverneurs-General*, I, 13–15.
[37] Meilink-Roelofsz, *Asian Trade and European Influence*, 245–54.
[38] Both to the Heren XVII, 18 July 1611, *Generale Missiven*, I, 6.

life." Nicolls regretted having come to a place where "the King and the people are devoid of all honesty."[39]

II

In the late twentieth century, it is easy enough to see that, though opposition from established Asian traders was often quite real, Europeans on the scene enveloped these commercial rivalries with anxieties that were proportional to the fragility of their own position in a vast and alien world. Nonetheless, until recent decades, scholarly understanding of Southeast Asian trade in the early modern centuries indirectly vindicated early modern European perceptions of an Asian hostility so implacabale it could only be broken down by force. The problem was not just that historians looked at Southeast Asia only through European eyes. Anyone who doubts the common view that Van Leur effected a change of perspective in this respect may wish to consult a work like E. S. De Klerck's *History of the Netherlands East Indies*, published in 1938 but based on twenty-year-old lecture notes. The brief section on "Native Organization" provides little more than local variations on the European convention of "Asian despotism," leading to the conclusion that "it is nonsense to speak of a native government," in the sense of rule for the common good, and that "*any* foreign government was better."[40] By contrast, Van Leur treated the history of the region in terms of processes common to other parts of the globe. He was, however, guided by certain assumptions about economic history that then had considerable currency, specifically that the free market is a phenomenon of recent historical vintage, and that trade in earlier periods was commonly regulated by state power in its own interest. This point of view had strong support in the early decades of the twentieth century,[41] but scholars nowadays would be more inclined to say that (relatively) free markets have a long history, and that state regulation of trade is a phenomenon of recent vintage. For example, although the close connection between trade and state

---

[39] *Calendar of State Papers, Colonial Series*, I, nos. 996, 1050, 1058, 1062, 1084, 1111, 1156, II, nos. 51, 119, 134, 136, 245. 384, 388, 760.

[40] De Klerck, *History of the Netherlands East Indies* (The Hague, 1938); see the comment in W. Ph. Coolhaas, *A Critical Survey of Studies on Dutch Colonial History* (2d. ed., revised by G. J. Schutte, The Hague, 1980), 23.

[41] See the comments on the work of Karl Polanyi in Professor Chaudhuri's chapter in this volume; and, on the influence of Gustav Schmoller and the German historical school, see Frederic C. Lane, *Profits from Power: Readings in Protection-Rent and Violence-Controlling Enterprises* (Albany, 1979), 4–5.

policy was long thought to be a common feature of ancient Mediterranean life, an important recent study finds that sea power was rarely used for strictly commercial aims; the famed "thalassocracy" of the Minoans was invented by Thucydides, and that of the Athenians by modern historians influenced by "the bellicose imperialism of the late nineteenth century." As for the Romans, having defeated Carthage, they disbanded their navy, and rebuilt it a century later only in order to suppress piracy.[42]

For present purposes, it will be convenient to take Van Leur's essay (published in Dutch in 1935) as representing the beginning of a scholarly generation that culminated in Meilink-Roelofsz's *Asian Trade and European Influence in the Indonesian Archipelago* (1962) – the scaffolding on which scholars writing in the last quarter century have begun to build a more nuanced picture of Southeast Asian trade in the early modern era. Van Leur distinguished the "bourgeois trade" of modern times from "ancient trade," the basic patterns of which had changed very little, he thought, in the 2,000 years before the coming of the Dutch. Ancient trade was characterized by "compulsory stapling," a concept familiar to Dutch readers because of constant efforts by towns in the medieval Low Countries to claim the "staple" or exclusive privilege of marketing certain classes of goods.[43] For the Indonesian archipelago, this general theory of early trade seemed to have been borne out by the trading kingdom of Srivijaya, based at Palembang in eastern Sumatra, the history of which had only recently been brought to light through the study of Malay inscriptions and Chinese texts. In one of the few explicit references to how trade functioned, Chou Ch'ufei, a twelfth-century Chinese traveler, remarked that warships patrolled the strait to ensure that merchant vessels that did not call voluntarily at Srivijaya's chief port would be forced to do so. In the fourteenth and fifteenth centuries, when Islam was spread throughout the archipelago by traders, the new Muslim rulers and their nobles enjoyed a "dominant" position in the economy, and maintained the practice of "compulsory stapling." Thus "the market continued to be small and unstable, regulated by political aims." By implication, anyone outside the system had no choice but to fight for a share of the goods to be had. Thus, in the Spice Islands, "Commercial shipping was of less importance than military and predatory expeditions, in which taking the heads of defeated enemies was the

---

[42] Chester G. Starr, *The Influence of Sea Power on Ancient History* (New York, 1989), 3–5, 12–13, 36–8, 47, 61–2, 73–4.

[43] The best known example is the Dodrecht staple, on which see B. van Rijswijk, *Het Dordtsche Stapelrecht* (The Hague, 1900).

custom. The people of Banda, especially, give the impression of having been bellicose."[44]

On the basis of years of archival research, as well as newly published primary sources, like Pires's *Suma Oriental*, Meilink-Roelofsz was especially critical of Van Leur for his dismissive comments about the significance of Portuguese trade in the archipelago.[45] Because of Pires, she focuses her discussion of Asian trade before the coming of the Europeans on the great entrepôt of Melaka, but some of Van Leur's thinking lives on in her belief that it was the only port in the region where trade was not controlled by the ruler, and where "individual merchants had a certain amount of influence, inconsiderable though this was compared with their position in Europe."[46] She is also willing to regard Melaka as a zone of free trade, though with a touch of doubt: if Pires can be believed, she says, Melaka enticed Javanese merchants (and their rice and spices) to its well-run market, rather than employing the coercive methods of Srivijaya. Comparison between Melaka and Srivijaya is inevitable because Malay sources agree with Pires in tracing the founding of Melaka to the ruling dynasty of Srivijaya, which in the 1390s was expelled from what was left of its territory in Sumatra by Javanese invaders. Thus, if Melaka was indeed open to all traders, Srivijaya's trade may not have been so coercive as pioneer students of the earlier kingdom had believed.[47] For the Spice Islands, Meilink-Roelofsz again uses Portuguese sources as a corrective to Van Leur. Warfare was indeed important, and a kingdom's position was measured by the number of its warships, as Pires seems to suggest: "Ternate owed its authority over the islands to the fact that it possessed the most kora-koras." But the Banda Islanders, unlike the Ternateans, had trading vessels (junks) of their own, and carried on an active commerce with points as far away as Melaka; they also required Javanese merchants in the Bandas to buy nutmeg as well as the more precious mace, and sometimes burned quantities of nutmeg to maintain the desired price ratio between the two.[48] With warriors one may have to do battle, but with traders one

---

[44] J. C. van Leur, *Indonesian Trade and Society* (The Hague, 1955), 66–7, 75, 92, 105, 141–2.

[45] Meilink-Roelofsz, *Asian Trade and European Influence*, 137–66; Bassett, "European Influence in Southeast Asia," thinks she overstates Portuguese activity in the archipelago.

[46] Meilink-Roelofsz, *Asian Trade*, 9, 46; both Meilink-Roelofsz (8) and Van Leur (72–3), citing Max Weber's *Wirtschaftsgeschichte*, make the point that there are no Asian equivalents for the corporate autonomy of European towns, in which merchants had a prominent political role.

[47] Meilink-Roelofsz, *Asian Trade*, 13–14, 16, 28, 33.

[48] Ibid., 94–7

can usually strike a bargain. Thus Meilink-Roelofsz, unlike most Dutch historians up until her time, has difficulty finding justification for the monopolistic tendencies of the VOC. At Bantam, for example, she finds that local nobles did not control the pepper trade, contrary to what was suggested by Dutch sources and by Van Leur. When the pangeran successfully asserted the state's right to preempt pepper, to prevent one set of foreign merchants (the VOC) from cornering the market, "the Dutch felt they were being victimized, but their moral indignation was not unmixed with envy."[49]

Since the publication of *Asian Trade and European Influence*, more specialized studies have made the notion of state-controlled trade seem even more unlikely. Perhaps the single most significant historiographical development in recent decades has been the emergence of an understanding that early Southeast Asian states made extensive use of ritual as a means of attracting and maintaining support. The king manifested his power by sponsoring rituals that reenacted a great cosmological drama, and satellite regions participated in the prosperity and the glory that were seen as flowing from the ruler's power by providing tribute, in order to support the activities of the great temples at the center of the realm. This flow of goods from periphery to center was separate from the mechanisms of market exchange in the same region, and should also be distinguished from the model of a command economy controlled by a powerful bureacratic state, on the order of T'ang China.[50]

In this view of monarchy, a ruler had trouble making himself accepted unless he came from a house perceived as having sacred power. Legitimism in this sense is now understood to have been one of the major elements of continuity in the history of Srivijaya and its successor state, Melaka. The ruler whom the Portuguese expelled from Melaka (1511) founded the Sultanate of Johor, a bit farther down the Malay peninsula; when the dynasty died out in the direct line in the seventeenth century, Johor's "men of the sea" (*orang laut*) offered their allegiance to the ruler of the former Srivijayan capital of Palembang – the place from which the founder of Melaka had come more than two and a half centuries earlier. Like Srivijaya, Melaka had possessions on Sumatra as well as on the peninsula, and it is clear that the Malay-speaking *orang laut* who kept the strait clear of pirates played a critical role in the com-

---

[49] Ibid., 196, 249–53

[50] There is a good summary of the literature on this theme in Kernial Singh Sandhu and Paul Wheatley, "The Historical Context," in Sandhu and Wheatley, *Melaka: The Transformation of a Malay Capital, c. 1400–1800* (Kuala Lumpur, 1980), 9–17.

mercial eminence of both states, just as they later did in Johor.[51] The rulers of seventh-century Srivijaya and fifteenth-century Melaka enjoyed legitimacy of a different kind through their connections with the Celestial Kingdom; both the T'ang and Ming dynasties preferred dealing with a single power in a given region, on which the emperor would confer a special status, and this tributary relationship to China gave first Srivijaya and later Melaka a tremendous advantage over other ports along the strait.[52] Taken together, these common threads in the history of the two states make Srivijaya seem more like the free port of Melaka, and less like a medieval European city striving for a "compulsory staple." To be sure, there are still the quotations from Chinese sources that speak of ships being forced to call at Palembang, and the great invasion of Srivijaya (1025) by a Chola fleet from the Coromandel coast seems to have been directed against a trading monopoly of some kind. But it is possible that coercive measures were adopted only in the centuries of Srivijaya's decline, and that the Cholas, as newcomers to the trade of this region, reacted to perceived hostility by mounting a great show of force, just as European interlopers would do many centuries later.[53]

Recent scholars seem agreed that the fourteenth century witnessed a great quickening in the production and circulation of the commodities that would henceforth seem typical of the archipelago: pepper, fine spices, and sandalwood. This growth in trade seems to have been due first to the eastward expansion of Muslim trading communities, and second to a renewed interest in oceanic commerce on the part of China's early Ming emperors, beginning in 1368. In turn, it had profound social and political consequences for the archipelago; an increase in the relative importance of coastal cities dependent on trade is detectable, perhaps as early as the thirteenth century; and by the fifteenth century Melaka was only the most prominent of a number of emporia that depended on international trade.[54] The rise of trading

---

[51] Kenneth R. Hall, *Maritime Trade and State Development in Early Southeast Asia* (Honolulu, 1985), 78–9; O. M. Wolters, *Early Indonesian Commerce: A Study of the Origins of Srivijaya* (Ithaca, 1967), 239–42; Leonard Andaya, "The Structure of Power in Seventeenth-Century Johor," in Anthony Reid and Lance Castle, eds., *Pre-Colonial State Systems in Southeast Asia* (Kuala Lumpur, 1975), 5–9.

[52] Andaya and Andaya, *History of Malaysia*, 28.

[53] George W. Spencer, *The Politics of Expansion: The Chola Conquest of Sri Lanka and Sri Vijaya* (Madras, 1983).

[54] Reid, "The Structure of Cities in South East Asia," 235–40. The policy of free trade was at times explicitly formulated, as at Makassar in the fifteenth century: Gilbert Hamonic, "Les Reseaux Marchands Bugis-Makassar," in Lombard, *Marchands et Hommes d'Affaires Asiatiques*, 253–65.

cities also meant rising social position and political influence for traders. In Denys Lombard's view, the elite of the new towns consisted
of the chief traders, not mandarins or nobles; and, as city-states became Muslim, and created an Islamic polity, it was often one of the
more prominent merchants who founded a new dynasty of sultans.
In the Banda Islands, where Muslim conceptions of monarchy had
not yet superimposed themselves on the traditional social organization, control of the nutmeg and mace produced by each village seems
to have been shared between a native *orang kaya* and a *shahbandar*, or
chief merchant, presumably of Javanese origin. By a subtle shift in
meaning, the very term *orang kaya* reflected the new conditions; it
seems originally to have had the sense of "men of the high country,"
or noble men, but by the time the Europeans arrived it meant "rich
men."[55]

The notion of state control of trade lingers on, and can lead to a
difference of emphasis among scholars. For example, although Anthony Reid sees the Sultanate of Melaka as different from earlier states
because the capital city lacked a substantial agricultural hinterland,
and thus depended on trade even to feed its population, Kenneth
Hall points to Melaka's pepper- and gold-producing dependencies
across the strait in order to suggest that the new, commercially oriented states of this era had a greater need than earlier states did to
exert effective control over "territory that produced marketable products."[56] But recent studies point to the conclusion that direct control
of trade by state functionaries – whether the prince or his officials –
is a reaction to European presence in Southeast Asia, not a condition
that the Europeans found on their arrival. The most striking example
of trade conducted in the name of the ruler is under Sultan Iskandar
Muda, mentioned earlier as the *bête noire* of EIC agents in his kingdom.
The Sultanate of Aceh passed quickly from being a pirate state to
being a major trading center and naval power; its attacks across the
strait often forced Portuguese Melaka and the Sultanate of Johor into

---

[55] Lombard, "Le Sultanat Malais comme modèle socio-économique," in Lombard and
Jean Aubin, eds., *Marchandes et Hommes d'Affaires Asiatiques dans l'"ocean Indien et la
Mer de Chine, 13e–18e Siècles* (Paris, 1988), 117–24; Villiers, "Trade and Society in the
Banda Islands;" J. Kathirithamby-Wells, "Royal Authority and the Orang Kaya in
the Western Archipelago, circa 1500–1800," *Journal of Southeast Asian Studies* 17 (1988):
256–67.

[56] Reid, "The Structure of Cities in South East Asia," 240, supported by Lombard, "Le
Sultanat Malais comme modèle socio-économique;" Hall, *Maritime Trade and State
Development*, 222–36, supported by Kathirithamby-Wells, "Royal Authority and the
Orang Kaya," 267.

an unwilling alliance with each other, and its direct shipments to the
Red Sea were principally responsible for reviving the fortunes of the
Muslim spice trade and its principal European customer, the Republic
of Venice. In this zealously Muslim state, there was a certain historical
logic to the process by which Iskandar Muda repressed the proud
orang kaya of his realm and took firm control of the pepper trade, the
better to use it as a weapon against the infidels.[57] State officials took
little part in trade under the sultans of Melaka – indeed they were
prohibited from doing so – but under the seventeenth century sultans
of Johor they became the leading figures in local trade because of
special privileges given them by the VOC, which found this procedure
a convenient way of gaining the cooperation of states that were not
under its authority.[58]

At the time the Europeans arrived, then, one may envision littoral
Southeast Asia as divided between zones of endemic warfare and
plunder, and zones surrounding trading emporia, where piracy was
kept more or less under control. Boundaries between the zones were
not fixed because plunderers could easily become traders, or vice
versa, but there were ports within whose sphere of influence a merchant and his goods were safe, and markets that were open to all
who came in peace, under terms that were widely known and generally accepted. In these circumstances, K. N. Chaudhuri's general
comment about the Indian Ocean can be reiterated for the Southeast
Asian portion of this vast trading region: "The phenomenon that is
in need of explanation is not the system of peaceful but of armed
trading."[59] How does one account for the combination, characteris-
ticially if not uniquely European, of state power and trading interest,
whether in the form of an arm of the state that conducts trade, or a
trading company that behaves like a state? Does this peculiar combination explain the eventual success of the Europeans in their commercial struggles with formidable indigenous rivals, especially in
Asia? Or might the policy of armed trading have served rather to
offset the benefits of dynamic innovations (such as the full-rigged
ship or new forms of commercial credit), which thus bore fruit only

---

[57] Denys Lombard, *Le Sultanat d'Atjeh au temps d'Iskandar Muda, 1606–1637* (Paris, 1967),
33–7, 72–123; Anthony Reid, "Trade and the Problem of Royal Power in Atjeh, c.
1550–1700," in Reid and Castle, *Pre-Colonial State Systems*, 45–53.

[58] Andaya, "The Structure of Power in Seventeenth-Century Johor," 6; L. F. Thomaz,
"Malaka et les communautés marchandes au tournant du XVIe siècle," in Lombard
and Aubin, *Marchands et Hommes d'Affaires Asiatiques*, 31–3.

[59] Chaudhuri, *Trade and Civilization in the Indian Ocean* (London and New York,
1985), 14.

in the eighteenth century, as Europe's warring nations gradually came
to recognize the freedom of the seas? Such are the questions that are
addressed in this volume.

III

Douglass North begins the discussion with an exposition of the concept of transaction costs, which can be used to account for the actual
historical vicissitudes of trade, and which views "protection" as one
kind of cost among others. The following four essays explore in various ways the connection between trading wealth and the armed
might of the state or its agencies. Michael Pearson's broad comparative
survey of state policies in regard to trade finds that, in contrast to
Mughal India, the European state system promoted competition, and
hence state interest in trading wealth, as well as the debatable proposition that armed trading was the best way of exploiting Europe's
new connection with the East. Focusing on the European background,
Thomas Brady argues that the framework of church law legitimized
a system of multiple small polities, especially in the fragmented central
zone north and south of the Alps, dotted with city-states whose commercial classes and commercial strategies would light the way for the
larger ambitions of Atlantic nations. Geoffrey Parker maintains that
Europe was finally able to dominate mainland Asia by exporting not
its mercantile institutions, but its revolution in military technology,
developed in the course of continuing warfare among the major states.
The fluid boundary between what was perceived as legitimate or
illegitimate force is explored in comparative terms by Anne Pérotin-
Dumon, who shows how European states labeled their enemies pirates, while using pirates for their own ends, until the time came
when pirates of all sorts had to disappear, to make room for a regime
of free trade. The next five essays deal with transaction costs other
than protection, or with indirect connections between state power
and the mercantile economy. Russell Menard undertakes a broad
survey of the history of shipping costs, and finds little support for
the view that this sector of the European economy underwent a
"transportation revolution," save to a limited extent in the eighteenth
century, when the benefits of safer seas supplemented the gains
achieved by technical improvements. Focusing on the north Atlantic
trade of the eighteenth century, Jacob Price shows how smaller firms
that lacked the overhead costs of monopoly companies were able to
make use of contemporary banking practice to develop new and more
serviceable forms of credit. Dennis Flynn argues that the global silver

market of the sixteenth and seventeenth centuries can best be understood by seeing silver as a commodity with its own demand structure, and not just as a means of payment; he suggests that, though Tokugawa Japan seems to have used its silver-production profits wisely, Habsburg Spain contributed to its decline by squandering these gains on European wars. On the other hand, in regard to a European state monopoly whose achievements have been underestimated, Sanjay Subrahmanyam and L. F. Thomaz present an *Estado da India* that shows favorable trade balances continuing through the sixteenth century, and that indirectly promoted the emergence of a vigorous private trade. Arguing for a different kind of connection between trade and state power, José Jobson de Andrade Arruda contends that, in the dawning era of free trade, Brazil's trade was profitable to some extent to Brazil itself, more so to the mother country, and most of all to capital-rich England. Finally, by way of conclusion to the major themes treated here, K. N. Chaudhuri offers a philosophical reflection on the social and political determinants of trade, and transaction costs, in world history.

Authors represented in this volume will at times disagree with one another, or with authors represented in *The Rise of Merchant Empires*. It has not been the purpose of these two volumes to simulate consensus where none exists. Rather, the aim has been to bring together scholars whose work has been setting agendas in their respective fields, for broad comparative essays on themes that now seem to matter most for an understanding of Europe's overseas trading empires. Whether this effort at collaboration among scholars of multiple perspectives is indeed a worthy approach to the rich and complex cross-cultural trade it seeks to elucidate, only the reader can judge.

CHAPTER 1

Institutions, transaction costs, and the rise of merchant empires

DOUGLASS C. NORTH

THE central purpose of this volume is to explore the role that merchant empires played in the evolution of Europe, from its position as a relatively backward part of the world to its preeminence in 1750. My assignment is not to focus on the evolution of superior military technology or on state-building, but to concentrate on the creation of institutions that permitted trading empires to exist and to be viable, that is profitable. I focus, therefore, on the costs of transacting, which are a function of the institutions and technology human beings create to interact with each other in repetitive dealings. But, of necessity, the analysis is concerned with politics, military technology, and so forth because they all interacted to determine the costs of transacting. In what follows, I state the issues from the perspective of an economist (Section I), explore the evolution of the state in its connection with trading empires (Section II), look at the innovation of commerical and financial instruments that lowered the costs of transacting (Section III), and then consider the development of institutions and enforcement procedures that made those instruments possible and effective (Section IV). Finally, I put this institutional evolution in historical perspective (Section V). An appendix elaborates the theoretical and technical issues.

I

The international trade model of the economist is the ideal foil against which to examine this evolution. The model is the ideal foil because

I am indebted to Michael Haupert for research assistance; to Elisabeth Case for editorial assistance; and to Larry Neal and Jim Tracy for valuable comments on the draft of this chapter presented at the "Rise of Merchant Empires" conference.

22

it is frictionless: all of the actors have perfect knowledge, there are no institutions or government, and therefore people interact purely on the basis of comparative advantage. The result is that one can clearly see the importance of these assumptions when one contrasts this model with the actuality that we perceive in historical research. The international trade model is built on the principles of comparative advantage, in which differential endowments of the factors of production – land, physical capital, and human capital – would lead each area and region to specialize and then trade with each other. It would be a world of interdependence, of specialization and division of labor, much as Adam Smith described in *The Wealth of Nations*. The model's implications have been explored at length in international trade theory. Factor and product prices tend to be equalized by trade and factor movements among all of the world's players. In this theoretical world, economic growth is not a problem because it is only limited by the tastes and preferences of individuals with respect to the number of children they have and the amount of savings they wish to create, which determine the rate of capital formation. Now, if one wishes to complicate this pure model with the cost of transportation, it changes the model only to the degree that positive transportation costs become a drag upon the relative comparative advantage of players in different parts of the world. But then, of course, as transportation costs fall through history, one would expect that trade and specialization and in consequence growth and prosperity would occur.

Now, if we take a long enough view of economic history, something like this process has occurred. Indeed, we do live today in a world of specialization, where trade and comparative advantage play something like the role described by the model. But for an economic historian the implications of the model do not accord with the evidence over most of the historical period we are concerned with. For most of history, international trade has been a relatively small part of economic activity. Autarky and self-sufficiency, or local trade, have dominated most of history; and only in rare periods, such as during the heyday of the Roman Empire in the Mediterranean world and a few other periods in early history, have we observed extensive amounts of trade occurring. Moreover, declining transportation costs have themselves not been a sufficient reason to induce the growth of international trade, though at times they have helped. And, even if we look at the world today, we see enormous disparity between the rich and the poor nations of the world; in the latter, patterns of economic activity and standards of living still exist that were paralleled by the

Western world centuries and even millenia ago. What is missing from this neo-classical model are transaction costs and the implications of transaction costs for economic growth.

Transaction costs are all the costs of human beings interacting with each other. They involve not only the economic costs of making bargains and enforcing contracts and agreements, but also the political costs of devising a framework of rules and enforcement so that bargains can be extended over time and space and therefore allow us to capture the gains from trade. If transaction costs were zero, then the world of the economist's model that I have been describing would obtain, but, in the presence of positive transaction costs, the world has looked extraordinarily different. Transaction costs include the costs associated with capturing the gains from trade: the costs of measuring and defining the attributes of the goods and services being exchanged and the performance of agents as well as the costs of enforcing agreements with respect to the contracts that are made. They interact intimately with production costs in that it is the two together that make up the total costs of economic activity and define therefore whether trade, specialization, and production and interchange will occur.

Once we introduce transaction costs into the story, we have to ask ourselves an entirely different set of questions than we find in the economist's model of pure international trade theory. How does a transaction-costs framework alter the way in which we explore the historical issues? First, we must continually look at both transaction and production costs to see when it becomes worthwhile for production to take place and for trade and exchange to occur. Throughout most of history, the insecurity and consequent risks have made the costs of transacting so high that trade has been very limited. Second, the role that the state plays then becomes an important part of our examination. Throughout most of history, the state has acted more like the Mafia than an organization that was concerned with economic growth. What made rulers of some states perceive that their interests lay in promoting trade rather than holding trade and economic activity to ransom? During the period we are examining in this volume, the role of the state in enforcing agreements and lowering the costs of transacting among merchants and individual actors is a central part of the story we wish to explore. At some point the state realizes economies of scale in violence or in enforcing agreements (the flip side of the same coin) and therefore begins to assume the role of contract enforcer between parties on an international level. Notarial records suggest that, at the local level in Italian city-states, the state played a role in enforcing local contracts and supplemented the role of merchants' legal relationships and merchant courts in enforcing property rights and agreements. How the state widens its role, what induces it to widen its role, and the degree to which it helps or frequently hinders the evolution of international trade and the fall of transaction costs, are central to the issues that we must explore.

A central actor in the evolution of international trade was the trading company, a quasi-independent voluntary organization that retained some coercive aspects. It was quasi-voluntary because it was certainly a trading company but frequently was endowed, empowered, and sometimes delegated by the state to have coercive force. Although it at times engaged purely in trade, it was not simply a passive trader, but frequently engaged in plunder and piracy. How did this particular form of voluntary organization evolve; and as it evolved, how did the costs of transacting change? Here the story becomes more complex because, as voluntary organizations evolved, they faced a complex of issues, from external threats of piracy or the inability to get agreements with traders in foreign countries, but also from the internal problems of agency, that is, the problems of constraining and controlling their own agents in international exchange. The agency problem became a central issue as voluntary organizations evolved through time. But they did evolve not only in ways by which to protect themselves against external threats, or achieve some degree of compliance in enforcing agreements in foreign political systems, but also in ways by which they could control the problems of internal organization. They did so, through the development of a succession of organizational and financial innovations, which over time lowered the costs of transacting.

II

What set off the expansion of Western Europe, which led to its ultimate hegemony in the world? A proximate part of the explanation, though certainly not a complete one, is the revolution in military technology that occurred in the late Middle Ages; the cross-bow, the long-bow, the pike, and gunpowder had implications for the organization and capital costs of warfare. The costs of warfare rose. So, accordingly, rose the costs of survival of political units. Because kings were supposed to live on their own, they were faced with devising ways to increase fiscal revenues. This "Crisis of the Tax State," to use the title of a celebrated essay by Joseph Schumpeter published in 1919, led to radical changes in the polities and economies of Western

Europe. A king's revenues from his own estates and other traditional rights he held from feudal obligations were nowhere near enough to be able to pay the armies and mercenaries necessary for survival. Of necessity, the king tapped the wealth and income of his constituents. This led to the creation of representative bodies of wealth-holders, who then traded tax revenues for rights received from the Crown.

At this point our story diverges radically. The Estates General of France and the Cortes of Castile in Spain gradually gave up the powers they had in initial bargains with the king and their role was reduced. In consequence the Crowns of France and Spain (and Portugal too) evolved into centralized monarchies. In order to control the economies and polities, and their overseas empires, they developed large, centralized bureaucracies. The result was an institutional path that was to shape the subsequent history of these polities and economies. The problems of control within this vast bureaucracy present a classic dilemma of agency.

An alternative path was pursued by the Netherlands and England, though certainly not by any intention (in the latter case) of the Crown. Gradually the Estates General in the Netherlands and the Parliament in England achieved a degree of control over fiscal matters and therefore over the polities themselves. The story in England in the revolutionary seventeenth century is a very familiar one; however, the issue of control remained in doubt through much of that century. By 1689 Parliament achieved supremacy, and the divergent path, in England as in the Netherlands, led to a radically different form of organization. From regulated companies to joint-stock companies, increasingly voluntary organizations evolved, more and more independent of government control.

Moreover, throughout the entire Western world, competition was playing a critical role. Polities and economies struggled, not only inside Europe for hegemony but also in the growing empires of the rest of the world, where competition played the critical role (in the decentralized parts of the system) of inducing increased efficiency, as it had in the Netherlands and England. On the other hand, in Spain, Portugal, and France, colonies were run by bureaucratic decree.

The importance of these diverging paths for the analysis in the following sections is clear. In the case of the Netherlands and England, decentralized control produced an adaptively efficient set of institutions that adjusted to changing needs; thus, competition gradually forced the development of more efficient institutions and instruments that promoted commerce and trade, and, in consequence, lowered transaction costs in these economies. The bureaucracies of Spain, Portugal, and France, on the other hand, lagged behind, stifling initiatives that would have induced increased productivity, and Spain and Portugal pursued a downward path that would continue for centuries.

III

Innovations that lowered transaction costs consisted of organizational innovations, instruments, and specific techniques and enforcement characteristics that lowered the costs of engaging in exchange over long distances. These innovations occurred at three cost margins: 1) those that increased the mobility of capital; 2) those that lowered information costs; and 3) those that spread risk. Obviously these are overlapping categories; however, they provide a useful way to distinguish cost-reducing features of transacting. All of these innovations had their origins in earlier times; most of them were borrowed from medieval Italian city-states or Islam or Byzantium and elaborated upon in subsequent development. Because there is already an immense literature on the specifics of these innovations and instruments, my task, as I see it, is to attempt to draw out the larger implications of the specific developments for economic growth. In this section, let me schematically order the innovations. In the next section, I will look at their implications.

Let me begin with innovations that affected the mobility of capital. The first of these were the techniques and methods evolved to evade usury laws. The variety of ingenious ways by which interest was disguised in loan contracts ranged from "penalties for late payment" to exchange-rate manipulation,[1] to the early mortgage, but they did increase the costs of contracting. The costliness of usury laws was not only that the need for disguising interest made the writing of contracts complex and cumbersome, but also that enforceability of such contracts had become more problematic. As usury laws gradually broke down and rates of interest were permitted, the costs of writing contracts and the costs of enforcing them declined.

A second innovation that improved the mobility of capital, and the one that has received the most attention, was the evolution of the bill of exchange and particularly the development of techniques and instruments that allowed for the negotiability of the bill of exchange

---

[1] Robert S. Lopez and Irving W. Raymond, *Medieval Trade in the Mediterranean World* (New York; 1955), 163.

and the development of discounting methods. Negotiability and discounting in turn depended on the creation of institutions that would permit their use and the development of centers where such events could occur, first in fairs, such as the Champagne fairs, then through banks, and finally through financial houses that could specialize in discounting. These developments were a function not only of specific institutions but also of the scale of economic activity. Increasing volume obviously made such institutional developments possible. In addition to the economies of scale necessary for the development of the bills of exchange, improved enforceability of contracts was critical, and the interrelationship between the development of accounting as well as auditing methods and their use as evidence in the collection of debts and in the enforcement of contracts was an important part of this process.[2]

Still a third innovation affecting the mobility of capital arose from the problems associated with maintaining control of agents involved in long-distance trade. The traditional resolution of this problem in medieval and early modern times was the use of kinship and family ties to bind agents to principals in ways that provided some assurance to the principal that the orders and directions of the principal were safely carried out (the church's greater success with agents probably reflected ideological commitment). However, as the size and scope of merchant trading empires grew, the extension of discretionary authority to others than kin of the principal required the development of sophisticated accounting and auditing methods and more elaborate procedures for monitoring the behavior of agents.

When we turn to information costs, the major developments were the printing of prices of various commodities as well as the printing of manuals that provided information on weights, measures, customs, brokerage fees, postal systems, and, particularly, on the complex exchange rates between monies in Europe and the trading world. Obviously these developments were primarily a function of the economies of scale resulting from the volume of international trade.

The final innovation consisted of the transformation of uncertainty into risk. By uncertainty, I mean here a condition wherein one cannot ascertain the probability of an event and therefore cannot arrive at a way of insuring against such an occurrence. Risk on the other hand implied the ability to make an actuarial determination of the likelihood

---

[2] B. S. Yamey, "Scientific Bookkeeping and the Rise of Capitalism," *Economic History Review* ser. 2 1 (1949): 99–113; Ross Watt and Jacob Zimmermann, "Agency Problems, Auditing, and the Theory of the Firm: Some Evidence," *Journal of Law and Economics* 26 (1983): 613–34.

of an event and hence insure against such an outcome. We think of insurance and portfolio diversification in the modern world as methods for converting uncertainty into risks and thereby reducing, through the provision of a hedge against variability, the costs of transacting. Indeed, when we look at the medieval and early modern world, we find precisely the same results. That is, marine insurance evolved from sporadic individual contracts covering partial payments for losses to contracts issued by specialized firms.

By the fifteenth century marine insurance was established on a secure basis. The wording of the policies had already become stereotyped and changed very little during the next three or four hundred years . . . In the sixteenth century it was already current practice to use printed forms provided with a few blank spaces for the name of the ship, the name of the master, the amount of the insurance, the premium, and a few other items that were apt to change from one contract to another.[3]

Marine insurance was one example of the development of actuarial, ascertainable risk; another was business organization that spread risk through either portfolio diversification or through institutions that permitted a large number of investors to engage in risky activities. The *commenda* itself, from its Jewish, Byzantine, and Muslim origins[4] through its evolution at the hands of Italians to the English regulated company and finally the joint-stock company, provides an evolutionary story of the institutionalization of risk (though, as discussed below, the developments created new problems of agency for the principals involved).

IV

The specific innovations and particular institutional instruments briefly described in the previous section evolved as a result of the interplay of two fundamental economic forces. One was the economies of scale associated with a growing volume of trade; the other was the development of improved enforcement mechanisms that made possible the enforcement of contracts at lower costs. Surely the causation ran both ways. That is, the increasing volume of long-distance trade raised the rate of return to merchants of devising effective mechanisms for enforcing contracts. In turn, the development

---

[3] Florence De Roover, "Early Examples of Marine Insurance," *Journal of Economic History* 5 (1945): 198.

[4] Abraham Udovitch, "At the Origins of Western Commenda, Islam, Israel, Byzantium?" *Spectrum* 37 (1962): 198–207.

of such mechanisms lowered the costs of contracting and made trade more profitable, thereby increasing its volume.

When we look at the development of enforcement mechanisms, we see first that the process was a long one. Although a number of courts handled commercial disputes, the development of enforcement mechanisms by merchants themselves is of particular interest. Enforceability appears to have had its beginnings in the development of internal codes of conduct in fraternal orders of guild merchants; those who did not live up to them were threatened with ostracism. More specialized, the law merchant evolved and was conveyed through long-distance trade codes of conduct, so that Pisan laws passed into the sea codes of Marseilles. Oleron and Lübeck gave laws to the north of Europe, Barcelona to the south of Europe, and from Italy came the legal principle of insurance and bills of exchange.[5]

The development of more sophisticated accounting methods and of the use of such methods and of notarial records for evidence in disputes permitted evidence to become the basis for ascertaining facts in disputes. The gradual blending of the voluntaristic structure of enforcement of contracts via internal merchant organizations with those of the state is an important part of the story of increasing the enforceability of contracts. The long evolution of merchant law from its voluntary beginnings and the differences in resolutions that it had with both the common and Roman law are a part of the story. The two types of law did not accommodate each other very well to begin with. This was particularly true in cases of moral hazard and asymmetric information in insurance contracts as well as those associated with fraud in exchange. The law merchant was assumed by the court of common law but continued to be administered in the original spirit of the law merchant, that is, as a law based on custom. At first, it still applied only to proven merchants, whether they were the plaintiff or defendant. Cases seldom laid down a particular rule because it was virtually impossible to separate custom from the facts. The habit was to leave the jury with the custom and the facts, and the judge would charge the jury to determine and apply the custom when supported by the facts. Eventually, this was changed. The turning point could be designated as 1756, the year Lord Mansfield became chief justice of the English court of King's Bench. He gave form to the existing customs. He established general principles that were to be used to rule future cases. He was not too fond of English common law and

---

[5] William Mitchell, *An Essay on the Early History of the Law Merchant* (New York: reprint edition, Burt Franklin, 1969), 156.

as a result he derived many of these principles from the writings of foreign jurists. "For instance, in his judgement in Luke v. Lyde, which raised a question of the freight due for goods lost at sea, he cited the Roman Pandects, the Consolato del Mare, laws of Wisby and Oleron, two English and two foreign mercantile writers, and the French Ordonnances, and deduced from them a principle which has since been part of the Law of England."[6]

The law merchant, besides providing a much-needed court of law especially suited to the unique needs of the merchant, also fostered some significant developments that aided in decreasing transaction costs of exchange. Among such developments can be included the recognition of the responsibility of the principal for his agent. This spawned both a benefit and a cost. It allowed the merchant to expand his scope of operation via a series of agents. At the same time, it created a principal-agent problem. Initially, this legal recognition was in effect only for well-known agents of the principal. The fact that credit was generally given to the agent because it was generally believed he was acting for his master provided an obvious opportunity for the agent to benefit himself. At the same time, however, the privilege was also used to control the principal-agent problem. By extending to his agent the privilege of using the merchant's credit for his own personal trading, the merchant was able to increase the opportunity cost to the agent of losing his position. If the agent abused his position, he would lose not only his job, but a valuable line of credit as well.

The effect of the merchant law on contracts and sales was especially encouraging to the expansion of trade. The existing Roman and Germanic laws did not give the security and certainty of bargains that merchants needed. Neither body of law protected them against the claims of the original owner of stolen or lost goods that the merchant had innocently purchased. The feudal lord recognized the value of fairs and markets as a revenue source and therefore the importance of protecting the honest purchaser. Under merchant law, the honest purchaser was allowed either to keep the goods or return them if the original owner refunded the purchase price.

Protection of the bona fide purchaser was not a part of the common law. But in commercial disputes the "good-faith" principle was used earlier and on a much wider scope (the basis of Roman contract law by A.D. 200). It evolved first out of the Fair Bonds, which validated

---

[6] Thomas E. Scrutton, *The Elements of Mercantile Law* (n.p.: Wm. Cloves & Sons, Ltd., 1891), 15.

sales at fairs by affixing a seal to the bond. Originally this was a voluntary measure – the custom of fairs allowed debts to be contracted by witness. Eventually though, the desire to avoid fraud and at the same time increase revenue led to a law requiring that all sales be recognized by a sealed bond. Once sealed, the bond could be invalidated only by proving that the seal had been forged.

The good-faith principle was extended to the area of insurance. Extreme good faith was required when writing out a marine insurance contract. Because the person wishing insurance had more knowledge, he must tell the underwriter the "whole truth and nothing but the truth." The law required this extreme good faith or the contract would be invalidated. Misrepresentation was a sufficient reason, even when not intended, to invalidate the contract, as opposed to ordinary contracts where intent to defraud was necessary in order to invalidate a contract.

Many rules of merchant law developed because common law interfered with trade. For example, the common law's failure to protect bona fide purchasers forced examining the title of goods all the way back to the original owner. This presented an obvious problem for merchants: the cost and time required to carry out such a search were prohibitive.

This problem caused the first exception to common law that the law merchant made. The evolution of the situation from the thirteenth to the sixteenth century can be measured by the manner in which purchasers of goods with fraudulent titles were treated. In the thirteenth century, the purchaser of such goods would be forced to return them upon the discovery of a discrepancy anywhere along the chain of ownership of the good. By the time Sir Edward Coke was appointed chief justice in 1606, the final (good-faith) purchaser of a good was recognized (in certain but not all courts) as having the only viable title to the good, making any legal purchase he made legal all the way back down the chain of ownership.

Another, similar example of the common law hindering the merchants was the common law's ruling that a "chose in action" was not transferable. This is the right to a thing as opposed to the thing itself; the separation of the property right from the property itself. This was inconvenient if the bearer of a bill of exchange had to check every endorser in the chain's credibility and furthermore was not able to sue in his own name, but would have to do so in the name of the man mentioned as payee on the bill. The law merchant established certain "choses in action" called negotiable instruments. The holder of a negotiable instrument could then sue in his own name. Also, he was not affected by the previous lack of title. The laws of negotiable instruments were almost entirely built on custom.

A major player in this whole process was the state, and there was continuous interplay between the fiscal needs of the state and its credibility in its relationships with merchants and the citizenry in general. In particular, the evolution of capital markets was critically influenced by the policies of the state because, to the extent that the state was bound by commitments that it would not confiscate assets or in any way use its coercive power to increase uncertainty in exchange, it made possible the evolution of financial institutions and the creation of more efficient capital markets. The shackling of arbitrary behavior of rulers and the development of impersonal rules that successfully bound both the state and voluntary organizations were a key part of this whole process.[7] In addition, the development of an institutional process by which government debt could be circulated, become a part of a regular capital market, and be funded by regular sources of taxation was a key part of this process.[8]

It was of course in the Netherlands, and Amsterdam specifically, that these diverse innovations and institutions were put together to create the predecessor of the efficient modern set of markets that make possible the growth of exchange and commerce. An open immigration policy attracted businessmen; and efficient methods of financing long-distance trade were developed, as were capital markets and discounting methods in financial houses that lowered the costs of underwriting this trade. The development of techniques for spreading risk and transforming uncertainty into actuarial, ascertainable risks as well as the creation of large-scale markets that allowed for lowering the costs of information, and the development of negotiable government indebtedness all were a part of this story.[9]

Equally well known is the evolution of this process in England. The political conflict of the seventeenth century that culminated in the triumph of Parliament in 1688 and the subsequent flowering of the capital market in the next twenty-five years in England,[10] the expansion of long-distance trade, the improved enforcements of contracting, and the reductions of uncertainty that came with the development

---

[7] Douglass North and Barry Weingast, "Constitutions and Commitment: The Evolution of Institutions Governing Public Choice in the Seventeenth-century England," *Journal of Economic History*, 49 (1989): 803–832.

[8] James D. Tracy, *A Financial Revolution in the Hapsburg Netherlands: Renten and Renteniers in the County of Holland, 1515–1565* (Berkeley, 1985).

[9] Violet Barbour, *Capitalism in Amsterdam in the Seventeenth Century* (Baltimore, 1950).

[10] Peter Dickson, *The Financial Revolution in England: A Study in the Development of Public Credit, 1688–1756* (New York; 1967).

of commerce and the joint-stock company were equally a part of the process in Britain.

Let me conclude this section by briefly assessing both the improvements in the costs of transacting that occurred in this period and the ongoing dilemmas. Perhaps the most striking feature that one can draw from transaction-cost stories of companies, such as the English East India Company,[11] the Hudson Bay Company,[12] or the Royal African Company,[13] all of which have been extensively documented in their historical evolution, was the degree of sophistication they brought to solving the problems they confronted in a world where information costs (at least by modern standards) were enormously high, where enforcement of contracts was, even at the end of the period, quite uncertain, and where problems of agency increased as the volume and size of the companies grew to previously unknown levels. These problems, particularly the latter, were major dilemmas.

Yet, what stands out in the history of these companies is how sophisticated they were in solving these problems. David Galenson's study of the slave trade and of the evolution of the Royal African Company provides us with a good case study of this process. He demonstrates conclusively that sophisticated techniques were used to make markets work efficiently, at least efficiently in comparison to previous notions of trading patterns. He also demonstrates that the Royal African Company, despite being granted a monopoly, was itself a victim of the dilemmas of the world of such uncertainty.

There were three major reasons for the failure of the Royal African Company. First was the lack of rapid communications technology, which hindered the ability of the firm to respond to changing market conditions and to monitor agents. Second, its charter imposed certain costs on the company in exchange for certain other benefits. The Royal African Company bore those costs, such as manning forts in Africa, but never did reap the promised benefits. These benefits included a grantable monopoly in the slave trade between England and the American colonies in the Caribbean. Third, England refused to allow the West Indian colonies to issue their own currency and the result was a chronic shortage that left the Royal African Company the major creditor of the colonies. All of the problems faced by the Royal African

---

[11] Gary Anderson, Robert McCormick, and Robert Tollison, "Economic Organization of the English East India Company," *Journal of Economic Behavior and Organization* 4 (1983): 221–38.

[12] Ann Harper-Fender and Elizabeth Mancke, "Hudson's Bay Company: Precursor to the Modern Corporation," unpublished manuscript.

[13] David W. Galenson, *Traders, Planters, and Slaves: Market Behavior in Early English America* (Cambridge, 1986).

Company might still have been overcome had it not been for the competition the firm faced. Even though it was granted the Crown monopoly, several competing firms existed. Some of these were foreign competitors, some British. Because the Royal African Company faced constraints (discussed below), while their competitors were free to operate without them, they were eventually driven out of business by more efficiently operating firms. It is an indication of the sophistication of the competing firms that they were able to overcome the problems of agency, long-distance communication, and so forth that all firms faced, and still fare better than the company protected by the Crown. The three agency problems the Royal African Company had to solve were those associated with ship captains, agents manning the forts, and sales agents in the West Indies. Monitoring the ship captains turned out to be extremely difficult and indeed led to the captain's taking advantage of the company at every turn. Similarly, agents manning the forts in Africa were a continual problem, a deadly combination of incompetence and dishonesty; again, the problems of monitoring them turned out to be an insuperable dilemma. A similar dilemma existed with agents who sold slaves in the West Indies. Perhaps the Royal African Company is the ideal illustration with which to conclude this section or because it indicates on the one hand how far company organization had come in its ability to engage in long-distance trade in the face of the dilemmas of high information costs and uncertain enforcement and on the other hand the road that lay ahead before further extension of such trade and commerce could occur.

V

What distinguished Western Europe from other places in the world, where persistent economic growth failed to occur, was that there gradually evolved a set of adaptively efficient institutions that persistently tended to lower the costs of transacting, producing, and transporting in a way that produced a continuous evolution of productivity increases in these societies (see appendix). We know all too little about this process, but clearly merchant empires were a step along the way. They were a step from autarky, localized trade, to larger trade and specialization, which at least for some economies, notably the Netherlands and England, were steps along the route to a persistent evolution of more efficient forms of economic organization. Perhaps the best way to look at this process is to reverse the perspective of Section I. There we used the neo-classical model, where all rights are perfectly specified and delineated and where parties engage in trade and exchange without facing problems of measurement or enforcement. The reverse is a world of complete anarchy and autarky, where no rights are recognized by the parties, and no enforcement mechanisms exist. Such a world never, in fact, really existed, because, even in tribal groups and primitive societies, some rights were at least implicitly recognized in small-scale exchange. Nevertheless, we do observe in early modern Europe a gradual growth in specialization and division of labor made possible by a variety of institutions and instruments that reduced the uncertainties associated with contracting and enforcing trade over long distance and with increasingly diverse and "unknown" trading partners.

As indicated above, two major influences were a part of this process. First were the economies of scale associated with the volume of exchange; and second was the development of improved methods of enforcing contracts. Although such economies of scale can be looked upon, in a sense, as an automatic consequence of this volume of exchange, political action by the state to encourage adaptively efficient instruments was anything but automatic. Indeed, the divergent paths of the Netherlands and England on the one hand, versus Spain and Portugal on the other, provide us with an important clue to resolving this issue. Clearly, the incremental change of institutions and the consequent path-dependent evolution, which take us down one road or another, were a major part of this process. Path-dependency suggests that we can learn as much from the dead-end path pursued by Spain and Portugal, with respect to institutional evolution, as we can from the successful paths to evolving more efficient institutions pursued by the Netherlands and England. We are a long way from completely understanding the interplay among institutions, transaction costs, and economic growth, but exploring changing transaction costs and their implications and consequences for institutional evolution is a major step ahead in improving our understanding.

APPENDIX: TRANSACTION COSTS AND PRODUCTIVITY INCREASES IN EARLY MODERN WESTERN EUROPE

The growth of Western Europe – indeed the rise of the Western world – was a consequence of the growing productivity of these economies and their relative rise was a consequence of the contrast in productivity growth between Western European countries and the rest of the world. The story I have recounted in the foregoing essay implies that declining costs of transacting brought about by the innovations of institutions played a key role in the process of growth. In the essay, I was primarily interested in telling a "plausible story." In this appendix, I wish to lay out the logic of my arguments, provide evidence consistent with them, and, most important, invite researchers to develop evidence systematically that will critically evaluate these hypotheses.

Productivity increase results from getting more constant quality output from given amounts of inputs of the factors of production. We customarily ascertain productivity increases by contrasting the inputs of land, labor, and capital required for a given amount of output in two different settings. Economists have traditionally conceived of the inputs of raw materials, labor, machinery, and so forth as being transformed into an intermediate or final good or service. In fact, concealed in this simple formulation were transaction as well as transformation costs, and accordingly we should have enlarged the argument to include the real resource inputs that went into both transformation (as a consequence of technology) and transaction (as a consequence of institutions) in order to get the total input costs associated with any given output. That is, the costs of production (inputs) are a function of the resources used in both transforming and transacting. Moreover, it is important to note that, just as a new technology (for example, the computer) might as easily have reduced the cost of transacting as the cost of transforming, so might an institutional change have reduced the cost of transforming (for example, unitizing an oil field through the allocation of property rights) as well as the cost of transacting. Clearly, the interdependence between transformation and transaction costs and between technological change and institutional change is complicated. And because it is complicated – and new to our understanding – we need to rethink a great deal of our understanding of economic history.

Interdependence makes the task of unambiguously measuring the role of transaction costs in productivity change much more difficult. Moreover, the difficulty of measuring variation in the quality of inputs and outputs and the dilemmas (also common to standard national income accounting) posed by costs of transacting that do not go through the market or are otherwise measured (queuing, waiting, bribery, quality deterioration, and so forth) complicate the task even further.

These problems are difficult but not insurmountable, and a major task of the economic historian is to attempt to get as good a measure as possible. Let me make some suggestions and then discuss some of the evidence we currently have to explore the issues raised in this essay. The ideal data would measure the cost-reducing consequences of a specific-institutional or technological change. Even more ideal for an economic historian is to know the sequence of changes and their cost effects because usually the consequence of a given institutional (or technological) change is to induce a technological (or institutional) change. The problems of imputing causation are always present. For example, to choose an illustration relevant to this essay, the triumph of Parliament in 1688 was followed in the next 25 years by what has been described as a financial revolution.[14] Not only did interest rates on government securities decline but so did interest rates of nongovernmental securities. The new institutions that played a part in this process were the Bank of England (1694), the creation of regular sources of tax revenue to finance government securities, and the development and expansion of other financial intermediaries. But the assumptions in this argument are 1) that the triumph of Parliament did induce the creation of these institutions; and 2) that these institutions were responsible for lowering interest rates by reducing the costs of transacting. Obviously we cannot prove the sequence of hypotheses to be true; however, we can at least test our confidence in them by examining alternative explanations, for example, checking that the interest-rate decline was not a consequence of changes in the price level (comparing real versus nominal interest rates) or of some other nontransaction cost change. Similar problems of measurement and causation are involved in the secular decline in marine insurance rates during this period. Perhaps the best evidence is found in the decline in ocean freight rates after 1600 that appears to have been a consequence of both institutional and technological change.[15]

An even more difficult but still critical issue, particularly with respect to the focus of this volume, is to explain the initiation of production and exchange where none existed before because a basic assertion of the transaction-costs approach is that it has been the

---

[14] Dickson, *Financial Revolution*.

[15] In "Sources of Productivity Change in Ocean Shipping: 1600–1850," *Journal of Political Economy* 76 (1968): 953–70, I maintained that the productivity increase over the period was solely due to institutional and not technological change, but more recent research by Knick Harley, "Ocean Freight and Productivity, 1740–1913: The Primacy of Mechanical Invention Reaffirmed," *Journal of Economic History* 68 (1988): 851–76, has demonstrated I was wrong for the later part of the study and that technological change was more important. However, the evidence for the seventeenth century does, I believe, support my argument. See also the chapter by Russell Menard in this volume.

insecurities and uncertainties of production and exchange that are the major stumbling blocks to economic growth, and it is their reduction that has led to development. But how can we know that an institutional change has induced a decline in transaction/transformation costs and subsequently led to production or exchange where none existed before? After all, any downward shift in the supply curve or demand curve for the good or service could explain its beginnings. Delving into the immense literature that exists in economic history on the question of whether a given expansion was demand- or supply-induced would take me too far afield. However, much of that literature, though inconclusive, does suggest some partial answers. On the supply side we can explore whether alternative technological explanations are possible, as was done in the case of ocean shipping. We can try to sort out the sources of productivity increases, whether economies of scale, technological change, institutional change. The most plausible explanation may be a sequential interdependent process embodying over time all three sources. (Again, however, it is true that our task of definitive measurement will be made vastly more complicated by the latter.)

Before turning to some of the specific issues in the foregoing essay, let me add one important point that cliometricians have tended to obliterate or at least ignore with their voluminous data sets. Qualitative evidence is immensely valuable. Used carefully to reflect the same concerns that plague us even with numbers, such evidence is frequently going to have to be the "only game in town." Do not misunderstand me. I think that there is vastly more statistical data out there, which, by asking the right questions, can be unearthed; and I strongly believe that even for the early period we can develop much improved quantitative measures. But we should also – indeed we must – judiciously employ qualitative evidence. For example, regardless of the deficiencies of quantitative data, the accounts we possess of the growth of the Dutch capital market, the consequent increased mobility, and the institutional structure that underpinned it are important. Even though we may suspect some of the real interest rate data, the widespread agreement that Dutch interest rates were lower than elsewhere appears to be solidly based. Moreover, the qualitative contemporary evidence overwhelmingly links them to low costs of transacting as a consequence of political stability and the underlying capital market institutions.

What kind of evidence do we possess to assess the three sources of transaction cost declines discussed in these pages? Consider first the mobility of capital. We do have interest rate series[16] that, whatever their substantial drawbacks, are consistent. We have a large volume of qualitative evidence on the evolution of the bill of exchange and the increased mobility that were made possible by improved negotiability and discounting. We have evidence on the development of a regular government capital market.[17] By the beginning of the eighteenth century we have quantitative evidence of the integration of London and Amsterdam financial markets.[18] The decline in information costs is recorded with the production of merchant manuals, the beginnings of "prices current" and the growth of a financial press.[19] The conversion of uncertainty into risk obviously is reflected in the growth of marine insurance, the development of a number of financial intermediaries, such as discount houses, and of course the development and spread of the joint-stock company.

I do not mean to imply that I have summarized all the evidence available. I do mean to conclude this appendix by inviting economic historians to attempt to systematically develop quantitative information and to pull together and synthesize qualitative information that will provide us with a surer sense of the roles transaction costs and institutions played in the evolution of early modern Europe.

[16] Sidney Homer, *A History of Interest Rates* (New Brunswick, 1963); Carlo Cipolla, *Before the Industrial Revolution: European Society and Economy, 1000–1700* (New York, 1980).

[17] Dickson, *Financial Revolution*; Tracy, *Hapsburg Netherlands*.

[18] Larry Neal, "Integration of International Capital Markets: Quantitative Evidence from Eighteenth to Twentieth Centuries," *Journal of Economic History* (1985): 219–26; Robert Eagly and Kerry Smith, "Domestic and International Integration of the London Money Market, 1731–1789," *Journal of Economic History* 46 (1976): 198–212.

[19] Neal, "The Rise of a Financial Press, London and Amsterdam, 1681–1796," unpublished manuscript, 1985.

CHAPTER 2

Merchants and states[*]

M. N. PEARSON

INTRODUCTION

ANY study of the effects of politics on economic life, especially long-distance trade, runs a grave danger of ratifying the present from the past. We know that one country which created a merchant empire also produced late in the eighteenth century the Great Transmutation of commercial, scientific, and industrial revolutions. There is the obvious danger of seeing the whole period from 1350 to 1750 as a prolegomena to this achievement, and merely looking for the processes in this long early modern period that contributed to the end result of British supremacy.[1] Such an approach can produce distortions of the actual experience of those centuries. Even European "expansion" was not new in the late fifteenth century. Relevant and cautionary here are works by Jones and Scammell;[2] they point to a very long history of European expansion, both internal and external, far predating 1492 or 1498. Scammell's whole book is designed to show elements of

*Several people made helpful comments on this chapter, but I am especially grateful to Jim Tracy for his useful critique, and to all the participants at the "Rise of Merchant Empires" conference. Initial bibliographical research was done by Martin Braach-Maksyvtis, supported by Special Research Grant funds from the Faculty of Arts, University of New South Wales.

[1] See, for example, an article by Jack A. Goldstone, "East and West in the Seventeenth Century: Political Crises in Stuart England, Ottoman Turkey, and Ming China," *Comparative Studies in Society and History* 30 (1988): 103–42, which traces similarities in mid-seventeenth century political crises in these three countries. This sort of comparison is much to be preferred to work such as that of Eric L. Jones, which is vitiated by his lack of comprehension of areas other than those in which the "European Miracle" occurred. See E. L. Jones, *The European Miracle*, (2d. ed., Cambridge, 1987). The editor of a recent outstanding collection on the Ottoman Empire notes that in too much of the literature "the West is viewed as the privileged domain of world-history characterized by change and development, and the East as the non-privileged, unchanging, therefore the *ahistorical* domain." Huri Islamoglu-Inan, "Introduction: 'Oriental Despotism' in World-System Perspective," in Huri Islamoglu-Inan, ed., *The Ottoman Empire and the World-Economy*, (Cambridge, 1987), 1. On the matter of the singularity of England see Thomas Brady's chapter in this volume.

[2] Jones, *European Miracle*: G. V. Scammell, *The World Encompassed: The First European Maritime Empires, c. 800–1650*, (London, 1981)

continuity in European expansion from 800 to 1650 (he should have gone on to 1750, for it is about then that we can begin to find generic change).

My contribution to this collection lies at the cutting edge of economic history today, for it tries to analyse the effect of one exogenous variable, namely politics, on economic behavior. Before World War II, at least in the English-speaking world, economic history was concerned with wider influences, with political, social, and even ideological and religious impacts on economic activity. Subsequently, economic historians did two things. As data bases expanded, and also in a quest to be more "scientific," they ignored policy and regulation and instead looked to the actual workings of the various units and segments of the economy. This trend meant that F. C. Lane was for long a prophet without honor, for he consistently stressed the connection between politics and economics, most notably in his concern to delineate protection costs. But over perhaps the last twenty years the pendulum has swung back, not exactly to replicate the studies done before World War II, but in the sense that economic historians again now are concerned with the "border-country between economic history and political history."[3] One of the first signs of this seems to have been Postan's declaration in the introduction (1963) to volume three of the *Cambridge Economic History of Europe*, where he stated that this volume dealt with "policy and organizations in relation to political and constitutional developments which do not commonly enter into the ken of economic history." Given this now dominant trend, it is not incumbent on me to justify a study of the connection between politics and economic development. But I am reluctant to say that politics is more important than economics in the rise of the merchant empires. It is impossible to quantify such a matter anyway, but certainly politics was important, and not necessarily just in the area stressed by my fellow contributor Douglass North. He emphasizes the state enforcement of property rights as a crucial precondition for "the rise of the west." No one would disagree with this, but, as I hope to show, states did many other things too, some helpful for growth, some not; and often they helped by doing nothing at all. Not however that we can yet issue declarative statements. I was favorably impressed by a casual remark by Eric Jones in the introduction to the second edition of his important *The European Miracle*. In the middle of a discussion on the role of the state, he noted that "the role of

---

[3] N. B. Harte, "State Control of Dress and Social Change in Pre-Industrial England," in D. C. Coleman and A. H. John, eds., *Trade, Government, and Economy in Pre-Industrial England* (London, 1976), 132–3.

government in economic development is thus more problematic than it seems."[4]

A focus on long-distance trade must not be allowed to blind us to the fact that vast areas of the early modern economy in both Europe and Asia were far outside the ken of government, except in the most indirect way. We are beginning now to understand the comparatively large extent of long-distance trade in such basics as rice and cloths in early modern Asia by both land and sea.[5] Peddling coastal trade done in small ships was often outside the cognizance of any political authority at all. In this largely anonymous and politically unregulated area, Europeans also participated on a basis of equality from the sixteenth century, fitting in as one more element in the complex fabric of early modern local trade in Asia, no different from the many other local and foreign groups and individuals who had done this trade for millenia. It was only in the command sectors, long-range trade in more valuable goods, that political figures participated, and when they could collected taxes, and even provided encouragement. This was also the arena where the official Europeans had their impact, where they participated, or even attempted monopolies.

The matter of terminology needs to be explicitly addressed. What, for example, is a "state," or a "government?" In Western Europe the problem begins to disappear as our period progresses, as local authorities and autonomies were curtailed or ended by advancing central governments, but in the fourteenth or fifteenth century the matter was still confused, and remained so in, say, India to the end of our period. Local power figures could still act independently, often in fact in defiance of the central government, most notably in fiscal matters such as collecting "illegal" tolls and transit duties. To be sure, central governments tried to curtail this, but often their efforts merely resulted in their recognizing these rights, in other words bestowing them on people who had them already. There is a large difference between a right created by a government, and a right recognized, either tacitly or more explicitly, by it, just as a clear distinction must be made between the position of a local authority figure who was appointed from above and from the outside, as compared with an existing locally rooted authority who was recognized by some central power. In early modern Europe, at least at first, a government could be an Italian city, a feudal principality, the Hanseatic League, or a more familiar empire or kingdom. Better perhaps to look at function,

[4] Jones, *European Miracle*, xxiv.
[5] For a recent case study, see S. Arasaratnam, "The Rice Trade in Eastern India, 1650–1740," *Modern Asian Studies* 22 (1988):531–50.

to see which person or body exercised coercive power, and could de facto at least allocate rights and collect taxes.

We need also to distinguish between despotic and interventionist governments. A despotic government has a more general character, and by definition is not freely chosen. An interventionist government may or may not be democratic, or rely on popular support. The first is perhaps more ideological than the latter, but we need to try and delineate very carefully how far the despotism penetrated. Was it just a matter of a cowed group of courtiers, or did the despotism impinge far down into society? An interventionist government was more discriminating. It intervened in defined areas of social, political, or economic life, it was less all-encompassing, more specific to selected sectors, than is a generally despotic government. A related problem is also important here, and will inform much of our discussion: this is the frequent gap between normative and actual behavior.[6] Early modern governments often made vast claims, expressed in decrees and fiats, that appeared to give them massive interventionist roles. Too often these central aspirations, set out in documents that have survived, have seduced historians and led them to believe that indeed these governments achieved all that they hoped to. But increasingly we are aware that many of these were aspirations only: expressions of intent, often benevolent, which however no early modern government could hope to make effective, if only because of the technological difficulties of enforcement in large states with primitive communications and rudimentary administrative machines.

The way to write global history that attempts to avoid invalid categories based on European experience has been brilliantly elucidated by Eric Wolf. Most relevant for our period is his concept of the "tributary mode of production." In this mode, political and military rulers extracted a surplus from primary producers, who in return for tribute were allowed access to the means of production. The central authority could be strong or weak, and the role of local power figures or intermediaries was correspondingly small or large. Where it was small, this mode is often described as an Asiatic mode, where large as feudal. But in fact these are merely "oscillations within the continuum of a single mode." Wolf acerbically comments that "Reification of 'feudalism' into a separate mode of production merely converts a short period of European history into a type case against which all other

[6] For a good discussion, see Huri Islamoglu and Caglar Keyder, "Agenda for Ottoman History," in Islamoglu-Inan, ed., *The Ottoman Empire*, 43–4; and M. N. Pearson, "Premodern Muslim Political Systems," *Journal of the American Oriental Society* 102 (1982): 47–58.

'feudal-like' phenomena must be measured. The concept of an Asiatic mode of production, in which a centralized state bureaucracy dominates unchanging village communities of hapless peasants, similarly suffers from an ahistorical and ideological reading of Asian history.'[7] Creative though Wolf's schema may be, it really is only a first step. He has transcended the problem of inappropriate transference of terminology, but at the expense of creating a category that is so all-encompassing as to have little heuristic value. The task now is to specify his "oscillations," to delineate important temporal and regional variations within the broad rubric of the tributary mode, and especially to recognize that the tributary *mode of production* included several different *systems of production* in different areas and historical times.

STATES AND ECONOMIES

Before turning to the precise question of overseas trade and the rise of merchant empires, it seems apposite to focus on the general question of the role of governments in economic development. This is, of course, a cosmic question, but an attempt at a global overview will help to put into context a more focused discussion of the role of long-distance trade. The basic point that justifies a fairly extended discussion of general state-economy connections is that long-distance trade cannot be taken as a discrete economic category. Government attitudes to it were conditioned by, often generally the same as, their attitudes to the economy generally.

European governments

In general accounts of European developments, such as those by Wolf, Jones, Wallerstein, Holton, Braudel, North and Thomas, and Baechler and his colleagues,[8] there is considerable agreement that the role of

---

[7] Eric R. Wolf, *Europe and the People without History* (Berkeley, 1982), 81–2.
[8] Wolf, *Europe*; Jones, *European Miracle*; Immanuel Wallerstein, *The Modern World-System*, (New York: 1974–89, 3 vols to date); Douglass C. North and Robert Paul Thomas, *The Rise of the Western World* (Cambridge, 1973); R. J. Holton, *The Transition from Feudalism to Capitalism* (London, 1985); Fernand Braudel, *Civilization and Capitalism, 15th–18th Century*, (3 vols., London, 1981–4). For a discussion of some of these works, especially Wallerstein, see M. N. Pearson, *Before Colonialism: Theories on Asian-European Relations, 1500–1750* (Delhi, 1988). Holton's excellent book provides a useful introduction to the literature, surveying works by Wallerstein, North and Thomas, Perry Anderson, Robert Brenner, Weber and Marx. He does not mention Wolf or Jones. He is particularly good when he discusses the unsatisfactory nature of nineteenth-century evolutionist universal theories. So there is and can be no transition

government is to clear away impediments and provide some basic infrastructure; an example is North and Thomas's stress on making legal contracts enforceable. Obstacles to development were many and various. Among them could be numbered excessive river tolls, which in backward Central Europe continued through the eighteenth century.[9] The Spanish *mesta* is often cited, or indicted, as a system where pastoralists, being nobles, dominated over more productive agrarian interests.[10] Guilds, backed by governments for fiscal reasons, imposed a dead hand on productive elements.[11] There were more subtle impediments too; Jones instances an excess of holy days, monasticism, and religious sanctions and restrictions.[12] These were eliminated in some countries, which had the largely unintended effect of giving the market a freer play.

This was not done by farsighted governments with coherent models of economic growth in their minds, but rather for quite pragmatic and even selfish reasons. Fiscalism, in the sense of "the attempt to raise money by any means that were to hand regardless of the social and

from feudalism to capitalism outside of Western Europe; nor is there any constantly valid and universal path from feudalism or any other mode to capitalism; nor is the development of capitalism a unilinear process governed by one prime mover. Even in Europe we need causal pluralism. Holton's overview is preferable to another recent effort, by Rosenberg and Birdzell, for they tend to see the economy as autonomous, and also to see Western growth and Third World poverty as essentially autonomous, with no connections between the two. See Nathan Rosenberg and L. E. Birdzell, Jr., *How The West Grew Rich: The Economic Transformation of the Industrial World* (New York, 1986). Finally, a very recent publication covers much of this ground in a stimulating way: Jean Baechler, John A. Hall, and Michael Mann, eds., *Europe and the Rise of Capitalism* (Blackwell, 1988). This collection is consciously comparative and global. Particular essays will be noted in subsequent footnotes, but it is fair to say that the overall thrust tends to agree with the present analysis. Most of them discuss connections between political power and economic change. Some of them, however, are dealing with very different periods from the early modern one I survey, and others try to explain why capitalism did not evolve in Asia; my concern is with the role of the state in economic change and development.

[9] C. H. Wilson, "Trade, Society and the State," in *The Cambridge Economic History of Europe*, vols. III–V (Cambridge, 1963–77), IV, 554; Karin Newman, "Hamburg in the European Economy, 1660–1750," *Journal of European Economic History*, 14 (1985):70–3; Jacques Bernard, "Trade and Finance in the Middle Ages, 900–1500," in Carlo Cipolla, ed., *The Fontana Economic History of Europe*, vols. I–III (London:1972–4), I, 313.

[10] Ralph Davis, *The Rise of the Atlantic Economies*, (Ithaca, 1973), 58.

[11] See North and Thomas, *Rise of the Western World*, 57, 126–7; A. B. Hibbert, "The Economic Policies of Towns," *Cambridge Economic History*, III, 157–229, esp. 198–229; C. H. Wilson, "Trade, Society, and the State" in ibid., IV, 491; Richard T. Rapp, "The Unmaking of the Mediterranean Trade Hegemony: International Trade Rivalry and the Commercial Revolution," *Journal of European Economic History*, 35 (1975): 514–15; M. W. Wood, "Paltry Peddlers or Essential Merchants? Women in the Distributive Trades in Early Modern Nuremberg," *The Sixteenth Century Journal* 12 (1981):4–8.

[12] Jones, *European Miracle*, 96.

economic consequences," was important right through our period.[13] The fiscal needs of the states determined that they trade off revenue for property rights, and indeed for other rights that also promoted growth, such as monopolies for trading companies, and a package of measures affecting trade summed up as mercantilism. The role of the government then, in successful countries like the Netherlands and England, was basically to provide the infrastructure, the preconditions, and thus give the market and economic forces the freedom to develop.

Similarly with the Industrial Revolution, where Supple's excellent summary stresses an important, but indirect, role for the English state, one restricted basically to providing some preconditions so that the market could function better. He finds generally that state action "may be needed to improve the 'non-economic' environment within which private agencies can allocate resources most effectively" and also provide parts of the necessary infrastructure that private enterprise cannot or will not undertake.[14]

It was not intervention per se that was important, but rather where it was directed. Positive intervention was designed to remove restrictive elements such as moribund guilds, and instead encourage, even legislate for, productive activity. The English wool trade was protected throughout, not surprising when around 1500 close to one-half of English government revenue came from taxes on external trade, in which wool was overwhelmingly dominant. Regulation in such developing countries as England and the Netherlands could be minute. To protect the English salmon fishing industry, it was decreed in 1714 that salmon were to be caught only between the beginning of August and 11 November. River salmon had to weigh at least six pounds. Similarly, lobsters had to be at least eight inches. The Dutch also laid down the extent of the fishing season, and even specified what type of salt was to be used.[15] English government policy affected the consumption of, and so trade in, such staples as tea and port wine. There was also some regulation in the interest of prevailing notions of eco-

---

[13] Betty Behrens, "Government and Society," in *Cambridge Economic History*, V, 578–9; B. A. Holderness, *Pre-Industrial England: Economy and Society, 1500–1750* (London, 1976), 173, 179–80.

[14] Barry Supple, "The State and the Industrial Revolution, 1700–1914," in Cipolla, ed., *Fontana Economic History*, III, 303; also 301–2, 315.

[15] W.M. Stern, "Fish Marketing in London in the First Half of the Eighteenth Century," in Coleman and Johns, eds., *Trade, Government, and Economy in Pre-Industrial England* 69—70; Charles Wilson, *Profit and Power: A Study of England and the Dutch Wars.* (2d ed., The Hague, 1978), 33; see also W. M. Stern, "Where, oh Where, Are the Cheesemongers of London?" *The London Journal* 5 (1979):228–48.

nomic justice, such as antimonopoly laws directed against the Fuggers.

The assumption is that growth only resulted when the opportunities provided by the government were taken up. Conversely, however, without these sorts of government policies growth was hampered or even blocked completely. Kriedte provides a useful summary of the whole matter. The state, not the feudal structure, because of the monopoly of violence that it claimed and slowly made effective, was able to "impose wage labour conditions upon the productive sphere, institutionally to guarantee the freedom of exchange of goods in the commercial sphere and, finally to formalize the legal framework without which the nascent capitalist society would not have been able to exist. Also, by expanding the transport infrastructure it promoted the general conditions required in an economy which produced goods for the market."[16]

The European state system

Another element of commonalty among scholars is the notion that these changes can only occur in a state system. No one has tried to quantify how big is too big, but the general idea is that the competitive state system of Europe was a vital variable because it led to healthy competition, and because only in units of this size were rulers forced to concede rights for revenue. As Jones and Wallerstein stress,[17] there were important interstate economic and social connections also. Further, in a state system, persecuted minorities could move and fulfil their potential in a different country. In an empire this was not possible, or at least such minorities had to move a very long way, such as the escape of most of Persia's Zoroastrians to India.

Take the position of Jews in several European countries. In the medieval period, discrimination against them in Western Europe had, as is well known, led to their assuming important roles in commerce, a process reified by Curtin as that of "cross-cultural brokers."[18] According to Wallerstein, the later waves of expulsions are to be seen

---

[16] Peter Kriedte, *Peasants, Landlords, and Merchant Capitalists: Europe and the World Economy, 1500–1800*, (Cambridge, 1983), 16.

[17] See also John A. Hall, "States and Societies: The Miracle in Comparative Perspectives," in Baechler, *Europe and the Rise of Capitalism*; and Holton, *Transition from Feudalism to Capitalism*, esp. 169–87, 203–5, for an excellent overview of the importance of the development of the state, and of a landed society; and 206–18 for a discussion of the importance of competitive states and exogenous influences, a discussion that curiously does not refer to Jones's earlier and very similar analysis.

[18] Philip D. Curtin, *Cross-Cultural Trade in World History*, (Cambridge, 1984).

not as essentially ideological or religious, but as part of a process aiming to homogenize the populations of these states, this in turn being part of the process of creating strong states in core areas. The expulsion of Jews from Spain had important, and deleterious, economic consequences; in 1492 some 150,000 were expelled, mostly from the south, where they had been important traders and artisans.

The Portuguese case is rather different. Those who chose not to convert were expelled at the end of the fifteenth century, and the confiscation of their goods provided capital for the Crown and possibly also opened up even more opportunities for nonindigenous financiers, notably those from Genoa. Conversion was much more of a possibility in Portugal than in Spain, and the Portuguese did not check too closely into its sincerity. But New Christians remained objects of suspicion and derision, and subject to the Inquisition. Thus vulnerable, in the sixteenth and seventeenth centuries crypto-Jews in Portugal were milch cows who could be milked at will.

The reverse of expulsions and prohibitions was that more tolerant states within a system received well-qualified or rich strangers and did well as a result, while bigotry could deny entry to economically useful minorities.[19] Cipolla stresses the vital role played in England by immigrants fleeing religious persecution in the period 1550–1650, especially French Huguenots and Walloons.[20] The Dutch did well from an enlightened attitude on religious matters. Although there was intolerance at home, all foreigners regardless of religion were welcomed. This brought great benefits up to the formal recognition of independence in 1648, and again after the revocation of the Edict of Nantes.[21] Hamburg has also been cited as an example of tolerance leading to benefits; similarly to the United Provinces, after the revocation of the Edict of Nantes several notable French Protestants moved there.[22] Yet, although the revocation may have benefited host areas, a major study of its economic impact on France claims that this politico-religious action did not have a sizable economic effect. French stagnation in the late seventeenth and early eighteenth centuries was not a result of the revocation.[23]

---

[19] For example, Richard Conquest, "The State and Commercial Expansion: England in the Years 1642–1688," *Journal of European Economic History* 14 (1985):165.

[20] Carlo M. Cipolla, *Before the Industrial Revolution: European Society and Economy, 1000–1700*, (2d ed., London, 1981), 283–5.

[21] B. H. Slicher van Bath, "The Economic Situation in the Dutch Republic during the Seventeenth Century," in Maurice Aymard, ed., *Dutch Capitalism and World Capitalism* (Cambridge, 1982), 27.

[22] K. Newman, "Hamburg in the European Economy," 83–4.

[23] Warren C. Scoville, *The Persecution of Huguenots and French Economic Development,*

The role of warfare

If, then, suspect minorities do better in a state system, can it be argued that a problem with states is that there is more chance of war within the system? What can be said of this general problem of the economic consequences of violence? There seem to be, analytically, two categories. There was obviously war done by a state or state agency, and this could include privateering. These wars might be waged for various reasons, not all of them economic, but my concern at present is not with the causes as much as with the economic consequences of war. State-sanctioned violence, waged for state concerns, needs to be differentiated from disorder, that is, violence not sanctioned by the state. This includes piracy correctly defined, that is, armed attacks at sea by ships that have no claim to operate on behalf of any government, and robbery or brigandage on land.[24] The sequence over our period was of states trying to limit the second category, in other words reserving to themselves a monopoly of the use of force and military coercion. Such an attempt has often been depicted as part of the creation of more effective and "modern" states, just as these states also tried to reduce the power of alternative sources of political and fiscal influence.

The achievement of this sort of monopoly was clearly a prime necessity for economic growth. True that a state could be extortionate in the extreme, yet its actions generally would be more predictable, and usually more subject to influence from commercial groups, among others, than would the actions of uncontrolled robbers, leviers of illegal tolls, and bandits in general. Indeed the point has often been made that states provided law and order, and other prerequisites for commerce and trade, and in return received taxation revenue. Protection costs were thus subsumed into general taxation payment, as compared with being separate and specific, as was the case, say, with caravans crossing the deserts of the Middle East, or local Asian traders paying the Portuguese in order not to be attacked by them.

Wars had to be paid for, and this could lead to increased taxation or government loans. In the short term, at least the latter option was most likely, for armies had to be paid at once or else they deserted. Raising extra revenue from taxation took time; loans, forced or oth-

1680–1720, (Berkeley, 1960). Recently Menna Prestwich, in "The Revocation of the Edict of Nantes," *History* 73, no. 237 (1988):73, claims that Scoville's conclusions "remain intact."

[24] For an extended discussion of piracy, see the chapter in this volume by Anne Pérotin-Dumon.

erwise, could be used instantly. As European armies increased in size between about 1500 and 1700[25] so too did government spending. (This is not to say, of course, that growing state penetration in the sixteenth and seventeenth centuries was a consequence of changes in military techniques and technology; the reverse seems to be the case.) The economic consequences have been much studied. In England between 1542 and 1550, some £450,000 was spent each year on wars with France and Scotland, at a time when the Crown's revenues were only £200,000 a year. The gap was filled by the sale of about two-thirds of the church lands recently confiscated by Henry VIII and by loans and higher taxes.[26] By the seventeenth century, however, the Crown was weaker in England, and was no longer allowed to spend huge sums on war.[27]

The immediate impact of war is a matter of controversy. It may be that the classical picture, derived I think from the English Civil War, of peasants continuing to plow while the agents of the elite battled in the next field, is too simple. K. N. Chaudhuri in an Asian context stresses the deleterious effects of wars, which extended right down in society.[28] Nonparticipants may not have been attacked directly, but they still could suffer. It has been claimed that premodern armies on the march were usually far more efficient in destroying crops and spreading disease, as well as commandeering livestock, than they were in waging war. At least in part as a result of Louis XIV's wars, France suffered great famines in 1692–4 and 1709–10, in which between 10 and 20 percent of the population died. The Thirty Years' War was notoriously devastating.[29]

ASIAN EMPIRES

A geographic area covered by an empire by definition did not have interstate wars. If this was a plus for an empire, the general question is then exactly what was wrong with being an empire? Were they inherently antithetical to the sorts of developments stressed especially

[25] Under Louis XII the French Crown had some 30,000 or 40,000 troops; under Louis XIV nearly 300,000. See Domenico Sella, "European Industries, 1500–1700," in C. Cipolla, ed., *Fontana Economic History*, II, 384–8; and Geoffrey Parker, *The Military Revolution: Military Innovation and the Rise of the West, 1500–1800*, (Cambridge, 1988), 45–6.

[26] Parker, *Military Revolution*. 62.

[27] R. Davis, *Rise of the Atlantic Economies*, 209–11.

[28] K. N. Chaudhuri, *Trade and Civilization in the Indian Ocean: An Economic History from the Rise of Islam to 1750*, (Cambridge, 1985), 33.

[29] Kriedte, *Peasants, Landlords, and Merchant Capitalists*, 61–2; R. Davis, *Rise of the Atlantic Economies*, 229; C. Cipolla, *Before the Industrial Revolution*, 135.

by Jones? Here it seems is where the Asian experience is relevant. What we find is that the crucial variables were revenue needs and resources, class structures, and ideological inputs, these last no doubt powerfully affected by the former. All of these were affected by the degree of heterogeneity of the population, and the degree to which either a common ethic or military force could integrate these populations.

Mughal India

The familiar case of Mughal India can be taken first. No apology is needed for this. A vast empire, with a standard of living comparable to Europe at the same time, with a population of over 100 million in 1600, and later as it expanded much more, an area acting as the center or fulcrum of a vast trading network all over the Indian Ocean (the Indian Ocean being, according to Wallerstein, a world economy or at least proto-world economy),[30] an empire where the ruler around 1600 had an income some twenty-five times that of James I of England; this is no trivial object of comparison! What then can be said of the role of government in economic development here?[31]

This was a state that played a very minor role indeed. There were reasons for this. Most important, the revenue needs of the empire, vast though they were, could be met from massive amounts of land revenue collected by a rather articulated and efficient chain of government officials. What could be easier than to tax a peasant population numbering many tens of millions, who by definition had to stay put and so could easily be taxed? Merchants, by nature mobile, were much less easy to get at. The amounts collected are a matter of debate. The dominant Aligarh school claims the state extracted a

---

[30] Pearson, *Before Colonialism*, 51–68; R. Palat, et al., "The Incorporation and Peripheralization of South Asia, 1600–1950," *Review* 10 (1986): 171–208.

[31] There has recently been much debate over the precise penetration of the Mughal state into Indian society, some seeing it as massive, others as minor. For the former claim, see the works of Irfan Habib, a recent example being "Classifying Pre-Colonial India," in T. J. Byres and H. Mukhia, eds., *Feudalism and Non-European Societies*, (London, 1985), 44–53, where *inter al.* he makes the extraordinary claim that towns and commerce in Mughal India "were then entirely dependent on the system of state-enforced agrarian exploitation," and he also talks of "centralised despotism" (48); for the latter, see M. N. Pearson, "Land, Noble and Ruler in Mughal India," in Edmund Leach, S. N. Mukherjee, and John Ward, eds., *Feudalism: Comparative Studies*, (Sydney, 1985), 175–96, or M. N. Pearson, *Merchants and Rulers in Gujarat: The Response to the Portuguese in the Sixteenth Century*, (Berkeley, 1976), chap. 6; and for an overview, which tends to support me rather than Habib, see Sanjay Subrahmanyam, "Aspects of State Formation in South India and Southeast Asia, 1500–1650," *Indian Economic and Social History Review* 23 (1986): 357–77.

colossal one-third or even one-half of the agricultural product. The sources on which this seemingly extravagant claim is based are mostly the normative accounts of the officials themselves, and these may express aspiration rather than real accomplishment. Were we to use bottom-up sources, such as inscriptions, we might get a very different picture of state revenue extraction, and state power in general. A further complication was that state power was geographically specific, in the sense that areas near the center, the *doab* in northern India, were much more tightly controlled and taxed than were more remote, and less productive, areas.[32]

Nevertheless, there is agreement that the state did extract vast amounts, as was witnessed by the obvious wealth and ostentation of the court, on which seventeenth-century European visitors commented in awe, and by the way vast resources of bullion could be released as military needs became more pressing later in the seventeenth century. It may be noted here, however, that Mughal India's ultimately destabilizing military campaigns from the second half of the seventeenth century, notably against the Marathas, are a prime example of the sort of inefficiencies that Wallerstein found to be characteristic of world empires. A single political entity, no matter how loosely integrated, must respond to such challenges. An India divided into several states, not necessarily nation states, could have ignored the Marathas, and let them control at least their remote and unproductive home area. Yet we must also remember that there was a pronounced tendency for merchants to ignore the wars of the elites, and trade on regardless. It is interesting that this was done not only by Indian merchants but also by Portuguese ones. In a period before the voracious demands for loyalty of the nation-state were in effect, wars were seen as something to be done by, and to effect, only the politico-military elite.

How can we explain the success of the revenue-raising efforts of the Mughals, and what were the consequences? The achievement was based on military and administrative effectiveness, with apparently an ideological underpinning. From the point of view of the state, its role was to protect the land and Islam. In return, it collected a share of the product of the land. This is of course a familiar enough equation. Those actually using the land did so under conditions of security, but with the obligation to pay one-third or more to the ruler in recompense.

[32] Yet, this said, the discussion in Shireen Moosvi, *The Economy of the Mughal Empire c. 1595: A Statistical Study* (Delhi, 1987), 126–49, is probably as convincing as we will ever get, and she broadly supports the earlier findings of her Aligarh colleagues.

The structure of the empire is best seen as consisting of a prebendal ruling group clustered around the emperor and bound to him by ties of patronage and more nebulous symbolic bonds, which were consciously promoted. This upper circle interfaced with locally grounded elites whose power was essentially patrimonial, and who were known as *zamindars*, literally land holders. Several levels of *zamindars* collected and passed on the land revenue until it reached the bottom of the prebendal hierarchy and passed into state control. This system seems to have worked relatively well, and was backed up by armed force. One of the prime objects of this sort of state, or indeed any state, was to secure a monopoly over the use of force. Mughal India's achievement here was only partial, a result it seems of the vast size of the empire, or, if one likes, the fact that it was an empire, not a state. *Zamindars* continued to have their own troops. The state, through lack of choice, tolerated this, but only if they were used to extract revenue from peasants and then pass this on to the state. If local troops were used to try and retain more than the accepted percentage of revenue, then centrally controlled armies were used to curb them. The central army, mostly levies raised by office holders, was overwhelmingly dominant, limited only by the size and diversity of the vast empire it tried to control.

The effects of this vast extraction of resources are difficult to portray.[33] Part of it was simply hoarded. Some was spent on extravagant consumption, though the effects of this are not really so easy to evaluate. The basic question is to try and work out whether or not the sums spent on monuments and luxuries were relatively large. In the case of Mughal India, they were not. The most celebrated monument of the empire, the Taj Mahal, was built over a period of seventeen years, and each year took less than 0.5 percent of the total revenue of the empire.

About 80 percent of the revenue collected by the state never went near the central treasuries,[34] but instead was allocated to officeholders as their salary, and to enable them to keep up their fixed quota of troops. From most of the land of the empire, revenue was collected from *zamindars* by agents of office holders, in accordance with centrally defined norms, and in cooperation with centrally appointed lower

---

[33] Our best quantitative evidence comes from Shireen Moosvi's recent book, *The Economy of the Mughal Empire*. She finds that, of the total agrarian surplus, *zamindars* took about one-fifth. The state took 60 percent of the total claimed land revenue, with the rest going to other right holders, that is *zamindars* primarily, and the costs of collection; see chaps. 5 and 7.

[34] Ibid., 272. And after this 80 percent, some 14 percent went for royal military and household expenses with the remainder being hoarded.

officials. And the officeholders spent about two-thirds of their receipts on maintaining their contingents. It became in fact a circular and essentially unproductive process, where revenue was used to pay troops who ensured the revenue was collected.

What role did merchants play in all this? Wolf's sketch is basically correct, if only because it is so general.[35] An important modification is the distinction between tribute and revenue payment, with the latter representing a considerable advance in terms of regularity and efficiency. There were variations in the way land revenue was collected, circulated and distributed. The elite very seldom consumed all the surplus, and similarly it was very unusual for officials to do all the actual collection and circulation of this surplus. Rather this surplus, together with its actual collection and transfer, was where commercial intermediaries played their role. Mercantile activity and tributary relationships were symbiotic. Mughal India was more bureaucratized than were many other states with tributary modes (so that, for example, at its height tax-farming was not common) and this decreased the role of the merchants. They played a part in collecting the revenue, in that they converted the actual crop into money with which peasants could pay their tax, they moved necessities like food around India, they imported bullion, they provided luxuries (significantly referred to in the English records as "toys") for the court, and they functioned in the interstices of the system to provide occasional financial services for the elite.[36] All of these functions, however, were undertaken for sound commercial reasons; and, though some had implications for the state, these did not establish any connection between economic and political power similar to that emerging in Western Europe at the same time.

Their major role was far away from the state. In their basic activities of exchanging, financing, and trading, they operated under conditions of freedom by and large. In these mercantile activities, they often did very well indeed. Seventeenth-century European accounts expatiate on the probity, and on the wealth, of India's great mer-

---

[35] I consider that Wolf's account of the role of merchants in the tributary mode is his main contribution. As regards the basic notion of the tributary mode, a little-known article by Kate Currie, "Problematic Modes and the Mughal State Formation," *The Insurgent Sociologist*, 9–21 anticipated his basic schema, though he does not list her work in his bibliography. But Currie, like for example Byres et al. (Byres and Mukhia, eds., *Feudalism and Non-European Societies*) and many others, is weak on the facilitative role of merchant groups within the tributary mode; here is where Wolf is truly innovative.

[36] For more on two merchant groups in India, see Irfan Habib's chapter in the preceding volume in this series, *The Rise of Merchant Empires*.

chants, some of whom could have bought and sold the European trading companies of the time. Older depictions of them being subjected to random or even routine extortion by members of the elite are wide of the mark. Professor Habib in his chapter in *The Rise of Merchant Empires* writes of the "indifferent neutrality" of the state toward merchants; there was no state support for them, but neither was there much oppression. The basic environment was one of openness and free competition.[37] Indeed, this land-based empire demanded very little revenue from them. Customs duties were low, about 5 percent ad valorem. Apart from this there were inland duties to be paid, some sanctioned by the state and some extorted by local controllers of passes and river crossings. These seem to have been relatively routine also, even if "illegal." Most *zamindars* controlling a choke point seem to have been too shrewd to risk their golden eggs by charging excessive rates.[38] Protection costs thus seem to be low. Some of them were met by merchants, others by state authorities who tried to curtail these instances of local autonomy. Those merchants who traded by sea, a minority, were in a rather different position, as we will see later.

It is quite incorrect to talk of a routine relationship between the state and the merchant. The only regular interaction that involved all merchants was the payment of various taxes. These, as noted, were low, and were usually collected by heads from within particular merchant groups who functioned in a role precisely analogous to that of *zamindars*. The merchant head, a person recognized by but not appointed by the state, then passed on the proceeds to an agent of the state. In juridical matters also, merchants had considerable autonomy, just as in medieval Europe; enforcement of contracts was done between the parties concerned, or between representative bodies encompassing the parties. The difference is that in Europe guilds were backed up by governments; in India merchant groups were not. A dispute between a cloth merchant and a supplier would be settled between these two individuals, or by the heads of occupationally specific groups of cloth merchants and cloth suppliers. It was only in extraordinary cases where a resolution was not reached that the state-appointed network of *qazis* had a role, especially because the vast

---

[37] For a good survey, see Tapan Raychaudhuri, "The State and the Economy: the Mughal Empire," in *The Cambridge Economic History of India*, (vol. I, Cambridge, 1981), 172–93.

[38] See ibid., 187–8, for a perhaps slightly exaggerated account of exactions on inland trade routes.

majority of India's merchants and artisans, like the whole population, were not Muslim.[39] Similarly, the state sometimes tried to provide security for dealers in credit, but here again the main enforcement mechanism did not involve the state. The credit system worked because it depended heavily on a reputation for honesty, rather than on any legal system.[40]

There are some obvious contrasts to be made with the situation in that part of Europe that was undergoing important changes at this time. The Mughals were concerned to reduce the independent power of local figures, just as were the new monarchies.[41] They were, however, less successful, a result mostly of environmental factors, in other words the size and complexity of the empire. In any case, their motivation for this seems to have been more a matter of prestige than of fiscal necessity. The basic problem was that the Mughals had too much money to need to trade off revenue for rights as European rulers had to do. Nor, unlike in China, was there any ideologically backed reason for them to get involved in the economy. The land-oriented ethos, and more important the source of most of their revenue, was too influential; there was no crisis of feudalism in India because the Mughal version of the tributary mode of production was more viable. Let me stress that this is not to say that the "East" was static and immobile and ahistorical. There were changes and movement; most obviously, the empire began to collapse in the second half of the seventeenth century; overseas trade certainly expanded greatly in this century; there was constant tension and jockeying for advan-

---

[39] This case is more fully set out in my *Merchants and Rulers in Gujarat*, chaps. 5 and 6. Although I no longer stand by everything in this piece of juvenalia, and in particular I now see merchants playing an important integrating role, I still like the basic schema sketched in chap. 6.

[40] Raychaudhuri in *Cambridge Economic History of India*, I, 347. We should note here a small debate over the role of "Great Firms" in Mughal India. Karen Leonard put forward a claim that these played a crucial role both in the functioning and decline of the empire. The reply by J. F. Richards was much more convincing; so far we have no evidence of these "Great.Firms" operating in the way described by Leonard in the sixteenth or seventeenth centuries. See Karen Leonard, "The Great Firm' Theory of the Decline of the Mughal Empire," *Comparative Studies in Society and History* 21 (1979): p. 151–67; a reply by J. F. Richards, "Mughal State Finance and the Premodern world economy," in the same journal, 23 (1981): p. 285–308, followed by Leonard, "Indigenous Banking Firms in Mughal India: A Reply," 309–13.

[41] I have sketched elsewhere a case for seeing the Mughals as concerned not only with horizontal expansion, but also with a limited amount of vertical expansion. These attempts, mostly unsuccessful, consisted of trying to keep more of the surplus for themselves, and reducing the role of the intermediaries or *zamindars*. See Pearson, "Land, Noble, and Ruler in Mughal India," in Leach et al., eds., *Feudalism: Comparative Studies*, p. 188–93.

tage between the state on the one hand and the intermediary layer on the other. But these were generically different changes and tensions from those occurring in Western Europe at the same time.

The Mughal state did take some measures to facilitate the working of this system; these were all to do with the land, and no doubt had an ideological dimension also in that a good ruler was one who ruled over a prosperous land populated by sleek and contented peasants. The state gave incentives for bringing new land into cultivation,[42] and sometimes sponsored the construction of new villages. In a land where the frontier was still open, peasants sometimes were forbidden to move. And the state sometimes did things that look like infrastructural development. A few canals and *caravansarais* were built, charity was dispensed in time of famine, and an attempt was made to provide security for travelers. These are, however, rather different from equivalent efforts in Europe. They were done either for the reasons of the state alone (such as to facilitate troop movements or the royal post system), with no thought to their possibly beneficial effects for commercial life; or they were done by people high in the state to be sure, but on an individual basis. These actions then were similar to the dispensation of charity at the time. Rich people, many of whom in this sort of system were members of the political elite, had a perceived obligation to help the less fortunate in time of distress; this, however, was done on a personalized basis, not a routine governmental one. As Marshall Hodgson put it in a general Islamic context, charitable actions were "looked on as private benevolence by the caliph or the vizier; benevolence incumbent on them no doubt, but as rich men rather than as officials."[43] Obviously there are flaws in such a personalized method of social security and infrastructural development, and similarly with the personal dispensation of justice, as seen in the common provision of a bell rope on the palace wall that when rung would immediately summon the ruler to give justice.

One aspect of the security of contracts, government backing of an economically productive legal system, is the development of a state-enforced system of private property in land. In England this change began as early as the thirteenth century, when we can find the be-

---

[42] This was done especially by providing loans and tax remissions so that peasants would repair embankments and excavate canals, but, as Habib notes, these efforts were not very important to the state, and the effects were only marginal. Habib in Byres and Mukhia, *Feudalism and Non-European Societies*; 48.

[43] Marshall G. S. Hodgson, *The Venture of Islam*, (3 vols., Chicago, 1974), I, 292–4. For a precise European comparison, concerning Charles the Good, see H. van Werveke, The Economic Policies of Towns: The Low Countries," in *Cambridge Economic History of Europe*, III, 341.

ginnings of the notion of private property in land, including the right to transfer it.[44] Mughal India had no such system. The effects of this have been much debated. A French doctor, François Bernier, after an extended stay in India (1659 to 1667), expatiated on the evils of the Mughal system, where there was no security of tenure and an arbitrary government could dispossess an occupant at any time.[45] Regrettably, this account was taken at face value by Marx, and has been influential on some of his followers.

In fact, there was privately owned land in Mughal India, at least in the cities; we have some mortgage and sale documents to prove this. Nevertheless, the vast bulk of the land was agricultural, and was held, not owned, by peasant cultivators. As noted, they paid a share of their produce to the state in return for being allowed to hold and use their land. The question here is whether the lack of private ownership along the lines on which it had evolved in the West was necessarily detrimental. It has been claimed that peasants who have *title* to the land can then use the land to obtain credit, as had been quite common in Western Europe since the twelfth century. Nevertheless, the key thing was not to be subject to arbitrary dispossession, regardless of the legal basis on which the land was held. If this be accepted, then the Mughal system seems to be not much different from, nor worse than, the European. Certainly there was nothing to stop a peasant from improving the land; indeed, the state sometimes encouraged this. The frontier was still open, so that peasants, far from being subject to expropriation, were in fact stroked by land controllers, and even encouraged to move from the land of one to another. We are sometimes told that power in India consists of control over land, and the people on it; this seems to be correct at least for our period. Thus, even apart from ideological barriers to oppressing peasants, there were sound pragmatic reasons to foster them and keep them happy. The issue of land ownership seems to be irrelevant in this context.

Bernier's depiction of the Mughal state was based on his experiences as a doctor at court, just as so many later historians look out from the perspective of the elite. The people he saw being dispossessed were the officeholders, or *mansabdars*. What he saw in fact was an Indian, or indeed Muslim, refinement of the tributary mode of production that was different from the operation of this mode in its feudal European variant. Mughal *mansabdars* were paid by being allocated

---

[44] North and Thomas, *Rise of the Western World*, p. 63–4.
[45] François Bernier, *Travels in the Mogul Empire*, (London, 1914).

by the emperor areas of land called *jagirs*, from which they collected the land revenue due to the state. Thus, over most of the empire the people who collected the land revenue were agents of *jagirdars*, and the revenue collected was used to pay them and their troops and staff. Only a relatively small amount of land was *khalsa*, or Crown land, where the revenue was collected by central officials and deposited in the state treasury. This method had some advantages, and at least one disadvantage. This was that, if *jagirdars* collected the revenue of an area, and also were the government officials administering this area, then there was a danger that they would acquire too much local power and finally be tempted to become independent. Such fissiparousness was a constant problem in Islamic agrarian empires.

To counter this threat, the Mughals did two things. First, they usually allocated *mansabdars jagirs* in areas other than that where they were the government agent. Second, nobles normally had their *jagirs*, and also their areas of governmental authority, transferred every three years. Thus, their tendency to build up local support was checked. Some have claimed this led to the nobles being extortionate, for if they were in an area for only three years they had no interest in long-term economic development but rather would squeeze the area and its peasants for all they were worth before their inevitable transfer. Such a claim, however, seems to be covertly racist, implying that all Mughal officials were inherently extortionate, and in any case is contradicted by the facts. We have little evidence of such extortion, and when it did occur the state, or the emperor, usually took prompt action to stop it. In any case, Bernier simply saw *jagirdars* being transferred and assumed that deleterious consequences followed. He, and those who have used his account since, are mistaken.

A modern follower of Bernier, W. H. Moreland, went even further than him and claimed that there was a rule of escheat in Mughal India; the property of nobles, and even merchants, was taken over by the state when they died. Apart from being unfair, this meant that there was no reason for nobles to invest in productive enterprises, for all would go when they died. Instead, they aimed to spend up to or beyond their incomes, there being no point in leaving anything behind them. If true, such a phenomenon was in direct contrast with the sort of legally guaranteed rights enjoyed in Europe; escheat in fact was the very reverse of government guaranteeing property rights that promoted economic efficiency. But this claim, which has had some influence on later writers, is totally false. Occasionally the state would sequester the property of nobles when they died until their debts to the state had been paid, but we have copious evidence of many nobles leaving large estates to their heirs, as did merchants.

Other Asian empires

For reasons of space, and a certain lack of expertise, our discussion of other non-European economies, and state impacts on them, will be much more synoptic than was the case for Mughal India. In any case, we have already made clear that we follow Wolf in seeing virtually all of Asia as being encompassed within a tributary mode of production. In many respects, the Mughal Indian data above can stand as a model that applies to all other areas. We will simply sketch some themes that appear from the literature on the Ottoman Empire and China, with a very brief side glance at Mamluk Egypt. The selection is, of course, arbitrary enough, yet I think it will suffice to make some general points. Smaller political units, such as the trade-dominated port cities of both India and Southeast Asia, will be discussed when the focus turns to trade alone. Arguably these states were too small, too lacking in indigenous resources, to have any chance of producing the sorts of changes that occurred in some states of Western Europe.

We can start by considering the Middle East, and specifically the Ottoman Empire. When we discussed Mughal India, we said little about ideological attitudes from the state impacting directly on merchants because in a society where the majority of the population were not Muslim the attitude of Islam to commerce seemed to be largely irrelevant. The Ottoman Empire, however, was a much more thoroughly Islamic state.

Unlike in Christianity, where traders and merchants had a low ideological position, their status in Islam was much more positive. Islam, or at least the tenets of the *Quran* and the sayings of the Prophet, was not inimical to commerce, nor indeed to capitalist development.[46] It is true that *riba*, the taking of interest on loans, was prohibited. Historically this seems to have been a result of the Prophet's problems with Medina's Jews, and in any case it could be circumvented by *commenda* and partnership arrangements, or indeed simply ignored.[47] Inalcik has shown how in Middle Eastern premodern societies three productive classes were recognized: farmers (*sc.* peasants), merchants, and craftsmen, with the last named being lower

---

[46] Maxime Rodinson, *Islam and Capitalism*, (London, 1977).
[47] A. L. Udovitch, *Partnership and Profit in Medieval Islam*, (Princeton, 1970).

in status than the first two. This position for merchants was bolstered, or perhaps caused, by basic Islamic doctrine. The *Quran*, reflecting Muhammad's own experience as a merchant, contains several *suras* recommending and encouraging merchant activity, and the Prophet himself is quoted as saying, "The merchant enjoys the felicity both of this world and the next" and, even more bluntly, "He who makes money pleases God."

This leads us into the matter of Ottoman intervention in the economy in general. Some of the historiography presents a very different picture from what we have just sketched for Mughal India. In the late sixteenth century, Jean Bodin wrote: "The king of the Turks is called the grand seigneur, not because of the size of his realm . . . but because he is complete master of its persons and property."[48] McGowan points out that to the extent that the Ottomans were interested in the economy, as opposed to mere fiscalism, their first priority was to ensure food supplies for Constantinople. This seems unexceptional, but he then goes on to claim that this "staple policy" was but one element in a command economy that also included price controls, controls over cráft guilds and merchants, a system of service villages and service groups, a commodity purchase scheme, and a prohibition on the export of war matériel and specie. He then, thankfully, backs off a little by acknowledging that this command economy has not yet been well specified.[49]

Inalcik goes even further. There were two groups in the Ottoman population: the rulers and the ruled. All classes were obliged to preserve and promote the power of the ruler. To increase their revenue, states developed economic activity and increased production, and to achieve this "all political and social institutions and all types of economic activity were regulated by the state"![50]

A much more sophisticated collection of essays in part seems to bolster these claims of a genuine Oriental Despotism.[51] Islamoglu-Inan is critical of the whole notion of an Asiatic Mode of Production,

---

[48] Quoted in Perry Anderson, *Lineages of the Absolutist State*, (London, 1974), p. 398.

[49] B. McGowan, *Economic Life in Ottoman Turkey: Taxation, Trade, and the Struggle for Land, 1600–1800*, (Cambridge, 1980), p. 11.

[50] Halil Inalcik, *The Ottoman Empire: Conquest, Organization, and Economy*, (London; 1978), p. v, 53–4.

[51] See Huri Islamoglu-Inan, ed., *The Ottoman Empire and the World Economy*. This collection marks a qualitative improvement in the literature available in English on the Ottomans. It is also important in terms of theory, for it is consciously oriented to Wallerstein's world-system theories, and makes clear the very great value of his work.

and of depictions of Ottoman society such as those of Gibb and Bowen, which are seen as "Orientalist."[52] Instead, it is claimed that "the state was the dominant structure that served to integrate the society and the economy," though this power group "had to reconcile its interests with those of other groups through the forging of ideological unity between the different groups."[53]

A whole range of evidence serves to modify these extravagant depictions. Merely to think of the extent of this empire in the sixteenth century, stretching to Basra, Aden, and far along the Maghreb and into southeastern Europe, is to raise doubts about how effective it could be. In empires of this size, the distinction between center and periphery is important, as it was in Mughal India. Thus, a case study by Islamoglu-Inan[54] indeed shows a very extensive penetration by the state into peasant society, one apparently much more massive than anything the Mughals achieved, but the point is that this was in Anatolia, the center in other words.[55] Whether this degree of penetration was realized in other parts of this vast empire is very much open to question. The administrative system seems to have been no better nor more efficient than that of Mughal India. Such inflated accounts of Ottoman effectiveness often seem to be derived from normative, top-down, accounts generated at court, and expressing not reality but aspiration. In theory the sultan was absolute, but in practice his aim, only partially achieved, was to preserve his rule and collect taxes from peasants as best he and his agents could. Indeed, this lack of fit between normative prescriptions and actual practice is acknowledged in the Islamoglu-Inan collection itself.[56]

The role of two social groupings in the empire serves to modify further the prevailing view. One was groupings called *millets*, semi-autonomous religiously based groups, including the overwhelmingly dominant Muslims, which enjoyed a considerable degree of internal authority in such matters as taxation collection, the settlement of legal disputes, and regulation generally of the lives of their members. Similarly with the Ottoman version of guilds. These appear to have been slightly more controlled by the state than was the case in Mughal

---

[52] See ibid., p. 3, 4–5, 45.
[53] Ibid., p. 19, 20; see also p. 48–51, 66–7.
[54] "State and Peasant in the Ottoman Empire: A Study of Peasant Economy in North-central Anatolia during the Sixteenth Century," in ibid., 101–59.
[55] As noted, the collection is oriented to Wallerstein's theory. It would be interesting to see whether his basic notion of core and periphery could be applied within one political unit, whether it be Ottoman Turkey or Mughal India.
[56] Huri Islamoglu-Inan, ed., *The Ottoman Empire and the World Economy*, 43–4.

India, but they still could set their own prices and chose their own heads.[57] It is possible that historians have been led astray by the fact that in the case of both *millets* and merchant and artisan groupings the head was recognized by the state. But there is a major difference between a state recognizing a leader who had evolved out of and been chosen by the members of a particular religious or occupational group, and a situation where a state had the power to impose a leader, perhaps from outside, onto such groups.

Other particular evidence makes me even more dubious about accepting the vast claims in Islamoglu-Inan's excellent collection. In the same book, Faroqhi presents a much different view of the power of the state.[58] In a specific case, when the authors talk of the state controlling internal trade, they sometimes are in fact merely talking of the state taking measures to ensure food supplies for the capital, Constantinople.[59] This has long been acknowledged as a prime aim of the Ottomans, but it alone is not enough to justify depictions of state control of all internal trade. Goldstone's recent excellent comparative article sketches a rather different system. He refers to the mid-seventeenth century as "an era when centrally appointed officialdom rarely penetrated below the county level," and notes that during this period in Turkey the percentage of land controlled by the state fell, and that a basic change was the rise of a class of landed magnates, called *ayans*, who competed with the palace officials and the central military.[60]

In sum, the matter is controversial. This may be because of the underdeveloped state of Ottoman historiography at present, and here the collection cited certainly marks a huge step forward. But to criticize those who, like myself, tend to see important limits on the power of the central Ottoman state as "Orientalists," or as unreconstructed Marxists, is to disguise the fact that there is not yet enough evidence to pronounce definitively either way. My own reading of the secondary literature makes me see this vast Muslim agrarian empire as structurally congruent with Mughal India, and one that fits perfectly

---

[57] See especially H. A. R. Gibb and Harold Bowen, *Islamic Society and the West*, (London, 1950); H. Inalcik, *The Ottoman Empire: The Classical Age, 1300–1600* (London, 1973); 150–62; Stanford Shaw, *History of the Ottoman Empire and Modern Turkey*, (vol. I, Cambridge, 1976), p. 134–5, 151–3; Pearson, "Premodern Muslim Political Systems."

[58] Suraiya Faroqhi, "The Venetian Presence in the Ottoman Empire, 1600–30," in Islamoglu-Inan, ed., *The Ottoman Empire and The World Economy*, p. 311–44, especially p. 314–5; and, for a good summary of this article, see Huri Islamoglu-Inan, "Introduction: 'Oriental Despotism' in World-System Perspective," in ibid., 19.

[59] *The Ottoman Empire and the World Economy*, 50, 90.

[60] Goldstone, "East and West in the Seventeenth Century," p. 105, 110–1, 121.

within Wolf's schema. Some details are different, but the basic structure looks very much the same. And we are then left with the same explanation of the failure to evolve; the state may not have impinged much on the subject population, but neither did it provide the sorts of preconditions that could have produced structural economic change. A possibly important variant in the Ottoman case is that this empire fought much bigger external wars than did the Mughals: a whole series of them with Safavid Persia, and then another lot with Russia. Apparently these could be paid for from existing, largely agrarian, sources, but the system seems to have been more strained than was the case in more peaceful India.

We have stressed the sizes of these two empires, and seen this as one more or less environmental factor which restricted their integration. It is instructive to compare these two with a much smaller Islamic state, that is, Mamluk Egypt between 1250 and 1517. What we find here is a much tighter society (whereas in the case of the empires we would have to talk of societies). Three groups contributed variously to achieve this. First was the power of the army. Lapidus tells us that the Mamluks and their slave armies were very dominant. "These superbly organized Turkish armies mastered the resources and people of the area and towered over the subject societies in power and wealth."[61] Second were the *ulama*. Most of the population in this relatively small state were Muslim, and the *ulama* could play a crucial integrating role. They themselves were heterogeneous, but their common socialization seems to have meant they had the best of both worlds. On the one hand their diverse origins meant they could relate to different groups in society, yet on the other they were teaching a common code to all. Third, there is clear evidence in Mamluk Egypt of much closer ties between merchants and rulers. In the fifteenth century more merchants were assimilated into state positions; official and merchant careers sometimes merged. There were various sorts of "official" merchants, and some of these even became Mamluks.

It seems that the underpinning of all this was that (albeit fortuitously) this was a very successful fiscal state. The bulk of spices bound for Europe passed through Mamluk territory toward Alexandria or the Levant, where Venetian merchants purchased them and arranged their distribution all over Europe. This trade was savagely taxed, and contributed very substantially to Mamluk revenues. Presumably this

---

[61] Ira M. Lapidus, *Muslim Cities in the Later Middle Ages*, (Cambridge Mass., 1967), p. 6, 77–8, 127–30. For a problem-oriented, rather conclusionless analysis of the Mamluk State, see Jean-Claude Garcia, "The Mamluk Military System and The Blocking of Medieval Islamic Society," in Baechler, *Europe and the Rise of Capitalism*, 113–30.

meant there was no need for many other sources of revenue, nor therefore was there any need for alternative economic forms. From the merchant angle, taxes were very high indeed, yet the profits from the spice trade were such that the trade continued despite this. In Mughal India, merchants were left alone because the state had other, easier, sources of revenue, while in Mamluk Egypt merchants were heavily taxed, yet in other respects again were not interfered with. What seems to be the achievement of equilibrium in Mamluk Egypt was shattered by a massive fall of revenue once the Portuguese diverted, for a time, a large part of the spice trade. This loss contributed importantly to making possible the Ottoman conquest of the area soon afterward, in 1516–17.

At first sight, it appears that Chinese empires should have much in common with the Mughals and the Ottomans. All three were large agrarian structures encompassing huge areas and with heterogeneous subject populations. There is indeed one important element of commonalty. These characteristics meant that vast areas of these empires, and the great bulk of their populations, were very lightly governed indeed;[62] communications were simply not efficient enough to enable tight control, even if this had been wanted.

It is here that there seems to be some difference, for the Chinese state did want to, and was able to, impact much more fully and successfully on some parts of the society under its rule than was the case in the other two empires. And the explanation for this seems to be at heart to do with ideology.[63] Confucianism in China, or more correctly Neo-Confucianism under the Ming and Qing dynasties, produced a mandarin class of administrators that was much more integrated, and much more all-encompassing in their power, at least when their dynasties were strong, than was the case with the administrations of Mughal India and Ottoman Turkey. In areas where the state wanted to intervene, which was far from being all areas, it could do so much more effectively than could the other two empires.

[62] See especially W. Eberhard, *Conquerors and Rulers: Social Forces in Medieval China* (2d. ed., Leiden; 1965), p. 1–17; similarly, Goldstone, "East and West in the Seventeenth Century," gives a picture of the considerable negative power of the Chinese gentry in the Ming period, with imperial orders being ignored or circumvented.

[63] Ideology has mostly been only tacitly present in my discussion, yet I am convinced of its importance. For an excellent discussion of the role of ideology in Ming China, Stuart England, and Ottoman Turkey, see Goldstone, "East and West in the Seventeenth Century," 129–31, 133. He stresses both similarities and differences, but does see ideology as significant. For a useful introduction to ideology in European development, see Herman Kellenbenz, *The Rise of the European Economy: An Economic History of Continental Europe from the Fifteenth to the Eighteenth Century*, (London; 1976), p. 7–9.

This is most clearly to be seen in the case of the economy. In the long period from the Sung to the late Qing, the Confucian ideal was powerful at least among the some 20 percent of the population who were not peasants. The general effect was to create loyalty to the dynasty of the time which was "a matter separate from one's origin or race . . . As a consequence, the Confucian monarchy had a basis more cultural than national. Under it might function all those who had assumed a proper place with reference to Confucian polity."[64] Confucian thought relegated merchants, and wealth, to a low level. "Like organized resort to armed force, private riches acquired by personal shrewdness in buying and selling violated the Confucian sense of propriety."[65] Fairbank writes of the "anti-commercial nature of the Confucian state, where the merchant was low in the social scale and nominally beneath both the farmer and the bureaucrat, who lived off the produce of the land."[66] The concrete results of this could be most detrimental to economic groups. The ethic dictated that the government could confiscate businesses, control them, or force manufacturers to sell at fixed prices. As a result, capitalists not surprizingly tended to invest in land rather than in fixed establishments. In Ming China (1368–1644) as in earlier times, the Confucian proagrarian and antibusiness ethic resulted in heavy restrictions on merchants and craftsmen. All craftsmen were registered, and had to work for the government in the capital for three months every three years. Their trades were hereditary, and craftsmen had to stay in their professions for life.[67]

This broad picture needs to be elaborated on a little. First, it seems that all dynasties, despite all in theory upholding Confucian ideals, were not equally interventionist. Qing China was less so than the earlier Sung, and even the Ming, dynasties. Second, the basic problem seems to be not government supervision, so much as actual government control, monopolization, of the production and distribution of various products, sometimes in alliance with cowed merchant groups. There were two aspects to this. First, manufactured goods used by the government were produced by it, such as cloths, pottery, and so on. The court was a great consumer, but private business was allowed no role here. Second, the government monopolized the production

---

[64] John K. Fairbank, *Chinese Thought and Institutions*, (Chicago, 1957), 211.

[65] William H. McNeill, *The Pursuit of Power*, (Chicago, 1982), 36; see also Wang Gung-wu's chapter in the preceding volume in this series, *The Rise of Merchant Empires*.

[66] John K. Fairbank, *Trade and Diplomacy on the China Coast*, (vol. I, Cambridge, Mass., 1953), 33; cf. 52: "the ancient domination of the mandarin over the merchant."

[67] W. H. McNeill, *Pursuit of Power*, p. 48–50; Wolfram Eberhard, *A History of China* (3d ed., Berkeley, 1969), p. 247–8, 276.

and distribution of many basic commodities, such as salt and iron. Workers were required to turn over their production to the government, which then sold them to private merchants on a quota basis.[68]

We can accept that the Chinese state in certain areas was more penetrative than were its Indian and Ottoman peers. Nevertheless, our earlier comments about theory and practice, about normative texts generated at court and actual practice on the ground need to be kept in mind. Students of Qing China (1644–1911) are now concerned not to be seduced by the pronouncements of the elite into believing that the edicts, whether brutal or beneficent, were uniformly enforced all over China, or indeed necessarily enforced at all. Thus, an edict to establish a state granary may or may not have resulted in a granary actually being built, and this may or may not have resulted in food being distributed in times of famine. As a related example, scholars now are trying to delineate the relationship, if indeed there was any, between agricultural treatises written by the elite and actual changes in Chinese agriculture over the centuries.

An alternative scenario has been put forward by Elvin.[69] His task is to explain why China at about 1100 was the most advanced economy in the world, yet after 1350 failed to maintain the pace of technological advance, even though it did progress economically. He denies that the role of the state was important, nor indeed does he see the state as very restrictive. He hardly mentions ideology or Confucius. Instead, he finds a "high-level equilibrium trap" that limited the chances of profitable technological inventions being made. There may well be a similarity here with Mughal India; both economies functioned well enough, so structural change was not needed. And, to the extent that there may have been impetuses for change, unlike in Europe these were not helped by the state – indeed in China were hindered.

Even accepting the gap between normative and actual, there seems to be a clear case for saying that the Chinese state, controlling a uniquely efficient administration, was able to enforce policies that did hinder innovation and economic change. This is not to say that there was no trade, nor indeed growth, but overall the state was too effective. If then we can say the state in India and Turkey did nothing to help, and in parts of Europe did underpin conditions that promoted

[68] See Braudel, *Civilization and Capitalism*, II, 586–94; Eberhard, *History of China*, p. 200–1, 276; J. R. Levenson, *European Expansion and the Counter-Example of Asia, 1300–1600*, (Englewood Cliffs, N. J., 1967), p. 94–7.

[69] Mark Elvin, *The Pattern of the Chinese Past*, (London, 1973). See also Elvin's overview. "China as a Counterfactual," in Baechler, *Europe and The Rise of Capitalism*, 101–12.

change, then in China it appears that the state to the contrary put into effect policies that hindered growth.

GOVERNMENTS AND TRADE

It would be unproductive simply to write of a whole range of different countries in turn, and the attitudes of their governments to long-distance trade. The result would presumably be to show that England's policies were the best of all, and so we have the success of the East India Company. Thus, the present is ratified by the past. Asian governments, we can clearly see in retrospect, had policies unsympathetic to trade, and deservedly fell behind, finishing up, as a fitting punishment, by being colonized. What I intend to do instead is to try and erect a typology that is explicitly comparative and that will try to bring out broad patterns of attitudes to trade, and their consequences, though I do intend to provide quite detailed case studies of particular countries and areas. The broad theme is that the crucial variable is sizes of states, class structure, and revenue resources. Controllers of small political units typically have to take much more interest, for better or worse, in overseas trade than do rulers with large peasant populations that can be taxed relatively easily. This theme, of course, ties in very closely with our earlier discussion of general government contributions and inhibitions toward economic development. We will also have to consider the role of ideological factors, which seem to either reflect or influence or correlate with the types of revenue resources enjoyed by different areas.

A basic conditioning element is size and population and resources. We do have some reasonable estimates of populations in the seventeenth century. China is put at about 150,000,000, the Indian subcontinent at 145,000,000, France at 20,000,000, England at over 5,000,000, the Netherlands at between 1,000,000 and 2,000,000, and Portugal at perhaps 1,500,000.[70] If we also consider the sizes of these countries, and their natural resources, we find a continuum that seems to reflect quite closely the degree to which trade was important in the economy, and more important was a crucial part of government revenue and so of government concern.

---

[70] See generally Braudel, *Civilization and Capitalism*, I, 31–103, but I have modified his figures for India, China, and England in accordance with Moosvi, *The Economy of Mughal India*, 405, and Goldstone, "East and West in the Seventeenth Century," 36.

Port cities

At one end of the scale are states or quasi-states whose whole existence is based on trade. The best examples from Asia are port cities either de facto or de jure independent of any inland political authority, and from Europe the Italian city-states and the cities grouped in the Hanseatic League. There are, however, important variations within this mode, for though all were based on trade, some governments played much more active roles in fostering and taxing trade than did others. These governments are to be seen as interventionist rather than despotic; they interfered only in selected areas of life, especially economic. The Asian examples point to a much more hands-off policy from the governments. In the classical port cities of Asia, such as Aden, Hormuz, Calicut, Melaka, Aceh, Bantam, and Makassar, several factors were crucial. By and large, these ports did not have access to hinterlands that produced items of long-distance trade; rather they were redistribution centers. They stood apart from the dominant mode of the time and area, the great tributary empires. Late fifteenth-century Melaka was a type case. This was the great center for products from China, such as silk and porcelain, for spices from the Moluccas, for cloths from India, and for some European products, such as some textiles, and bullion. The only fairly local trade item was pepper from Sumatra and Malaya. In many cases, location was all important. Aden and Hormuz and Melaka were all situated on or near choke points; Cairo and Alexandria controlled one of the two possible overland routes for trade between Asia and the Mediterranean.

The crucial point is that all of these Asian port cities prospered not by compulsion, but by providing facilities for trade freely undertaken by a vast array of merchants. What the rulers provided was really opportunities, fair treatment, an infrastructure within which trade (but not, of course, large-scale internal development) could take place. They ensured low and relatively equitable customs duties, and a certain law and order, but did little else. Visiting merchants (to call them foreign would be redundant at this time) enjoyed considerable juridical autonomy, and typically lived in defined areas with their fellows and handled most of their legal and commercial matters for themselves. Officials concerned with trade were instructed to encourage and welcome visitors.

State revenue in these independent cities did not come from land revenue, if only because these were territorially very small states; rather it came from commodity taxes, taxes on professions and the various communities, and especially from taxes on trade, and from the rulers' own participation in trade. As to the last, however, it was unusual for rulers to use their position to give themselves particular advantages. On reflection this is not to be wondered at, for such an attempt would simply lead to merchants taking their trade elsewhere. The initiative was very much with the merchants.

There are however some variations to be noted, especially in the case of Southeast Asia.[71] The historiography on this area for our period has been dominated by the notion of a dichotomy between inward-looking, agrarian-based, inland mini-empires and outward-looking maritime port cities.[72] In terms of our discussion, the difference in this area seems to consist of a much more extensive trade by the rulers of these Southeast Asian port cities than was the case in other Asian and European ports, and the fact that they were not just exchange and redistribution centers but also engaged in quite important production.

Sometimes these mini-states intervened more actively. The earlier state of Srivijaya had pursued a much more discriminatory and oppressive policy, actively trying to control and direct trade. This model turned out to be unworkable, and the empire (not, be it noted, the port city) collapsed under its own contradictions. A better example, and a more positive one, is the port city of San Thomé on the Coromandel coast. Located four miles away from the major English settlement of Madras (and today a suburb of this same city), in the early eighteenth century this port boomed. This was largely because of the policies of its controller, the Nawab of Arcot, and despite the strong opposition of the English. A mint was established in San Thomé, and low customs duties of 2 1/2 percent on both imports and exports were levied. For a time no inland duties at all were charged. This "tax holiday" policy worked well; it was undercut by English competition and military opposition that, however, had nothing to do with the intrinsic merits of the policies.[73]

---

[71] Anthony Reid has been the main scholar here. See his article "The Organization of Production in the Pre-colonial Southeast Asian Port City," in Frank Broeze, ed., *Brides of the Sea*, (Sydney, 1989), and many other articles conveniently cited and evaluated in Sanjay Subrahmanyam, "Aspects of State Formation in South India and Southeast Asia," which article provides a good overview of the whole matter, and which also tries to decrease the extent of the gap between inland and port states by pointing to the existence of "portfolio capitalists" in both. Reid's latest thoughts on the matter will be summarized in the second volume of *Southeast Asia in the Age of Commerce, 1450–1680*, forthcoming.

[72] See J. Kathirithamby-Wells, "The Islamic City: Melaka to Jogjakarta, c. 1500–1800," *Modern Asian Studies* 20 (1986): 333–51 for a recent re-endorsement of this position.

[73] Sinnappah Arasaratnam, *Merchants, Companies, and Commerce on the Coromandel Coast, 1650–1740*, (Delhi, 1986), 169.

The next step along our continuum is port cities in Asia that jur-idically were part of large empires, and yet had some degree of au-tonomy. There is in fact a mini-continuum here. Using Indian data, we find some port cities that, though part of an inland state, achieved considerable autonomy, but others were more closely integrated. Diu and Cambay can stand as types. Diu, until its conquest by the Por-tuguese in 1535, was part of the large Sultanate of Gujarat, but thanks to its geographic isolation, and the astute policies of its controller for much of this time, Malik Ayaz, it was able to function relatively independently. The port boomed under his control, attracting large numbers of merchants, especially Turks, and becoming the center of a massive entrepôt trade. Here also geography was important, for Diu could draw on the great contiguous, and politically common, production area of Gujarat.

Malik Ayaz himself was a great trader and shipowner, but we have no evidence that he tried to use his political position to foster his own trade. At the least, he cannot have pursued policies that were so advantageous to himself as to be detrimental to other traders, for the foreign merchant community grew greatly under his rule. The other point to make is that the fact that Diu was part of Gujarat did make a difference. Malik Ayaz had to keep up his influence at court, es-pecially to counter projected policies there that reflected the interests of the vast majority of Gujarat's nobles, who were land-oriented. At times, the court seemed likely to favor the Portuguese, who desper-ately wanted to control Diu for themselves in the interest of their trade-control policies. These policies impinged very little on the mind-sets, or interests, of most of the nobility and the sultan. But they did affect Malik Ayaz, and he was forced to undertake massive bribe-giving to ward off these threats to his own, peculiar, interests.

Other port cities were much less autonomous. Cambay was located in the heartland of the Sultanate of Gujarat, and was much more fully controlled by its rulers. The governors of the port were appointed from the center, and routinely replaced from the center. They were able to achieve much less freedom of action than did Malik Ayaz. In this and comparable cases, we find even less participation in merchant affairs by the political elite, for here the ethos and interests of the court were better reflected. Thus, merchants traded more or less free from political interference, just as in the formally independent port cities. The important difference lies in the fact that, though the ruler of Calicut, let us say, encouraged merchants to call because they were needed, there being plenty of competitors along the Malabar coast, in the case of Cambay merchants called but were not encouraged in quite the same active and positive way. But they called anyway, simply because they were still well treated, and especially because in Cambay were to be found all the products of Gujarat, and indeed north India generally. Given its location, Cambay or some adjacent port could hardly help but prosper; unlike in San Thomé or Calicut, active encouragement was not needed.

The majority of the trade in all these port cities was handled by the famous pedlars, small-scale and largely autonomous and unorganized petty traders who traveled from port to port with a few goods and had no control over either production or transport. Curtin has recently studied what he calls "trade diasporas," but there is a difference between these and pedlars. Indeed, the whole concept of a diaspora seems problematic, for many of the groups he classifies in this way in fact did retain strong ties with some base or home area; this certainly applied to India's Hindu and Muslim overseas traders, and even to Armenians, who had no country but did have centers, notably Julfa in Isfahan.[74]

Occasionally, however, trade was dominated by a more organized group of merchants, the solidarity tie being either religion or place of origin. In fifteenth-century Melaka, three groups were important: Gujaratis, merchants from Coromandel, and those from Java. In fifteenth-century Calicut, it was merchants from the Red Sea and Cairo who held the cream of the trade. This did not lead to their attempting any sort of political control in the port, but the ruler, called the Zamorin, was obviously aware of their vital role in the port and so in his revenues. When the Portuguese told him to expel these commercial and religious opponents, he refused, pointing out that they had been there for years, and had contributed importantly to his revenues. Indeed, this was the pattern at several of these port cities at the time. The Portuguese, with very different ideas about how trade should be conducted, achieved their ends by force, for they were unprepared, at an official level, to participate on a basis of equality and open competition in Asian trade.

This is the place to deal with the matter of protection rent and protection costs. This notion is derived from Karl Polanyi's fundamental belief that the price-fixing market is a recent phenomenon. In earlier times, economic processes were embedded in noneconomic institutions, and nonmarket exchanges based on reciprocity and redistribution were important. Long-distance trade was closely con-

---

[74] See Curtin, *Cross-Cultural Trade in World History,* and Chaudhuri, *Trade and Civilization,* 224–6.

trolled by the state and subordinated to state ends. The state established terms of exchange and fixed prices; no price-fixing market was allowed. This then was the situation in the port of trade. From this Frederick C. Lane went on to create his influential concept of protection costs. As noted, his work is important in the history of economic history, for it reintroduced political factors into the agenda for economic historians. The concept of protection costs is a powerful and important one for a discussion of the Mediterranean city-states and their trade policies, and Steensgaard has shown how useful it is to analyze the activities of the Portuguese in the Indian Ocean in the sixteenth century, a point I will return to.[75] It is not, however, of any utility in a discussion of the port cities of Asia. As described above, these operated on a basis of freedom, where merchants were encouraged to call. A crucial element in the encouragement was the very existence of free markets, which were precisely not embedded in any political system but rather operated free from political interference. Merchants paid taxes in return for the facilities provided, not as protection rent. The most sustained attempt to apply Polanyi to the pre-Portuguese Indian Ocean arena is Leeds's article. Although he claims that his data "unequivocally" shows ports of trade, his evidence is limited and flawed, and ignores masses of evidence to the contrary. He uses data selectively, jumbles in material from many different centuries, puts meanings on his long quotations that they will not bear, and often what he calls "administered" trade is merely the provision of facilities by port controllers.[76] Protection rent came into Indian Ocean trade with the Portuguese.

Asian port cities sooner or later were undercut by the activities of Europeans, whether the Portuguese or later the Dutch and English. Armed force played a large role here. In the European equivalents, the Italian cities and the Hanseatic League, the decline ironically stemmed from competition from the same countries; in other words,

---

[75] See Dietmar Rothermund, *Asian Trade and European Expansion in the Age of Mercantilism*, (New Delhi, 1981), p. 8–10; Curtin, *Cross-Cultural Trade*, p. 13–14, 41–2; F. C. Lane, *Profits from Power: Readings in Protection Rent and Violence-Controlling Enterprises* (Albany, 1979), and "The Role of Governments in Economic Growth in Early Modern Times," *Journal of European Economic History* 35 (1975): 8–17; Niels Steensgaard, "Violence and the Rise of Capitalism: Frederick C. Lane's Theory of Protection and Tribute," *Review* 5 (1981): p. 247–73; Niels Steensgaard, *The Asian Trade Revolution of the Seventeenth Century* (Chicago; 1974), 60–113; Douglass C. North, "Markets and Other Allocation Systems in History: The Challenge of Karl Polanyi, *Journal of European Economic History*, 6 (1977): 703–16; Karl Polanyi et al., *Trade and Market in the Early Empires*, (New York; 1957).

[76] Anthony Leeds, "The Port-of-Trade in Pre-European India as an Ecological and Evolutionary Type," *Proceedings of the American Ethnological Society* (1961): 26–48.

they were unable to compete with merchants based in new centralized states.

An important part of the position of merchants from both the Italian cities and the Hanseatic League was based on the desire of elites in late medieval Europe for luxuries and for revenues from trade. Italian merchants provided the former, the Hanse merchants more basic, but still taxable, commodities. Italian merchants, with their access to the products of the Levant and Asia, were patronized and given special privileges in less developed areas like France, Germany, and England. This was seen especially in the great fairs of the twelfth to fifteenth centuries. The desire for luxuries interacted with fiscal needs to promote very favourable conditions for Italian merchants, especially in the Champagne fairs. Law and order was scrupulously maintained, and safe-conducts were given to Jews and Italians. Similarly, in the fifteenth century French government policy resulted in success for the great fairs held at Lyons, and the decline of Geneva. Lyons was allowed free trade for the period of the fair, and foreign money was allowed to circulate freely. The safe passage of foreign goods and merchants was guaranteed by the French Crown.[77]

All this is strongly reminiscent of the Asian port cities, and of the later "free" ports, such as Antwerp, in Europe. But French policy at the fairs contrasts strongly with the policies of the beneficiaries of these actions, that is, the strong and exclusionist policies pursued by both the Italian cities and the Hanseatic League. In both there was almost an identity between trade and government. In the Italian cities, traders were forced to call, forced to pay taxes, forced to trade, forced to use local merchants to sell their goods, and the role of foreigners was very closely regulated so that the natives would make the profits. The state-merchant connection in the Mediterranean was perhaps most clearly seen in the case of Venice, where indeed there was little difference between the state and merchants. All was subordinated to trade. As Scammell puts it, "though other imperial powers might devote much of their energies and resources to the defence of some particular monopoly, with none, except Venice, did its running and protection become in effect the whole purpose of their being, with the state providing the ships for its operation and a navy and empire for its safeguard."[78]

[77] O. Verlinden, "Markets and Fairs," in *Cambridge Economic History of Europe*, III, 127–34; J. N. Ball, *Merchants and Merchandise: The Expansion of Trade in Europe, 1500–1630* (London, 1977), 31–2.
[78] Scammell, *The World Encompassed*, 116; cf. A. B. Hibbert, "The Economic Policies of

The Hanseatic League was in many ways comparable, indeed economically even more exclusionist even if commercially less advanced, and benefiting from the fact that, though its seventy or eighty towns cooperated, the Italian cities usually competed with each other. The league had a loose formal structure to be sure, but very great commercial power, and policies almost totally dominated by merchants and reflecting merchant interests. Apart from defending the privileges of their members in such outposts as Bergen, Bruges and London, all the cities of the league enforced a "guest law," which forbade direct trade between noncitizens in their towns; thus locals prospered as middlemen.[79]

It does seem that there is a very clear difference between Asian and European cases at this level. It is true that there is a similarity in the fact that both really existed only on sufferance. As powerful regional governments arose in Europe, their merchants, backed by these governments, eroded the position of these port cities; indeed, the Hanseatic League was created only because in its area there was no government. In Asia the landed empires had no reason to interfere; it was the arrival of the Europeans, with exclusionist economic and political notions deriving in part from the experience of the Italian city-states, that ended this freedom. But the differences are more important. In the Asian port cities, outside merchants were dominant, and the governments did nothing to hinder this; indeed, it was encouraged. In the European examples, government policy was precisely the opposite, and acted powerfully to help locals. The broad difference between the Asian and European cases is difficult to explain. It seems to reflect wider societal changes leading to a larger role for governments in general in Europe than in Asia, and with a more proto-nationalist, more competitive, attitude from European governments that were concerned to help their own burghers, though Asian governments did not do this for their subjects. European governments were becoming more exclusionist. This in turn seems to reflect different class positions. Merchants in Europe were, as a class, more powerful, and could influence or control governments more

Towns," in *Cambridge Economic History of Europe*, III, 159–72; Braudel, *Civilization and Capitalism*, III, 125.

[79] Scammell, *The World Encompassed*, 536; Ball, *Merchants and Merchandise*, 36–40; Edward Miller, "Government Economic Policies and Public Finance, 1000–1500," in Cipolla, ed., *Fontana Economic History*, I, 360–7; R. de Roover, "The Organization of Trade," in *Cambridge Economic History of Europe*, III, 105; Jan K. Federowicz, The History of the Elbing Staple: An Episode in the History of Commercial Monopolies," *Jahrbücher für geschichte Osteuropas* 27 (1979): 220–1.

directly and easily than could merchants in Asia, whose lack of class solidarity did not allow them any political influence.

The Portuguese

Portugal operated in a much wider arena than had the Italian city-states, establishing a worldwide empire of sorts, but there are important elements of continuity between Portugal's policies and those pursued by, say, Venice. Portugal's role was to introduce to Asia European notions, specifically Mediterranean notions, of trade control and monopoly. In short, the protection system developed by Venice was applied to the Indian Ocean. At the official level, then, there was a very tight connection between the Crown and trade. This in turn can be correlated with Portugal's resources. In a poor country, with a population of less than 1,000,000 in 1500, and with almost no natural resources, trade had to be important; it was the only method for the Crown to achieve profit and status.[80]

This central state role applies particularly at the intercontinental level. Trade with Asia was funneled through the *Casa da India*, on the Tagus downstream from Lisbon. All imports and exports to and from Asia were stored there for registration, customs clearance, and payment of freight. Officials there sold the pepper and other goods brought in for the Crown, supervised the loading and unloading of ships, checked for contraband, paid the crews, and kept a register of all sailings and all people on board ships. From 1506 the Crown claimed a tight monopoly on the provision of ships for the *carreira*, or passage to India, and on the trade in precious metals from Portugal and imports of pepper and spices.[81] For a time, the results were impressive indeed. As early as 1506, the spice trade produced 27 percent of royal income in Portugal, and in 1518 some 39 percent, which was more than the Crown's income from metropolitan Portugal. In Asia all trade in spices, and a few other products, were declared to be Portuguese Crown monopolies. No one else was to trade in these products, under pain of confiscation or worse. Even more grandiloquently, the Portuguese Crown claimed to control and

---

[80] For this whole section, see M. N. Pearson, *The Portuguese in India*, (Cambridge, 1987). The overview of the Portuguese in the sixteenth century by Professors Subrahmanyam and Thomaz in this volume raises important new questions, and is particularly successful in the attempt to investigate change, both in Portugal and in Portugal's Asian Empire.

[81] A. R. Disney, *Twilight of the Pepper Empire*, (Cambridge, Mass., 1978), 71–2, 86–7.

tax all other sea trade in Asia. No trade in any product was to take place except in ships that had taken a pass from the Portuguese, which in turn obligated these ships to call at Portuguese ports and pay customs duties. This policy in Asia was backed up by extensive naval patrolling and a string of forts around the littoral of the Indian Ocean, among them several of the great port cities we have already mentioned: Melaka, Diu, and Hormuz.

The aspiration was vast, but in several areas this picture of a royal monopoly applied both in Portugal and in Asia is subject to major modifications. We can find in both Asia and Europe economic groups apart from the Crown participating and profiting under the very leaky umbrella of royal monopoly. Thus, although spices coming into Portugal were nearly all owned by the Crown, their distribution and sale once they left the *Casa da India* was handled by others. They were sent to Antwerp, and from there were distributed by Germans, Florentines, and ironically Jews recently expelled from Portugal. Right from the start there was substantial private involvement in Portuguese long-distance trade, and many of these people were not Portuguese. In 1454 a young Venetian, Cadamosto, asked how he could participate in the Portuguese expeditions to west Africa. He was told that he either could fit out his own caravel, load it with his own goods, and pay one-quarter of the proceeds to Prince Henry, the so-called Navigator, who controlled this trade, or he could go in one of Henry's own caravels and pay him one-half of his proceeds.

The actual "discoveries" down the Africa coast were at times contracted out. In 1469 Fernão Gomes was given a five-year monopoly to trade in areas south of where the Portuguese had so far penetrated. In return he was to pay the king 200 milreis a year, and "discover" a minimum of 100 leagues of coast each year.[82] Nor was the vital pepper trade with Asia conducted completely autonomously by Portugal's Grocer Kings. Private shipping was often used, some privileged groups were themselves allowed to trade in goods normally monopolized by the Crown, there was very substantial private trade in nonmonopoly goods, and a vast "illegal" trade. In the 1560s the Crown, faced with liquidity problems, encouraged private participation in the spice and pepper trade from Asia. From the mid 1570s it was contracted out to several private syndicates, some German, some Italian, some Portuguese. Dutch and English competition in the

---

[82] Lyle N. McAlister, *Spain and Portugal in the New World, 1492–1700*, (Oxford, 1984), 252; B. W. Diffie and G. D. Winius, *Foundations of the Portuguese Empire, 1415–1580*, (Minneapolis; 1977), p. 96–7, 146.

early seventeenth century reduced the profits, the private contractors lost interest, and the Crown was reluctantly forced back to doing the trade itself.

Part of the problem seems to have been that the Crown was not rigorously economic, as indeed presumably Crowns never can be. The anti-Jewish policy overall was detrimental economically, and was a result of religious bigotry and of a marriage contract with the even more intolerant Spanish Crown. Religious bigotry also played a role in the central effort to monopolize the spice trade, for this was controlled by Muslims. Although Portugal avoided the sort of European involvement that was fatal for Philip II's Spain, the monarchy still spent vast sums of money on marriage dowries, on bloody and pointless wars in north Africa, and on conspicuous consumption in Portugal. Similarly, the voyages down the Africa coast reveal a strange mixture indeed of piracy, corsairing, and slave-trading, all solemnly dressed up in the official chronicles with a veneer of chivalry.[83]

As for the Asian end of things, Steensgaard and Rothermund have demonstrated clearly the continuities with Mediterranean practice.[84] At the official level of monopolies and passes, this was an empire that used military coercion to try and achieve a strictly noneconomic advantage. Basically a tribute was demanded from Asian trade; the Portuguese created de novo a threat of violence to Asian shipping, and then sold protection from this threat, as seen in the requirement to take passes and pay customs duties. No service was provided in return; in modern terms this was precisely a protection racket. As we know, the effort failed anyway. By mid-century more spices and pepper were coming to Europe via the Red Sea and the Mediterranean than via the Cape. Within Asia the Portuguese were able to make the need for protection effective only at certain choke points, most notably the entrance to the Gulf of Cambay. Over most of the vast and intricate sea trade of the Indian Ocean at the time they had no control and no influence. The central flaw was in fact the nature of the whole policy, whose aims were too ambitious for such a small state to hope to achieve. It is arguable that, had they wanted to, they could have done better by using the cost advantages of the Cape route to undercut the traditional trade with Europe by purely economic means. This is a debateable claim no doubt, and counter-factual anyway, yet what is not in doubt is that the mixture of politics with trade, indeed the

---

[83] See M. D. D. Newitt, "Prince Henry and the Origins of Portuguese Expansion," in M. D. D. Newitt, ed., *The First Portuguese Colonial Empire*, (Exeter, 1986).
[84] Rothermund, *Asian Trade and European Expansion*; Steensgaard, *Asian Trade Revolution*.

subordination of trade to politics, resulted in a ramshackle, unsuccessful, and insolvent empire.

This can be further demonstrated if we look at areas where the Portuguese did better, which turn out to be the same as areas where there was less Crown interference. Leaving aside the intercontinental trade, much local country trade in Asia made large profits both for the Portuguese state and for private Portuguese. The voyages between Japan and China, and on to Melaka and India, made vast profits, and these were not based on the sort of exclusionism characteristic of the *carreira* back to Portugal. In many ways, the Asian empire operated independently of the metropole, self-financing and self-controlled. Right outside of it thousands of private Portuguese trafficked more or less successfully as part of the rich warp and weft of traditional Asian trade, participating on a basis of equality with the vast array of others engaged in the same sorts of trade, with no particular advantages or disadvantages. And if the Asian empire, at least internally, was tacitly allowed to go its own way, this applied more formally in some other parts of the empire. In the Atlantic islands, feudal rights were sold off, and central control or interference was minimal. In Brazil also rights to vast territories were sold off to various captains in the donatory system; these essentially feudal lords then in effect ruled these areas for themselves. Arguably the success of the Brazilian sugar industry from late in the sixteenth century owed much to this very freedom from Crown control. In short, the attempt to imitate Venice in a much larger arena failed, and the crucial failure was caused by the very link between politics and trade.

Spain

The Spanish case presents important differences, and some similarities. Several contrasts are immediately apparent. Spain was much bigger, but also much less united; regionalism and local rights remained important throughout our period. Spain was much more pastoralist than tiny Portugal, as seen in the dominance of the *mesta* for so long. More important, Spain's rulers, and especially Charles V and Philip II, had many more fish to fry than did Portugal's. For them European concerns, and wars, were central. The results are well known. Wars took large proportions of the income of the Crown, more indeed than was available, so that late in Philip II's reign interest payments on his debts took two-thirds of his income.[85] The Spanish

---

[85] Ralph Davis, *Rise of The Atlantic Economies*, 68.

Empire was much less central, and was left alone much more. Yet, in the broadest structural terms, the end-result of empire was the same for both. In the Spanish case, most imports of manufactured goods for the Americas came from Europe outside Spanish areas, and even the imports from there to Spain were usually sent on to other Europeans. This trend existed in the sixteenth century but was writ very large by the late seventeenth. In 1670 the Mexican fleet brought in 8,500,000 pesos. The Genoese took 1,500,000, French 1,300,000, Dutch 700,000, Germans 500,000, and English 300,000. Just under half remained in Spain. In 1691 foreigners engrossed 90 percent of imports from America.[86] As Anderson, Wallerstein, Wolf, and many others have noted, both Portugal and Spain became in effect conveyor belts that transported spices and bullion to Europe and then sent them on to the north and east. In Portugal, empire did not lead to internal economic change; royal power was too great, so that a nascent bourgeoisie was unable to flourish and ended up in a comprador role facilitating the exploitation of Portugal by foreigners, especially the English. The Spanish case is at present much discussed. It seems clear that local mercantile groups did better here than in Portugal, but this is not to say that they were able to flourish in the way English merchants did in the early modern period; in other words, they may have done better than we once thought, but they still did not do nearly well enough.

Given the manifold other preoccupations of the Spanish Crown, the system it put into effect was very different from the official system in Portugal. The context also was quite different, for in America Spain ruled over territorial colonies and had virtually a free hand. At first sight, the Spanish imperial trade seemed to be as centralized as was the Portuguese one. All fleets to and from America had to go to Seville only. The *casa de la contratacion de las Indias* oversaw all colonial trade, fitted out all the royal fleets, and regulated all private trade. But in fact the Spanish Empire was really merely a vast contracting-out system, the *casa* a regulating, not a trading, organization. Even the pioneering voyages, and the conquests, were not financed by the Crown; rather, licences were provided by the Crown, and Castilian or Genoese bankers, or other private individuals, put up the money. Adventurers and explorers were given state licenses, but not Crown support. Similarly, in the colonies most territory was divided into

[86] McAlister, *Spain and Portugal in The New World*, 375. On Spain's economy in this period, and especially the presence of at least some bourgeoisie, see an important overview by Carla Rahn Phillips: "Time and Duration: A Model for the Economy of Early Modern Spain," *American Historical Review* 93 (1987): 531–62.

rather loosely supervised *encomiendas*.[87] As Davis puts it, the Crown's role in America "did not extend far beyond giving its formal sanction to exploration and settlement projects, covering them with the mantle of Castilian authority and setting up a framework of government within which orderly development could proceed. Resources for conquest and settlement came for the most part from private individuals."[88]

This is not to say that the Crown did not do well from America. It received between one-quarter and one-third of the bullion coming in from America; at its peak this made up 25 percent of the royal income. And this revenue source, being bullion, was readily negotiable. Nor is this to say that the Crown was totally distanced from America. There was indeed a royal structure of controls and administrators; royal decrees from Madrid by and large were obeyed. This was a centralized, bureaucratic empire, modified however by distance and slow communications.[89] The worst abuses, such as the inhuman treatment of indigenes, were checked at least to some extent by Crown decrees. The fatal flaw clearly was the European military and diplomatic preoccupations of Spain's rulers.

The Portuguese and Spanish cases, then, present rather different paradigms of government effects on long-distance trade. In the Portuguese case, at least in the command sector, intercontinental trade, one can see too much state involvement both in Europe and Asia, an overly ambitious attempt to reorient Asian trade, and at home policies that denied the chance of internal economic development. In the Spanish case, one sees rather looser control, and vast profits again being made in the empire, and by other Europeans, but not by the Crown. A looser system worked no better in terms of the development of the metropole, and for the same basic reasons, to do with the way the windfalls were used.

Japan

A comparison with Japan is instructive here. The country's size, population, and resources had certain similarities with Portugal, yet its development was quite different, and this seems to have been very much a consequence of government policy, with a strong ideological input. In the so-called feudal and warring state periods, through to

[87] J. H. Parry, *The Spanish Seaborne Empire* (London, 1966), 54, 243.
[88] Davis, *Rise of the Atlantic Economies*, 39–42.
[89] Parry, *Spanish Seaborne Empire*, 192 ff.; McAlister, *Spain and Portugal*, 182–9; 203–7; 423–6; 435–9.

the end of the sixteenth century, foreign trade expanded considerably. This often merged into piracy, such as the Wako traders-pirates who operated off the Chinese coast. A quite substantial overseas trade was possibly facilitated by internal developments. During the sixteenth century, warring *daimyos*, or land controllers, attempted to develop their areas, and as part of this put into effect policies designed to attract trade and merchants. The older monopolies on many goods were abolished and trade was freed, even to the extent of not being taxed.[90]

The change, as in general in Japanese history, came with the To-kugawa creation of unity. At first, Ieyasu and his successors were anxious to encourage foreign trade. This implied close government supervision of it, and this in turn seems to mark the influence of Confucian notions in Japan. Foreign trade was closely controlled, especially after about 1600, partly by officials and partly by responsible merchant organizations or licensed merchants who had a monopoly on foreign dealings. In 1604 the shogun got silk merchants in Kyoto, Sakai, and Nagasaki to form a group, and they then bought silk from the Portuguese at an agreed price, divided it among themselves, and sold it. The authorities in Nagasaki themselves often traded in silk, or interfered in its trade.[91]

For reasons that are basically environmental, a country like Japan appears to need foreign trade, as twentieth-century history demonstrates, but the strength and effectiveness of government policy in the early seventeenth century dictated a different result. An official awareness of the importance of trade, and indeed governmental interference in it, was outweighed by ideological and political factors, which led to the so-called "closed-country era." In this decision, one in theory antithetical to foreign trade, general Confucian notions, now strong in Japan, played a part, at least in the broad sense of allocating a low-status position to economic activity generally, and rather giving primacy to peasants and rulers.

More specifically, Tokugawa Ieyasu became exclusionist after an influx of Spanish clergy from the Philippines began in 1592. These were feared as being a fifth column that would lead to a Spanish invasion. The success of missionaries before and after this time in converting masses of Japanese aroused more fear of foreign influence and even control. The result was the well-known persecution of local

[90] E. Reischauer et al., *East Asia: The Great Tradition*, (London, 1960), 560–5; Peter Duus, *Feudalism in Japan* (New York, 1969), 68–80.
[91] See Kristof Glamann, "The Changing Patterns of Trade," in *Cambridge Economic History of Europe*, V, 281.

and foreign Christians, and very strict, almost total, curtailment of foreign trade. The persecution of Christians began in 1597. In 1606 Christianity was proscribed, in 1623 the English left Japan, in 1624 the Spanish were expelled, and in the 1630s Japanese were officially forbidden to travel or trade overseas. In 1639 the Dutch were moved to Deshima island, in Nagasaki harbor, and from there undertook for some two centuries a very closely supervised and regulated trade in those few imports that the Japanese rulers considered to be essential. Recent research by Toby has modified this standard depiction to an extent, in that he stresses that Japan *did* retain ties with Asia, even if not with the Europeans.[92] One can then see the notion of the closed country being another example of Eurocentrism, for it was closed only to Europeans. Nevertheless, this contact was controlled in most respects by the state, so that the point to be made is that the Japanese case is a very clear example of an effective government attitude to foreign trade, an extreme one no doubt, but very successful in terms of the government's own political and ideological concerns.

The Dutch

The comparison to be made now is with the role of the government of the United Provinces in overseas trade. Portugal, Japan, and the Netherlands can be seen as comparable in size, population, and lack of domestic resources, though certainly not in terms of the class composition of the population. How then are we to explain the success of the last as compared with the failure of Portugal and the exclusionist policy of Japan? The answer harks back very clearly to our earlier discussion of the general role of the state in economic development; it seems that the Dutch state provided the infrastructure, but not tight control, provided in fact a favorable environment in which merchant groups could operate effectively. Underpinning the whole matter was the strong class position of Dutch merchants as compared with those in Japan and Portugal. Dutch economic elites were so powerful as to almost control the state.

The rather bizarrely constituted central government was notoriously weak; indeed, Klein, in his explicit attack on Wallerstein's claim that core states by definition have strong governments, says that this was deliberate. Wallerstein on the surface agrees, saying that

---

[92] Ronald P. Toby, *State and Diplomacy in Early Modern Japan*, (Princeton, 1984), xiv–xviii; 22.

this was "a jerry-built and seemingly ineffectual state machinery."[93] There is however a difference between a strong government and one that intervenes selectively and effectively in defined areas of an economy, just as there is a difference between a generally despotic and a selectively interventionist state. In the case of the Netherlands, the government could be very effective at times when it was necessary. Thus, Dutch foreign policy was "an undisguised assistance to trade." Dutch carrying trade with Western Europe and the Baltic, and its fishing in the North Sea, were much more important than its intercontinental trade. The prosperity of the seventeenth century was based on the earlier acquisition of dominance in the Baltic trade, where the Hanseatic League was supplanted. In 1666 three-quarters of the capital active on the Amsterdam bourse was engaged in the Baltic trade.[94] Consequently, relations with Denmark and Sweden were totally governed by the need to secure shipping through the sound. In 1645 a Dutch fleet intervened in a war between Sweden and Denmark in the Baltic for precisely this reason. Similarly with the wars with England in the same century; this was a state that could intervene, and usually successfully, when it was needed.

This government attitude is most clearly and relevantly seen in the state's role in the founding and functioning of the Dutch East India Company (VOC). Competition among the early individual companies was fierce. As early as January 1598 the States General suggested that a merger would be worthwhile. Later, the important statesman Johan van Oldenbarnevelt pushed for unity, and even Prince Maurice lent a hand at a critical point in the negotiations. The result was the forming of the VOC in March 1602. The company was given very extensive powers overseas, to the extent of the right to make war and peace and treaties. At first the States General did exercise some control, so that for example initially instructions to governors from the Heren XVII were approved by the States General. But by mid-century the nexus between government and company was so tight that this was not necessary. The oligarchy and the Heren XVII were one and the same, indistinguishable from each other and indeed often consisting of the same people. This was the reason for the apparent autonomy from metropolitan political control that the VOC enjoyed;

[93] See B. H. Slicher van Bath, "The Economic Situation," in M. Aymard, ed., *Dutch Capitalism and World Capitalism*, 31; Peter Wolfgang Klein, "Dutch Capitalism and the European World-Economy," in ibid., 85; and Immanuel Wallerstein, "Dutch Hegemony in the Seventeenth-Century World-Economy," in ibid., 95.

[94] C. R. Boxer, *The Dutch Seaborne Empire* (London, 1965), 43.

because the VOC was identical with the state, this was really no abdication by the state.

The relationship was, of course, reciprocal. Thus, the state helped in the formation of the VOC in part because such a united company could attack the Spanish and Portuguese far from home.[95] In the wars of the late seventeenth century, the VOC lent money and ships to the States General: twenty, for example, during the second Anglo-Dutch War. Similarly, every time the VOC's charter was renewed, it paid for the privilege of having its monopoly confirmed. Here, as in the cases of Spain and England, we can see the age-old notion of an exchange, of a privilege being granted in return for a fiscal benefit to the state.

In its Asian operations, the VOC acted rather differently from the Portuguese. There was an ongoing debate over the role of force and its contribution to profit, but in general military action was used in a more discriminating way than the blanket claims and actions of the Portuguese. Unlike the Portuguese, commerce was always central. As Steensgaard put it, "The VOC integrated the functions of a sovereign power with the functions of a business partnership. Political decisions and business decisions were made within the same hierarchy of company managers and officials, and failure or success was always in the last instance measured in terms of profit."[96] Further, a more rational and advanced business structure, a company as opposed to a state, was able to exercise much tighter control. Not only the intercontinental trade, but also the intra-Asian trade, was tightly centralized. Basically the VOC in Asia internalized its protection costs, and here the contrast with the Portuguese again is clear. "Estado da India was a redistributive enterprise, which traded in order itself to obtain the full benefit of its use of violence, whereas the Companies were associations of merchants which themselves used violence and thereby internalized the protection costs."[97]

What then of the difference between this and the Spanish Empire?

---

[95] The commercially unsuccessful Dutch West India Company is an example of the dangers of this symbiosis. It was founded in 1621 not really as a commercial venture – indeed private investment was slow to come forward – but rather as an instrument to help in the war against Spain. The States General was forced to invest money in it, in order to encourage private investors, and the Dutch admiralty even lent warships to the company.

[96] Niels Steensgaard, "The Dutch East India Company as an Institutional Innovation," in Aymard, ed., *Dutch Capitalism*, 237.

[97] Steensgaard, *Asian Trade Revolution*, 114. As we know, the Dutch in the eighteenth century did less well. For an overview of their failure, see the chapters by Steensgaard, Bruijn, and Neal, in *The Rise of Merchant Empires*.

It could be argued that the Spanish Empire was much more closely supervised from the metropole, but if one accepts the line of argument above which sees the state and the company as more or less identical in the Netherlands then this is a false distinction. The real difference is that the whole operation of the Spanish long-distance trade system allowed the benefits to pass through and out of Spain, and in the classic Dutch redistributive empire the benefits remained very firmly in the country. In one, the state allowed merchants, often non-Spanish, to operate in the entrails of its empire; in the other, indigenous merchants were the empire and were the state. We see here, in fact, a much tighter connection between merchants and states than we do in England, where we must now turn.

England

The broad contrasts are clear enough. English government had more concern with nontrade and noneconomic matters than did the Dutch. Yet, this said, it is clear that English policies, sometimes deliberately, more often inadvertently, were much more sympathetic to long-distance trade, to economic enterprize generally, than was the case with Spain; the reason for this has much to do with less European entanglements for England, and a government that as compared with Philip II was much more answerable to the public generally, and especially to important merchant groups. Their class position, and political influence, seems to be midway between the Dutch as compared with the Spanish and Portuguese. Fiscal needs, of course, lay at the heart of this responsiveness. The contrast with Portugal also is clear; royal power there was too strong, and too unenlightened, too illiterate in economics, for her grandiose projects to be successful.

The broad strands of state concern with trade can be quickly sketched. Basically the Crown gave a privilege, or a franchise, giving special advantages to a particular group; the trading companies are an apposite example, and by 1603 all areas of English overseas trade were subject to company regulation. These privileges were supported, when it suited the government, by diplomacy, and by an evolving consular service. The culmination was the Navigation Acts. What was not to be seen, however, was a conscious government policy over any long period that put overseas trade and its development and protection at the center. Unlike in the Netherlands and Portugal, at least to 1630 "the evidence we have hardly ever shows the crown – or ministers on its behalf – taking the initiative, but rather responding more or less helpfully to private projects."[98] Andrews's whole book is a vigorous setting-out of this thesis. Overseas trade and expansion was seen by Elizabeth as part of the power game of Western Europe. Efforts overseas were welcomed, but were seen as secondary; the initiative, especially on the financial side, was left to others. The broad context of state encouragement, or more often acquiescence, in foreign voyages was opposition to Spain. Even James I, despite being much more subservient to Spain, still denied its exclusionist claims in both America and the East. Hakluyt and other propagandists notwithstanding, it is false to think that "some grand mercantile and imperial strategy was at work, and that the founding of this essentially commercial empire was a royal achievement, inspired by a coherent policy of economic nationalism."[99]

The point is an important one, for it shows elements of continuity right through. The joint-stock companies of the seventeenth century obviously constituted a commercial innovation, but in terms of relations with the state the mix was as it had been under Elizabeth, and indeed earlier. State involvement with the regulated companies, and then with the joint-stocks, was not generically different from the sorts of restrictions and opportunities that had previously been laid down by guilds and backed by English governments. In both cases corporate bodies – guilds or companies – received the privilege of being allowed to engage in a particular activity to the exclusion of others. The Crown was paid in one way or another for granting this right to the body concerned.

The regulated companies were groups of merchants who operated individually, and at their own risk, not a corporate one. There was, however, a framework of collective discipline, which was designed to reduce or eliminate competition within the company, while the Crown, by bestowing a monopoly, prevented competition from other English nationals. Take the Eastland Company. In 1579 England's Baltic trade was in difficulties. A possible solution was to end competition within England, so Elizabeth gave the company a monopoly charter on this trade. The company could now regulate its members closely; times of sailing were specified, ships sailed in convoys, and the amount of debt incurred by each participating merchant was checked.[100] The Crown, of course, was merely telling these merchants to trade and profit if they could; the political contribution was to

---

[98] K. R. Andrews, *Trade, Plunder, and Settlement: Maritime Enterprise and the Genesis of the British Empire, 1480–1630*, (Cambridge, 1984), 360.
[99] Ibid., 16, and generally 10–17.
[100] J. K. Fedorowicz, "The History of the Elbing Staple," 220–4.

eliminate intra-English competition, but usually nothing could be done about non-English rivals.

For the Crown, one advantage of encouraging trade was that a stronger merchant marine had naval implications. Walsingham noted in 1578 that a trade to Turkey will "sett a grett nomber of your grettest shippes a worke wherrby your navie shalbe mainteyned." But the more important payoff for the Crown was financial, in other words the expectation that increased trade would promote general prosperity in England, and more specifically increase royal customs duties. The Levant Company was formed in 1581, with a patent and monopoly from Elizabeth I. But its monopoly for seven years was dependent on its trade after the first year producing customs revenues of £500 each year. More direct financial benefits were also demanded by the Crown; the Levant Company's monopoly was renewed in 1600 for fifteen more years, but only on payment of £2,000 each six months. The Turkey Company patent of 1581, which reserved the whole of the Middle East trade to just twelve merchants, was granted partly because the merchants concerned were rich and influential, and partly because they gave the queen £5,000.[101]

Occasionally, at times when it fitted with more general diplomatic strategies, the Crown would do more than simply tell merchants to go ahead. To promote English trade with Turkey, Elizabeth sent with a merchant traveling to Constantinople a letter of support, and in 1580 he was able to get capitulations for all English merchants in Turkey. When the Levant Company was formed next year, it decided to appoint an agent in Constantinople. To give him status, Elizabeth made him her ambassador to the sultan. The mix here is clearly to be seen; the merchant-cum-ambassador, Harborne, was paid by the company. He helped the interests of his fellow merchants, but also pushed English interests in general, for example anti-Spanish measures.[102]

Ai.drews's claim of continuity up to at least 1630 seems valid. The history of state involvement with the early years of the East India Company (EIC) shows very much a continuation of the Elizabethan mix. We know, of course, that as a joint-stock company, with a permanent capital from 1623, the EIC was in commercial and financial terms innovatory, but this did not alter the attitude of the state to it.

---

[101] William Foster, *England's Quest of Eastern Trade*, (London, 1933), 69–70, 76; Robert Brenner, "The Social Basis of English Commercial Expansion, 1550–1650," *Journal of Economic History* 32 (1972): 369.

[102] Andrews, *Trade, Plunder, and Settlement*, 91–2; Foster, *England's Quest of Eastern Trade*, 69–73.

(This is not to say that this commercial change did not have important repercussions on the effectiveness of this company in Asia; we will discuss this matter later.)[103]

The mix is clearly seen in the founding of the company at the end of 1600. After the death of Philip II in 1598, Elizabeth hoped for peace with Spain, and so voyages to the East were discouraged. But, after negotiations broke down in the middle of 1600, the Privy Council wrote encouraging the leaders of the movement to extend English trade to the East. The famous Charter of 1600 gave a monopoly on trade to the East for fifteen years, for four years there were to be no customs duties on exports, reexports were to be free of duties, and importantly the company could export bullion worth up to £30,000 a year.[104] But the vast powers to make war and peace and treaties that the VOC got two years later were not granted by Elizabeth. In structural terms, this was because there was not the identity between merchants and state in England that there was in the Netherlands. The VOC could be trusted with these extraordinary privileges precisely because it was unlikely it would do anything incompatible with the interests of the state with which it was so closely merged; this assumption could not necessarily be made in the English case.

The Crown's interests were various. In general terms a prosperous English trade to the East would be good for reexports, and Eastern goods would now arrive in English ships. Customs duties would rise, and it was hoped (correctly as it turned out) that the company could be milched for loans to the government. But in broad terms the state was merely again letting a group of merchants proceed. Some assistance was provided, but commercial success or failure was a matter for the company itself. Nor did the company want closer control disguised as assistance. When the Privy Council gave the all clear for the formation of the company in September 1600, it also suggested that the commander of the initial voyage should be Sir Edward Michelborne, a courtier friendly with the influential Earl of Essex. The merchants' reply was a request to be allowed "to sort ther busines with men of ther owne qualety . . . lest the suspition of the imploy-

---

[103] See esp. Holden Furber, *Rival Empires of Trade in the Orient, 1600–1800*, (Minneapolis, 1976). The works of K.N. Chaudhuri are fundamental for all this; see *The English East India Company* (London, 1965), *The Trading World of Asia and the English East India Company, 1660–1760*, (Cambridge, 1978); *Trade and Civilisation*. For summaries of his work, see his chapters in the *Cambridge Economic History of India*, vol. I, and in Leonard Blussé and Femme Gaastra, eds., *Companies and Trade*, (Leiden, 1981).

[104] Chaudhuri, *The English East India Company*, 3–69; Foster, *England's Quest*, 150–1; for the text of the charter, see G. Birdwood and W. Foster, eds., *The First Letter Book of the East India Company, 1600–1619*, (London, 1893), 163–89.

ment of gents . . . do dryve a great number of the adventurers to with-
drawe ther contributions." The inappropriately titled, "adventurers,"
really merchant investors so opposed to adventure or risk-taking as
to insist on monopoly rather than competition, were worried that
such a person would want to do a Drake-like "warfare voyage."[105]
Such a response from the VOC could never have happened, for men
like Michelborne were irrelevant in Dutch politics and certainly would
never have been considered for command of VOC ships. Nor could
this have happened in France; the state there took a close interest in
the personnel employed by French companies, and would not be
brooked of this right.

Many other examples of this relationship could be quoted. In September 1601 the EIC was trying to raise money for the second voyage
(it should be remembered that until 1612 the company sent out separate, and separately financed, voyages). Because the results of the
first were not yet known, very little money was promised by the
members. This annoyed the court, and a month later the Privy Council
wrote a scolding letter that held up the example of the Dutch, and
hinted strongly at an end to the company's monopoly if it could not
keep the voyages going.

The influence of wider diplomatic concerns can also be seen in
events after the Persian-English capture of Hormuz from the Portuguese in 1622, as also can the opportunism (or fiscalism) of the state.
England and Spain, then ruling Portugal, were now at peace in Europe, but even so James I was prepared to back the company against
Portuguese protests. But he and his favorite, Buckingham, also used
the opportunity to squeeze the company. Buckingham, as Lord High
Admiral, demanded a share of the spoils – one-tenth of the claimed
booty of £100,000. The company had already given his wife £2,000 as
a sweetener, and now protested that it had not been operating under
Buckingham's authority but rather as a trading company. His response was to say that in that case the company's action had been
piratical. Caught between two stools, the company chose the lesser
evil and paid up to Buckingham. James I extorted a similar amount
of £10,000, the occasion of his memorable question "Did I deliver you
from the complaint of the Spaniard and do you return me nothing?"[106]

The primacy of European diplomatic concerns in the minds of the
government was often seen. After several EIC servants were killed
by the Dutch at Amboina in 1623, and again after the Dutch took the

---

[105] Foster, *England's Quest,* 149; Andrews, *Trade, Plunder, and Settlement,* 262.
[106] Foster, *England's Quest,* 311; Chaudhuri, *East India Company,* 64.

important port of Bantam in 1682 and expelled the English from it, the EIC was keen to retaliate. On both occasions, it was stopped by the Crown, which for its own diplomatic ends wanted peace with the Dutch. But, as Chaudhuri notes, the financial connection was the key: at home "its monopoly and other commercial privileges were upheld by the state largely as a result of the financial payments received by the Crown."[107] This was a constant in the seventeenth century. The Protectorate in 1659 asked for a loan of £30,000, and finally was bought off with £15,000. Charles II squeezed out £10,000 in 1662, £50,000 in 1666, and next year £70,000. Even more ominous, in 1698 a rival company was allowed after it had lent the government £2,000,000. After the successful merger of old and new in 1709, the whole capital of the United Company of £3,000,000 was lent to the government, and the company operated on borrowed funds.

What did the company receive in return for this virtual extortion? The short answer is, as noted above, the freedom to make the best it could of its monopoly in the East, though even this was twice breached by the government. But it did receive some other help. On occasion the state lent diplomatic support: Sir Thomas Roe and later negotiators with Indian political powers were royal ambassadors, even if they were paid by and acted for the company. More generally, it seems that the state was aware that the successes of the company, to be seen especially, after a slow beginning, in the second half of the century, did indeed increase England's prosperity, and did raise customs revenues for the Crown. A sign of this government appreciation is that, even in this mercantilist age, it was prepared right from the start to allow the company to export vast amounts of bullion. In the second half of the century, never less than two-thirds of the company's visible exports were precious metals.

Chaudhuri has written that, "if there was a perfect example of what we today understand as the spirit of mercantalism, the East India Company embodied it in its policy of harnessing political power and privileges to commercial purpose."[108] Implicitly this applies to the company from its foundation, and in fact mercantilism as such, in the broad sense of political actions that were designed to foster the trade of one's own country, has a long history in England, indeed in Europe. It is, after all, really just a policy of economic nationalism, in a context of new powerful territorial states an obvious matter of each for itself, designed especially to build up the supply of bullion.

[107] Chaudhuri, *Trading World of Asia*, 120.
[108] Ibid., 20.

In this general sense, English governments, whose financial resources were to an important extent dependent on customs revenues (as long ago as Henry VI, nearly one half of public revenue came from duties on external trade), had always been mercantilist. The legislation of the mid-seventeenth century can be described not as totally innovative, but as an effort to consolidate and regulate privileges and monopolies so as to serve better the interests of the state.

Nevertheless, the scope was extended considerably in England around the middle of the seventeenth century; the Navigation Acts mark a quantitative, even if not qualitative, change. The reason seems to be that commerce was becoming more important and commercial interests less subservient to the previously overwhelmingly dominant landed interest. And, although one can see the EIC as mercantilist to be sure, the Navigation Acts had little to do with English activities in the East. Rather, they stemmed from the fact of territorial colonies in America, and from the need to make the best use of these.

It is no more correct to see these colonies as instances of powerful and theoretically conscious state direction than it would be as regards the EIC. Similarly to Spain, the Crown merely issued a charter, normally either in return for a payment, or to a favorite, more often both together, and then let private capital get on with it. The extreme examples are the North American proprietary companies in, for example, Barbados and Maryland; or for that matter similar ventures in Ireland. The important consequence was that the existence of these colonies was taken advantage of, enhanced, by the Navigation Acts. The aim was to build up English exports, reduce imports from noncolonial sources, and for both strategic and economic reasons build up the trade carried in English ships. In short, the Navigation Acts aimed at "the twin goals of strategic power and economic wealth through shipping and colonial monopoly."[109] This, of course, is not to say that here either was there a consistent body of doctrine that found expression in legislation. To the extent that mercantilism is heuristically a useful concept, this is thanks to the work of later commentators, and especially Adam Smith, who reified a rather inchoate and ad hoc body of policy into a system merely in order to denounce it.[110]

---

[109] C. H. Wilson, "Trade, Society and the State," in *The Cambridge Economic History of Europe*, IV, 520–1, 496.

[110] The literature is, of course, vast. I have found the following most useful: Richard Conquest, "The State and Commercial Expansion: England in the Years 1642–1688," *Journal of European Economic History* 14 (1985): 155–71; Lars Magnusson, "Eli Heckscher, Mercantalism, and the Favourable Balance of Trade," *Scandinavian Economic History Review* 31 (1978): 103–27; Ball, *Merchants and Merchandise*, 44–9; Salim

The legislation on its own was not sufficient; it was backed up by force as needed, most obviously in the three Anglo-Dutch wars, and in the eighteenth century by wars against France. The fruition came only in the eighteenth century, when England's trade did expand enormously; as one measure, the tonnage of the English fleet rose by 326 percent between 1702 and 1788.[111] As Coleman notes,[112] government regulation remained important throughout. Less restrictions in the nineteenth century were a result of English dominance, not its cause. But, as we noted above, the role of the government in this triumph was facilitative rather than causative or directive; and secondly the role of overseas trade, at least to the eighteenth century, does not seem to have been particularly important or generative in terms of the total economy. Trade expanded after, and as a result of, the Industrial Revolution.[113]

France

France is often quoted as an awful warning of the consequences of too much state concern with trade. As compared with a positive merchant-state nexus in the Netherlands, and a rather fortuitously beneficial relationship in England, in France the state pushed too hard, was so directive as to stifle what indigenous forces there may have been. The difference with England lay in France's much greater natural resources, so that overseas trade was less important in the total economy, and hence merchant interests were less influential, their class position fragmented by the overweening power of the state. Indeed the basic political context was quite different, being characterized by *étatisme* and economic autarky.[114] One comparison then is with Spain and Portugal, and the important similarity with Spain has to do with territorial extent, and with the European ambitions of kings

---

Rashid, "Economists, Economic Historians, and Mercantilism," *Scandinavian Economic History Review* 28 (1980): 1–14; D. C. Coleman, "Mercantalism Revisited," *Historical Journal* 23 (1980): 773–91.

[111] R. P. Thomas and D. N. McCloskey, "Overseas Trade and Empire, 1700–1860," in R. Floud and D. McCloskey, eds., *The Economic History of Britain Since 1700*, (vol. I, 1700–1860, Cambridge, 1981), 92.

[112] Coleman, "Mercantilism Revisited."

[113] See Thomas and McCloskey, "Overseas Trade and Empire," 87–102; Cipolla, *Before the Industrial Revolution*, 292–4. Patrick O'Brien in his important article "European Economic Development: The Contribution of the Periphery," *Economic History Review* 2d ser., 35 (1982): 1–18, notes that even in 1790 only about 4 percent of Europe's GNP was exported across national boundaries.

[114] C. H. Wilson, "Trade, Society and the State," in *Cambridge Economic History of Europe*, IV, 522–30.

in both countries. Another, difficult, comparison could be made between French and Asian land-based empires, for in Europe only France was close to these in terms of extent, population, and numbers of peasants waiting to be taxed.

The policies associated with Colbert and Louis XIV had quite hoary antecedents. Even in the first half of the sixteenth century, when France was moving to greater unity but the administration was still underdeveloped, the state undertook as best it could intervention designed to help local manufactures. Impressively long lists laid down which goods were to be imported, where they were to come from, and through which French town they were to enter. Similarly, Richelieu made trade agreements with Denmark and Sweden, and with Turkey. These trends found fruition in Colbert's policies in the 1660s and 1670s. While in England the internal economy was freed up, in France industry was closely regulated by the state, a top-down rather than bottom-up strategy. There were incentives, such as interest-free loans and land and buildings at low rents. State workshops were set up for some luxuries, and to produce others monopoly rights and subsidies were allocated, but with rigorous state inspection.

Colbert, despite France's greater internal resources, did see overseas trade as important. Classic mercantilist policies were followed. Raw-material imports were tax-free, imported manufactures were taxed, and the export of French manufactures was subsidized. In 1673 foreign ships were excluded from French colonial trade. The policies are familiar enough, as was military help, for example in the wars with the Netherlands, which were meant to back up legislative assistance. Similarly with the many overseas trading companies. Unlike in England and the Netherlands, they were largely state controlled. The government was active in their formation, recruited members, appointed directors, provided capital. State political concerns had priority; business was to be under the control of, even at the mercy of, the state and its concerns. These concerns were typified by Versailles and the vastly expensive wars of Louis XIV; in the 1700s some 75 percent of his revenue went to war.[115] This is not, however, to say that private merchants always suffered. In a manner a little analogous to Spain, French merchants could in effect sit back and let the state finance trading companies, and then plunder them, as in pursuing their own trading interests under the umbrella of a company.[116] However, this sort of individual profit-making is very different from the

---

[115] Geoffrey Parker, *The Military Revolution*, 62.
[116] Pierre H. Boulle, "French Mercantilism, Commercial Companies, and Colonial Profitability," in Blussé and Gaastra, eds., *Companies and Trade*, 97–117.

activities and profits of the Dutch and English companies as corporations. French companies always lost money. Had the state not needed such vast resources to support its military operations, it is at least possible that the French economy generally would have been less subject to government control and so could have done better. But *dirigisme* designed to finance unproductive state expenditure resulted in the eighteenth century in ossified industry, unsuccessful trading companies, and a generally stagnant economy.

A final point to clarify here is one that relates to the general matter of the impact of overseas trade on general economic development. The literature mostly sees this impact as small indeed.[117] Spain's overseas trade expanded greatly in the sixteenth and seventeenth centuries, and Professor Butel's excellent chapter in *The Rise of Merchant Empires* shows for the first time how greatly France's did too, from Colbert's time onward. But the point is first that this trade was small in terms of the total economies of these two countries, and especially of France's; and second that this trade did not, for the reasons we have sketched, lead to any important expansion of the home economy in general. It is not the fact of overseas trade, or even its growth, that is important, but rather the uses to which it is put.

If we now turn to Asian land-based empires we see a very different picture. It seems that ideological factors make at least some difference, which can help to explain rather different attitudes to trade in Mughal India as compared with Ming and Qing China. In China we find a strong state, which either interfered in, or even forbade, foreign trade. In the case of India, the state was little interested, and neither helped nor hindered trade very much.

India

The pronounced difference in the Asian case is between the port cities strung all around the littoral of the Indian Ocean, and the territorially based tributary agrarian empires. The whole mind-set of the Mughal emperors and their nobles was land-based. Prestige was a matter of controlling vast areas on which were located fat, meek peasants. Glory was to be won by campaigns on land, leading one's contingent of cavalry, galloping over the plains. To courtiers, including the emperors, the sea was a marvel, a curiosity, a freak. This was not an arena where power and glory were to be won. Numerous elite aphorisms make this point: "Merchants who travel by sea are like silly

---

[117] See references cited in note 113 above.

worms clinging to logs." "Wars by sea are merchants' affairs, and of no concern to the prestige of kings." Tied up with this, a causative matter perhaps, was revenue. As we noted, the Mughal empire taxed its peasants rigorously and successfully, even if not to the extent laid down in the official manuals. Sea trade and merchants were grossly undertaxed. Peasants were required to pay one-third, even one-half, of their production to the state; customs duties were around 5 percent.

In this context, merchants were not hindered very much, but neither were they helped. The Mughal state saw no need, either fiscal or ideological, to pass the sorts of legislation, create the sorts of infrastructures, that occurred in the Netherlands and England. As in England, merchants were welcome to get on with it and do the best they could, but unlike in England the state did nothing at all to help.

This broad picture does need to be modified a little. Particular nobles at particular times did have more interest in sea and trade matters. A noble who drew his revenue, in other words held a *jagir*, at a port was concerned to increase the trade of this port; hence, at times complaints from local merchants could lead to the local political authority in, say, Surat restricting the trade of the Europeans. But such officials did not have a continuing and generative interest in sea trade. Like all the others, they were rotated every three years or so, and from Surat could be posted far inland and away from any concern with sea trade. In any case, these temporary port controllers were still subject to the authority, and norms, of their land-based and land-oriented emperors, just as we noted earlier of the governor of the great port city of Cambay.

In their own way, the emperors were as bullionist as were Europeans in the seventeenth century. They had no theoretical underpinning for this, but they were concerned to see continue the age-long flow of precious metals into India. Some 80 percent of Mughal India's imports were bullion, mostly silver.[118] To this end, the Europeans in the early seventeenth century paid duties of 3.5 percent on goods, but only 2 percent on bullion. Too much cannot be made of this, however; the emperors were also keen to get curiosities from overseas, and the importation of these was also encouraged, in much the same way as was bullion. We are not here dealing with some sort of embryonic mercantilism. The Mughals never tried to restrict what export of bullion there was, nor indeed any other product, not even foodstuffs or military matériel.

Third, many of the Mughal elite traded on their own behalf. This

---

[118] Moosvi, *Economy of the Mughal Empire*, 381 and footnotes.

was seen as a quite acceptable way to increase private incomes. Merchants were usually used as agents to handle the mechanics of this trade. Nobles and members of the royal dynasty owned their own ships, and traded in very substantial quantities. For much of the seventeenth century in Bengal, overseas trade was largely in the hands of the elite.[119] At times, political powers used this to give themselves an extra advantage in trade, such as in instructing a local port official to coerce merchants into selling cheap to them, or to hinder the trade of merchant rivals. In the late seventeenth century in Bengal, a new *subahdar*, a grandson of the emperor Aurangzeb, was a very active trader, to the extent of making compulsory purchases at low prices. The point, however, is that once his grandfather heard of this he was reprimanded and demoted.[120] Similarly with other more flagrant cases of abuse; there was a fairly effective state authority, and this intervened as best it could to check abuses generally, not just those dealing with overseas trade. Such rectifications often resulted from complaints from merchants who had been detrimentally affected by these actions; when merchants felt really oppressed, they could even threaten to leave a port where an official was behaving badly and take their trade to another. A noble whose basic income came from customs payments obviously was suspectible to such threats, and usually responded by ending the abuse.

The final modification as regards the Mughals has to do with a different sort of ideological factor, that is, religion. To varying extents, the Mughals were concerned to safeguard, and even promote, the pilgrimage to Mecca. In Mughal times, as a result of tense political relations and also dogmatic disputes with *shia* Safavid Persia, this was normally done by sea through the great port of Surat. Europeans in both the sixteenth and seventeenth centuries were sometimes able to pressure the Mughals by threatening to block this pious passage. Here is the one area where the sea impinged decisively on the Mughal consciousness, though even here the sea route needs to be seen as merely a necessary link to enable a land-based activity, the *hajj*, to take place.

If we look south, to the sultanates of Bijapur and Golconda, we find a slightly different picture; rulers here were a little closer to the position of the port city rulers. These states, independent until they were conquered by the Mughals in the 1680s, were smaller and for

---

[119] Om Prakash, *The Dutch East India Company and the Economy of Bengal, 1630–1720* (Princeton, 1985), 229–34.

[120] Ibid., 214; Satish Chandra, "Commercial Activities of the Mughal Emperors during the Seventeenth Century," *Bengal Past and Present* 78 (1959): 92–7.

this reason gave greater attention to sea trade. As Subrahmanyam notes, there was more "interpenetration of the worlds of merchants and politico" in Golconda; in Mughal Surat "the worlds of merchant and politico appear far more disjunct than on Coromandel."[121] We lack precise data, but the strong possibility is that revenue from overseas trade, both customs duties and participation by the elite, made up a higher proportion as compared with land-based sources than was the case in Mughal India. Two outstanding recent books[122] make a strong case for the existence of an important connection between the court and the sea. The great Coromandel port of Masulipatnam, for example, was dominated by the trade and ships of the Golconda royalty and elite. These sultans encouraged the development of ports, and the linkage of them with inland areas. Merchants, on the other hand, had considerable control over the administration and revenues of ports and coastal villages, and in return lent large sums of money to the elite. Subrahmanyam has pointed to the existence of "portfolio capitalists," people who straddled inland and ports, who linked the land and the sea.[123]

We are not here being given a picture of a relationship like that in, say, Venice or the Netherlands. The point seems to be that, though for fiscal reasons there was much more state involvement in sea trade, this seldom led to too much interest, along the lines of France. There were connections no doubt, but this did not mean that nobles consistently abused their position; they were too tied in with powerful merchants to be able to do this. Nor, on the other hand, did this lead to the sorts of infrastructural or legislative encouragements one finds in England. As a telling example, in England at this time a more powerful central authority was freeing up the internal economy, but in Golconda the state was unable or unwilling to do precisely this. Trade in the hinterlands of the ports was subject to numerous road taxes and tolls "because of the historic rights of taxation accruing to a variety of authorities."[124] The sorts of generative policies pursued by the Nawab of Arcot, which we sketched earlier, make the matter

---

[121] Sanjay Subrahmanyam, "Persians, Pilgrims and Portuguese: The Travails of Masulipatnam Shipping in the Western Indian Ocean, 1590–1665," *Modern Asian Studies* 22 (1988): 530 and footnote, and also 505, 511, 513–4 for closer merchant-politics connections.

[122] S. Arasaratnam, *Merchants, Companies, and Commerce*; S. Subrahmanyam, *The Political Economy of Commerce: Southern India, 1550–1650* (Cambridge and New York, 1990).

[123] Subrahmanyam, "Aspects of State Formation," 370–2.

[124] S. Arasaratnam, "European Port-Settlements in the Coromandel Commercial System, 1650–1740," *Proceedings of the Second International Conference on Indian Ocean Studies*, (Perth, 1984): 4.

clear. As ruler of a tiny state, he was very dependent on revenue from trade, and took innovative steps to encourage this; the rulers of the much larger mini-empire of Golconda were not in this position. Merchant influence, and state-merchant interaction, was greater, or at least more visible, than was the case in the Mughal empire, but this was not a matter of a generic or structural difference.

Persia and Turkey

Much the same can be said of the other two great agrarian Muslim tributary empires of the time, Turkey and Persia. In the case of the latter, there are some indications of a slightly more interventionist role from the court, based, however, completely on fiscal and political factors. As one example, Shah Abbas I early in the seventeenth century was anxious to encourage European traders to use his ports; indeed, he even used one European against another, for he called in the English in 1622 to help take Hormuz from the Portuguese. The shah intervened for two reasons. First, Safavid Persia was locked in a virtually unending battle with the Ottomans, and the shah hoped that the Europeans could help him with military technology; hence the favoring, and the embassies, of the Sherleys. Second, Persia's main export was silk. An important destination for the silk was Europe, and this trade passed through Turkey and, of course, was taxed on the way. The shah then was anxious for this trade to bypass his enemy, and instead go by sea to Europe. Similarly, he imported Chinese silk-weavers so that Persia could export manufactured rather than raw silk. But this was not a matter of state encouragement of general economic development, for the silk trade in Persia was more or less a royal monopoly, and the shah's actions were thus merely fiscal. General Persian policy seems to be remarkably congruent with that of the Mughals and the Ottomans.

In Turkey, merchants again were left alone to trade and pay taxes. Nevertheless, it is necessary to stress the very large extent of trade in this vast empire. McGowan estimates that, while the Baltic grain trade in the late seventeenth century was valued at 78 million grams of silver, Ottoman exports were worth 292 million grams. Even late in the next century, the figures were 63 as compared with 290.[125] As in Mughal India, the revenue needs of the state could be largely met from taxes on the produce of the land. Merchants were conspicuously undertaxed. Ottoman aphorisms reflect exactly the same ethos as that

---

[125] McGowan, *Economic Life in Ottoman Turkey*, 16.

of the Mughals. Again as in India, we do have some evidence of relations between merchants and the state, and indeed the connection may have been slightly tighter here. At least in Constantinople, merchants cooperated with nobles, who used funds from the treasury together with their own resources, and the approval of the sultan, to export grain. Ordinary people were prohibited from doing this, and the nobles and their merchant partners made huge profits as the Ottomans kept the domestic price of grain low. Similarly, low taxes often meant big profits for merchants, and some of this wealth was lent to nobles, and even to the government itself.[126]

This, however, does not mean that the government did much to help merchants. We must note again the revisionist interpretation put forward in the collection edited by Islamoglu-Inan. The editor in the Introduction to this fine collection puts forward a case for a very large state role in controlling trade and merchants; the state, for example, could "direct the flow of goods."[127] As I noted in my comments on the general discussion by these authors of the connections between state and the economy, I feel that their case is at best not proven, and that two crucial distinctions, between normative and actual, and between the center and the periphery, must always be kept in mind. As should be clear, I follow Wolf in seeing merchants playing an essential role in the functioning of these large tributary empires, but am unable to accept claims as grandiose as those put forward in the Islamoglu-Inan collection. But we must await further empirical research before we can pronounce with any finality. Certainly there are instances of military intervention for what at first sight may seem to be economic reasons. In 1538 a large naval contingent was sent to attack the Portuguese in the Indian Ocean, at their port of Diu. To counter pirates on the important Alexandria-Constantinople route, merchant ships sailed in convoy and were protected by state warships. And generally, the aphorisms to the contrary, the Ottomans, unlike the Mughals, did possess and use a very large and effective navy. Yet this was perhaps large and effective only when compared with other navies in the Mediterranean at the time. As Braudel noted of the Ottoman defeat at Lepanto, so cataclysmic a victory for the Christian forces, in terms of total Ottoman interests this was a minor matter; the sultan could simply withdraw to his vast landed empire and concentrate on more important matters, such as wars with Persia.

As for the particular cases cited above, to which could be added

---

[126] S. Shaw, *History of the Ottoman Empire*, I, 158–9.
[127] H. Islamoglu-Inan, "Introduction," in H. Islamoglu-Inan, ed., *The Ottoman Empire and the World Economy*, 10.

many others, what we have here is really just the state looking after its own interests. The attack on Diu was motivated in part by anti-Christian feeling, and in part was an attempt to dispossess the Portuguese so that the spice trade through Ottoman territory would rise to pre-Portuguese levels and so increase customs payments to the state; in other words, the expedition was basically fiscal. As for convoying ships to Constantinople, matters of prestige must have played some part here, but probably more important was the constant Ottoman preoccupation with food supplies for the capital; and here they seem, as in the Italian cities, to have been influenced by notions of the common good – residents of the capital at least should be fed – and by the converse, the threat of disorder if food ran out.

China

Chinese state attitudes to foreign trade were also affected by fiscal and politico-military factors, with an ideological input that is now a matter of some discussion. The emphasis that Fairbank put on this, such as the ideological influences that determined the tribute system, seem now to be less stressed in the historiography. Fairbank's case for a massive ideological input runs as follows:[128] foreign trade "was officially regarded as a boon granted to the barbarian, the necessary means to his sharing in the bounty of China, and nothing more. No doubt, this quixotic doctrine reflected the anticommercial nature of the Confucian state, where the merchant was low in the social scale and nominally beneath both the farmer and the bureaucrat, who lived off the produce of the land." True, he then allows the influence of less mystical factors: "It was strengthened perhaps by the self-sufficiency of the empire, which made supplies from abroad unnecessary. At all events, it was the tradition that foreign trade was an unworthy objective for high policy and this dogma was steadily reiterated in official documents down into the nineteenth century. Meanwhile, foreign trade developed and grew even larger within its ancient tributary framework."[129]

The precise ideological underpinning of all this was the Confucian notion of superiority, especially cultural. The emperor's virtue inevitably attracted foreign barbarians, and tribute was a ritual expression of this inferiority, and of the beneficence of the emperor. Beneath the ritual umbrella of the tribute system much ordinary, commercially

---

[128] See especially Fairbank, *Trade and Diplomacy*, 3–38; 46–7, 51–2. Professor Wang in his contribution to *The Rise of Merchant Empires* follows Fairbank on this matter.

[129] Fairbank, *Trade and Diplomacy*, 33.

based, trade took place. Trade that was not incorporated in the tribute system was carried on under very controlled conditions, this being a consequence of the low status of merchants in the Confucian ethic.

Yet the actual conduct of foreign trade seems to have been influenced by other, much more pragmatic, factors. The states of south China from the tenth century controlled insufficient productive land to be indifferent to overseas trade, so state involvement was substantial. Trade was encouraged because it yielded large customs revenues. At times, government funds were even invested in voyages overseas. Trade was handled mostly by foreigners, especially Koreans and Arabs, and they were both controlled and helped. In the ports a special office handled customs and registration matters, supplied interpreters, received them officially, and gave them a farewell dinner when they left.[130] An edict of 1146 from the southern Sung runs: "The profits of foreign trade contribute much to the national income. We ought to continue the old system by which people of faraway countries are encouraged to come and abundantly circulate goods and wealth."[131] The echoes here are of Golconda, or the littoral port cities of the same and later periods; the contrast with, say, the Mughals could hardly be sharper.

The big change came with the Ming, and then Qing, dynasties. There were three reasons for their generally hostile attitude to foreign trade. Ideology, that is Neo-Confucianism, no doubt played a part. More important was the size of these empires, much bigger than, say, the southern Sung, and much more agrarian based. Finally, the continuing threat from the Mongols and their successors in the northwest dictated a state concentration on land matters, and on defense, at the expense of trade. The first Ming emperor (r. 1368–98) banned all overseas travel for all Chinese, and restricted all maritime trade to foreign tributary missions. Similarly, increased piracy off the coast fostered a withdrawal from trade, the tactic being to starve them out. The effects could be devastating, literally. The new Qing dynasty was faced by a successful revolt by the Ming loyalist Cheng Ch'eng-kung (1624–62). His illicit trade with southeast China was the basis of a large maritime empire centered on Taiwan. The Qing response was massive. Thousands of villages and towns along the coast were forcibly evacuated. Although not always strictly enforced, this policy remained in effect for twenty years, and, if it did lead finally to the defeat of Cheng and his followers, it also had very obviously detri-

---

[130] McNeill, *Pursuit of Power*, 41; Reischauer, *East Asia: The Great Tradition*, 211–7; Eberhard, *History of China*, 198; Chaudhuri, *Trade and Civilization*, 55.
[131] See Elvin, *Pattern of The Chinese Past*, 215–25.

mental effects on those dispossessed.[132] The decline of the Chinese navy was also important; one reason for this was that, after the Grand Canal to Beijing was reopened in the early fifteenth century, rice supplies for the capital, a preoccupation for Chinese emperors as for many other rulers, could come this way instead of by coastal shipping. Thus, private trade was officially prohibited, or at least discouraged.

This is not to say that all trade outside of the tribute system was ended. There is evidence of considerable trade, legally smuggling, but in fact often protected by, and making large profits for, officials in the southern ports. An example is the large trade in silk for silver between Canton and Manila, which began in the late sixteenth century and flourished for two centuries, and Portuguese trade between Macao and Japan, which ended in the 1630s. Indeed it seems the official ban was supported by local gentry and officials precisely because within the context of a not very well enforced ban they could do very well from smuggling.[133]

The most quoted case concerns the end of the voyages associated with the Muslim eunuch Cheng Ho. Indeed, Jones choses to cite this as a prime example of the problems of empires; they can make these prohibitions and can enforce them, whereas in the state system of Europe such a ban would not have such a universal currency. As is well known, between 1405 and 1433 Cheng Ho led seven expeditions, which got as far as Jidda and east Africa. These were major feats; the first had 62 vessels and 28,000 men. Their motivation was traditional. The object was not exploration as such, nor trade for profit, but rather to incorporate South and Southeast Asia into the tribute system. These voyages were ended because they were expensive, because of the threat from the north, and because Cheng Ho as a eunuch and a Muslim was part of the emperor's circle at court, and was opposed by the mandarins. Not just these expeditions were stopped; it is from this time that blanket bans on overseas trade were imposed. Three years after the expeditions were stopped the building of new seagoing ships was also forbidden.

Several eminent historians, including Fernand Braudel, Immanuel Wallerstein, Joseph Needham, and W.H. McNeill, have been struck by the parallels between these voyages and the contemporary early expeditions of the Portuguese down the west African coast. We are told that the Chinese had the capacity to round the Cape and discover

[132] William S. Atwell, "Some Observations on the Seventeenth-Century Crisis in China and Japan," *Journal of Asian Studies* 45 (1986): 234.

[133] Elvin, *Pattern of the Chinese Past*, 215–25; Reischauer, *East Asia*, 324–37; Chaudhuri, *Trade and Civilisation*, 13; Levenson, *European Expansion*, pp. 82–3.

Europe; world history would have been stood on its head. Although this sort of attitude at least is a useful corrective to older Eurocentric versions of the inevitable advance of the West, the moral usually drawn is that it was the power of the Chinese state that ended the voyages; denunciations of empires, or of Confucianism, then follow. But this is only part of the explanation. To be sure, state involvement generally in overseas trade, characterized by tight controls, the tribute system, and at times prohibitions, was clearly detrimental, and reflects the interests of an elite that had political, resource, and ideological reasons for these attitudes. It is for this reason that the Cheng Ho expeditions must not be seen as an aborted thrust that could have led to the creation of a world system. They were rooted in Chinese society, were intricately bound up with the tribute system, and so have to be seen as totally different in character even from the halting expansion of the Portuguese at the same time, let alone as compared with the later Dutch and English. They were more like the French East India Companies, and would have gone nowhere for the same reasons, concerning the interests and the role of the state.

ASIAN RESPONSES TO THE MERCHANT EMPIRES

Finally, we turn to an analysis of the responses of local states to the trading activities of the merchant empires in their areas. What we have said about the attitudes of various Asian states to trade in general, and about the roles of home governments in the actions of the companies, is all relevant to understand the nature of the relationship up to the middle of the eighteenth century. Thus, a distinction has to be made between the responses of port city controllers and rulers of tributary empires, just as the policies and ambitions of the various Europeans need to be differentiated.

When we disaggregate the data in this way we find a very varying, but in general minor, European role. Om Prakash has been a leader in this effort. He finds, for example, that in the late seventeenth century the VOC was taking some 30 percent of the refined saltpeter produced in Bengal. In this same area, 10 percent of employment in textiles was created by European demand.[134] In the sixteenth century, Asian spice and pepper production roughly doubled, thanks to increased demand both in Asia and Europe. These data mark a step toward greater specificity to be sure, but their evaluation is not always

---

[134] Prakash, *Dutch East India Company*, 60, and "Bullion for Goods," *Indian Economic and Social History Review* 13 (1976): 159–87.

an easy task – is 10 percent a lot or a little? What can be said is that there is no sign that these and other examples of increased demand produced any structural change in the industries concerned; this may have been a result of there being such slack in the local economies that this increased demand could be met without changing existing productive techniques. Yet there is good evidence of Asian trade expanding greatly in the seventeenth century, and of Europeans playing a larger role in this trade, especially in transporting it;[135] and it is hard to see there being such slack in the Indian economy that this apparently large increase could continue to be met merely by taking up unused capacity. Again we need much more empirical research; in the meantime, it does seem that Asian trade and Asian production changed *quantitatively*, but in Europe at this same time there were *qualitative* internal changes occurring.

Three other general points must be made before we proceed to cases. First is to stress again that we must not see the European presence as completely innovatory. There had, after all, been foreigners trading all around the Asian littoral for millenia before 1500. European activities after this time and until the mid-eighteenth century can in many ways be seen as different only in degree, not in kind. Similarly with the Europeans themselves. Just as we depicted Portuguese methods as really being a continuation of Venetian policies in the Mediterranean, the notion of trading posts in foreign areas goes back to the Mediterranean. One can see a line of progression from the *fondachi*, the residential quarters, of the Genoese, Venetians, and other Italians in the ports of north Africa and the Levant, to Portuguese factories in west Africa and then in Asia, and so on to the factories of the Dutch and English. This is the sort of point stressed in Scammell's attempt[136] to find continuity from 800 to 1650. Similarly, the fact of long-distance trade was not new for either the Dutch or the English; indeed, Dutch financial strength in 1600, as seen in the capital available for the VOC, was built precisely on long-distance trade, to the Baltic and the Atlantic fisheries, and throughout the seventeenth century this European trade was far more important for the Dutch than was the Asian trade.

Second, Steensgaard[137] has made a strong case for seeing a dis-

---

[135] See Subrahmanyam, "Persians, Pilgrims, and Portuguese;" Arasaratnam, *Merchants, Companies, and Commerce*; Niels Steensgaard, "Asian Trade and World-Economy from the 15th to 18th centuries," in T. R. de Souza, ed., *Indo-Portuguese History: Old Issues, New Questions* (New Delhi, 1985), 225–35.

[136] Scammell, *The World Encompassed*.

[137] Steensgaard, *The Asian Trade Revolution*. For a critique of the "Steensgaard thesis," see also the chapter by Subrahmanyam and Thomas in this volume.

junction at the time of the arrival of the companies. They represent, he says, a generically different economic force as compared with the pedlars and the Portuguese. At least potentially this is true, though the full implications of this were revealed, I would argue, only in the eighteenth century. In any case, this difference had much to do with European methods of commercial organization, but did not mark a major change in terms of political and economic impacts in Asia, and Asian responses to the European presence. As Steensgaard notes, the Dutch were able to lower their protection costs, but the fact of protection, and its being demanded or sold, was common to the sixteenth and seventeenth centuries, and indeed had been levied by some controllers of choke points on land for centuries.

A more important difference for our period may have to do with the fact that the Dutch early on acquired a territorial base, in Indonesia, but the English were slower to do this. Although there were differences between the various Europeans, as there were between their Asian interlocutors, these should not be overemphasized, especially if by doing this one ends up merely finding reasons for the final dominance of the English.

Responses to the Dutch and English

The Dutch had much more capital behind them than the English, and their early actions were more thoroughgoing and decisive. The Dutch moved vigorously against the Portuguese, and to establish control over spices. They soon conquered the main production areas in the Moluccas, and then pursued a rigorous policy of limiting production and trying, much more successfully than had the Portuguese, to control all the spice trade. They were less successful in monopolizing pepper, for it came from several different production areas, but in the 1650s after they took Sri Lanka from the Portuguese they were able to monopolize cinnamon also. They immediately raised the price from 15 stuivers a Dutch pond to 50, and later in the century to 60. The Dutch also acquired a firm territorial base by taking the port city of Djakarta, renamed Batavia.

These sorts of monopolies were, however, only a part of Dutch activities in Asia. Two other strands were equally important. In many areas of Indonesia, the Dutch did not conquer, but instead imposed treaties on controllers of port cities that gave the VOC particular privileges, even monopolies, over trade in desired products, especially pepper. Finally, and for our purposes most important, over vast areas of Asia the Dutch participated in the country trade on a basis of political and commercial equality. In this trade, as Arasaratnam has shown in the case of Coromandel, the Europeans had no particular commercial advantage; indeed, they were usually outtraded by the locals, except where they had some politico-military advantage, as in trade from here to Dutch-controlled areas in Indonesia. Nor can one see the early European settlements on the Indian coast as introducing positive European notions such as the rule of law that by providing security for property and persons inevitably attracted merchants from the surrounding Asian-ruled, and so implicitly less lawful, areas. Quite the contrary, as the earlier example of San Thomé seems to show, and as Arasaratnam has also shown in the case of Madras. Indians settled in this English town preferred not to use English courts, but rather their traditional systems of arbitration by caste elders.[138]

This country trade done by the companies was quite separate from the private country trade that some Dutch and many English company servants indulged in. The latter could, it is true, sometimes use company facilities and even backing, but these individuals were not organized, grouped, in the way the official country trade of the companies was. The point of the country trade was that the Dutch, like the English, found that the way to avoid having to pay for Asian products with bullion from Europe was to trade and profit in all sorts of goods within Asia, and use the profits from this to pay for goods bound for Europe. Not that this was totally successful, for both companies still did have to export large, and politically damaging, amounts of specie from their metropoles; the annual average of bullion imported just to Bengal by the Dutch alone was Fl.1.28 million in the 1660s, and steadily rose thereafter to Fl.2.87 million in the 1710s.[139] Steenagaard's chapter in *The Rise of Merchant Empires* makes the important point that European exports to Asia consisted of 10 percent for commodities, 30 percent for bullion, and a large 60 percent for services, such as technical, especially navigational, know-how, transportation, and even piracy. This somewhat nebulous category, like the inter-Asian trade, reduced the amounts of bullion needed to be exported, yet even so in European eyes the amounts exported remained very large indeed.

Our focus is on the political relations consequent on this trade, and we can select certain case studies to illustrate the process. We do not need to differentiate very much between the Dutch and English here,

---

[138] Arasaratnam, "European Port-Settlements," 11, and *Merchants, Companies, and Commerce*

[139] Prakash, *Dutch East India Company*, 249.

for though the English did not have the territorial base which the Dutch had, in China, India, and Japan the two were faced with similar problems and similar opportunities. And it is their contacts in India that are most relevant. China and Japan were less open to them, while except for the VOC in Indonesia their contacts with Southeast Asia at this time were rather peripheral. It was from India that they could get the vital trade items, especially cloths, that could be used in the country trade.

Some controllers of ports that were not linked to land empires saw that the Europeans could increase the trade of their ports, and so their customs revenues. So long as the Europeans did not try to obtain political control they were happy to have them call. In 1610 the raja of Vellore, who controlled the Coromandel port of Pulicat, even gave the Dutch a quasi-monopoly control over the trade of his port. He soon realized that this was not in his interests, and became concerned to get the English to trade there too. In 1614 he sent the English a letter "written uppon a leafe of golde, wherein hee excused the former faulte done to us in Paleacatte, desiring that nowe wee woulde come into his countrie and chuse a place to our beste lyking, and that there wee shoulde builde a howse or castle according to our owne lyking." Similarly, in 1639 a petty ruler in the same area of Coromandel invited the English to his village of Madraspatam, where they were allowed to build not just a factory but a fortified one. Thus was Fort St. George, soon to be surrounded by the town of Madras, acquired by the English. Such were the advantages of dealing with petty port city controllers; the Europeans could hope to get much better facilities there than in areas controlled by the empires. The Mughals would never have allowed European forts in their territories.

In north India the Dutch and English quickly realized that they were dealing not with petty port controllers but with a large and centralized empire. Hawkins, on the third English voyage, was told in Surat in 1607 that, though local officials could allow his ships to trade on a one-time basis, continuing trade needed permission from the emperor. He, therefore, went off to talk to Emperor Jahangir. What he, and his many successors, wanted was not just permission to trade, but more extensive privileges. They hoped to gain from the Mughals the sorts of advantages they had at home. They were prepared to pay money in return for getting privileges. They wanted formal, binding, treaties that would regulate and recognize the trade of their company in Mughal territories; later they asked for lower customs duties and no payment of internal duties. At first these sorts of claims were met by incomprehension at court. The Mughals had no concept of making treaties for trade at all, and certainly not with a group of merchants; as the Portuguese took great delight in pointing out at court, this was, as compared with their status as representatives of a real king, all that the Dutch and English were. For this reason, the companies used ambassadors accredited by their rulers, though they were paid by, and acted on behalf of, the companies.

Even this did not solve all the companies' problems. They were asking for privileges that had been granted to no other foreign traders. The Mughals were happy enough to see foreign traders call at their ports, but requests to make treaties with them, and later to give them rights that were not available to local traders, were incomprehensible. It was a true case of a failure to understand the most basic under-pinning of the Europeans' requests. The Mughals had no precedent for the sort of privileges-for-money equation that had for so long been the basic merchant-ruler connection in Europe. Nor do the early English embassies figure at all largely in the Indian accounts, even if we have voluminous documentation from the English side. Emperor Ja-hangir's copious *Memoirs* make hardly any reference at all to these early English embassies. And even the English accounts make clear the lack of interest of the court in their presence, much to the disgust of the self-important Sir Thomas Roe. He spent two years and nine months trailing around India with the court, in the end getting only a *farman*, an order, that gave good conditions for trade, but which, as the English later found out, had currency only for the reign of the emperor who had issued it and which was not always observed any-way. An earlier envoy, Canning, had been ignored by the emperor, who however was fascinated by a cornet player who was part of Canning's suite, this being a new instrument at court. The Jesuits, upset at this English advance, produced a European conjurer as a counter-attraction. Similarly, the English were disgusted that their prized broadcloths found no sale in India, and were insultingly used merely as covers for elephants. It is at this petty level of a search for novelties to catch the attention of the Great Mughal that early Eu-ropean intercourse with India proceeded. The parallels with Chinese attitudes then and much later are very clear.

What happened in India, however, was that the Europeans did make some advance over the seventeenth century.[140] This is not to say that the court became obsessed with foreign trade, even if Eu-ropean accounts sometimes give this impression. Mughal interests remained firmly land based. But the decline of Mughal authority later

---

[140] See the references in note 135, and also Chaudhuri, *Trading World* of Asia, 109–27.

in the seventeenth century provided opportunities for the Europeans, and their use of force on occasion produced advantages.

Professor Parker's chapter in this volume skillfully covers the use of force, and Asian responses to it. The English and Dutch were soon able to show that they were in fact not just yet another two groups of foreign merchants, like say Armenians, or Jews, or Cairo-based Muslims. They were backed up by much more organized and coherent trading companies, and they could use force selectively to get advantages. Like the Portuguese, they sold protection from their own violence, and sometimes from the violence of others. They issued passes, but these did not have the effectiveness of the earlier Portuguese ones because now there were at least three bodies issuing them; the Portuguese success, very partial anyway, had been based on their monopoly. And there were two more important differences. First, the companies did better than the Portuguese in that they used force in a much more selective, in fact rational, way; it was used only for commercial ends. Unlike the Portuguese, the bottom line was always the balance sheet. Second, a negative factor, their operations extended far inland. This meant that their servants in say Surat or Agra could be seized in retaliation for an attack on Indian ships at sea. The equation then was a delicate one. And the companies had to keep in mind their wider interests. If the Dutch tried to monopolize the trade between Gujarat and the Red Sea, this could hinder their other trade in the area. The companies needed Gujarat as an area to which they imported copper and spices, and from which they got cloths and indigo to send all over Asia and to Europe.[141]

A continuing problem was to get local officials to agree to enforce concessions acquired at court; this problem became greater as central authority declined. Partly as a result of this decline, the English in 1717 secured major advantages from the emperor. These can be seen as the achievement by the company of privileges comparable to those they enjoyed at home: concessions in return for money. They got the right not to pay duties on both external and internal trade, in return for the payment of fixed sums each year of Rs.10,000 at Surat and Rs.3,000 in Bengal. However, getting local authorities to agree to this took extra effort; the governor of Surat had to be given Rs.70,000 before he would confirm this concession. Such port officials, and also the myriad collectors of official and semiofficial inland duties, were obviously detrimentally affected by these imperial concessions, and

---

[141] H. W. van Santen, *De Verenigde Oost-Indische Compagnie in Gujarat en Hindustan, 1620–1660* (Leiden, 1982), English summary on 206–12, esp. 208–9.

had to be put right before they would agree to enforce them; all the more so as unscrupulous Europeans often sold off their rights to Indian colleagues too.

The use of force in fact went both ways. The lack of any Mughal navy, arguably a cost-effective decision, did mean that the Europeans could use selected naval actions to get advantages or secure redress. Late in the seventeenth century, European pirates operated in the Arabian Sea, much to the disgust of the companies, which were sometimes punished for their actions, the Mughals usually not differentiating between one lot of *farangis* and another. Finally, a pirate seized a large ship owned by Emperor Aurangzeb. His mind thus concentrated on sea matters, he got the companies to agree to provide escorts to Indian ships on the Red Sea route; the Dutch, for example, were to provide two armed escort vessels, and their crews, and were to beat off pirates. In return they got Rs.40,000 for each ship, one-half coming from the Surat customs house, and one-half from the merchants whose ships were thus protected.

Other individual actions by Mughal nobles could be less advantageous, though never so much as to lead to the companies giving up on the trade with India, just as Stuart extortion at home never really threatened the continuance of the EIC. Sometimes nobles acted to protect the interests of local merchants, no doubt after some sweeteners had been provided. In 1619 Surat merchants were alarmed that the English trade with the Red Sea, and especially the port of Mocha, was undercutting their own participation on this important route. Matters came to a head when the English brought in a cargo of Mediterranean coral, which previously had been imported from the Red Sea in Indian ships. Prince Khurram, later Emperor Shah Jahan, was quoted by an English agent as saying "He absolutelye tould mee wee should not trade to the Red Sea . . . nor bringe anye corrall into these partes to sell; and yf [we] could not be contented to have free trade for all but Mocha, wee might goe out of the countrye yf wee would, for [he] must not beggar his people for us." His solicitude for "his" merchants may well have been a gloss to cover his own extensive trading interests; certainly some years later when he was emperor he used his position to secure a noncommercial advantage. In 1643 the English had trouble getting freight for a ship of theirs bound for the Red Sea, because the governor of Surat had prohibited merchants, under great penalties, from lading goods on any vessel "untill the Kings great jounck was full." In other words, Mughals could be as thoroughly fiscal as could European rulers.

The Levant Company trading in the Ottoman Empire often had to put up with similar problems. When it was a matter of a prince or emperor, the companies could do little about it, just as they could not at home either; and, even when it was merely some local official, the cost of complaining at court and getting redress was often greater than the cost of ending the problem with a bribe. In any case, it is clear that these sorts of difficulties for the Europeans could be overcome. They were disadvantages no doubt, but not insuperable ones, and certainly they were outweighed by the advantage of having access to the valued trade goods of the Mughal empire.

These examples do not point to a coherent Mughal policy designed to cope with the presence of European traders in their ports. We must stress again that sea matters, sea trade, were peripheral for the Mughals. Occassionally they would give short-term advantages to the Europeans for short-term ends, but what they were really doing in the seventeenth century was building the Taj Majal, fighting wars of succession, defending Islam, coping with the Maratha revolt, squeezing the peasantry – land matters entirely. When we look at China and Japan, however, we find a rather more coherent policy affecting the Europeans.

Although in south China local gentry and officials were happy to allow foreign trade, and profit from the bribes involved, the official Chinese policy was one of exclusion and discouragement of foreigners in general. The authorities got suspicious if Europeans tried to venture beyond a tacitly tolerated position near the southern ports, and they were subjected to all sorts of indignities and restrictions. This is reflected in the vicissitudes of the Jesuit missionary and savant Ricci. He got to the Portuguese settlement of Macao in 1582, but like all other Europeans was not allowed to go farther into China. Finally, he received permission to travel to Beijing, and at last in 1601 was allowed to live in the capital. Similarly with the famous Macartney mission of 1793. His presents, worth a substantial £15,000, were labeled by the Chinese as "Tribute from the Kingdom of England." He was commended for his "respectful spirit of submission" but told "our celestial empire possesses all things in prolific abundance." But the emperor charitably added, "I do not forget the lonely remoteness of your island, cut off from the world by intervening wastes of sea."

These sorts of attitudes combined with other factors to reduce, until the eighteenth century, the role of the companies in south China. There was only a minor commercial push until tea drinking caught on in Europe; and, when efforts were made to investigate the possibilities of trade, they were met with firm rebuffs. English and Dutch exploratory voyages to south China in the first decade of the seventeenth century were simply told to go away. It was only in 1699 that an English factory was allowed in Canton; from then to about 1760 was the time of the Canton system.[142] From the Chinese end, the so-called Hoppo, the superintendent of maritime customs in Canton, used Chinese merchants as agents, this group being known to Europeans as the Cohong. The system was formalized in 1720. There were in fact other hongs dealing with other trade, and the origin of these groups goes back some centuries. Nor indeed were they, in Chinese terms, structurally very innovative. For example, they were similar to salt brokers who were licensed to supervise this monopoly, or indeed the traditional Chinese "guilds." As Fairbank puts it, "Through this merchant guild the Chinese state applied to the European traders the same type of regulatory mechanism that it used for merchants in China – a guild monopoly licensed by and responsible to the officials."[143]

In this system, European merchants, just like their Chinese competitors, were very closely supervised. The history of the system is one of tension and bargaining among the three parties involved, the Europeans, the Cohong, and the officials. The three standard Chinese demands were that all European ships should surrender their guns, powder, and sails while they were in Canton; that they should pay a series of taxes and duties; and that they should deal only with the Cohong. Europeans were also subject to Chinese law and, among more minor restrictions, they could not bring wives with them, nor use sedan chairs, nor enter the walled city of Canton.

This situation of total subordination, a very different context from that found in India and southeast Asia, was writ even larger in Japan once the "closed-country era" began. Toby has cast doubt on whether this policy affected Japan's relations with other areas in East Asia, but, as regards our present concern, the Europeans, after 1639 only the Dutch were allowed, and they were confined to Deshima island. Here they operated under even more tight restrictions than those later imposed in Canton. Few Japanese were allowed to have dealings with the Dutch; Japanese were not to learn Dutch, nor the Dutch Japanese (Portuguese was used instead); exports of gold were not allowed; goods were to be sold only on set days, and the main import, Chinese raw silk, was sold at a price more or less arbitrarily determined by Japanese merchant groups. The position of the Dutch was well reflected in the instructions the VOC sent to their agents there

---

[142] See Reischauer, *East Asia*, 71–4; *Trade and Diplomacy*, 47–50; Chaudhuri, *Trading World*, 55, 399–401.

[143] Reischauer, *East Asia*, 73.

in 1650. They must "look to the wishes of that bold, haughty, and exacting nation, in order to please them in everything."[144]

CONCLUSION

The general theme that can be extracted from all these data is clear enough, as is the value of even this sketchy attempt at a comparative exercise. Even if we are careful always to avoid ratifying the past from a basis of later events, even if we take pains to avoid trivializing the Asian experience by merely trying to find out what went wrong, we can still look at broad reasons for European advance, and at their attitudes to long-distance trade, and find useful comparisons. In the case of England, the trend in the literature is clear. The contribution of long-distance trade to development is problematic at best, and basically seems to be minor. As for the role of its government in intercontinental trade, this seems to reflect the state's role in the economy generally, a role that was at best facilitative, helpful, but not determining or interventionist, at least not on the basis of any coherent body of doctrine.

This broad conclusion can illuminate usefully the experience both of other European states, and also states in Asia. There are reasons why both the Chinese and the Indian states did not pursue the sorts of policies that contributed to development in England, though these reasons are not completely identical. And it must be stressed again that, even if they did not change in the same way as Europe did, this does not mean that "Asia" was inert, unchanging, ahistorical. Three scholars who have contributed to these volumes even doubt that European dominance had much to do with its commercial and industrial development; they see the beginning of European dominance in the eighteenth century as being a result of military advantage, and nothing more.[145] This is a classic chicken-and-egg question; did gun and shot make possible economic control, or was this military superiority a symptom of the qualitative commercial and economic changes occurring in Europe at this time? In any case, the logic of my argument is that Asia's failure, explicable though it may be in terms of the internal needs and interests of these states, did mean that they did not develop along English lines. These broader attitudes

---

[144] Prakash, *Dutch East India Company*, 119–20; C.R. Boxer, *The Dutch Seaborne Empire*, (London, 1965), 94–5.

[145] See Geoffrey Parker's chapter in this volume; Irfan Habib's chapter in *The Rise of Merchant Empires*; and Subrahmanyam, "Persians, Pilgrims and Portuguese," 530, where he finds the beginnings of a difference in Coromandel as early as 1655–65.

were reflected in the smaller, indeed peripheral, arena of overseas trade. An alternative argument, if this one is seen as being too uni-directional, too captivated by the largely fortuitous story of the development of Western Europe, would have to put forward a scenario for development in, say, China or India generically different from the European model. At the present stage, all we can say is that they had the choice of following the European model, a choice that for all the reasons given above was virtually impossible, or of developing on some other basis and so being able to compete with a Europe that was advancing in the way with which we are familiar. It is not my task to try to suggest such an alternative path to a status that could meet the European challenge. But only thus could they avoid being incorporated as peripheries in the world economy, avoid being under-developed, avoid suffering as merchant empires turned into much more ominous territorial empires backed by an economically dominant Western Europe.

CHAPTER 3

The rise of merchant empires, 1400–1700: A European counterpoint

THOMAS A. BRADY, JR.

Glory of empire! Most unfruitful lust
After vanity that men call fame!
It kindles still, the hypocritic gust,
By rumor, which as honor men acclaim.
What thy vast avengeance and thy sentence just
On the vain heart that greatly loves thy name
What death, what peril, tempest, cruel woe,
Dost thou decree that he must undergo!
     —Luis Vaz de Camoëns

Pride in their port, defiance in their eye,
I see the lords of human kind pass by.
     —Oliver Goldsmith

Where is the flag of England?
Go East, North, South or West;
Wherever there's wealth to plunder
Or land to be possessed;
Wherever there's feeble people
To frighten, coerce or scare;
You'll find the butcher's apron,
The English flag is there.
     —Derek Warfield of "The Wolfe Tones"

ON July 8, 1497, as Vasco da Gama's men were embarking at Lisbon's Belem docks, an old man, a soothsayer out of Greek drama, warned the departing adventurers that the pursuit of glory, wealth, and power in the East would doom their own souls. The Christian West would lose its soul in the East – or at least that is how Luis Vaz de Camoëns told it, many years later.[1] Da Gama's voyage and that of Columbus,

---

[1] Luis Vaz de Camoëns, *The Lusiads*, IV, 95, in Leonard Bacon's translation.

117

five years earlier, set Europeans on the path to global unification through the rise of merchant empires. The transformation of Europe from a lesser civilization perched on the western point of Eurasia into a cluster of empires brawling for domination of world trade is widely held to mark a turning point in world history. From the events of the 1490s thus come the currently popular divisions of the world into "developed" and "underdeveloped," "First World" and "Third World," "North" and South," and "white" and "colored." Although commonly employed today to criticize Europe, these pairs derive from a European vision of the post–1490s world. The Scottish philosopher Adam Smith proclaimed it in the birth year of the American Republic: "The discovery of America, and that of the passage to the East Indies by the Cape of Good Hope, are the two greatest events recorded in the history of mankind."[2] Today, as this vision shoulders aside a rival that claims "affiliation with a tradition of Western Civilization that ran back through modern and medieval Europe to the ancient Greeks and Hebrews,"[3] the rise of merchant empires is coming to mark the inception of modern history.

As they knitted the globe together, the European merchant empires affected different parts of the world in different ways. In parts of the Americas, ecological exchange made the initial contacts catastrophic; in other parts of the Americas and some of Africa and Oceania, peoples were drawn into the global trading system at a pace that allowed for adaptation and even some control; and in much of Asia the Europeans caused few important economic and political changes until the eighteenth century.[4] Then, however, "institutional changes in the international economic order speeded the process in banking, finance, transportation, and communication," and their source, industrial technology, "made it virtually impossible for any non-Western society to resist Westernization, at least in the field of trade and exchange."[5] The rise of merchant empires, therefore, formed the first stage of European penetration of and continuous interaction with the wider world, which led to radical transformations only after 1750.

More controversial is the merchant empires' part in the making of

[2] Quoted by André Gunder Frank, *World Accumulation, 1492–1789* (London, 1978), 25.
[3] William H. McNeill, "Mythistory," in his *Mythistory and Other Essays* (Chicago and London, 1986), 10.
[4] Alfred W. Crosby, *Ecological Imperialism: The Biological Expansion of Europe, 900–1900* (Cambridge, 1986); Eric R. Wolf, *Europe and the People without History* (Berkeley and Los Angeles, 1982), 131–231; Paul E. Lovejoy, *Transformations in Slavery: A History of Slavery in Africa* (Cambridge, 1983), 103–34; Michael N. Pearson, *Before Colonialism: Some Theories on Asian-European Relations, 1500–1750* (New Delhi, 1988).
[5] Philip D. Curtin, *Cross-Cultural Trade in World History* (Cambridge, 1984), 251.

modern Europe.[6] According to its usual plot, the story of modern Europe as "development" begins in Portugal around 1450 and migrates northward to find its proper home in England and the Netherlands around 1600, where it settles down to wait for the great transformation around 1750. The story of Europe can also be plotted, however, from the experiences of the peoples who did not go over the sea, as Bernal Diaz del Castillo once wrote, "to serve God and His Majesty, to give light to those who were in darkness, and to grow rich, as all men desire to do."[7] This chapter's goal is to replot the story from their perspective.

MERCHANT EMPIRES AND EUROPEAN HISTORY

Silks and cottons, coffee and tea, tobacco and opium, tomatoes and potatoes, rice and maize, porcelain and lacquerware – the impact of the merchant empires on European material culture proved profound and permanent. No less striking were the mental changes, beginning with wonder at strange plants, beasts, and men and culminating in the fruitful cultural relativism that sprouted from European encounters with Americans, Africans and Asians.[8] The merchant empires' contribution to European economic development is more controversial, though the dominant opinion now seems to be that, whatever the vital role played by American silver in greasing the wheels of European trade in Asia, the share of imperial profits in the capitalization of the Industrial Revolution was not very great.[9] Much of em-

---

[6] The leading works are Immanuel Wallerstein, *The Modern World-System*, vol. 1: *Capitalist Agriculture and the Origins of the European World-Economy in the Sixteenth Century* (New York, 1975); Eric L. Jones, *The European Miracle* (Cambridge, 1981); Eric R. Wolf, *Europe and the People without History* (Berkeley and Los Angeles, 1982); Peter Kriedte, *Peasants, Landlords, and Merchant Capitalists: Europe and the World Economy, 1500–1800*, trans. V. R. Berghahn (Cambridge, 1983), 162–84; R. J. Holton, *The Transition from Feudalism to Capitalism* (New York, 1985); *The Brenner Debate: Agrarian Class Structure and Economic Development in Pre-Industrial Europe*, edited by T. H. Aston and C. H. E. Philpin (Cambridge, 1985).

[7] Quoted by J. H. Parry, *The Age of Reconnaissance: Discovery, Exploration, and Settlement, 1450–1650* (Berkeley and Los Angeles, 1963), 19.

[8] Anthony Pagden, *The Fall of Natural Man: The American Indian and the Origins of Comparative Ethnology*, (Cambridge, 1982), 209; Donald F. Lach, *Asia in the Making of Europe*, vol 2: *A Century of Wonder*, 3 parts (Chicago and London, 1970–77) 3:565.

[9] Wolfgang Reinhard, *Geschichte der europäischen expansion*, vol. 1, *Die alte Welt bis 1818* (Stuttgart, 1983), 157–70; Ward Barrett, "World Bullion Flows, 1450–1800," *The Rise of Merchant Empires*, edited by James D. Tracy (Cambridge, 1990), 224–54. Reinhard's judgment (p. 232) is that "Die Gewinne aus dem Überseehandel waren zu gering, um als entscheidende Ursache für das beschleunigte wirtschaftliche Wachstum und die Industrialisierung Großbritanniens nach 1750 in Frage zu kommen." Kriedte, *Peasants, Landlords, and Merchant Capitalist*, 160, and Holton, *Transition*, 207, agree;

pire's profits flowed into the upkeep and expansion of the merchant empires themselves, which gradually merged into a single vast system of accumulation, out of which the Industrial Revolution fashioned a global domination. The relationships between these two processes – the formation of the world economy and the coming of industrial capitalism – form the topic of the hottest debates between proponents respectively of "endogenous" and "exogenous" origins of European capitalism.[10] The debate contrasts with a hardening consensus about the European political order – a competitive system of small, centralized states – that seems to have promoted the rise of merchant empires. More and more, the roots of Europe's distinctiveness are being sought in political formation rather than in social structure; indeed, the proposition that Europe's social evolution may be seen as the paradigm of global social history is now under attack.[11] The shift of perspective toward state-building, however, merely poses the old question in a different form: Why did Europe diverge from world patterns of empire?

Empire, runs one useful definition,

> is a political system encompassing wide, relatively highly centralized territories, in which the center, as embodied both in the person of the emperor and in the central political institutions, constituted an autonomous entity. Further, ... empires ... have often embraced some idea, a potentially universal political and cultural orientation that went beyond that of any of their component parts.[12]

Neither in the age of merchant empires nor earlier did Europe produce any empires of this kind. Indeed, there is growing agreement that the failure of empire in Europe made possible the European pursuit of empire abroad, and that the most important agent of this change was the European "nation state." E. L. Jones attributes Europe's hegemony to its polycentric, competitive state system, and Immanuel Wallerstein identifies the absence of true empire in Europe as the absolute precondition of the European seaborne world economy.[13]

and the issue is reviewed by Patrick O'Brien, "European Economic Development: The Contribution of the Periphery," *Economic History Review* 35 (1982): 1–18.

[10] There is a recent survey by William W. Hagen, "Capitalism and the Countryside in Early Modern Europe: Interpretations, Models, Debates," *Agricultural History* 62 (1988), 13–47.

[11] See Wolf, *Europe and the People without History*, 79–88, whose concept of "tributary society" is the most important contribution to this shift.

[12] Shmuel N. Eisenstadt, "Empires," *International Encyclopedia of Social Sciences* 5 (1968): 41. Michael Doyle, *Empires* (Ithaca, 1986), 45, overemphasizes the concept of sovereignty.

[13] Jones, *European Miracle*, 85, 89–90, 93–5, 104–24; Wallerstein, *Modern World-System* 1:15–18.

Paul Kennedy, finally, concludes that the dynamic expansion of late medieval Europe continued into the modern era because "the manifold rivalries of the European states, already acute, were spilling over into transoceanic spheres."[14]

The full realization of the potential for expansion came in one form, the nation-state, and in one region, northwestern Europe. As V. G. Kiernan writes, "among the various components making up the unique amalgam of modern north-western Europe, none was more important than its political component, the loosely named 'nation-state,' " which was a "political organization of society of a kind distinct from any other in history."[15] It arose not in Europe as a whole or even at its heart but on its far northwestern corner. There, in the Low Countries but above all in England, occurred the events that prompt all of the debates about what is variously called "the transition to capitalism," "the European advantage," or "the rise of the West."

ENGLAND, EUROPE, THE WEST: A SYNECDOCHE

A synecdoche is a figure of speech in which a part stands for the whole.[16] The part, the essential locus of European modernity, was its northwestern corner, which became "leading part" or "leader" in the race for development, into which it drew much of the rest. Kiernan puts the notion as well as it can be put:

> In the seventeenth century there began that diffusion of ideas and technology from a corner of north-western Europe which is still continuing . . . Within another century or two the southern part of this [Atlantic] region had dropped out, as Spain and Portugal sank into hopeless decadence, and the northern area – corresponding fairly closely with the one dominated or most strongly affected by Protestantism in its more active forms – went far ahead. This is how it has come about that in nine contexts out of ten today, when the world talks of something as "European," it means something that originated in this one small area, or growing-point of Europe.[17]

A strict review of the ingredients of development, indeed, reveals that only one country, England, produced all the requisites: a strong state without competing structures, an important seaborne empire,

---

[14] Paul Kennedy, *The Rise and Fall of the Great Powers: Economic Change and Military Conflict from 1500 to 2000* (New York, 1987), 29.

[15] V. G. Kiernan, "State and Nation in Western Europe," *Past and Present* no. 31 (July 1965): 20–38, here at 20. And see Holton, *Transition from Feudalism to Capitalism*, 208.

[16] Arthur Quinn, *Figures of Speech: 60 Ways to Turn a Phrase* (Salt Lake City, 1982), 56–58.

[17] Kiernan, "State and Nation," 20.

an agriculture transformed by capitalist investment, and its own Industrial Revolution.

England may be regarded as the only complete case of "development" in European history. In every account, England sets the pace and fixes the norms, flanked by the Netherlands and France, and trailed by Spain and Portugal. Germany and Italy, once in the van, after 1500 or so gallop to the rear, where they ride herd on the clouds of barbarian auxiliaries—Scandinavia, Eastern Europe, and the Muslim world. This hierarchy is reproduced from a wide variety of perspectives, from the consistently Marxist arguments of Maurice Dobb and Robert Brenner to the neo-classical exchange model of Douglass C. North and Robert Paul Thomas.[18]

In recent years, the discussion has begun to shift from economic development to state formation, which tends to relieve the blinding Anglocentrism of the transition debate and makes different accounts defensible.[19] From within the broadly Marxist discourse, for example, Perry Anderson follows the trajectories of a romanized and a non-romanized Europe into a dynamic West and an imitative East.[20] Greater emphasis on government also tends to magnify the importance of French and German (usually Prussian) history,[21] and thus to turn attention away from what Marx called the first or "really revolutionary" path to capitalism, in which producers become capitalists, toward the second, less revolutionary path, in which merchants assume control of production.[22] It may well be that in Europe the first, "really revolutionary," way could and did occur only once; and that the second, less revolutionary, way has been the paramount one. If so, it suggests that the two ways were not alternatives at all, and that the unique English invention of capitalism transformed other societies by replicating its outcome but not its formative experience. In this

---

[18] Maurice Dobb, *Studies in the Development of Capitalism*, rev. ed. (New York, 1963); Robert Brenner, "Agrarian Class Structure and Economic Development in Pre-Industrial Europe," and "The Agrarian Roots of European Capitalism," in *Brenner Debate*, 54–62, 213–327; Douglass C. North and Robert Paul Thomas, *The Rise of the Western World: A New Economic History* (Cambridge, 1973), 103, who classify England and the Netherlands as "winners," France as an "also ran," and Spain, Italy, and Germany as "clear losers."

[19] See Theda Skocpol, "Bringing the State Back In: Strategies of Analysis in Current Research," in *Bringing the State Back In*, edited by Peter B. Evans, Dietrich Rueschemeyer, and Theda Skocpol (Cambridge, 1985), 3–43, here at 4–8.

[20] Perry Anderson, *Lineages of the Absolutist State* (London, 1974).

[21] Gianfranco Poggi, *The Development of the Modern State: A Sociological Introduction* (Stanford, 1978), 17.

[22] There is a good discussion of Marx's concept of two paths to capitalism by Kohachiro Takahashi, "A Contribution to the Discussion," in *The Transition from Feudalism to Capitalism*, edited by Rodney H. Hilton (London, 1976), 68–97, here at 88–97.

view, what has happened to the world is not a social evolution toward "modernity" but the spread of capitalism as a kind of global "maladie anglaise."

One reason for the transition problem's intractability is its focus on the passage from feudal governments before the fourteenth-century crisis to absolute monarchies in the sixteenth.[23] The debate lacks the perspective of medieval Christendom's heartlands, based on a line running roughly from Cologne to Rome, where the failure of medieval imperial tendencies at the center enabled smaller, more efficient empires to form later at the western, especially the northwestern, periphery. The heartlands did produce rulers who aimed to unite Christendom into an empire of a classic sort, but they failed.[24] One reason for their failure was that, down to the end of the medieval era, much of the ideological and religious ground on which empire had to be built – and not a little of its material basis – served an institution which made rival imperial claims. I refer, of course, to the Latin church in general and to the Roman papacy in particular.

But, if empire in the heartlands fell victim to particularism the very success of this particularism held significance for the rise of Western Europe's merchant empires because among the small powers of Italy and Germany were to be found the pioneers of an especially European kind of dominion. At Venice and Genoa, at Lübeck and Hamburg, warrior-merchants pioneered seaborne raiding-and-trading empires; and, though they had all plunged into deep decline before 1500, their operations provoked emulation on a grander, oceanic scale by Portugal and Spain and the Netherlands and England respectively. The warrior-merchant, who is surely one of Europe's most distinctive social types, first appeared not in the western tier but in the Italian and German heartlands.

THE CHURCH AS EMPIRE

At the fall of the Roman power in the West, it has long been recognized, some imperial functions passed to the Latin Christian church. Some, but not all, for the church's authority was essentially spiritual or ideological, not military, and its claims were embodied in law, not

---

[23] Paul Sweezey, "A Critique," and Takahashi, "Contribution To The Discussion," in ibid., 46–52, 83–7.

[24] The will, if not the means to dominate Europe in this way, certainly existed. See, e.g., Hermann Wiesflecker, *Kaiser Maximilian I. Das Reich, Österreich und Europa an der Wende zur Neuzeit*, vol. 5: *Der Kaiser und seine Umwelt. Hof, Staat, Wirtschaft, Gesellschaft, und Kultur* (Munich, 1986), 445–7, 641–42.

in armies.[25] From the eleventh century onward, the church provided central leadership, models of bureaucratic government, a vocabulary of authority, association, and power, a common language and institutions for the spread of high culture, and an ecumenical ideology. Its center, the papal monarchy, grew as an essentially European creation to fill essentially European needs, and in its mature, twelfth-century form the papal monarchy may have been the most peculiarly European institution Europe ever knew. The language, symbols, and law that linked the papacy to the Roman imperium contained more shadow than substance, except in the sense that the papal monarchy filled a role that was in some respects similar to the one the Roman monarchy had filled. Some who recognized this fact could nevertheless hardly separate its functional aspect – Europe's need – from the historical one: the Roman heritage. Thomas Hobbes, for example, wrote that "the Papacy is no other than the ghost of the deceased Roman empire, sitting crowned upon the grave thereof."[26] This is the historical aspect, but Hobbes also recognized the functional aspect – the need that had given room to ecclesiastical authority – when he warned that "it is not the Roman clergy only, that pretends the Kingdom of God to be of this world, and thereby to have a power therein, distinct from that of the civil state."[27] He might have meant Calvin's Geneva,[28] he certainly meant the English Puritans, and he abhorred the idea that such forces might offer something that "the civil state" could not supply.

The papal monarchy flourished and must therefore be associated with European needs in the era from 1050 to about 1300, when the popes claimed the supreme lordship of Christendom and made their claim credible through victories over the Holy Roman emperors. Although armed by 1200 with a full theory of an imperial papacy, the thirteenth-century popes were unable to translate the theory into practice. The crucial test came under Pope Boniface VIII, whose great bull "Unam Sanctam" (1302) delivered "a fine [Augustinian] summary of the political consequences of that hierarchy of being where peace and justice in the world are derived from the sacred, from sanctification and legitimation through the sacraments and the jurisdiction

---

[25] See, for a general statement, John A. Hall, *Powers and Liberties: The Causes and Consequences of the Rise of the West* (Berkeley, 1985): 120–1. See also Robert G. Wesson, *The Imperial Order* (Berkeley and Los Angeles, 1967), 416–24.

[26] Thomas Hobbes, *Leviathan or the Matter, Forme, and Power of a Commonwealth, Ecclesiastical and Civil*, chap. 47 (edited by Michael Oakeshott [Oxford, 1960], 457).

[27] Ibid., 459.

[28] Harro Höpfl, *The Christian Polity of John Calvin* (Cambridge, 1982), 188–206.

of the Church."[29] His defeat by the French king, however, proved a turning point in the doctrine's application, and thereafter "the facade of Christian control over Europe was maintained . . . in large part because the secular powers of society had come to learn how the papal machine could in fact be operated to their best advantage."[30] Despite its imperial failure, the papacy played "a very notable role in making a secular empire impossible" because "the church refused to serve as a second fiddle in an empire equivalent to those of China and Byzantium, and thus did not create a Caesaropapist doctrine in which a single emperor was elevated to semi-divine status."[31]

Full recognition of the church's imperial role in the governance of Christendom has been hindered by the tired convention of treating religion as ideology or, more commonly, "mere ideology." This habit mars some of the best contributions to the transition debate, whose authors generally treat European Christianity as though it were significant only for changes in the attitudes of individuals, such as merchants.[32] All that must change, however, once we admit the lesson, drawn from the study of ancient religions, that religion is initially ritual and social and only secondarily mythic and individual, and that religion forms a part of every social order's definition.[33]

Christendom resembled its sister civilization, Islam, far more than it did the disintegrated religious cultures of modern Europe and North America. Whatever else they attempted, Christendom's leaders aimed to perform for many peoples the essential task of a religious system: to reveal the connections between the invisible and the visible worlds

---

[29] Heiko A. Oberman, "The Shape of Late Medieval Thought," in his *The Dawn of the Reformation: Essays in Late Medieval and Early Reformation Thought* (Edinburgh, 1986), 32.

[30] Hall, *Powers and Liberties*, 134.

[31] Ibid., 134–5.

[32] See, e.g., Frank, *World Accumulation*, 269–70, who is still mired in the debate about Weber and Tawney. The deficit is not made good by Wallerstein, though there are promising signs in Wolf's *Europe and the People without History*. There are several ways to attack the veil of mystery, which this convention draws across Europe before 1450 or so, among them Perry Anderson's revitalization of the view that the peculiarities of medieval European civilization arose from a "synthesis" of Roman and Germanic institutions. See Anderson, *Passages from Antiquity to Feudalism* (London, 1974), esp. 128–42.

[33] Eugene D. Genovese, *Roll, Jordan, Roll: The World the Slaves Made* (New York, 1972), 161, muses that "few tasks present greater difficulty than that of compelling the well educated to take religious matters seriously." The tide has, however, turned in studies of premodern Europe, as witness, e.g., Robert W. Scribner, "Cosmic Order and Daily Life: Sacred and Secular in Pre-industrial German Society," and "Ritual and Popular Belief in Catholic Germany at the Time of the Reformation," in his *Popular Culture and Popular Movements in Reformation Germany* (London and Ronceverte; 1987), 1–16, 17–48.

and to make the former's power available for strengthening the latter's order. Most medieval Christian thinkers could have heartily endorsed the view expressed by the Muslim philosopher Ibn Khaldūn: "Only by God's help in establishing His religion do individual desires come together in agreement to press their claims, and hearts become united."[34]

Christendom had its peculiarities, of course, and one of them arose from its ordering of the relationship between religion and government. Their institutional separation was not in itself distinctive, for in Islam, contrary to what is often said, by 1100 "the bifurcation of the Islamic structure of domination into caliphate and rulership had become fully established."[35] This arrangement permitted Islamic states to function with legitimacy in the absence of any successor (caliph) to the Prophet; and the postclassical "gunpowder empires" – Ottoman Turkey, Safavid Persia, and Mughal India – all practiced the de facto separation of religious from military authority.[36] Some Christian civilizations, notably the Byzantine, evolved a very similar pattern: a highly centralized monarchy and a clerical hierarchy, each recognizing the divine origin of the other's authority.

The rise of the papal monarchy blocked a similar solution in the Christian West, where the church evolved its own system of authority as well as its own imperial claims and sought to deny divine legitimacy to all other rulers. Tendencies of this sort appeared already in the late Roman era, when St. Augustine provided the normative doctrine of a world divided into two realms – being a Roman, he called them "cities" – but the full arrangement did not emerge until the eleventh and twelfth centuries. Then began the stupendous transformation of a fragmented, agrarian Europe into Latin Christendom, a civilization that came to rival and resemble its elder Islamic sibling. Between 1050 and 1250, under the Roman bishops' leadership, the church struggled "against domination of the clergy by emperors, kings, and lords and for the establishment of the Church of Rome as an independent,

---

[34] Ibn Khaldūn (= 'Abd-ar-Raḥmân Abû Zayd ibn Muhammad ibn Muhammad ibn Khaldūn), *The Muqaddimah: An Introduction to History*, trans. Franz Rosenthal, abridged edition by N. J. Dawood (Princeton, 1957), 125. See Thomas A. Brady, Jr., "Godly Republics: The Domestication of Religion in the German Urban Reformation," in *The German People and the Reformation*, edited by R. Po-Chia Hsia (Ithaca, 1988), 14–32, here at 15.

[35] Said Amir Arjomand, *The Shadow of God and the Hidden Imam: Religion, Political Order, and Societal Change in Shi'ite Iran from the Beginning to 1890*, Publications of the Center for Middle Eastern Studies, vol. 17 (Chicago and London, 1984), 94.

[36] Marshall Hodgson, *The Venture of Islam: Conscience and History in a World Civilization*, vol. 3: *The Gunpowder Empires and Modern Times* (Chicago and London: 1974), 16–133, from whom the quoted phrase is taken.

corporate, political and legal entity, under the papacy." The church thus won the liberty to "work for the redemption of the laity and the reformation of the world, through law,"[37] and, beneath the umbrella of its titanic clash with the emperors, there sprouted the legal autonomy of kings and princes, the self-confidence of thousands of more or less self-governing cities, and the ambitions of the universities, with their new sciences of theology and law.

The Roman papacy emerged from this history as chief claimant to hegemony over the peoples who made up "Christendom (*christianitas*)," a term that came into common use just in this era.[38] Its church alone mediated among these peoples and engaged in both the fundamentally religious task of "the redemption of the laity" and the fundamentally political one of "the reformation of the world." The church had become one of those "superstructures" that "necessarily enter into the constitutive structure of the mode of production."[39]

By A.D. 1200, therefore, the Roman papacy had grown into an incompletely articulated imperial power. Its lords' claims, most boldly stated in Pope Gregory VII's "Dictatus papae" (1075), held that the Roman church alone was founded by God, that the pope alone is called "universal," that he alone may make new laws and wear the imperial insignia, that he may depose emperors, and that he may revise the judgments of all other rulers and absolve subjects from their oaths of fealty. In principle, at least, these claims represented "a massive shift in power and authority both within the church and in the relations between the church and the secular polities."[40]

How could an imperial papacy make good such claims? Not through feudal lordship, for despite papal assumption of feudal lordship over a few realms, such as Sicily, England, and the lands of the Teutonic Order, feudal contract offered no very promising basis for imperium. Nor through military might, for, despite the popes' role in provoking the Crusades, they did not control the crusading forces. Some power accrued from papal assumption of the right to appoint to benefices, called "reservations,"[41] though the benefice system left most eccle-

---

[37] Harold J. Berman, *Law and Revolution: The Formation of the Western Legal Tradition* (Cambridge, Mass., 1983), 520.

[38] Bernard Guénée, *States and Rulers in Later Medieval Europe*, trans. Juliet Vale (Oxford, 1985), 2.

[39] Anderson, *Lineages of the Absolutist State*, 403. The point is made, though in different language, by Hall, *Powers and Liberties*, 20–21.

[40] Berman, *Law and Revolution*, 100. A useful, if one-sided, special study is Walther Ullmann, *The Growth of Papal Government in the Middle Ages: A Study in the Ideological Relation of Clerical to Lay Power* (London, 1955).

[41] Geoffrey Barraclough, *The Papal Provisions: Aspects of Church History, Constitutional, Legal, and Administrative in the Late Middle Ages* (Oxford, 1935).

siastical property in local hands.[42] Then, too, the Roman popes contested possession of the symbols and vocabulary of Roman imperial authority with, first, the Holy Roman emperors, and, later on, the kings and princes.[43]

The most effective instrument of the sacerdotal imperium was neither military force nor Roman regalia but the idea of universal jurisdiction and universal law: God had set a law over the world, and the Roman bishop was the supreme judge. The definition of ecclesiastical jurisdiction and canon law "was a matter not merely of convenience but of principle, and of deep principle, for which men were ready to fight, bleed, and die."[44] The principle's popularity, in turn, depended on a broad sense of Christian community, of the (Latin) Christians as a *populus christianus*, which drew both from the communitarianism of Germanic folk culture and from the powerful, even predominant, socioreligious metaphor of the family.[45] Encompassing this whole community of peoples – Swedes and Sicilians, Celts and Croats, Portuguese and Poles – was the church, "a single state structure, governed by a single system of law, the canon law." The one church's universality firmly sanctioned the plurality of polities against all other claims to absolute or universal authority. Not only did the popes of the twelfth and thirteenth century defeat the German emperors, their rivals for the imperium, but the theory of imperial sacerdotium extended the principles of reason and redeemability to all other bodies of law, whether customary or statutory, royal, regional, or local. Above them all stood the church's canon law, which

> was, to be sure human law; yet it was supposed to be also a reflection of natural law and divine law. The secular order, however, was less perfect, more primitive, more earthbound. Its law was, therefore, more tied to irrational factors, to power, to superstition, to decadence. Yet it was capable of being regenerated; it was redeemable; it had positive significance. The church could help to make it conform more fully to natural law and ultimately to divine law. The canon law could serve as a model for the secular legal orders.[46]

Under the church's sponsorship, therefore, emerged Latin Christendom's ecumenical idea, universal law, which held that the universe

---

[42] Jörn Sieglerschmidt, *Territorialstaat und Kirchenregiment. Studien zur Rechtsdogmatik des Kirchenpatronatsrechts im 15. und 16. Jahrhundert*, Forschungen zur kirchlichen Rechtsgeschichte und zum Kirchenrecht, vol. 15 (Cologne and Vienna, 1987), 7–28.

[43] Wesson, *Imperial Order*, 423–5; Roy Strong, *Art and Power: Renaissance Festivals, 1450–1650* (Berkeley and Los Angeles, 1984), 65–81.

[44] Berman, *Law and Revolution*, 531.

[45] Ibid., 528; John Bossy, *Christianity in the West, 1400–1700* (Oxford, 1985), Chap. 2.

[46] Berman, *Law and Revolution*, 531, See note 86 below.

itself was subject to law, that the duality of temporal and spiritual authorities placed limitations upon the power of each, that the supremacy of law was rooted in the plurality of secular authority within kingdoms and within Christendom, and that mutual obligation existed between superiors and inferiors, between central and local authorities, and between official and popular agencies of government.[47]

The idea of universal law helped to sustain an ecumenical sense of the church during the fourteenth and fifteenth centuries, when the papal monarchy reeled from one disaster to another: the transfer of the papacy to Avignon in 1309; quarrels with the Spiritual Franciscans and with the Holy Roman emperor; the dissident movement of the Lollards in England and the Hussites' armed revolt in Bohemia; and the Great Western Schism of 1378–1415. These shocks eased the appropriation of legitimacy by the kings and princes and drove the Roman papacy to become locally more secular and universally more spiritual. Locally, the fifteenth-century popes began to form the Patrimony of Peter into a territorial state, the Papal State, the organization, symbols, and political culture of which exerted the profoundest influence on the other monarchies of the early modern era.[48] Ernst Kantorowicz formulated splendidly the effects of this influence: "Under the *pontificalis maiestas* of the pope, . . . the hierarchical apparatus of the Roman Church tended to become the perfect prototype of an absolute and rational monarchy on a mystical basis, while at the same time the State increasingly showed a tendency to become a quasi-Church or a mystical corporation on a rational basis."[49] In its union of temporal and spiritual government, the Renaissance papacy produced "a cultural typology which was to serve as a model of excellence for the whole of Europe of the ancien regime."[50]

The church's official reaction to the Reformation reaffirmed this

---

[47] Ibid., 536–7. The papalist doctrine, which "designated the Pope as the *homo spiritualis*, the spiritual man, who cannot be judged by anyone and who judges everything in both realms of Church and State," was but one interpretation of the common view "that without the *vera iustitia* of the Church, the State has to disintegrate, can only become a latrocinium, a robber-state–as St. Augustine put it:" Oberman, "The Shape of Late Medieval Thought," 32. Against this view, the canon lawyers developed the position that the pope also stands under the law. See Francis W. Oakley, *The Western Church in the Later Middle Ages* (Ithaca, 1979), 159–74.

[48] Paolo Prodi, *The Papal Prince, One Body and Two Souls: The Papal Monarchy in Early Modern Europe*, trans. Susan Haskins (New York, 1987), 6, sees in the early modern Papal State a prototype of the way "in which some tendencies of the management of power made themselves known in a dialectical relationship . . . with the evolving states on the one hand, and with the papacy's primatial call . . . on the other."

[49] Ernst Kantorowicz, *The King's Two Bodies: A Study in Medieval Political Theology*, 3d ed. (Princeton, 1973), 194.

[50] A. Quondam, quoted by Prodi, *Papal Prince*, 47.

union, and the Council of Trent proclaimed that "the Church is un-questionably a visible, jurisdictional institution, the structure and traditions of which are derived directly from the inspiration of the Holy Ghost."[51] Catholic theologians of the sixteenth century nevertheless adjusted theory to practice. Robert Bellarmine (1542–1621), for example, struck "a middle road" between the extreme theocratic doctrine of direct papal sovereignty and the denial of all papal authority, holding "that there should be power of indirect intervention exceptionally where spiritual welfare is concerned and because the problem of salvation affects all mankind."[52] In Spain some advanced theologians, such as Francisco Vitoria (ca. 1485–1546), affirmed the papal supremacy within the church but denied that the pope, or anyone else, could have supreme, direct, and absolute governance over the whole world, for no power on this earth could dispense from the natural law or the law of nations.[53] The lawfulness of the universe, once an ecclesiastical instrument against the Holy Roman emperor's superior might, had taken on a life of its own.

The papacy's local retreat into the Papal State, plus the Catholic retrenchment on the issue of direct papal sovereignty, encouraged the growth of a new universalism, more religious and spiritual and less political than the theory of direct papal monarchy. Partly this arose from the fact that the Roman church became, just at the moment of its greatest losses in Europe, a global institution. The change may be illustrated by a contrast between Pope Alexander VI's (r. 1492–1503) imperial demarcation of the globe between Portugal and Spain in 1493 and Pope Paul III's (r. 1534–49) pastoral "Sublimis Deus" of 1537, which forbade Christians to enslave the newly discovered peoples beyond the sea.[54] As the church voyaged out with the merchant adventurers, traders, and conquerors, its agents expanded the Christian universalism far beyond the old boundaries.[55]

---

[51] Quentin Skinner, *Foundations of Modern Political Thought*, 2 vols. (Cambridge, 1978), 2:144.

[52] Prodi, *Papal Prince*, 26.

[53] See Venancio D. Carro, "The Spanish Theological-Juridical Renaissance and the Ideology of Bartolomé de Las Casas," in *Bartolomé de Las Casas in History: Toward an Understanding of the Man and His Work*, edited by Juan Fried and Benjamin Keen (DeKalb, Ill., 1971), 236–77, here at 250–63. For the intellectual context, see Skinner, *Foundations of Modern Political Thought*, 2:151.

[54] Guenée, *States and Rulers*, 10, believes that the demarcation "was already arbitration within the jurisdiction of the law of nations rather than a sovereign decision of the Pope." On Paul III's bull, see Lewis Hanke, *All Mankind Is One: A Study of the Disputation Between Bartolomé de Las Casas and Juan Ginés de Sepúlveda in 1550 on the Intellectual and Religious Capacity of the American Indians* (DeKalb, Ill., 1974), 17–22.

[55] See, e.g., Jonathan D. Spence, *The Memory Palace of Matteo Ricci* (New York, 1984).

To this more universal universality is linked the growth of a more spiritualized form of papal supremacy, the doctrine of papal infallibility. The teaching that the pope cannot err in matters of doctrine is more a repudiation, than a confirmation, of Christendom's ecumenical ideology of universal law. It originated not with canon lawyers but among the mendicant orders of the thirteenth and early fourteenth centuries, especially the Franciscans, whose late thirteenth-century theologians evolved an increasingly radical doctrine of papal infallibility. Itself a sign of radical skepticism about the church's ability to govern the world through law, infallibility came to be taught by some of the papacy's fiercest enemies, such as William of Ockham (d. ca. 1349), who clung to the idea that, even if popes could err, the true church could not. After a long life on the margins of orthodoxy, "only in the sixteenth century did the doctrine of the pope's personal infallibility begin to find considerable acceptance in Catholic theology."[56]

The intensification of papal monarchy over the Papal State, the theoretical backpedaling to the Bellarminian doctrine of indirect power, the development of the notion of a global religious mission, and a growing orthodox acceptance of papal infallibility – these were all signs that the sixteenth-century papacy was no longer a European imperial monarchy. The pope's two new roles, local monarch over the Papal State and leader of a global religious community, framed the papacy's postmedieval history until 1870. On July 18, 1870, the First Vatican Council proclaimed the dogma of papal infallibility; two months later, on September 20, Italian troops invaded the Vatican and ended the Papal State. The church had failed to become a true empire; it had briefly become a state; it remained a global religious organization.

One of the imperial papacy's most enduring political legacies to Europe was the idea of Rome as a paradigm of imperial rule. The Roman heritage, long contested between popes and emperors, acquired new vigor through the literary and artistic culture of the Renaissance. This can be illustrated by the clash of claims. At the court of Pope Julius II (r. 1503–13), an orator promised that, though Julius Caesar merely thought he ruled the world, Pope Julius II in fact did.[57]

[56] Brian Tierney, *Origins of Papal Infallibility, 1150–1350: A Study on the Concepts of Infallibility, Sovereignty, and Tradition in the Middle Ages,* Studies in the History of Christian Thought, vol. 6 (Leiden, 1972), 57, 92–109, 171–237, 271, with the closing quote at p. 271.

[57] John W. O'Malley, "Giles of Viterbo: A Reformer's Thought on Renaissance Rome," *Renaissance Quarterly* 20 (1967): 1–11, here at 10 (reprinted in John W. O'Malley, *Rome and the Renaissance: Studies in Culture and Religion* [London, 1981]).

132   *Thomas A. Brady, Jr.*

A few years later, as if in reply, the imperial grand chancellor, Mercurino Arborio di Gattinara (d. 1530), trumpeted grandiosely that the work begun by Charles the Great would be completed by Charles the Greatest, giving the world "one pastor and one flock."[58] Such bombast may have charmed the humanist literati who flocked to the Hapsburg courts from lands, such as Germany, Italy, and the Netherlands, which lacked large, strong states, but they soon learned to venerate the particular monarchies as worthy successors to Rome.[59] Roman imperial language and symbols became tools in the kits of the Renaissance Italians, Burckhardt's "first-born among the sons of modern Europe,"[60] who poured forth an army of artists and architects, rivers of symbols, and a creeping wave of taste to feed the tastes of the powerful in all the European capitals.

The coming of the large states meant the doom of many smaller units, and a look backward from around 1600 teaches us how vital were the great universalist structures of medieval Europe to the peculiarly European success of very small political units.[61] This was true of the Italian communes, in which the bishops personified local autonomy, while the papacy sponsored anti-imperial urban leagues.[62] And it was sometimes true of the Holy Roman Empire's lands, where small semisovereignties flourished under what an early sixteenth-century Austrian official called "both wings of the [imperial] eagle."[63]

The old universalisms nevertheless proved ever more difficult to sustain, as fighters moved in to serve the papacy as it had served the Holy Roman Empire. Some did so in the belief that an imperial papacy hindered, even shackled, the church's efforts to preach the redemption of the world.[64] Others did so on behalf of the most powerful and ultimately most successful gravediggers of the papal imperium – the kings and princes, whose confidence and independence had earlier waxed under its protection of the church.[65] By the fifteenth century,

[58] John M. Headley, "The Habsburg World Empire and the Revival of Ghibellinism," *Medieval and Renaissance Studies* 7 (1978): 93–127, here at 97–102.
[59] Skinner, *Foundations of Modern Political Thought*, 1: chap. 9; Thomas A. Brady, Jr., *Turning Swiss: Cities and Empire, 1450–1550* (Cambridge, 1985), 22–8.
[60] Jacob Burckhardt, *The Civilization of the Renaissance in Italy*, trans. S. G. C. Middlemore, revised by Irene Gordon (New York, 1961), 121.
[61] Wallerstein offers this insight in *Modern World-System*, 1:172–3.
[62] J. K. Hyde, *Society and Politics in Medieval Italy: The Evolution of the Civil Life, 1000–1350* (New York, 1973), 58–9; Daniel Waley, *The Italian City-Republics* (New York and Toronto, 1969), 127.
[63] Quoted by Brady, *Turning Swiss*, 78.
[64] For orientation, see Oakley, *The Western Church*, 178–259; and idem, *Omnipotence, Covenant, and Order: An Excursion in the History of Ideas from Abelard to Leibniz* (Ithaca, 1984), 55–65, 77–84, for William of Ockham's role.
[65] The inability to grasp the influence of the church on the political evolution of Europe

the structures that had helped them to become more than tribal paramount chiefs or feudal tenants-in-chief, stood in their way, and the assault on the papacy's material foundations began well before there erupted, sparked by quite different forces, the Protestant Reformation. Well before that time, Emperor Frederick III (r. 1440–93) summed up Austrian practice in a sentence: "What the priests own, belongs to us."[66]

Legitimate or not, the European state, or nation-state, is the imperial papacy's true successor. It grew up in the house of Christendom, a space the Latin church had helped to create, it grew strong by feeding on the church's temporalities, and it eventually appropriated the spiritual claim to be the true foundation of human community. It became "one body and two souls,"[67] both empire and nation. Not, however, without a struggle, for the same forces that unsettled the feudal order – urbanization, trade, plague, and depression – opened space for a very different kind of voice, the demand for corporate-communal rule.

THE COMMUNAL WAY – ALTERNATIVE TO THE STATE?

A state, to use the term in its sixteenth-century meaning, "is a political body subject to a government and to common laws." Although medieval Europeans hardly used the word (status, *état*, *estado*, *stato*, *Staat*), the patterns of governance that produced the European type of state – smaller and better integrated than an empire, larger and more powerful than a city-state – reach far back into the twelfth and thirteenth centuries.[68] Public opinion in Christendom nonetheless long held that "the peace of the world could only be safeguarded by the existence of a single universal power."[69] Down at least through Dante Alighieri (d. 1321), the vision of a neo-Roman universal monarchy became a major weapon against those who, like Giles of Rome (ca. 1246–1316), were beginning to argue that all political authority and even the ownership of property (*dominium*) depended on loyal

---

is the greatest weakness of Reinhard Bendix's *Kings or People: Power and the Mandate to Rule* (Berkeley and Los Angeles, 1978).

[66] "Pfaffengut ist Kammergut," quoted by Wiesflecker, *Kaiser Maximilian I.*, vol. 1: *Jugend, burgundisches Erbe und Römisches Königtum bis zur Alleinherrschaft, 1459–1493* (Munich, 1971), 79; and in a slightly different form, "Pfaffenhab ist unser Kammergut," in ibid., vol. 5:156.

[67] Prodi, *Papal Prince*, 185.

[68] Joseph R. Strayer, *On the Medieval Origins of the Modern State* (Princeton, 1970), 12.

[69] Guenée, *States and Rulers*, 7.

membership in the church.[70] Lawyer-popes, indeed, proved more flexible than imperial propagandists, and the theory of papal monarchy allowed them to argue, as Pope Innocent III (r. 1198–1216) did in 1202, that kings and princes were not units of the Roman imperium and thus did not have to recognize a temporal superior, that is, the emperor. One party of the church's lawyers, it has been said, "held the national state over the baptismal font."[71]

With the *regnum*, the realm of well-defined boundaries associated with a strong core region, such as the king of France's Ile-de-France, the political future truly lay. By the fourteenth century, old-fashioned vassalage no longer supplied a sufficient basis for monarchy, not least because the economic crisis was steadily undermining the governmental functions of landlordship, on which feudal governance depended. Kings and princes came to deal with powerful subjects not as individuals but as members of corporate assemblies, called "estates." The dualistic state (*Ständesstaat*), a nearly universal phenomenon in Latin Christendom by the fourteenth century, formed a major transition stage between the feudal monarchy of the past and the centralized monarchy of the future.[72] Such corporate institutions formed and flourished during the 250 years after about 1250, beginning as "tools of government" through which kings and princes sought consent from the "politically active, propertied classes," and ending sometimes as their rivals, sometimes as their creatures.[73]

The passage from these dualistic governments of kings-and-parliaments to centralized monarchy unfolded since 1450 in Europe's western tier, often in ways that now seem inevitable.[74] That centralization of power proved more fundamental than its monarchical representations is proven by the case of England, where the ultimately successful assault on royal absolutism between 1640 and 1688 hardly challenged the centralized state's supremacy – any more than the French Revolution would in France. The true anomaly among the

---

[70] John B. Morrall, *Political Thought in Medieval Times* (London, 1958; reprinted, New York, 1962), 86–86.

[71] "Cum rex superiorem in temporalibus minime recognoscat," quoted by Guenée, *States and Rulers*, 7.

[72] Poggi, *Development of the Modern State*, 36–59, summarizes the data and the theories; and see Guenée, *States and Rulers*, 171–87.

[73] Strayer, *Medieval Origins of the Modern State* 66–67.

[74] See now, however, the very important volume edited by Helmut G. Koenigsberger, *Republiken und Republikanismus im Europa der Frühen Neuzeit*, Schriften des Historischen Kollegs, Kolloquien, vol. 11 (Munich, 1988), which shows that premodern republicanism remained an oppositional current that never developed a theoretical position, and that all tendencies to republicanism on a national level – England, Sweden – failed to come to fruition.

empire-building peoples is not England but the Netherlands, which, because of its failure to centralize, is sometimes regarded as a case of "failed development."[75] The Netherlands, however, belonged by heritage and experience to the old Central European heartlands, where particularism had prevailed, and, though the experience of empire strained the older corporate structures, it did not smash them to make way for a thoroughly centralized state.

The Netherlands form the transition from the western states, whose experience shapes most accounts of European history in the early modern era, to the lands that had been the heartlands of medieval Christendom but became the semiperiphery of modern Europe. The experience of these lands, especially Germany and Italy, makes it unlikely that wholly endogenous causes produced the large, centralized nation-states of the West. Indeed, history written from the perspective of the Central European heartlands of Christendom reveals what is sometimes called "Old Europe," the continuity of whose life from about 1000 to about 1800 depended on its corporately organized society, a vast, bewildering welter of assemblies, foundations, guilds, societies, and other corporate institutions of every conceivable type.[76] European history since 1800 can then be seen as the conformity, forced and induced, of this old society to the new type of the centralized, imperial European nation-state. One of the great values of the heartlands' premodern history is to show us a political experience that was relatively undisturbed by the experience of empire. Although this history has remained largely hidden from the centralist-developmentalist perspective, its recovery can throw a new and powerful light both on what Christendom was and on what Europe became.

Between 1250 and 1500, much of Europe witnessed innovations in governance that, in the absence of merchant empires, could sometimes allow an exit from feudal governance quite different from absolute monarchy. First came a general devolution of political power: corporate bodies of powerful subjects came to play an important role in the government of kingdoms, duchies, and other principalities; guilds came to play an important role in the governments of some cities; and in a few places even villages gained a significant measure

---

[75] Frederick Krantz and Paul M. Hohenberg, eds., *Failed Transitions to Modern Industrial Society: Renaissance Italy and Seventeenth-Century Holland. First International Colloquium, April 18–20, 1974* (Montreal, 1975); Strayer, *Medieval Origins*, 91.

[76] See Dietrich Gerhard, *Old Europe: A Study of Continuity, 1000–1800* (New York, 1981). For the present state of discussion on corporate society, see Winfried Schulze, ed., *Ständische Gesellschaft und soziale Mobilität*, Schriften des Historischen Kollegs, Kolloquien, vol. 12 (Munich: 1988).

of self-administration. Second, the sense of place, of country, began to form and become the object of people's loyalties, as they began to identify themselves with their homelands. Gradually, as the sense of political community became more concrete, it attached to language as well, and political and ethnic communities (*populus* and *natio*) began to take shape.[77] The growing strength of such identifications made ever more remote the possibility of resubmerging them in an imperial loyalty of civilizational scale. Third, this era seethed with corporate ideology, ideas of community, of togetherness, of the whole superseding the parts, and of the common good that transcends ever particular good.[78] Although these three developments are often called "feudal," they represented a massive shift of governance away from government by contract and vassalage and toward participation in government by the body of subjects, or the *melior pars* thereof. Indeed, the community of the *populus* or *natio*, though not so comprehensive as the church, was far more so than the old assemblies of vassals. We find everywhere and on all levels of political life and thought this broadening, by means of which political life burst the lower bounds of the feudal age's concept of a society divided into clergy, nobility, and "workers," that is, the urban rich.[79] In a few places, this devolution brought even peasant householders into the political assemblies, while in civic governments the lesser merchants, shopkeepers, and artisan masters sometimes pushed their way into the town halls. At Florence in the 1370s, the political success of such folk even inspired the wool workers, called the *Ciompi*, to imitate them; and at Basel in 1521 the guildsmen briefly pushed the greater merchants out of government altogether.[80] The extreme examples of devolution, however, came in certain, naturally favored corners of the Central European countryside, especially the central Alpine lands. Here armed farmers and stockmen ruled themselves and answered with

[77] Guénée, *States and Rulers*, 49–55.
[78] Antony Black, *Council and Commune: The Conciliar Movement and the Fifteenth-Century Heritage* (London, 1979); idem, *Guilds and Civil Society in European Political Thought from the Twelfth Century to the Present* (Ithaca, 1984).
[79] Georges Duby, *The Three Orders: Feudal Society Imagined*, trans. Arthur Goldhammer (Chicago and London, 1980), 5.
[80] See Hans Füglister, *Handwerksregiment. Untersuchungen und Materialien zur sozialen und politischen Struktur der Stadt Basel in der ersten Hälfte des 16. Jahrhunderts*, Basler Beiträge zur Geschichtswissenschaft, vol. 143 (Basel, 1981). On the political movements of south German journeymen, and on the fall of real wages that undermined them, see Knut Schulz, *Handwerksgesellen und Lohnarbeiter. Untersuchungen zur oberrheinischen und oberdeutschen Stadtgeschichte des 14. bis 17. Jahrhunderts* (Sigmaringen, 1985); Jean-Pierre Kintz, *La société strasbourgeoise du milieu du XVIe siècle à la fin de la Guerre de Trente Ans 1560–1650. Essai d'histoire démographique, économique et sociale* (Paris, 1984).

pike and sword all who challenged their right to do so. "The Swiss," as Machiavelli noted, "are best armed and most free."[81]

The popularization of corporate institutions and ideas aroused contempt and sometimes fear in the traditional elites. It was not enough to shout at the newcomers, "Canaille! Canaille! Canaille! May you die of starvation," or call them "these craftsmen of shit!" – as fourteenth-century Florentine aristocrats did.[82] Whole new terms had to be invented for groups whose voice had now and then to be heard, but who, by the lights of their betters, had no right to voice at all. This new actor on the political states, the Common Man (*popolo minuto, menu peuple, gemeiner Mann*), threatened to play an unpredictable role: he was stupid, he was cunning; he was docile, he was dangerous; he was subservient, he was sullen; he was hardworking, he was lazy; he was the wisest beast in the farmyard, he was a dangerous rebel. He and his comrades acted, as Emperor Maximilian sneered at the Swiss in 1499, like "wicked, crude, stupid peasants, in whom there is neither virtue, noble blood, nor proper moderation, but only immoderate display, disloyalty, and hatred for the German nation."[83]

Two features of the spread of corporate thinking through Europe merit special attention. First, it bore intimate connections to what was happening in the church, for not only did it draw vitality from the corporate-familial images that animated late medieval religious consciousness, it also expanded in a moral room created by the eleventh-century investiture controversy's "radical reappraisal of the relationship between church and state."[84] Second, corporate ideas came to serve the vast communal movement, which arose in the European cities during the twelfth and thirteenth centuries, and the outcome of which, most pronounced in Central Europe, brought elements of self-government into the hands of the Common Man.

The political Golden Age of the Common Man coincided with the depressed, stagnant, troubled, and disrupted fourteenth and fifteenth centuries. How were economic depression and political emancipation related? Economic dislocation, followed by famine and plague and a hundred years of economic stagnation, undermined both the economic viability of the manorial estates and the political vitality of the

---

[81] Machiavelli, *The Prince*, chap. 12.
[82] G. A. Brucker, *Florentine Politics and Society, 1343–1378* (Princeton, 1962), 52–53.
[83] Quoted by Guy P. Marchal, "Die Antwort der Bauern. Elemente und Schichtungen des eidgenössischen Geschichtsbewußtseins am Ausgang des Mittelalters," in *Geschichtsschreibung und Geschichtsbewußtsein im späten Mittelalter*, edited by Hans Patze, Vortnäge und Forschungen, vol. 31 (Sigmaringen, 1987), 757–90, here at 757.
[84] Black, *Guilds and Civil Society*, 62. The corporate character of medieval religion is a principal theme of Bossy, *Christianity in the West*.

seigneuries – the two foundation stones of feudal government. On the land, some of the lords' administrative functions devolved upon the villages, while in the towns, the rise of real wages – commodity prices fell faster than wages – lent new political force to the craftsmen and laborers. The advance of market forces, which the depression accelerated rather than stemmed, lent new value and hence new power to human labor and new voice to those who labored, the commons, and this at a time when no new form of the state had definitively replaced feudal monarchy.[85]

The great devolution took many forms in many places. An immense wave of rural revolts began in England in 1381 and culminated in the great German Peasants' Revolt of 1525. In the cities, too, political agitation came in waves: guild revolts laced with anti-Jewish riots in the Rhenish towns in the mid-fourteenth century; terrible pogroms in the Castilian towns in the 1380s and a communal revolt in the early 1520s; and a tremendous wave of riots, revolts, and coups in the Italian cities during the first third of the sixteenth century. In Bohemia, revolt developed on a much greater scale: slashing, brutal campaigns in which Hussite armies, armed with religious enthusiasm, patriotism, wagon-forts, and cannon, held off one imperial army after another.[86]

All of this appeared as disorder, as chaos, as the unfortunate consequences of government's inadequate finance and military force – but only if seen from throne and castle. Seen from below, the same

---

[85] This paragraph recapitulates an argument I make in "Der Gemeine Mann und seine Feinde: Betrachtungen zur oberdeutschen Geschichte im 15. und 16. Jahrhundert," in *Stände und Gesellschaft im Alten Reich. Beiträge des zweiten deutsch-amerikanischen Kolloquiums zur frühneuzeitlichen Reichsgeschichte*, edited by Georg Schmidt, Veröffentlichungen des Instituts für Europäische Geschichte Mainz, 85 (Wiesbaden, 1988), 50–6. It agrees closely with Peter Blickle, *Die Gemeindereformation. Die Menschen des 16. Jahrhunderts auf dem Weg zum Heil* (Munich, 1985), 165–204. Closer study may uncover politically significant communalism in other parts of Europe. See the suggestive comment by Marc Bloch, *French Rural History: An Essay on Its Basic Characteristics*, translated by Janet Sondheimer (Berkeley and Los Angeles: 1966), 167. Although Emmanuel Le Roy Ladurie notes in passing "the universal strength of peasant communalism" in France, he calls it merely "colourful." Emanuel Le Roy Ladurie, *The French Peasantry, 1450–1660*, trans. Alan Sheridan (Berkeley and Los Angeles, 1987), 384, 391.

[86] Peter Blickle, "Peasant Revolts in the Late Medieval German Empire," *Social History* 4 (1979): 223–39; Peter Bierbrauer, "Bäuerliche Revolten im Alten Reich. Ein Forschungsbericht," in *Aufruhr und Empörung? Studien zum bäuerlichen Widerstand im Alten Reich*, edited by Peter Blickle (Munich, 1980), 1–68; R. H. Hilton, *Bond Men Made Free: Medieval Peasant Movements and the English Rising of 1381* (London, 1979); Lauro Martines, *Power and Imagination: City-States in Renaissance Italy* (New York, 1979), 295–6. See, in general, Guénée, *States and Rulers*, 192–7; Michael Mollat and Philippe Wolff, *The Popular Revolutions of the Late Middle Ages*, trans. A. L. Lytton-Sells (London, 1973).

movements posed a corporate defense of local and regional rights, of the subjects' purses, and of the cause of law and justice.[87] Much of later fourteenth- and fifteenth-century Europe faced two possible political paths: "one, emancipation of the small producer, the peasant and the craftsman, from the higher classes in church and state; the other, reorganization of the higher classes, moral rearmament, pruning of excrescences, concentration of power."[88] By the first half of the sixteenth century, this choice was clearly resolved, at least in Europe's western tier, in favor of concentration, the road to the "national state."

The new state differed from the old monarchies in several ways: first, it controlled a well-defined, continuous territory; second, it was relatively centralized; third, it was differentiated from other organizations; and fourth, it reinforced its claims through a tendency to monopolize the concentrated means of physical coercion within its territory.[89] Such states possessed standing armies, bureaucracies staffed by lawyers, regular taxation, mercantilist trade policies, diplomatic services, and an ideology of sovereignty drawn more or less from Roman law.[90] Thus armed, states tackled the twin traditional tasks of government – the administration of justice and defense of the realm – in new and more effective ways. Royal law, codified in innovative lawbooks and administered by Latin-speaking lawyers and judges, became the knife that cut away at the vast riot of corporate immunities, privileges, and liberties.

Nowhere in Europe did the problem of reconstructing authority pose itself more acutely than in the German-speaking world, where in 1525 political devolution culminated in the greatest mass rebellion of premodern European history.[91] The rebels opposed not law but alien law – the book-based laws of the empire and the territorial states, against which so many bitter jokes circulated – in favor of their own "old law" and the "godly law."[92] They wanted government, but of

---

[87] Peter Blickle, "Communalism, Parliamentarism, Republicanism," trans. Thomas A. Brady, Jr., *Parliaments, Estates, and Representation* 6 (1986): 1–13.

[88] Kiernan, "State and Nation," 28.

[89] Charles Tilly, "Reflections on the History of European State-Making," in *The Formation of National States in Western Europe*, edited by Charles Tilly (Princeton, 1975), 27.

[90] Anderson, *Lineages of the Absolutist State*, 24–38. In the Holy Roman Empire, by contrast, the idea of sovereignty took no root before the eighteenth century. Helmut Quaritsch, *Souveränität. Entstehung und Entwicklung des Begriffs in Frankreich und Deutschland vom 13. Jahrhundert bis 1806*, Schriften zur Verfassungsgeschichte, vol. 38 (Berlin, 1986).

[91] Peter Blickle, *The Revolution of 1525: The German Peasants' War from a New Perspective*, trans. Thomas A. Brady, Jr., and H. C. Erik Midelfort (Baltimore, 1981).

[92] Gerald Strauss, *Law, Resistance, and the State: The Opposition to Roman law in Reformation Germany* (Princeton, 1986), esp. 3–30.

their own choosing: where effective territorial governments existed, the rebels of 1525 proposed a new role in them for the commons; in hopelessly fragmented regions, they proposed new states based on popular representation; and everywhere they demanded an end to political privilege based on property in land and labor.[93] Sometimes they got their wishes. Rural householders came to sit in the parliaments (*Landschaften*) of many small Swiss and south German lands, and where there was little or no landed nobility, as in Chur and the Valais, they pushed their demands toward truly republican government.[94] The uplands of the German-speaking world's southern tier formed the freest political zone in Europe, and the liberties of its armed, self-governing commoners exercised a powerful demonstration effect far beyond the Swiss Confederacy's borders. Deep in the heart of south Germany, it was said that the common folk wanted "to be free, like the Swiss" and "be their own lords."[95]

In very few places had the commons any real chance of becoming "free, like the Swiss," for the prospect of an empowerment of the primary producers sufficed to rally the elites to the early modern state. The landed nobles clearly had little choice, for the traditional combination of government with landlordship had failed, leaving rural society open to freeholding, wage labor, and representative government. Hence the aristocracies, and not only in the German-speaking world, supported "a *displacement* of politico-legal coercion upwards towards a centralized, militarized summit."[96] In lands where the urban element was weak, such as the Duchy of Upper Austria, the alliance between landed nobility and the Hapsburg state operated in just this way. Taking advantage of rural overpopulation, the state guaranteed succession rights to the inheriting farmers, who helped to guard law and order among their less fortunate kinsmen and kinswomen.[97]

Urban elites, too, longed for law and order, even at foreign hands. In northern Italy between 1494 and 1530, for example, the ruling classes of the city-states "could not command enough support or loyalty from the subject communities to have any firm faith in sur-

---

[93] Blickle, *Revolution of 1525*, 125–45.

[94] Peter Blickle, *Landschaften im alten Reich. Die staatliche Funktion des gemeinen Mannes in Oberdeutschland* (Munich, 1973); idem, "Communalism, Parliamentarism, Republicanism," 1–13.

[95] Brady, *Turning Swiss*, 34–40.

[96] Anderson, *Lineages of the Absolutist State*, 19–20 (emphasis in the original).

[97] Hermann Rebel, *Peasant Classes: The Bureaucratization of Property and Family Relations under Early Habsburg Absolutism, 1511–1626* (Princeton, 1983).

vival."[98] It is no wonder, then, that the Genoese elite in particular found the Spanish hegemony as tolerable as it was lucrative.[99] Even in the great ramshackle structure that was the Holy Roman Empire, "the machinery of the imperial constitution played a crucial role in regulating and shaping the course of urban conflicts."[100]

Rural pacification lay at the core of the state's situation. The surest way to rural peace lay in the fixity and security of peasant property rights and tenures, a step with which not all landlords agreed. Indeed, in England the landed class split over centralization, and in France for a long time the process aroused powerful noble resistance.[101] In the long run, however, enhanced peasant property rights helped to pacify the countryside and forced landlords to rely on the state for continued extraction of the agricultural surplus.[102] In some countries, therefore, the state became the lord of all peasants and burghers, both now "subjects," and at least in some respects the guarantor of their property rights. The new pacification and security came at a very high price, for all the old rights, the entire "old law," became vulnerable to invasion by the king's or prince's law. Theirs was a written law preached by learned lawyers, "the priests of this law and the political theologians of the new state," whose gospel held that "princes and magistrates are called 'the living law.'"[103]

Two things about this process strike the eye. First, though it is sometimes argued that the early modern state's protection of property rights promoted economic development,[104] this is true only of certain types of rights, such as contracts, for wherever the state pacified the countryside by securing peasant property rights – the classic case is

---

[98] Martines, *Power and Imagination*, 288.

[99] Wallerstein, *Modern World-System*, I: 171–3.

[100] Christopher R. Friedrichs, "Urban Conflicts and the Imperial Constitution in Seventeenth-Century Germany," *The Journal of Modern History* 58, Supplement (December 1986), S98–S123, here at S123.

[101] Brenner, "Agrarian Class Structure and Economic Development in Pre-Industrial Europe," in *Brenner Debate*, 54–62. On peasant property rights and the growth of the French state, see William H. Beik, *Absolutism and Society in Seventeenth-Century France: State and Provincial Aristocracy in Languedoc* (Cambridge, 1985), esp. chap. 1; Hilton Root, *Peasants and King in Burgundy: Agrarian Foundations of French Absolutism* (Berkeley and Los Angeles, 1987).

[102] See Brenner, "The Agrarian Roots of European Capitalism," in *Brenner Debate*, 286–91.

[103] Strauss, *Law, Resistance, and the State*, 164.

[104] This is the principal argument of North and Thomas, *Rise of the Western World*, though occasionally (see, e.g., 29–30) they acknowledge that the market had to be helped by force. For critiques, see Brenner, "Agrarian Class Structure," 16n12; Charles Tilly, "War Making and State Making as Organized Crime," in *Bringing the State Back In*, 169–91.

France – it did so at the expense of economic development. Economic development ultimately required a massive expropriation of the peasantry, which happened in the fullest sense only in England. "Ironically," concludes Robert Brenner, "the most complete freedom and property rights for the rural population meant poverty and a self-perpetuation cycle of backwardness. In England, it was precisely the absence of rights that facilitated the onset of real economic development."[105]

A second point about rural pacification is that more secure rights for peasants limited the extraction of the surplus and diminished the state's revenues. Rural pacification thus affected kings' and princes' ability to pursue what since about 1500 had become their leading enterprise: the business of war.

THE STATE AS MILITARY ENTERPRISE

One view of European history holds that the emergence of strong states encouraged and, indeed, proved vital to, something called "development."[106] This, if true, was the furthest thing from their builders' minds. State-building aimed to enhance the rulers' power to make war. "The new monarchy," Kiernan writes, "bore an essentially warlike character that it was never to lose. War for it was not an optional policy, but an organic need, . . . [and] the whole state apparatus that rulers were putting together piecemeal was largely a by-product of war."[107] Political consolidation began with conquest and ended with "an exchange of resources, including plunder, to merchants in return for goods and credit."[108] War and trade were complementary ways of gaining control of what belonged to others.

The European state's growth as a military enterprise shaped the rise of merchant empires, which were made possible by "the absolute or relative superiority of Western weaponry and Western military organisation over all others."[109] The formation of the imperial arsenal began at home with the evolution of a new system of warfare that replaced an older pattern in which war might described as a kind of

---

[105] Brenner, "Agrarian Class Structure," 52.
[106] Guénée, *States and Rulers*, 20–21, cites the French version, but there are others.
[107] Kiernan, "State and Nation," 31.
[108] Wolf, *Europe and the People without History*, 105. As Charles Tilly so pungently puts it, "war making and state making – quintessential protection rackets with the advantage of legitimacy – qualify as our largest examples of organized crime." Tilly, "War Making and State Making," 169.
[109] From Geoffrey Parker's chapter in this volume, "Europe and the Wider World, 1500–1700: The Military Balance."

"violent housekeeping."[110] It emerged in full flower during the 1490s – the decade of Columbus and Da Gama – when the Italian Wars became the laboratory for a new style of land warfare, the essentials of which did not change for three hundred years.

Europe's "military revolution" began with innovations in management, organization, and weaponry.[111] The management of war as an enterprise bloomed in fourteenth-and fifteenth-century Italy, whence it spread across Europe.[112] By 1451 the rulers of its homeland could establish a structure of collective security, which enabled them to gain control over the enormously expensive system of mercenary warfare.

The chief organizational innovation, the renaissance of infantry, began in 1302 at Courtrai, when the Flemish guild militias defeated a French feudal army. After the Burgundian Wars of 1474–7, when the Swiss and Upper Rhenish forces smashed the Burgundian army in three stunning victories, the revival took on "world-historical influence, as the other peoples, recognizing the superiority of the Swiss way of war, began to imitate it."[113]

Guns, the new weaponry, had been known in Europe since around 1330, but 150 years passed before artillery and muskets became indispensable to field armies.[114] The Swiss used them sparingly, but during the Italian Wars Gonzalo Hernandez de Cordoba (1453–1515), Castile's "Great Captain," began to pack his infantry formations with gunners. By this time, too, every European warlord had invested heavily in cannon, especially after Charles VIII's French guns battered one fortress after another in his progress to Naples in 1494. Thereafter, as Spanish, French, and Italian gunners demonstrated the obsolescence of all older fortifications, a new system, the wickedly expensive *trace italienne*, began to spread across Italy and then into the rest of

---

[110] John R. Hale, *War and Society in Renaissance Europe, 1450–1620* (Baltimore, 1985), 13, 15. See also Kennedy, *Great Powers*, 36–7, 41–6. Like most accounts, Kennedy's focuses too much on Charles V vs. Francis I and too little on the previous generation, when the French invasion of Italy in 1494 provoked the transformation of a Franco-Burgundian struggle into a European one. See Wiesflecker, *Kaiser Maximilian I*, 5:410–47.

[111] See the masterful synthesis by Geoffrey Parker, *The Military Revolution: Military Innovation and the Rise of the West, 1500–1800* (Cambridge, 1988); also William H. McNeill, *The Pursuit of Power: Technology, Armed Force, and Society Since A.D. 1000* (Chicago and London, 1982), 79–81.

[112] Michael Mallet, *Mercenaries and their Masters: Warfare in Renaissance Italy* (Totowa, N.J., 1974), 76–145.

[113] Hans Delbrück, *Geschichte der Kriegskunst im Rahmen der politischen Geschichte*, vol. 4, *Neuzeit* (Berlin, 1920; reprinted, Berlin, 1962), 1. See Parker, *Military Revolution*, 16–17.

[114] Carlo M. Cipolla, *Guns, Sails, and Empires: Technological Innovation and the Early Phases of European Expansion, 1400–1700* (New York, 1965), 21–31.

Europe.[115] Cannon won their place on the battlefield, too, and at Marignano in 1515, under the walls of Milan, a French army taught the Swiss what even the best infantry could expect, if they gave battle without them.

The Italian Wars were the laboratory of early modern warfare,[116] which, along with painting, architecture, classical scholarship, and music, belonged to the Renaissance culture that spread across Europe during the sixteenth century. Warfare's scale grew enormously: between 1530 and 1710 the total numbers of armed forces paid by the European states and the total numbers involved in European battles increased about tenfold.[117] The states passed these costs on to their subjects, who "paid higher taxes, and, thanks to higher imposts on commodities, they paid more for what they wore, ate and drank. The increased size of armies was passed on still more personally through the voracious appetite of the recruiting process."[118] Still more went into fortifications, the bottomless hole into which the peoples' substance disappeared.[119]

Early military enterprising suffered from primitive bureaucracies and poor field commanders, but most of all from lack of money. One aggravating condition of the latter was corporate liberties, the growth of which over the previous 150 years had made a narrow passage for the royal fist into subjects' purses. Taxation without consent generally passed for a mark of tyranny, as Philippe de Commynes (ca. 1447–1511) wrote: "Is there any king or lord in this world who has the power, outside of his own domain, to levy a single *denier* on his subjects without the approval and consent of those who are to pay it, unless he does it by tyranny or violence?"[120] As the states grew stronger and sought more powerfully and effectively after their subjects' wealth, corporate institutions provided just about the only instruments of resistance. In no other large state was this truer than in the Holy Roman Empire, where under Emperor Maximilian I (r. 1493–1519) the imperial diet contributed so little to his Italian Wars that in compensation he squeezed Austria dry: between 1508 and 1517, the

[115] Parker, *Military Revolution*, 9–16.
[116] Mallet, *Mercenaries and their Masters*, 231–8. On the wider background, see Philippe Contamine, *War in the Middle Ages*, trans. Michael Jones (Oxford, 1984), 119–72.
[117] Geoffrey Parker, "The 'Military Revolution, 1560–1660' – A Myth?" in his *Spain and the Netherlands, 1559–1569* (London and Short Hills, N.J., 1979), 86–103, here at 95–96. See now Parker, *Military Revolution*, 45–46.
[118] Hale, *War and Society*, 47. See Parker, *Military Revolution*, 61–4.
[119] Parker, *Military Revolution*, 39, on the relative costs of offense and defense.
[120] *The Memoirs of Philippe de Commynes*, edited by Samuel Kinser, trans. Isabelle Cazeaux, 2 vols. (Columbia, S.C., 1969–73) 1:358 (Book V, chap. 19).

modestly endowed Austrian lands produced perhaps twenty times as much revenue per year (about 1,000,000 florins per year) as did the entire remainder of the empire.[121] A similar disparity, arising from similar causes, existed between the Hapsburgs' two European milch cows, Castile and the Netherlands.[122] The common folk of Castile, where corporate powers of resistance were weak, shouldered an ever greater burden of regressive, indirect taxes, despite the rivers of American bullion that flowed through Spain into foreign hands. In the Hapsburg Netherlands, by contrast, the regent and the estates cooperated in funding the public debt in such a way that for "the first time in European history . . . the future revenues of whole provinces could be mobilized for present needs through the mechanism of credit."[123] After the Dutch revolt, this innovation worked against the Hapsburgs rather than for them.

Few European populations would tolerate the levels of taxation needed to pay for Europe's sixteenth-century wars, and few royal warlords could finance their enterprises of their own. The rulers turned, therefore, to Europe's merchant-bankers for the freedom to make war on credit.[124] The Germans led the way. Emperor Maximilian I raised two German infantry regiments, which were drilled and armed in the Swiss manner. To pay them he had to borrow often from the Fuggers and the other Augsburg firms, who financed his wars.[125] This alliance between banking and war-making fostered the rise of the German military enterprisers, who helped the German lansquenets replace the Swiss as kings of Europe's battlefields and promoted, a generation later, a parallel transformation of German cavalry (*Reiter*). The emperor's lack of regular taxes or a standing army made the Holy Roman Empire a fertile pasture for both the south German bankers and the military enterprisers. To them was owing

---

[121] Wiesflecker, *Kaiser Maximilian I.*, 5:572–4.
[122] This is based on John H. Elliott, *Imperial Spain, 1469–1716* (New York, 1964), 191–9; and M. R. Rodriguez-Salgado, *The Changing Face of Empire: Charles V, Philip II, and Habsburg Authority, 1551–1559*, Cambridge Studies in Early Modern History (Cambridge, 1988), 50–72. The latter points out (p. 60) that the Aragonese were thoroughly protected from taxation by their corporate liberties. Paul Kennedy's account of Habsburg resources in *Great Powers*, 43–44, suffers from too modern a view of "incomes." The banking houses were not a "major source of income" but a means for anticipating income from taxes at the cost of incomes from the domain and regalian rights.
[123] James D. Tracy, *A Financial Revolution in the Habsburg Netherlands: Renten and Renteniers in the County of Holland, 1515–1565* (Berkeley and Los Angeles, 1985), 221. See Geoffrey Parker, "Spain, Her Enemies, and the Revolt of the Netherlands," in *Spain and the Netherlands*, 17–42, here at 21–2.
[124] McNeill, *Pursuit of Power*, 102–16.
[125] Wiesflecker, *Kaiser Maximilian I.*, 5:545–54.

much of the debt Maximilian left behind: 6,000,000 florins, or eighteen times his annual income, half of it to the Augsburg bankers.[126]

The German military enterprisers arose to meet the need to coordinate command with credit during the first half of the sixteenth century; they organized armies under contract, extended credit to equip and pay them, led them on campaign, and commanded them in battle.[127] In their ranks ranged some old-fashioned, hell-raising nobles, such as Count William IV of Fürstenberg (1491–1541), but also men who combined military with entrepreneurial talents, such as Georg von Frundsberg (1473–1528), the south German warlord whose 10,000 lansquenets helped to sack Rome in 1527. No Welser or Fugger ever prepared his son more carefully to enter the family business than he did his son, Caspar. Such men raised and financed German mercenaries for wars from Russia to America and from North Africa to Scotland. The Germans spread through Europe a practice that the more centralized western monarchies put to more efficient use than any German ruler could, giving rise to "the seemingly symbiotic relationship . . . between the state, military power, and the private economy's efficiency in the age of absolutism. Behind every successful dynasty stood an array of opulent banking families."[128]

The merchant empires gave new scope and opportunities to military enterprising and found new uses for its practices and skills. The Iberian conquests employed specialists from among all the peoples who made a business of war, and no conquistador would have felt strange in Frundsberg's army. It was chiefly Germans and Italians who developed "the absolute or relative superiority of Western weaponry and Western military organization,"[129] while Portuguese, Spaniards, Frenchmen, Dutchmen, and Englishmen took this superiority over the sea into the wider world.

The state's growth as a military enterprise accelerated its appropriation of church property in the wake of the Reformation. In the Holy Roman Empire, the century of religious wars (1546–1648) wedded the "confessions," religious alliances of small states, to military enterprising, while the confessional systems protected each state's

[126] Brady, *Turning Swiss*, 80–90. See Wiesflecker, *Kaiser Maximilian I.*, 5:566–70; Peter Schmid, "Reichssteuern, Reichsfinanzen und Reichsgewalt in der ersten Hälfte des 16. Jahrhunderts," in *Säkulare Aspekte der Reformationszeit*, edited by Heinz Angermeier, Schriften des Historischen Kollegs, Kolloquien, vol. 5 (Munich and Vienna, 1983), 153–98.

[127] I draw details from Fritz Redlich, *The German Military Enterpriser and His Work Force: A Study in European Economic and Social History*, 2 vols. (Wiesbaden, 1964).

[128] Jan de Vries, quoted by Tilly, "War Making and State Making," 179.

[129] From the chapter by Geoffrey Parker in this volume.

appropriation of its church's wealth, personnel, and means of social discipline.[130] Elsewhere, the advance of the Reformation quickened the state's appropriation of the identification of church and people, which had so powerfully supported both local and universal corporate feeling during the preceding era.[131] Reforming kings marshaled local patriotism (the sense of *natio*) for their own ends by merging it with a wider, sacral sense of community, which they wrested from the papacy.[132] As the identification of people and church ripened in kingdoms, such as England, and city-states, such those of Switzerland, the identity between "the church" and the subjects of a single ruler or regime became a mental habit.[133]

The Reformation and the imitative side of the Counter Reformation thus eased the church's passage from Christendom to the large but particular communities created by the states. This process, legitimated by the doctrine of sovereignty, occurred most completely in the states that competed for merchant empires, for competition and rule over non-Europeans provoked the growth of a sense of community in something called the "nation." In Germany and Italy, by contrast, states rarely if ever created communities of this sort before the nineteenth century. There never was a Prussian nation, and the German, Austrian, and Italian nations of today arose much later than the western imperial nations.[134]

---

[130] Hale, *War and Society*, 35–9.
[131] In England, at least, the process began well before the Reformation, as Walter Ullmann shows in " 'This Realm of England is an Empire,' " *Journal of Ecclesiastical History* 30 (1979): 176–91. The growth of rulers' practical authority over the church has been studied with special intensity in Germany. See Heinz Schilling, "The Reformation and the Rise of the Early Modern State," and Karlheinz Blaschke, "The Reformation and the Rise of the Territorial State," both in *Luther and the Modern State in Germany*, edited by James D. Tracy. Sixteenth Century Essays and Studies, vol. 7 (Kirksville, Mo., 1986), 21–30, 61–76. For Spain, see Elliott, *Imperial Spain*, 204–41.
[132] The best study is Ullmann's " 'This Realm of England is an Empire,' " esp. 199–203. There is a good insight into how it worked in Gillian E. Brennan, "Papists and Patriotism in Elizabethan England," *Recusant History* 19/1 (May 1988): 1–15.
[133] On the German-speaking free cities, see Gottfried W. Locher, *Die zwinglische Reformation im Rahmen der europäischen Kirchengeschichte* (Göttingen, 1979), 167–71; Brady, "Godly Republics," 14–32. This identity, as Bernd Hamm cogently argues, found its legitimacy in Huldrych Zwingli's rejection of Luther's doctrine of "two kingdoms" in favor of a one "kingdom" or "city" and a convergence of civil and Christian freedom. See Bernd Hamm, *Zwinglis Reformation der Freiheit* (Neukirchen-Vluyn, 1988), 100–17.
[134] The formation of confessional networks supplied the German-speaking world with some of the sense of community that elsewhere the sense of nationality provided. See Wolfgang Reinhard, "Zwang zur Konfessionalisierung? Prolegomena zu einer Theorie des konfessionellen Zeitalters," *Zeitschrift für Historische Forschung* 10 (1983): 257–77.

The sovereign national state thus succeeded the papal imperium as the form of government; and the nation, the state's moral creature, succeeded the church as the ultimate community of fortune. Nations are postecclesiastical Europe's solution to the problem of mobilizing populations for imperial and other purposes.[135] The first nations were the first imperial peoples – England, Spain, Portugal, the Netherlands, and France – and other peoples invented nations either to imitate the imperial states or to get free of them. Examples of the former are the Germans and Italians, of the latter the Poles and the Irish. Each of Europe's old imperial nations, however, arose from a state that undertook imperial enterprise beyond the seas, and their sense of themselves fed from their feelings of linguistic, cultural, and racial superiority over European rivals and European and non-European inferiors.[136]

Such were some of the military and ideological links among military enterprising, state-building, and overseas empire. To them we may add another, social, link: the quintessentially European figure of the warrior-merchant.

THE MERCHANT AS WARRIOR

As a historical problem, the rise of merchant empires intersects the debate about the transition from feudalism to capitalism in Europe. The debate's least tractable sector concerns the relationship of the merchants to the feudal order, on the one hand, and the capitalist bourgeoisie, on the other. Few discussions of the merchants' role in preindustrial Europe are free from thoughts about their connections to modern business classes. The notion that Europe witnessed the replacement of land-based feudal warriors by city-born business elites is very deeply rooted in European historiography, and a durable apologetic contrasts the merchant as bearer of peaceful trade with the noble as bearer of war.[137] It is an old idea, celebrated

---

[135] See Kiernan, "State and Nation," to whose view my own is indebted.

[136] Although the literature on early modern Europe emphasizes the strength of Spanish racialism, in modern times the leaders in racial thought have been Northern Europeans. See Hugh A. MacDougall, *Racial Myth in English History: Trojans, Teutons, and Anglo-Saxons* (Hanover, N.H., and London, 1982); Roger Chickering, *We Men Who Feel Most German: A Cultural Study of the Pan-German League, 1886–1914* (Boston, 1984), chap. 4.

[137] John Merrington suggests why this is so: "... to read the progressive role of the urban bourgeoisie backwards into history is to pose the market as the only dynamic force, the principle behind all movement, all change." John Merrington, "Town and Country in the Transition to Capitalism," *in Transition from Feudalism to Capitalism*, edited by R. H. Hilton, 170–95, here at 173.

long ago by the English clergyman Edward Young (1683–1765) in these words:[138]

> Merchants o'er proudest heroes reign;
> Those trade in blessing, these in pain,
> At slaughter swell, and shout while nations groan
> With purple monarchs merchants vie;
> If great to spend, what to supply?
> Priests pray for blessings; merchants pour them down.
>
> Kings, merchants are in league and love,
> Earth's odours play soft airs above,
> That o'er the teeming field prolific range.
> Planets are merchants; take, return,
> Lustre and heat; by traffic burn:
> The whole creation is one vast Exchange.

How utterly this notion of the world as "one vast Exchange" contrasts with our image of the early medieval merchant, who huddles – harmless and ghostlike, though pregnant with mighty revolutions – at the foot of castles in which barbarian kings hold sway. This image – it is Henri Pirenne's – haunts us still, even in our knowledge of how neatly the merchant, his trade, and his cities nestled in the violent bosom of feudal Europe. Once grown rich, the merchant strove upward into the warrior classes because, as a fifteenth-century Strasbourgeois insisted, "he whom God has granted wealth, also wants honor."[139]

War and trade, K. N. Chaudhuri writes, "are the two indivisible symbols of man's basic desire to look beyond his inner self and of the urge to master the constraints of immediate natural environment."[140] The great contemporary Asian empires – Ottoman Turkey, Mughal India, and Ming China – are said to have separated government from trade and warriors from merchants.[141] This was certainly not true in Europe, where from an early time merchants governed

---

[138] Edward Young, "To a Solemn Musick," in *The Stuffed Owl: An Anthology of Bad Verse*, edited by D. B. Wyndham Lewis and Charles Lee (London, 1962), 72.

[139] Quoted by Thomas A. Brady, Jr., *Ruling Class, Regime, and Reformation at Strasbourg, 1520–1555*, Studies in Medieval and Reformation Thought, vol. 22 (Leiden, 1978), 49.

[140] K. N. Chaudhuri, "The Organising Principles of Premodern, Long-Distance Trade, Merchants, and Objects of Trade," a paper presented at the "Rise of Merchant Empires" conference, Minneapolis, October 1987.

[141] See the grand overview by Michael N. Pearson in his chapter in this volume, where he writes that in Mughal India "mercantile activity and tributary relationships thus function side by side," though "it is . . . quite incorrect to see [the merchants] as other than passive vis-à-vis the elite." But the chapter by K. N. Chaudhuri, also in this volume, expresses doubt on this point.

and made war. States ruled by merchants or by merchants and land-owners arose in Italy very shortly after A.D. 1000. Pisa, Genoa, and Venice led the pack, but all up and down Central Europe, from Tuscany to Flanders, from Brabant to Livonia, merchants not only supplied warriors – as they did all over Europe – they sat in governments that made war and, sometimes, buckled on armor and went into battle themselves. Such places make a long list: not only Florence, Milan, Venice, and Genoa, but also Augsburg, Nuremberg, Strasbourg, and Zurich; not only Lübeck, Hamburg, Bremen, and Danzig, but also Bruges, Ghent, Leiden, and Cologne. Some of them – Florence, Nuremberg, Siena, Bern, and Ulm come to mind – built considerable territorial states; Genoa and Venice acquired Europe's first merchant empires; and the German Hansa dominated the northern trade and stimulated the commercial rise of the Dutch.[142] In very many respects, such as the organization of slave labor, management of colonies, imperial administration, commercial institutions, maritime technology and navigation, and naval gunnery, the Italian city-states were the direct forerunners of the Portuguese and Spanish empires, to the shaping of which the Italians contributed so heavily, and in the profits of which they so largely shared.[143]

By 1500 only rags and tags remained of the Italian seaborne empires. The Genoese position in the East quickly crumbled before the Ottoman advance, whereupon the Genoese merchants – "a Genoese and therefore a merchant," the saying went – turned to feed at the Iberian trough.[144] The Venetian seaborne empire held out longer, but well before 1500 Venice began to build a compensatory empire on *terra ferma*. Supremacy in the European long-distance trade and banking had by this time passed to the south Germans.[145] The remarkable continuity between big Italian and big south German trade and banking is hardly surprising in a purely institutional and technical sense

---

[142] G. V. Scammell, *The World Encompassed: The First European Maritime Empires, c. 800–1650* (Berkeley and Los Angeles, 1981), gives this dimension its full due; Philippe Dollinger, *The German Hansa*, trans. D. S. Ault and S. H. Steinberg (Stanford, 1970), 62–84, 281–329.

[143] As Chaudhuri says in his chapter in this volume: "With the rise of the trading republics in Italy, the professional skills of their merchants gradually became an integral part of western social self-awareness and acceptance."

[144] Carla Rahn Phillips, "The Growth and Composition of Trade from Southern European, 1350–1750," in *Rise of Merchant Empires*, 34–101; Herman Van der Wee, "Structural Changes in European Long-Distance Trade, and Particularly in the Reexport Trade from South to North, 1350–1750," in *ibid.*, 33.

[145] Jean-François Bergier, "From the Fifteenth Century in Italy to the Sixteenth Century in Germany: A New Banking Concept?" in *The Dawn of Modern Banking*, edited by the Center for Medieval and Renaissance Studies, University of California, Los Angeles (New Haven and London, 1979), 105–30.

because the Italians were the Germans' teachers, but it also had an ideological side.

Christianity is sometimes said to have been hostile to merchants and commerce, and it is true that "the Scholastic Doctors of the Middle Ages looked with favor upon husbandry but regarded trade with distrust because it was an occupation which, although not wicked in itself, nevertheless endangered the salvation of the soul."[146] The explosive expansion of trade, however, brought radical changes, and by the fifteenth century Italian writers, such as Bernardino of Siena (1380–1444) and Antonino of Florence (1389–1459), were wrestling realistically with economic issues and practices. Some humanists went further than that. In his *De avaritia* of 1428–9, the Florentine humanist Poggio Bracciolini (1380–1459) rejected the ideal of evangelical poverty. He argued that wealth is a sign of divine favor, and that "everything we undertake is for the sake of money, and we are all led by desire for gain."[147]

Such arguments built self-confidence in men and families whose power came from trade rather than birth, status, or vocation. At Augsburg in the first half of the next century, the humanist politician Conrad Peutinger (1465–1547) set out to defend his Welser in-laws and the other big firms against the powerful German antimonopoly movement. He argued that the very pursuit of profit promoted the common good and should therefore be free of all restrictive legislation.[148] Although still a far step from viewing the world as "one vast Exchange," Peutinger's argument lies on the same path toward the idea of a world governed by the market.

Like their Italian counterparts, the south German merchant-bankers had to grapple with the disparity between their political power and their economic interests. Genoa and Venice proved too weak to hold

[146] Raymond de Roover, "The Scholastic Attitude toward Trade and Entrepreuneurship," in *Business, Banking, and Economic Thought in Late Medieval and Early Modern Europe: Selected Studies of Raymond de Roover*, edited by Julius Kirshner (Chicago and London, 1974), 336–45, here at 336, and see 339–45 for what follows.

[147] Poggio Bracciolini, "On Avarice," translated by Benjamin G. Kohl and Elizabeth B. Welles, in *The Earthly Republic: Italian Humanists on Government and Society*, edited by Benjamin G. Kohl and Ronald G. Witt (Philadelphia, 1978), 231–89. See Hans Baron, "Franciscan Poverty and Civic Wealth as Factors in the Rise of Humanistic Thought," *Speculum* 13 (1938): 1–37, and more generally, Eugenio Garin, *Italian Humanism: Philosophy and Civic Life in the Renaissance*, trans. Peter Munz (New York, 1965).

[148] Erich Höffner, *Wirtschaftsethik und Monopole im 15. und 16. Jahrhundert* (Jena, 1941; reprinted, Stuttgart, 1969); and, on the context, see Brady, *Turning Swiss*, 120–30. My point is hardly weakened by Raymond de Roover's doubt about the novelty of Peutinger's argument. Raymond de Roover, "Monopoly Theory Before Adam Smith," in his *Business, Banking, and Economic Thought*, 285–7.

what their merchant-warriors had seized; the military power of Augsburg and Nuremberg hardly reached a half-day's ride from their walls. The really big firms, such as Augsburg's Fuggers, grew much too large for the protection such city-statelets could supply and cultivated a way of life too grand for their merchant colleagues. Sometimes they conducted separate foreign policies against their own governments or against their natural allies. The war between Charles V and the German Protestants in 1546–7 and its aftermath supply some telling examples. At Augsburg the Fuggers stayed loyal to the emperor, but their government supported the Protestant league; at Nuremberg the big families, all Lutherans, kept the entire city loyal, despite the entreaties of their fellow Protestants; and at Strasbourg, the threat of outlawry if Charles won the war drove the Protestant merchants to face exile rather than resistance and ruin.[149] The lesson is clear: the great south German firms, having outgrown their hometowns, gravitated toward the monarchy for protection and favor.

This mismatch between commercial enterprise and political base presents a south German variation on an Italian theme and a foretaste of a Dutch one, for the government of the United Provinces of the Netherlands proved itself unable to supply the political and military weight the Dutch merchants required in order to keep up with the English.[150] The north Italian, south German, and Dutch cases lead to a single conclusion: the expansion of long-distance trade required, sooner or later, a strong, highly centralized and militarized state, and the minimum size – in area, population, and wealth – of that state grew larger with each passing century. City-states simply could not command sufficient force in the changed world of the sixteenth and seventeenth centuries.

The association of the big merchants with the centralized monarchies, it is sometimes argued, promoted economic development because the state provided security to private property, especially to contracts.[151] This is no doubt true so long as we recognize that, though it may have helped to assure private property rights of the domestic elites, the union of warfare and trade was bound by no law in dealings with other peoples. Indeed, the securing of some private property rights in the core countries of Europe went hand in hand with massive

---

[149] Olaf Mörke, "Die Fugger im 16. Jahrhundert. Städtisches Elite oder Sonderstruktur?" *Archiv für Reformationsgeschichte* 74 (1983): 141–61; Brady, *Turning Swiss*, 202–21.

[150] See Peter Wolfgang Klein, "Dutch Capitalism and the European World-Economy," in *Dutch Capitalism and World Capitalism*, edited by Maurice Aymard (Cambridge, 1982), 75–91, who believes that this weakness was deliberate.

[151] See note 104 above.

invasion of nearly every other form of property right in the world: communal and corporate rights in European lands; and ancient forms of land tenure in Ireland and Scotland, the Canary Islands, Mexico, and British North America.[152]

The rise of merchant empires thus continued a European union of trade and warfare, the continuous history of which had begun with the Italian maritime empires. The business of war on land flowed into the war of business at sea and across the seas, and it is often very difficult to separate them, for "in every instance European ventures on the oceans were sustained by a combination of public, quasi-public, and relentlessly private enterprise."[153] The entire English operation in the Atlantic prior to 1630, writes Kenneth R. Andrews, was a "predatory drive of armed traders and marauders to win by fair means or foul a share of the Atlantic wealth of the Iberian nations."[154] A Drake, a Fenner, or a Hawkins, to name but three of the great English families who lived from maritime plunder, can hardly be distinguished from some of the leading German military enterprisers.[155] And they were all fellows to the Portuguese Da Gamas, who traded spices in India in one generation and crusaded in Ethiopia in the next.[156] Such men continued a long European tradition of the union of warfare and trade. What was new in the sixteenth century was the immense power of the relatively small imperial states they served, as they served themselves.

The Portuguese, first Europeans to go over the sea, partly grabbed and partly built an Asian trading network based on the cooperation of private traders with the Crown, on convincing naval superiority, and on the successful seizure of strategic ports. The role of the Crown, which managed trade through royal officials and the sale of licenses (*cartazes*), loomed greater than it would in the later Asian systems of the Dutch and the English, but it remained within the limits of the European type of seaborne empire.[157]

---

[152] Such invasions lay behind a fundamental change in the notion of property. See Winfried Schulze, "Vom Gemeinnutz zum Eigennutz. Über Normenwandel in der ständischen Gesellschaft der frühen Neuzeit," *Historische Zeitschrift* 243 (1986): 591–626; Renate Blickle, "Nahrung und Eigentum als Kategorien in der ständischen Gesellschaft," in Schulze, ed., *Ständische Gesellschaft und soziale Mobilität*, 73–93.

[153] McNeill, *Pursuit of Power* 103.

[154] Kenneth R. Andrews, *Trade, Plunder, and Settlement: Maritime Enterprise and the Genesis of the British Empire, 1480–1630* (Cambridge, 1984), 356.

[155] David B. Quinn and A. N. Ryan, *England's Sea Empire, 1550–1642* (London, 1983), 69.

[156] Bailey W. Diffie and George D. Winius, *Foundations of the Portuguese Empire, 1415–1580* (Minneapolis, 1977), 354–8.

[157] Niels Steensgaard, *The Asian Trade Revolution of the Seventeenth Century: The East India*

When, as in England, the state could not pay the costs of empire, or, as in the Netherlands, it would not, the imperial division of labor evolved a new form: the chartered company, in which the merchants themselves both conducted trade and policed the trading system. The vigorous young English seaborne empire was managed ashore by "men who had participated in the promotion of the drive for trans-oceanic trade and plunder; afloat its conduct was largely in the hands of men whose maritime experience had been accumulated in the same movement."[158] They and their Dutch counterparts had to shift from prevailing European methods of making war, which would not do in Asia, where Europeans could not transform the terms of trade through brute force. The more efficient kind of political management of trade, which they required, was supplied by the chartered companies.

The Dutch East India Company (VOC) and English East India Company (EIC) were just as closely linked to government and war as the Portuguese *Estado da India* had been.[159] Their Asian trade, according to Chaudhuri, "could not be strictly separated from the conduct of national foreign policy, and reasons of state dictated that the merchants should look to the government for a large measure of political support."[160] Although their centralization of the distribution of Asian commodities in merchants' hands proved more efficient than the Portuguese system, the East India companies essentially extended and adapted the historic European union of warfare and trade. They functioned in many respects like states, but the kind of states Europe might have had, had merchants ever gained a completely free hand to manage the state as a profit-making enterprise. The companies built, maintained, and used fleets, organized and maintained armies, and conducted diplomacy, and their budgeting, accounting, and communications were far more efficient than those of any European state. Free of the cares of noncommercial, nonmilitary affairs, which so weighed down the merchants who ruled European city-states, for a long time the chartered companies had no subjects to manage. They drew from the wealth produced by hundreds of peoples, without the

Companies and the Decline of the Caravan Trade (Chicago and London, 1974), 85, 95–113; Diffie and Winius, *Foundations*, 301–37; K. N. Chaudhuri, *Trade and Civilisation in the Indian Ocean: An Economic History from the Rise of Islam to 1750* (Cambridge, 1985), 63–79. For a critique of Steensgaard's thesis, see Sanjay Subrahmanyam and Luís Filipe F. R. Thomaz's chapter in this volume; they emphasize the dynamism and adaptability of the Portuguese system in Asia.

[158] Quinn and Ryan, *England's Sea Empire*, 69.
[159] See Chaudhuri, *Trade and Civilisation*, 80–97.
[160] K. N. Chaudhuri, *The Trading World of Asia and the English East India Company, 1660–1760* (Cambridge, 1978), 455.

expenses, troubles, and dangers of managing the primary extraction of surplus.

Protected by guarantes of law at home and attracted by freedom from laws abroad, the company merchants resembled Spanish conquistadors or German military enterprisers more than they did the Fuggers of Augsburg or the Strozzi of Florence. They lived in two worlds: a home world in which the growing security of property protected their accumulations from the type of behavior they exhibited abroad; and a wider world that afforded release from restraints on freedom at home.

CONCLUSION

The rise of European merchant empires capitalized on certain features of Christendom: the separation between ecumenical integration and military force, the success of small governments, the close integration of trade and government, and the operations of the warrior-merchants. These characteristics arose since 1000 in Christendom's heartlands, roughly the lands of Italy and the Holy Roman Empire; their consequences developed most freely between 1450 and 1650 in Europe's western tier, where the combined enterprises of governmental centralization, war-making, and overseas adventure and conquest began to transform the old kingdoms into the early modern states. From this time onward, Italy and Germany began to become "backward," while Portugal, Spain, France, England, and the Netherlands marched or trudged on the path to imperial-national statehood. In the nonimperial heartlands, the fundamental lines of medieval European development continued: the centrality of religious institutions and culture, the fragmentation of government, and the preservation of traditional property rights against capitalist invasion.

"Development," therefore, as defined by the experience of northwestern Europe, and more especially by that of England, meant the transformation of European civilization through the acquisition of seaborne empires into new patterns, which were not simply extensions of earlier European ones. The acquisition of power over non-Europeans abroad encouraged the European elites to integrate their realms into civilizations – called "nations" – a process that began with language and ended with biology.[161] The belated efforts, moreover,

---

[161] "Nations," writes Ernest Gellner, "can be defined only in terms of the age of nationalism," which is, "essentially, the general imposition of a high culture on society [and the] generalized diffusion of a school-mediated, academy-supervised idiom, codified for the requirements of reasonably precise bureaucratic and tech-

of the "backward" peoples to catch up, compete with, and surpass the Western European imperial nation-states on the stage of world history, prepared the ground for some of our own century's greatest tragedies.

The great going-out over the sea did not change everything, but it changed everything it touched. It did not create the warriors' quest for new lands or the merchants' for new markets, but it did open to European warrior-merchants realms where laws were less strict, less enforceable, or simply absent, and where popular resistance to invasion of rights was less effective than at home.[162] The merchant empires afforded new freedoms in new lands, where men could obtain greater wealth, prestige, and power than they could have won at home. If they did so at the expense of Africans, Amerindians, and other peoples, who cared, especially after death stilled Las Casas's bold tongue? Who abhorred the buying and selling of human beings, so long as it was not done at London, Paris, Seville, or Amsterdam – cities whose merchants bought and sold more Africans in three-and-a-half centuries than the Islamic world did in more than a millennium?[163] Slavery, that ultimate human lordship over the socially dead,[164] completed the gradient of contempt which – to take the English example – "civilised and prosperous Englishmen" felt "for the vagabonds of their own country, for the customs of the most backward parts of England, and for the dirty, cowkeeping Celts on its fringes."[165] This gradient, boundless in its expansibility, began at home and spread its shadow from nearby hearts of darkness to those far over the sea.

The merchant empire-builders' freedom of action arose from European superiority in the organization and execution of war by land and by sea, and of commerce. This "eccentric departure from the human norm of command behavior," to use McNeill's language,[166] may be associated with "the rise of capitalism," providing that certain qualifications are respected. First, the rise of merchant empires does not signal a victory of a mercantile bourgeoisie over a warrior nobility.

---

nological requirements." Gellner, *Nations and Nationalism* (Ithaca and London, 1983), 55, 57.

[162] Tilly, "War Making and State Making," 183, notes that "popular resistance to war making and state making made a difference."

[163] Lovejoy, *Transformations in Slavery*, 24–45, 44–47.

[164] Orlando Patterson, *Slavery and Social Death: A Comparative Study* (Cambridge, Mass., 1982).

[165] Angus Calder, *Revolutionary Empire: The Rise of the English-Speaking Empires from the Fifteenth Century to the 1780s* (New York, 1981), 25.

[166] McNeill, *Pursuit of Power*, 116.

The European nation-state was militarized and expansionist, it policed agriculture, it allied with merchants bent on overseas profits and plunder, and it articulated itself through the growth of civil and military bureaucracy.[167] It generally acquired these characteristics, moreover, before it became genuinely national, and perhaps the possession of overseas empire made the passage to nationhood possible or at least easier. This possibility is strongly supported by the one case in which a centralized, militarized state created a nation in the absence of foreign empire. In the Prussian creation of modern Germany, foreign empire seemed very useful, even necessary, to the stability of the state and social order. Whether German "social imperialism" owed more to a realistic appraisal of social strains in the new Germany or to the German bourgeoisie's envy of the British Empire, the point remains that empire seemed necessary to nation-building.[168]

A second qualification to the association of merchant empires with capitalism concerns the imperial contribution to European development. Apart from the grease that American bullion supplied to the Europeans' Asian trade, the importance of the non-European world's contribution to the capitalization of industrialism in Europe is still quite controversial. It may well be, however, that this contribution came not just as capital accumulated through exchange but as the vaulting confidence of Europe's rulers and elites in knowing history's blessing upon their rule.

Once firm limits are fixed to the merchant's role, two neglected aspects of the transition to capitalism emerge from obscurity. The first aspect, the continuity of imperial enterprise from home to the colonies, helps to ease the sometimes acrimonious conflict between proponents respectively of endogenous and exogenous theories of capitalist development.[169] Much can be clarified by glancing underneath the Europe organized by states to see the correspondences between colonizations at home and abroad. The pursuit of profit, which led some merchants to seek fortunes in the colonies or in the Asia trade, led others to find the areas within Europe that were less resistant to the controlling power of merchant capital than were the guild-bound cities.[170] The export of commodity production into the

---

[167] Wolf, *Europe and the People without History*, 110.

[168] My thinking on this point owes a good deal to Geoff Eley, "The British Model and the German Road: Rethinking the Course of German History Before 1914," in David Blackbourne and Geoff Eley, *The Peculiarities of German History: Bourgeois Society and Politics in Nineteenth-Century Germany* (Oxford, 1984), 39–155.

[169] The best overview is provided by Pearson, *Before Colonialism*. For the basic schema, see Wallerstein, *Modern World-System* 1:349–50.

[170] On rural industry and proto-industrialization, see Kriedte, *Peasants, Landlords, and*

European countryside meant that the growth of the merchants' hegemony over production, which perhaps ended in Bengal, Java, and Martinique, began just outside Bristol, Haarlem, and Rouen. Warfare underwent a similar change, driven by the restless search for new sources of money, guns, and men. Propelled by these forces of war and trade, market relations penetrated the European "hinterlands" in every possible geographical and social sense of the term: the urban commons, the countryside, the backward sectors of core countries, relatively backward countries (Wallerstein's semiperiphery), and the seaborne empires. In this sense, European societies were also colonized and plundered, less catastrophically than the Americas but more so than most of Asia. The rise of the enterprising classes from military and mercantile backgrounds suggests that Marx's second, "non-revolutionary" way to capitalism was Europe's journey, to which the first, "really revolutionary," English way gave a massive impulse. The rapid economic development yielded by the English path proved extremely destructive, both of traditional property rights at home and of institutions and cultures throughout the world.

The second aspect of the transition that this account brings to the fore, concerns the role of the Latin church in the origins and growth of the state system. Arguments about the origins of the European difference, whether conceived as "capitalism," "modernity," or "development," commonly cultivate a stubborn ignorance of the role of the Latin church in the governance of feudal Europe. Partly this stems from a retrograde mentality that deals with religious systems as "mere" ideology, but partly it reflects bewilderment at the spectacle of a civilization governed as was no other in world history. Once recognized, this fact in itself disqualifies European "feudalism" to serve as a stage in any universal scheme of social evolution.

To a very great degree, it was the popes' sacerdotal imperium that the European states came to ape, with this difference: the communities they created, the nations, were exclusive rather than universal. Above the national claims, of course, the ruling elites long claimed to represent more universal values embodied in something they called "civilization." That quickly fell by the wayside, however, when the imperial struggles came home, and World War I found each belligerent defining itself as a "civilization." Such definitions merely completed the logic of the European state system. If empire consists in

Merchant Capitalists, 74–8; Myron P. Gutmann, *Toward the Modern Economy: Early Industry in Europe, 1500–1800, New Perspectives on European History* (New York, 1988), 5–6, 8–11, 94–5.

centralized rule over disparate peoples, combined with an encompassing, integrative ideology and a circulation of wealth to the center and force to the periphery, then the major states of early modern Europe were all empires before they were national states, and the modern European nations are mostly their creations.

Imperial operations of the European type first attained full scope in the merchant empires constructed by Western Europeans during the early modern era. In their forefront was the warrior-merchant, whose presence reminds us how much the merchant empires owed to their predecessors, the seaborne raiding-and-trading empires built by small urban powers in the heartlands of medieval Europe.

Three things, therefore, seem to have determined that Central Europe and Western Europe would move since about 1450 on different paths: the temporary but decisive success of the imperial papacy in sheltering politico-military particularism in the heartlands; the greater scope afforded warrior-merchants by the kingdoms of the west; and the attainment of empire in lands that lay far beyond the restraints which old European institutions and habits – corporate governance, communal ideals, collective holding of property, governance split between civil and ecclesiastical authority – placed on the management of trade and property to utmost advantage.

The early commercial empires of Central European city-states therefore, grew into nothing; the later commercial empires of Western European kingdoms grew into imperial nations. The latter came to compare themselves to the classical empires, though they never lost a faint, ghostly sense of forming a civilization – the "West" as opposed to all the "Easts."

All of the "Easts" participate in the history of the "West." The seaborne empires served, for example, to dampen for a time the scale and consequences of warfare in metropolitan Europe. For about 350 years before 1914, Europe exported some of its competitive struggles into the wider, colonial world, though, when this relief valve failed, the old pattern of perennial intra-European strife, which had first appeared in the Italian Wars, reestablished itself in Europe in new and terrible forms. The stakes, of course, were infinitely higher now – domination not just of Europe but of the world – and the costs had grown astronomically through the industrialization of war. The warring powers, however, remained what they had become in the era of merchant empires: morally autarchic entities, the military-commercial competition among which was unrestrained by any principles of law. Despite a vague allegiance to "civilization," their elites respected no ecumenical ideology but the doctrine of the market, no common ritual but the business of exchange, and no common morality but the pursuit of profit.

This is one way of looking at the European consequences of the rise of merchant empires. There are others. One of them, starting from the neo-classical theory of international trade, tends to park most other historical forces – church, states, empires; religion, patriotism, racial consciousness; government, war, plunder – under the ledger heading of "transaction costs."[171] From this perspective, the merchant empires represent "a step from autarky, localized trade, to larger trade and specialization, which at least for some economies . . . were steps along the route to a persistent evolution of more efficient forms of economic organization." Two changes, in this view, made greater efficiency possible: "economies of scale associated with the volume of exchange" and "improved methods of enforcing contracts."

Despite its very different language and assumptions, the trade-based account of the rise of merchant empires does not differ so radically from the one I have sketched above. Each emphasizes a valuable perspective on the process: European trade expanded its scope through military enterprising on a global scale; the security of contracts grew out of the state's tendency to favor merchant property over other forms of property right. And these two changes – expansion abroad, security of property at home – reveal the two faces of Europe's empire-builders: plunderers, slavers, and extortioners abroad; prudent, law-abiding businessmen at home. It is nonetheless worth considering, whether the term "transaction costs" expresses adequately these two roles.

The end returns us to the beginning, where the old Portuguese soothsayer stood at the Belem docks on that fateful July day in 1497. He charged Da Gama with turning his back on Christendom for the sake of profit, glory, and empire. Ahead, the oceanic revolution opened to Europe's warrior-merchants worlds in which they could pursue these goals with a freedom Europe often denied and an efficiency it rarely tolerated. Their escape into the "Easts" from custom, law, and obligation gave them a taste of power they would crave forever more. At Sao Tomé and Mombasa, at Goa and Macao, at Jakarta and Malacca, at Cuzco and Tenochtitlan, and at Calcutta and Hanoi, Europeans finally learned to walk the earth as "the lords of human kind."

---

[171] This is explained very lucidly by Douglass C. North, in his chapter in this volume. The remaining quotes in this paragraph are from the same source. See the critical remarks on North's views by Tilly, "War Making and State Making," 177.

CHAPTER 4

Europe and the wider world, 1500–1750: the military balance.*

GEOFFREY PARKER

In the Victoria and Albert Museum in London, there is an ivory chess set, made for Tippu Sultan of Mysore during the late eighteenth century. One set of chessmen represents an Indian princely army, whose soldiers wield swords and hold shields; their adversaries, however, are the European officers and native infantry of the British East India Company – all in uniform, and all impressively equipped with firearms.[1] This contrast neatly symbolizes a central feature of European overseas expansion since the Middle Ages: namely, the absolute or relative superiority of Western weaponry and Western military organization over all others. Amid the wealth of statistics on Europe's import of Asian spices, on the silver production of colonial America, or on the export of African slaves, it is easy to forget that each of these lucrative economic enterprises rested in the last analysis upon force. Although other chapters in this volume stress lower transaction costs as a key explanation of Europe's commercial expansion, it was often a minor consideration overseas, where even the sharpest and most sophisticated business methods would scarcely have been competitive without the sanction of superior force on the part of the Western merchants. As Irfan Habib put it in his perceptive contribution to *The Rise of Merchant Empires*:

'Could it be that the European triumph over Indian (and Asian) merchants was not, then, one of size and techniques, of companies over peddlars, of

---

*This paper draws heavily on G. Parker, *The Military Revolution. Military Innovation and the Rise of the West, 1500–1800* (2nd edn., Cambridge, 1990). I am grateful for important corrections and additional material to Jean Aubin, David W. Baeckelandt, William J. Hamblin, Teresa A. Hiener, Sanjay Subrahmanyam, and Ronald P. Toby.
[1] Victoria and Albert Museum (London), Catalogue no. I. M. 42-1910. See the reproduction in Parker, *Military Revolution*, 116.

joint-stock over atomized capital, of seamen over landsmen? Might it not have been more a matter of men-of-war and gun and shot?'

Indeed, Frederick C. Lane and Niels Steensgaard have gone even further, and suggest that the principal export of preindustrial Europe to the rest of the world was violence, and that the *fidalgos*, the *conquistadores*, the *vrijburghers*, and the *nabobs* were (in effect) warrior nomads who differed little from the Mongols or the Mughals.[2] Even the contrasting styles of conquest, with the Europeans commanding from the quarterdeck while the Asians rode on horseback, were more apparent than real, for the major gains of both were all made on land; and to acquire and preserve a territorial base overseas required fortifications and armies as well as ships.

It follows that, if the dynamics of European overseas expansion are to be fully comprehended, a study of the changing military balance between the West and the rest is essential. But, almost immediately, a major paradox appears. In Central and South America, small groups of Westerners in the first half of the sixteenth century caused the collapse of the mighty Inca and Aztec empires, which (between them) had ruled over nearly one-tenth of the world's population; yet in India, until the mid-eighteenth century, the Europeans made virtually no impact on even the minor states of the subcontinent. Indeed, the sudden progress of Western military methods there after the 1740s was so rapid that it left many Europeans bewildered. When, for example, Edmund Burke spoke in December 1783 in a debate in the English House of Commons on Fox's India Bill, he interrupted his tirade on the injustices and humiliations inflicted upon the Mughal emperor by officers of the Honorable East India Company to observe:

It is impossible, Mr. Speaker, not to pause here for a moment to reflect on the inconsistency of human greatness and the stupendous revolutions that have happened in our age of wonders. Could it be believed, when I entered into existence or when you, a younger man, were born, that on this day, in this House, we should be employed in discussing the conduct of those British subjects who had disposed of the power and person of the Grand Mogul?[3]

---

[2] I. Habib, 'Merchant communities in precolonial India' in J. Tracy, ed., *The Rise of Merchant Empires*. (Cambridge, 1990), 371-99, at p. 399; F. C. Lane, *Venice and History* (Baltimore, 1966), chaps. 23 and 24; N. Steensgaard, "Violence and the Rise of Capitalism: F.C. Lane's Theory of Protection and Tribute," *Review* 5 (1981): 247–73. See also the perceptive sociohistorical analysis of G. B. Ness and W. Stahl, "Western Imperialist Armies in Asia," *Comparative Studies in Society and History* 19 (1977): 2–29.
[3] P. J. Marshall, ed., *The Writings and Speeches of Edmund Burke*, V (Oxford, 1981), 392.

No, indeed: in 1727, the year of Burke's birth, it *had* been unimaginable, for the Europeans in India were still confined to a handful of fortresses and factories huddled around the coasts of the subcontinent.

It used to be fashionable to attribute the rapid transformation of this situation either to the innate moral superiority of the white man, or to the added strength afforded him by the Industrial Revolution. But unfortunately there is little evidence that Britons were more virtuous in 1800 (when they held much of India in their power) than in 1700 (when they held very little) or in 1600 (when they held none at all); and proof that the factory system played a major role in conquering the non-Western world before the nineteenth century is either ambiguous or absent. Although the Machine Age helps to explain how the Europeans extended their control over the total land area of the globe from 35 percent in 1800 to 84 percent in 1914, it cannot explain how they managed to acquire that initial 35 percent.[4] By 1800 white colonists ruled all of Siberia, large parts of America and India, several enclaves in Southeast Asia, and a few outposts along the coasts of Africa; but in East Asia, by contrast, they had still scarcely made any impact. These striking differences can only be understood if the "rise of the West" is broken down into a number of distinct geographical and chronological components.

I

By 1650 the West had already achieved military mastery in four separate areas: central and northeast America; Siberia; some coastal areas of sub-Saharan Africa; and in some parts of the Indonesian and Philippine archipelagoes. Different as these regions, and their inhabitants, undoubtedly were, their experience of the European invaders was, in one crucial respect, identical: the white men, they found, fought dirty and (what was worse) fought to kill. Thus the Narragansett Indians of New England strongly disapproved of the colonists' way of making war. "It was too furious," one brave told an English captain in 1638, "and [it] slays too many men." The captain did not deny it. The Indians, he speculated, "might fight seven years and not kill seven men." Roger Williams, a colonial governor, likewise admitted that the Indians' fighting "was farre lesse bloudy and devouring than

---

[4] D. R. Headrick, *The Tools of Empire: Technology and European Imperialism in the Nineteenth Century* (Oxford, 1981), passim.

the cruell warres of Europe."[5] Meanwhile, on the other side of the world, the peoples of Indonesia were equally appalled by the all-destructive fury of European warfare. The men of Java, for example, were "very loth to fight if they can choose." According to Edmund Scott, who lived among them between 1603 and 1606, the reason was simple: "They say . . . their wealth lyeth altogether in slaves; so that, if their slaves be killed, they are beggared."[6]

Scott had noted a vital and unusual feature of military organization in Southeast Asia that was shared (though he probably did not know it) with America and sub-Saharan Africa: native wars in these areas were almost always fought to enslave enemies rather than to exterminate them, to control labor rather than land, to gain men rather than territory. Of course, there were exceptions. Some Amerindian tribes, such as the Algonquin, tortured their defeated enemies to death in a prolonged and painful ritual; the Zulus in the nineteenth century killed their enemies indiscriminately; and the Igorots of central Luzon in the Philippines remained, until modern times, more interested in collecting heads than slaves.[7] Conversely, the European, for their part, sometimes enslaved defeated enemies. Thus, in the 1650s, the survivors of the Scottish armies captured by the English

[5] Quotations from J. L. Axtell, *The European and the Indian: Essays in the Ethnohistory of Colonial North America* (Oxford, 1981), 140; and F. Jennings, *The Invasion of America* (New York, 1976), 150. Admittedly in some Mesoamerican societies those spared in battle were later slaughtered in religious rituals. The "Flower Wars" of the later Aztec Empire, for example, involved few deaths precisely because all those captured were required for sacrifice. See C. M. Maclachlan and J. E. Rodríquez O, *Forging of the Cosmic Race: A Reinterpretation of Colonial Mexico* (Berkeley, 1980), 38 ff.; and I. Clendinnen, "The Cost of Courage in Aztec Society," *Past and Present* 107 (1985): 44–89.

[6] Edmund Scott, "An Exact Discourse of the Subtilties of the East Indies," in W. Foster, ed., *The Voyage of Sir Henry Middleton to the Moluccas, 1604–1606* (London, 1943; Hakluyt Society, 2d ser., LXXXVIII), 142. Of course, all testimony by Europeans on the *motives* of people from different cultures must be treated with some caution: The Europeans' view of the "savages" was often insensitive and not infrequently confused. Take, for example, the assertion of the French missionary in seventeenth-century Canada, Louis Hennepin, who claimed that when the Indians went to war "'tis commonly to recover satisfaction for some injury that they pretend has been done to them. Sometimes they engage in it upon arrival of a dream; and often as Fancy takes 'em." (quoted in C. J. Jaenen, *Friend and Foe: Aspects of Franco-Amerindian Cultural Contact in the Sixteenth and Seventeenth Centuries* (Ottawa, 1976), 129.)

[7] Jaenen, *Friend and Foe*, 138–41; D. R. Morris, *The Washing of the Spears. The Rise and Fall of the Great Zulu Nation* (London, 1966), 47, 108, 389; W. H. Scott, *The Discovery of the Igorots: Spanish Contacts with the Pagans of Northern Luzon* (Quezon City, 1974), 48–50, 52. A. Reid, *Europe and South-East Asia: The Military Balance* (James Cook University of North Queensland, South-East Asian Studies Committee: occasional paper XVI [1982]), 1–2, notes that some Indonesian battles ended with a suicidal charge by a few of the defeated, but this practice, known as "running amok," was merely a token of the mettle of the vanquished before the rest became slaves. It did not herald a mass slaughter.

were condemned to permanent servitude (usually in Barbados, though sometimes at home: the members of a parliamentary delegation sent to congratulate Oliver Cromwell on his victory at Worcester were each given a horse and two Scotsmen by the Lord General "for a present" to do with as they pleased.[8] But the Scots were regarded as rebels and were treated accordingly; and, even in the case of this and other civil conflicts, the *aim* of making war in Europe was never to secure slaves, as it was in the non-European areas under consideration.

Another distinctive common feature of these regions lay in their settlement patterns. In America, although the Aztec and Inca empires possessed some walled cities, the less civilized peoples to the north and south of them did not. This dearth, of course, facilitated the initial conquest because the natives lacked defensible bases to fall back on, but it complicated consolidation. As Increase Mather, of New England, complained in 1675: "Every swamp is a castle to them, knowing where to find us; but we know not where to find them!" And there are innumerable examples of colonial soldiers marching out with drums beating and colors unfurled in order to destroy an Indian "town" – only to find it gone. The logic of Western superiority in fixed encounters had been thoroughly digested by the Indians: after their costly initial defeats, they were scrupulously careful to avoid pitched battles – much to the fury of the Europeans – because they always lost them. "They doe acts of hostility without proclaiming war; they don't appear openly in the field to bid us battle," was the lament of another irate New England preacher.[9] Only gradually did the Europeans recognize that the only way to beat the Indians was to adopt those same guerilla methods. The serious native rising of 1675 in New England, known as King Philip's War, was only suppressed when the colonists followed the advice of Captain Benjamin Church and fought in small units, armed with hatchets, dogs, and knives as well as firearms, which operated in open formation rather than in lines or columns.[10]

---

[8] Whitelocke, *Memorials of the English Affairs*, III (Oxford, 1853), 351. The author claimed to have set his Scotsmen free at once.

[9] Quotations from Axtell, *The European and the Indian*, 145, 142. For the Indians' guerrilla tactics, see K. F. Otterbein, "Why the Iroquois Won: An Analysis of Iroquois Military Tactics," *Ethnohistory* 11 (1964): 56–63; and F. R. Secoy, *Changing Military Patterns on the Great Plains (17th through early 19th century)* (New York, 1953: Monographs of the American Ethnological Society, XXI), 52ff.

[10] For Benjamin Church, see Axtell, *The European and the Indian*, 146f.; and R. Slotkin and J. K. Flosom, eds., *So Dreadfull a Judgment: Puritan Responses to King Philip's War 1676–7* (Middletown, 1978), 370–470, which provides a critical edition of Church's *Entertaining Passages Relating to Philip's War*.

But the Indians of New England were also learning fast. From the 1640s they managed to acquire an adequate supply of guns from the French, the English and (until the collapse of New Netherland in 1664) the Dutch; and they used them to deadly effect – soon realizing that a musket ball traveled with more force, and faster, than an arrow, and was less likely to be deflected by leaves or undergrowth. Furthermore, the Narragansetts in King Philip's War took refuge in "the Great Swamp" behind the walls and bastions of a European-style fortress that claimed the lives of seventy colonists before it was taken. In the end the "Red Indians" lost ground not so much through any technical inferiority as because their numbers dwindled throughout the seventeenth century (largely thanks to the inroads of European diseases), while those of the Westerners (largely thanks to immigration) relentlessly increased.[11]

The situation in Siberia was not dissimilar. The Cossacks who crossed the Urals into Siberia in the 1580s made excellent use of both firearms and forts to expand eastward, reaching the Pacific by the 1630s in their headlong search for furs. But their rapid progress was due also to the relative absence of concerted opposition: the native population of Siberia at the time was, after all, probably less than 200,000.[12]

Black Africa, however, was a complete contrast. In the first place the Europeans remained, until the nineteenth century, largely confined to their necklace of forts around the coast. The African interior remained inhospitable, if not impenetrable, and many of its states possessed armies that were both numerous and well disciplined. Until the mass manufacture of quinine, the Europeans possessed little defense against the malaria that raged throughout the "dark continent";

---

[11] Details from Secoy, *Changing Military Patterns*, 68 ff.; P. M. Malone, "Changing Military Technology among the Indians of Southern New England 1600–77," *The American Quarterly* 25 (1973): 48–63; H. Lamar and L. Thompson, eds., *The Frontier in History: North America and Southern Africa Compared* (New Haven, 1981), chaps. 5 and 7; and F. Jennings, *The Ambiguous Iroquois Empire: The Covenant Chain Confederation of Indian Tribes with English Colonies from its Beginning to the Lancaster Treaty of 1744* (New York, 1984), 80ff. Much the same sequence of events had already taken place farther south. See the accounts offered by P. W. Powell, *Soldiers, Indians, and Silver: The Northward Advance of New Spain, 1550–1600* (2d ed., Berkeley, 1969); I. Clendinnen, *Ambivalent Conquests. Maya and Spaniard in Yucatan, 1517–1570* (Cambridge, 1987); A. Jara, *Guerre et société au Chili: essai de sociologie coloniale* (Paris, 1961); and E. Cabral de Mello, *Olinda restaurada. Guerra e açúcar no Nordeste 1630–1954* (Rio de Janeiro, 1975) – especially chapter 7.

[12] Details from D. W. Treadgold, *The Great Siberian Migration* (Princeton, 1957); and G. V. Lantzeff and R. A. Pierce, *Eastward to Empire: Exploration and Conquest on the Russian Open Frontier to 1750* (London, 1973).

and, until the invention of the machine gun, their armament may have been enough to win battles, but it was seldom sufficient to win wars. Indeed, several African rulers, from the mid-sixteenth century onward, could match Western firepower with guns of their own – especially after the 1650s, when the Dutch began a direct exchange of guns for slaves. Some 8,000 muskets were sent to the Gold Coast for trade in the three years following July 1658, for example, exchanged at the rate of twelve per slave; a century later, the total number of firearms exported every year was around 400,000, exchanged at the rate of 4, 5, or 6 per slave. And yet, in most areas, this inflow of Western technology scarcely affected most African military techniques.[13] As late as 1861 an English officer in Nigeria who observed the Yoruba at war noted that the native troops in battle still "spread themselves out anyhow into open order, and skirmish away until their ammunition is exhausted, upon which they return to replenish." He added that "though thousands of rounds be fired, the killed may be counted by units and the wounded by tens."[14] Tactics like these would clearly prove ineffective against highly trained European forces. But Black Africa did not import guns for this purpose: wars continued to be fought for slaves, not territories, and the irrelevance of musketry salvoes to operations aimed at securing fit and healthy slaves is obvious. Smoothbore weapons were far too inaccurate to be used with precision to wound rather than to kill; and, in any case, the injuries inflicted by lead shot, however slight, often smashed bones and created wounds that turned gangrenous and caused death. In the eighteenth century, the use of pellets rather than bullets overcame this problem in part – which perhaps explains the

[13] However, the possession of firearms certainly influenced the rise and fall of such west African states as the Asante, whose expansion from the late seventeenth century onward seems to have been based on the gun. See I. Wilks, *The Asante in the Nineteenth Century* (Cambridge, 1975), 20, 110ff. But this is a highly controversial subject, for which much conflicting evidence has been unearthed. See R. Kea, *Settlements, Trade, and Politics in the Seventeenth-Century Gold Coast* (Baltimore, 1982), 158f.; idem, "Firearms and Warfare on the Gold and Slave Coasts from the Sixteenth to the Nineteenth Centuries," *Journal of African History* 12 (1971): 185–213; K. Y. Daaku, *Trade and Politics on the Gold Coast, 1600–1720* (Oxford, 1970), 149–53; J. E. Inikori, "The Import of Firearms into West Africa, 1750–1807: A Quantitative Analysis," *Journal of African History* 18 (1977), 339–68; and W. Richards, "The Import of Firearms into West Africa in the Eighteenth Century," ibid., 21 (1980): 43–59.

[14] J. F. Ade Ajayi and R. Smith, *Yoruba Warfare in the Nineteenth Century* (Cambridge, 1964), 31, 50. In east Africa, it has been suggested, wars in the immediate precolonial period became largely ritualized for lack of manpower: see J. de V. Allen, "Traditional History and African Literature: The Swahili Case," *Journal of African History* 23 (1982): 227–36, at p. 234.

dramatic increase in musket imports – but this did nothing to facilitate the adoption of Western methods of musketry in warfare, for guns simply did not fit into most African military traditions at all.[15]

It was much the same story in the Indonesian archipelago. Sultan Iskandar Muda, of Aceh, for example, had by 1620 accumulated some 2,000 artillery pieces from various Ottoman and European sources. But it led nowhere: the guns proved inferior in action against the Portuguese and almost all were lost at the unsuccessful siege of Melaka in 1629. In reality, firearms never fully replaced Aceh's 900 war elephants as the front line of defense; and such cannon as remained after 1629 were reserved for ceremonial purposes.[16] In part this victory of tradition over innovation is explained, as in America, by the relative infrequency of walled towns. Indeed, in some cases, the boundary between town and country could be hard to find. A French visitor to the capital of Aceh in the 1620s claimed that it was despised by most Europeans "because it is a town undefended by any wall, resembling more an open village in Normandy than a city".[17]

In these areas, naturally, siege warfare was a new experience. Because wars had previously been fought to secure slaves or tribute, rather than to annexe more territory or acquire new specific strategic

---

[15] On the muted impact of the gun, which was repeatedly introduced into African societies only to fall out of use again, see (apart from the sources quoted above): H. J. Fisher and V. Rowland, "Firearms in the Central Sudan, "*Journal of African History* 12 (1971: 215–39; G. White, "Firearms in Africa: An Introduction," ibid., 173–84; R. Oliver, ed., *The Cambridge History of Africa*, III (Cambridge, 1977), 305–12; H. A. Gemery and J. S. Hogendorn, "Technological Change, Slavery, and the Slave Trade," in C. Dewey and A. G. Hopkins, eds., *The Imperial Impact: Studies in the Economic History of Africa and India* (London, 1978), 243–58; and above all, J. K. Thornton, 'The art of war in Angola, 1575–1680', *Comparative Studies in Society and History*, XXX (1988), 360–78; and R. Elphick, *Kraal and Castle: Khoikhoi and the Founding of White South Africa* (New Haven, 1977), 53ff.

[16] See D. Lombard, *Le Sultanat d'Atjeh au temps d'Iskandar Muda (1607–1636)* (Paris, 1967), 83–100; and C. R. Boxer, "The Achinese Attack on Malacca in 1629," in J. Bastin and R. Roolvink, eds., *Malayan and Indonesian Studies* (Oxford, 1964), reprinted in Boxer, *Portuguese Conquest and Commerce in Southern Asia* (London, 1985), chap. 4; D. K. Bassett, "Changes in the Pattern of Malay Politics, 1629–c.1655," *Journal of South-East Asian History* 10, no. 3 (1969): 429–52; and A. R. Reid, "Sixteenth-Century Turkish Influence in Western Indonesia," ibid., 395–414. For similar evidence of poor use of Western guns and military techniques by another Malayan native state, see I. A. Macgregor, "Johore Lama in the 16th century," *Journal of the Malayan Branch of the Royal Asiatic Society* 28, no. 2 (1955): 48–125.

[17] On the typology of towns in Southeast Asia, see the excellent studies of A. R. Reid, "The Structure of Cities in South-East Asia, 15th–17th centuries," *Journal of South-East Asian Studies* 10 (1980): 235–50; idem, "Southeast Asian Cities before Colonialism," *Hemisphere* 28, no. 3 (1983): 144–9; and R. Reed, *Colonial Manila: The Context of Hispanic Urbanism and Process of Morphogenesis* (Berkeley, 1978), 1–3. The Philippines on the eve of Spanish conquest in the 1560s possessed no towns at all. Beaulieu's contempt for Aceh is quoted by Lombard, *Sultanat*, 45n2.

bases, the best defense against attack was either immediate surrender (when the enemy appeared in overwhelming strength) or temporary flight (at all other times). Thus, the last Muslim ruler of the thriving port city of Melaka was not unduly alarmed by the arrival of a small Portuguese squadron in 1511. After some resistance, he and his men withdrew inland "a day's journey" thinking (according to the *Commentaries* of Bras de Albuquerque) that the Portuguese "simply meant to rob the city and then leave it and sail away with the spoil." But, instead, they built the powerful fort known as *A Famosa*, constructed (typically) on the ruins of the Great Mosque with stones gathered from the sacred hill where the sultan's ancestors lay buried. Eventually the walls of Portuguese Melaka stretched for two kilometers and withstood some ten sieges.[18] One of these, in 1629, was undertaken on a heroic scale: Iskandar Muda, of Aceh, led in person a besieging force of 20,000, supported by 236 boats and artillery. They erected siegeworks around Melaka so well that, according to a Portuguese account, "not even the Romans could have made such works stronger or more quickly." But it was not enough to secure victory – on the contrary, the sultan eventually lost 19,000 men and his two senior commanders, as well as most of the ships and guns. In the same year, an equally formidable siege was begun by the ruler of Mataram against the Dutch fortified port of Batavia, which the sultan correctly identified as a "thorn in the foot of Java" that had to be "plucked out, for fear the whole body should be endangered." The sultan's forces, like the troops of Aceh, managed to dig trenches in the European fashion; but they made no impression against the massive moat, wall, and bastions of the new Dutch settlement.[19]

The Europeans erected many other fortifications in Southeast Asia: numerous small citadels in the "Spice Islands" (as at Ternate, Tidore,

[18] Bras de Albuquerque, *The Commentaries of the Great Alfonso Dalboquerque*, III (London, 1880; Hakluyt Society, LXII), 129. See also G. Irwin, "Malacca Fort," *Journal of South-East Asian History* 3, no. 2 (1962): 19–44. The article is reprinted, with some additional material, in K. S. Sandhu and P. Wheatley, eds., *Melaka: The Transformation of a Malay Capital c. 1400–1980*, I (Oxford, 1983), 782–805. This admirable two-volume work contains much else on the subject, though unfortunately there is no chapter on Portuguese Melaka. Today only one gate (the so-called Porto de Santiago, which is in fact Dutch) and some rubble remain on the site of "A Famosa."

[19] See the sources quoted in note 16 above and C. R. Boxer, "Asian Potentates and European Artillery in the 16th–18th Centuries," *Journal of the Malayan Branch of the Royal Asiatic Society* 27, no. 2 (1965); 156–72 (reprinted in Boxer, *Portuguese Conquest and Commerce*, chap. 7). There is a fine painting of the siege of 1629 in the Museum "Old Batavia" in Jakarta. See also the description in H. J. de Graff, *De Regering van Sultan Agung, Vorst van Mataram 1613–1645* (The Hague, 1958), 144–63; and the similar conclusion of R. Maclagen, "On Early Asiatic Fire-Weapons," *Journal of the Asiatic Society (Bengal)* 45, no. 1 (1876): 30–71.

or Amboina) and the Philippines; Fort Zeelandia on Taiwan; the Monte fortress in Macao; and defensible factories in other places – Ayutthia, Bantam, Pegu.[20] But there was only one other fully fortified city to compare with Batavia and Melaka: Manila in the Philippines. Shortly before the arrival of the Spaniards in the 1560s, Muslims from Borneo and the Moluccas had introduced the art of fortification to the islands, but only in wood: a small fort near Puerta Galera (on Mindoro island) was the only stone building known to have existed in the pre-Hispanic Philippines. And neither that, nor the larger wooden stockade at Manila, could resist Spanish artillery and attack. But on the site of that Muslim stockade the Spaniards built massive defenses that defied all assaults for over two centuries. The citadel of Santiago itself was not much bigger than other forts (such as St. Pedro at Cebu), but it was connected to the vast stone wall, eight-feet thick and studded with bastions, which surrounded the Spanish city (known as Intramuros) and it dominated the finest natural harbor in East Asia.[21]

Impressed – or intimidated – by these developments, a few local rulers began to follow the European example: Bantam, Pati, Japura,

---

[20] Excavations of the fort at Cebu and the factory at Ayutthia reveal a great deal about sixteenth-century European construction techniques in the tropics: see M. Maceda, 'Preliminary Report on the Excavation at Fort San Pedro, in Cebu City, Philippines," *Fu-Jen Studies* (Taipei, 1973), 45–59; and *The Portuguese and Ayutthaya* (exhibition catalogue, Bangkok, Portuguese embassy, 1985). It seems clear that the Iberians intended to create a fourth fortified port city, at Nagasaki, but the Japanese government refused to allow bastions to be built: see D. Pacheco, "The Founding of the Port of Nagasaki and Its Cession to the Society of Jesus," *Monumenta Nipponica* 25 (1970): 303–23; and G. Elison, *Deus Destroyed: The Image of Christianity in Early Modern Japan* (Cambridge, 1973: Harvard East Asian Series, LXXII), 133f. The Dutch, for their part, created a "colonial city" at Zeelandia after 1624, with its own town hall, weighhouse, hospital, orphanage, and even a house of correction for fallen women, but they only fortified the citadel and one outlying redoubt. The city itself was not provided with walls, and so it was captured in 1662 (after a lengthy siege) by the Ming loyalist forces commanded by Coxinga (Cheng Ch'eng-Kung). See R. G. Knapp, *China's Island Frontier: Studies in the Historical Geography of Taiwan* (Honolulu, 1980), 3–29; and J. L. Oosterhoff, "Zeelandia: A Dutch Colonial City on Formosa (1624–62)" in R. Ross and G. Telkamp, eds., *Colonial Cities: Essays on Urbanism in a Colonial context* (Leiden, 1985: Comparative Studies in Overseas History, V), 52–63.

[21] Details from Reed, *Colonial Manila*, chap. 3 ("Intramuros: A City for Spaniards"); and C. Quirino, *Maps and Views of Old Maynila* (Manila, 1971). But not everyone was impressed by Intramuros. One Spanish official in Manila told the king in 1588 that the fortifications then being built were "a disgrace" and "a waste of time and money, because . . . they are made with round bulwarks in the old fashion;" and the military commandant three years later regretted that because the Spanish architect who designed them had remained in Europe, the defenses were "somewhat out of proportion, being made without architect, advice or plan." (Quotations from the excellent study of M.L. Díaz-Trechuelo Spínola, *Arquitectura española en Filipinas (1565–1800)* [Seville, 1959], 43f. See all of chaps. 2, 3, 6, 7, 12, 13.) The walls built in the 1650s, however, were more formidable.

and Surabaya all acquired brick or stone walls in the sixteenth century; the sultans of Makassar (in south Sulawesi) built a brick wall and three redoubts around their capital in the mid-seventeenth century.[22] But in vain: the keys to the long-distance trade of East Asia remained in European hands: Manila for the trans-Pacific link with America; Melaka and Batavia for commerce with India and beyond. All three quickly acquired large populations of both natives and Chinese, but they remained in Western hands (albeit not always in the same Western hands) until 1942; and, with the wealth conferred by their possession, the Europeans could exercise a maritime hegemony over all other major ports in the region and prevent any rival state from mounting an effective challenge. They were also ideally placed to use the resources extracted from the area to extend that hegemony wherever an opportunity presented itself. Increasingly, their gaze was directed toward the territories, and the riches, of the Muslim rulers of India, Persia, and the Levant.

II

Slaves also played an important role in determining the Muslim response to Europe's military challenge, for they were likewise central to Islamic warfare. In the early ninth century, the Muslim states of North Africa, Spain, and Egypt began to use slave soldiers to defend themselves; by the middle of the century, the caliphs of Baghdad had followed suit; and the practice soon spread further. But the slave soldiers were not kidnapped and conscripted as adults: instead, they were recruited while still children (often as a form of tribute paid by non-Muslims to their conquerors) and brought up in the ruler's household with his own children, so that they learned the ways of Islam as well as the art of war. The Mamluks of Egypt, mostly recruited in the Crimea, and the Ottoman Janissaries, mainly recruited in the Balkans, are merely the best known examples of these elite slave warriors. They were part of a military system that was unique to the

---

[22] See the important studies of C. R. Boxer, *Francisco Vieira de Figureido. A Portuguese Merchant-Adventurer in South-East Asia, 1624–1667* (The Hague, 1967); A. Reid, *South-east Asia in the Age of Commerce. I: The 'Lands below the Winds'* (New Haven, 1988), 121–9; A. Reid, "The Rise of Makassar," *Review of Indonesian and Malaysian Affairs* XVII (1983): 117–80; L. Andaya, *The Heritage of Arung Palakka: a History of South Sulawesi (Celebes) in the Seventeenth Century* (The Hague, 1981), chap. 3; J. A. J. Villiers, "Makassar and the Portuguese Connexion, 1540–1670" (paper presented at the *Symposium on South-East Asian Responses to European Intrusions* [Singapore, 1981]); and D. de Iongh, *Het Krijgswezen onder de Oostindische Compagnie* (The Hague, 1950), 36f. and 102–13.

world of Islam. Even the Muslim states of Indonesia had them: in the early seventeenth century the sultans of Aceh were served by 500 royal slaves born abroad and trained in warfare since their youth.[23] And, although the Islamic states of India placed less reliance on slave soldiers, in compensation the sultans of the Deccan made extensive use in the fifteenth and sixteenth centuries of foreign mercenaries, particularly those from the Ottoman empire and Persia (referred to in the Portuguese records as *a gente branca* [white men] because they looked pale in comparison with the native Indians).[24] The character of Islamic warfare was thus consistent and clear: the core of every major army was composed of men lacking any local ties, devoted entirely to fulfilling their government's wishes, and fighting in the traditional manner. As a historian of Islamic institutions has written: "Mamluks were not supposed to think, but to ride horses; they were designed to be not a military elite, but military automata." The Mamluk aristocracy, like several other elites elsewhere, strongly opposed the proliferation of new weapons that threatened to erode the basis of their military predominance – thus although they eventually tolerated the use of firearms for sieges they refused to deploy them in battle.[25] And so in 1517 the imperious Mamluk knights were overthrown by the soldiers of the Ottoman Turks, whose commanders lacked such high principles.[26]

[23] See P. Crone, *Slaves on Horses: The Evolution of the Islamic Polity* (Cambridge, 1980); D. Pipes, *Slave Soldiers and Islam: The Genesis of a Military System* (New Haven, 1981); and R. Irwin, *The Middle East in the Middle Ages: The Early Mamluk Sultanate, 1250–1382* (London, 1986). On the slave soldiers of Aceh, see Reid, *Europe and Southeast Asia*, 7.

[24] See details in J. Aubin, "Le royaume d'Ormuz au début du XVIe siècle" in *Mare Luso-Indicum*, II (Paris, 1972), 77–179, at 175–9. For the pre-European period, see S. Digby, *War-Horse and Elephant in the Delhi Sultanate: A Study of Military Supplies* (Oxford, 1971); and M. Habib, *Politics and Society during the Early Medieval Period*, II (New Delhi, 1981), 144–8 ("Heritage of the Slave Kings") with the chronicle of Alauudin Khalji that follows (149–270).

[25] Crone, *Slaves on Horses*, 79. European elites had also opposed the use of gunpowder, but with rather less unanimity: see J. R. Hale, 'Gunpowder and the Renaissance: an Essay in the History of Ideas' in Hale, *Renaissance War Studies* (London, 1983), 389–420.

[26] See the classic account of D. Ayalon, *Gunpowder and Firearms in the Mamluk Kingdom: A Challenge to Medieval Society* (London, 1956). See also the similar situation in North Africa described by A. C. Hess, "Firearms and the Decline of Ibn Khaldun's Military Elite," *Archivum Ottomanicum* 4 (1972): 173–99. Ayalon argued that Safavid Iran was defeated by the Turks at Chaldiran because her forces were unfamiliar with firearms, but it has recently been shown that this was not so. Rather, as with the Mamluks, the Persian army sometimes used guns – but only with reluctance, and (even then) only in siege warfare: see R. N. Savory, *Iran under the Safavids* (Cambridge, 1980), 42–4; and the observations (made in the 1620s) that the Persians long continued to "detest the trouble of the cannon, and such field peeces as require carriage," in T.

At first sight, the Ottoman army appears to have adopted and mastered Western military technology with remarkable speed and thoroughness. Handguns, field guns and siege guns were all rapidly imitated by the Turks after their appearance in the West; advanced siege techniques of both offense and defense were evident from the 1520s; and, for a century and a half following this, the Turks were clearly equal to all but the largest forces that the West could throw against them.[27] And yet there were important respects in which the military revolution was imperfectly practiced by Europe's most dangerous neighbor. First, and best known, was the Ottoman decision to build their artillery big, whereas the Western powers concentrated on increasing the mobility and numbers of their guns. In part this may have been because the Ottoman Empire (not unlike the "socialist" countries of Eastern Europe today) experienced difficulty in mass producing and stockpiling manufactured items in order to build up a surplus. It must have seemed easier to produce a handful of big guns that delivered a few decisive shots than a multitude of quick-firing small ones. But, whatever the reason, it proved to be a mistake. The great Christian victory over the Ottoman army outside Vienna in 1683 came about partly because the Turks had directed all their heavy guns against the city, and could not maneuver them round in time when a large relief army, its field artillery at the ready, charged unexpectedly out of the Vienna Woods.[28] But the Turkish defeat before Vienna was the product of other factors, the chief of which was the failure to fortify their siege camp. It had become standard military practice in the West to build two sets of siege works: one against the beleaguered town, the second around the siege works to guard against

Herbert, *Some Yeares' Travels into Divers Parts of Asia and Afrique* (4th ed., London, 1677), 232, 298ff. Conversely, parts of the Ottoman army – the *sipahis* – refused to use the gun, or else used it unwillingly: see R. C. Jennings, "Firearms, Bandits and Gun-Control: Some Evidence on Ottoman Policy towards Firearms in the Possession of Reâya, from Judicial Records of Kayseri 1600–27," *Archivum Ottomanicum* 6 (1980): 339–80, at 340f.

[27] See on all this the important articles of G. Káldy-Nagy, "The First Centuries of the Ottoman Military Organization," *Acta Orientalia Academiae Scientiarum Hungaricae* 31, no. 2 (1977): 147–83; and D. Petrović, "Firearms in the Balkans on the Eve of and After the Ottoman Conquests," in V. J. Parry and M. E. Yapp, eds., *War, Technology, and Society in the Middle East* (Oxford, 1975), 164–94. Sultan Mohammed the Conqueror brought 62 guns against Constantinople in 1453, but almost 200 against Belgrade three years later.

[28] On the general issue, see C. M. Cipolla, *Guns and Sails in the Early Phase of European Expansion, 1400–1700* (London, 1965), 90–9. On the siege of Vienna, see P. Broucek, *Historischer Atlas zur zweiten Turkenbelagerung Wien* (Vienna, 1983) – in which all the prints and maps show the Turkish camp undefended against attack by a relief army; and J. Stoye, *The Siege of Vienna* (London, 1964), 157–9, 255–7.

any attempt at relief. That the Turks did not trouble with this elementary precaution in 1683 may have been mere carelessness by their commander on that occasion, the ill-fated Grand Vizier "Black Mustafa," but it fits in with other evidence that Ottoman troops embraced the gunpowder revolution with less enthusiasm than their Christian adversaries. Some contemporaries observed that, although Turkish craftsmen could copy any new western weapon that they found on a battlefield or that a renegade brought to them, it usually took them a long time; and that, even then, gunpowder weapons remained largely confined to the infantry.[29] But this merely reflected differences in military traditions: cavalry in Europe had not normally used missile weapons, so that adopting the gun represented a threat to which it was imperative to respond; but Muslim armies still relied heavily upon the mounted archer, whose military effectiveness would in fact have been reduced by using single-shot firearms. Given its enormous size, and its proven success, the early modern Ottoman army had no real incentive to abandon its traditional military methods. It should be remembered that the great siege of 1683 saw the Turks beneath the walls of Vienna and not the Christians beneath the walls of Istanbul.

So the Turks continued to fight, even in the eighteenth century, exactly 'as in the days of Suleiman the Magnificent', two hundred years before. The Maréchal de Saxe in 1732 offered the following explanation:[30]

'It is hard for one nation to learn from another, either from pride, idleness or stupidity. Inventions take a long time to be accepted (and sometimes, even though everyone accepts their usefulness, in spite of everything they are abandoned in favour of tradition and routine) . . . The Turks today are in this situation. It is not valour, numbers or wealth that they lack; it is order, discipline and technique.'

Nevertheless, the more the Europeans improved these qualities, the greater became their superiority over the forces of Islam, until the spectacular victory of Napoleon Bonaparte at the battle of the Pyra-

---

[29] *Encyclopaedia of Islam*, I (2d ed., Leiden and London, 1960), 1055–69 (article on "barūd" – gunpowder – by D. Ayalon, V. J. Parry, and R. N. Savory), notes *inter alia*, that the Turks still had no pistols by the 1590s, were slow to adopt new siege techniques, and, even in the 1600s, had no 'good powder but that whyche they gett from overthrone Christians, or els is broughte them out of Englande." See also some similar observations that the Turks used their handguns inefficiently in H. Inalcik, "The Socio-Political Effects of the Diffusion of Firearms in the Middle East" in Parry and Yapp, *War, Technology and Society*, 195–217.

[30] Saxe, *Rêveries*, (written 1732, published 1757), quoted by V. J. Parry, "La manière de combattre' " in Parry and Yapp, *War, Technology, and Society*, 218–56 at 256.

mids in 1799 heralded the opening of the entire Levant to western exploitation.

By this stage, however, industrial power had transformed the quality as well as the quantity of European gunpowder weapons. Even in the sixteenth century, contemporary sources almost invariably claimed that arms and armour taken from Islamic forces were of no use to westerners. Thus, after the Christian naval victory at Lepanto in 1571, some 225 bronze guns were captured by the Venetians alone, but almost all were melted down and recast (with reinforcement) because, according to the Council of Ten, "the metal is of such poor quality." That is, Ottoman naval artillery was found to be too brittle for safe and effective use.[31] This may have been mere chauvinism, but it is indirectly supported by a recent chemical analysis of the composition of some other Muslim weapons and armor from the Middle East which showed that Western iron and steel was indeed notably stronger than the Islamic equivalents. Admittedly the sample submitted to analysis was somewhat small – because few museums will consent to the mutilation of their exhibits in the cause of science – but the results were both consistent and convincing.[32]

Much the same technological inferiority was reported from India. Artillery had been in use in the north of the subcontinent from about 1440 and in the Deccan from about 1470 and yet, in the late eighteenth century, the Europeans still considered all "country" artillery (as they called it) to be unserviceable for their needs.[33] Although the native

[31] Order of the Council of Ten, 28 November 1572, quoted in M. E. Mallett and J. R. Hale, *The Military Organization of a Renaissance State: Venice c. 1400–1617* (Cambridge, 1984), 400; and Luis Collado, *Manual de artillería* (Milan, 1592), fo. 8v. (guns "founded by the Turks are usually poor and flawed, even though the alloy is good"). Of course, a slight technical inferiority did not normally matter to the Turks: the Ottoman fleet dominated the Mediterranean neither by virtue of superior commanders (most of their admirals were relatively inexperienced graduates of the palace school) nor through superior organization. They won thanks to greater resources. Their empire had more men, more ships, and more equipment at its disposal than any enemy, and all were directed by a unified supreme command. Minor defects in individual items scarcely mattered when the Turks could send 250 galleys against Christian adversaries who possessed only 100.

[32] See A. Williams, *The Metallurgy of Muslim Armour* (Manchester, 1978: Seminar on Early Islamic Science, monograph III), 4, 5, 11.

[33] On the introduction of ordnance to India, see B. Rathgen, "Die Pulverwaffe in Indien," *Ostasiatische Zeitschrift* 12 (1925): 11–30, 196–217; I. A. Khan, "Early Use of Cannon and Musket in India, AD 1442–1526, "*Journal of the Economic and Social History of the Orient* 24 (1981): 146–64; and idem, "Origin and Development of Gunpowder Technology in India, AD 1250–1500," *Indian Historical Review* 4, no. 1 (1977): 20–29. But the quality was often poor. When, for example, in 1525 the government of Portuguese India was computing the total quantity of ordnance available for defense, they noted: 'We make little mention of moorish guns, because they are no good on our ships; however if the metal is melted down, better guns can be cast." See R. J.

rulers had plenty of guns, these were found to be poorly cast (even in the eighteenth century, some Indian guns were still made of iron strips held together with metal bands), poorly maintained, and too heavy to move. According to an Indian writer in the 1780s, the native artillery was as "cumbrous, ill-mounted and ill-served as was the artillery of Europe three hundred years ago." Many European sources bear him out. A report on the copious brass ordnance of the pro-British nawab of Oudh in 1777, for example, ruled 90 percent of the guns to be unfit for service, due either to metal fatigue or to rotten carriages; and the artillery captured from Tippu Sultan, of Mysore, in the 1790s was likewise reckoned by Sir Arthur Wellesley, later Duke of Wellington, to be suitable only for scrap. It was much the same with "country" handguns, which were normally of limited useful-ness, either because they wore out quickly and could not easily be replaced; or because they did not conform to a single size, so that the shot often failed to fit the barrel; or because they had a shorter range than European muskets.[34]

Before the eighteenth century, however, the Europeans were not always so contemptuous. As the Portuguese in India never tired of pointing out, Asia was not like America: adversaries there were armed with firearms and steel swords, not with wooden clubs and obsidian knives. It was simply not possible for 168 men with 67 horses to destroy the Mughal empire, as Pizarro and his Spanish companions had brought down the Incas in the 1530s, for the Mughal army had almost limitless military resources. The total manpower available for the army of the emperor Akbar in the 1590s was estimated by one expert at 342,696 cavalry and 4,039,097 infantry – many of them armed with muskets.[35] Moreover the principal Indian rulers (including the

de Lima Felner, ed., *Subsídios para a história da Índia portuguesa* (Lisbon, 1868), part III, 12. Matters do not seem to have improved in the seventeenth century. The European traveller Jean de Thevenot noted in 1666–7 that 'The swords made by the Indians are very brittle', and that 'They have cannon also in their towns, but since they melt the metal in diverse furnaces, so that some of it must needs be better melted than others when they mingle all together, their cannon commonly is good for nothing'. (See S. Sen, ed., *Indian travels of Thevenot and Careri* [New Delhi, 1949], 61–2. Careri, who visited India in 1695, made much the same comments – see *ibid.*, 242–5.

[34] Details from W. Irvine, *The Army of the Indian Moghuls: Its Organization and Admin-istration* (London, 1903), 114–17; B. P. Lenman, "The Weapons of War in Eighteenth-Century India," *Journal of the Society for Army Historical Research* 46 (1968): 33–43; and S.N. Sen, *The Military System of the Marathas* (2d ed., Calcutta, 1979), 103.

[35] See references in Boxer, "Asian potentates," 161. On the difficulty of estimating accurately the size of Indian armies, see D. H. A. Kolff, 'An armed peasantry and its allies. Rajput tradition and state formation in Hindustan, 1450–1850' (Leiden

Mughals) became increasingly reliant on the advice of foreign military experts, at first by the Turks (particularly in Muslim states) but later also by the Europeans. As early as 1499 two Portuguese deserted from Vasco da Gama's fleet in order to serve native rulers for higher wages. They were soon joined by others—two Milanese gunfounders to Calicut in 1503; four Venetian technicians to Malabar in 1505—until by the year 1565 there may have been as many as 2000 European renegades serving the various native rulers of South and East Asia. By the early seventeenth century the total may have risen to 5000.[36]

And yet the impact of the 'foreign experts' was often far from decisive. Thus Prince Dara, one of the contenders for the Mughal throne in the 1650s, employed perhaps 200 Europeans and Turks, yet still lost every battle that he fought and was at length captured and executed by his rival, Aurangzeb, who eventually became emperor and took most of the Europeans into his service.[37] But Aurangzeb, too, seems to have derived little direct benefit from their presence, for field artillery and musketry volleys simply did not fit easily into

University Ph.D. thesis, 1983), 11–17; and R. K. Phul, *Armies of the Great Mughals (1526–1707)* (New Delhi, 1978), 125–34. Phul estimates Akbar's campaign army in the later sixteenth century at some 50,000 men, and Prince Dara's in 1653 at 90,000. But there were also provincial armies, garrisons and feudal levies. In addition almost all peasants, carters and camel-drivers bore arms (and knew how to use them), raising the number of men capable of serving in the Mughals' armies to the huge figure, derived from Abū'l Faẓl's *Ā'īn-i Akbarī*, quoted in the text (Kolff, *op. cit.*, 13ff).

[36] Details from Irvine, *Army*, 152ff.; Boxer, "Asian potentates," 158; M. A. Lima Cruz, 'Exiles and renegades in early sixteenth-century Portuguese Asia', *Indian Economic and Social History Review*, XXIII (1986): 249–62; and S. Subrahmanyam 'The *Kagemusha* effect: the Portuguese, firearms, and the state in early modern South Asia', *Môyen Orient et Océan Indien*, IV (1987), 97–123. See also the admirable general discussion of J. N. Sarkar, *The Art of War in Medieval India* (New Delhi, 1984), 76–89. There was, of course, nothing new in Christian military personnel taking service with Muslim rulers: El Cid and many others in Spain, like numerous Franks in north Africa and the Near East, had done so in the Middle Ages (see J. Richard, *Orient et occident au moyen âge: contacts et relations (XIIe–XVe siècles)* [London, 1976], chap. 13).

[37] We know a great deal about two of Prince Dara's European military experts: see P. H. Pott, "Willem Verstegen, een extra-ordinaris Raad van Indië, als avonturier in India in 1659," *Bijdragen tot de Taal, Land- en Volkenkunde* 112 (1956): 355–82; and N. Manucci, *Storia do Mogor, or Mogul India 1653–1708* (4 vols., ed. W. Irvine, London, 1906–8). There are also numerous references to European military experts in Mughal service in F. Bernier, *Travels in the Mogul empire, AD 1656–1668* (London, 1891), e.g., 31, 47–56, 93. On 55 Bernier, writing in the 1660s, ventured the opinion that "I could never see these [Mughal] soldiers, destitute of order, and marching with the irregularity of a herd of animals, without reflecting upon the ease with which 25,000 of our veterans from the [French] Army of Flanders, commanded by the Prince of Condé or Marshal Turenne, would overcome these armies, however numerous." The problem, however, was to get so many Europeans (to say nothing of Condé or Turenne) to India at the same time.

local traditions of warfare. As one of the "experts," Niccolo Manucci, perceptively observed of a battle between Dara and Aurangzeb in 1658:

Be it known to the reader that these two armies were not ordered in the disposition obtaining in Europe. But one division was close to another, as the trees of a pinewood . . . I saw in this action, as in so many others where I was afterwards present, that the only soldiers who fought were those well to the front. Of those more to the rear, although holding their bared swords in their hands, the Moguls did nothing but shout *Bakush, bakush* and the Indians *Mar, mar* – that is to say "Kill, kill". If those in front advanced, those behind followed the example; and if the former retired, the others fled – a custom of Hindustan quite contrary to that of Europe.[38]

Manucci was right: Indian armies may have been huge, but they remained, essentially, aggregations of individual heroic warriors. Their principal ambition was to close with as many enemies as possible in single combat and, unless they achieved this quickly, their overall strength soon disintegrated. The drill, tactics, and disciplined volley fire of Europe were, to them, irrelevant.

It is more surprising to find that the Mughals, like other South Asian rulers, never attempted to imitate European techniques of fortification, with the bastions, ravelins and defenses in depth that had proved highly effective both in Europe and overseas. But it must be remembered that many of the larger Indian fortresses were already so huge that even the heaviest early modern artillery bombardment could make little impression on them: thus, the fourteenth-century walls of Gulbarga in the Deccan were seventeen meters thick, and those of the Purana Qila at Delhi, built between 1530 and 1545, were the same; the walls of Agra, rebuilt between 1564 and 1574, consisted of two revetments of dressed red sandstone blocks ten meters apart, filled in with sand and rubble. They lacked bastions because, on such a scale, they scarcely needed them: sieges in early modern India were

---

[38] Manucci, *Storia do Mogor*, I, 276, 278. For the introduction of regular European military practice to Portuguese India see, for example, clause 53 of the royal Instructions to Viceroy Redondo, going to India in 1617: "We have tried many times to reorganize our troops in India according to the European manner, since experience has shown that without it we have suffered several important losses, and now that we are at war with the Dutch, who are disciplined soldiers, it is more important than ever" (R. A. Bulhão Pato, ed., *Documentos remetidos da India ou Livros das Monções*, IV, [Lisbon, 1893], 168–9). See also 287–8 (royal letter of 1618) and others in later years on the same subject. An interesting insight into Portuguese military practice in India in the early seventeenth century is offered by G. D. Winius, *The Black Legend of Portuguese India: Diogo de Couto, His Contemporaries and the 'Soldado Prático'* (New Delhi, 1985).

decided by blockade and mines rather than by cannonade. Even in the late eighteenth century, the Europeans could not take any of these strongholds by bombardment.[39]

But, until the late eighteenth century, the Europeans – for the most part – did not even try. Recent research has stressed how anachronistic it is to see the West as bent upon world domination from the voyage of Vasco da Gama onward.[40] In fact, the Europeans originally came to Asia to trade, not to conquer, and most of them only undertook military expenditure either to coerce reluctant buyers or in order to safeguard themselves against attack from their European rivals; the cost of defense would otherwise have eaten up all trading profits. The Dutch were, however, an exception to this rule: They were already fighting a bitter war in Europe and they aimed straight for the overseas bases of their Spanish and Portuguese enemies, trying to destroy them, as well as usurping their trade. Heavy military spending was therefore, for them, essential and (according to an official investigation in 1613) even the "voorcompagnieën" (the rival associations of Dutch merchants who traded in Asia before the foundation of the United East India Company) spent over 30 percent of the running costs of each voyage on war-related items. After the formation of the United Company in 1602, the annual figure rose to 50, 60, and even 70 percent. Indeed, the total cost of building Dutch forts on the principal islands of the Moluccas between 1605 and 1612 amounted to no less than 1.72 million florins, almost one-third of the company's initial capital.[41] This was because most Dutchmen in the East were utterly convinced that no profit was to be had without power, and no trade without war. In the terse (and oft-quoted) letter of Governor-General Jan Pieterszoon Coen to his directors in 1614: "You gentlemen ought to know from experience that trade in Asia should be conducted and maintained under the protection and with the aid of your own weapons, and that those weapons must be

[39] For details, see the description of sites such as Golconda, Gulbarga, and Delhi Fort in S. Toy, *The Strongholds of India* (London, 1957); idem, *The Fortified Cities of India* (London, 1965); V. Fass, *The Forts of India* (London, 1986); and Sarkar, *Art of War*, 126–74.

[40] See, in particular, P. J. Marshall, "Western Arms in Maritime Asia in the Early Phases of Expansion," *Modern Asian Studies* 1 (1980): 13–28. The following part of my argument owes much to discussions with Professor Marshall, whose generous aid I gratefully acknowledge.

[41] Figures from P. J. N. Willman, "The Dutch in Asia, 1595–1610" (St. Andrews University M.A. thesis, 1986), 21–2, 26: based on private calculations made by Grotius from the companies' own papers, and preserved in the Rijksarchief Van Zuid Holland, The Hague, *Collectie Hugo de Groot*.

wielded with the profits gained by the trade. So trade cannot be maintained without war, nor war without trade."[42]

Some of the British in the Far East during the seventeenth century thought that their East India Company should follow the Dutch model. Dr. John Fryer, for example, a company surgeon in Surat during the 1670s, observed that the Dutch were "as powerful for men, riches and shipping in Batavia, as in Europe"; and continued:

[Their strategy] is grounded on a different principle from our East India Company, who are for the present profit, not future emolument. These [the Dutch], as they gain ground, secure it by vast expences, raising forts and maintaining souldiers: ours are for raising auctions and retrenching charges, bidding the next age grow rich as they have done, but not affording them the means.[43]

But the comparison was unjust. The British, after some initial failures, preferred to concentrate their trade in areas where the native Indian states were relatively small and weak, and European competitors were not already entrenched: Golconda, the Carnatic, Bengal.[44] The directors of the company could therefore take pride in their ability to avoid hefty military expenditure. "All war is so contrary to our constitution as well as [to] our interest," they informed their officials in 1681, "that we cannot too often inculcate to you an aversion thereto." Or, in a rather more succinct message sent in 1677: "Our business is trade, not war."

As late as 1750, the directors still reproached their officials in the field for seeming "to look upon yourselves rather as a military colony than [as] the factors and agents of a body of merchants;" and in 1759

---

[42] Coen to Heren XVII, 27 December 1614 (from Bantam in Java), quoted by H. T. Colenbrander, *Jan Pieterszoon Coen. Levenbeschrijving* (The Hague, 1934), 64. It should be noted, however, that Coen's advice was not always followed. In 1622 he was rebuked by the directors for fighting too much. Violence, they told him, should be used only in the service of profit: "One must avoid and eschew war if it is at all compatible with the preservation and safety of our state . . . No great attention should be paid to questions of 'reputation' . . . for we are mere merchants." Quoted by Steensgaard, "The Dutch East India Company As an Institutional Innovation," in M. Aymard, ed., *Dutch Capitalism and World Capitalism* (Cambridge, 1982), 235–57 at 255. The directors had good reason for concern: many of their forts and factories in the Orient were returning a loss! See M. A. P. Meilink-Roelofsz, *Asian trade and European influence in the Indonesian Archipelago between 1500 and about 1630* (The Hague, 1962), 386.

[43] John Fryer, *A New Account of East India and Persia, Being Nine Years Travels, 1672–1681*, I (London, 1909: Hakluyt Society, 2d ser., XX), 124.

[44] There were some company officials who agreed with the Dutch view, and in the 1680s some of the directors supported them. Several apposite quotations will be found in I. B. Watson, "Fortifications and the 'Idea' of Force in Early English East India Company Relations with India," *Past and Present* 88 (1980): 70–87.

they dismissed the strategic designs of the governor of Madras on the grounds that "Were we to adopt your several plans for fortifying, half our capital would be buried in stone walls."[45] But, by then, the directors were seriously out of date. The arrival of the French on their doorsteps – at Pondichéry, close to Madras, in 1674; at Chandernagore, upstream from Calcutta, in 1686 – was bad enough. But after the reorganization of the *Compagnie des Indes* in 1719 these modest toeholds on the subcontinent suddenly became threatening bridgeheads from which French territorial influence in India might be extended. It became inevitable that, whenever Britain and France went to war in Europe, the conflict would now spread to their colonies. But still the directors of the East India Company failed to see the need for change. As late as 1740, when the War of the Austrian Succession broke out, British forces in India totaled less than 2,000 men, widely distributed over the subcontinent in decrepit, poorly defended fortresses. And so, when the French in the Carnatic launched an attack on Madras in 1746, the 200 guns of Fort St. George still had only 100 men to serve them and the chief gunner, a man named Smith, died of a heart attack when he saw the French approaching. The fortress fell. Then, later that same year, the victorious French went on to defeat a superior army of Britain's Indian allies at the Battle of Adyar River with the classic European technique of the musketry salvo: 300 Europeans and 700 native troops, drawn up in three ranks, moved forward against their 10,000 adversaries firing successive volleys of shot. Almost immediately, they were masters of the field.[46]

The Battle of Adyar River was a turning point in Indian history. Admittedly, the combination of a core of European soldiers with a larger number of European-trained Indian troops was not new. All the Western powers in the Orient, from the Portuguese in the sixteenth century onward, had tried to compensate for their great numerical weakness by recruiting members of the "martial races" of Asia, such as the Ambonese in Indonesia or the Pampangas in the Philippines. They had also made use of native converts to Christianity

---

[45] Quotations from East India Company records in G. J. Bryant, "The East India Company and Its Army, 1600–1778" (London University Ph.D. thesis, 1975), 10, 31, 74, 138. There was a brief period of belligerence in the 1680s, under the leadership of Josiah Child, but it failed (see Bryant, 32–3; interestingly, it coincided with a similar assertiveness by England in its American colonies – S. S. Webb, *The Governors-General: The English Army and the Definition of the Empire. 1569–1681* [Chapel Hill, 1979], 447–55).

[46] The Battle of the Adyar River (7 November 1746) was well described by the Tamil factor of Dupleix at Pondichéry: J. F. Price, ed., *The Private Diary of Ananda Ranga Pillai*, III (Madras, 1914), 94–5 and 444–52.

(often descended from a European father), such as the "topazes" in British India and the "mardijkers" in Dutch Java.[47] But these various recruits served as auxiliaries, not regulars: they fought in their traditional fashion, with their traditional weapons, and in their traditional formations. The French, however, trained native troops to fight in the European fashion with European weapons and European uniforms; and after 1751 they supplied them with European officers and noncommisioned officers too.[48] In that same year, the French governor in Pondichéry informed his superiors in Europe that: "All my efforts are directed towards attaining for you vast revenues from this part of India, and consequently placing the Nation in a position to maintain itself here even when it may lack support from Europe."[49]

His British rival was well aware of the threat. "Since the French have put themselves in possession of extensive domains," Governor Saunders wrote to his superiors in February 1751, "and have raised their flag at the bounds of our territory and have striven to constrain our settlements to such an extent that they can neither receive supplies nor goods, it has been judged essential to thwart their designs, lest their success render our situation worse during peace than in time of war . . . We shall therefore oppose them to the greatest extent of which we are capable." In this, the British held one decisive advantage: their superior financial resources in the subcontinent. It was not merely that the volume of British trade in Asia by 1750 was roughly four times that of France; there was also the fact that, from the 1680s onward, the company's agents in Madras accepted substantial deposits in cash from both Indian and European merchants and officials.

---

[47] See the interesting remarks on this theme by J. A. de Moor, "Militaire Interdependentie tussen Europa en de Derde Wereld. De Geschiedenis van 'Johnny Gurkha,' " *Internationale Spectator* 37 (1983): 356–64; de Iongh, *Het Krijgswezen*, chap. 4; and Marshall, "Western Arms in Maritime Asia," 25f.

[48] Exactly how this happened is something of a mystery. A. Martineau, *Dupleix et l'Inde française*, III (Paris, 1927), devoted a few pages to the sepoys (62–72), but filled them with a sustained diatribe about the shortcomings and vices of all Asian races! E. W. C. Sandes, *The Military Engineer in India*, I (Chatham, 1933), 64–5, claimed that the French trained some 5,000 Muslims as regular troops in 1741 in order to oppose an invasion of the Carnatic by the Marathas, but Dupleix himself later stated that sepoys were first used by the French only in 1746. This contradiction is resolved by the records at Pondichéry, which reveal that two companies of "cypahes" were raised by the French in January 1742 and were drilled, armed, and paid in the European manner. But they were disbanded at the end of the year, and so Dupleix in 1746 had to start all over again. See H. H. Dodwell, *Sepoy Recruitment in the Old Madras Army* (Calcutta, 1922); Studies in Indian Records, I), 3–7; and S. C. Hill, 'The Old Sepoy Officer," *English Historical Review* 28 (1913): 260–91, 496–514.

[49] Dupleix to the Directors of the Compagnie des Indes, 15 February 1751, quoted by H. Furber, *Rival Empires of Trade in the Orient, 1600– 1800* (Oxford, 1976), 156.

In normal times, most of this was remitted back to London in bills of exchange, but when war threatened, or erupted, these deposits provided a useful capital fund from which to finance military expenditures. And, as the trade and population of Madras grew, so the capital on deposit increased.[50] By the 1740s, it was sufficient to allow the company to follow the French example and raise their own companies, battalions, and eventually regiments of "sepoys" (as these troops were known, from *sipahi*, the Persian word for soldier). There were two sepoy battalions in the company's service by 1758, five by 1759, and ten – some 9,000 men – by 1765. With numerical strength such as this, enhanced by the new, more reliable flintlock muskets and the quick-firing field artillery exported from Europe, it was now possible for the company to challenge not only its French rivals, but also the smaller native states of India with some chance of success.[51]

The first major opportunity occurred in Bengal in 1757. The Mughal empire in its prime had been able to mobilize perhaps a million warriors, but, after the death of Aurangzeb in 1707, a number of satraps on the imperial frontier had broken away and created their own separate states.[52] Nevertheless, the military strength of these rulers remained formidable, compared with the Europeans. The decision to send an army of sepoys and British troops to Bengal in 1757, under the command of Robert Clive, was something of a wild gesture. Admittedly the new nawab of Bengal had given provocation by taking Calcutta, and demanding increased payments from the Company in

[50] Details from Furber, ibid., 147–69 (Saunders quoted at 156); idem, *John Company at Work: A Study of European Expansion in India in the Late Eighteenth Century* (Cambridge, Mass. 1948), 204f; and A. das Gupta and M. N. Pearson, eds., *India and the Indian Ocean, 1500–1800* (Calcutta, 1987), 311ff. I am most grateful to Professor Blair B. Kling for these references and for invaluable help in formulating the argument of this paragraph.

[51] Figures from Bryant, "The East India Company and its Army," 299f.; P. Mason, *A Matter of Honour: An Account of the Indian Army, Its Officers and Men* (2nd ed., London, 1976), 62f. I am grateful to Dr. Bryant for sending me further material and additional references on this matter. See also the new insights on the social world of the sepoys in M. P. Singh, *Indian Army under the East India Company* (New Delhi, 1976); and Kolff, 'An armed peasantry', 123–56.

[52] The Mughal army was probably the same size – around a million men – in circa 1700 as in circa 1600: see Kolff, 'An armed peasantry', 13. There is a tendency to write off the military strength of the native states of India in the early eighteenth century, perhaps because of the evident collapse of native seaborne trade at the same time. But this is wrong: see A. das Gupta, *Indian Merchants and the Decline of Surat, c.1700–1750* (Wiesbaden, 1979), introduction. See also das Gupta's perceptive further thoughts in 'Asian merchants and the western Indian ocean: the early seventeenth century', *Modern Asian Studies*, XIX (1985), 481–99; and in T. Raychaudhuri and I. Habib, eds., *The Cambridge Economic History of India*, I (Cambridge, 1982), 425–33.

return for trade, but his army was ten times the size of Clive's 2,000 sepoys and 900 Europeans, and was assisted by French military advisers.

But, at the Battle of Plassey, Clive won. The nawab, Siraj-ud-Daulah, was executed and a replacement more acceptable to the British set up in his place. After some years of further hostilities and negotiation, in 1765 the Mughal emperor and the new nawab finally recognized the right of the British company to collect all state revenues in the provinces of Bihar, Orissa, and Bengal. It was wealth beyond the dreams of avarice: the "Net amount of territorial revenues and customs, clear of charges of collection" received officially by the company leapt from nothing before 1757 to almost £2 million in 1761–4, and to almost £7.5 million in 1766–9. With the aid of these funds (all paid in silver), it proved possible to build impregnable fortresses and to raise armies large enough to intervene effectively in the Deccan, in Mysore – indeed, anywhere in the subcontinent.[53] By 1782 the British were able to maintain 115,000 men in India (90 percent of them sepoys) and reduce the odds against them in battle from the 10 to 1 of Plassey to only 2 to 1 against states such as Mysore. The prospect of the European domination of India, to match the European domination of America, had become a real possibility.[54] And the military resources of India, once under European control, were to prove decisive for the further rise of the West. As early as 1762, a detachment of 650 sepoys was sent to assist the British to capture Manila; and, during the nineteenth century, such foreign service became com-

---

[53] *Reports from Committees of the House of Commons*, IV (1804), 60–1. My thanks go to Professor P. J. Marshall for this reference. The figures are all the more striking when it is remembered that the company *lost* £2.5 million between 1753 and 1760. The massive new Fort William at Calcutta, built between 1765 and 1771 at a cost of £1 million, is just one example of how the Bengal settlement allowed the Europeans to change the art of defensive warfare in India. See P. J. Marshall, "Eighteenth-Century Calcutta," in Ross and Telkamp, *Colonial Cities*, 90.

[54] See Ness and Stahl, "Western Imperialist Armies in Asia"; J. P. Lawford, *Britain's Army in India from Its Origin to the Conquest of Bengal* (London, 1978), 72–81; Bryant, "The East India Company and its army," chaps. 3–5; and R. Callahan, *The East India Company and Army Reform, 1783–98* (Cambridge, Mass., 1972), 6. The Dutch East India Company also began to train its Asian troops to fight like Europeans in the 1740s, under Governor-General van Imhoff: see de Iongh, *Het Krijgswezen*, 165–8. In the first years of the nineteenth century, the Maratha Confederation secured sufficient European advisers and European-designed field guns to launch attacks on the British in India that came within an ace of success, but they came too late. See J. Pemble, "Resources and Techniques in the Second Maratha war," *Historical Journal* 19 (1976): 375–404; and D. H. A. Kolff, 'The end of the Ancien Régime: colonial war in India, 1798–1818' in J. A. de Moor and H. L. Wesseling, eds., *Imperialism and War. Essays on Colonial Wars in Asia and Africa* (Leiden, 1989: Comparative studies in overseas history, VIII), 22–49.

monplace – in Burma, in East Africa, above all in East Asia. For the Europeans now possessed the means to challenge even their most powerful opponents. The Western armies that invaded China in 1839–42, 1859–60, and 1900 all included important Indian contingents. Immediately after the Boxer Rising, even the traffic of Peking was directed by Sikhs. In the words of the distinguished Sinologist Louis Dermigny: "It was as if the British had subjugated the Indian peninsula simply in order to use its resources against China."[55]

III

If, therefore, the native peoples of America, Siberia, Black Africa and the Philippines lost their independence to the Europeans because they had no time to *adopt* western military technology, those of the Muslim world apparently succumbed because they saw no need to integrate it into their existing military system. But the peoples of East Asia, by contrast, were able to keep the West at bay throughout the early modern period because, as it were, they already knew the rules of the game. Firearms, fortresses, standing armies, and warships had long been part of the military tradition of China, Korea, and Japan. Indeed, both bronze and iron artillery were fully developed in China before they spread westward to Europe around 1300. However, after the mid-fourteenth century, contact between the Far East and the Far West diminished, and the subsequent evolution of firearms in the two areas took a somewhat different course. By 1500 the iron and bronze guns of Western manufacture – whether made by Turkish or Christian founders – proved to be both more powerful and more mobile than those of the East, so that when they were brought to the Orient in the sixteenth century they attracted both attention and imitation. They may have arrived in China as early as the 1520s, perhaps with one of the numerous Ottoman diplomatic missions to the Ming Court, but, if so, knowledge of them seems to have remained confined to government circles. For most Chinese, Western-style firearms were first encountered in the hands of pirates operating from Japan against Fukien in the late 1540s.[56]

---

[55] On the sepoys in the Philippines, see Mason, *A Matter of Honour*, 68, 242. On China, see L. Dermigny, *La Chine et l'Occident. Le commerce à Canton au XVIII- siècle, 1719–1833*, II (Paris, 1964), 781. Later, in the nineteenth century, sepoys were sent to conquer both Java (1811–15) and East Africa for Britain. See also the general remarks of A. J. Qaisar, *The Indian Response to European Technology and Culture, AD 1498–1707* (Oxford, 1982), 46–57, 144–6.

[56] The suggestion that the Turks introduced Western firearms to China before the Europeans was first made by P. Pelliot, "Le Hoja et le Sayid Hussain de l'Histoire

Although guns were not widely employed by Ming forces against the *wakō* pirates, they were introduced shortly afterward on China's northern frontier for use against the nomads of the steppe. In 1564, for example, the Peking garrison replaced their clay-cased cannonballs with lead; and in 1568 these too were abandoned in favor of iron. Then, in the 1570s, under the direction of Ch'i Chi-kuang (who had masterminded the defeat of the pirates), the Great Wall was rebuilt with pillboxes to shelter musketeers, and the reserve units of the northern army were strengthened with small carts (known as "battle wagons"), each carrying breech-loading light artillery and served by twenty men.[57]

A remarkable source that illustrates the degree to which European weaponry had been adopted on China's northern frontier under the late Ming is the illustrated *Veritable Records of the Great Ancestor (T'ai-tsu Shih-lu)*, compiled in 1635 to record the deeds of Nurhaci, founder of the Ch'ing dynasty. It is significant that in the pictures of the "Great Ancestor's" early victories all the guns are on the side of the Ming: the imperial armies are shown deploying field guns, mounted either on trestles or on two-wheeled "battle wagons", while the northern warriors seem to rely on their horse-archers.[58] But in 1629, the Ch'ing attacked and annexed four Chinese cities south of the Great Wall: in one of them, Yung-p'ing, a Chinese artillery crew "familiar with the techniques of casting Portuguese artillery" was also captured. By 1631 some forty of the new European-style artillery pieces had been made by the captives and, directed by men who had received either first-or second-hand training from Portuguese gunners, they were soon in action against Ming positions. Gradually, as shown in later illustrations from the *T'ai-tsu shih-lu*, they appeared on the Ch'ing side.

But firearms remained only a minor part of the armament of Chinese armies. After all, the Ming supported (in theory at least) some 500,000 men and 100,000 horses on the northern frontier, and the Ch'ing army that entered Peking in 1644 probably num-

des Ming," *T'oung Pao* 38 (1948): 81–292, at 199–207. See also J. Needham, Ho Ping-Yü, Lu Gwei-Djen, and Wang Ling, *Science and Civilization in China*. Volume V part vii: *Military Technology – The Gunpowder Epic* (Cambridge, 1986), 440–9.

[57] Details from R. Huang, "Military Expenditures in Sixteenth-Century Ming China," *Oriens Extremus* 17 (1970): 39–62; idem, *1587: A Year of No Significance: The Ming Dynasty in Decline* (New Haven, 1981), chap. 6; A. Chan, *The Glory and Fall of the Ming Dynasty* (Norman, 1982), 51–63; and the important new study of A. Waldron, *The Great Wall of China. From History to Myth* (Cambridge, 1990).

[58] *T'ai-tsu shih-lu* (facsimile edition, Mukden, 1931: reproduced from an edition of 1740 that seems to be based, in turn, on an illustrated chronicle compiled in 1635 – that is, by and for those who might themselves have seen the events they described).

bered 280,000 warriors: It would have been almost impossible to equip all these troops with Western-style firearms.[59] So the soldiers of the new dynasty continued to fight in the traditional manner until the nineteenth century. It is true that, in 1675, the Chinese imperial army was supported by 150 heavy guns and numerous batteries of field artillery, cast under the direction of Jesuit missionaries in Peking, but this was a specific campaign against dangerous domestic enemies (the "Three Feudatories" and their supporters). At other times, the main strength of the Ch'ing lay in the overwhelming numbers of their armed forces.[60]

The Japanese, however, whose armies in the mid-sixteenth century were considerably smaller than those of their great continental neighbour (even though much larger as a percentage of the total population), made far more use of Western firearms. It is generally accepted that they were first introduced by some Portuguese castaways in 1543 on the island of Tanegashima, south of Kyushu, and that they were quickly copied by Japanese metalsmiths (which is why they were commonly known as *Tanegashima*).[61] Muskets were used effectively

[59] The exact size of the Ch'ing army was an official secret, but it would seem that a campaign army in the later seventeenth century might number 150,000 men, with up to 40,000 men directly involved in battles. See C. Fang, "A Technique for Estimating the Numerical Strength of the Early Manchu Military Forces," *Harvard Journal of Asiatic Studies* 13 (1950): 192–215.

[60] Although the efforts of the Jesuits and other Europeans in Macao and Peking to supply first the Ming and then the Manchu with guns usually monopolize the limelight, this is just another case of Eurocentrism. The bulk of Chinese artillery was produced by Chinese craftsmen: see Needham, *The Gunpowder Epic*, 392–414; and Chan, *Glory and Fall*, 57–63. The same was definitely true in Japan, where production by local workshops far surpassed European imports: see K. Itakura, "The First Ballistic Laws by a Japanese Mathematician, and its Origin," *Japanese Studies in the History of Science* 2 (1963): 136–45. The only East Asian country that seems to have been heavily dependent on weapons imported from the West was Vietnam: the Nguyen of the north relied heavily after the 1620s on bronze guns either cast by Westerners living in Hué, or else imported from Macao, in their wars against the Tring of the south, who received (in their turn) supplies from the Dutch in Batavia. But even in Vietnam, local production continued: a French visitor to Hué in 1749 saw 800 bronze and 400 iron guns, by no means all of which were of European manufacture. See P. Y. Manguin, *Les Portugais sur les côtes de Viêtnam et du Campa* (Paris, 1972), 206–8; L. Cadière, "Le quartier des Arènes. I. Jean de la Croix et les premiers Jésuites," *Bulletin des amis du Vieux Hué* 11 (1924): 307–32 (La Croix resided in Hué and cast guns for the Nguyen from the 1650s to 1682); and C. R. Boxer, "Macao as a Religious and Commercial Entrepôt in the Sixteenth and Seventeenth Centuries," *Acta Astatica* 31 (1974): 64–90.

[61] For the precise manner in which Western guns were introduced into Japan, see the definitive account, together with a German translation of Japanese sources, in G. Schurhammer, *Gesammelte Studien, II. Orientalia* (Rome, 1963: Biblioteca Instituti Historici Iesu, XXI), 485–579. There is an English translation of one source – the *Teppō-ki* of Nampō Bunshi (1606) – in Tsunoda Ryusaku et al., eds., *Sources of Japanese Tradition*, I (New York, 1964) 308–12. It should be noted that the island of

in battle by the army of Takeda Shingen in 1555, but a more spectacular demonstration of the power of Japanese musketry occurred on 21 May 1575 at the battle of Nagashino. The warlord Oda Nobunaga deployed his musketeers in 23 ranks in this action, having trained them to fire in volleys so as to maintain a constant barrage – 1,000 rounds every 20 seconds according to one source. The opposing cavalry – ironically of the same Takeda clan that had pioneered the use of the gun – was annihilated. The battle scene in Kurosawa's film *Kagemusha* (*The Shadow Warrior*) offers a credible reconstruction, for the action is intended to represent Nagashino.[62]

The originality of Japan's rapid adoption of the gun has perhaps not always been fully appreciated. In the first place, whereas Europe concentrated on increasing the speed of reloading, the Japanese were more interested in improving accuracy. So Western military manuals explained primarily how a soldier could recharge his weapon more rapidly, and Japanese treatises – from the 1550s onward – gave instruction on how he could take better aim. The *Tanegashima* were, for their day, remarkably accurate. But this in fact accentuated the crucial defect of the muzzle-loading musket: the length of time required to recharge it. Now the only way to overcome this disadvantage was to draw up the musketeers in ranks, firing in sequence, so that the front file could reload while the others behind fired. This solution was not even suggested in Europe until 1594, and it did not pass into general use there until the 1630s. Yet Oda Nobunaga had experimented with musketry salvoes in the 1560s, and he achieved his first major victory with the technique in 1575, twenty years before the Europeans – starting with Maurice of Nassau and the army of the Dutch Republic – invented it themselves.[63]

Tanegashima, where the first Portuguese guns arrived, was an ideal spot for copying them. It was, in 1543, not only an established center of trade but a major center of sword production; it was relatively easy for the sword-smiths to turn out musket barrels instead, ready for the merchants to distribute.

[62] In 1549 Oda Nobunaga was apparently asked to provide "500 musketeers and bowmen," which does not necessarily mean – as many scholars have said – 500 men with muskets (Hora Tomio, *Tanegashima-jū. Denrai to sono eikyō* [Tokyo, 1958], 157). But in 1555 Takeda Shingen definitely deployed 300 musketeers at the Battle of Shinano Asahiyamajō (Nagahara Keiji, *Sengoko no dōran. Nihon no rekishi*, XIV [Tokyo, 1975], 947; and Hora, *op. cit.*, 144–54). Nagashino is depicted in a marvelous series of screen paintings, reproduced in *Sengoku kassen-e Byōbu Shūsei. I.i Kawanakajima kassen-zu Nagashino kassen-zu* (Tokyo, 1980). However, because the screens were all painted several decades after the battle, they may depict later Japanese military practice rather than the actual techniques employed by Nobunaga at Nagashino.

[63] The general account of N. Perrin, *Giving up the Gun: Japan's Reversion to the Sword, 1543–1879* (New York; 1979), though interesting and provocative, is based almost entirely on Western sources and pushes some of the evidence too far. Greater reliance

By the time Nobunaga was assassinated, in 1582, he had conquered about half of the provinces of Japan; after a brief hiatus of disorder, the work was continued by two of his most brilliant generals, first Toyotomi Hideyoshi and then Tokugawa Ieyasu. As further provinces were brought under central authority, the size of the main army was swollen by contingents from Hideyoshi's new vassals and allies. In 1587, when he decided to invade the island of Kyushu, almost 300,000 troops were mobilized. The island was conquered in a matter of weeks. The reunification of Japan might perhaps have been achieved without the gun, but the ability to turn large numbers of men into effective musketeers certainly accelerated the process. By 1610 Tokugawa Ieyasu could write: "Guns and powder . . . are what I desire more than gold."[64]

Nobunaga and his successors also saw the usefulness of the heavier guns used by the Westerners, and they seem to have realized immediately that artillery would render indefensible almost every existing castle and fortress in Japan because any wall that was built high, in order to keep besiegers out, was thereby rendered vulnerable to the impact of artillery bombardment. A new sort of defensive fortification therefore emerged, situated on a ridge and encircled by stone walls, creating a solid mass of rock and soil. A prototype was built by Nobunaga himself beside Lake Biwa at Azuchi, between 1576 and 1579, using the combination of hilltop and thick stone walls to produce a virtually solid bailey, surrounding a seven-story keep of unparal-

may be placed on D. M. Brown, "The Impact of Firearms on Japanese Warfare, 1543–98," *The Far Eastern Quarterly* 7 (1948): 236–53. Hora, *Tanegashima*, 21–3, shows that firearms, almost certainly imported from China, were used in Japan before 1543. They were, however, few in number and limited in effect. The exact nature of early Japanese guns is difficult to establish because so few survive – perhaps only ten *Tanegashima* from the sixteenth century are known today (personal communication from Dr. Yoshioka Shin'ichi of Kyoto in 1984). And much the same is true of artillery: very few early modern pieces survive – though here the culprit (at least according to Japanese sources!) was the "liberation" of most of the beautiful guns collected in the Kudan Museum in Tokyo by American forces after 1945. Only a few firearms are to be found today in the military museum attached to the Yasakuni shrine in Tokyo. There is a concise discussion of the sources and problems in Needham, *The Gunpowder Epic*, 467–72, which relies (perhaps too heavily?) on the utopian vision of Noel Perrin. Finally, on the military changes in early modern Europe, see G. Parker, *The Military Revolution* (Cambridge, 1987), chaps. 1–2.

[64] Quotation from E. M. Satow, "Notes on the Intercourse between Japan and Siam in the Seventeenth Century," *Transactions of the Asiatic Society of Japan* ser., 1 13 (1884–5). 139–210 at 145. Army size figures in G. B. Sansom, *A History of Japan, 1334–1615* (Stanford, 1961), 322. A recent consideration of the armies commanded by Hideyoshi – which reached a total strength of 280,000 for the invasion of Korea in 1593 – is provided by B. Susser, "The Toyotomi Regime and the Daimyō," in J. P. Mass and W. B. Hauser, eds., *The Bakufu in Japanese History* (Stanford, 1985), 129–52, at 135ff.

leled beauty.[65] But Azuchi was almost totally destroyed after its creator's murder in 1582 (though the ruins of the outer walls and the surviving foundations of the keep are still impressive). Even less remains of another massive fortress of this period: Odawara, the stronghold of the Hojo clan, large enough to shelter 40,000 warriors and surrounded by twenty outlying forts. It required an army of over 100,000 men to starve it out in the summer of 1590 and was destroyed after its capture by Toyotomi Hideyoshi – giving rise to a popular doggerel the following year:

> So what's the use of hauling rocks and building castles?
> Just look at Azuchi and Odawara![66]

Rather more exists today of the even larger citadels built by Hideyoshi and his followers, who preferred to fortify isolated hills on the plain. There is a remarkable homogeneity about the sixty or so surviving castles built in Japan between 1580 and 1630 from Sendai in the north to Kagoshima in the south, even though some were bigger than others. Kato Kiyomasa's castle at Kumamoto, for example, was twelve kilometers in circumference (with forty-nine turrets and two keeps); Ikeda Terumasa's beautiful "White Heron castle" at Himeji, almost as large, was constructed with an estimated 103,000 tons of stone; and the walls of Tokugawa Hidetada's vast citadel at Osaka extended for over thirteen kilometers. Some of the individual stones used to build the defenses of Osaka weighed 120 and 130 tons each and were brought to the site from all over Japan by feudatories anxious to prove their loyalty to the regime; even today each daimyo's mark can still be seen, affixed to "their" rocks (which were also given special auspicious names). With such blocks, more appropriate to a pyramid than to a castle, walls were built that were in places nineteen meters

---

[65] Kodama Kōta et al., eds. *Nihon jōkaku taike*, XI (Tokyo, 1980), 261–9 on Kannonji; ibid., 254–60 on Azuchi; plus Naitō Akira, 'Azuchi-jō no kenkyū', *Kokka*, LXXXIII (nos. 987–8; 1976), with a brief English summary. A review of Naitō is also helpful: Takayanagi Shun'ichi, "The glory that was Azuchi, "*Monumenta Nipponica* 32 (1977): 515–24. See also G. Elison and B. L. Smith, eds., *Warlords, Artists and Commoners: Japan in the Sixteenth Century* (Honolulu, 1981), 62–6; and M. Cooper, *They Came to Japan: An Anthology of European Reports on Japan, 1543–1640* (London, 1965), 134–5.

[66] The verse is quoted by George Elison in Elison and Smith, *op. cit.*, 66. On the siege of Odawara, see Sansom, *A History of Japan, 1334–1615*, 326–7. Concentrations of troops on this scale caused severe logistical problems and placed an almost intolerable strain on the Japanese economy, weakened by over a century of civil strife. On the link between castle size, army size, and tax demands under Hideyoshi, see the richly documented article by G. Moréchand, "'Taikō kenchi': le cadastre de Hideyoshi Toyotomi," *Bulletin de l'École française de l'Extreme Orient* 53, no. 1 (1966): 7–69, esp. 12–13. For a recent biography of the remarkable *Taikō* – Japan's only commoner ruler before modern times – see M. E. Berry, *Hideyoshi* (Cambridge, Mass., 1982).

thick.[67] Quite possibly (as Professor J. W. Hall pointed out some years ago) these Japanese castles had "no peers in terms of size and impregnability" anywhere else in the early modern world.[68]

Once again we find that, though the Japanese leaders were perfectly prepared to take over Western military innovations, they always adapted them to local conditions in a distinctive way.[69] Early modern China, however, had no need of Western examples in the art of defensive fortification: its rulers had already been living with gunpowder for centuries, and the massive fortifications erected under the Ming dynasty had been designed to resist both artillery bombardment and mining. It is true that the Chinese had no castles, preferring to fortify whole towns – indeed the Chinese use the same character (*ch'eng*) for both "walled city" and "rampart" – but these towns were surrounded by massive walls (fifteen meters thick in places) that could withstand even modern shells. Thus in 1840, during the Opium Wars, a two-hour battery from a seventy-four-gun Royal Navy warship on a fort outside Canton "produced no effect whatever," according to an eyewitness. "The principle of their construction was such as to render them almost impervious to the efforts of horizontal fire, even from the 32-pounders." Likewise, the British expeditionary force sent to China in 1860 found the walls of Peking impregnable. According to the British commander, General Knollys:

Ancient history tells us the walls of Babylon were so broad that several chariots could be driven abreast on top of them; but I really think those of Peking must have exceeded them. They were upwards of 50 feet in breadth,

[67] Kodama, *Nihon jōkaku*, XII (1981): 152–81; Okamoto Ryōichi, *Nihon jōkaku-shi kenkyū sōsho VIII: Ōsaka-jō* (Tokyo; 1982). Both works are fully illustrated. See also the plates in K. Hirai, *Feudal Architecture in Japan* (New York, 1973), chap. 4; the account of W. B. Hauser, "Osaka Castle and Tokugawa Authority in Western Japan' " in Mass and Hauser, *The Bakufu*, 153–72; and the description of the Maeda stronghold at Kanazawa in J. McClain, *Kanazawa: a Seventeenth-Century Japanese Castle Town* (New Haven, 1982), 33f.

[68] J. W. Hall, "The Castle Town and and Japan's Modern Urbanization," *Far Eastern Quarterly* 15 (1955), a classic article reprinted in J. W. Hall and M. B. Jansen, eds., *Studies in the Institutional History of Early Modern Japan* (Princeton, 1968), 169–88 quotation at 177. Possibly the Dutch fortifications at Galle, in southern Ceylon, were in fact larger: see W. A. Nelson, *The Dutch Forts of Sri Lanka: The Military Monuments of Ceylon* (Edinburgh, 1984), 48–51.

[69] Although we know from several sources that military conversation was one of Nobunaga's chief passions, the Westerners with whom he conversed were mainly regular clergy whose knowledge of military architecture would normally not have extended to the intricacies of defensive architecture. See A. Valignano, *Sumario de las Cosas de Japón* (1583: ed. J. L. Álvarez-Taladriz, Tokyo, 1954), 152. It is true that some Jesuits in the Far East became skilled in metal casting, but this did not necessarily make them into reputable military engineers.

very nearly the same in height, and paved on the top where, I am sure, five coaches-and-four could with a little management have been driven abreast.[70]

Thus, the scale of fortification in East Asia in effect rendered siege guns useless. That may be why indigenous heavy artillery never really developed there: In Japan, it was only seriously deployed against Osaka in 1615 and against the Shimabara rebels in 1636–7 (and on both occasions it proved indecisive); in China, it was seldom used offensively except during the 1670s. In both empires, sieges were usually decided by mass assaults, mining, or blockades rather than by bombardment.[71] Heavy guns, both of traditional and of Western manufacture, were certainly employed to defend the massive walls, but, otherwise, the use of artillery in the land warfare of East Asia was confined to the field.

Even so, the great states of East Asia paid more attention to the military innovations of the Europeans than to any other aspect of Western culture (except, perhaps, for astronomy and the clock). But this paradox may easily be explained when it is remembered that the seaborne arrival of the Europeans in the far East coincided with a period of sustained political disintegration in both China and Japan. In the former, instability lasted roughly from the renewal of pirate attacks on Fukien in the 1540s to the suppression of the last of the Ming loyalists in the 1680s; in the latter, the era of civil war lasted from the start of the Ōnin war in 1467 to the fall of Odawara in 1590. Throughout this long period, every military innovation was naturally accorded close attention, but, once stability was restored, the value of such things as firearms diminished. In China, they were largely confined to the frontiers; in Japan, most were kept in government arsenals and throughout the century the production of guns (which could only be made under license) was steadily reduced.[72]

But Japan did not only "give up" the gun. After 1580 successive central governments carried out a series of "sword hunts" aimed at

---

[70] Quotations from J. Ouchterlony, *The Chinese War* (London, 1844), 174–5; and H. Knollys, *Incidents in the China War of 1860* (Edinburgh; 1875), 198–9. See also Headrick, *The Tools of Empire*, 90–1; S. D. Chang, "The Morphology of Walled Capitals," in G. W. Skinner, ed., *The City in Late Imperial China* (Stanford, 1977), 75–100; and H. Franke, "Siege and Defence of Towns in Medieval China," in F. A. Kierman and J. K. Fairbank, eds., *Chinese Ways in Warfare* (Cambridge, Mass., 1974), 151–201.

[71] The new study of Needham, *The Gunpowder Epic*, replaces all earlier accounts as far as China is concerned. But see also C. R. Boxer, "Early European Military Influence in Japan (1543–1853)," *Transactions of the Asiatic Society of Japan* 2d ser., 8 (1931): 67–93; idem, "Portuguese Military Expeditions in Aid of the Mings and against the Manchus, 1621–1647," *T'ien Hsia Monthly* 7, no. 1 (August 1938): 24–36; and Cipolla, *Guns and Sails*, 114–17.

[72] Perrin, *Giving up the Gun*, 64–5.

removing *all* weapons from the temples, the peasants, the townsmen – from anyone who might try to resist the administration's taxes or policies. Some of the confiscated swords were melted down to make a great metal Buddha at Kyoto, and others were kept in state arsenals for use in emergencies (for instance, during the invasions of Korea during the 1590s), until in the end wearing the sword became largely confined to the hereditary arms-bearing class (the samurai). However, although the samurai might be left with their swords, they were deprived of most of their castles: starting (again) in 1580, the central government commenced a systematic destruction of the fortifications belonging to its defeated enemies. Then, in 1615, the shogun decreed that each lord could thenceforth maintain only one castle: All the rest should be destroyed. Thus, in the western province of Bizen, for example, where there had been over 200 fortified places at the end of the fifteenth century, there were only 10 by the 1590s, and after 1615 only 1: the great "Raven Castle" at Okayama. This "demilitarization" of Japan even affected literature. For some decades after 1671, the importation of all foreign books concerning military matters (and Christianity) was forbidden; and the *Honcho Gunki-ko* (*On the Military Equipment of Our Country*), completed in 1722 and published in 1737, contained only one chapter on firearms, and that was brief.[73]

But by that time the West had also largely lost interest in Japan, for the European presence in East Asia had changed substantially. The Dutch had been expelled from Taiwan in the 1660s, and their factory in Japan no longer yielded vast profits; the Iberian powers had lost much of their trading empire in the Orient; and the English East India Company still traded relatively little in the Far East. So China and Japan remained largely outside the West's sphere of influence throughout the early modern period.[74]

IV

The almost constant wars fought by the Europeans overseas during the period 1500–1800 were entirely different from those fought at

---

[73] Data taken from Itō Tasaburo, "The Book-Banning Policy of the Tokugawa Shogunate," *Acta Asiatica* 12 (1972): 36–61; B. Susser, "The Toyotomi Regime," 140–5; Fujiki Hisashi and George Elison, "The Political Posture of Oda Nobunaga," in J. W. Hall, Nagahara Keiji, and Kozo Yamamura, eds., *Japan Before Tokugawa: Political Considerations and Economic Growth, 1500–1650* (Princeton, 1981), 149–93, at 186–93; and J. W. Hall, *Government and Local Power in Japan, 500 to 1700: A Study Based on Bizen Province* (Princeton, 1966), 248, 316.

[74] See the radically new assessment of the development of East Asian history in early modern times offered by R. P. Toby, *State and Diplomacy in Early Modern Japan; Asia in the Development of the Tokugawa Bakufu* (Princeton, 1984).

home. In the first place, whereas wars in Europe normally involved limited aims and ended with the transfer of only small portions of territory and assets, those fought abroad aimed at the permanent and total subjection of the enemy population, the destruction of their political system, and the appropriation and exploitation of as many of their assets as possible. In the second, although the aims of colonial wars were unlimited, the means deployed to fight them were not. Thus, in the wars of Europe, the investment of resources became steadily more massive, while overseas the numbers of the combatants and the means for conquest at their disposal remained exiguous almost until the end of the period. Colonial wars were, as the title of the best military manual on the subject proclaimed, "small wars".[75] In the sixteenth century, Cortés conquered Mexico with perhaps 500 Spaniards; Pizarro overthrew the Inca empire with less than 200; and the entire Portuguese overseas empire, from Nagasaki in Japan to Sofala in southern Africa, was administered and defended by less than 10,000 Europeans. In the seventeenth century, when the number of Europeans in Portuguese Asia had dwindled to perhaps 1500, those involved in the Dutch enterprise in the East involved fewer than 10,000 whites; and even in the eighteenth century, the Dutch East India Company employed in Asia an average of only 20,000 Europeans.

So by the year 1800 the West had expended, in relative terms, remarkably little effort in order to gain control of more than a third of the globe. Admittedly it then proved rather more difficult to subjugate those people who had previously escaped (or successfully resisted) the European embrace. Thus it took the construction and despatch of an ironclad steamship, the *Nemesis*, to reduce the Central Kingdom to reason during the first Opium War (although the ship's two pivot-mounted 32-pounders managed to destroy, in just one day in February 1841, nine war-junks, five forts, two military stations and a shore battery in the Pearl River); and likewise, in 1863, the defeat of a belated attempt by the Tokugawa regime to exclude Western warships from Japanese waters required an attack on Kagoshima by a full flotilla of the Royal Navy during a typhoon, and the combined efforts of French, British, Dutch and American warships in order to silence the modern gun batteries in the straits of Shimonoseki.[76] Mean-

---

[75] C. Callwell, *Small Wars: Their Principles and Practice* (3rd edn., London, 1906). See also the excellent general remarks of de Moor and Wesseling, *Imperialism and War*, 1–11.

[76] For the fascinating story of the *Nemesis* see Headrick, *The Tools of Empire*, chap. 2 (details quoted from 47 and 50); for the 1863 naval campaign, see G. A. Ballard, *The*

while, not until the industrial production of effective prophylactics against tropical diseases could the Europeans bring enough of their well-armed troops into the African interior to secure the subordination of the 10,000 or so political units of the continent.

Nevertheless, although in terms of the number of combatants and the scale of resources deployed in European conflicts, this dramatic overseas expansion continued to be the product of 'small wars', it still relied critically upon the constant use of force. In the nineteenth century, as before, the West's advantage in the global 'military balance' was still vital: it was thanks to their military superiority, rather than to any social, moral or natural advantage, that the white peoples of the world managed to create and control, however briefly, the first global hegemony in History.

Influence of the Sea on the Political History of Japan (London, 1921), chap. 4 On the later episodes in the military rise of the West, see L. S. Stavrianos, *The World Since 1500: A Global History* (3d. ed., Englewood Cliffs, 1966), chaps. 13–14; and W. H. McNeill, *The Pursuit of Power: Technology, Armed Force and Society since A.D. 1000 (Oxford, 1982).*

CHAPTER 5

The pirate and the emperor: power and the law on the seas, 1450–1850

ANNE PÉROTIN-DUMON

"For elegant and excellent was the pirate's answer to the great Macedonian Alexander, who had taken him: the king asking him how he durst molest the seas so, he replied with a free spirit, 'How darest thou molest the whole world? But because I do with a little ship only, I am called a thief: thou doing it with a great navy, art called an emperor.' "

St. Augustine, *The City of God*, Book IV, Chapter IV.

I

There is a description of piracy that spans the ages: illegal and armed aggression at points of maritime traffic that are important but under weak political control. The aggression is committed by the marginal who seek to appropriate the wealth of the more affluent, or by new-comers desiring to force their way into preexisting trade routes.[1] This elementary description tells us about plundering and illegality; it tells us about immediate causes and motivations. But it leaves out the questions of what law is invoked against the pirate, and behind the law, of what power is involved in this maritime confrontation over matters of trade.

In the rise of merchant empires at the beginning of the modern era that is the focus of this book, what is called piracy is also easily recognizable. From sea to sea and age to age, we observe the same phenomena appearing – at once picturesque, violent, and sordid. From the Barbary Coast to the Rio de la Plata, from Madagascar to the Chinese Coast of Fukien, we could sketch a sort of sociology of

[1] C. R. Villar, *Piracy Today: Robbery and Violence at Sea Since 1980* (London: Conway Maritime Press, 1985).

196

piracy: by examining where pirates were based (retreats lodged in sheltered but deserted bays or on islands all along the coasts near frequented routes); by describing their behaviors in a single-sex society (verbal exaggeration, eccentricity in clothing, and infantilism); and finally by analyzing pirates' methods (raiding along the coasts or intercepting ships, living in complicity with the local inhabitants or exercising tyranny over them and so forth). Similarities exist also in how different authorities reacted, even down to the very expressions they used for their policies against pirates: to "cleanse the sea" and then to grant pardon, whether it was in the Low Countries, whose North Sea fishing fleets suffered the assaults of Norman and Scottish pirates during the sixteenth century, or the Ching dynasty facing a confederation uniting several thousand pirates along its southern coasts at the beginning of the nineteenth century.[2] These commonalities suggest collective patterns that, with the question of the damage done to commerce, have been the main subjects of work on piracy and its repression in the age of European expansion.

This chapter considers the other issue raised by piracy, one that has received little attention (and that with erroneous premises): the political significance of piracy and its repression. To understand piracy in the era of Europe's overseas commercial expansion, we must begin by considering the choices and conflicts that arose around control of the seas and trading routes: whether to aim for monopoly over Atlantic Routes, as in the Iberian, and later English and French, cases, or to work to keep them free and open, as in the Dutch case; whether to suppress Europeans who rebelled against this control or to eliminate non-European rival trading networks. These were all political decisions and policies expressing state power. The political will and policies that created merchant empires at the same time produced the piracy of that age. The common view that pirates existed "where commerce is active" is incomplete because it fails to consider the crucial political factor. Active commerce is indeed a necessary precondition for piracy, but it is not a sufficient one. Rather, the history of piracy in this period shows that it arises above all from change in the political realm – either the will of a state to establish commercial hegemony over an area where it had previously been weak or nonexistent, or from the conflict between two political entities, one an

---

[2] James D. Tracy, "Herring Wars: Sea Power in the North Sea under Charles V," under consideration by a journal; *Calendar of State Papers, Colonial Series, 1574–1660*, W. Noël Sainsbury ed. (London: Public Record Office, 1860) and *C.S.P., America and West Indies, 1661–1668*, W. Noël Sainsbury ed. (London: P.R.O., 1880); Diane Murray, *Pirates of the South China Coast, 1790–1810* (Stanford: Stanford University Press, 1987).

established trading power and the other a newcomer. The prize of piracy is economic, but as a historic phenomenon, the dynamic that creates it is political.

Most of the literature on this "imperial" piracy has retained a legalistic approach. It has considered what laws were used against pirates; it has assessed the wrongs done according to these laws. It has not inquired into what authority made the laws in the first place, and has failed therefore to identify what power was at stake in such maritime confrontations over trade. Moreover, a legalistic approach runs into the fact that there is not, and never has been, an authoritative definition of piracy in international law. The historiographical limitations of our topic and ambiguities around the notion of piracy in law and politics are analyzed in the second section of this essay.

In the third, fourth, and fifth sections of this chapter we deal successively with three episodes of piracy related to the rise of European merchant empires. The third section treats the first of these (1520–1650), when Iberians declared pirates other Western Europeans with whom they came into conflict in regions where they had asserted initial imperial dominion. This piracy was especially characteristic on the Atlantic routes to America, where the Iberian trade had not needed to supplant an indigenous trade but quickly experienced competition from other European merchants who organized trading voyages to America. French and later English "pirates" were, as the Greek word suggests, adventurers who wandered the seas in contempt of sixteenth-century Spanish monopolies that refused them license to trade beyond the Canary Islands. They are of special interest because of their role in expanding and intensifying European seaborne trade beyond the Iberian domain.

The second episode of piracy, analyzed in the fourth section, hit territorially based merchant empires that excluded foreigners. This piracy can be seen in two subepisodes. The first of these (1660–1720) concerns the well known cases of France and England. During this period, in which they established their own trading and colonial power, they outlawed cosmopolitan gangs of freebooters that challenged their new commercial regulations and drove away the Dutch, whose entrepôt-based empire in the Atlantic was premised upon free trade.[3] French and English courts of admiralty tried their own na-

---

[3] Jonathan I. Israel, *Empires and Entrepots: The Dutch, the Spanish Monarchy, and the Jews, 1585–1713* (London: Hambledon Press, 1990), after Peter W. Klein, *De Trippen in de 17e eeuw: een studie over het ondernemersgedrag op de Hollandse stapelmarkt* (Assen: Van Gorcum, 1965).

tionals as pirates. This suppression of piracy within national frameworks is important as an indicator of new state power; in particular the array of policies used to subdue pirates – including punishment or pardon, regulation or toleration – shows the concrete limits within which a state was able to assert itself.

In the second subepisode (1714–50), pirates resurface to challenge established commercial hegemonies. The fourth section of this chapter also deals with this case, when smugglers resist Spanish efforts to reimpose their claims over trade routes and networks. This outbreak of piracy is worthy of attention because it reflects the vicissitudes in control of large-scale commerce by merchant empires, not simply according to their laws on the matter, but rather to their political strength or weakness. Here historians have often failed to differentiate simple contraband from piracy. What created the shift from the former to the latter was the effort of a state power to control trading routes. Where previously a weak or tolerant state had tolerated smugglers, now their resistance made them pirates.

A third type of piracy can be seen in the conflicts between Europeans and non-Europeans from 1500 on. These encounters, analyzed in the fifth section of this chapter, are particularly prominent in the Indian Ocean, where the European newcomers met an armed resistance to their prohibitions from the established indigenous traders. The sixteenth-century Portuguese, for example, to impose a monopoly over the pepper trade in India, treated the people of Malabar as pirates.

Even circumscribed into these three broad episodes, the field of the phenomenon remains vast. It would be wonderful to accomplish what Samuel Johnson proposes in the opening verses of "The Vanity of Human Wishes":

> Let observation with extensive view
> Survey mankind from China to Peru;
> Remark each anxious toil, each eager strife
> And watch the busy scenes of crouded [sic] life.

Reality, however, requires a compromise between breadth and precision. Our focus here will be the Atlantic route to the East Indies and the Caribbean, regions that were hotbeds of world piracy between 1520 and 1820. The questions that most clearly emerged from this Atlantic piracy are then addressed comparatively in other specific situations where pirates and growing merchant empires faced off on other seas.

II

Most of what has been written on piracy is part of the body of work done on the naval and commercial expansion of Europe linked to the formation of modern states. Because of a nationalistic bias in the literature of the time, the studies done of European sixteenth- and seventeenth-century piracy failed to inquire into its political significance. They assumed the legitimacy of European states rather than considering how those states were formed and then established legitimacy over pirates as parts of the historical process to be studied. This literature focuses on English pirates and Dutch sea rovers more as national heroes against Catholic Hapsburgs than as instruments to the achievement of English and Dutch state power. Later, when France and England hung their most notorious freebooters, the legal apparatus for doing this is studied, not its political roots. As Kenneth Andrews has noted, this approach has obscured the international dimension of Caribbean piracy.[4]

The historiography of piracy, which flourished particularly between 1880 and 1940, was contemporary with the second wave of European expansionism, after a victory over indigenous piracy that was considered definitive.[5] It was influenced by the belief that the progress of "civilization" was served by commercial expansion. This framed an interpretation of piracy along cultural lines, distinguishing indigenous piracy from Western civilization. The suppression of non-European piracy became the equivalent on the sea of the "civilizing mission" in French colonial territories (even for the English, who

---

[4] Kenneth R. Andrews, "The English in the Caribbean, 1560–1620," in *The Westward Enterprise: English Activities in Ireland, the Atlantic and America, 1480–1650*, K. R. Andrews, N. P. Canny and P. E. H. Hair, eds. (Detroit: Wayne State University Press, 1979), p. 104.

[5] Several examples will illustrate how a Eurocentric interpretation of piracy developed following its "suppression" by regular naval forces in the nineteenth century. About Caribbean piracy in the 1820s, in the aftermath of the wars of Spanish American independence, Francis B. C. Bradlee wrote a hundred years later: "Revolutionary governments are, at best, generally attended by acts of violence, but when undertaken by the ignorant and depraved people of the South American colonies, it . . . led to rapine and piracy" (*Piracy in the West Indies and its Suppression* [Salem, Mass.: Essex Institute, 1923], p. 1). For Admiral Jurien de la Gravière, the conquest of Algiers in 1830 was the ultimate triumph of a *Gallia victrix* that "avenges Christendom" (*Les corsaires barbaresques et la marine de Soliman le Grand* [Paris; E. Plon, 1887], last chapter.) This judgment was also echoed by the English historian Stanley Lane-Poole in *The Story of the Barbary Corsairs* (New York: G. P. Putnams's Sons, 1890), 3: "For more than three centuries, the trading nations of Europe were suffered to pursue their commerce or forced to abandon their gains at the bidding of pirates. Nothing but the creation of the large standing navies crippled them. Nothing less than the conquest of their too convenient coasts could have suppressed them."

sought, in contrast to the French, to maintain local indigenous institutions). Only the era of decolonization made it possible to begin to approach the history of piracy critically, at the same time the history of European expansion was being revised. In the decade of the 1960s, the work of Nicholas Tarling on British imperialism in Malaysia, with its maritime implications, illuminated the colonialist premises that had caused non-European rivals to be designated as pirates.[6]

The older historiography of European piracy tied to the rise of merchant empires is marked in other ways by the frame of reference of nineteenth-century expansion. What was a novelty of the time – powerful states endowed with naval forces that kept the great oceanic routes open – was projected onto the past. This led to an anachronistic conception of the power of the state in the naval realm, and of the relationship between war and commerce in the sixteenth and seventeenth centuries. The meaning of piracy at the beginning of the modern era came to be implicitly assessed against these notions of an all-powerful state, of a public sector quite distinct from the private sector, and of a navy serving the glory of the nation by suppressing pirates.

Nation-states in the process of formation were capable of none of this, especially because these states were engaged in expensive wars among themselves. With the means of the time, they were incapable of sending strong fleets frequently enough to control seas far away from their European bases. It was not until the nineteenth century that first England, and then the United States, strove to apply the doctrine of total mastery of the seas, justifying vast naval forces.

One must also note the subtle but enduring error of perspective that consists in treating war and commerce as if they had always been incompatible. In sixteenth-century Europe, war and commerce went together, like mathematics and astrology, or physics and alchemy. For a long time, only those prepared to defend themselves could undertake any long-distance voyage. If they were also ready to go over to the attack, they were suited to a form of trade that could require the use of force, or the threat to do so, at any point. When Northern European pirates entered the Mediterranean and targeted the Venetians in the late sixteenth and early seventeenth centuries, Alberto Tenenti observes that their combination of commercial and aggressive operations was new for the region.[7] Northern European

---

[6] Nicholas Tarling, *Piracy and Politics in the Malay World: A Study in British Imperialism in Nineteenth-Century South-East Asia* (Melbourne: F. W. Cheshire, 1963).
[7] Alberto Tenenti, *Naufrages, corsaires et assurances maritimes à Venise, 1592–1609* (Paris: S.E.V.P.E.N., 1959), 39–40.

merchant empires initially arose in close association with both war and commerce; when the two elements were combined in a predatory and aggressive trade, it was piracy. And commerce was equally nourished when the cargo sold in home ports had been seized rather than bought!

Violence then was not a trait of piracy but more broadly of the commerce of that age. Commercial profits were linked pragmatically to considerations of war and aggression, though at the same time the state could be expected to put protective formations in place, like convoys that became a regular practice in the seventeenth century. The Dutch theoreticians Grotius and De la Court who, already in the seventeenth century, insisted that war was harmful to commerce and put their hopes in free trade rather than control of the seas, were exceptions. Similarly, merchants were more likely to arm their vessels than, like those of the Low Countries or Japan, to opt to purchase a safe-conduct.[8]

Let us examine now the question of the legal authority by which police power and justice pursued pirates. In the age that concerns us piracy was rarely limited to the simple case of a state with the right to use force against a few isolated wrongdoers captured near its coasts. More often the crime occurred far from territorial water (or, before this notion existed, far from the coasts) and belonged to the international domain. Whether national or international, piracy was the object of numerous codes and legal treaties, especially from the time when European states began to authorize and regulate attacks on the sea in the form of privateering wars. But crimes of piracy were always handled within a national legal framework. Although they belonged more properly to the domain of international law, they were brought before national admiralty courts or commerce jurisdictions.[9]

The difficulties that have historically surrounded the international crime of piracy in maritime law are no different in essence from those encountered by twentieth-century jurists. Piracy raises the question of what sort of power and order can ever be enforced on the sea, an area not settled by human societies and therefore not carved into political units. The sea falls de facto into the international domain; it lies in between nations. But judicial institutions belong to land communities; consequently, they lack legal authority to judge crimes occurring on the sea. Even in our day, international law has not

---

[8] Tracy, "Herring Wars."

[9] In studying naval wars, even the best historians have succumbed to the temptation to take the letter of these laws and their jurisprudence at face value. See Richard Pares, *Colonial Blockade and Neutral Rights, 1739–1763* (Oxford: Clarendon Press, 1938).

progressed very far; the notion of an overall legal imperative by which all are bound remains in its infancy.[10] Its application is limited by numerous obstacles, like the fact that it requires voluntary cooperation of states that in practice refuse to submit to international law (for example, the outlawing of war) because they perceive it as an infringement of their national sovereignty.

Since antiquity, there has been a consensus that the pirate should be considered as an *hostis humani generis* and his offense an attack on the law of nations. But this general opinion has not been concretized as a tool of law; a proper "law of nations" never existed. Humanity is not a wielder of law – only states are – and there is no international tribunal of a supra-national entity with coercive authority at its disposal to try the offenders. Among the matters under study by the Commission of International Law (appointed by the UN General Assembly), there is a proposed code of crimes against the peace and security of humanity that is supposed to deal with piracy. So far, it appears that the conclusion of experts who discussed this at the time of the League of Nations remains valid: There is no authoritative definition of international piracy.[11]

The lack of a legal definition for international piracy shows in the relativity that has always characterized the identity of the pirate (consequently, the terms employed in this chapter – pirate, privateer, corsair, freebooter, and so forth – are used not in reference to ideal categories but following our sources). Consider the case of Jean Florin, one of the Norman captains who ventured to attack the Spanish monopoly over the wealth of the Indies. As early as 1523, lying in wait between the Canary Islands and the Azores, Captain Florin captured two vessels returning from Mexico. In the eyes of the Spanish, this man was a pirate if ever there was one! But in Normandy in the church of Villequier, of which he was the lord, beautiful stained glass windows recount this local hero's capture of Montezuma's treasure. In Malaysia around 1830, the sailor whom the officials of the English trading company called a "ruffianly pirate," was a hero to local Malay merchants. The same relativity has affected judgments on the repression of piracy. At the very end of the seventeenth century, Bellomont was appointed governor of the colony of New York, with a mission to put an end to the activity of pirates along the coast. Referring to

[10] Monique Chemillier-Gendreau, "Fragilité et carence du système juridique mondial. L'état souverain aurait-il peur du droit international?" *Le Monde diplomatique* no. 422 (May 1989): 24–5.

[11] Barry Hart Dubner, *The Law of International Sea Piracy* (The Hague: M. Nijhoff Publishers, 1980), 41–55.

differing opinions that were expressed on the way he carried out his charge, the governor wrote: "They say I have ruined the town by hindering the privateers (for so they called the pirates)."

However, the epigraph at the beginning of this chapter about the pirate and the emperor (an anecdote borrowed by St. Augustine from an ancient writer) makes clear that the dispute about whether someone should be called a pirate or not is really about who has the power.[12] In our own century, the anticolonial wars have exhibited a similar dynamic of "pirate and emperor," translated into disputes over recognition or illegality. In the 1930s the Nicaraguan patriot Augusto Sandino was a bandit in the eyes of the North Americans, and in the 1940s the German authorities of occupied France viewed as terrorists the *résistants* loyal to *France libre*.

The parallels with native or creole resistance against European conquest or dominance are legion throughout the era of European expansion. On the Malabar coast of India in the sixteenth century, the Kunjalis were the main adversaries of the Portuguese, who treated them as *cossarios*; for the Zamorin princes of Calicut, the Kunjalis were their naval force and were patriots *avant la lettre*. During the wars of Spanish American independence between 1810 and 1830, when there were important actions at sea, royalists long insisted on labeling the *corsarios insurgentes* simply as pirates. These examples illustrate another political dimension of piracy to which we will later return: A dynamics of power is at play between an established power of superior strength and a newcomer of lesser, lacking recognition, that challenges it.

Confrontations at sea were both an important instrument of state power and of a measure of the degree to which state authority was actually established. Gaston Zeller some time ago noted that the development of nationalism in the sixteenth century started with the conquest of the seas and was most often exerted in the economic domain in the form of protectionist and exclusionist commercial legislation.[13] Western Europe state-building and commercial expansion were parallel developments that fed each other; hence the influence of politics in defining piracy at the time and, conversely, the role of piracy in the nation-building process.

---

[12] On echoes of the pirate's response in popular English satire in the early eighteenth century, emphasizing the relativity of the claims made by empires, see Joel H. Baer, "The Complicated Plot of Piracy: Aspects of the English Criminal Law and the Image of the Pirate in Defoe," *The Eighteenth Century: Theory and Interpretation* 23 (1982): 20–1.

[13] Gaston Zeller, *Histoire des Relations commerciales*, Vol. 2, *Les temps modernes de Christophe Colomb à Cromwell* (Paris: Presses Universitaires de France, 1953).

The sixteenth and seventeenth centuries witnessed an extraordinary debate over the state's lawmaking power and the political foundations of law, over the questions of warfare and violence. This was the time when a Francisco de Vitoria could claim that the Hapsburg monarchy's right to conquest ended where the natural rights of Amerindian societies began; when a Montaigne could write that "laws maintain their credit not because they are just, but because they are laws. This is the mystical basis of their authority; they have no other, and this serves them well."[14] That Augustine's anecdote about a confrontation between Alexander the Great and a pirate provided the setting for a reflection on the foundations of political power is perhaps revealing of the unique relationship between politics and the sea that then existed.[15]

Jurists like Bodin and Suárez, Grotius and Pufendorf were indeed dumbfounded by the conflicts brought on by the rise of states and their commercial expansion. Confronted by the powerlessness of diplomacy to resolve problems caused by the arrival of European newcomers in so many lands and on so many seas, they sought to regulate relations in a world composed of new states. A few even believed with Grotius that the sea should be open and long-distance trade free of all conflict. The propositions of many remained utopian: As mentioned, it is within a national framework that laws dealing with international matters were elaborated, among them those on navigation and trade that dealt with piracy. Different laws supported differing policies: either, as in the case of English and French monarchies after the Iberians, to control trading routes and monopolies; or, as in the case of the Dutch Republic, to keep trade open and free – save in regions where the Dutch themselves claimed a monopoly. Both types of policies, however, involved the power of a state.

The fact that public authorities decided on matters of navigation and trade ultimately sealed the fate of pirates, even when, as in the Dutch case, the state opted for freedom of trade and the seas. When the Dutch economist De la Court included the assertion that "seas must be kept free and open" among his general maxims for the welfare of humankind, it was, he said explicitly, in the interests of the Hollanders, who "are the great, and indeed only carriers of goods throughout the world; catching herring, haddock, cod and whale, making many sorts of manufactures and merchandize [*sic*] for foreign

---

[14] Michel de Montaigne, *Essais* (1580–1595); English trans., George B. Ives, *Essays* (New York: Heritage Press, 1946), Book III, Chapter XIII, 1464.

[15] Baer, "Complicated Plot."

parts.''[16] De la Court called for a fleet that would serve only to protect
Holland merchantmen from Flemish or English rovers and robbers.
In fact, however, privateering as an activity required immediate material rewards for those who carried it out; Dutch privateers, their
compatriot observed, tended not to defend their own merchant fleet
but to attack the enemies' ships and to take prizes, a modus operandi
that fell short of clearing the sea from *hostes humani generis*.[17]

III

A captain of Honfleur, Gonneville, left in 1503 to trade with the
Indians along the coast of Brazil; he carried a cargo of knives, mirrors,
and other "trinkets of Rouen." The hides, bird feathers, and dyewood
that he brought back were lost in the storm encountered on the home
journey of the ship *l'Espoir*. But the "relation" of his voyage was
preserved, and begins thus:

> Trafficking in Lisbon, Gonneville and the honorable men Jean l'Anglois and
> Pierre le Carpentier, having seen the beautiful riches of spice and other rarities
> coming into this city on the Portuguese ships going to the East Indies, dis-
> covered several years ago, made a pact together to send a ship there, after
> making a thorough enquiry of several who had made such a voyage, and
> having hired at high wages two Portuguese who had come back from there
> . . . in order to help them with their knowledge on the route to the Indies.[18]

In a few lines, the captain from Honfleur describes the careers of
thousands of his kind, from 1500 until around 1700, whose activities
were carried on with the sponsorship of the merchants of French and
English ports: learning in the principal Iberian commercial centers of
the existence of new resources, going in search of them oneself, by-
passing the Iberian intermediary, finding a pilot who knew the route
to these riches, and leaving, finally, on a venture with one's cargo of
trumpery wares. These men were convinced that, in spite of Iberian
claims, the sea and the riches of "Peru" or "Brazil," unlike those of
the Mediterranean and the Indian Ocean, were free and open to their
enterprises. The Dutch – who persisted in these views (and acted on

---

[16] Pieter de la Court, *Het interest van Holland, ofte grond van Hollands welwaren* (Amsterdam, 1662); Engl. trans., *Political Maxims of the Republic of Holland* (1743, New
York: reprint Arno Press, 1972), 48.

[17] De la Court, *Political Maxims*, Part II, Chapter 1, "The Necessity of Clearing the Seas
from Pirates," *passim*.

[18] Published by Charles-André Julien in *Les Français en Amérique pendant la première
moitié du XVIe siècle* (Paris: Presses Universitaires de France, 1946), 26.

them) later than other Northern Europeans – coined an appropriate name for themselves and others of their kind: *vrijbuiter*, or freebooter.

Such pirates, explorers, and traders prepared the way for regular maritime connections across the Atlantic and for the rise of new merchant empires following those of the Iberians. From Newfoundland to Brazil, their innumerable "trafficks, trades and barters" of manufactured goods and trumpery wares for exotic products constituted the main form of exchange between the Old World and the New (with ecological consequences that in our own times are receiving increasing attention). As Spain succeeded in keeping the hands of pirates off its principal Atlantic sealanes and mainland American empire, petty exchanges concentrated on the margins. On North American and Brazilian coasts and in the Carribean region, this petty commerce brought new societies into being initially based on plunder and smuggling. Atlantic and American piracy expanded to an intercontinental scale established exchanges between Northern and Southern Europe, fish and forest products for sugar and dye products. According to the distinction proposed by Robert López between the "inner" and "outer" areas of large-scale commerce, the Atlantic and the Caribbean were still an "outer area" for those pirate explorers, but their actions nonetheless foretold the creation of a new "inner area," with regular routes and with predictable costs and profits.[19]

The role pirates could play as adventurous merchants and explorers for new routes and commercial goods, in defiance of empires, may be seen in East Asia, where they challenged the Ming. The *wakō* (or *wokou* for the Chinese, meaning "Japanese bandits") started spreading along the Korean and then Chinese coasts at the end of the thirteenth century. Their plundering marked the beginning of a remarkable Japanese expansion toward mainland Asia that would lead them on to Java and Manila.[20] Later, seeking to escape the constrictive policy of the Ming empire that banned trade with foreigners, Hokkien merchants, studied by Wang Gungwu, left the coasts of China to settle overseas, some of them in Manila like their Japanese counterparts. Between the fourteenth and eighteenth centuries, they formed prosperous communities that defied the agrarian-bureaucratic orientation of the Chinese Empire.[21] Ironically, European intruders would rely

[19] Chapter by Russell R. Menard in this volume, note 11.
[20] Paul Akamatsu, "Le décollage des grands marchands japonais au 17e siècle," in *Marchands et hommes d'affaires asiatiques dans l'Océan Indien et la Mer de Chine 13e–20e siècles*, Denys Lombard and Jean Aubin eds. (Paris: Editions de l'Ecole des Hautes Etudes en Sciences Sociales, 1988), 128–9.
[21] Wang Gungwu, "Merchants without Empire: The Hokkien Sojourning Communities," in *The Rise of Merchant Empires: Long-Distance Trade in the Early Modern*

on these Chinese and Japanese overseas merchant communities to establish themselves commercially on the margins of the Chinese and Japanese trading systems.

In the second half of the sixteenth century, the English followed French incursions into Iberian America. The first "privateering voyage" of John Hawkins in 1562 is well documented.[22] Through his long term correspondents in the Canary Islands, the Englishman learned of the Guinea trade and of sugar in the Spanish Greater Antilles: Slaves instead of knives and mirrors and sugar rather than feathers and shells were the basis for a potentially much more substantial venture. After bribing a Spanish pilot, Hawkins sailed for the west African coast, where he was able to buy 300 slaves "partly by the sword, partly by other means." The slaves he sold at Hispaniola, in exchange for sugar as well as hides, ginger, gold, and pearls. As he had hoped, Hawkins obtained a trading license from local officials, after a sufficient show of force to provide the excuse they would need to explain, in reporting to the king, why they had been constrained to admit a foreign vessel.

Voyages like this were more or less repeated for half a century (1560s–1630s) by other intruders. Once the facade of hostility had been displayed, the Spanish governor could close his eyes and allow inhabitants to trade with the English, bringing them wares they needed anyway because they were rarely visited by their national merchants. Sometimes a fort would threaten to shell the English ship, forcing it to retreat to an undefended (and thus more hospitable) site nearby. There business could be conducted peacefully at night with inhabitants who came down from the capital. Sometimes French and

---

World, 1350–1750, James D. Tracy ed. (New York: Cambridge University Press, 1990), 400–21.

[22] *The Hawkins Voyages during the Reigns of Henry VIII, Queen Elizabeth, and James I,* Clements R. Markham ed. (London: Hakluyt Society, 1878). English and Spanish sources referring to English privateering voyages have been published by Irene A. Wright, *Spanish Documents Concerning English Voyages to the Caribbean, 1527–1568* (London: Hakluyt Society, 1929, 2d ser., no. 62; Kraus reprint, 1967), and *Documents Concerning English Voyages to the Spanish Main, 1569–1580* (London: Hakluyt Society, 1932, 2d ser., no. 71; Kraus reprint, 1967); and by Kenneth R. Andrews, *English Privateering Voyages to the West Indies, 1588–1595* (Cambridge: Hakluyt Society, 1959). Andrews has studied English piracy extensively in *The Spanish Caribbean: Trade and Plunder, 1530–1630* (New Haven: Yale University Press, 1978); *Trade, Plunder, and Settlement: Maritime Enterprise and the Genesis of the British Empire, 1480–1630* (New York: Cambridge University Press, 1984); and "The English in the Caribbean," in *The Westward Enterprise.* Spanish treatments include Antonio Rumeu de Armas, *Los viajes de John Hawkins a América, 1562–1595* (Seville: Escuela de Estudios Hispano-Americanos, 1947) and *Piraterías y ataques navales contra las islas Canarias* (Madrid: Consejo Superior de Investigaciones Científicas, 1947–50).

English corsairs carried out joint operations, and the display of superior forces would convince local officials to grant them a trading license. Simply by being continuously present and scaring other ships off, English pirates managed to force locals to trade with them. "Coming or going, we always have a corsair in sight . . . If this continues . . . they will compel us to do business with them rather than with Spain," complained a Spanish official from Hispaniola in 1595.[23]

After a trip of several months, a pirate was anxious to get rid of his cargo (if, for example, as in the case of Hawkins, some slaves had fallen ill), and it was necessary to force the exchange and make use of cannon against the colonists. This kind of exchange Spaniards would also accept, but "whether by consent, or by compulsion, I can't say," as one pirate boasted of this method in *History of the Pyrates*, attributed to Defoe.[24] At times, even under those conditions, no exchange would be possible, but pirates would still need return merchandise or simply fresh provisions and water. This could lead them then to loot the churches, official buildings, and private houses of Spanish American towns, though pirates were often content to attack unprotected settlements along the coasts, sugar mills, and cattle farms.

Before there were North European pirates, the first Castilian enterpreneurs operating in America had also sometimes been traders and sometimes raiders. The two words "raiding" and "trading" appear over and over in the literature to describe these two modes of operation.[25] Whether pirates chose one mode or the other depended on a variety of circumstances, such as whether or not one was familiar with potential local partners, far from or close to one's base, at the beginning or the end of one's venture, and so forth. What mattered was to be ready for either option. When the Dutch West Indies Company was founded in 1621 as a joint-stock freebooting venture to compete with the Spanish trade, it set for itself the dual objectives of commerce and privateering raids. The freebooter admiral Piet Heyn quickly made his presence felt in the Greater Antilles and on the Spanish Main; he captured the Mexican fleet at Matanzas Bay, in Cuba, in 1627.

[23] Quoted in Andrews, "The English in the Caribbean," 119–20.
[24] *A General History of the Robberies and Murders of the Most Notorious Pyrates* (London, 1724; New York: reprint Garland Publishers, 1972).
[25] John H. Elliott, "The Spanish Conquest and Settlement of America," *Cambridge History of Latin America*, Vol. 1, 156; Paul E. Hoffman, *The Spanish Crown and the Defense of the Caribbean, 1535–1585: Precedent, Patrimonialism, and Royal Parsimony* (Baton Rouge: Louisiana State University Press, 1980); Andrews, *The Spanish Caribbean* and *Trade and Plunder*.

The mixture of seduction, distrust, and violence visible in the dealings of pirates with Spanish officials and colonists was a common combination in early encounters between people of mutually exclusive cultures. The emergent nationalism of the time was often defined by cultural differences. When all was said and done, the pirate was the "other"; he was a problem because he was culturally different. The Spanish Crown reacted with hostility when non-Spaniards tried to create free zones in the east of Cuba and in the northwest of Hispaniola at the beginning of the seventeenth century. The presence of the "other" was as much a cause of annoyance as the losses represented by those *rescates*, or illicit transactions with foreigners. The "age of great piracy" is also that of Reformation: cultural differences came to crystallize around confessional ones. For Catholic Spaniards, contacts with "Huguenots" and "Lutherans" were unacceptable and had to be furtive.[26] As the American trade was increasingly threatened by intrusions of non-Spaniards in the second half of the sixteenth century, the Inquisition expanded to the New World. Its role would often be essential in the pursuit of intrusive traders like Hawkins.

Lacking precise estimates of the damages that pirates inflicted on trade in European waters prior to 1500, there has been a tendency to consider as unprecedented the piracy that accompanied overseas expansion. A brief glance at the past makes one skeptical, however, about whether it is possible to speak of increasing insecurity on the sea.[27] There are the several thousand letters of the fourteenth and fifteenth centuries preserved in the Archives of Arles (in Provence), which document how the city was then part of a typically Mediterranean network of information and on the alert against Catalan, Saracen (Moorish), Pisan, and Genoese pirates. Before 1500, there were Breton, Norman, Welsh, and Cornish pirates who threatened regular traffic between the main English and French ports, kidnapping travelers and holding them for ransom, just as Barbary pirates would continue to do for centuries in the Mediterrenean. In ports that lacked the rich export merchandise of a Bordeaux or Plymouth, men could just as easily be pirates as carriers, or both, as were the Bretons.

Writing on the export of French wines to England, Russell Menard

---

[26] Arturo Morales Carrión, *Puerto Rico and the Non Hispanic Caribbean: A Study in the Decline of Spanish Exclusivism* (Río Piedras: University of Puerto Rico Press, 1952), and Rumeu de Armas, *Piraterías*.

[27] For European piracy before the European expansion, see Michel Mollat, *Le commerce normand à la fin du Moyen-Age* (Paris: E. Plon, 1952); and D. Mathew, "The Cornish and Welsh Pirates in the Reign of Elizabeth," *English Historical Review* 39 (1924): 337–48. On piracy in the coastal towns of Provence, see Philippe Rigaud, *Letras de la Costiera: La Provence et la guerre de course, XV-XVIes siècles*, forthcoming.

notes that the problem of insecurity was of long standing: As reflected in the cost of transportation, troubles began at the time of the Hundred Years' War and continued intermittently through the sixteenth century, when France and England were too weak to police their seas.[28] Trading and raiding were already alternatively practiced in the Atlantic and the Channel, but in the sixteenth century the patterns of European piracy spread like a turbulent climatic front. Shortly after 1500, the front of this tornado was already at the Azores and the Canary Islands, a third of the way toward America; by the middle of the sixteenth century, it had reached the Greater Antilles. A century later, European pirates had touched the coasts of north Africa, where they occasionally allied with native pirates. By the end of the seventeenth century, European pirates were at Madagascar and southern Africa; and then they reached India, operating from the south of Bombay, the Malabar coast, and as far as the Gulf of Bengal.

In *The Military Revolution*, Geoffrey Parker describes the developments that were a prerequisite for this Western hegemomy: the great progress in the domain of armament and strategy made by Europeans on both sea and land at the beginning of the modern era.[29] When the freebooter Captain Fleury sailed from Dieppe in 1618, to carry on trade with the "continent of Peru," he had not left Norman waters before he was busy fighting with Dutch, Breton, and English ships. We are fortunate to have an extremely evocative account of his two-year expedition, which took the Frenchman to Cape Verde, Brazil, the Caribbean, Central America, and Florida.[30] After describing the Indian communities that received the freebooters, saving them from exhaustion and starvation, the anonymous narrator enthusiastically refers to "rounds of cannon, catapults and muskets" fired by Fleury's men and the prizes they took of "powder, leads and guns." A few decades later, in 1642, Captain William Jackson sailed from London to raid on the Spanish Main. He enlisted almost a thousand men between the islands of Barbados and St. Christopher (today St. Kitts). "Commanders and officers spent their time in exercising their souldiers [sic] to make them more ready and expert on all occasions." The English corsair proudly listed his stock of "muskitts, carbines, fire-

---

[28] Menard, "Transport Costs," note 45.
[29] Geoffrey Parker, *The Military Revolution: Military Innovation and the Rise of the West, 1500–1800* (New York: Cambridge University Press, 1988). See also J. R. Hale, "Sixteenth-Century Explanations of War and Violence," *Past and Present* no. 51 (May 1971); 3–26.
[30] *Un flibustier français dans la mer des Antilles en 1618–1620*, Jean-Pierre Moreau ed. (Clamart, France: Ed. J.-P. Moreau, 1987).

locks, halfe-pikes, swords, cutlases & ye like offentius weapons."[31] Thus, an old phenomenon, the long-term insecurity of the seas, was aggravated by a new development, the improvements in naval gunnery that gave the advantage to aggressive merchants. Violence could spread more easily because European navigation brought previously separate trading zones into contact with one another.

While the front of European piracy reached shores ever more distant, Japanese wakō pirates and their Chinese accomplices were breaking into the defenses of a declining Ming empire. In the Indian Ocean between 1650 and 1750, Mughal forces were held in check on the Malabar coast by a force of their own former corsairs. What we have here are the signs of a changing political dynamic, of new powers seeking to gain control of large-scale commerce and of new commercial hegemonies being established. "Whether it was at the beginning, the middle, or the end [of the seventeenth] century," wrote Louis Dermigny, "pirates developed everywhere on the flanks of massive mainland empires in crisis or decline: the Spanish empire, the Mughal empire and the Chinese empire."[32]

Fernand Braudel, among others, has brought to light the function piracy played culturally as well as economically.[33] Running through a multitude of examples with an encyclopedic faith less in evidence today, the historian of the Mediterranean rightly perceived that armed trade was just as important as peaceful trade, and that both of these vast movements of exchange promoted conflict as well as contact between cultures. With particular insight, Braudel explained the spread of aggression to the seas as an encounter between different kinds of merchant states, those in the process of formation and expansion and others losing momentum and influence. Thus, in Braudel's terms, the assaults of Northern European pirates on Spanish and Venetian commerce at the beginning of the seventeenth century were "the sign of a recent arrival." Venetian regular forces and Spanish Caribbean squadrons, as the instruments of established commercial powers, treated the newcomers – the French, English, and Dutch

---

[31] "The Voyages of Captain William Jackson," in *Colonizing Expeditions to the West Indies and Guyana, 1623–1667*, Vincent T. Harlow ed. (London: Hakluyt Society, 1925, 2d ser., no. 56,), 2–3.

[32] Louis Dermigny, *La Chine et l'Occident: Le commerce à Canton au XVIIIe siècle, 1719–1833* (Paris: S.E.V.P.E.N., 1964). See in particular the chapter entitled "Piraterie et conjoncture", 92–103.

[33] Fernand Braudel, *La Méditerranée et le monde méditerranéen à l'époque de Philippe II* (Paris: A Colin, 1949); English trans., Siân Reynolds, *The Mediterranean and the Mediterranean World in the Age of Philip II* (New York: Harper Torchbooks, 1975), Vol. 2, 865–91.

who challenged them – as pirates. In practice, however, the forces of both powers displayed lethargy and defeatism toward the intruders; they remained in port or gave themselves up without battle.[34] It is as if they were vaguely aware that the dynamic of change was no longer on their side (while also knowing that galleys and galleons do not easily flight pirate ships).

The Europeans denounced indigenous piracy, but Braudel's remark is equally apt for this phenomenon, that it was the "sign of a recent arrival." The process was the same – attacks on established merchant powers by outsider competitors – but the main actors exchanged dramatic *personae*: In the Indian Ocean, the newcomers were the ones to accuse the long-term occupants of piracy. Thus, in the Indian Ocean the Portuguese claimed a commercial monopoly and treated as pirates the Malabar sailors who resisted them along the southern coasts of India, which they defended for the Mughal emperor. In the Mediterranean the established Venetian and Spanish traders were the ones to bar North European competitors from their monopoly and treat them as pirates. Whether they were pirates or not, the intruders from Northern Europe challenging old Mediterranean powers and the Asiatic merchant communities resisting the intrusion of Europeans represented two sides of the same coin. By insisting on their hegemonic pretensions, the Spaniards in the Mediterranean and the Portuguese in Asia were both attempting to compensate for their lack of effective control, a point to which we return later. The second imperialist push of Europe in the nineteenth century would reproduce situations in which non-European merchants were pursued as pirates by Europeans, now backed by better naval forces. So it happened with the Qawasim, seafarers from a commercial emirate that stubbornly refused to cede the English control over the entry to the gulf in the course of the nineteenth century.[35]

When situations of piracy reveal that shifts in power are occurring and new hegemonies are being established, what starts as a dispute over trade may ultimately become one over political control. A case in point is the Mappila merchant community in sixteenth century Calicut, studied by Geneviève Bouchon. Unlike other Muslim merchant communities that dominated long-distance trade in Calicut, the

---

[34] Alberto Tenenti, *Venezia e i corsari, 1580–1615* (Bari, 1961); English trans., Janet and Brian Pullan, *Piracy and the Decline of Venice, 1580–1615* (Berkeley and Los Angeles, University of California Press, 1967); Enriqueta Vila Vilar, *Historia de Puerto Rico, 1600–1650* (Seville: Escuela de Estudios Hispano-Americanos, 1974).

[35] Sultan Muhammad Al-Qasimi, *The Myth of Arab Piracy in the Gulf* (London: Croom Helm, 1986).

Mappila were native and specialized in the South Indian coastal trade and the Java Trade. The arrival of the Portuguese caused the departure of the Arabs at the beginning of the sixteenth century. In a context of war brought about by Portuguese intrusion, Mappila power rose in Calicut. They started fitting out their privateers, which regardless of official conflicts, would, throughout the century, relentlessly attack Portuguese spice trade circuits. Such piracy had a clear political outcome: the Mappila came to dominate Calicut and for a time threw off the yoke of the Zamorin.[36]

The Malay seafarers resisting the English who were in the process of replacing the Dutch domination in the 1830s and 1840s offer another example. Before the coming of the English, it was customary for maritime adventurers progressively to extend their commercial control over an area from which over time they would dislodge the previous political power. During the time Malay sultanates were created, piracy provided the basic mechanism for shifts in political control. Between the fifteenth and the eighteenth centuries, these sultanates, as studied by Denys Lombard, displayed an astonishing similarity to their Dutch foes: they, too, were maritime states centered around port cities and their merchant elites.[37] European intrusion and naval control interrupted this dynamic of state-building. Pirates were now condemned to remain pirates instead of evolving toward the creation of a maritime state. "If this has been called piracy," writes Tarling, "it was also an aspect of the political dynamics of this part of the world."[38]

IV

Turning to English and French piracy in the seventeenth century, we leave the global stage to consider markedly national episodes that would be remembered as the "the suppression of piracy." The excesses of a last generation of pirates, those who were gradually outlawed, have with reason inspired much romantic fiction.[39] Life had

---

[36] Geneviève Bouchon, "Un microcosme: Calicut au 16e siècle," in Lombard and Aubin eds., *Marchands et hommes d'affaires asiatiques,* 55–56.

[37] Denys Lombard, "Le sultanat malais comme modèle socio-économique," in Lombard and Aubin eds., *Marchands et hommes d'affaires asiatiques,* 117–24.

[38] Tarling, *Piracy and Politics,* 4.

[39] Scholars like Clarence H. Haring, *The Buccaneers in the West Indies in the XVII Century* (New York: E. P. Dutton, 1910), I. A. Wright, and later K. A. Andrews (see note 22) have been exceptions in the literature on sixteenth- and seventeenth-century European pirates, which remains nationalistic and largely anecdotal because it is strictly based on pirates' narratives. The best-known of these narratives include Alexander Olivier Exquemelin, *De Americaensche zee-roovers* (Amsterdam, 1678), a

become extremely difficult for the last freebooters; nothing could be taken for granted any more. "My commission is large and I made it myself," proclaimed Captain Bellamy in *History of the Pyrates;* "I am a free prince and I have much authority to make war on the whole world," says a couplet of the ballad of Captain Avery. As they faced growing hostility, pirates dispersed, carrying their enterprise to its greatest geographic extension at the beginning of the eighteenth century, as already noted. Fleeing a Caribbean that was becoming less hospitable, they made for the coasts of North America, Africa, and the Indian Ocean.

Near the end of the eighteenth century, pirates were depicted as a social plague in a new literature, especially in English, with titles such as *Piracy Destroy'd; or, A short discourse shewing the rise, growth and cause of piracy of late; with a sure method how to put a steady stop to that growing evil.*[40] "The pirate," wrote Daniel Defoe in this spirit, "destroys all government and all order, by breaking all those ties and bonds that unite people in a civil society under any government." The pirate is barbarous and antisocial, and must therefore be destroyed. One finds here the ancient accusation against the pirate as *hostis humani generis.* The practices of such folk were, of course, delinquent and violent, but they had long been so. The appearance of this negative campaign against them in public opinion was not accidental. It coincided with the launching of a new commercial policy of the state, which was directed against French and English pirates naval and judiciary "campaigns" (the word is in itself a clear indication of state action) that would be sustained over several decades.

Individual operations of "gentlemen of fortune" were ridiculed as

best-seller in its time that was adapted in English under the title *The Buccaneers and Marooners of America: Being an Account of the Famous Adventures and Daring Deeds of Certain Notorious Freebooters of the Spanish Main* (1684); *The Life and Adventures of Capt. John Avery* (1709?), *The Successful Pirate Charles Johnson* (1713), Joel H. Baer ed. (Los Angeles: The Augustan Reprint Society, Williams Andrews Clark Memorial Library, University of California, 1980). *The Successful Pirate* was reworked by Defoe in his *General History . . . of the Pyrates,* published in 1724 (see note 24). A recent innovative approach has been in labor history: Marcus Rediker, *Merchant Seamen, Pirates, and the Anglo-Maritime World, 1700–1750* (New York: Cambridge University Press, 1987), and "The Anglo-American Seaman as Collective Worker, 1700–1750," in Stephen Innes, ed., *Work and Labor in Early America* (Chapel Hill: University of North Carolina Press, 1988). Another insightful study of pirates in political history is Robert C. Ritchie, *Captain Kidd and the War Against the Pirates* (Cambridge, Mass.: Harvard University Press, 1986). By Ritchie, see also *Pirates: Myths and Realities,* The James Ford Bell Lectures No. 23 (St. Paul: The Associates of the James Ford Bell Library, University of Minnesota, 1986)
[40] *Piracy Destroy'd* (London: J. Nutt, 1701). A copy is at the John Carter Brown Library, Providence, R. I., D 701/P 667 d.

archaic and unresponsive to the laws of the market, which required information, provisions, investments, and so forth. "He could have made a great profit on indigo, but he wanted nothing but gold, silver or jewels," noted the Jesuit missionary and historian Charlevoix, writing of l'Olonois. The "freebooter admiral," whose forces from Tortuga Island began to abandon him after a defeat in Puerto Rico in 1669, did not understand that the future was in plantation economy.[41] For the governor of the Isle of Bourbon (today Réunion), the *forbans* of Madagascar whom it was his responsibility to repress were equally *passés*: They possessed diamonds in the rough, but to no use, because they had not "a penny's worth of capital."[42]

In his *History of the Pyrates* Defoe superbly recast an earlier narrative, *The Successful Pirate Charles Johnson* (1713). One revealing change introduced by Defoe is that pirates are no longer successful. His novel is the account of commercial ventures that failed because they were itinerant and improvised – not only illegal but carried out "like a lottery." Facing repression by the merchant empires, fugitives from the Caribbean almost succeeded in establishing a trading circuit to supply New York with slaves, parallel to the Royal African Company, and they made of their Malagasy hideaways an entrepôt dealing in goods between Europe, Asia, and America, in contempt of the East India Company. Baldridge, a Madagascar pirate of Anglo-Saxon stock, in 1691 received an order for 200 slaves from a New York merchant specializing in the slave trade; Baldridge, however, turned out to be incapable of furnishing more than thirty-four.[43] His failure illustrates the fact that it was becoming increasingly difficult to maintain independent trade circuits parallel to those controlled by a mercantilist state; pirates were turning into mere parasites.

Islands that had begun as cosmopolitan rendezvous for pirates (who counted Flemish, Germans, Portuguese, and Maltese in their ranks) were now turned into export colonies exclusively linked to metropolitan merchants. The pirates failed to understand the change and clung to free trade and outmoded depredation. They tended to sell their prizes and spend their profits elsewhere than on their island, contributing to a national trade deficit. In a report of 1685, colonial authorities of the French island of Martinique observed that pirates

---

[41] Pierre-François-Xavier de Charlevoix, *Histoire de l'isle espagnole ou de Saint-Dominque* (Paris: F. Barois, 1730–31), Vol. 2, p. 73.

[42] Albert Lougnon, *L'île Bourbon pendant la Régence: Desforges Boucher, les débuts du café* (Nérac, France: Couderc, 1956), 244, n. 10.

[43] Jacob Judd, "Frederick Philippe and the Madagascar Trade," *The New York Historical Society Quarterly* 55 (October 1971): 354–74.

"go to buy their weapons, nautical equipment and munitions in Jamaica, where they bring absolutely all the money they make, which considerably prejudices the colony."[44] Or they brought back booty that was unmarketable. Because piracy depended on rumors telling of the success of this or that venture, accumulating disappointments led to a thinning of the ranks. The last outlaw holdouts could only declare a paranoid war against the human race.

To these Don Quixotes of piracy, Defoe contrasts the merchant of the future:

Every new voyage the merchant contrives is a project, and ships are sent from port to port, as markets and merchandizes [sic] differ, by the help of strange and universal intelligence; wherein some are so exquisite, so swift, and so exact, that a merchant sitting at home in his counting-house, at once converses with all parts of the known world. This and travel, makes a true-bred merchant the most intelligent man in the world, and consequently the most capable, when urged by necessity, to contrive new ways to live.[45]

Heralded by such outstanding pamphleteers as Defoe, a whole new era was under way: Large-scale commerce and colonies had become national objectives for France and England. The state assumed control of long-distance seaborne trade and of overseas settlements where agricultural export commodities were now being produced. In England a new class of merchants arose who had made their wealth in the West Indian trade, that is, outside of the framework of chartered commercial companies. With influence in political circles, these merchants oriented the trade policy of the state toward excluding foreigners and retaining for themselves the monopoly of provisioning and marketing in the colonies.[46] The state now financed embryonic national fleets to protect convoys of merchant ships and attack the enemy at sea.

As several chapters of this book make clear, there was a general trend in Western European countries in the course of the seventeenth century: Merchants laid down their weapons and accepted that the state would protect their business in exchange for regulating and

---

[44] Governor Bégon and Intendant Saint-Laurens of Martinique, January 25, 1685 (National Archives, France, Series Colonies C 8A/4, 67–85).

[45] Daniel Defoe, *An Essay Upon Several Projects: Or, Effectual Ways for Advancing the Interests of the Nation* (London, 1697), quoted in Thomas L. Haskell, "Capitalism and the Origins of the Humanitarian Sensibility," Part II, *American Historical Review* 90, no. 3 (June 1985): 558.

[46] Robert Brenner, "The Social Basis of English Commercial Expansion, 1550–1650," *Journal of Economic History* 32 (1972): 361–84.

taxing it.[47] There would have been no "suppression of piracy" without this change in relationship between merchant and state. Free-lancers who would not, or could not, adapt themselves to the new commercial age would be declared pirates. As trade carried by caravan merchants was displaced to the profit of transoceanic commerce in the course of the seventeenth century, so were small ventures of merchant captains forced out by the merchant houses allied to a mercantilist state that were to make the eighteenth century the golden age of Atlantic trade.

The actual policy put into effect at the end of the seventeenth century had a more modest goal than the "destruction of piracy" advertised: It was, as worded in the Jamaican Act of 1683, "the restraining and punishing of privateers and pirates." As mentioned earlier, the more ambitious tactics of protecting ships through convoys and cleaning out the freebooters' retreats could only be realized with much difficulty over an extended period of time. What appears to have been more effective in practice was attracting merchants into the commercial orbit of the state. In order to work, the measures and privileges described above had to make commerce more profitable and safer with rather than without the tutelage of the state. Further, the state had to encourage the formation of political blocs that were hostile to pirates and had an interest in their repression.

The recent study by Robert Ritchie, *Captain Kidd and the War against Pirates*, shows that punishment and repression were effective because the powerful East India Company succeeded in making Kidd a political issue in the conflict between Whig and Tory factions, and because the Tories had a stake in the operation of repression against pirates.[48] Unlike many superficial accounts of Kidd's adventures, Ritchie sheds new light on the subject because he analyzes the political circles involved in the case in England and in the colonies, whose influence led to the pirate's execution in 1701.

Few pirates, however, were, like Kidd, sent back to the metropolis. Repressing them was left in the hands of local authorities where they were operating. There *raison d'état* alone was not enough; local public opinion and local considerations had to be taken into account. One is reminded of the way local authorities have dealt in our century with guerrillas in the Philippines or in Colombia. The law authorized

---

[47] By accepting the protection sold by modern states, merchants returned to a formula that had been used for centuries in the Mediterranean. See Frederic C. Lane, "The Economic Meaning of War and Protection," in *Venice and History: The Collected Papers of Frederic C. Lane* (Baltimore: Johns Hopkins University Press, 1966), 383–98.

[48] See note 39 above.

an arsenal of pardons and rewards, amnesties and punishments; implementing it successfully required dextrous use of both positive and negative instruments. In 1720 the governor of the Isle of Bourbon received an order from Versailles to obtain the surrender of French elements among the pirates' nest of Madagascar.[49] When the hostility they encountered from native Malagasy appeared to make pirates receptive to the king's request, the governor offered them amnesty. With the consent of Bourbon colonists, repentant *forbans* who had made the trip from Madagascar were received, at first on a trial basis. On condition that they burn their fleet and deliver their treasure to the authorities, the *nouveaux habitants* were divided among different parishes; they were married off, and given pensions and land grants. Those found undesirable were allowed to return to Europe. It was not long, however, before Labuse – their leader – and a few recalcitrants took to the sea again, soon to be captured and hung. This news was widely publicized to emphasize the efficiency of royal justice against piracy.

Beyond repressing pirates, however, remained the task of implementing the exclusive commerce in the colonies themselves. This proved arduous in part because the new arrangements were less beneficial to colonists than to metropolitan merchants. Both the Navigation Acts as well as Colbert's edicts caused riots in the colonies, at about the same time as fiscal measures caused a revolt in French Brittany. Although the latter was severely crushed, freebooters in Saint-Domingue (today Haiti) received surprising clemency. The reason for this milder reaction in the colony, Charles Frostin wrote, was that "reprisals could strangle a young economy."[50] The governor had to keep a balance between local and metropolitan interests, a point that we examine below.

The official correspondence of French and English colonial authorities reveals that they faced the same dilemma with freebooters at the end of the seventeenth and beginning of the eighteenth centuries: If repression were too severe, it would only encourage freebooters to try their chances elsewhere, thus depriving the island of hands badly needed for both the economy and defense. Jamaican officials feared that disgruntled freebooters would go to swell the ranks of others

[49] Lougnon, *L'Ile Bourbon.* On the last Madagascar pirates in 1710–17, Lougnon writes: "A bout de souffle, très pauvres, ils soupiraient après l'amnistie" (164–5).

[50] Charles Frostin, *Les révoltes blanches à Saint-Domingue aux XVIIe et XVIIIe siècles (Haïti avant 1789)* (Paris: L'Ecole, 1975), 111. On mercantilism calling for smuggling and piracy, see also Shirley Carter Hughson, *The Carolina Pirates and Colonial Commerce, 1670–1740* (Johns Hopkins University Studies in Historical and Political Science, ser. 12, no. 5–7, Baltimore, 1894).

on the island of Tortuga or Curaçao, while at the same time the governor of Saint-Domingue imagined that they might already be sailing for Jamaica. For both the French and English, an incipient public sector experienced the limitations of state economic intervention and risked undermining prosperity by encouraging evasion.[51]

Being so close to the riches of the Spanish Main, Jamaica and Saint-Domingue would harbor incorrigible *forbans* for several generations. And colonial officials themselves were not completely prepared to give up the freebooter economy of free trade for that of plantations. Governor Modyford, of Jamaica, was one of these figures incurably attached to the old ways. In March 1665 he offered a grim picture of an island deserted by freebooters: defense forces reduced to one-fifth of what they had been, merchants leaving Port Royal or withdrawing credit, and so forth. When rumors of war against the Spanish arose, Modyford seized upon them to grant letters of marque – in other words, to return to the golden age of freebooter commerce. He described how this transformed the despairing mood of the island: "Your Lordship cannot imagine what an universal change there was on the faces of men and things, ships repairing, great resort of workmen and laborers, many returning, many debtors released out of prison and the ships from the Curaçao voyage . . . brought in and fitted out again, so that the regimental forces at Port Royal are near 400."[52]

The *guerre de course* of the seventeenth and eighteenth centuries played an ever-increasing role in international conflicts; colonial authorities used privateers to supplement the chronically short regular forces sent from Europe. As Modyford made clear, freebooters were encouraged to "render their bravery useful to the prince." Enlisting in wartime, they could raid and take prizes under conditions that were now codified: licences were issued for a given length of time, action was limited to the official period of conflict, rules were established to divide the booty after the state got its percentage, and so forth. To remain within their chosen vocation, many freebooters sub-

---

[51] See C. S. P., *Col. Ser.* (London, Public Record Office) and political and administrative correspondence from the French Caribbean islands, Col. Ser., C7A, 8A, and 9A (Paris, National Archives).

[52] Governor Modyford, August 21, 1666 (C. S. P., *Col. Ser.*, America and West Indies, 1661–1668), 406. To justify the fact that he was giving freebooters arms instead of disarming them, Modyford displayed the same logic as those who today oppose reduction in armaments because it would put them in an inferior position toward an enemy who is not going to disarm: "Had it not been for that reasonable action, I could not have kept my place against the French buccaneers."

mitted themselves to colonial authorities. The new framework allowed what proved to be the largest of all freebooting operations in the second half of the seventeenth century: the sack of Panama by the English pirate Morgan in 1670, and the raid on Cartagena during the War of the League of Augsburg (King William's War) in 1697, a joint operation of freebooters commanded by the governor of Saint-Domingue, Du Casse, with a fleet sent from France under Pointis, a naval officer.

Numerous complaints were raised, however, against freebooters: They were undisciplined under command, mediocre in military performance, and insatiable on payday. But they had to be taken as they were, remarked Exquemelin, who wrote perhaps the most famous buccaneer's memoirs of the seventeenth century, "for they are so accustomed to the buccaneering life [that] it is impossible for them to give it up."[53] One had no choice but to allow them to mount operations of plunder, even though their strategic value was doubtful. At any rate, this way of dealing with pirates had proved more successful than encouraging them to become planters, and the level of disorder on the seas had undoubtedly been reduced.

Although arming and enlisting freebooters under the legal cover of privateering war did curb piracy, it did not eradicate it. Corsairs could not be easily demobilized after peace was concluded. In Defoe's words, "privateers are a nursery for pyrates against a peace." The years following the wars of the League of Augsburg (1689–97) and of the Spanish Succession (Queen Anne's War, 1702–13) witnessed a new growth of piracy. More broadly, privateering wars prolonged the functional association between war and commerce. Indeed, during the wars of American independence, attacking the commerce of the metropolis – for North American and Spanish American colonists lacking regular navies – remained the preferred way to make war at sea.

Things began to change with the nineteenth century. Now, the idea was that "civilized nations" should not allow private individuals to wage wars, and that trade should not be a military target. Napoléon (whose insight was informed by the existing English mastery of the seas) is credited to have remarked:

A time may come . . . when the great belligerent powers may carry on warlike operations against each other, without the confiscation of merchant ships, or treating their crews as legitimate prisoners of war; and commerce would

---

[53] Exquemelin, 225.

then be carried on, at sea, as it is carried on by land, in the midst of the battles fought by their armies.[54]

In order fully to extinguish European piracy (and the American piracy that derived from it), it was thus necessary both to abandon commercial exclusivism in favor of free commerce and to replace privateers by regular navies. At the Paris peace conference ending the Crimean War in 1856, privateering was "abolished." The British delegate thought that "our state of civilization and humanity required that an end should be put to the system which no longer belongs to our time." Although the decision (which was not ratified by the United States, Mexico, and Spain) closed off about two centuries of established privateering, or *guerre de course*, between "civilized" nations of the Western world, at the same time it legitimated the campaigns the same nations would undertake against indigenous "pirates" in the second push of imperialism that was underway. Once again, as mentioned at the beginning of this chapter, non-European commercial competitors would be eliminated under the accusation of piracy.

V

If one considers how seventeenth- and eighteenth-century European monopolies functioned in various trading regions of the world, their weakness at the local level is striking. Ports that had direct, exclusive relations with European metropolises formed a very loose network of control. Only the main ones were fortified, and these were often paired with smugglers' retreats, like Baru near Cartagena or El Garote near Portobello. Secondary ports, for example in the French or Spanish Caribbean, had practically no direct relationship with metropolitan ports but were linked by coasting trade to the main ones feeding transatlantic commerce. Contraband had to make up for the chronic undersupply and exorbitant prices imposed by chartered commercial companies and state-controlled trade circuits. As early as 1619, Governor Nathaniel Butler, of Bermuda, laid out the situation candidly. Within a month after the only ship sent that year by the company had departed, colonists began to lament. Butler was forced to authorize trade with a "a Dutch gentleman from Middleborough" who had timely offerings of "victuals, courne, shoues [sic], shirts and the like."

[54] General Count Montholon, *History of the Captivity of Napoléon at St. Helena* (London: Henry Colburn, 1846), Vol. 2, 288.

Noble Sir, it is noe small advantage that a very mean conceit hath over the perfectest judgement in the world, when the one worcks upon the ground of experience, this other from a discourse of reasonable apprehension only. Being therefore thus advantaged, let me tell you that ther is not a securer nor speedier waye to firm this plantation and to refine it from the miscarriages that maye betide it by accidental meanes [referring to hurricanes] than the discreet admittance and kind wellcome of such as shall warrantably passe in course this waye.[55]

Contraband used cabotage routes along with monopoly trade. Foreign schooners sailed to French or Spanish colonies, bringing cargo to and from large vessels bound for Europe that operated from their neutral entrepôts, like the Dutch islands of St. Eustatius and Curaçao, or from New England ports. Coasting trade and smuggling existed in a symbiotic relationship; exclusive trade and the one with foreign entrepôts de facto coexisted at the local level.[56] Smuggling between islands was particularly important in wartime, when legal transatlantic trade with the metropolis was interrupted. Frequent wars between European merchant states were a principal factor in keeping monopolistic barriers permeable at the local level.

European commercial monopolies functioned differently in Asia, but they were equally weak at the local level. Recent scholarship, such as that of Denys Lombard and Michael Pearson, has corrected previous exaggerated assumptions about European control over Asiatic trade and shown how preexisting networks of merchant communities from the Near East and east Africa to India and the Chinese Sea remained powerful and resisted European intrusion.[57] The permea-

---

[55] *The Rich Papers: Letters from Bermuda, 1615–1646: Eyewitness Accounts Sent by the Early Colonists to Sir Nathaniel Rich*, Vernon A. Ives ed. (Toronto: University of Toronto Press, 1984), 179–80.

[56] Anne Pérotin-Dumon, "The Informal Sector of Atlantic Trade: Cabotage and Contraband in the Port of Guadeloupe (1650–1800)," in *Atlantic Port Cities: Economy, Culture, and Society in the Atlantic World*, Franklin W. Knight and Peggy K. Liss, eds. (Knoxville: University of Tennessee Press, 1990), pp. 58–86.

[57] Denys Lombard, "Y a-t-il une continuité des réseaux marchands asiatiques?" in Lombard and Aubin, eds., *Marchands et hommes d'affaires asiatiques*, 11–17; Michael N. Pearson, *The Portuguese in India*, New Cambridge History of India (New York: Cambridge University Press, 1987), passim. On the local weakness of European monopolies in Asia, see also K. N. Chaudhuri, *Trade and Civilization in the Indian Ocean: An Economic History from the Rise of Islam to 1750* (New York: Cambridge University Press, 1985), 72–73; Niels Steensgaard, *The Asian Trade Revolution of the Seventeenth Century: The East India Companies and the Decline of the Caravan Trade* (Chicago: Chicago University Press, 1974); *Companies and Trade: Essays on Overseas Trading Companies during the Ancien Regime*, Leonard Blussé and Femme Gaastra, eds. (Leiden: Leiden University Press, 1981), in particular, Pierre H. Boulle, "French Mercantilism, Commercial Companies, and Colonial Profitability," 102–5; Pieter Emmer, "The West India Company, 1621–1791: Dutch or Atlantic," 84–6; D. Lombard, "Questions on

bility of the Portuguese monopoly over the Malabar pepper trade is a well-documented example.[58] Pilferage of part of pepper production (sometimes the best quality) as well as armed resistance to Portuguese pretensions, particularly by the Zamorins of Calicut, never stopped. The Portuguese had no control over areas where the pepper was grown; they could only impose contracts on suppliers at low price and sell Portuguese passes to carriers to the main port. In K. N. Chaudhuri's phrase, the Portuguese had "to strike a compromise" with non-European merchants and carriers whose local channels of supply continued to function beyond Portuguese control. As in the case of the Java and Malaysia spice trade, smuggling and legal trade were imbricated.

In every case, the acceptance of a monopoly over the main routes required a state's tolerance of smuggling outside them. To maintain a certain equilibrium between the official exclusive circuits and informal smuggler trade was an important task for colonial administrators. In American colonies, they did this by protecting the functioning of transatlantic trade for the metropolis, while regularly permitting the importation of foreign products under the pretext of scarcity caused by a war or a hurricane. Officials even encouraged their own subjects to engage in smuggling if it produced a greater benefit than loss for the economy of a colony as a whole, as was the case for the French Caribbean with Spaniards who paid in silver. Such strategy might even meet with royal approval: There were companies chartered for contraband, like the Portuguese Companhia do Graõ-Pará e Maranhaõ, which carried commerce between Brazil and the Spanish American province of Quito, via the Amazon and the Mato Grosso.[59] There are even examples of colonial authorities who had to arbitrate between the interests of a contraband company and those of freelance smugglers, as in the case of the South Sea Company and private smugglers of Jamaica, both interested in cutting into Spanish-Caribbean trade.

For local authorities, the key was keeping complicity between royal

the Contact between European Companies and Asian Societies," 183–7; and Om Prakash, "European Trade and South Asian Economies: Some Regional Contrasts, 1600–1800," pp. 194–5; M. N. Pearson, *Merchants and Rulers in Gujarat: The Response to the Portuguese in the Sixteenth Century Western India* (Berkeley: University of California Press, 1976).

[58] Michael N. Pearson, "Corruption and Corsairs in Sixteenth-Century Western India: A Functional Analysis," in *The Age of Partnership: Europeans in Asia Before Dominion*, Blair B. King and M. N. Pearson, eds. (Honolulu: University Press of Hawaii, 1979), 15–41; M. N. Pearson, *Portuguese in India*, 44–51.

[59] Dauril Alden, "Late Colonial Brazil, 1750–1808," *Cambridge History of Latin America*, Vol. 2, 622.

officials and foreign merchants within acceptable limits. "To understand service in hot climate," to use the euphemism of an English governor, was to know how to harmonize legal and illegal trading interests: on the one hand, metropolitan merchant houses and transatlantic exclusive trade; on the other hand, local merchants involved with foreigners. Sent on mission throughout Spanish America in the middle of the eighteenth century, Spanish officials Jorge Juan and Antonio de Ulloa emphasized the laxity of appointed authorities, who camouflaged their excesses with similar euphemisms. On the situation in Guayaquil, the main port in the province of Quito and center of Pacific smuggling for the viceroyalty of Peru, they noted: "In those areas, acquiescing to or patronizing smugglers is generally labelled 'to live and let live'; officials who allow the trade to go on in return for payment of a bribe for each fardo are called men of good will who will harm no one."[60] This chronic fragility of European trade monopolies was never more obvious than when piracy periodically resurfaced, when a policy of control called previous tolerance into question. Suddenly the equilibrium between exclusion and permeability would be shattered because one of the two sides had gone too far: Either a state had imposed an exorbitant control that killed illegal but necessary alternatives; or contraband had developed into a full-fledged counter-system that evidently threatened official trade.

The policy of the Ming dynasty, between the fourteenth and the seventeenth centuries, exemplifies an exorbitant state control that led to a resurgence of piracy, when it sought repeatedly to impose strict control over international trade.[61] This policy threatened the activities of Japanese merchants (the wakō mentioned above) who had penetrated the Chinese coasts, along with their Chinese partners. A well-known episode of this struggle took place in the second part of the sixteenth century: for twenty years, there was a rash of kidnappings, raids, and plunderings from the coast of Cheking in the north to Fukien in the south. These were Japanese raids of defense against a ruinous state policy of a declining imperial power. Ming emperors proved incapable of deploying the measures of control and defense

[60] Jorge Juan and Antonio de Ulloa, *Discourse and Political Reflections on the Kingdom of Peru, their Government, Special Regimen of their Inhabitants, and Abuses which have been Introduced into One and Another, with Special Information on Why They Grew up and Some Means to Avoid Them*, John J. TePaske and Besse A. Clement, trans., (Norman: University of Oklahoma Press, 1978), p. 50.
[61] Wang Gungwu, "Hokkien Sojourning Communities"; Kwan-wai So, *Japanese Piracy in Ming China during the 16th Century* (East Lansing: Michigan State University Press, 1975); Ray Huang, *1587: A Year of No Significance: The Ming Dynasty in Decline* (New Haven: Yale University Press, 1981).

that their policy would have required. To reestablish their sway, they had to use both the carrot and the stick (as would the French and English in their campaigns against pirates a century later), reinforcing the presence of the state on the coasts while loosening the ban on Chinese trade with foreigners.

The Caribbean provides an example of how state power, reacting to full-blown contraband, could trigger a cycle of piracy. Acting on the warranties of the Treaty of Utrecht (1713), Spain began to organize a better resistance against companies of smugglers that had routinely cut into its colonial trade with impunity.[62] It established naval patrols and mobilized corsairs for Puerto Rico and for Venezuela against English smugglers from Jamaica and Dutch ones from Curaçao; and, for the Pacific coast of South America, against Spanish smugglers who, with French and English accomplices, maintained a trade network parallel to the legal one between Lima and Panama. Although it was a time of peace, Spanish pursuit of the smugglers was conducted on a true war footing, "como si hubiese guerra viva." In turn, those whose smuggling had been disturbed resisted with arms and resorted to "forced exchange." In imposing its interests by force, Spain induced the smugglers to return to piracy; confronting them in this form, it had some success in curbing the large-scale contraband that had plagued official trade.

Thus, ironically, the hegemonic nature of some merchant empires did much to keep piracy alive. As long as monopolies went along with commercial wars, piracy simply fluctuated according to the degree of a state's authority at sea. It was the linkage among trade, war, and hegemonic policies that engendered a cycle in which smuggling and piracy alternated. Enlisting European pirates into a *guerre de course* did keep them under control. To eliminate piracy as a phenomenon, however, trade monopoly had to be given up altogether. This was a policy toward which England, France, and Spain only gradually moved in the second half of the eighteenth century.

The episodes of world-scale piracy that we have examined in the sixteenth and seventeenth centuries are indicative of important shifts in world powers that took place then. Piracy was identified with

---

[62] Pares, *Colonial Blockade*; Vicente De Amezaga Aresti, *Vicente Antonio de Icuza, comandante de corsarios* (Caracas: Comisión nacional del Cuatricentenario de Caracas, 1966); Fernando Serrano Mangas, "Contrabando en las costas y corrupción administrativa en el comercio de indias, 1700–1760," *Revista del Archivo nacional* (Ecuador) 5 (1985): 53–63; J. C. M. Ogelsby, "Spain's Havana Squadron and the Preservation of the Balance of Power in the Caribbean, 1740–1748," *Hispanic American Historical Review* 49 (1969): 473–88; Angel López Cantos, *Historia de Puerto Rico, 1650–1700* (Seville: Escuela de Estudios Hispano-Americanos, 1975).

ventures that opened up new trading areas and broke into old established circuits. It emerged more specifically as a response to territorially based merchant empires with hegemonic commercial policies – first Spain and Portugal, then England and France – as opposed to "entrepôt-based empires" such as that of the Dutch in the Atlantic. There are clear parallels between European patterns surrounding piracy in this period and those in Asiatic trade: Spanish hegemonic policy recalled that of the Ming engaged in pursuing pirates; French and English freebooters resembled the sixteenth-century Japanese wakō in opening spheres to new trading powers; and Dutch port cities and merchant political elites had similarities to those of Malay sultanates. Behind variations in forms of piracy were differences in the political economy of various merchant empires.

CHAPTER 6

Transport costs and long-range trade, 1300–1800: Was there a European "transport revolution" in the early modern era?

RUSSELL R. MENARD

INTRODUCTION

It is now a commonplace among economic historians to argue that long-distance trade has been overemphasized by students of the early modern period. The international economy was poorly integrated before 1800, and trade between the numerous units (however defined) participating in long-range commerce was rarely a central dynamic in any of them. Some scholars even deny the utility of the concept of a world economy until more recent times, insisting that we have been misled by the relatively ample documentation generated by international, transoceanic, cross-cultural exchange to exaggerate its importance. We would be better advised, the argument runs, to focus on the internal organization of smaller-scale regional economic units, for it is in the everyday lives of ordinary people far removed from the glamor of the high seas and the counting houses of the great merchants that the roots of modern economic growth must be sought.[1]

I would like to thank Bernard Bachrach, Paul Bamford, Stanley Engerman, and Kathryn Reyerson for comments on an earlier version of this chapter. Research support was provided by the Graduate School and the Undergraduate Research Opportunities Program, University of Minnesota. Susan Cahn, Brigitte Henau, and Virginia Jelitis assisted with the research.

[1] The literature on this question is too large to discuss in detail here, but, for a convenient summary from the perspective of the new economic history, see Patrick O'Brien, "European Economic Development: The Contribution of the Periphery," *Economic History Review* 2d ser., 35 (1982): 1–18. The debate over the arguments advanced by Eric Williams in *Capitalism and Slavery* (Chapel Hill, 1944) is a good point of entry into the issue. The essays in Barbara L. Solow and Stanley L. Engerman,

That message has much to recommend it, but it too can be exaggerated. It is a mistake to argue that long-range trade and long-range trade alone drove the process of economic modernization, provided the capital and the markets necessary to industrialization. But it is also an error to dismiss long-distance trade altogether and to claim that a purely "internal" view is adequate to economic history. It is a mistake to argue for a perfectly integrated world market by 1800, but no one can deny that the enormous increase in long-range trade during the past four centuries had produced a good deal more integration than had been the case in 1400. Long-distance trade must have its due.

So, too, must the cost of transport. Long-distance trade across political, geographic, and cultural barriers is an ancient phenomenon. Before the early modern era, however, most of that trade was in what are commonly called "luxury" or "elite", goods, products that commanded high prices relative to their bulk. Commodities, as Eric Wolf has noted, "tended to move in two different spheres. There was a sphere of local trade and exchange, in which goods for everyday life moved among villages and towns within restricted regions; and the sphere of long-distance trade in valuables, produced for consumption by elites and serving to underline their positions of political and economic domination."[2] This was in large part a function of the high price of transport that limited the movement of bulky, cheap commodities across great distances. By the eighteenth century, those spheres were no longer so clearly demarcated. Luxury goods still played a large role in long-range commerce and in the calculations of international merchants, but so too did food, clothing, tools, and utensils. A major decline in transport costs – one is tempted to call it a "transport revolution" – lay at the center of that change.

Or so it would seem. However, just as one can question the contribution of long-range trade to economic development, one can minimize the contribution of falling transport costs to the growth of commerce. Certainly transport was slow, inefficient, and costly in the centuries before 1400, wasteful of labor and capital, and strapped by primitive technology. But so, too, as Michael Postan has pointed out, was agriculture and industry. By modern standards "the making and growing of goods for sale may well have been costlier than the carrying of goods to the consumer. To put it more abstractly," Postan continues, "the proportion of trading costs to total costs was probably

eds., *British Capitalism and Caribbean Slavery* (Cambridge, 1987), provide an introduction.

[2] Wolf, *Europe and the People without History* (Berkeley, 1982), 32.

less in the Middle Ages than it is now."[3] The growth of trade facilitated by improved transportation did not fuel economic modernization, Postan implies. Rather, productivity gains in industry and agriculture within various regional economies permitted long-range commerce among them despite the persistent inefficiency of transportation. Cheaper goods more than cheaper transport provided liberation from "the tyranny of distance."[4] This chapter addresses that issue by asking if the notion of a "transport revolution" contributes to an understanding of the dynamics of commercial expansion during the early modern age.

Approaches to early modern transport history

The literature on the role of transport in early modern commerce falls into four broad categories. The most venerable tradition, with roots in both Adam Smith and Karl Marx, places the subject within the context of discovery and exploration – particularly the discovery and exploration of the sea – and emphasizes innovations in ship design and navigational techniques. It finds such improvements most impressive, argues the centrality of gains in transportation to the expansion of trade, and favors the notion of a "transport revolution."[5] A second tradition, less venerable but now more widely accepted, embeds trade and transport in a broad historical context, finds technological gains less impressive, and stresses larger social, economic, and political processes in accounting for the growth of long-range commerce.[6]

The issues between these two approaches are most clearly joined in studies of exchange between Europe and Asia, particularly of the displacement of overland commerce by the Cape route in the spice trade. For historians of the "expansion of Europe" tradition, the question was why the Portuguese replaced Levantine merchants as the dominant figures in the spice trade around 1500. Their answer lay in innovative ship design and improved navigational techniques that

---

[3] "The Trade of Medieval Europe: The North," in M. Postan and E. E. Rich, eds., *The Cambridge Economic History of Europe*, vol. II, *Trade and Industry in the Middle Ages* (Cambridge, 1952), 155.

[4] The phrase is Fernand Braudel's, who considers inefficient transport a major "brake" on the early modern economy. *Civilization and Capitalism, 15–18th Century*, vol. 1, *The Structures of Everyday Life: The Limits of the Possible* (New York, 1979), 428–9.

[5] J. H. Parry is perhaps the most distinguished modern practitioner of this tradition. See, especially, his *The Discovery of the Sea* (New York, 1974).

[6] Niels Steensgaard, *The Asian Trade Revolution of the Seventeenth Century: The East India Companies and the Decline of the Caravan Trade* (Chicago, 1974), is a distinguished work in this tradition.

permitted the Portuguese to exploit the inherently superior Cape route, the first step in a process that would move the center of European economic activity from the landlocked Mediterranean to the maritime countries of Atlantic Europe, culminating in the creation of great seaborne commercial empires by the Dutch and English.[7] This view was challenged in the 1940s, most notably by Fernand Braudel and Frederick Lane, who pointed out that the Portuguese dominated the spice trade only briefly and that by the 1530s it was back in the hands of Levantine and Venetian merchants. It was only after 1600 that the Cape route became dominant, a shift that had less to do with European technological superiority or the inherent advantages of ocean transport than with political considerations, commercial structures, and force.[8]

A third group of works on the role of transport in early modern commerce consists of studies of particular trades, ports, or commodities. These rarely take transport costs as their central concern and they seldom address directly the larger issues raised in the approaches just discussed. However, they often report evidence bearing on transport charges, they have implications for those issues, and they bring detail and precision to a debate that is too often general and vague.[9] Finally, there is a literature that addresses the issues of the contribution of transport costs to the growth of commerce directly. Such studies – one thinks especially of Douglass North and his students – attempt to measure productivity gains in transportation. Although plagued by conceptual difficulties and a paucity of evidence on crucial points, studies of transport productivity formulate the issues with precision and provide direction to research.[10]

This essay fits within that final tradition. Its goals are: to identify the magnitude, pace, and pattern of productivity gains in transport

---

[7] See, for an early example, J. R. Seeley, *The Expansion of England* (1895).

[8] Braudel, *The Mediterranean and the Mediterranean World in the Age of Philip II* (New York, 1972), I, 543–70; Lane, "The Mediterranean Spice Trade: Its Revival in the Sixteenth Century," *Venice and History* (Baltimore, 1966), 25–34. For a recent summary of the issues, see Peter Musgrave, "The Economics of Uncertainty: The Structural Revolution in the Spice Trade, 1480–1640," in P. L. Cottrell and D. H. Aldcroft, eds., *Shipping, Trade, and Commerce: Essays in Memory of Ralph Davis* (Leicester, 1981), 9–21.

[9] The literature in this category is large and portions of it are cited below, in examinations of specific trades. I would include studies of transport as an industry under this heading, though at their best, as in Ralph Davis, *The Rise of the English Shipping Industry in the Seventeenth and Eighteenth Centuries* (London, 1962), such works certainly address the major issues in the history of early modern trade.

[10] North, "Sources of Productivity Change in Ocean Shipping, 1600–1850," *Journal of Political Economy* 76 (1968): 953–70; James F. Shepherd and Gary M. Walton, *Shipping, Maritime Trade, and the Economic Development of Colonial North America* (Cambridge, 1972).

during the early modern era; to identify the sources of those gains; and to assess the contribution of improvements in transport to the expansion of commerce. At the same time, this essay builds on the larger literature. It pays particular attention to the relative role of technological improvement (narrowly defined) and structural change in fostering productivity gains. And it focuses on several specific trades well suited to illustrate more general processes or blessed by good data and detailed scholarship.

A focus on productivity gains suggests the possibility of resolving the debate over the relative importance of technology and structure by viewing both as part of an integrated process. Although there were some leaps forward in ship design and navigation, technical advance during the early modern era was often a slow process of accumulating small innovations and subtle adjustments that were then gradually diffused through the world of long-range trade. It is in the process of diffusion that the link between technology and structure is most clearly revealed. Often, the most efficient techniques were specific to certain structural conditions and could spread to other trades only after those structural requirements were met. Further, although this is more difficult to demonstrate, it is likely that the structure-technology link extends beyond diffusion to the process of technical innovation. Trades that were safe and operated on a large scale under competitive conditions for long periods permitted the acquisition of knowledge and encouraged the experimentation necessary for technical improvements.

A distinction between what Robert Lopez called the "inner" and "outer" areas of long-range trade is useful in this context. The "outer" area, Lopez notes, "was a field of large risks and large profits, a frontier where good luck was almost as important as good management," and where commerce was an "adventure." In the "inner" area, by contrast, regular trade functioned competitively and "success depended mainly on efficiency, quickness and almost meticulous weighing of transport charges . . . and marketing conditions."[11] Although it is important to think of this distinction as a spectrum rather than a dichotomy and to remember that the vague boundary could move rapidly with shifting political conditions, the categories help sort out changes in the costs of early modern transport. The most important changes in technology were first developed in "inner trades" that encouraged innovation and placed a premium on effi-

---

[11] Robert S. Lopez, "The Trade of Medieval Europe: The South," in Postan and Rich, eds., *Cambridge Economic History of Europe*, vol. II, *Trade and Industry in the Middle Ages*, 333–4.

ciency. They were then spread more broadly as ever larger portions of the globe were incorporated into an increasingly integrated world economy orchestrated out of Europe's great metropolitan centers.

This chapter opens with a discussion of the concept of productivity and its application to transport history. It then presents a series of case studies: of the wine trade between England and the continent; of the trade between Europe and Asia; and of trade across the North Atlantic during the seventeenth and eighteenth centuries. A concluding section offers an overview of productivity gains in the movement of goods by way of determining whether there was a European "transport revolution" during the early modern era.

Measuring productivity in transport

There are several ways to approach the question of changing productivity in transport. Ideally, one would like to construct a measure of "total factor productivity" for all routes across the entire period by comparing the value of the output (in this case the movement of a commodity across space) to the value of all inputs. One would then go on to apportion changes in the index among the relevant variables. Even if the conceptual difficulties in such an approach are ignored, the task is impossible. Obviously, the data needed for such a measure are simply unavailable even if comprehensiveness is abandoned in favor of a focus on a handful of the better-documented trades. Although total factor productivity in early modern trade cannot be measured directly, the approach has the virtue of identifying precisely the desired result. It thus implies a research strategy by identifying what we need to know to describe changing transport costs.[12]

Fortunately, there are ways of approximating a measure of total factor productivity. One close proxy compares output prices (or freight rates) to an index of input prices.[13] Another assumes that input prices fluctuate with all prices and compares freight charges to the price level in general.[14] A third proxy calculates what Douglass North calls the "freight factor" by constructing an index that compares the

---

[12] The literature on productivity is large, but Richard R. Nelson, "Research on Productivity Growth and Productivity Differences: Dead Ends and New Departures," *Journal of Economic Literature* 19 (1981): 1029–64, provides an accessible introduction.

[13] See Dale Jorgenson, "The Embodiment Hypothesis," *Journal of Political Economy* 74 (1966): 1–17.

[14] Shepherd and Walton, *Shipping, Martime Trade, and the Economic Development of Colonial North America*, 62n2.

price of freight to the total price of a delivered commodity.[15] All of these measures assume competitive industries, which is not unreasonable for most of the trades discussed in this essay. A more important limit is the inability of these various measures to separate changes in transport from more general improvements in productivity. All they can capture are relative changes in the productivity of shipping. Although such a limit may be acceptable in the short term, we are examining more than four centuries characterized by major changes in basic economic organization.

If these general conceptual difficulties are not sufficiently discouraging, there are also major problems specific to the analysis of transport costs and to early modern economic history. Several of these will be encountered in the examination of particular trades, but it is useful to mention some by way of introduction to illustrate the magnitude of the obstacles to precise measurement. Currency is a major barrier. Freight charges and the cost components of voyages are expressed in a bewildering variety of monies that must be transformed into constant values before comparisons across time or between trades are possible.[16]

Weights and measures are another difficulty. Freight charges were levied on numerous units – firkins of butter, tons of tobacco, hogsheads of sugar, barrels of rice, butts of wine, pieces of cloth, and so forth – that confound efforts at comparison. Even apparently standard units can conceal considerable variability.[17] The "ton," for example, seems a precise measure but is in fact quite slippery, changing from commodity to commodity and port to port. A "ton" of sugar contained sharply different weights in Barbados and Jamaica during the late seventeenth century.[18] The Chesapeake tobacco trade illustrates the dimensions of the problem. During the colonial period, for purposes of charging freight a ton equaled four hogsheads of tobacco. Peacetime freight rates were fairly constant at £7 sterling per ton from the bay to England. The unwitting researcher might quickly conclude that

---

[15] North, "The Role of Transportation in the Economic Development of North America," in *Les Grandes Voies Maritimes dans le Monde, XV–XIX Siècles*, (Paris, 1965), 214.

[16] John J. McCusker, *Money and Exchange in Europe and America, 1600–1775: A Handbook* (Chapel Hill, 1978), assembles evidence on exchange rates for the North Atlantic world, and numerous other scholars have produced time series for other regions and earlier times. The work of econmic historians would be much easier if someone followed McCusker's lead and compiled those series in a single publication.

[17] John J. McCusker, "Weights and Measures in the Colonial Sugar Trade: The Gallon and the Pound and Their International Equivalents," *William and Mary Quarterly* 3d ser., 30 (1973): 599–624, suggests the complexities of this issue.

[18] Davis, *Rise of the English Shipping Industry*, 284.

real freight charges changed little. Not so! In 1630 a hogshead of tobacco weighed roughly 250 lbs; by 1770, a consequence of larger casks and tighter packing, a hogshead weighed ca. 1,000 lbs. Far from being constant, the real cost of shipping in the tobacco trade fell at about 1.5 percent per year.[19]

This list does not exhaust the difficulties. Shipping contracts, for example, were often written in such a way as to defy precise calculations of costs and to subvert efforts at comparison, so that some otherwise well-documented trades reveal little about transport charges.[20] Compensation for crew members often included shares in voyage earnings and freighting privileges as well as wage payments, confounding attempts at measurement.[21] Descriptions of ship sizes, critical to the analysis of transport efficiency, are imprecise, inconsistent, and at times simply misleading.[22] All of which serves as a warning: The pages that follow are full of numbers, but they must be read with due attention to "the quality of the quantities."[23]

That is not to say that the questions raised in this chapter are unanswerable. The major cost components of shipping are well known, and it is possible to piece together evidence on passage and port times, crew and ships sizes, capacity utilization, insurance rates, construction and maintenance costs, and the like. These make it possible to describe the direction of change, estimate its magnitude, and identify its major sources. And some trades, particularly those of the Atlantic in the seventeenth and eighteenth centuries, are sufficiently well documented to permit at least an approximation of total factor

[19] See Russell R. Menard, "The Tobacco Industry in the Chesapeake Colonies, 1617–1730: An Interpretation," *Research in Economic History* 5 (1980): 146–9; Shepherd and Walton, *Shipping, Maritime Trade, and the Economic Development of Colonial North America*, 65–76. Freight charges in the tobacco trade are discussed more fully below.

[20] See, for example, the discussion of the payment of freight costs by the Royal African Company in the slave trade in David W. Galenson, *Traders, Planters, and Slaves: Market Behavior in Early English America* (Cambridge, 1986), 15–16.

[21] Dorothy Burwash, *English Merchant Shipping, 1460–1540* (Toronto, 1947), 42–60; Davis, *Rise of the English Shipping Industry*, 133–52. As the early modern era progressed, payments to crew members came to focus almost exclusively on wages, making it possible for shipowners (and historians) to calculate labor costs with more precision.

[22] The literature on this issue is large. F. C. Lane, "Tonnages Medieval and Modern," *Economic History Review* 2d ser., 17 (1964): 213–33, is the best starting point, and John J. McCusker, "The Tonnage of Ships Engaged in British Colonial Trade during the Eighteenth Century," *Research in Economic History* 6 (1981): 73–105, provides a guide to more recent work. Throughout this chapter, I have reported ship sizes as tons burden, deadweight tonnage, or carrying capacity (synonymous terms) rather than in measured tonnage determined by rules developed by shipwrights.

[23] The phrase is Herbert Heaton's, from "Thomas Southcliffe Ashton, 1889–1968: A Memoir," *Journal of Economic History* 29 (1969): 265.

productivity. It is impossible to construct indices of transport productivity in long-range trade for the entire early modern period, but we can assess the extent of the European transport revolution and its contribution to the growth of commerce.

THE ENGLISH-CONTINENTAL WINE TRADE, 1300–1550

The wine trade is a good place to begin. It lacks the drama of the great voyages of discovery or of transoceanic intercontinental commerce, but its ordinary character is a considerable virtue. The trade in wine, as Henri Pirenne long ago noted, was one of the major commercial enterprises of the medieval world.[24] Documentation, at least for the shipment of nonsweet wines from Gascony to England, is fairly rich, sufficient to describe transport costs from the late thirteenth century onward. It was a regular, large-scale, well-developed trade between distinct but relatively integrated economies. Given those characteristics, it is likely that the wine trade approached the "best practices," and thus the lowest transport costs, achieved in the long-distance trade of the region at the end of the Middle Ages. It provides a baseline, as it were, for the European North Atlantic against which the gains of the early modern era can be measured. And it demonstrates that, during the late Middle Ages, "long-range trade" did not require great distance.

The export of French wines to England is an ancient business extending back to the late Saxon period, though the wines then came from the Seine basin, Burgundy, and perhaps the Rhineland, all by way of Rouen. With the rise of the Angevin Empire and the union of England and Gascony, southwest France became a more important supplier. By the thirteenth century, Gascony dominated the English market for foreign wines, and Bordeaux had emerged as the major port. The trade was at its peak from the late thirteenth through the first third of the fourteenth century, when it was generally stable and prosperous despite occasional disruptions produced by warfare (1294–1303, 1324–7), poor crops (1310–12), pestilence (1315–17), and a gentle decline in volume. During this period, exports from Gascony at times reached 100,000 tons, and an average of 170 ships sailed from the region to England each year.

The beginning of the Hundred Years' War (1337) and the visitations

---

[24] "Un grand commerce d'exportation au moyen age: les vins de France," *Annales d'histoire économique et sociale* 5 (1933): 225–43.

of plague to Gascony that quickly followed (in 1348–9, 1362–3, 1373–4, 1411–2) devasted the wine trade, producing a sharp contraction from which it never fully recovered. In 1336–7 Gascon wine exports fell to less than a quarter of their total in the previous year. The trade occasionally rebounded during the following century, particularly during periods of truce, but even at its best the volume failed to reach half the levels exported in the earlier peak years. Nor did the end of the Hundred Years' War permit a full recovery. Rather, the trade stabilized at a low level, with much higher prices and greatly reduced volume when compared to the early fourteenth century. It was also victim of warfare, plague, and the general contraction of economic activity as the North Atlantic moved from the late Middle Ages to the early modern era. Only in the sixteenth century did Gascon wine exports expand steadily, finally approaching the volume of ca. 1300 in the 1560s.[25]

Generalization regarding the design and size of the ships in the wine trade is hazardous. The evidence is thin, inconsistent, and at time contradictory, plagued by the bewildering variety of names used to identify vessels, the imprecision of tonnage measurements, and the lack of specialization common in medieval shipping. Still, the ships of the wine trade seem altogether typical of those used in ocean commerce by the merchants of Atlantic Europe from the end of the thirteenth to the mid-sixteenth centuries. In the peak years of the trade at the beginning of the fourteenth century, the most common vessel was a "round" ship of a type developed by Flemish and Hanse shipbuilders more than a hundred years earlier. For convenience sake, this ship can be called a "cog," recognizing that this is an expansive use of the term and includes vessels variously described by contemporaries that shared a generally similar design.[26] Clinker-built with a

---

[25] This description of the wine trade is based on Margery Kirkbridge James, *Studies in the Medieval Wine Trade* (Oxford, 1971), 1–69; E. M. Carus Wilson, "The Effects of the Acquisition and of the Loss of Gascony on the English Wine Trade," in *Medieval Merchant Venturers: Collected Studies* (London, 1954), 265–78; Y. Renouard, "Le grand commerce des vins de Gascogne au Moyen Age," *Revue Historique* 221 (1959): 261–304; H. L. Gray, "English Foreign Trade from 1446 to 1482," in Eileen Power and M. M. Postan, eds., *Studies in English Trade in the Fifteenth Century* (London, 1933), 13–14, 31–2; and Theophile Malvezin, *Histoire du commerce de Bordeaux depuis les origines jusqu'à nos jours* (Bordeaux, 1892), I, 333–7, II, 222–7.

[26] Burwash found forty-three different terms used to describe English ships during the period 1400 to 1550; her discussion, in *English Merchant Shipping*, 101–44, suggests just how complex the subject is, as does that of Jacques Bernard, *Navires et gens de mer à Bordeaux* (Paris, 1968), 219–377. J. H. Parry uses the term "cog" in a similarly expansive fashion in *The Age of Reconnaissance* (London, 1963), 60–1. On the slipperyness of the concept of ship type, see Archibald R. Lewis and Timothy J. Runyon, *European Naval and Martime History, 300–1500* (Bloomington, 1985), xii.

straight keel, flat bottom, and stern rudder, with a broad beam relative to its length, the cog carried a single mast with one massive spar and a large square sail.[27] Such ships were "bouyant and tubby," which made them clumsy, slow, and difficult to maneuver, but suited them for carrying large, bulky cargoes with fairly small crews in the "rough and unpredictable" North Atlantic seas.[28] During the prosperous years of the early fourteenth century, the cogs working the wine trade were quite large, averaging 120 tons, though ships of only 40 to 50 tons were common. War and the contraction of trade forced a sharp decline in average size, to about 70 tons in ca. 1410, followed by a slow rise to roughly 100 tons in 1450.[29] Despite these shifts in tonnage, round ships of this design dominated the wine trade until the middle to late fifteenth century.

Such primitive ship design joined with equally primitive navigational techniques to impose severe restrictions on ocean commerce. Medieval ships were not fit to face severe storms at sea, nor were they able to drive effectively against contrary winds. Medieval mariners relied more on "pilotage" than on "navigation": Whenever possible, that is, they coasted, taking ships from one place to another within sight of land rather than across open seas.[30] And even the pilotage of the North Atlantic was relatively primitive before the sixteenth century, usually performed without detailed charts, written sailing directions, or even a compass, dependent on dead reckoning, experience, and slowly accumulated knowledge passed on in an almost entirely oral culture.

These limitations forced the ships of the wine trade to hug the

---

[27] The literature on late medieval and early modern ship design is large. I found the following especially helpful: Richard W. Unger, *The Ship in the Medieval Economy, 600–1600* (London, 1980); Unger, *Dutch Shipbuilding Before 1800: Ships and Guilds* (Amsterdam, 1978); Carlo Cipolla, *Guns and Sails in the Early Phase of European Expansion, 1400–1700* (New York, 1965); G. V. Scammel, *The World Encompassed: The First European Maritime Empires, c. 800–1650* (Berkeley, 1981); Lewis and Runyon, *European Naval and Maritime History;* Parry *Discovery of the Sea;* Parry, *Age of Reconnaissance.* The notes and bibliographies of these books provide a guide to more specialized studies.

[28] Parry, *Age of Reconnaissance,* 60.

[29] Jean-Christophe Cassard, "Les flottes du vin de Bordeaux au début du XIVe siècle," *Annales du Midi* 95 (1983): 121; Bernard, *Navires et gens de mer à Bordeaux,* I, 307. Malvezin, *Histoire du commerce de Bordeaux,* I, 276, presents much different tonnage figures but on less comprehensive evidence.

[30] The distinction between pilotage and navigation is Parry's. *Discovery of the Sea,* 24. On pilotage and navigation see, in addition to the works cited in note 4 above, E. G. R. Taylor, *The Haven-Finding Art: A History of Navigation* (New York, 1957); D. W. Waters, *The Art of Navigation in England in Elizabethan and Early Stuart Times* (London, 1958); and J. B. Hewson, *A History of the Practice of Navigation* (2d ed., Glasgow, 1963).

coast, even though this increased the likelihood of encountering pirates, and despite the prevailing southwesterlies that drove many ships to destruction against the rocky shoreline. For the same reasons, master mariners would "wait any length of time to secure favourable winds" and duck into the closest safe harbor at first sign of bad weather. As a result, "medieval voyages varied greatly in length, often taking many months over a voyage which should only have taken a few days."[31] Long voyages of uncertain duration contributed to the high price of transport, forcing up wage bills and victualing costs, raising port charges, limiting the efficient use of ships on multiple voyages over a year, and prohibiting the careful calculation of freight costs as well as a quick response to market opportunities.[32]

Many of these limitations were overcome in the middle decades of the fifteenth century with the emergence of the "full-rigged," or "Atlantic" ship. The literature on this subject is large and the outlines of its development familiar: A brief summary of the main points will suffice here. The full-rigged ship – that "great invention of European ship designers" – was an innovation of such significance that it is sometimes used to mark the transition from the medieval to the early modern age.[33] It developed out of the convergence of the two great shipbuilding traditions of medieval Europe: the clinker-built, square-rigged ship of the North Atlantic; and the carvel-built, lateen-rigged vessel of the Mediterranean. Until the late fourteenth century, those traditions remained distinct, "like oil and water" in J. H. Parry's analogy. Then, a consequence of lengthy commercial contact, they began to interact in the shipyards of Portugal, west Andulusia, and in the Basque region along the Bay of Biscay, "to produce efficient and fertile hybrid combinations" during the fifteenth century.[34]

Despite its name, the full-rigged ship involved improvements in all three of the major categories of ship design: the method of propulsion; the systems that controlled direction; and the construction and shape of the hull.[35] The ships were carvel-built around a skeleton in the Mediterranean tradition, but the hull contained several features associated with northern design, particularly a tall stem, marked sheer,

[31] James, *Medieval Wine Trade*, 119.
[32] The complex methods of paying mariners and masters during the Middle Ages may reflect these uncertainties because shipowners, unable to anticipate the costs of a voyage with any certainty, spread the risks (and the returns) among all participants in the venture.
[33] Unger, *Ship in the Medieval Economy*, 216.
[34] Parry, *Discovery of the Sea*, 21. For the development of the full-rigged ship, see the works cited in note 27 above.
[35] For the categories, see Unger, *Ship in the Medieval Economy*, 29.

and straight keel. They also had higher length-to-breadth ratios than usually found on medieval cargo carriers, a ratio that rose over time as the "long ship" gradually replaced the "round ship" as Europe's principal vessel for long-range trade. Control came from a stern-post rudder not unlike that used on the cog, though the development of a high, square stern forced some changes. By and large, however, improvements in control came from the new hull design and, especially, from changes in the rig. After nearly a century of experimentation, the common full rig "with a spritsail, one squaresail on the foremast, two square sails on the mainmast and a lateen mizzen" emerged as the standard in the North Atlantic by ca. 1500.[36] The full-rigged ship was more seaworthy than its predecessors, could sail closer to the wind, and could be more easily maneuvered, and it could do all this at less risk while sailing at faster speeds with smaller crews. By 1500 such ships were becoming the dominant carriers in the Anglo-Gascon wine trade.

Improvements in ship design were accompanied by better navigational techniques, again reflecting a combination of Mediterranean and north European traditions. For the wine trade, the most important gains were the spread of the compass, the publication of marine charts and sailing directions or "rutters" reporting detail on tides, coastal features, and the depth of the ocean floor; and the use of hourglass, log, and traverse board to estimate speed and distance covered. The most familiar innovations of the age of discovery, the development of "latitude sailing" and celestial navigation, were of little interest to those whose voyages were confined to the passage between France and England.

The most attractive feature of the wine trade for the purposes of this study is the existence of a series of freight charges extending from the late thirteenth to the mid-sixteenth centuries. The data are summarized in Table 6.1, which presents freight rates for shipping a ton of wine from Bordeaux to London in shillings sterling and as a standardized set of index numbers. There are, of course, dangers in constructing a series that spans so long a time, but in this case the underlying evidence seems strong enough to justify the attempt. Wine was shipped in standard containers at two pipes to a ton throughout the period and nothing indicates a shift in measurement or trade conventions sufficient to distort the series.[37] Further, the main con-

---

[36] Ibid., 219.

[37] On measures in the wine trade, see two essays by Y. Renouard, "La capacité du tonneau bordelais au Moyen Age," *Annales du Midi* 65 (1953): 395–405, and "Recherches complémentaires sur la capacité du tonneau bordelais au Moyen Age,"

Table 6.1. *Freight Charges on Wine, Bordeaux to London 1290–1669*

Date	Price per ton	WPI	Freight index
1290–94	8.3(3)	97	80
1295–99	8.0(1)	106	70
1310–14	13.0(1)	116	104
1315–19	6.0(1)	167	33
1320–24	8.0(1)	134	56
1325–29	10.0(1)	112	83
1330–34	10.0(1)	119	78
1335–39	7.3(3)	94	73
1350–54	13.0(7)	130	93
1370–74	22.0(1)	147	139
1380–84	23.0(1)	112	191
1385–89	14.3(2)	104	128
1390–94	14.5(4)	109	124
1395–99	11.6(3)	108	100
1400–04	12.5(2)	116	100
1410–14	21.6(8)	111	181
1415–19	8.5(7)	115	69
1455–59	16.7(1)	96	162
1465–69	15.0(1)	108	129
1470–74	20.0(1)	100	186
1475–79	17.9(4)	88	189
1480–84	25.0(1)	131	178
1485–89	20.8(9)	101	192
1490–94	18.8(4)	107	164
1495–99	18.7(6)	96	181
1500–04	15.2(19)	109	129
1505–09	14.1(10)	100	131

clusions suggested by these data are robust enough to tolerate a considerable margin of error.

The most striking aspect of these data is the long-term pattern they describe. Ignoring for the moment short-term fluctuations (already concealed in the table by the use of five-year averages), it is possible

ibid., 68 (1956): 195–207. Additional data on freight costs in the wine trade appear in Jacques Bernard, "The Martime Intercourse between Bordeaux and Ireland, c. 1450–c. 1520," *Irish Economic and Social History* 7 (1980): 7–21; and Jan Craeybeckx, *Une grand commerce d'importation: les vins de France aux anciens Pays-Bas, XIIIe-XVIe siècle* (Paris, 1958), 161–3.

Table 6.1 (*cont.*)

Date	Price per ton	WPI	Freight index
1510–14	14.2(14)	108	122
1515–19	12.6(23)	115	102
1520–24	12.2(2)	147	77
1535–39	20.3(3)	147	128
1540–44	17.3(3)	169	95
1550–54	40.2(3)	272	138
1616	30.0	562	50
1623	24.0	588	38
1630–49	27.5	617	41
1660s	37.5	646	54

Notes and sources:

Price per Ton. Cost in shillings sterling of shipping a ton of two pipes of wine. I included only quotations in sterling for shipments from Bordeaux to London except for those periods when no such rates were available. Thus, the rate for 1290–94 is for Oleron to England; 1295–99, Bordeaux-Boston; 1315–19, Bordeaux-Newcastle; 1330–39, Bordeaux-Hull; 1395–1404, Bordeaux-Chester; 1455–59, Bayonne-Southampton; 1480–84 and 1616–69, Bordeaux-England. For 1465–79, the price was reported in ecus and has been converted into sterling at the rate of 1 ec. to 3.3 shillings. The number of observations is reported in parentheses. Compiled from Margery K. James, *Studies in the Medieval Wine Trade* (Oxford, 1971), 151–153; Jacques Bernard, *Navires et gens de mer à Bordeaux* (Paris, 1968), II, 598–606, III, *passim*; and Ralph Davis, *The Rise of the English Shipping Industry in the Seventeenth and Eighteenth Centuries* (London, 1962), 210.

WPI. A wholesle price index for consumables in England from Henry Phelps Brown and Sheila V. Hopkins, *A Perspective of Wages and Prices* (London, 1981), 44–53.

Freight Index. An index number constructed by dividing the price per ton by the wholesale price index, setting 1395–1404 = 100.

to identify five stages in the movement of freight charges. Freight rates were at their lowest in the first period, from the late thirteenth century to the 1330s, when the wine trade itself was at its peak and prevailing conditions supported an efficient transport system despite the primitive underlying technology. The beginning of the Hundred

Years' War and the general contraction of trade that accompanied it forced freight costs sharply upward during the second period until, by the early 1380s, they reached roughly three times the level prevailing before 1340. The general reduction in hostilities after the truce of 1383 led to a substantial recovery of trade and a major decline in freight costs during the third period, which lasted at least until 1420 and perhaps to the late 1430s. Although freight charges were much lower than in the early 1380s, they rarely approached the level achieved before 1340.

Freight charges were again high by the late 1450s and they remained so until 1500, despite the end of the Hundred Years' War. The early sixteenth-century recovery of the wine trade brought much lower freight charges during the fifth and final period (1500–1554). However, the improvements in ship design and navigational technique evident in this stage of the trade were not sufficient to produce a return to the levels of the early fourteenth century. On average, freight charges in the fifth period were roughly 50 percent higher than in the first. If there was a "transport revolution" in early modern Europe, it either bypassed the wine trade or occurred after 1550 and the major technological innovations in the shipping industry.

Although it is impossible to construct a formal index of shipping productivity from the available evidence, it is useful to compare freight charges to other prices, to wages, and to the cost of wine. Table 6.2 reports the percent change in wages and prices from the early fourteenth to the early sixteenth centuries. These suggest a real decline in shipping productivity over the period: freight charges rose less than textiles or than meat and fish products, but more than grains, drink, fuel and light, and the general price level. Wages outstripped freight rates, and rising labor costs may have been one source of the industry's problems. Freight charges increased more rapidly than the price of wine, and the "freight factor" in the wine trade (the freight charge divided by the C. I. F. value of the product) rose by about one-fourth.[38] It is worth noting, however, that freight charges fell sharply from the late fifteenth to the early sixteenth centuries, a pattern that does not appear in any of the other price series. Apparently there were real improvements in shipping productivity at the end of our period, though the industry remained less efficient than it had been between 1290 and 1340.

How can we account for this movement of freight charges? Clearly,

[38] Wine prices are reported in James, *Medieval Wine Trade*, 37, 64–9, and in James E. Thorold Rogers, *A History of Agriculture and Prices in England*, vol. 4 (London, 1882), 652.

Table 6.2. *Percent Change in Freight Charges on Wine and in the Prices of Other Products 1300–1349 to 1500–1549*

Freight Charges	+51%
Grains	+24%
Meat, Fish	+81%
Drink	−4%
Fuel and Light	−31%
Textiles	+106%
Wholesale Prices	+16%
Wages, Craftsmen	+79%
Wages, Laborers	+128%
Wine	+29%

Sources: Table 6.1, above; Henry Phelps Brown and Sheila V. Hopkins, *A Perspective of Wages and Prices* (London, 1981), 11, 44–51; Margery K. James, *Studies in the Medieval Wine Trade* (Oxford, 1971), 37, 64–69; James E. Thorold Rogers, *A History of Agriculture and Prices in England*, vol. 4 (London, 1882), 652.

warfare and, more generally, security at sea, played a major role. The impact of war is readily observable in freight charges and accounts for much of their short-run volatility. Indeed, throughout the early modern era, short-term shifts in freight rates were much larger than secular changes over a century or more because the outbreak of war doubled and tripled freights in a matter of months or even weeks, but the end of hostilities returned them to earlier, peacetime levels just as quickly.[39]

War increased the risk of trade by adding the danger of capture to the already considerable perils of ocean travel. Merchants and shippers in the wine trade responded to those risks in several ways, all tending to raise the costs of transport. They sailed in groups rather than singly, sometimes in government convoys, sometimes in informal associations, which lengthened voyages and increased port times because all had to wait for the slowest sailers and loaders.[40] They carried additional guns and men for defensive purposes, thus raising capital and labor costs. At times, such added burdens were substantial indeed: in 1372, for instance, a year of great danger at sea, four ships

[39] Davis, *Rise of the English Shipping Industry*, 315–37, provides several examples while offering the best general discussion of the impact of war on freight charges.
[40] James, *Medieval Wine Trade*, 124–33.

in the wine trade increased their normal complement of men from 34 to 60, 26 to 50, 32 to 60, and 26 to 48. At 22 shillings per ton for the voyage from Bordeaux to London, the freights charged by those ships were among the highest recorded in the fourteenth century.[41] Wine merchants also favored smaller and apparently less efficient ships during wartime, perhaps sacrificing cargo space for faster, more maneuverable vessels that might escape capture, perhaps simply reducing the capital and cargo carried by a single ship to minimize losses should the attempted escape fail.[42] Finally, wine merchants often laded ships to only half their capacity and increased their use of expensive overland routes over coastwise transport.[43] In addition to the higher costs imposed by strategies designed to minimize risks, wartime freights were also driven up by shortages of crews and ships as these were captured by the enemy or diverted to battle and as shipowners and sailors demanded premiums to compensate for the heightened dangers.[44]

Although the increased incidence of warfare accounts for some of the rise in freights in the wine trade after 1340, it does not account for all of it. Freights fell during periods of peace, but they rarely reached the levels of the early fourteenth century. In part the problem is resolved if we think of formal warfare as a particularly intense manifestation of a general political crisis that marked the shift from the medieval to the early modern eras. Simply put, from the 1330s to the 1480s the governments of England and France were too weak to police the seas effectively. Despite reprisals, safe conducts, the convoy system, and royal sea-keeping fleets, piracy was endemic throughout the period, at certain times and places – around 1400 and

[41] Ibid., 25–6.
[42] Bernard, *Navires et gens de mer à Bordeaux*, I, 307. Although the other responses to war discussed in this paragraph seem nearly universal, this was not. The average size of ships often changed with the outbreak of hostilities, but sometimes it fell, as merchants searched for speed, and at others it increased as they sought security in size. The behavior of the Royal African Company is particularly interesting in this regard. During wartime, it reduced the number of medium-sized ships, those too large to easily escape the enemy but too small to effectively defend themselves, and delivered slaves in vessels that were either very small or very large. Thus, mean tonnage did not change with the shift from peace to war, but the variation about the mean increased substantially. K. G. Davies, *The Royal African Company* (London, 1957), 192–3; Galenson, *Traders, Planters, and Slaves*, 30–32.
[43] James, *Medieval Wine Trade*, 17–18.
[44] Just how severe those shortages could be is suggested by Timothy J. Runyon's report that more than 1,000 ships were impressed into the royal service during the 1340s and 1350s. "Ships and Mariners in Later Medieval England," *Journal of British Studies* 16 (1977); 3. See, in addition, M. M. Postan, "The Costs of the Hundred Years' War," *Past and Present* 28 (1964): 34–53; and James W. Sherborne, "The English Navy: Shipping and Manpower, 1369–1389," ibid., 37 (1967): 163–75.

again in ca. 1450, off the Norman and Breton coasts and near the Channel Islands – reaching such intensity as to obliterate the distinction between war and peace. Piracy contributed to the persistence of high freight rates, keeping merchants and shippers on the defensive during times of peace. The more effective policing of the sea routes achieved in the late fifteenth century permitted carriers to relax their defensive posture and operate at lower costs.[45]

Labor costs are the main variable charge faced by shippers, and it is likely that these rose sharply from 1340 to 1550. Certainly wages increased, though this rise was partially offset by the costs of provisions, which were generally cheaper after 1340 than before, at least until they began a sustained rise in the early sixteenth century. One would expect shippers to counter rising wages by reducing crew size, but the need of extra men for defensive purposes in the long era of insecurity may have made such a response impossible. Unfortunately, evidence on manning ratios (usually expressed as tons served per man) is scarce. Jacques Bernard has assembled scattered observations for ships operating out of Bordeaux from the 1380s to the 1490s. Although these describe a few ships as grossly overstaffed (1.7 tons per man) and others with barely enough men to sail them (25 tons per man), most of the vessels operated at about 5 tons per man, and the data show no trend. Although it seems likely that crews were relatively smaller before 1340 and after 1500, when, except during times of active warfare, the seas were more secure, I have yet to find evidence to test that proposition.[46]

Evidence is even thinner for other crucial components of transport costs in the wine trade. We know little about what it cost to build and maintain ships or how long they lasted,[47] about passage or port times, or about how fully merchants were able to use the capacity of

---

[45] Wendy R. Childs, *Anglo-Castilian Trade in the Later Middle Ages* (Manchester, 1978), 43, 48, 161–2; James, *Medieval Wine Trade*, 122–3, 125–6; Bernard, *Navires et gens de mer à Bordeaux*, II, 765–79; C. F. Richmond, "The Keeping of the Sea during the Hundred Years War, 1422–1440," *History* 49 (1964): 283–98; Richmond, "English Naval Power in the Fifteenth Century," ibid., 52 (1967): 1–15; Richmond, "The War at Sea," in K. Fowler, ed., *The Hundred Years War* (London, 1971), 96–121; C. J. Ford, "Piracy or Policy: the Crisis in the Channel, 1400–1403," in *Transactions of the Royal Historical Society* 5th ser., 29 (1979): 63–78.

[46] Bernard, *Navires et gens de mer à Bordeaux*, I, 396n. On wages and provisions costs, see Brown and Hopkins, *Perspective of Wages and Prices*, 11, 28–9. G. V. Scammell provides a brief survey of manning ratios in "Manning the English Merchant Service in the Sixteenth Century," *Mariner's Mirror* 56 (1970): 131–2. See also Child, *Anglo-Castilian Trade*, 166–7.

[47] Unger, *Ship in the Medieval Economy*, 225, suggests that the shift to full-rigged ships of the type described above brought lower construction and maintenance costs and longer-lasting vessels to the shipping industry.

the ships they employed. Nevertheless, some speculation is possible. As Ralph Davis has shown, there were definite advantages to shippers who operated in a large-scale, regular, stable, and dependable trade.[48] Such a trade facilitates the flow of information regarding prices and supplies, encourages the use of specialized vessels suited to the demands of route and cargo, fosters the emergence of experienced masters and mariners, reduces dead times in port, and permits the full utilization of a ship's carrying capacity. Thus, the sharp contraction and heightened fluctuation in the wine trade that followed the beginnings of the Hundred Years' War and the devastations of the plague must have pushed up transport costs. In turn, the steady expansion of the early sixteenth century must have reduced them.

Occasional reports of freight charges on wine shipments from Bordeaux to England survive for the first three quarters of the seventeenth century, before the trade was prohibited in 1678. These are reported in Table 6.1, both in shillings sterling and as an index number to permit comparison with the earlier figures. Clearly, freight was by then cheaper than it had been in the early to middle fifteenth century. Indeed, transport costs had fallen below the prevailing rates of the high Middle Ages, though they were not yet consistently under the lowest prices charged in that era. Apparently, the advance in shipping productivity evident after 1500 had continued into the seventeenth century, finally returning the wine trade to the level of efficiency it had achieved during its golden age. What had happened?

Technical change is one possibility. During the sixteenth century, Dutch shipbuilders reacted to the opportunities presented by the north European trades in wheat, timber, salt, and fish by designing a new type of bulk cargo-carrier, the *fluyt*, or flyboat. Sacrificing speed and defensibility for carrying capacity and low running costs, the *fluyt* had a hull shaped like a long, narrow box, giving it a high stowage factor, and carried a relatively small area of sail, permitting it to operate with a small crew.[49] During the seventeenth century, manning ratios of 15, 20, and even 22 tons per crew member prevailed in England's North Sea, Baltic, and coastal trades, where variations on the *fluyt* were the dominant carriers.[50] Had such ships penetrated the Anglo-Gascon wine trade, a sharp reduction in freights would have quickly followed. Unfortunately, there is little evidence on the issue,

---

[48] Davis, *Rise of the English Shipping Industry*, 380–1.
[49] Unger, *Dutch Shipbuilding*, 35–8; Violet Barbour, "Dutch and English Merchant Shipping in the Seventeenth Century," *Economic History Review* 2 (1929–30): 261–90.
[50] Davis, *Rise of the English Shipping Industry*, 60–1; T. S. Willian, *The English Coasting Trade* (Manchester, 1938), 16.

but nothing suggests that the *fluit* was responsible for the low freights. The Channel trades seem to have favored small, fast, heavily manned ships: Even in the eighteenth century, crew sizes in Anglo-French commerce were much higher than in other trades.[51] Apparently, larger, more efficient markets and greater security at sea rather than technical improvements in shipping permitted the lower freights of the seventeenth century.

The history of freight charges on the movement of wine from Gascony to England demonstrates the utility of the distinction between "inner" and "outer" areas of long-range trade advanced by Lopez. In its peak years of the early fourteenth century, the commerce in wine exhibited the characteristics of an "inner trade," a comparatively safe, predictable business where competition demanded close attention to detail and efficient operation promoted low freight costs. The slow, painful transition from the high Middle Ages to the early modern era disrupted the wine business, turning it into a risky adventure with the features of an "outer trade." Only in the sixteenth century, when the seas became more secure and trade grew, did the wine business again become an "inner trade." Only in the seventeenth century did conditions permit a return to the levels of efficiency in transport achieved 300 years earlier. It was such broad political and commercial developments, not technical innovations in ship design or navigation, that governed the movement of freight charges in the wine trade at the dawn of the early modern age.

THE SPICE TRADE, 1600–1775.

The development of the full-rigged ship and of improved navigational techniques did not lead to a marked decline in freight charges in the wine trade before 1550. Those innovations did have an impact on relations between Europe and the wider world, however, an impact that can be traced, in part, by examining commerce with Asia.

There are two issues in the history of the spice trade that are central to the role of improved transport in the rise of the great merchant empires of the early modern era. The first turns on the competition between sea and land routes, roughly speaking during the sixteenth century. Did the development of the full-rigged ship that permitted the use of the Cape route lower transport costs sufficiently to shift control of the spice trade toward the maritime nations of Atlantic Europe? The second focuses on the movement of freight charges in

---

[51] Davis, *Rise of the English Shipping Industry*, 71.

the seventeenth and eighteenth centuries. Did lower transport costs contribute significantly to the great expansion of trade between Europe and Asia after 1600? A positive answer to either question would provide powerful support for the notion of a European transport revolution in the early modern era.

Recent historiography demonstrates that the answer to the first question is "no," on two counts. In the first place, if shipments by way of the Cape had been inherently superior to the overland route, a permanent shift would have occurred in the early sixteenth century rather than at the beginning of the seventeenth. However, the ascendancy of the Portuguese and the Cape route proved brief, and control of the spice trade was quickly recaptured by Venetian and Levantine merchants. The Dutch and English East India companies took control of that trade not because they managed to lower transport costs but because of institutional innovations that permitted them to internalize the business of protection and to create a more "transparent" market.[52]

Secondly, it is not clear that transport costs on the Cape route were lower than shipments overland. Niels Steensgaard has shown that freight charges in the caravan trade were so small a proportion of the selling price of pepper and silk that even major reductions in transport costs could have had little impact on marketing decisions. However, even if freight charges were important in the calculations of merchants, the data suggest the rather surprising conclusion "that the transport by ship was more expensive than the caravan transport."[53] The full-rigged, Atlantic ship made use of the Cape route possible, but it did not lower freight charges in the Euro-Asian spice trade. The notion of a transport revolution finds little support here.

The answer to the second question is less certain. Was there a major decline in freight charges after the early seventeenth century that fueled the expansion of trade? Freights on the shipment of pepper from India to England and Holland did fall at first, by roughly one-third between 1620 and 1650. Because this was a period in which

[52] See notes 6 and 8 above. C. H. H. Wake has recently challenged this view, arguing that for "the greater part of the sixteenth century – up to about 1550 and again in the 1570s and 1580s – the Portuguese accounted for upwards of 75 percent of Europe's pepper imports and probably as much or more of the spices imported from the East." He concludes that it is necessary "now to re-affirm the reality of Portugal's dominance of the carrying trade between India and Europe and to re-assess the economic and political significance of the Cape route in the sixteenth century. "The Changing Pattern of Europe's Pepper and Spice Imports, ca 1400–1700," *Journal of European Economic History* 8 (1979): 394–5.
[53] Steensgaard, *Asian Trade Revolution of the Seventeenth Century*, 40.

declining prices made pepper more affordable and led to a sharp rise in European consumption, the evidence seems to provide some support for the notion of a transport revolution. However, the lower freights did not result from more efficient ships or improved navigational techniques but rather from structural changes in the organization of trade that reduced the length of voyages and thus lessened costs.[54]

Nominal freight rates on shipments between India and England describe a curious pattern after the initial fall. Freight charges stabilized in the 1650s, hovering about £20 per ton for the next thirty years. Freights were, of course, higher during the turn-of-the-century wars, though they did not rise as sharply as in England's Atlantic trades. Rates were higher in the 1720s and 1730s than they had been in the 1660s and 1670s and they took another step upward in the 1760s, when they returned to the levels prevailing in the early seventeenth century. Although input prices rose between 1650 and 1775, the pattern in freight charges hardly describes a transport revolution.[55]

Unfortunately, the relationship between the nominal freight rates and the real cost of transport to the English East India Company is not clear. Indeed, the operation of some rather complex trade conventions, the details of which need not concern us, rather than a real deterioration in shipping productivity, may account for much of the steep rise in quoted freight rates after 1750. Nevertheless, Ralph Davis suggests, "it may be doubted whether the average rates paid from India in 1770–2 or 1753–5 were as low as those paid on the same voyage in the 1730's or even half a century earlier still."[56]

A look at the characteristics of shipping in Dutch trade with Asia supports Davis' argument. Table 6.3 describes the size of ships and crews on the outward voyage from Holland over the years 1615 to 1775. It shows that the ships in that trade were always large and tended to increase over time, averaging 1,000 measured tons after 1750. Greater size did not bring greater efficiency. The ratio of tons served per crew member rose slowly until the early to middle eighteenth century and then declined. By 1775 the ratio had returned to its level in 1625. The contrast with the Atlantic trades of the Dutch and English is striking. There the prevailing ratios were 15, 20, and

[54] Niels Steensgaard, "Freight Costs in the English East India Trade, 1601–1657," *Scandinavian Economic History Review* 13 (1965): 143–62; Wake, "Changing Pattern of Europe's Pepper and Spice Imports," 389–91.

[55] For freight charges, see Davis, *Rise of the English Shipping Industry*, 262–4; and Bal Krishna, *Commercial Relations between England and India, 1603–1757* (London, 1924), 321–3. On input prices, see below.

[56] Davis, *Rise of the English Shipping Industry*, 264–5.

Table 6.3. *Characteristics of Ships in the Dutch-Asiatic Trade 1615–1775*

Date	Number of ships	Average tonnage	Average crew	Tons per man
1615	2	235	44	5.3
1625	3	620	146	4.2
1665	9	445	88	5.1
1675	24	695	140	5.0
1685	12	753	121	6.2
1695	24	664	114	5.8
1705	23	717	114	6.3
1715	26	756	117	6.5
1725	25	764	116	6.6
1735	30	718	133	5.4
1745	26	768	119	6.5
1755	16	991	173	5.7
1765	24	1011	187	5.4
1775	6	1000	233	4.3

Notes and Sources: Includes all ships on the outward bound voyage from Holland for which both the tonnage and the number of seafarers were reported. Soldiers and craftsmen were not counted as part of the crew. Compiled from J.R. Bruijn, *et al.*, eds., *Dutch-Asiatic Shipping in the 17th and 18th Centuries*, volume II, *Outward-bound voyages from the Netherlands to Asia and the Cape (1595–1794)* (The Hague, 1979).

even 25 tons per crew member.[57] This evidence suggests that there were no gains in shipping productivity along this route in the seventeenth and eighteenth centuries and no fall in the real cost of freight. Other measures of performance in Dutch-Asian trade bolster this conclusion: Travel and port times did not decline over the period (indeed, they were slightly higher in the eighteenth century than in the seventeenth); the rate at which ships were lost at sea showed some tendency to rise, particularly on the return leg of the voyage across the Indian Ocean; and crew mortality increased, again especially on the return trip.[58] The trade between Europe and Asia pro-

[57] See below.
[58] J. R. Bruijn, F. S. Gaastra, and I. Schoffer (with assistance from A. C. J. Vermeulen), *Dutch-Asiatic Shipping in the 17th and 18th Centuries*, Volume I (The Hague, 1987), 67, 69, 72–5, 82–6, 89, 91, 163–4.

vides no support for the notion of an early modern transport revolution.

As we shall see, the poor performance on this route stands in sharp contrast to the experience of other trades where impressive productivity gains were recorded and where the cost of transport fell. Why was the Asian trade an exception? Davis thinks the failure was an organizational one rooted in the monopoly position of the companies. He may be correct. Perhaps the Dutch and English East India companies were guilty of that "negligence and profusion" that Adam Smith attributed to all regulated monopolies, which, spared from competition, paid slight attention to detail, discouraged innovation and experiment, and had little incentive to adopt the best practices of the shipping industry.[59] Although this is a compelling argument, it is not supported by detailed studies of the business practices of the two companies. Those find that the companies were carefully administered and sensitive to costs, characterized by "competition and changeableness rather than monopoly and constancy."[60] Perhaps, on the other hand, the problem lay in the structure of the trade. Ventures to the East, involving voyages often lasting two years, troubled by disease, adverse weather, piracy, and warfare, always remained uncertain and hazardous. Under early modern conditions, exchange between discrete world economies could not acquire the characteristics of an inner trade and thus lacked the essential structural requirements of an efficient system of transport.

ENGLAND'S NORTH ATLANTIC EMPIRE, 1600–1775.

One of the great achievements of the early modern age was the transformation of the North Atlantic ocean into an English inland sea. England's North Atlantic empire is also one of the better-documented commercial systems of the preindustrial era. Its records are sufficient to permit some rough estimates of productivity gains in shipping and the apportioning of those gains among various sources. It is a good arena in which to chart the progress of European transport during the seventeenth and eighteenth century. This section explores freight

---

[59] Smith, *An Inquiry into the Nature and Causes of the Wealth of Nations*, Cannan ed. (New York, 1937), 700; Davis, *Rise of the English Shipping Industry*, 260–1, 265.

[60] K. N. Chaudhuri, *The Trading World of Asia and the English East India Company, 1660–1760* (Cambridge, 1978); Chaudhuri, "The 'New Economic History' and the Business Records of the East India Company," in Cottrell and Aldcroft, eds., *Shipping, Trade, and Commerce*, 45–59; Kristof Glamann, *Dutch-Asiatic Trade, 1620–1740* (Copenhagen, 1958), quotation p. 265.

charges in several of the major trades of that empire, beginning with a lengthy discussion of the tobacco trade, where truly impressive savings in transport costs were recorded, before moving on to shorter comments on the rice and sugar trades and a general assessment of the sources and consequences of the growth of a more efficient shipping industry.

Throughout this section, I report freight charges in sterling without adjustments for changes in other prices. However, in an effort to construct a rough measure of changes in the productivity of shipping, I also report freight charges adjusted by the Phelps Brown and Hopkins wholesale price index, setting the decade 1700 to 1709 at 100. In effect, this assumes that the Phelps Brown and Hopkins series is a reasonable proxy for a weighted index of shipping input prices. North and Walton have attempted a more refined adjustment by contructing such a weighted index. Although theoretical considerations might suggest that I use their measure, there are reasons to prefer the general price series to the more specialized index offered by North and Walton. Over the long haul, both indices change at roughly the same rate and it matters little which is used to assess secular movements in shipping productivity. However, the underlying data on input prices gathered by North and Walton are too crude to capture short-term shifts, forcing them to assume that input prices changed at a constant rate. In practical terms, use of the North and Walton index lets fluctuations in freight charges govern changes in measured productivity over short periods and spreads the rather sharp rise in costs that occurred in the twenty-five years before the American Revolution across an entire century. The Phelps Brown and Hopkins index seems a more realistic proxy for the movement of shipping prices in the short term.[61]

Tobacco

The best documented of these well-documented trades is the shipment of tobacco from the Chesapeake colonies of Maryland and Virginia to England. The tobacco trade grew mightily during the colonial period, with two long upward swings sandwiching a shorter period

---

[61] Henry Phelps Brown and Sheila V. Hopkins, *A Perspective of Wages and Prices* (London, 1981), 52–5; North, "Sources of Productivity Change in Ocean Shipping," 953–70; Shepherd and Walton, *Shipping, Maritime Trade, and the Economic Development of Colonial North America*, 69–72. Over the period 1675 to 1775, both Walton's index of shipping input prices and the Phelps Brown and Hopkins WPI rise at a rate of 0.2 percent per year. Although the pages that follow often criticize Walton's use of evidence, I hope my debt to his pioneering work is clear.

of stagnation. Following the beginnings of commercial cultivation along the bay in 1616, British imports of Chesapeake tobacco surpassed 10 million pounds in the 1660s and 25 million in the 1680s. The trade stagnated from the mid–1680s to ca. 1715 and then began another sustained increase, approaching 50 million pounds by the 1730s and 100 million by the eve of the Revolution.[62]

The measurement of freight charges in the tobacco trade is difficult, requiring more than a series of money rates for freight and some elementary arithmetic. During the colonial period, freights on tobacco were usually levied by the ton, which, by convention, contained four hogsheads of tobacco. Freights were levied on volume, not weight. The cost of shipping four hogsheads of tobacco from the Chesapeake to England remained fairly constant during the seventeenth and eighteenth century, seldom varying substantially from the normal rate of £7 sterling per ton except in time of war when the price jumped sharply, often to more than twice its peacetime level. The amount of tobacco in a hogshead did increase over the period, however, from less than 200 pounds in the 1620s to around a thousand pounds by the Revolution, and the real cost of shipping the crop fell.

Although regional and varietal differences in hogshead weights compound the difficulties, it is possible to create a precise measure of freight charges on Maryland tobacco after 1700; and, with some reasonable assumptions, to extend it backward to the early seventeenth century. The resulting series, the cost of shipping a pound of tobacco from the Chesapeake to London between 1619 and 1775, appears in Figure 6.1.[63]

Ignoring, for the moment, the sharp, short-term fluctuations that were largely the product of war, freight charges reveal an impressive secular decline. The real cost of shipping a pound of tobacco from the Chesapeake to England during time of peace fell from about 3d in the 1620s to less than half a penny by the mid-eighteenth century. Over the entire colonial period, from 1619 to 1775, the average annual rate of decline was an impressive 1.4 percent. The decline was not

[62] McCusker and Menard, *Economy of British America*, 117–43, provides an introduction to the literature on the tobacco trade and the Chesapeake colonies.

[63] For the evidence underlying Figure 6.1, see Russell R. Menard, "Economy and Society in Early Colonial Maryland" (Ph.D. diss., University of Iowa, 1975), 480–4; Menard, "Tobacco Industry in the Chesapeake Colonies," 147; John M. Hemphill II, "Freight Rates in the Maryland Tobacco Trade, 1705–1762," *Maryland Historical Magazine* 54 (1959); 36–58, 153–87; Vertrees J. Wyckoff, "Ships and Shipping of Seventeenth Century Maryland," *Maryland Historical Magazine* 33 (1938): 334–42; and Shepherd and Walton, *Shipping, Maritime Trade, and the Economic Development of Colonial North America*, 191–2.

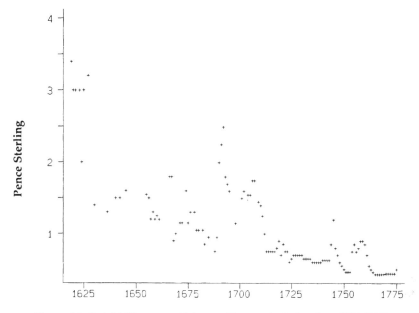

Figure 6.1. Freight Charges on Tobacco, Chesapeake to London, 1618–1775

steady, however. Most of the savings were captured in the seventeenth century. From 1619 to the mid–1680s, shipping costs fell at an annual rate of 2.1 percent; from the mid–1680s to 1774, the rate of decline averaged only 0.8 percent. The gains, furthermore, occurred in a series of brief spurts sandwiched between much longer periods of little or no change.[64]

The first and most substantial savings in shipping costs were captured between the mid–1620s and the mid–1630s, when the price of moving a pound of tobacco from the Chesapeake to London fell from 3d to just above 1.25d: Using 1624 and 1636 as benchmarks, the average annual rate of decline was 7.6 percent. Forty years of stability followed this substantial improvement as freight charges fluctuated gently around 1.3d per pound of tobacco from the middle 1630s to the late 1670s. A second spurt began just before 1680, when the price of freight fell sharply at a rate of more than 5 percent annually, reach-

[64] Adjusting for changes in the general price level in order to more closely approximate changes in shipping productivity yields similar results. Freight rates adjusted by the Phelps Brown and Hopkins wholesale price index fell at an annual rate of 1.6 percent over the entire colonial period, 2.3 percent from the 1620s to the 1680s. amd 1.1 percent from the 1680s to the 1770s. See above, Figure 6.1 and note 63, and Phelps Brown and Hopkins, *A Perspective of Wages and Prices*, 52–6.

ing its seventeenth-century low of .75d per pound in 1688. This falling trend was interrupted in 1690 with the outbreak of war. Freight charges rose sharply to levels not reached since the 1620s and, with a brief exception when peace intervened at the turn of the century, they remained high until the signing of the Treaty of Utrecht in 1713. Freight charges were slightly lower after the quarter century of warfare than they had been before, in large part because planters had countered high shipping costs with larger, more tightly packed hogsheads. In the late 1710s, the price of shipping a pound of tobacco hovered around 0.7d in contrast to the rate of about 0.85d in the middle and late 1680s. Freight charges then fluctuated moderately around .7d per pound before beginning a gentle decline during the 1730s. This decline, like that of the 1680s, was interrupted by warfare, though the rise of freights was less sharp than before, and the return of peace again witnessed lower shipping costs. That gain proved the last captured during the colonial period. From 1750 to 1774 the cost of shipping a pound of tobacco to London during peacetime moved within a narrow range of 0.42d to 0.46d. That stability may conceal a substantial improvement in shipping productivity, however. The general price level, after roughly 120 years of little secular change (despite considerable short-term volatility), jumped by more than a third in the quarter-century following 1750. Holding freight charges steady in the face of so sharp a rise in costs was no mean achievement.

The tobacco trade, it would seem, provides support for the notion of an early modern transport revolution. An average annual decline of 1.4 percent over more than 150 years is an impressive achievement, and the pattern of change – a series of short bursts of improvement punctuating an otherwise steady state – suggests the possibility of several technical innovations in shipping rapidly diffused through a highly competitive trade. Further, given the intense competition between Chesapeake and continental leaf for the European market, the fall in freight costs permitted lower prices and thus helped fuel the expansion of the British American tobacco industry. Perhaps we have found our European transport revolution after all. Closer inspection reveals that this prospect, too, is illusory. Although the tobacco trade did witness some improvements in shipping productivity rooted in technical changes, the major gains had other sources.

Why did freight charges fall? Precise answers are not possible, but we can make some progress by distinguishing between improvements in packaging tobacco and increases in the efficiency of shipping. The most dramatic fall in shipping costs, that of the late 1620s and early 1630s, when freight charges fell by more than half, was chiefly the result of the introduction of standard containers. In the years immediately following the introduction of commercial tobacco cultivation in Virginia, the staple was shipped in bulk, either loose or wrapped in rolls called "hands," or packed in whatever bag, box, or barrel could be found. By the 1630s, although one encounters shipments in bulk or in packages of various shapes, sizes, and construction throughout the colonial period, most tobacco was shipped in hogsheads. This led to a more efficient use of the available space within ships and a substantial savings in freight. Although it is clear that improvements in packaging were the major source of the initial decline in freight charges, it would be an error to dismiss the possibility of greater efficiency in shipping beyond that attributable to the more effective use of space following the introduction of standard containers. Whereas there is no evidence of technical improvements, perhaps experience in the trade led to shorter turn-around times, faster crossings, and lower risks.

The possibility of a technically driven transport revolution in the tobacco trade now seems less likely. The dramatic fall in freight costs of the early seventeenth century reflected changes in packaging rather than improvements in shipping, and we are left with only the more modest gains of the years after 1675. As Walton has noted, we can segregate the impact of improvements in packaging on freight costs from that of improvements in shipping by distinguishing changes in the weight of hogsheads from changes in their size. Between the 1670s and the 1750s, the weight of hogsheads in the Maryland tobacco trade increased by about 250 percent, while the size of casks grew by just under 70 percent. This suggests that more than three-quarters of the savings in freight after the first sharp decline was the product of tighter packing.[65] The case for a transport revolution has almost vanished.

Almost, but not quite. Walton, noting the constant peacetime freight rate for four hogsheads of tobacco and a rise in input prices, argues that the growth in the size of casks provides a lower bound estimate of the gain in shipping productivity. Over the period 1676 to 1776, he concludes, this implies an annual average gain of at least 0.5 percent in the productivity of shipping in the Maryland-London tobacco trade; adjusting for rising input prices increases that rate to 0.7 percent.[66] This is much lower than the figure we began with, but

---

[65] Shepherd and Walton, *Shipping, Maritime Trade, and the Economic Development of Colonial North America*, 65–8; Menard, "Tobacco Industry in the Chesapeake Colonies," 148–9.

[66] Shepherd and Walton, *Shipping, Maritime Trade, and the Economic Development of Co-*

it does leave open the possibility that technical change made an important contribution to the fall in transport costs.

Walton argues that this was not the case. He examined the cost determinants of shipping in an effort to locate the sources of improved productivity. A variety of evidence describes the following pattern for the principal cost components of a voyage: "crew size, armaments, and port-times declined precipitously; moderate reductions occurred in insurance costs; and, in contrast, ship size, seamen's wages, and ship speed remained stable, while shipbuilding costs and victualling costs rose over the period."[67] This pattern, Walton contends, suggests that technical change was not an important source of productivity advance, for improvements in technology would have been reflected in larger, faster ships. Rather, the major sources of change were in larger, better organized markets in the colonies that permitted a reduction in turn-around time, and in the elimination of piracy that permitted a reduction in crew size, armaments, and insurance rates. These were sufficient to produce an impressive rise in shipping productivity despite the absence of technical improvements.

Although Walton is correct that improved markets and increased security were major sources of the productivity gains, he is too quick to dismiss technical changes in ship design and navigation. The difficulty stems from a reliance on evidence that does not measure directly the performance of ships in the Chesapeake tobacco trade. Data on ship size, on ratios of tons, guns, and men, and on port times are compiled for all vessels in the Chesapeake trade rather than for only those ships that carried tobacco to London, and data on voyage times are presented only for vessels moving between the northern colonies and the West Indies. The failure to distinguish the London tobacco trade from other Chesapeake trades introduces a series of distortions in the analysis, several of which exaggerate the role of the market and security in accounting for the observed gains in productivity.

Port times, particularly time spent in foreign ports when crews had to be paid and fed, were a major cost of shipping in the early modern period. Improvements in market organization that permitted ships to turn around more quickly could lead to major savings. Walton over-

lonial North America, 69; Walton, "Sources of Productivity Change in American Colonial Shipping," *Economic History Review* 2d ser., 20 (1967): 67–78; Walton, "A Measure of Productivity Change in American Colonial Shipping," *Economic History Review* 2d ser., 21 (1968): 268–82.
[67] Shepherd and Walton, *Shipping Maritime Trade, and the Economic Development of Colonial North America*, 74.

estimates the decline in port times (and thus the contribution of more efficient markets to transport productivity) in the Chesapeake tobacco trade. He reports a decline of just over 50 percent in the time ships spent in port during the eighteenth century, from an average of 99.9 days in 1694 to 1701 to only 47.1 days in 1762 to 1768. The measure is distorted in two ways. First, it contrasts a period of war, when fully laden ships were forced to wait for later arrivals to complete their cargoes in order that all could sail home under convoy, with years of peace, when no such wait was necessary. Second, it reflects a major increase in the coastal and West Indian trades and thus a rise in the proportion of small ships that took less time to load and spent less time in port. Davis suggests that the decline in port times for ships in the tobacco trade was much smaller, perhaps thirty days rather than fifty, all of it captured by the 1720s. London tobacco ships registered no change in port times from the 1720s to the 1760s, though outport and, especially, Glaswegian, vessels do show some improvements.[68]

Walton also missed a decline in running time by relying on evidence from American coastal voyages. It was not that ships improved their speed under constant conditions but rather that they shifted their routes and thus encountered different conditions. There were two stages to the process. The earliest ships in the tobacco trade followed the tropical routes developed by the Spanish, sailing in a great arc by way of Madeira to Barbados or the Leewards before heading north to the Chesapeake. Although some ships still followed this route, by the middle of the seventeenth century most headed directly west from Madeira to the Bahamas before running up to the bay, followed "the bow" by sailing in a shallow by arc way of the Azores, or ran "the string" along a direct WSW line to Virginia. All these saved a week or more on average over the great southerly arc. The second stage witnessed the development of a route around the north coast of Ireland by merchants from Liverpool, Whitehaven, and Glasgow during the early eighteenth century, which shaved a further week or more in crossing time. The rise of these northerly routes was at least in part dependent on technical changes, in particular the development of the jib and headsails and of the helm wheel, which improved the

[68] Ibid., 198; Davis, *Rise of the English Shipping Industry*, 285–90, 378; Christopher J. French, "Productivity in the Atlantic Shipping Industry: A Quantitative Study," *Journal of Interdisciplinary History* 17 (1987): 623; Richard F. Dell, "The Operational Record of the Clyde Tobacco Fleet, 1747–1775," *Scottish Economic and Social History* 2 (1982): 1–17.

ability of ships to sail into the westerlies that prevailed in that part of the Atlantic.[69] Together with the savings in port times, these shifts in routes produced a substantial decline in the average length of voyages in the tobacco trade, from perhaps nine months in the 1630s, to eight months in the 1680s, to seven months in the 1720s.[70]

Walton's evidence is particularly misleading on the characteristics of ships, the key to his argument that technical improvements were not important in the tobacco trade. Walton describes a sharp decline in the average size of ships trading to the Chesapeake, from 113 tons in the 1690s to 77 tons in the 1760s; a modest rise in tons served per man, from 7.1 in the 1730s to 10.2 in 1768; and the virtual disappearance of guns by the 1760s.[71] All of this is a function of the growth of coastwise trade carried out in ships that were small, heavily crewed, and unarmed. If we concentrate on ships taking tobacco to London a very different picture emerges (Table 6.4).

If size and the ratio of tons served per man are adequate guides, the efficiency of shipping in the London tobacco trade actually declined between the 1680s and the 1720s. Ralph Davis thinks this reflects the changing the role of Dutch-built ships in the Chesapeake. "Large ships," Davis notes, "were always quite common in this trade," and the "lightness of the commodity gave a special advantage to the Dutch flyboat, designed to give high stowage in relation to tons burden."[72] The Dutch were active in the tobacco trade around mid-century, and after their exclusion English shipowners relied heavily on prizes taken in the three Dutch wars fought between 1652 and 1674. As these were used up, merchants returned to English-built ships, sizes fell, and crews increased. However, it is important

---

[69] Ian K. Steele, *The English Atlantic, 1675–1740: An Exploration of Communication and Community* (New York, 1986), 45–50, 90–1; Arthur Pierce Middleton, *Tobacco Coast: A Maritime History of Chesapeake Bay in the Colonial Era* (Newport News, Va., 1953), 8–11; Jacob M. Price, "The Rise of Glasgow in the Chesapeake Trade, 1707–1775," *William and Mary Quarterly* 3d ser., 11 (1954): 179–99.

[70] Davis, *Rise of the English Shipbuilding Industry*, 370. Shorter voyages lowered wage bills and provisioning costs, but it is not clear that they permitted a more efficient use of ships, at least in the London trade. Davis (ibid., 287) reports that London tobacco ships made only one voyage a year and were rarely used for other operations, except for an occasional run to the continent with tobacco where some cargo for the colonies might be picked up. Some Glasgow ships, on the other hand, regularly made two round trips per year to the Chesapeake on the eve of the Revolution. Jacob M. Price and Paul G. E. Clemens, "A Revolution in Scale in Overseas Trade: British Firms in the Chesapeake Trade, 1675–1775," *Journal of Economic History* 47 (1987): 38.

[71] Shepherd and Walton, *Shipping, Maritime Trade, and the Economic Development of Colonial North America*, 195, 196.

[72] Davis, *Rise of the English Shipping Industry*, 286.

Table 6.4. *Characteristics of London Ships in the Tobacco Trade*
1686–1769

Date	Average tonnage	Tons per gun	Tons per man
1686	209		9.8
1715–17	192		
1725–27	138	27.7	8.1
1749–55	168	57.3	11.7
1764–69	182	681.2	13.9

Notes and Sources: Ralph Davis, *The Rise of the English Shipping Industry in the Seventeenth and Eighteenth Centuries* (London, 1962), 71, 299; Christopher J. French, "Productivity in the Atlantic Shipping Industry: A Quantitative Study," *Journal of Interdisciplinary History*, 17 (1987), 630. Davis reports slightly different ton/man ratios than French, whose figures are reported here: 10.8 tons per man in 1726, 13 in 1751, and 15.6 in 1766.

to note, freight costs actually fell during this period of declining efficiency, from 1.3d per pound in the 1670s to about 0.7d per pound in ca. 1720. Apparently, merchants and planters were able to counter the effect of transporting tobacco in smaller, more heavily crewed ships by reducing voyage and port times and by packing the crop more tightly.

Both ship sizes and ton/men ratios rose markedly after the 1720s. Walton attributes the larger ships to improved markets, the smaller crews to safer seas. However, Chesapeake markets had proved capable of handling larger ships earlier, and vessels remained heavily armed in the 1750s, suggesting that the seas were not yet fully secure. Further, the decline in crew size was a general one, occurring in all the major London trades excepting that with Norway, where satisfactory manning ratios were achieved in the seventeenth century. "This dramatic reduction in crew size," Davis argues, "bespeaks a technical advance of some magnitude."[73]

Two improvements are especially notable. First, ships, and especially large ships, were being designed along the lines of the Dutch flyboats, approximating, that is, the shape of an oblong box and thus increasing their carrying capacity relative to their other dimensions. Secondly, there were major changes in rig design, difficult to describe

[73] Ibid., 71.

in brief, but chiefly involving the breakup of total sail area into smaller units and an increase in the number of sails. The result was ships with an improved capacity for sailing close to the wind that could be handled by smaller crews while making faster, safer voyages.[74]

The reduction in crew sizes of the eighteenth century played a major role in lower freight costs. It would be useful to apportion that reduction among the factors responsible for it and thus resolve the debate between Davis, who attributes it to technical improvements, and Walton, who assigns it to safer seas. Data on crew sizes in the Atlantic trades describe an increase in tons served per man during the eighteenth century of 50 to 70 percent (Tables 6.4, 6.7, and 6.9). Evidence gathered by Walton shows that unarmed ships had tons per man ratios that were ca. 25 percent higher than on ships carrying guns.[75] This suggests that roughly 40 percent of the reduction in crew size can be attributed to safer seas, 60 percent to better ships. It is useful to translate these numbers into more concrete terms. In 1725 a 200-ton ship in the tobacco trade would carry a crew of 25; in 1765, it would have 14 men. We can attribute the disappearance of 4 or 5 of those men to more secure seas, of 6 or 7 to more efficient ships.

Finally, it is possible that Walton underestimated the rise in shipping productivity relative to improved packaging in accounting for the decline of freight charges in the tobacco trade. The change in the volume of a hogshead (and thus of the space it would occupy in a ship's hold) is a critical figure in Walton's analysis, serving as the basis for his lower-bound estimate of shipping productivity. There is no direct evidence on the issue, forcing Walton to rely on legislation setting the maximum dimensions of hogsheads. These describe a rise from 13.2 to 22.2 cubic feet, all of it occurring between 1692 and 1694, after which date the maximum legal size did not increase.[76] However, there is some indirect evidence that the size (and not only the weight) of tobacco hogsheads rose in the eighteenth century. Christopher French reports that the number of hogsheads carried on ships in the London tobacco trade declined from 3 to 1.9 between the 1720s and the 1760s.[77] This is a rather puzzling pattern contradicting all the

---

[74] These changes have not received as much attention as those surrounding the development of the full-rigged ship, but see Davis, *Rise of the English Shipping Industry*, 72–3; and J. H. Parry, *Trade and Dominion: European Overseas Empires in the Eighteenth Century* (London, 1974), 278–80.

[75] Shepherd and Walton, *Shipping, Maritime Trade, and the Economic Development of Colonial North America*, 201–3.

[76] Ibid., 66–8. The legislation is summarized in Lewis C. Gray, *History of Agriculture in the Southern United States to 1860* (Washington, D.C., 1933), I, 220–1.

[77] French, "Productivity in the Atlantic Shipping Industry," 636.

Table 6.5. *Estimated Sources of Lower Freight Costs in the Chesapeake to London Tobacco Trade, 1620–1775*

Better Packaging	80%
Better Ships	8%
Bigger Markets	6%
Safer Seas	6%

Source: See text.

evidence indicating a growing efficiency of shipping, unless two hogs-heads in 1760 occupied as much space as three had in 1720. If that were the case, the rise of shipping productivity – and the impact of technical change on freight costs – was greater than Walton allowed.

Can we apportion the decline in tobacco freights among its various sources? Not precisely, but orders of magnitude can be suggested. Freight costs fell from 3d per pound in 1620 to .4d in 1770, a decline of 2.6d. All of the savings before 1635 and, a conservative estimate, half of those after, reflected better packaging, accounting for ca. 2.1d, or 80 percent of the fall. That leaves a half penny for distribution among the remaining sources of improvement: better markets, safer seas, and more efficient ships. The analysis of changing crew size presented above suggests the relative role of better ships and more secure seas, and it seems reasonable to assume that improved markets were as important as the elimination of pirates in lowering freights. Given that assumption, the ratio of better ships to more efficient markets to safer seas as sources of productivity gains in transport was 4:3:3. The results of this exercise, admittedly fanciful but surely not wildly misleading, are summarized in Table 6.5.

Freight charges declined considerably in the Chesapeake tobacco industry, but there was no transport revolution led by technical changes that drove the expansion of long-range trade. The bulk of the savings were achieved by the rather simple practice of using standard containers and taking care to pack them tightly. There were real gains in shipping productivity achieved in the trade, but, though Walton underestimates the role of techincal change, he is probably correct that most of those gains reflected more efficient markets and safer seas. This is not to deny that lower transport costs were im-portant in the tobacco trade. The freight factor in that trade fell sub-stantially in the century after 1670, from some 60 to 80 percent of the planter's English selling price to only 10 to 20 percent of it.[78] Given the importance of continental markets to the growth of the tobacco industry in the eighteenth century and the role of lower prices in the penetration of those markets, it is clear that lower freight charges were critical to the expansion of this particular branch of long-range commerce. However, it is to deny that the history of shipping in the tobacco industry supports the notion of a European transport revolution in the early modern age.

Sugar

The sugar trade was the most valuable of Britain's American trades. The pattern of growth bears at least a rough resemblance to that of the tobacco industry. British imports of muscavado sugar describe a rapid increase to the last decade of the seventeenth century, a fourfold rise in fifty years, followed by stagnation at around 40 million pounds in the quarter century of war after 1689. British muscavado sugar imports doubled between 1710 and 1730, declined slightly until the late 1740s, and then doubled again in a sustained rise that lasted until the Revolution.[79]

Measuring freight costs in the sugar trade is complex. Again, the problems stem from trade conventions and hogshead weights. Sugar, like tobacco, paid freight on a customary ton of four hogsheads during the seventeenth century. Sugar planters followed tobacco growers and increased the size and weight of casks in order to lower freight charges. Sugar was a heavy product, however; and, unlike tobacco, freights were levied on weight rather than volume. This forced merchants to abandon the trade convention, by 1697 on most of the islands, somewhat later at Jamaica.[80] Armed with this information, data on hogshead weights, and a series of nominal freight rates, it is possible to compute the real cost of shipping sugar to England.

The results, presented in Table 6.6, are surprising, for they show generally stable freight costs over the long term.[81] One would not

---

[78] Davis, *Rise of the English Shipping Industry*, 290.

[79] McCusker and Menard, *Economy of British America*, 144–8, provides an introduction to the literature on the sugar trade and the British West Indies.

[80] John J. McCusker, "The Rum Trade and the Balance of Payments of the Thirteen Continental Colonies, 1650–1775" (Ph.D. diss., University of Pittsburgh, 1970), 768–878, provides a clear guide through these complexities.

[81] Walton reports a substantial decline in freight costs in the sugar trade over the period 1678 to 1717 based on different assumptions about hogshead weights and the size of the ton. Shepherd and Walton, *Shipping, Maritime Trade, and the Economic Development of Colonial North America*, 68–9.

Table 6.6. *Peacetime Freight Charges on Sugar*
Barbados and Jamaica to London, 1650s to 1760s

	Barbados				Jamaica			
Date	Price per ton	Hogshead weight (in pounds)	Price per pound	Adj price	Hogshead weight (in pounds)	Price per ton	Price per pound	Adj price
1650–70	77.5s	784	.30d	.28d				
1678–82	79.0	896	.26	.26	896	124.0s	.42d	.42d
1683–88	91.0	1050	.26	.26	966	104.0	.32	.32
1698–02	61.0		.33	.29	1064	161.0	.45	.39
1714–17	72.0		.39	.36	1386	186.0	.40	.37
1760s	65.0		.35	.29		73.8	.40	.34

Notes and Sources: The price per ton is in shillings sterling. The price per pound is in pence sterling. The adjusted price is the price per pound divided by the Phelps Brown and Hopkins wholesale price index, setting 1700–1709 to 100. Henry Phelps Brown and Sheila V. Hopkins, *A Perspective of Wages and Prices* (London, 1981), 52–55. Ralph Davis, *The Rise of the English Shipping Industry in the Seventeenth and Eighteenth Centuries* (London, 1962), 282–285; John J. McCusker, "The Rum Trade and the Balance of Payments of the Thirteen Continental Colonies, 1650–1775" (Ph.D. diss., University of Pittsburgh, 1970), 768–878.

Table 6.7. *Characteristics of London Ships Trading to Jamaica 1686–1766*

Date	Average tonnage	Tons per gun	Tons per man
1686	214		8.7
1717	178		
1726	168		8.6
1752–55	153	39.8	10.5
1764–65	198	92.0	11.9

Sources: Ralph Davis, *The Rise of the English Shipping Industry in the Seventeenth and Eighteenth Centuries* (London, 1962), 71, 298; Christopher J. French, "Productivity in the Atlantic Shipping Industry: A Quantitative Study," *Journal of Interdisciplinary History*, 17 (1987), 631.

expect the real cost of shipping sugar to fall as sharply as in tobacco: The gains from packaging that played the major role in reducing freight costs in the tobacco trade were simply not available to sugar planters. However, one would expect the more efficient markets, safer seas, and technical improvements in hull construction and rig design that led to higher shipping productivity in the Chesapeake trade to operate in the Caribbean as well. Indeed, the evidence indicates that they did so operate: data on ship sizes, armaments, and manning ratios in the sugar trade replicated the pattern of change over time observed on the tobacco route (compare Tables 6.4 and 6.7). Why didn't sugar freights fall?

Ralph Davis suggests one answer: "The economies of larger and cheaper ships," he argues, were not "passed on to sugar planters . . . because the demand for shipping in this trade was rising very fast in the middle decades of the eighteenth century."[82] The high share of England's American fleet needed to bring the sugar crop home provides support for that contention, though it is surprising that persistently higher earnings did not call forth more ships. Security at sea is another possibility. Piracy was always a greater danger in the Caribbean than in North America and it remained a persistent threat around the islands long after it had been nearly eradicated along the continental coast. Perhaps continued dangers in the West Indian trade prevented shippers from taking full advantage of the technical improvements of the eighteenth century. This suggestion finds support in the evidence that sugar ships carried more guns and larger crews

[82] Davis, *Rise of the English Shipping Industry*, 284.

than ships trading to North America. Finally, constant freight costs do not mean there were no improvements in shipping productivity. Input prices went up during the colonial period: Seamen's wages rose slightly, while shipbuilding and victualing costs rose sharply.[83] Apparently, in the sugar trade the gains in productivity were just adequate to hold freight charges steady in the face of rising costs. Whatever the explanation, the sugar trade offers little support for the notion of a European transport revolution.

Rice

Commercial rice cultivation began in the Carolina low country during the 1690s. The crop "soon became the chief support of the colony, and its great source of opulence," "as much their staple Commodity, as Sugar is to Barbados and Jamaica, or Tobacco to Virginia and Maryland." The pattern of rice exports resembles that of the other great American colonial staples, rising in two long upward sweeps sandwiching a much shorter period of stagnation. Rice exports grew at a rapid but steadily decelerating pace, reaching six million pounds in 1720 and 40 million by 1740. More than a decade of stagnation from the early 1740s to the 1750s was followed by a fairly steady expansion. By the eve of independence, rice was one of America's most valuable crops, ranking third among exports from the British continental colonies, behind tobacco and wheat products, accounting for 10 percent of the value of all commodities shipped from British North America.[84]

In contrast to sugar and tobacco, where trade conventions and changing hogshead weights confound the historian of freight charges, measuring transport costs in the rice trade is straightforward. Freight rates were levied per ton of rice, and nothing suggests that the real weight of a ton in this trade changed over the colonial period. Unfortunately, few observations of freight rates have turned up for the early eighteenth century, but a nearly continuous series is available

[83] On wages, see ibid., 135–7; Gary B. Nash, *The Urban Crucible: Social Change, Political Consciousness, and the Origins of the American Revolution* (Cambridge, Mass., 1979), 392–4; and Billy G. Smith, "The Material Lives of Laboring Philadelphians, 1750–1800," *William and Mary Quarterly* 3d ser., 38 (1981): 191–2. On shipbuilding costs, see Davis, *Rise of the English Shipping Industry*, 372–5; and Robert G. Albion, *Forests and Sea Power* (Cambridge, Mass., 1926), 92–3. On victualing costs, see Shepherd and Walton, *Shipping, Maritime Trade, and the Economic Development of Colonial North America*, 69–71.

[84] Alexander Hewatt, *An Historical Account of the Rise and Progress of the Colonies of South Carolina and Georgia* (London, 1779), I, 119; [James Glen], *A Description of South Carolina* (London, 1761), 87. McCusker and Menard, *Economy of British America*, 169–88, introduces the rice trade and the low country.

Table 6.8. *Freight Charges on Rice, Charleston to England 1698–1774*

Date	Rate per Ton (in shillings)	Adjusted Rate (in shillings)
1698	100.0	77.0
1700	100.0	88.0
1726	60.0	55.7
1730	50.0	49.3
1739	56.3	60.8
1740	80.2	73.6
1741	84.4	70.0
1742	70.0	65.5
1743	80.0	81.6
1744	73.2	83.5
1745	120.0	134.2
1747	100.0	102.8
1748	130.0	128.2
1751	52.5	51.6
1755	76.7	78.4
1756	90.0	88.3
1757	95.0	76.6
1759	120.0	105.4

from 1739 to 1774. The evidence is summarized in Table 6.8. It shows, in addition to the usual war-induced fluctuations, an impressive decline in freight charges over the eighteenth century, from 100 shillings per ton around 1700 to 60s in the 1720s, 50 to 55 in the early 1750s, 40 to 45 in the 1760s, and 32 to 38 (and even to 20 shillings at their lowest) by the early 1770s. Given the rise in input prices in the eighteenth century, this is clear evidence of a substantial improvement in shipping productivity. Indeed, adjustments for changes in the general price level imply that productivity grew at roughly 1.4 percent per year from 1700 to the eve of the Revolution.

Converse Clowse has assembled data on the characteristics of Charleston shipping that helps to identify the sources of the gain in productivity (Table 6.9). Although the trends were reversed by warfare (note the figures for 1758), ship sizes grew by more than half over the period, while crews and armaments fell sharply. Although Charleston ships carried larger crews and more guns than was common in the tobacco and sugar trades, suggesting that the seas there were less safe than on the northern route or even in the Caribbean,

Table 6.8 (*cont.*)

Date	Rate per Ton (in shillings)	Adjusted Rate (in shillings)
1762	103.6	95.9
1763	73.5	66.3
1764	46.2	38.3
1767	45.0	33.7
1768	41.2	31.2
1771	20.0	15.2
1772	43.3	29.9
1773	39.6	27.3
1774	46.5	31.8

Notes and Sources: This is a preliminary table drawn chiefly from *The Papers of Henry Laurens*, ed. by Philip M. Hamer, *et al.* (Columbia, S.C., 1968–); *The Letterbook of Robert Pringle, 1737–1745*, ed. by Walter B. Edgar (Columbia, S.C., 1972), and The Records of the Secretary, South Carolina Department of Archives and History, Columbia, South Carolina. A more complete series will appear in Russell R. Menard, "Freight Charges in the Carolina Rice Trade," forthcoming. The rate per ton is given in shillings sterling. The adjusted rate is the rate per ton divided by the Phelps Brown and Hopkins wholesale price index, setting 1700–1709 to 100. Henry Phelps Brown and Sheila V. Hopkins, *A Perspective of Wages and Prices* (London, 1981), 54–55.

the changes are remarkable. Again, we can attribute the improvements to larger, better organized markets, more secure seas, and more efficient ships, though in what proportions it is impossible to say.

Making the North Atlantic an English sea

It was not only in the great staple trades in tobacco and rice that English shippers recorded impressive productivity gains. As Gary Walton has shown, major improvements were also achieved in the shipment of oil and bullion from the northern colonies to London and in the American coastwise trade with the West Indies, and somewhat smaller gains appear in the Anglo-Portuguese wine trade.[85] There

---

[85] Shepherd and Walton, *Shipping, Naritime Trade, and the Economic Development of Colonial North America*, 69.

Table 6.9. *Characteristics of Ships Clearing Charleston 1724–1766*

Date	Average tonnage	Tons per gun	Tons per man
1724	92	18.4	8.4
1731	96	19.2	8.7
1738	112	18.7	10.2
1758	161	16.1	7.0
1766	149	37.2	12.4

Source: Converse D. Clowse, *Measuring Charleston's Overseas Commerce, 1717–1767: Statistics from the Port's Naval Lists* (Washington, D.C., 1981), 112–114. Clowse organized the data by vessel type. The table reports data on "ships," the largest vessels clearing Charleston, most of which carried rice to Europe.

was, apparently, a general increase in the productivity of shipping in Britain's north Atlantic empire during the colonial period. How can it be explained? And what role did it play in that great transformation that marks the end of the early modern age: the English Industrial Revolution?

One way of approaching the sources of productivity change in the English Atlantic is to look at trades where no gains were captured or where improvements were minimal. The timber trade with Norway meets those conditions: As Ralph Davis notes, "there was no substantial change in peacetime timber freights from Norway during more than one-and-a-half centuries – between the 1620s and 1790s."[86] The trade was large and stable, conducted across safe seas except in wartime in specially designed ships that turned around quickly, made four to five voyages per year, were always loaded to capacity, and carried small crews. There was little room for improvement in the Norway trade: It operated at peak efficiency under early modern conditions from at least the beginning of the seventeenth century. The Norway trade provides powerful support for Walton's contention that better markets and safer seas rather than technical improvements in ship design drove down the cost of transport in England's long-range commerce. The history of freight charges in the Atlantic trades involved extending the commercial and political conditions that prevailed in the North Sea to the American colonies, turning the north Atlantic ocean into an English inland sea. As that broad political and

[86] Davis, *The Rise of the English Shipping Industry*, 223.

economic process developed, the technical accomplishment of the Norway trade – the "best practices" of the shipping industry – spread to other parts of Britain's commercial empire.

At best, the sugar trade also shows only minor gains in productivity, but it is more puzzling. The characteristics of shipping changed during the eighteenth century: Ships became larger and carried fewer guns and smaller crews. One would expect these developments to generate improved productivity and lower freights, but they did not. Perhaps the sugar trade defines the limits of the process. English merchants transformed the north Atlantic into an inland sea while building their Old Empire, but the Caribbean remained "beyond the line."

The trade in slaves also shows no improvement in shipping productivity. Indeed, as David Richardson has shown, freight charges nearly doubled in the century after 1680 and the productivity of shipping probably fell. Slavers were unable to capture the efficiencies gathered in other Atlantic trades for two reasons. For one thing, turn-around times on the African coast rose during the eighteenth century, adding roughly two months to average voyage length, as the increase in the volume of the trade stretched the capacity of suppliers to fill ships quickly. For another, the need to control slaves during the middle passage made it impossible for shippers to reduce crew sizes. In the late eighteenth century, when the other Atlantic trades operated at ratios of 15 and even 20 tons per crew member, Bristol and Liverpool slavers ran at only 3 to 5 tons per man.[87] We are again at the limits of the process. Slaving was always too violent and bloody a business to become an "inner trade."

Although commercial and political developments deserve the major credit for reducing freight costs in England's Atlantic empire, technical changes in ship design played a part. Improvements in rigging and the development of the helm wheel, for example, permitted the use of shorter routes that required sailing close to the wind while allowing the major reduction in crew sizes apparent in the eighteenth century. Further, it is a mistake to view commercial practices, political change, and technology in isolation from one another. Clearly, they interacted as merchants applied the appropriate technology to shifting conditions. It was not simply that markets grew, the seas became more

[87] David Richardson, "The Costs of Survival: The Transport of Slaves in the Middle Passage and the Profitability of the 18th-Century British Slave Trade," *Explorations in Economic History* 24 (1987): 178–96. For the case that there were productivity gains in this trade, see H. A. Gemery, and J. S. Hogendron, "Technological Change, Slavery, and the Slave Trade," in C. Dewey and A. G. Hopkins, eds., *The Imperial Impact: Studies in the Economic History of Africa and Asia* (London, 1978), 243–58.

secure, and freights fell. Rather, larger markets and safer seas encouraged innovation and promoted the diffusion of the most efficient shipping technology – the "best practices" – across ever larger portions of the globe.

"What part did the shipping industry play in preparing for the greatest of all changes, the Industrial Revolution of the late eighteenth century?" The question is from Ralph Davis, as is the answer: "a very small part indeed."[88] Cheaper freights were helpful to the growth of the English economy, but they were not essential. They provided consumers cheaper goods and permitted a greater volume of trade than would have been the case had transport costs not fallen, but they touched off no fundamental transformation. It was only when industrialization was in full swing, in the century after 1775, that a truly dramatic fall in freight costs occurred.[89] If there was a transport revolution that drove the growth of trade and promoted industrial development, it happened then, in the nineteenth century. The great merchant empires of the early modern era had other sources.

CONCLUSION

It is useful to end where we started, with the wine trade. A long series of freight charges stretching from the 1590s to 1783, is available for wine shipments from southern Europe – Malaga, Cadiz, Lisbon, and Oporto – to England, and appears in Table 6.10. Reducing those rates by a constant to account for the greater distance, it is possible to splice this series with that for Bordeaux to London and construct an index of freight charges in the wine trade that extends from the late thirteenth to the late eighteenth centuries (Figure 6.2). Although the index ought to be approached cautiously, it does provide a grand overview of the movement of freight charges in a major trade across the entire early modern period and thus permits an assessment of the extent of the "European transport revolution."

Clearly, starting points are crucial. If one begins in the late fifteenth century the case for a European transport revolution – of major gains in shipping productivity driven by the improvements in ship design and navigational techniques of the age of discovery – is strong. From the late fifteenth to the mid-eighteenth centuries, the freight index fell at a rate of 0.7 percent per year, an impressive performance by pre-industrial standards. The major gains, furthermore, were cap-

---

[88] Davis, *Rise of the English Shipping Industry*, 391.
[89] C. Knick Harley, "Ocean Freight Rates and Productivity, 1740–1913: The Primacy of Mechanical Invention Reaffirmed," *Journal of Economic History* 48 (1988): 851–76.

Table 6.10. *Freight Charges on Wine, Southern Europe to London*
1590–1783

Date	Price per ton	From	WPI	Freight index	Adjusted index
1590s	47.5	Malaga	472	94	54
1604–49	77.5	Malaga	524	137	79
1660s	65	Malaga	646	94	54
1684	71.2	Malaga	570	116	67
1685–86	68.1	Malaga	605	105	61
1696	160	Cadiz	697	213	124
1700–02	90	Lisbon	613	136	79
1720s	40	Lisbon	608	61	35
1730s	30	Oporto	553	50	29
1740–41	90	Oporto	678	123	72
1754–55	30	Oporto	596	47	27
1757–58	80	Oporto	732	102	59
1760–62	62.5	Oporto	632	92	53
1764–66	36.2	Oporto	733	46	27
1783	40	Oporto	869	43	25

Notes and sources: WPI. A wholesale price index for consumables in England from Henry Phelps Brown and Sheila V. Hopkins, *A Perspective of Wages and Prices* (London, 1981), 44–55.

Freight Index. An index number constructed by dividing the price per ton by the WPI, setting 1395–1404 = 100.

Adjusted Freight Index. The Freight Index multiplied by a constant (.574, the ratio of freight charges from Bordeaux to London to freight charges from Southern Europe to London during the 1660s) to account for the difference in distance.

Price per ton. Cost in shillings sterling of shipping a ton of two pipes of wine. Compiled from Ralph Davis, *The Rise of the English Shipping Industry in the Seventeenth and Eighteenth Centuries* (London, 1962), 210; James F. Shepherd and Gary M. Walton, *Shipping, Maritime Trade, and the Economic Development of Colonial North America* (Cambridge, 1972), 193; and H.E.S. Fisher, *The Portugal Trade: A Study of Anglo-Portuguese Commerce, 1700–1770* (London, 1971), 121–122.

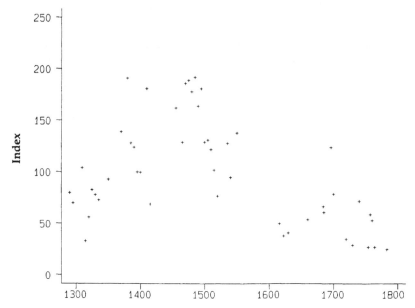

Figure 6.2. Index of Freight Charges on Wine, Continental Europe to England, 1290–1783.

tured early, before 1650, at precisely the time when the new, full-rigged, Atlantic ship came to dominate commerce. From the 1480s to the 1620s, the freight index fell at an annual rate of 1.2 percent, an impressive performance by *any* standard. Here is the case for the centrality of technical improvements in shipping to the rise of Europe's merchant empires during the early modern age.

Things look much different with a longer view. If we begin in the early fourteenth century, the case for a European transport revolution led by technical innovations vanishes. Freight charges in the mid-eighteenth century were only slightly lower than in the best years of the high Middle Ages; productivity gains in transport were not impressive compared to advances in agriculture and manufacturing. Perhaps Postan was correct: Insofar as improvements in productivity fueled the growth of long-range trade, it was cheaper goods more than cheaper transport that liberated the early modern world from the tyranny of distance. More likely, productivity gains rooted in better techniques played only a minor role in the growth of trade. Broad political and commercial developments fostered the safe shipment of large quantities across great distances by turning the oceans of the world into a vast inland sea dominated by Europe's major metropolitan capitals. That process rather than technical improvements in transportation drove the rise of merchant empires.

It will not do to dismiss improved transport entirely. It was cheaper to ship commodities across great distances in 1750 than in 1500 or during the high Middle Ages. And, even if cheaper freights were mostly a function of smoother markets and safer seas, better ships and better navigators were a part of the process. Indeed, the marked increase in the integration of the world's economies over the years 1500 to 1800 could not have occurred without dependable ships and competent sailors. Technical achievements may not have made long-range trade much cheaper before the rise of industry, but they did bring the merchant empires of the early modern age within the realm of the possible.

CHAPTER 7

Transaction costs: A note on merchant credit and the organization of private trade

JACOB M. PRICE

DOUGLASS North has very ably sketched some of the key problems involved in evaluating the role of declining transaction costs in creating the viability of the commercial networks that held together the merchant empires of early modern Europe. Because there are separate papers in this and the preceding volume on many related topics, particularly shipping, I shall confine my remarks to the problems of smaller-scale commercial firms and credit in the British and French "mercantile empires" of the seventeenth and eighteenth centuries.

By conquest, peaceful penetration, or otherwise, the British and French acquired dominion over considerable territories that, unlike those of the Spanish or Portuguese to the southward, contained no mines of precious metals. Many could, however, with the addition of capital and labor, produce commodities for which they seemed to have a comparative advantage, products, that is, which could be sold advantageously in Europe in exchange for European or Asian products. The principle of comparative advantage did, however, take a long time to work itself out. For the first century after the discovery of America, direct European, primarily Iberian, exchanges with the new wider world were restricted to a fairly limited list of commodities centering on the silver forcibly extracted from Mexico as well as South America and the pepper and spices of the East. A wider range of exchanges began with the Dutch penetration of the Indian Ocean after 1590 and the English and French settlements in North America and the West Indies in the new century.

The trades in different directions were not unconnected. Europeans had difficulty finding enough of their own produce to exchange for Asian goods (textiles joining pepper and spices) and had to make up the difference with silver, primarily from the New World. The English, French, and Dutch colonies in America lacked Spain's mines of silver, which they could only get by trade. By trial and error, though, the early settlers gradually found markets in Europe for furs, fish, tobacco, dyestuffs, and sugar. In return they received European textiles and metalware, wine, and some Asian products, including eventually tea, coffee, cotton, and silks. The products of the more northerly colonies (fish, forest products, provisions) could also be exchanged for the sugar, dyestuffs, and so forth of the more southerly.

Production of most export products in the Americas was seriously limited by labor shortage. The Spaniards tried enslaving the indigenes, with but limited and short-run success. After an initial bonus of voluntary emigration, the English and French colonies depended increasingly in the seventeenth century on indentured servants. Population pressure in Europe facilitated their recruitment at first, but their supply became more exiguous after 1688. In the colonies south of Pennsylvania, their place came increasingly to be taken by African slaves.[1] The procuring and transporting of both indentured servants and slaves became an entrepreneurial activity of those trading to the new colonies – whether chartered companies, partnerships, or individuals (or at least some of each).

Few would challenge the utility of organizing the history of European trade with Asia after 1600 around the history of the Dutch, English, French, and other East India companies. But the joint-stock chartered company did not have an unbroken record of success in all fields. After 1624 English trade to the Americas was almost exclusively organized around the private, unincorporated, unchartered concern. The South Sea Company was the principal exception that proved the rule. Chartered in 1711, it for a moment promised dazzling returns from semilegal circumvention of the trade exclusiveness of the Spanish American Empire. The collapse of the South Sea Bubble in 1720 marks the beginning of a process of disillusionment and realistic reappraisal that led to the abandonment of the company's trade after 1739.

---

[1] The process of the transition from indentured servants to slaves has been studied most carefully for the Chesapeake colonies. An overall survey and excellent bibliography of the topic can be found in John J. McCusker and Russell R. Menard, *The Economy of British America, 1607–1789* (Chapel Hill and London, 1979). See in particular the works cited therein by Lois Carr, Allan Kulikoff, Gloria Main, and Russell Menard, plus Allan Kulikoff, *Tobacco and Slaves: The Development of Southern Culture in the Chesapeake, 1680–1800* (Chapel Hill and London, 1986). An equivalent interest in the same phenomenon in the French colonies filled the work of Gabriel Debien. See in particular his *Les esclaves aux Antilles françaises (xvii–xviiie siècles)* (Basse-Terre and Fort-de-France, 1974); *Etudes antillaises (XVIIIe siècle)* (Paris, 1956); *Le peuplement des Antilles françaises au XVIIe siècle: les engagés partis de La Rochelle (1683–1715)* ([Cairo, 1942]); *Plantations et esclaves à Saint-Domingue* (Dakar, 1962); "Les engagés pour les Antilles (1634–1715)," *Revue d'Histoire des Colonies* 38 (1951): 5–274.

The illicit commerce to Spanish America thereafter reverted to the private traders of the British and Spanish Caribbean colonies to whom it had belonged before the company came on the scene.[2] In the African slave trade, too, the private traders or interlopers were able in the end to defeat the chartered Royal African Company. For only a few years did the government try to enforce the company's monopoly or give it compensating help. After 1712 the company was increasingly on its own and increasingly languished. After 1750 it was dissolved and its place taken by a new African regulated company composed of private traders of London, Bristol, and Liverpool.[3] The burglars had bought the closed police station. The end of the Royal African Company bore some similarities to the fate of chartered but nonjoint-stock companies that monopolized England's European trade. In the later seventeenth century, the Merchant Adventurers, Eastland, and Russia companies had been thrown open to all Englishmen on payment of a modest fine – and a similar fate befell the Levant Company in 1754.[4] In the French Empire, too, after the collapse of Law's schemes, the American trades were increasingly dominated by private traders,[5] and the Asian rump of Law's company was ended in 1768 after its military defeats in the Seven Years' War.

Compared with the East India companies, the private firms that dominated the American trades seem picayune and unstructured. How did such small concerns operate over such great distances? Douglass North has perceptively stressed the problem of "agency."

[2] There is a very full bibliography of publications relating to the company in John G. Sperling, *The South Sea Company: An Historical Essay and Bibliographical Finding List* (Boston, 1962). See also Colin Palmer, *Human Cargoes: The British Slave Trade to Spanish America, 1700–1739* (Urbana, 1981).

[3] Most of the now voluminous literature on the British slave trade is listed in the bibliographies in McCusker and Menard (note 1) and in Roger Anstey, *The Atlantic Slave Trade and British Abolition, 1760–1810* (Atlantic Highlands, N.J., 1975), 426–43. See also David W. Galenson, *Traders, Planters, and Slaves: Market Behavior in Early English America* (Cambridge and New York, 1986); Philip D. Curtin, *Economic Change in Precolonial Africa: Senegambia in the Era of the Slave Trade* (Madison, 1975); Henry A. Gemery and Jan S. Hogendorn, eds., *The Uncommon Market: Essays in the Economic History of the Atlantic Slave Trade* (New York, 1979), esp. 303–30 (article by D. Richardson); Adam Anderson, *An Historical and Chronological Deduction of the Origin of Commerce*, 2 vols. (London, 1764), II, 387–8, 395–6; and K. G. Davies, *The Royal African Company* (London, 1957).

[4] E. Lipson, *The Economic History of England*, 3d ed., 3 vols. (London, 1943), II, 265–6, 315–60. See also R. W. K. Hinton, *The Eastland Trade and the Common Weal* (Cambridge, 1959).

[5] Recent studies of the private firms in French colonial trade include J. F. Bosher, *The Canada Merchants, 1713–1763* (Oxford, 1987); Paul Butel, *Les négociants bordelais, l'Europe et les îles au XVIIIe siècle* (Paris, 1974); Charles Carrière, *Négociants marseillais au XVIIIe siècle* (Marseille, 1973); and John G. Clark, *La Rochelle and the Atlantic Economy during the Eighteenth Century* (Baltimore and London, 1981).

There were basically two ways in which an English, French, Dutch, or comparable merchant firm could be represented overseas or anywhere at a distance: by an *employee* or by a *correspondent*. An employee-agent (who could be a ship captain or supercargo as well as a storekeeper) could buy and sell for his firm, which was responsible for his actions. A correspondent was (formally) an independent merchant trading on his own and alone responsible at law for his action, even when acting as a factor on commission for another. Merchants acting as factors (*commissionaires*) charged their correspondents or principals a fixed percentage commission for executing almost any charge. In the late seventeenth and eighteenth centuries, this was normally 2 percent for buying and selling in Holland; 2 1/2 percent in the colonial trades of England and France, but 5 percent in the British or French colonies of North America and the West Indies. Lesser commissions were charged for handling bills of exchange and insurance. Almost anything that a merchant could do for himself he could do on commission for a correspondent. At law, though, he was acting for himself when dealing with others: he entered goods at the customs house in his own name and was responsible for the duties and all attendant regulations. When he bought goods for a correspondent, he himself was responsible for paying for them. The seller had no way of knowing for whom the merchant-factor was buying, any more than customs had of knowing who really owned the goods he entered.[6]

For students of transaction costs, the interesting thing about the merchant correspondent system is its low cost and flexibility. There were considerable overhead costs in maintaining an employee in a foreign port. Such overheads were usually unacceptable except in the area of one's primary concern. But a merchant could have correspondents all over Europe and in many colonies without overhead and need pay commission only when he used a correspondent. Much depended on the reliability of such correspondents and the degree of trust inherent in the correspondence. Reflecting the need for trust, many networks of correspondence followed family and religious-ethnic connections,[7] but such bonds were not absolutely necessary.

---

[6] The various functions of a factor (*commissionaire*) are discussed in Jacques Savary, *Le Parfait Negociant*, 2d ed., 2 vols. (Paris, 1679), II, 209–45. Commissions are discussed by Henry Roseveare, *Markets and Merchants of the Late Seventeenth Century: The Marescoe-David Letters, 1668–1680* (*Records of Social and Economic History*, n.s., XII), 19–22. This suggests that the 2.5-percent commission common in colonial trade may have originated as a 2-percent commission and separate one-half percent brokerage fee.

[7] For examples of religious-ethnic "networks," see Herbert Lüthy, *La banque protestante en France de la révocation de l'Edit de Nantes à la Révolution* (*Affaires et Gens d'Affaires*, XIX), 2 vols. (Paris, 1959, 1961); and Jacob M. Price, "The Great Quaker Business

However, a successful merchant had to inherit or acquire good correspondents one way or another.

Because it was difficult or impossible to find "good" correspondents in strange and distant markets, the big chartered companies trading to remote corners of the earth (remote, that is, for Europeans) almost always started with and continued using employees both in their commercial and their military activities. This, of course, added to the overhead that troubled them so much.

The smaller British and French private merchants trading to the New World experimented with trading through employees, particularly ship captains and supercargoes who returned home periodically and thus could be kept under closer supervision. However, by the middle of the seventeenth century it was increasingly realized that resident factors could trade more efficiently than ship captains, whose "time in the country" was greatly and expensively extended by commercial responsibilities. In the seventeenth century, these factors or *commissionaires* were in form petty commission merchants buying and selling for a correspondent or principal in Europe. However, they differed significantly from European commission merchants in that most of them started with little or no capital of their own and were charged by their principals with doing little but selling European goods and buying sugar, tobacco, and so forth. Some of these "Sotweed Factors," however, managed to accumulate some capital and metamorphosed into a class of indigenous merchants or "merchant-planters" in North America or the West Indies. As substantial independent merchants, they could deal with European merchants more nearly on the parity of status implied by the merchant correspondent system.[8]

Ca. 1740, or shortly thereafter, some of the big Scottish firms trading

Families of Eighteenth-Century London: The Rise and Fall of a Sectarian Patriciate," in Richard S. Dunn and Mary Maples Dunn, eds., *The World of William Penn* (Philadelphia, 1986) 363–99.

[8] On the emergence of local merchants in the colonies, see Gary B. Nash, "The Early Merchants of Philadelphia: The Formation and Disintegration of a Founding Elite", in Dunn and Dunn, *World of William Penn*, 338–62; Bernard Bailyn, *The New England Merchants in the Seventeenth Century* (Cambridge, Mass., 1955); Carville Earle and Ronald Hoffman, "Urban Development in the Eighteenth Century South," *Perspectives in American History* 10 (1976): 7–78; Edwin J. Perkins, *The Economy of Colonial America*, 2d ed. (New York, 1988) ch. V; Alain Buffon, *Monnaie et crédit en economie coloniale: Contribution à l'histoire économique de la Guadeloupe, 1635–1919* (Bibliothèque d'histoire antillaise, 8) (Basse-Terre, 1974) 107–10; Adrien Dessalles, *Histoire générale des Antilles*, 5 vols. (Paris, 1847–48), IV, 592; Louis-Philippe May, *Histoire économique de la Martinique (1635–1763)* (Paris, 1930), 208–9; and Françoise Thésée, *Négociants bordelais et colons de Saint-Domingue ... la maison Henry Romberg, Bapst et Cie 1783–1793* (Bibliothèque d'Histoire d'Outremer, Nouvelle Serie, Travaux, 1) (Paris, 1972), esp. 29–32.

to the Chesapeake and North Carolina reverted to salaried employees to operate their "stores." Such large firms, however, normally had a partner resident in the colony who could supervise salaried employees. Such a system, practical in the booming and thickly settled Chesapeake of 1750, would have been much too top-heavy with overhead in the more lightly settled colonies seventy or eighty years before. The large Glasgow firms of 1750–75, with capitals of £50–100,000, were in scale unlike anything known in the previous century. Their size required practices in accounting and cost control much more systematic than those expected in ordinary private firms.[9] However, the resident partner was also known in French trade to Canada and the West Indies.[10]

There was, though, one traffic, the slave trade, in which the ship captain continued to have major responsibilities for buying and selling. This was particularly evident in the French version of the trade, in which the slaving vessel carried two captains outbound. The senior, or first, captain was normally responsible both for buying slaves on the West African coast and for selling them in the West Indies – mostly *on credit*. As soon as sales were completed, the second captain sailed the vessel home to France, and the first captain remained behind in the islands up to a year more to collect the slave sale debts. If he left before all the debts were collected, he had to share his sales commission with the local merchant-factor responsible for collecting the balance still owed.[11] English slave traders, particularly those of Liverpool, also experimented with the two-captain system, but by the mid-eighteenth century had generally been persuaded to entrust American sales to resident merchant-factors who could give surety for the prompt remittance of all the slave debts. Although these factors' combined commission for slave sales and guaranteed timely

---

[9] T. M. Devine, *The Tobacco Lords: A Study of the Tobacco Merchants of Glasgow and their Trading Activities ca. 1740–90* (Edinburgh, 1975); idem, ed., *A Scottish Firm in Virginia 1767–1777: W Cunningham & Co.* (Scottish History Society 4th Ser. 20) (Edinburgh, 1984); Jacob M. Price, *Capital and Credit in British Overseas Trade: The View from the Chesapeake, 1700–1776* (Cambridge, Mass., 1980) 20–43, 152–5; idem, "Buchanan & Simson, 1759–1763: A Different Kind of Glasgow Firm Trading to the Chesapeake," *William and Mary Quarterly* 3d ser. 40 (1983): 3– 41.

[10] See French works cited in note 8 above and works by Bosher and Butel in note 5 above.

[11] On the French slave trade, see Robert Louis Stein, *The French Slave Trade in the Eighteenth Century* (Madison, 1979); Jean Meyer, *L'armement nantais dans la deuxième moitié du XVIIIe siècle* (*Ports-Routes-Trafics*, XXVIII) (Paris, 1956); and the valuable works of Father Dieudonné Rinchon, particularly *Les armements négriers au XVIIIe siècle d'après la correspondance et la comptabilité des armateurs et des capitaines nantais* (Académie royale des sciences coloniales, Classe des sciences morales et politiques, *Mémoires*, VII:3) (Brussels, 1956).

remittance – 10 percent – was high, the slave traders found it less costly than alternatives at final reckoning.[12]

The gradually emerging indigenous merchants of America were not the only ones there who could take advantage of the merchant correspondent system. If merchants in London and Bristol could sell sugar and tobacco for their merchant correspondents in North America and the West Indies, why could they not also sell for planters? The line between merchant and planter was not always too clear. Many of the larger merchants were also planters and some of the larger planters were also merchants. If such hybrids could consign colonial goods to commission merchants for sale in England, why couldn't pure planters, too? Much the same held true in the French islands, whose large planters learned soon enough when it was convenient to consign to Bordeaux, Nantes, and so forth. This does not mean that all or most planters consigned. Only a minority did: perhaps 10 percent in the early eighteenth-century tobacco colonies, more in the sugar colonies. (The rest of the planters dealt with local merchants or the local agent or employees of metropolitan firms.) When shipping was available in abundance at relatively low peacetime rates, the planter-consigner system was a relatively efficient, low-overhead mode of trade, though disappointing in years of glut, when sales prices fell and overheads (including freights and part of commissions) remained relatively constant. In wartime, freight rates could more than double and insurance rates go through the roof – but the expected enhanced gap between American and European prices made consignment still attractive to the more adventurous planters.[13]

The eighteenth century saw the growth in both the British and

[12] There are many documents relating to the slave selling factors, their commissions, etc., in Elizabeth Donnan, ed., *Documents Illustrative of the History of the Slave Trade to America*, 4 vols. (Washington, D.C., 1930–5), esp. vols. III and IV; and in Philip M. Hamer et al., eds., *The Papers of Henry Laurens*, 11 + vols. (Columbia, 1968-). See also S. G. Checkland, "Finance for the West Indies, 1780–1815," *Economic History Review* 2d ser. 10 (1958): 461–9; Richard B. Sheridan, "The Commercial and Financial Organization of the British Slave Trade, 1750–1807," ibid., 11 (1958): 249–63; idem, *Sugar and Slavery: An Economic History of the British West Indies, 1623–1775* (Baltimore, 1973), 292–94; Leila Sellers, *Charleston Business on the Eve of The American Revolution* (Chapel Hill, 1934) chap. VII; and Elizabeth Donnan, "The Slave Trade in Charleston Before the Revolution," *American Historical Review* 32 (1928): 804–28.

[13] On consignment, see Richard Pares, *Merchants and Planters* (*Economic History Review, Supplements*, 4) (Cambridge, 1960); idem, "A London West-India Merchant House, 1740–1769," in R. Pares and A. J. P. Taylor, eds., *Essays Presented to Sir Lewis Namier* (London, 1956), 75–107; Sheridan, *Sugar and Slavery*, chaps. 12 and 13; Jacob M. Price, "The Last Phase of the Virginia-London Consignment Trade: James Buchanan & Co., 1758–1768", *William and Mary Quarterly* 3d ser. 43 (1986): 64–98; Elizabeth Donnan, "Eighteenth-Century English Merchants: Micajah Perry," *Journal of Economic and Business History* 4 (1931): 70–98.

French sugar colonies of a significant class of absentee estate owners that had no equivalent in the tobacco or more northerly colonies. If the absentee owner was a merchant or partner in a merchant house, such consignments would be made to that house. Credit could also be arranged by the absentee at the European end.[14]

The bilateral sugar and tobacco trades were relatively simple compared with some of the more northerly trades. Wheat and flour from Pennsylvania or the Chesapeake and fish from New England were sent on account either of American or British merchants to their correspondents in ports in southern Europe (particularly Iberia); part of the proceeds from such sales was commonly remitted to London – usually in bills of exchange – to pay for imports from the mother country. Similarly, New England fish, livestock, provisions, and forest products were sent to the West Indies for sale there with returns made partly in West Indian products and coin to New England and partly in bills of exchange on London. Some of these transactions could be handled by ship captains or supercargoes, but the more complex dealings, particularly in Iberia, required merchant correspondents.[15]

The full complexity and efficiency of the merchant correspondent system can most readily be seen in the ubiquitous use of the bill of exchange in the Atlantic mercantile world of the seventeenth and eighteenth centuries. To minimize the need for scarce metallic currency, to avoid risks of loss by the dangers of the road and sea, and to avoid immobilizing monetary resources during long overland or ocean voyages, merchants during the Middle Ages had used the bill of exchange whenever possible to shift money or credits from place to place. By the second half of the seventeenth century, its use had become universal in western and central Europe, with Amsterdam the center point for all transactions where direct remitting was not possible because of the absence of a current market and market rate for transfer between other points. In such cases, Amsterdam merchants accepted bills drawn on them for the account of others and

---

[14] On absenteeism, see Sheridan, *Sugar and Slavery*, 385–7; Richard Pares, *A West-India Fortune* (London, 1950); and Lowell Joseph Ragatz, *The Fall of the Planter Class in the British Caribbean, 1763–1833: A Study in Social and Economic History* (New York, 1928).

[15] For the British colonies' trade with Southern Europe, see Thomas M. Doerflinger, *A Vigorous Spirit of Enterprise: Merchants and Economic Development in Revolutionary Philadelphia* (Chapel Hill, 1986), 97–122; Virginia D. Harrington, *The New York Merchant on the Eve of the Revolution* (New York, 1935), 200–02; Converse D. Clowse, *Economic Beginnings in Colonial South Carolina, 1670–1730* (Columbia, 1971), 122, 219–20, 243–4; and James F. Shepherd and Gary M. Walton, *Shipping, Maritime Trade, and the Economic Development of Colonial North America* (Cambridge, 1972), passim. Cf. also Sellers, note 12 above.

covered themselves by redrawing. For example, the Stockholm correspondent of a Scottish firm received orders to purchase copper, getting funds for the same by drawing and selling bills on the Scottish firm's Amsterdam correspondent. Properly instructed, the Amsterdam firm accepted the bills when they appeared and, if not supplied in time, obtained funds to pay the same by selling their own bills on Scotland or more likely on the Scottish firm's London correspondent. In this, the Amsterdam firm was playing the role of a nineteenth-century "accepting house."[16]

Theoretically all bills should have been sold at a discount because the drawer-seller got his money immediately and the buyer-remitter or his assignee would only collect at the other end after the passage of many weeks or months. In fact, when the demand for any particular bills was keen (as was usually the case in the colonies for bills on the metropolis), the discount could be turned by the market into a premium.[17] In the colonies, there was usually only one way to remit money home by bills, just as, in the Swedish example given above, there was in the seventeenth century only one feasible way to remit money from London to Stockholm, that is, via Amsterdam. However, there were frequently *several ways* available to make remittances between places in Europe. For example, a merchant in London wishing to remit to Hamburg could use any of the following methods: 1) buy a bill on Hamburg in London; 2) buy a bill on Amsterdam in London and instruct one's Amsterdam correspondent to remit the proceeds to Hamburg; 3) if speedier remittance was needed, instruct one's Hamburg correspondent to draw a bill on London and sell it for cash locally; or 4) instruct the Hamburg correspondent to draw and sell a bill on Amsterdam, with one's Amsterdam correspondent obtaining cash to pay said bill by drawing and selling in Amsterdam a bill on

[16] For bills of exchange in England, see J[ames] Milnes Holden, *The History of Negotiable Instruments in English Law* (London, 1955); for France, see Charles Carrière, Marcel Coudurie, Michel Gutsatz and René Squarzoni, *Banque et capitalisme commercial: La lettre de change au XVIII siècle* (s.l., 1976); for legal aspects, see also Henri Lévy-Bruhl, *Histoire de la lettre de change en France aux xviie et xviiie siècles* (Paris, 1933). For multilateral remitting via Amsterdam, see J. M. Price, "Multilateralism and/or Bilateralism: The Settlement of British Trade Balances with 'The North' c. 1700" *Economic History Review* 2d ser. 14 (1961): 254–74.

[17] The fluctuations in exchange rates between the colonies, British and French, and Europe are conveniently tabulated in John J. McCusker, *Money and Exchange in Europe and America, 1600–1775: A Handbook* (Chapel Hill, 1978). The significance of the fluctuations in the British colonies is discussed in Joseph Albert Ernst, *Money and Politics in America, 1755–1775* (Chapel Hill, 1973). For some post–1775 exchange rates, see Jean Bouchary, *Le Marché des changes de Paris à la fin du XVIIIe siècle (1778–1800)* (Paris, 1937); and T. S. Ashton, *An Economic History of England: The 18th Century* (London, 1955), 253.

one's self in London. The precise method chosen would depend on the urgency with which the cash was needed in Hamburg and on the exchange rates prevailing between London, Hamburg, and Amsterdam. Indirect or multilateral remittances were called by contemporaries "arbitrage" or "arbitration." They have in common with modern ideas of arbitrage their dependence on variations in prices for the same good between different markets and their tendency to bring such prices closer together. They were feasible because all over Western and Central Europe newspapers and specialized publications reported weekly or daily fluctuations in rates of exchange between different centers. Technical assistance could also be obtained from exchange brokers, whose function it was to bring together buyers and sellers of bills. To perfect the market there were also exchange dealers who bought and sold bills.[18]

In Amsterdam, all bills were payable "at the bank," that is, by check-type transfers from one account to another at the Bank of Amsterdam, primarily a bank of deposit.[19] At London, by contrast, the whole complex bill of exchange system was operated through most of the seventeenth century without the necessary intercession of banks. On its establishment in 1694, the Bank of England immediately issued bank notes that replaced similar goldsmiths' notes as the preferred way to settle bills of exchange in London. A "drawing office" was set up by the bank in 1698 offering deposit and check-type facilities comparable to those of the Bank of Amsterdam.[20] Many merchants, however, preferred to deal with private bankers, some of whom issued "notes of deposit"; all, however, eventually came to handle transfers by checks similar to those of the Bank of England. The diversity in London of deposit banks handling the collection of bills of exchange made the creation of the London clearing house another necessary invention of the eighteenth century.[21]

Because bills on Amsterdam, London, and other major centers could in law and in fact be readily sold and bought, they became

---

[18] Many contemporary commercial manuals explain *arbitrage* or *arbitration* transactions. For example, see Patrick Kelly, *Universal Cambist*, 2 vols. (London, 1811), II, 135–57; Samuel Ricard, *Traité général du commerce*, 3 vols. (Paris, an VII), II, 317–434. Perhaps the fullest treatment is in Isaac Wiertz, *Traité des arbitrages* (Basel, 1728).
[19] J. G. Van Dillen, "The Bank of Amsterdam," in J. G. Van Dillen, ed., *History of the Principal Public Banks* (The Hague, 1934; London and New York, 1964), 79–123, esp. 84, 105–6.
[20] Sir John Clapham, *The Bank of England: A History*, 2 vols., (Cambridge, 1966), I, chap. III.
[21] Philip W. Matthews, *The Bankers' Clearing House* . . . (London, 1921), 8–12.

"negotiable instruments"; their "negotiation" enabled merchants and manufacturers to realize assets otherwise frozen for the time being as goods in transit or merchandise or credits in the hands of others. Such "negotiation" (normally at a discount reflecting the duration of the bill and the market for bills on its place of payment) commonly took one of three forms: 1) the bill might be "passed" by the holder to a creditor to help settle a debt; 2) the bill might be sold to someone needing a remittance to the bill's place of payment; or 3) the bill might be bought before maturity as a short-term investment by a bank or moneyed man at its place of payment.

The key technical advance of the Bank of England on the Bank of Amsterdam was discounting, that is, the purchase at a discount of accepted bills of exchange prior to their maturity. Goldsmith-bankers had been discounting for some time and the bank added it as a service for depositors in a very hesitant way in the 1690s. At first the bank insisted on scrutinizing almost every bill and the volume of discounting was relatively small. In the next few years, with favorable legal decisions on transferability and with more experience, the bank moved toward a policy of almost automatic discounting for regular customers. The volume of discounting rose steadily through the eighteenth century, particularly after the Seven Years' War.[22] In 1782 the bank was discounting nearly 10,000 bills per month with a mean value of about £175 each, for a total of almost £1,750,000 monthly.[23] In addition, there were still other bills being discounted by the increasingly prosperous and numerous private bankers. Merchants trading to America preferred these private bankers in part because they were more flexible on loans other than by discounting. Such emergency credit was extremely important to such merchants because some of the bills they received from America would not be accepted; it took many months to send such protested bills back to America and have better bills returned. Private bankers would cover them in such straits.[24]

In Britain, Ireland, and the British colonies, remittances from place to place were commonly made by bills on London. Even the much-discussed small bills used as currency in Lancashire were bills on London.[25] When the representative in America of Glasgow, Liverpool, or Bristol firms had to draw on his "home office," he made his bills

---

[22] Clapham, *Bank of England*, I, 122–30, 301–2.
[23] Bank of England Archives, G8/1** Committee of Treasury Minutes, 1779–1781.
[24] Price, *Capital and Credit*, chap. 5.
[25] Henry Thornton, *An Enquiry into the Nature and Effects of the Paper Credit of Great Britain (1802)*, ed. F. A. von Hayek (London, 1939), 94n.

payable in London; otherwise they would most often have had to be sold at a discount. The British colonial bill market was unbalanced in another respect: There was an active market in all major American colonies for bills on London, but before the American Revolution there was no market in London for bills on American centers. This had to wait till the nineteenth century.[26]

In general terms, the use of bills of exchange was as normal in the French ports as in the English. In the northern and western ports, which handled most of France's colonial trade, bills to be fully negotiable had to be drawn on Paris or payable in Paris. (Lyons was a lesser center for bill operations in the south, but its role in bill movements there was of minimal importance for colonial trade.) Colonial bills were, of course, frequently drawn on merchants in the western French ports but would have to be made payable in Paris to be fully negotiable just as colonial bills on British ports were made payable in London.[27] Although the practice of discounting was well known in France, I have seen nothing to suggest that it was anywhere near as routine there as in England. Hence the desire for the *Caisse d'Escompte* at the end of the *ancien régime*. Once established, this institution (founded in 1776) had a significant if not brilliant growth, the value of its discounts by 1781 reaching 30 percent of those of the Bank of England that same year.[28]

The bill of exchange was primarily an instrument to transfer and thus realize credits at a distance. However, because bills could as noted also be drawn against the value of goods in transit or not yet sold, the sale of such bills was a way to realize the worth of distant non-cash "effects." Their use as instruments of pure credit was derivative and secondary. Of course, the selling of a bill of exchange on a distant point inevitably involved an element of credit for the time elapsing between the sale of the bill in one place and its eventual payment in another. But more obvious credit uses were also possible. Bills of exchange in Holland and England were normally due thirty or sixty days (one or two *usances*) after presentation ("sight"). Bills drawn in the English colonies on London were most often for two months, though one month and three months' sight bills were not

---

[26] For an example of the operation of the bill market in North America, see Devine, ed., *A Scottish Firm in Virginia*, 32. On the eve of the American Revolution, some use was being made of bills on Philadelphia in the Chesapeake colonies.

[27] Stein, *French Slave Trade*, 149. Cf. also Bosher, *Canada Merchants*, 195–201.

[28] Robert Bigo, *La Caisse d'Escompte (1776–1793) et les Origines de la Banque de France* (Paris, [1928]), 64; Bank of England Archives, G8/1**. This calculation is based on the assumption that Bigo's figures refer to total bills discounted in the year and not to discounted paper held at the year's end.

uncommon. In the French West Indian colonies, however, bills could be made payable six months or a year after date (not sight) and much longer bills were known. Perhaps the longest bills routinely handled were those of up to two years (and more) used in British slave sales. In such transactions, the credit role of the bill was much more pronounced.

Within Europe, desperate and somewhat unscrupulous merchants could conspire to raise money rather expensively by drawing and redrawing on each other though no conventional mercantile transaction had taken place. Bankers discounting bills had to keep their eyes open for such "kiting" operations. They were not, however, feasible in bill operations between America and Europe because, though there was always a market and a rate in the colonies for bills on the metropolis, there was as noted no market in the metropolis for bills on the colonies.

Bills of exchange were known in Asia, but were not as commonly used in European-Asian trade as in European-American trade. When we begin to find more numerous references to them ca. 1750–90, they are likely to be associated with the movement homeward of funds irregularly acquired by the "servants" of one of the East India companies, movements which the remitter wished to keep secret from his employer.[29]

Discounting then was a conventional credit operation for the banker or other discounter buying accepted bills at less than face value, but its primary importance to merchants was its help with liquidity. The same result could be attained by passing an endorsed bill to one's own creditor. When not thirsting for liquidity, merchants often chose to save on interest and hold bills to maturity. But the mere knowledge that one could, in an emergency, discount most accepted bills and thereby improve one's liquidity greatly facilitated merchant's planning and the economies made possible by planning.

Also relevant for bill operations, though less obviously so, was the development of marine insurance. The insurance idea goes back several centuries; its practice was well known in the great commercial centers of the seventeenth century, particularly Amsterdam; yet it was not universally available then nor universally used when available. In England, war rates were very high, particularly during the 1690s. Many venturers by sea chose instead to self-insure by dividing their risks. An investor might acquire one-

---

[29] Holden Furber, *John Company at Work* (Cambridge, Mass., 1948), esp, 45–50, 79–80, 89–96, 114–28; Lüthy, *La banque protestante*, II, 376–81.

sixteenth of sixteen ships rather than a whole ship. Instead of sending one parcel of goods abroad to an American colony, a merchant similarly might take shares in several "adventures" with other merchants. But the dividing of risks increased transaction costs in supervision and bookkeeping. It might also slow the turnaround of vessels and thus affect their earnings and in the long run raise freight costs. In the eighteenth century, insurance became cheaper and more generally available: Peacetime insurance between Britain and North America was only 2 1/2 percent. With the use of insurance becoming more routine, we find more ships owned or chartered by a single firm. It was now safer at least for a British merchant to put all his eggs in one basket. In the wars of mid-century, of course, insurance was much more expensive than in peacetime for everyone, with French rates reaching astronomic levels.

In London, marine insurance after 1720 was divided between the two new insurance companies started then and the famous insurance exchange at Lloyd's Coffee House, where private underwriters could be found as needed by the efficient brokers. In Scotland, the English outports and some ports in Britain's northern colonies, there was some local underwriting managed by a few specialist brokers; but when, as frequently happened in wartime, sufficient insurance could not be obtained locally, recourse was had to London or even Amsterdam for the balance. In France in the mid-eighteenth century, some insurance was available in the principal ports from local underwriters or companies, but in wartime here too recourse had to be had to Paris or Amsterdam.[30]

The importance of insurance for bill of exchange operations is frequently overlooked. When a merchant or planter in an American colony of Britain or France consigned local produce (sugar, tobacco, furs, and so forth) to a metropolitan merchant, he not infrequently shortly afterward drew a bill upon that same merchant. If the goods arrived before the bill, the merchant with "effects in hand" would

---

[30] On insurance, see Frank C. Spooner, *Risks at Seas: Amsterdam Insurance and Maritime Europe, 1766–1780* (Cambridge, 1983); L. A. Boiteux, *La Fortune de mer, la besoin de sécurité et les débuts de l'assurance maritime* (Paris, 1968); Clark, *La Rochelle and the Atlantic Economy*, chap. 9; J. F. Bosher, "The Paris Business World and the Seaports under Louis XV: Speculators in Marine Insurance . . . ," *Histoire Sociale*, XII (1979), 281–97; Charles Wright and E. Ernest Fayle, *A History of Lloyd's . . .* (London, 1928); Barry Supple, *The Royal Exchange Assurance* (London, 1970); A. H. John, "The London Assurance Company and the Marine Insurance Market of the Eighteenth Century," *Economica* 25 (1958): 126–41; and Lucy S. Sutherland, *A London Merchant, 1695–1774* (Oxford, 1933) chap. III.

usually accept the bill. To cover other contingencies, the consigner might write to the merchant by another vessel – the earliest possible – enclosing a copy of the bill of lading and asking the merchant to insure the consigned cargo (if not taken care of by earlier correspondence). With the bill of lading in hand (assuring him the cargo when and if it arrived) and with insurance made (assuring him of equivalent value should ship or cargo be lost), the merchant was safe in accepting the bill though he had not yet received the cargo concerned. Failure to execute these linked steps could have the most disturbing results, as was shown during the War of the Spanish Succession. Numerous bills were drawn by Virginians on London firms to whom goods had been sent in uninsured vessels. When the ships were lost at sea, the merchants were forced to refuse to accept the related bills; hundreds were returned protested to Virginia, spreading commercial chaos on both sides of the Atlantic.[31]

Even with insurance, the trade to America remained rather risky, what with the dangers of the sea, frequent wars, and the need to deal with people who, though one's own compatriots, lacked either the capacity or the inclination to repay the debts they so eagerly incurred. In countries where fertile lands could be obtained for almost nothing, but labor and capital were very scarce, quite modest amounts of wealth could in the long run normally be most advantageously invested, whether in land, buildings, slaves, servants, livestock, trading goods, or ships. The settlers knew this and quite rationally and deliberately tried to get as much credit as they could from traders, whether local or metropolitan. (Shifting current consumption onto credit might free other resources to buy servants, slaves, or land.) Successful firms consciously offered easy credit to attract customers, but tried to keep totals outstanding within the customer's ability to pay. Collecting could be very difficult. Even when the debtor (planter or local trader) had the greatest goodwill, a decline in market prices might have rendered him incapable of paying for several years. Uncollectable debts from planters helped finish the Royal African Company and many private concerns, small and large.[32] The risk of nonpayment is too often the transaction cost least visible to the historian, but the successful merchant had to allow for that risk (whether arising from human frailty or the fluctuations of the market). After

---

[31] Examples can be found in PRO (Public Record Office) H.C.A.13/83 ff. 575, 578 and T. 70/278 and 279.

[32] On slave debts, see Davies, *Royal Africa Company*, 316–25, 346. On the broader problem of business failure, see Julian Hoppit, *Risk and Failure in English Business* (Cambridge, 1987).

normal deduction on their balance sheets for desperate debts (100 percent) and doubtful debts (50 percent), Glasgow firms trading to the Chesapeake deducted another 10 to 20 percent on overseas accounts receivable for good measure.[33]

In the first two-thirds of the seventeenth century, with so little known about the American colonies, and that not all good, very few men of substance were interested in trading thither on any but the most modest, experimental scale. Yet profits on individual transactions could be high, and adventures were undertaken. This was the age when both the English and French trades seem to have attracted many small men. The decline in tobacco prices in the later seventeenth century as well as the establishment of the French tobacco monopoly in 1674 and of radically higher tobacco duties in England in 1685 started a process in which small men were squeezed out of the tobacco trade in both Britain and France and their place taken by fewer and bigger firms. The same process proceeded less urgently but just as certainly in the sugar trade.[34]

These bigger firms had the resources to own or charter whole vessels and thus realize some of the economies in shipping discussed elsewhere in this and the preceding volume. Insurance eliminated the risks of concentrated investment in a few ships. The size and reputation of the greater firms attracted consignments of sugar and tobacco and made it easier for their agents and correspondents in America to raise money by selling bills of exchange on them. This same reputation made such bills easier to discount or pass from hand to hand as quasi-money. The same reputation made it easier for them to raise additional working resources by borrowing on bond. In fact, in Scotland and the English outports, where investment opportunities were somewhat limited, trustees of widows and orphans sought out big merchants and asked them to take the trust's money on bond loans. Finally, their standing enabled them, at least in England, to obtain export goods from wholesalers on long credits. There is, of course, no such thing as a free lunch and the British credit price then was at least 10 percent p.a. above the cash price. (But, when money was easy, this made it attractive for an exporter to borrow at the legal

---

[33] Examples of further markdown of value of debts (after normal deductions for doubtful and desperate debts) can be found in PRO T. 97/7 ff. 368–369; T.79/18 (Donald, Scot & Co.); T.79/22 (Oswald, Dennistoun & Co.); T.79/23 (Colin Dunlop & Co.); and T.79/31 (John Ballantine & Co.).

[34] Jacob M. Price and Paul G. E. Clemens, "A Revolution of Scale in Overseas Trade: British Firms in the Chesapeake Trade, 1675–1775," *Journal of Economic History* 47 (1987): 1–43.

maximum of 5 percent to repay his wholesalers early and obtain a greater refund.)[35]

There were, of course, differences in the specific credit conditions in different countries. In Holland, we are told, merchants could borrow money at the lowest interest rates in Europe and were expected to buy goods for cash or short credit at the cash price.[36] Purchases on longer credits were well known in France – though not on such long credits as in Britain and not by persons not domiciled in France. Three to six months' credit on export sales may well have been normal in France.[37]

There were also interesting differences in partnership law and practice in different countries. In England, partnerships were rather small and unstructured; sleeping partners were known but uncommon in the American trades. By contrast, Scottish firms often involved much larger numbers of partners, some of them inactive investors. To reassure the latter, Scottish partnership contracts were long and complicated documents establishing societies with carefully defined procedures. The formal meetings and decisions of the partners were recorded in sederunt books, and entries therein signed by a majority of the partners (by value) were binding on the rest.[38] In France and other continental countries, this was carried further in the *société en commandite*, which provided for the admission of inactive and limited partners. This would appear to have been attractive to investors at a distance who could not supervise the affairs of the firm closely.[39] British capital mobilization suffered from the lack of equivalent facilities for unincorporated partnerships though Britain, like the continental countries, knew the bottomry loan in which the lender, in return for a very high rate of interest, agreed to forgive a loan if the ship on which it depended failed to complete its voyage. This type of loan incorporated some features of insurance and was apparently

---

[35] Price, *Capital and Credit*, chaps. 4 and 6.
[36] John Hope, *Letters on Credit*, 2d ed. (London, 1784), 9–10.
[37] Butel, *Négociants bordelais*, 258–9. At Rouen in the 1660s and 1670s, three or four months credit appears to have been normal on sales of imported raw materials. Roseveare, *Marescoe-David Letters*, 86, 185, 241, 390.
[38] Price, *Capital and Credit*, 24.
[39] Savary, *Le Parfait Negociant*, 2d ed., II, 1–25, esp. 17. See Henri, Lévy-Bruhl, *Histoire juridique des sociétés de commerce en France aux xvii et xviii siècles* (Paris, 1938). The *société en commandité* permitted investors in Paris and other inland towns to take shares in partnerships in French port towns trading to the colonies, and metropolitan firms to take shares (sometimes major) in partnerships in the French colonies. The latter arrangement was also known in Scotland but without any hint of limited liability.

the only type of high risk-high interest loan that escaped the restrictions of the British usury laws limiting interest to 6 or 5 percent.

The influence of the state on transaction costs was somewhat ambiguous. The most important and pervasive activities of the state in the seventeenth and eighteenth centuries were waging war and raising taxes to pay for current and previous conflicts. Wars stimulated the shipbuilding and naval stores trades as well as the manufacture of munitions and almost every branch of the iron and steel trade. Hostilities, however, were very burdensome for maritime commerce. A major merchant fleet like that of Britain, France, or Holland could lose thousands of vessels to the enemy in the course of a long war. Freight and insurance rates soared while the press gangs made sailors scarce and expensive. By making colonial products costlier in Europe, wars also tended to check growth of demand – at least in the short run.[40]

To finance these wars, the state, of course, had to increase taxes. Because many colonial and Asian products, particularly tobacco, tea, calicoes, pepper and rum, were considered luxuries, they attracted particularly high levels of taxation. Tobacco in all countries led the way in establishing the feasibility of ever higher rates of impost. Such high levels were not only a burden on the consumer but also greatly increased the working capital and credit needed by importers and processors of affected colonial products. There is considerable evidence that higher taxes tended to discourage small men from entering some trades and thus encouraged dominance therein by fewer and larger firms.

To finance wars, the early modern state had also to borrow ever larger amounts. The seventeenth and eighteenth centuries saw the emergence of something approaching a national debt in most European states. (Municipal and provincial debts were older.) This made the state a rival in the capital markets of the borrowing sectors of the landed and business communities. Usury laws prevented the private sector from outbidding the state for loans and also protected landed borrowers from having to pay mortgage rates that they considered too high.[41]

---

[40] On the economic burden of war, cf. J. S. Bromley and A. N. Ryan, "Navies" in J. S. Bromley, ed., *The New Cambridge Modern History*, VI (Cambridge, 1970), 790–833, esp. 800–05; A. H. John, "War and the English Economy, 1700–1763", *Economic History Review* 2d ser. 7 (1955), 329–44; and James C. Riley, *The Seven Years War and the Old Regime in France: The Economic and Financial Toll* (Princeton, 1986).

[41] See Riley (note 40); P. G. M. Dickson, *The Financial Revolution in England* (London

It is difficult to assess the influence of the usury laws on the availability of credit to businessmen. The impact was undoubtedly restrictive, particularly for new and marginal concerns. In Scotland post–1714 bonds were normally at the full legal rate of 5 percent. In England some well-established firms were able to borrow on bond at below the legal maximum, but new firms or houses of uncertain repute had to pay the top legal rate if they could get such loans at all. Paying an illegal rate might be a short-term solution, useful in a crisis, but unlikely to produce the long-term credits that many businesses needed.[42] The usury laws must also have tended to deepen short-term financial crises. (Because they could not raise discount rates above 5 percent after 1714, British banks anticipating a crisis could only restrict or cease discounting.) Such laws also affected competition between old established firms of repute and newer firms whose reputations were yet to be established. In an open capital market, new firms can compete for loans by offering a higher rate of interest. That was only minimally possible under the usury laws. Firms could really compete for loans only on the basis of the reputation and the pledges or sureties they could offer. That gave a substantial advantage to larger, reputable firms and contributed further to the concentration of the colonial trades in fewer and larger firms as the eighteenth century progressed.[43]

Although the state competed with private businessmen for the funds of lenders, in some respects state debt in those countries where state credit was strongest could sustain and help expand semiofficial and private credit. The parliamentary guaranteed debt held by the Bank of England was part of the congeries of "authority" that helped attract deposits and sustain the credit of its note issue, just as the same debt held by the new and United East India companies should have made it easier for them to borrow on bond. (In fact, United East India Company bonds were held in the highest esteem by London bankers of the later eighteenth century.)[44] What is less well understood is that government "stock" belonging to private individuals could also be used as the basis for credit. For example, Scottish and English provincial merchants and bankers deposited government securities as well as shares and bonds of the three "great moneyed

and New York, 1967); Marcel Marion, *Histoire financière de la France depuis 1715*, 6 vols. (Paris, 1914–31), vol. I.

[42] Price, *Capital and Credit*, chap. 4.

[43] See Price and Clemens, "A Revolution of Scale."

[44] K. N. Chaudhuri, "The English East India Company in the 17th and 18th Centuries..." in Leonard Blusse and F. Gaastra, eds., *Companies and Trade* (Leiden, 1981) 45.

companies" as pledges with their London correspondents (both merchants and bankers) to support their bill of exchange operations.[45] The London correspondent would feel more content in accepting bills on him if he had in his strong box some security of his provincial correspondent to fall back on should bills sent him not be honored. Thus, government securities held by bankers in eighteenth-century London tended to increase the volume of bills of exchange in circulation in ways that have modern parallels.

The most basic role of the state was, of course, the preservation of law and order and the enforcement of contracts. The state's role in the enforcement of contracts was not always exemplary when its own contracts were concerned. But the overseas orientation of this chapter makes it necessary to omit such topics as the Stop of the Exchequer in England and the currency debasements of Louis XIV. More immediately relevant for maritime empires was the extension of the idea of law and order to the high seas. Considerable naval effort was undertaken by the maritime powers to repress piracy in the West Indies and North American waters and to extract respect for their flags from the rulers of north Africa, controllers and eventually owners of the corsairs. This was a classic area in which merchants organized to bring pressure on their own governments and thereby reduce the risks of the sea for sailors, shipowners, shippers, and insurers.[46]

Part of the enforcement of contracts inevitably involved the state in the disputes between settlers (particularly plantation owners) and their creditors. The resulting experience of Britain and France was different. Planters everywhere wanted protection for their lands, their slaves, and their livestock from the claims of creditors. In the French island colonies, by the *Code Noir* of 1685, Negro field-hand slaves could not be seized for debt and compulsorily removed from the land they cultivated. By the letter of the law, a total plantation or farm, including its slaves, could be seized for debt, but the procedure was so difficult that such seizures were virtually impossible. Such remained the case even under the Napoleonic Code.[47] In the British colonies, planter-dominated legislatures, particularly in Jamaica and Virginia, passed measures impeding the collection of debts and mak-

---

[45] E.g., Price, *Capital and Credit*, 88.
[46] Useful modern studies include Robert C. Ritchie, *Captain Kidd and the War against the Pirates* (Cambridge, Mass., 1986); and Paul Butel, *Les Caraïbes au temps des flibustiers* (Paris, 1982).
[47] Lucien Peytraud, *L'esclavage aux Antilles françaises avant 1789* (Paris, 1897) 160, 164, 245–65; Buffon, *Monnaie et credit*, 97–122; Louis-Philippe May, *Histoire économique de la Martinique (1635–1763)* (Paris, 1930), 264–66; Dessalles, *Histoire générale des Antilles*, III, 243–9.

ing slaves the equivalent of landed property that could only be seized for debts if mortgaged. Merchant-creditors were, however, able to obtain relief from Parliament in the Colonial Debts Act of 1732, which made the land, houses, chattels, and slaves of debtors in the colonies liable for the satisfaction of debts "in the like Manner as Real Estates are by the Law of *England* liable to the Satisfaction of Debts due by Bond or other Specialty." The law was furiously unpopular in Virginia, but, in the long run, probably encouraged the expansion of credit to the Virginians, particularly bond debt for the purchase of slaves.[48] In thinly populated areas, the right to seize slaves was probably more attractive to a potential creditor than the right to seize land. The difference between the influence of merchant-creditors in Britain and France is striking.

In other respects, as Douglass North has pointed out, the internal legal systems of modern West European states were progressively "modernized" to reflect mercantile practice and mercantile needs. Most merchants, however, avoided where possible recourse to formal ordinary legal procedures, preferring to trust the less formal law and custom of merchants. In France, this meant settling through the consular courts controlled by merchants. In England, merchants preferred arbitration or (more frequently) equity proceedings in the courts of Chancery and Exchequer. In Scotland there appears to have been a marked preference for arbitration with merchant-officials, such as the Dean of Gild and Lord Provost of Glasgow, frequently acting as third man or "umpire" in the arbitration proceedings. Recourse to arbitration was frequently mandatory in Scottish partnership and other contracts.

All these evolutions seem slow to modern eyes. Yet the general tendency in the total system toward increased efficiency or lower transaction costs seems undeniable. However, whenever credit enters the picture, one must possibly qualify one's generalization. Credit historically has been an absolute essential for the development of frontier economies where labor and capital are scarce. But the excessive use of credit for current consumption or to finance imprudent investments can alter the final balance of gain and loss. If traders had

---

[48] John M. Hemphill II, *Virginia and the English Commercial System, 1689–1733* . . . (New York, 1985), 150–89; Jacob M. Price, "The Excise Affair Revisited: The Administrative and Colonial Dimensions of a Parliamentary Crisis," in Stephen B. Baxter, ed., *England's Rise to Greatness, 1660–1763* (Berkeley, 1983), 257–321, esp. 272–3, 277–9, 284–8, 306–7; Sheridan, *Sugar and Slavery*, 289; Edward Long, *The History of Jamaica*, 3 vols. (London, 1774), I, 546.

to base their cost calculations on exceptionally high expected losses through uncollectable debts, then contemporaries would through the price system have lost a possibly significant share of the advantages otherwise accruing through increased efficiency.

CHAPTER 8

Evolution of empire:
The Portuguese in the
Indian Ocean during the
sixteenth century

SANJAY SUBRAHMANYAM

LUÍS FILIPE F.R. THOMAZ

INTRODUCTION

A better understanding than obtains at present of the nature of the
Portuguese imperial enterprise in the sixteenth-century Indian Ocean
depends on the resolution of a paradox: If it is poorly understood,
this is because the principal "facts" of the matter are apparently so
well known. Every schoolboy knows – or is supposed to know – of
Vasco da Gama's voyage of 1497–9, and of Afonso de Albuquerque's
acts of empire-building. Thereafter, at least in popular imagination,
the Portuguese Empire in Asia disappears into historical mists, until
it reemerges in the early seventeenth century as the rival of the East
India companies.

Historians, too, seem to have been seduced into thinking along
these lines. The best known recent characterization of the sixteenth-
century Portuguese Asian Empire is self-confessedly "structural" in
its construction, and the purpose of its author Niels Steensgaard is
to use this characterization as part of an exercise in Institutional Darwinism, wherein the organizational superiority of the East India companies may be inferred from the very fact of their "triumph."[1] To this
end, the essence of the Portuguese presence is extracted from a sample
of documentation drawn indifferently from various parts of the sixteenth century; the chief elements that emerge are, at the Asian end,

[1] Niels Steensgaard, *The Asian Trade Revolution of the 17th Century* (Chicago, 1974) 120,
126, 141, 151–3 passim.

298

"constitutionally determined corruption" and a "redistributive enterprise," while at the European end we are informed that the Portuguese ran what was in sum a "customs-house operation."

This approach, attractive to the adherents of the New Institutional Economic History (not surprisingly, in view of their own commitment to Institutional Darwinism, with a dash of Pangloss thrown in for good measure), seems to have superseded to a large extent earlier constructs in which the Portuguese enterprise in the Indian Ocean was permitted to *evolve* over the sixteenth century.[2] This evolution, in the writings of late nineteenth and early twentieth-century historians, took the form of one half of a sine wave. From the tenuous beginnings under Da Gama, a peak was reached in the second quarter of the sixteenth century, succeeded in turn by a decline in economic, political, and moral terms. Thus, the Portuguese were apparently internally undermined long before the companies came along to deliver the coup de grâce. Such a view of a brief florescence and a long decline is remarkable in its similarities to conventional views of Ottoman history before and after the reign of *kanuni* Suleiman, and this may be no coincidence because both came to be seen as poor relations of Europe.[3]

In this chapter, we present a rather different interpretation of how the Portuguese presence in the Indian Ocean evolved in the sixteenth century. The principal elements we intend to stress are four in number: (1 the evolution of imperial ideology in the metropolis, and its effects on the way empire was conceived; (2 the evolution of the economic context, both in metropolitan Portugal and the Indian Ocean region; (3 the structure of society in Portuguese Asia, and the role of local initiatives as opposed to central drives; and (4 the spatial dynamic, as new Asian regions entered the ambit of Portuguese trade. It is obviously impossible to do full justice to these themes in the space available, and hence we must content ourselves with outlining the essentials in each case.

---

[2] For a critique, see K. Basu, E. Jones, and E. Schlicht, "The Growth and Decay of Custom: The Role of the New Institutional Economics in Economic History," *Explorations in Economic History* 24 (1987), esp. 8–19.

[3] For such views of the Portuguese Empire, see António Baiao et al., *História da Expansão Portuguesa no Mundo*, vol. II (Lisbon, 1939); and in English R. S. Whiteway, *The Rise of Portuguese Power in India, 1497–1550* (London, 1899); more recently, George D. Winius, *The Black Legend of Portuguese India* (New Delhi, 1985). On the Ottomans, see Bernard Lewis, "Ottoman Observers of Ottoman Decline," *Islamic Studies* 1 (1962): 71–87; also see V. J. Parry, "The Successors of Suleiman, 1566–1617," in M. A. Cook, ed., *A History of the Ottoman Empire to 1730* (Cambridge, 1976), 103–32.

I

Historians of Portuguese Asia frequently treat Vasco da Gama's arrival in Calicut in May 1498 as the very beginning of the Portuguese Asian enterprise. In doing so, they neglect the important role played by three-quarters of a century of expansion in north Africa and the Atlantic in influencing Portuguese designs in Asia. Over the period 1415 to 1500, the Portuguese had developed three distinct models of imperial organization. First, in north Africa, they held a network of coastal fortresses in a more or less endemic state of war, which were dominated for the most part by the Portuguese military nobility and its bellicose ideology. Second, in the Atlantic islands, they developed a system appropriate to that context, namely agrarian and territorial colonization and settlement, an experience that seems fundamentally to have shaped their later policies in Brazil. Third, on the coast of Guinea, the Portuguese developed a coastal network once again, but here their expansion was largely (though not wholly) commercial and peaceful, with a minimum of territorial occupation, settlement, or direct control of the means of production.

In the initial phase of their Asian venture, which is to say from roughly 1500 to 1530, the Portuguese tendency was to apply variants of these inherited models to different parts of Asia. Under Albuquerque, the north African model was applied to the western Indian Ocean, and from category of the *fronteiro* (frontiersman settler) was developed the Asian notion of the *casado* settler. East of Melaka, on the other hand, the Guinea model tended to dominate, with dispersed settlements linked by maritime threads, and apparently less conflictual in character than on the Indian west coast, in the Persian Gulf, the Red Sea, or East Africa. As for the Bay of Bengal, it remained for the most part a *mare incognitum* for Portuguese officialdom in the pre–1530 period, linked to the rest of the enterprise by commercial *carreira* voyages it is true, but for the greater part the domain of the Portuguese deserter and disreputable private trader.

The first three decades of the sixteenth century also constitute a more or less distinct phase for other reasons. This is the period in which the characteristic Manueline imperial ideology finds expression in Portugal, only slowly giving way in the late 1520s to its Joanine successor. To understand this ideology and its world view, it is necessary to read with great attention the letters addressed by D. Manuel to the pope and to the king of Castile describing the acts of his agents in Asia, the *regimentos* (instructions) of the king to these same agents (in particular D. Francisco de Almeida and Diogo Lopes de Sequeira), and the writings of D. Manuel's courtiers such as Duarte Galvão and Duarte Pacheco Pereira, even when they refer not to the king himself but to his ancestors.[4] From these sources, a curious and complex picture emerges. On the one hand, we have the "Portuguese monarchic capitalism" of the period, as so ably set out by Manuel Nunes Dias, and as manifested in trade on the Cape route, the functioning of the Flanders factory, and the structures of the Casa da India and the Casa de Guiné.[5] On the other hand, the Manueline imperial concept is clearly distinguished by other elements that are usually little analyzed. These include the central position given to *pareas* – a sort of tribute notionally rooted in the *taifa* that was extracted by the Iberian Islamic states of the Middle Ages – as well as an attachment to the medieval view of the emperor as quite literally the "king of kings." It is known that D. Manuel contemplated acquiring the title of emperor, and in fact appears to have been awaiting the accomplishment of his pet project before doing so. This project, though rarely discussed by historians of early sixteenth-century Portuguese expansion, is in fact very probably the key to his policies, without which one can understand neither his Asian projects nor his actions in north Africa: we refer here to the conquest of Jerusalem. Indeed, the repeated blockades of the Red Sea and the resources devoted to this end were justified precisely on these grounds: the need to strangulate the Islamic economy centered around the Holy Land, in order to facilitate its reconquest through a pincer movement from the south and the west.[6] The ideological statements of the period of D. Manuel are characterized moreover by Messianic overtones, with the mention of the accomplishment of prophecies, and a great significance given to the fact that D. Manuel – despite his great distance in genealogical terms from the throne – had become the king of Portugal in the first

[4] For a more detailed exposition of these ideas, see Luís Filipe Thomaz, "L'idée imperiale manueline," in J. Aubin, ed., *La Découverte, le Portugal et L'Europe* (Paris, in press). For some of the sources on which they are based, see Duarte Galvão, *Crónica de D. Afonso Henriques*, ed. J. de Bragança (Lisbon, 1950); Duarte Pacheco Pereira, *Esmeraldo in Situ Orbis*, ed. A. E. da Silva Dias (Lisbon, 1905); S. J. Pacifici, ed. and trans., *Copy of a Letter from the King of Portugal Sent to the King of Castile concerning the Voyage and Success of India* (Minneapolis: 1955); "Epistola ad Leonem X. Pont. Max. de victoriis habitis in India et Malacha," in *Novus Orbis Regionum ac Insularum Veteribus Incognitarum*, ed. Simon Grynaeus (Paris, 1532).

[5] Cf. Manuel Nunes Dias, *O Capitalismo Monárquico Português* (1415–1549), 2 vols. (Coimbra, 1963).

[6] Thomaz, "L'idée imperiale manueline;" on the Middle Eastern question, also see A. H. Lybyer, "The Influence of the Rise of the Ottoman Turks upon the Routes of Oriental trade," *English Historical Review*, 30 (1915): 577–88; for the post-Manueline period, also see Salih Özbaran, "The Ottoman Turks and the Portuguese in the Persian Gulf, 1543–1581," *Journal of Asian History* 6 (1972): 45–87.

place. This was seen as proof of a divine design, wherein "the humble and the small are chosen to confound the powerful."

Several characteristics distinguish Manueline ideology from that under his son and successor D. João III (r. 1521–57). In the latter reign, and especially from the end of the 1520s, Castilian influence becomes noticeably stronger, with the twin-marriage alliance between D. João and Charles V serving to reinforce this to a considerable extent. The Joanine period is, as is well known, that in which the phase of monarchic capitalism is on the wane with the shutting down of the Flanders (Antwerp) factory in the late 1540s being one significant landmark in this process.[7] Equally, it is the period when the Counter Reformation gains force in Portugal, and the Society of Jesus now makes its presence felt not only in the metropolis but also in the Asian empire. Once again, the rapid strides made by these forces – and the curious abortion of the Portuguese renaissance – may be at least partly attributed to the growing Hapsburg shadow, in evidence already in the period 1528 to 1532 in the letters of Lope Hurtado de Mendoza, Castilian ambassador to the Portuguese court, who dealt *inter alia* with the Moluccan question.[8] Equally, the abandoning in the second half of D. João III's reign of a good part of the north African network, especially Alcacér-Ceguer and Arzila in 1549–50 (besides Safi in 1542), is of some significance, signaling the giving up in explicit terms of the Jerusalem enterprise of D. Manuel. In Asia, one sees a decline in this same period in direct participation by the Crown in the commerce of the intra-Asian *carreiras*, which have by the 1540s often become purely freight-trade enterprises. In Asia, the Counter Reformation has other consequences as well, including the formulation of a clear policy of discrimination in the trading privileges given to Christians (as opposed to Muslims or Hindus) in Portuguese customs houses.[9]

The Joanine period therefore marks, according to some authors,

---

[7] Nunes Dias, *O Capitalismo Monárquico,* passim. For a discussion of the rise of the Flanders factory and the shift from Bruges to Antwerp early in the sixteenth century, see A. H. de Oliveira Marques, *Ensaios da História Medieval Portuguesa* (Lisbon, 1980), 159–93; also see the general discussion in Virgínia Rau, *Estudos sobre História Económica e Social do Antigo Regime,* ed. José Manuel Garcia (Lisbon, 1984), 143–60.

[8] Cf. Aude Viaud, "La cour de Portugal vue par Lope Hurtado de Mendoza (1528–1532)," in J. Aubin, ed., *La Découverte, le Portugal et L'Europe;* for the ambience of this period, also see José Sebastião da Silva Dias, *A Política Cultural da Época de D. João III,* (2 vols., Coimbra, 1969). For Portuguese-Spanish political relations, also see A. W. Lovett, *Early Habsburg Spain, 1517–1598* (Oxford, 1986), 169–71.

[9] Luís Filipe Thomaz, "Les Portugais dans les mers de l'Archipel au XVIe siècle," *Archipel* 18 (1979): 105–25; Vitorino Magalhães Godinho, "Fluctuações económicas e devir estrutural do século XVI ao século XVII," in Godinho, *Ensaios,* II, (sobre história de Portugal) (Lisbon, 1968).

the beginnings of a structural change in Portuguese society, both in the metropolis and overseas. The decline of monarchical capitalism is also the proximate cause of the beginnings of a deterioration in the position of the middle bourgeoisie, which had been closely associated with the state; and, as the state begins to see commerce as "beneath the dignity of the royal estate," there is equally a strengthening of the hand of the trading *fidalgo* and the internationally connected mercantile capitalist. The first clear signs of this appear however only in the reign of D. Sebastião, or perhaps during his minority; the period after 1580 (and the Hapsburg "capture" of the Portuguese monarchy) then serves to strengthen the tendency further. In an illuminating essay on the Philippine period in Portugal, Vitorino Magalhães Godinho suggests that Portuguese expansion had, by 1580, produced as a social type the *fidalgo tratante*, who was "linked to the cosmopolitan capitalist, in detriment of the middle bourgeoisie which was geographically dispersed," and goes on to add that "contrary to what has been supposed, the oceanic and overseas expansion wound up consolidating the position of the nobility: to their revenues from land, which may at times have been affected by the spectacular rise in prices, there are added the settlements, pensions, dowries etc."[10] Indeed, if one reads popular tracts written in support of D. António, prior of Crato and pretender to the Portuguese throne in the early 1580s, these often make the point that Castilian rule is bad for Portugal precisely because it would continue to strengthen the purely fiscal or "customs house" character of the royal role, as opposed to direct Crown involvement in trade.[11]

Over the period from 1500 to 1580 then, imperial ideology tended to shift quite clearly in respect of both trade and empire: on the one hand, the Crusade and the projected conquest of the Holy Land is abandoned: on the other, monarchical capitalism is abandoned for a more straightforward semi-Absolutist conception of the state's relationship to trade, in which trade was seen as beneath the dignity of the royal estate. Within this broad line of development, things did not always proceed smoothly of course; for instance, it may be argued that the 1570s mark a return to Manueline-style involvement in north Africa, though this was to end very soon in the sands of El-Ksar El-Kebir. But all in all, the general tendency appears clear enough, if to the elements outlined above we add one more: the creeping domi-

---

[10] Godinho, "1580 e a Restauração," in *Ensaios*, II, 268.
[11] Cf. J. M. Queiros Veloso, *O Interregno dos Governadores E O Breve Reinado de D. António* (Lisbon, 1953); Joaquim Veríssimo Serrão, *O Reinado de D. António, Prior de Crato* (Coimbra, 1956).

nance in the last quarter of the sixteenth century of an increasingly territorial conception of empire in Asia. We have already seen that the two models of empire espoused in Asia early on, in the period 1500 to 1530, were both based on conceptions of a network or thalassocracy. The one, more purely Manueline in its character perhaps, was what obtained east of Melaka in imitation of the Guinea coast pattern. The other, for which Albuquerque appears to have been principally responsible, obviously reflected his own experiences in north Africa, but was still based on the idea of a network, though a military one to be sure. It is noteworthy that both these models differ substantially from that adopted in Brazil in the first major phase of expansion; in the latter case, the system of *capitanias* is introduced in the 1530s in an effort at conquering territorial space. Early Portuguese imperial structures in Asia are also in marked contrast to Castilian empire-building principles, whether in Nueva España, Tierra Firme or – later in the sixteenth century – in the Philippines. Initially basing themselves on a tenure termed *repartimiento*, the Castilians soon adopted the famous *encomienda* system, which – despite later attempts at reform – remained their basic building block overseas in the sixteenth and early seventeenth century.[12] Theirs was a concept of empire then that was territorial to the core, and even if trade was in a sense centralized after the initial period (so that ships could set sail only from Seville), private participation was crucial to maritime commerce in all phases. Thus, in the forms in which they existed ca. 1550, Castilian-style empire demanded the subordination of the sea to the land, and Portuguese-style empire *in Asia at least* reversed the relationship: in the first half of the sixteenth century, "Portuguese India" did not designate a space that was geographically well defined but a complex of territories, establishments, goods, persons, and administrative interests in Asia and East Africa, generated by or subordinate to the Portuguese Crown, all of which were linked together as a maritime network.

Could these two distinct concepts survive the union of the two Crowns in 1580? Most historians, like J. H. Elliott, have argued that they must have done so, mainly because Philip II, at the Cortes of Tomar, held in April 1581, agreed to keep Portuguese affairs overseas separate from those of Castile.[13] However, we know now that this promise was in some respects a dead letter from the moment it was

---

[12] Cf. James Lockhart, *Spanish Peru, 1532–1560* (Madison, 1968); L. B. Simpson, *The Encomienda in New Spain* (Berkeley, 1950); and Nicholas P. Cushner, *Spain in the Philippines* (Quezon City, 1971).

[13] J. H. Elliott, *Imperial Spain, 1469–1716* (London, 1963), 264–5.

uttered, for Philip had agreed to turn a blind eye to Portuguese (and especially New Christian) participation in Spanish America, as the price to be paid for the support of the trading *fidalgos* and upper bourgeoisie. Thus, by the 1630s, the Portuguese had penetrated the economies of both the Peru viceroyalty and Mexico to a substantial extent, and only the repression of the post–1635 period could manage to undo this.[14] On the other hand, trade between Manila and the Macao was winked at; later, the Spanish even entered into a series of territorial adventures in mainland Southeast Asia.[15] Further, because under Hapsburg rule the governing council of Portugal was dominated by men who, even when Portuguese, were noted for their loyalty to Castile, and who had often spent substantial parts of their lives in Spain (like Cristôvão de Moura, Marquês de Castel Rodrigo), it is questionable whether they would have been free of Castilian influence in their own thinking on empire-related questions.[16]

At any rate, it is remarkable that the last two decades of the sixteenth century see a succession of attempts in Asia, with either prior or post facto sanction from Philip II, to create an empire of large territorial units. In east Africa, this period is marked by several farfetched schemes to conquer Monomotapa, which would eventually result (it may be argued) in the creation of the *prazos* of the region; the 1580s and 1590s also witness a bitter series of struggles between the *Estado da India* and local powers over control of the island of Sri Lanka, which the Portuguese now attempt to conquer in its totality; equally, there are attempts in Burma and Cambodia to create land-based imperial structures.[17] Even though these did not result primarily from central initiatives, it is evidently no coincidence that such a rash of "territoriality" occurred even as the Hapsburgs gained control of the Portuguese Crown.

---

[14] Cf. Harry E. Cross, "Commerce and Orthodoxy: A Spanish Response to Portuguese Commercial Penetration in the Viceroyalty of Peru, 1580–1640," *The Americas* 35 (1978): 151–67; also, the poorly argued but well-documented study of Gonçalo de Reparaz, *Os Portugueses no Vice-Reinado do Peru (Séculos XVI e XVII)* (Lisbon, 1976).

[15] On Manila-Macao trade in the early 1590s, see Viktor von Klarwill, *The Fugger News-Letters*, trans. Pauline de Chary (London, 1924), 143–6. On Spanish ambitions in Southeast Asia, see Charles R. Boxer, "Portuguese and Spanish Projects for the Conquest of Southeast Asia, 1580–1600," *Journal of Asian History* 3 (1968): 118–136.

[16] On Moura, see Lovett, *Early Habsburg Spain*, 171–4; for a general biographical study, see Alfonso Danvila y Burguero, *Don Cristóbal de Moura, Primer Marqués de Castel Rodrigo, 1538–1613* (Madrid, 1900).

[17] For a more extensive discussion of these questions, see Boxer, "Spanish and Portuguese Projects"; also Sanjay Subrahmanyam, "The Tail Wags the Dog: Some Aspects of the External Relations of the *Estado da India*, 1570–1600," *Moyen Orient et Océan Indien*, V (1988).

II

Turning from imperial ideology and the metropolis to the empire as it appeared on the ground, we come up against a near-insuperable problem, for the statistical information that one needs to analyze the evolution of the Portuguese Asian economy in the sixteenth century is hard to some by. Such information as is available tends to appear in specific contexts: first, there is some data on shipping and trade on the Cape route; second, financial statistics exist, on customs house revenues and expenditures, for various years in the sixteenth century, at times in the form of budgets (or *orçamentos*); third, we have in the last quarter of the sixteenth century some statistical data on the so-called concession system of voyages, which were introduced when the Portuguese Crown reduced its involvement in intra-Asian commerce. Apart from these data, statistical and economic information tends to be scattered, and limited to the odd account-book (*livro de receita e despesa*), giving details of the functioning of a factory or of a set of voyages on Crown shipping, but more often than not fragmentary and concerned with a limited period.

Portuguese and more recently foreign scholars have struggled manfully to squeeze blood from these turnips, and in the forefront of this struggle has been V. M. Godinho. Where trade on the Cape route is concerned, he was able to put together fairly convincing statistics on the numbers of ship arrivals and departures, at both the European and Asian ends, as well as losses en route.[18] It is only very recently that his work has been superseded, by the American historian T. Bentley Duncan, who provides us not only with more complete data on shipping, but also estimates of tonnage. His findings on sixteenth-century traffic on the Cape route are summarized in Table 8.1.[19]

It emerges quite clearly from Table 8.1 and from Duncan's plausible reconstruction of the tonnages that the substantial increase that took place over the sixteenth century in the tonnage of individual vessels compensated for the decline in the numbers of thè vessels themselves on the Cape route. This therefore helps lay to rest one myth: that Portuguese trade on the Cape route declined substantially after the mid-sixteenth century.

[18] V. M. Godinho, *Os Descobrimentos e a Economia Mundial*, 2 vols. (Lisbon, 1963–5), II, 77–8.
[19] T. Bentley Duncan, "Navigation between Portugal and Asia in the Sixteenth and Seventeenth centuries," in E. J. Van Kley and C. K. Pullapilly, eds., *Asia and the West : Encounters and Exchanges from the Age of Explorations* (Notre Dame, 1986), 3–25.

Table 8.1. *16th Century Portuguese Shipping on The Cape Route*

Period	Europe-Asia				Asia-Europe			
	Departures		Arrivals		Departures		Arrivals	
	Ships	Tonnage	Ships	Tonnage	Ships	Tonnage	Ships	Tonnage
1501–10	151	42,775	135	38,695	88	26,085	73	21,115
1511–20	96	38,690	87	35,830	60	26,060	59	25,760
1521–30	81	37,720	67	32,290	55	28,520	53	27,020
1531–40	80	44,660	76	42,610	61	39,110	57	36,410
1541–50	68	40,800	56	34,100	58	34,550	52	30,550
1551–60	58	39,600	46	32,500	47	33,650	35	25,750
1561–70	50	37,030	46	35,580	45	36,250	40	32,150
1571–80	50	42,900	48	40,800	42	38,250	39	35,150
1581–90	59	55,420	45	42,870	51	48,450	42	39,290
1591–1600	43	49,200	39	42,540	40	45,350	22	25,000

Source: T. Bently Duncan, "Navigation between Portugal and Asia in the sixteenth and seventeenth centuries," in E. J. Van Kley and C. K. Pullapilly, eds., *Asia and the West: Encounters and Exchanges From the Age of Explorations* (Notre Dame: 1986), 3–25.

To round out the picture, detailed figures on cargoes are necessary. However, these are available to us in the case of the Asia-Europe run (the more interesting from this viewpoint) for only thirty-one years in the sixteenth century, and with large gaps. The largest of these gaps extend from 1531 to 1547, and again from 1549 to 1580, but even in years when figures are available they may be incomplete, and sometimes only partially take account of private trade on the Cape route.[20] One of the much-debated questions in this context is the extent to which Portuguese return cargoes on the *Carreira da India* were able to meet European demand for pepper and spices. Since F. C. Lane's classic paper on the revival of the Mediterranean spice trade in the last third of the sixteenth century, it has increasingly passed into conventional wisdom that the Portuguese domination of the European pepper and spice market lasted only a few decades. Thereafter, it is argued, either on account of Portugal's lack of resources, or because the Portuguese were by nature or preference tax-gatherers, the older route between Asia and Europe via the Levant revived. According to some, like Niels Steensgaard, this meant that at the close of the sixteenth century, the Portuguese supplied a mere half of European imports of pepper and spices, and this even before their northern European rivals appeared on the Asian scene.[21] This argument has been severely criticized though in recent times, not least of all on account of its tenuous statistical basis. As a result of the work of C. H. H. Wake, a more complex view of the role of the Cape route has arisen, and it is argued that Levant-route imports into Europe became significant only in such years when the Portuguese failed, for whatever reason, to meet European demand.[22] For the most part, trade from Malabar, Aceh, and other pepper- and spice-producing areas in Asia to the Red Sea may have been intended to supply Middle Eastern and north African markets.

Recent writings have also begun to stress the changing commodity composition of Portuguese trade on the Cape route in the course of the sixteenth century. At the European end, as the century progresses, the emphasis on bullion exports (particularly in the form of rials of eight) becomes stronger, though it is very likely that bullion domi-

---

[20] For details of such cargoes, see, besides Godinho, *Os Descobrimentos*, Geneviève Bouchon, *Navires et Cargaisons Retour de L'Inde en 1518* (Paris, 1977), and *L'Asie du Sud à L'Epoque des Grandes Découvertes* (London, 1988).

[21] F. C. Lane, "The Mediterranean Spice Trade: Its revival in the Sixteenth Century," reprinted in Lane, *Venice and History* (Baltimore, 1966); also Steensgaard, *Carracks, Caravans, and Companies*, 168–9.

[22] See C. H. H. Wake, "The Changing Composition of Europe's Pepper and Spice Imports, ca. 1400 to 1700," *Journal of European Economic History* 8 (1979): 361–403.

Table 8.2. *Composition of Imports Into Lisbon From Asia (% weight)*

Period	Pepper	Ginger	Cinnamon	Spices	Textiles	Indigo	Other
1513–19	80.0	7.3	2.1	9.0	0.2	0.0	1.4
1523–31	84.0	6.1	3.3	6.2	0.0	0.0	0.4
1547–48	89.0	4.2	0.9	4.5	0.0	0.0	1.4
1587–88	68.0	3.7	6.3	1.6	10.5	8.4	1.5
1600–03	65.0	2.5	8.7	5.0	12.2	4.4	2.2

Source: Neils Steensgaard, "The Return Cargoes of the *Carreira da India* in the Sixteenth Century," in T. R. De Souza, ed., *Indo-Portuguese History: Old Issues, New Questions* (New Delhi: 1984), 13–31.

nated Portuquese exports to Asia even in the early sixteenth century. The evolution of the return cargoes is more interesting, for here, though pepper, spices, and to an extent lac are of significance in the early 1500s, cinnamon, indigo, and above all textiles come to account for a significant share of cargo space in the last quarter of the sixteenth century (Table 8.2).[23]

However, in addition to the changes shown in Table 8.2, some writers have posited a phenomenal increase in the last decades of the sixteenth century in terms of *value* in private trade in silks, cottons, and jewels. These, it is suggested by James Boyajian, could between them have accounted for consignments worth some 2.25 million *cruzados* by the early seventeenth century![24] Although the particular figure cited here may be something of an exaggeration, there is no gainsaying that important shifts do occur in the composition of trade, whether seen in value or volume terms. In part, such shifts reflect changes in European tastes, but they also reflect the rise of a new class of substantial and well-connected private traders, like the trading *fidalgos* mentioned somewhat earlier. Late sixteenth-century governors and viceroys like Manuel de Sousa Coutinho (1588–91) and D. Francisco da Gama (1597–1600) made substantial private fortunes, and there is considerable documentation linking them to the pepper contractors and their agents in Asia, including the wealthy Augsburger

[23] Cf. the thought-provoking synthesis by Niels Steensgaard, "The Return Cargoes of the *Carreira da India* in the Sixteenth Century," in T. R. De Souza, ed., *Indo-Portuguese History : Old Issues, New Questions* (New Delhi, 1984), 13–31.

[24] See James C. Boyajian, *Portuguese Bankers at the Court of Spain, 1620–1650* (New Brunswick, 1983), 220–1.

Ferdinand Cron and the "Lusitanian Sinbad," Duarte Gomes Solis; these *fidalgos* thus set the trend that was later followed by other trading viceroys like D. Miguel de Noronha in the 1630s and D. Filipe Mascarenhas in the 1640s.[25] The rise in the value of private trade is reflected in the growing amounts paid per Cape route vessel by customs-farmers in Lisbon: 23 million *reis* in the 1580s, 30 million *reis* in the 1590s, and 50 million *reis* in the period 1600–1624.[26]

Over the course of the sixteenth century, trade on the Cape route was organized under various different regimes, reflecting in large measure the Crown's perception of its commercial and economic role. In the early decades, the Crown itself organized most shipping, with some conspicuous exceptions. For example, in the period 1497 to 1510, several Florentine merchant houses with interests in Lisbon were actually permitted to send vessels to Asia as part of a larger fleet; these ventures probably reach their height with the fleet that sailed in 1510 under the command of Diogo Mendes de Vasconcelos, and which was largely staffed and financed by the commercial house of Sernigi and its associates.[27] Such a form of enterprise seems to have become more rare in later years, though it should be conceded that our information on the trade of the Cape route is quite deficient for the middle decades of the sixteenth century. From the 1560s, however, the winds of change had most definitely begun to blow. In 1564 the first of a whole series of contracts was signed, giving over trade on the Cape route to private parties. This move was retracted though in 1570, when D. Sebastião introduced a set of wide-ranging if short-lived changes, including the freedom of commerce, save for silver and copper exports and pepper imports. This may be seen as an incipient hands-off policy in respect of trade, as well as an assertion of the essentially military and revenue-gathering character of the

---

[25] For a general overview on these and related questions, see Frédéric Mauro, "La bourgeoisie portugaise au XVII siècle," in Mauro, *Études Économiques sur L'Expansion Portugaise* (1500–1900) (Paris, 1970), 15–35. On Solis, see the excellent but little-known study by José Calvet de Magalhães, "Duarte Gomes Solis," *Studia* 19 1966: 119–71 ; on Cron, see *inter alia* Charles R. Boxer, "Uma raridade bibliográfica sobre Fernão Cron," *Boletim Internacional de Bibliografia Luso-Brasileira* 12 (1971): 323–64. On D. Miguel de Noronha, see A. R. Disney *Twilight of the Pepper Empire* (Cambridge, Mass., 1978), which will soon be superseded on this issue by Disney's forthcoming biography of this *fidalgo*. Finally, for a glimpse of D. Filipe Mascarenhas's activities, see George D. Winius, *The Fatal History of Portuguese Ceylon : Transition to Dutch Rule* (Cambridge, Mass., 1971), 99–100, 109–13.

[26] See Boyajian, *Portuguese Bankers*, 220.

[27] See Carmen M. Radulet, "Girolamo Sernigi e a importância económica do Oriente," *Revista da Universidade de Coimbra*, 1984, 67–77 ; also Sanjay Subrahmanyam, " 'Um bom homem de tratar': Piero Strozzi, a Florentine in Portuguese Asia, 1510–1522," *Journal of European Economic History* 16 (1987): 511–26.

state.[28] It is difficult to sort out the tangled threads of policy in this period, for we must also bear in mind that the same decade sees a revival of interest in the north African outposts abandoned under D. João III – which does suggest a harking back in part at least to Manueline thinking.

But the period of D. Sebastião certainly sees no efforts to revive monarchical capitalism; on the contrary, in 1576, there is once again a reversion to the contract system on the Cape route with the beneficiary being the Augsburg merchant Konrad Rott. With the folding up of Rott's enterprise a few years later, however, the system of contracts did not end; if anything it was strengthened under Philip II. In the period 1581 to 1586, the Crown continued to retain control of trade in cinnamon and Chinese silk, giving over the pepper trade to the Augsburg firms of Fugger and Welser; then, in 1586, the Milanese Giovanni Battista Rovellasca – earlier one of Rott's associates – took on a contract of six years duration, in association with Giraldo Paris of Limbourg. The contract required Rovellasca to finance the fitting out of five ships a year to Asia, and to dispatch to Asia some 170,000 *cruzados* a year to buy 30,000 *quintais* of pepper.[29] Later contracts with other firms such as the Ximenes d'Aragão, the Fuggers, and the Welsers, as well as the Malvenda, endured to 1598, when the Crown – apparently anticipating a quickening in rivalry on the Cape route with northern European rivals – reverted to direct control.[30]

Thus, even on the Cape route, the regime of traffic evolved over the sixteenth century, reflecting changes in the Crown's self-perception, the extent of its involvement with international banker firms, as also possibly the fact that – as the century wore on – more and more administrative attention had to be devoted to Brazil rather than India. As for trade within Asia, the participation of the Portuguese Crown therein also followed distinct phases over the sixteenth century. In an initial period, from 1511 to 1520, a whole series of Crown routes (or *carreiras*) were created, many emanating from Melaka and created in cooperation with Tamil-speaking Kling merchants

---

[28] For a general discussion of these changes, see A. H. de Oliveira Marques, *História de Portugal*, I (Lisbon, 1976), 464–5.

[29] For details, see Hermann Kellenbenz, "Les frères Fugger et le marché international du poivre autour de 1600," *Annales* E.S.C. 11 (1956): 1–28.

[30] Cf. José Gentil da Silva, *Contratos de Trazida de Drogas no Século XVI* (Lisbon, 1949); also the discussion in Kellenbenz, "Les frères Fugger et le marche' international dupoivre." For further details of shipping and pepper cargoes, see Luíz de Figueiredo Falcão, *Livro em Que Se Contem Toda a Fazenda e Real Património de Portugal* (Lisbon, 1859).

resident there, but also others involving ports like Goa, Bhatkal, and Hormuz.[31] By around 1530, however, a dual process had begun to change this system piecemeal: on the one hand, the first moves occur toward substituting privately owned vessels for the Crown's own; on the other, a shift takes place – even on *carreiras* operated with Crown shipping – of reducing the investment of Crown capital in the cargo to a minimum, and pursuing a form of freight-trade. This style of commerce, it was often declared in the 1540s and 1550s, benefited the Crown less than the royally appointed captain and scrivener, who held sections of the cargo space as perquisites and arranged to have the choicest goods (with the highest value to volume ratio) stowed in their *agazalhados*, or "liberty-chests."[32] Although reforms of this system were discussed through the 1540s, action seems to have been taken only in the next decade, by which time the structure of the entire Portuguese enterprise had undergone a convulsion.

This mid-century crisis has been pointed to by several historians, most notably V. M. Godinho, who sees it as nothing less than a *viragem estrutural* (structural break, or reversal of conjuncture) lasting from 1545 to 1552, and consequently far more serious than earlier financial and commercial crises such as those of 1521–4 and 1531–5. His evidence for the seriousness of the crisis is fairly strong at the European end, but in the case of Asia stems fundamentally from customs house records, which show that the principal collection points in Portuguese Asia witnessed a severe contraction in receipts, some in the mid–1540s, some in around 1550.[33] It may be suggested that the serious agrarian crisis that besets peninsular India in the early 1540s, with consequences ranging as far as the Red Sea, is the beginning of the problem. We are aware that mortality was severe, and D. João de Castro even claimed (though this is hardly to be taken literally) that two-thirds of the inhabitants of the Deccan died as a result of the famine and associated epidemics.[34] As a study of other crises on which

---

[31] See Luís Filipe Thomaz, *De Malaca a Pegu : Viagens de um Feitor Português* (1512–1515) (Lisbon, 1966); Thomaz, "Nina Chatu e o comércio português em Malaca," *Memórias do Centro de Estudos de Marinha* 5 (1976): 3–27. Also more recently, Jean Aubin, "Un Voyage de Goa à Ormuz en 1520, "*Modern Asian Studies* 22, no. 3 (1988): 417–32.

[32] See the discussion of the Bengal and Coromandel *carreiras* in Sanjay Subrahmanyam, "The Coromandel-Malacca Trade in the Sixteenth Century: A Study of Its Evolving Structure," *Moyen Orient et Océan Indien*, III (1986): 55–80; Sanjay Subrahmanyam, "Notes on the 16th century Bengal trade," *The Indian Economic and Social History Review* 25 (1987): 265–89.

[33] Godinho, "Fluctuações económicas e devir estrutural," in *Ensaios*, II, 177–205.

[34] Letter from D. João de Castro to the Infante D. Luís, 30 October 1540, in Elaine Sanceau, ed., *Cartas de D. João de Castro* (Lisbon, 1954), 49–50. Also see the remarks

Table 8.3. *Customs Collection in Melaka and Hormuz*
(in thousands of serafins)

Period	Melaka	Period	Hormuz (average)
1542	100.0	1524–28	100.0
1543	96.5	1529–33	98.5
1544	85.7	1534–38	98.5
1550	40.6	1539–43	105.5
1555	169.0	1544–48	82.6
1568	202.8	1549–51	120.2
1574	160.7	1574	169.8
1581	150.1	1588	168.5
1586	202.8	1605	174.3
1590	176.4	1610	179.0

Source: For these figures, see V. M. Godinho, *Les Finances de L'État Portugais des Indes Orientales (1517–1635)*, (Paris: 1982) 47–49, 96, 115. On Melaka, also see Thomaz, "Les Portugais dans les mers de l'Archipel."

clearer evidence exists, like that of the early 1630s, brings home, such agrarian contractions were apt to be reflected in sharp drops in trade and consequently in customs collections.[35] Evidently, this had a considerable impact on the finances of Portuguese India, especially when taken together with the threat posed by Ottoman expansion in the western Indian Ocean in the same decade.

As Table 8.3 indicates, customs collections in Hormuz and Melaka dropped sharply; in the case of Goa, figures are not available for the first half of the sixteenth century, but a comparison between mid-century and the early 1570s does suggest – as in the other two cases – a quite considerable expansion of customs collection, which may hence be taken to imply that here too the period around 1550 was something of a low-water mark.[36]

in Gaspar Correia, *Lendas da India*, ed. R. J. de Lima Felner, vol. IV (Lisbon, 1864), 131–2.

[35] Cf. Sanjay Subrahmanyam, *The Political Economy of Commerce : A Study of Southern India*, 1500–1650 (Cambridge, in press), Chaps. IV and VI ; W. S. Atwell, "Some Observations on the 'Seventeenth Century Crisis' in China and Japan," *Journal of Asian Studies* 45 no. 2 (1986): 223–44.

[36] For these figures, see V. M. Godinho, *Les Finances de L'État Portugais des Indes Ori-*

Other sources independently corroborate that the 1540s and early 1550s were bad years financially for the Portuguese Asian enterprise. Shipping tonnage sent out on the Cape route from Asia to Europe, which had steadily expanded from 1510 through to 1540 (as Table 8.1 shows), contracts slightly in the 1550s and 1560s, to recover thereafter in the last three decades of the century. The letters and extensive reports of the *vedor da fazenda* Simão Botelho seem also to point in this direction because they are very largely concerned with financial reorganization and potential new sources of revenue.[37] Finally, the policies followed by governors of the 1540s such as Martim Afonso de Souza, raiding temples and the like, were – at least in the Goan rumor-mills that were tapped by Gaspar Correia – attributed to the unsound state of official finances.[38] The defense of Diu undertaken by D. João de Castro later in the same decade can only have added to this imbalance between expenditures and receipts.[39]

Thus, in the 1550s and more rapidly still in the following decade, Portuguese Crown participation in intra-Asian commerce shrank to a considerable extent. Of the intra-Asian *carreiras* of the mid-sixteenth century, only one survived intact into the 1580s, that from Goa to the Banda Islands. For the rest, the *carreiras* now gave way to the *viagens*, or concessionary-voyages, of which there were in 1580 some thirty, roughly a half involving Melaka either as destination or point of departure. In some cases, a *carreira* route was simply transformed into a *viagem*, but some major new voyages were also created, notably from Goa to Nagasaki via Macao (the so-called Great Ship from Amacon), and the Goa-Moçambique voyage created after 1580.[40] The concessions of these voyages were typically given out as rewards to the nobility, or to soldiers of long service, and fairly soon most of them acquired a waiting list, which could be of several decades duration. On occasions of exceptional financial stringency, such as once

---

entales (1517–1635) (Paris, 1982), 47–9, 96, 115. On Melaka, also see Thomaz, "Les Portugais dans les mers de l'Archipel."

[37] Botelho's correspondence and report may be found in R. J. de Lima Felner, ed., *Subsídios para a História da Índia Portuguesa* (Lisbon, 1868).

[38] Correia, *Lendas*, IV, 299–305, 324–30.

[39] For further details, see J. B. Aquarone, *D. João de Castro, Gouverneur et Viceroi des Indes Orientales* (1500–1548) (Paris, 1968), 2 vols.

[40] On the Macao voyage, see the classic study by C. R. Boxer, *The Great Ship from Amacon: Annals of Macao and the Old Japan Trade, 1555–1640* (Lisbon, 1959); on the other voyages, see "Livro das cidades e fortalezas que a Coroa de Portugal tem nas partes da India," ed. F. P. Mendes da Luz, *Boletim da Biblioteca da Universidade de Coimbra* 21 (1953), 1–144. For the concession-system in the early seventeenth century, and the *venda geral*, see Biblioteca Nacional de Lisboa, Fundo Geral, no. 1540, f. 89–91v; also Arquivo Nacional da Torre do Tombo, Lisbon, Documentos Remetidos da Índia, no. 38, f. 334–45.

Table 8.4. *Returns From Major Intra-Asian Voyages, c. 1580*

Route	Net Average Profit (in cruzados)	Auction Price (in cruzados)
Goa-Macao/Nagasaki	35,000	20,000
Goa-Moluccas		
: captain	9,500	
: scrivener	3,000	
Malaka-Macao	10,000	5,500
Coromandel-Melaka	6,000	
Coromandel-Cosmin	6,000	
Melaka-Pipli	9,000	
Melaki-Sunda	10,000	5,500
Melaka-Borneo	5,500	
Maco-Sunda	6,500	

Source: Thomaz, "Les Portugais dans les mers de l'Archipel," which is based in turn on the "Livro das Cidades e Fortalezas."

in the early seventeenth century, they were all sold in auction (the famous *venda geral*), with the purchasers getting precedence over regular grantees. The voyages were broadly of two types: the complete monopolies, which excluded all other shipping on the concession route; and grants of the position of captain-major over all trading vessels on a given route with certain additional perquisites. Although some of the more lucrative concessions – like those from Coromandel to Melaka, or from Coromandel to Cosmin (in Burma) – were given out as such, others sometimes came attached to official positions. The captains of Melaka in the 1580s thus enjoyed the right to a good number of concession-voyages, in the Bay of Bengal and the Indonesian archipelago. Often, these concessions acquired a resale value, and the captains of Melaka usually sold theirs to the highest bidder, rather than troubling to make the voyage themselves (Table 8.4).[41]

In sum then, the structure of Crown participation, both on the Cape route and in trade within Asia, had changed considerably between about 1520 and 1580 (from the death of D. Manuel to the accession of D. Felipe). Equally, that part of trade within Asia that was *not* in official Portuguese hands had changed over the same period. One

[41] Thomaz, "Les Portugais dans les mers de l'Archipel," which is based in turn on the "Livro das Cidades e Fortalezas."

fairly well-recognized development is the rise of trade from the north Sumatran port of Aceh to the Red Sea, a process that begins around 1530 but gathers momentum only in the 1560s.[42] Equally, Aceh became a center of great importance for trade and Islamicization in Indonesia, thus inheriting to an extent the mantle of the old Sultanate of Melaka. Less well known but equally important is Aceh's trade within the Bay of Bengal, to the ports of lower Burma, Arakan, Bengal itself, and Coromandel ports such as Masulipatnam. A network of trade developed in this maritime region over the last third of the sixteenth century that was outside the control of the Portuguese *Estado da India*, though private traders and renegades of Portuguese origin were at times involved in it.[43] This network, and others like it in Indonesian waters, thus constitutes an alternative system to the concession-voyages mentioned above. A third set of routes existed that is also worth mentioning, these dominated by the Portuguese *casados* resident in the cities and settlements of the *Estado da India*. This network will be discussed at greater length in the next section.

As a consequence of the changes in administrative and commercial structure made over the sixteenth century, the Portuguese Asian enterprise remained a solvent one, when seen in terms of the official calculus. The Crown kept two sets of books: one with respect to trade on the Cape route; the other the balance sheet of the *Estado da India* itself (Table 8.5). An examination of the latter, the so-called *orçamentos*, shows that the receipts from customs and other revenues (including the so-called *páreas*, or tribute), usually exceeded officially stated expenditures, thus yielding a surplus (*saldo*). It should be noted that there are some reasons for treating these figures with caution, for they do not always account for nonroutine expenditures (toward defending a settlement against siege, or sending a special expeditionary fleet). There may also be some suspicion that they do not represent a statement of fact, but rather some combination of ideas of the normal and the ideal. What they do testify to is that when things were proceeding normally, no deficits were experienced – a statement that does not rule out the possibility of deficits occurring in actual fact, as in the mid-sixteenth century.[44]

Within this structure, there were, however, areas of normal deficit

---

[42] C. R. Boxer, "A Note on the Portuguese Response to the Revival of the Red Sea Spice trade and the Rise of Atjeh, 1540–1600," *Journal of Southeast Asian History* 10 (1969): 415–28.

[43] Cf. Sanjay Subrahmanyam, "The Portuguese Response to the Rise of Masulipatnam, 1570–1600," *The Great Circle* 8 (1986): 127–30.

[44] A. T. de Matos, "The financial situation of the State of India during the Philippine Period (1581–1635)," in De Souza, ed., *Indo-Portuguese History*, 90–101.

Table 8.5. *Budget Figures For The Estado Da India*

(a) Receipts and Expenditures, 1581–1609, in reis

Year	Receipts	Expenditures	Surplus
1581	263,036,953	242,784,701	20,252,252
1588	303,051,620	259,949,854	43,101,766
1607	355,530,600	235,677,600	120,153,000
1609	249,780,000	156,627,088	93,152,912

(b) Chief Revenue-collection points (%)

Location	1581	1588	1607	1609
Goa	26.3	28.5	34.2	34.3
Hormuz	21.3	18.2	16.6	17.9
Bassein	17.9	14.1	10.4	9.8
Diu	15.0	17.5	18.1	19.1
Melaka	7.0	8.3	7.4	7.0
Daman	6.5	6.5	5.0	4.3
Others	6.0	6.9	8.3	7.7

Source: A. T. de Matos, "The financial situation of the State of India during the Philippine period (1581–1635)," in De Souza, ed., *Indo-Portuguese History*, 90–101.

and surplus. In the 1574 *orçamento*, for example, Hormuz, Diu, Daman, Bassein, and Chaul are shown as surplus centers (where revenue collection exceeds local expenditures), as is Melaka.[45] On the other hand, the Moluccas, Sri Lanka, Goa, and the Indian southwest coast show a deficit.

Reconciling these figures with those for trade on the Cape route can prove difficult. In a sense, the maintenance of a fort at, say, Cochin was in part an expenditure that helped guarantee a certain level of return to trade on the Cape route, even if it is shown as part of the *orçamento* of the *Estado da India*. Yet, at the same time, one is never sure precisely what proportion of the Cochin expenses could reasonably be attributed to the "pepper account." Moreover, because the Portuguese Crown saw fit to keep the two accounts separate, we

[45] Cf. Godinho, *Les Finances de L'État Portugais*, passim.

would not be justified in pooling them indiscriminately either. This is a problem that must remain central to any discussion of the "contribution" of the Asian empire to the Portuguese state.

III

It is common enough in the existent historiography to compare the massiveness of the Asian population to the smallness of that of Portugal in the sixteenth century. In about 1527, Portugal had a population of at most 1.4 million, and by 1640 that number had increased to about 2 million.[46] But of even these, a relatively small proportion reached the overseas possessions in the sixteenth century because colonization based on mass emigration was a phenomenon that largely post-dated 1600. V. M. Godinho has suggested that emigration from Portugal in the fifteenth century was of the order of 50,000; the pace then increased, so that the figures for 1500–1580 and 1580–1640 are respectively 280,000 and 300,000 to 360,000. He goes on to posit that in the late sixteenth century, there were between 100,000 and 150,000 Portuguese resident overseas, be it in Brazil, Africa, the Atlantic islands, or Asia.[47]

What proportion of these is Asia likely to have accounted for? In 1513, Godinho notes, it was suggested that there were in Asia some 2,500 Portuguese capable of bearing arms; this number had increased already by 1516 to around 4,000. The increase continued, albeit in a gradual fashion, in the succeeding decades. According to D. João de Castro, writing in 1539, there were at that time "between Sofala and China" some 6,000 to 7,000 Portuguese, but thereafter an acceleration is perceptible. Estimates for the last quarter of the sixteenth century tend to hover between 14,000 and 16,000, which is to say somewhat over double what obtained in mid-century.[48] At most then, less than 1 percent of the Portuguese population was resident in Asia at any point in the century; and, until the mid-century, the number was closer to 0.6 percent. In addition to the population resident in Asia on a medium- to long-term basis, there was also a substantial turnover, serviced by the Carreira da India. According to recent rough

---

[46] Godinho, "Os Portugueses e o Oriente," in Ensaios, II, 209–10.
[47] V. M. Godinho, "L'émigration portugaise (XVe–XXe siècles) – Une constante structurelle et les réponses au changements du monde," Revista de História Económica e Social 1, (1978): 5–32, esp. 8–9. On the population of the Atlantic islands, also see T. Bentley Duncan, Atlantic Islands: Madeira, The Azores and the Cape Verdes in Seventeenth-Century Commerce and Navigation (Chicago, 1972), 255–8.
[48] Cf. Godinho, "L'émigration portugaise" see also his, "Os Portugueses e o Oriente."

Table 8.6. *Movements of Persons By The Cape Route (decennial average)*

Period	Europe-Asia		Asia-Europe		Net additions
	Departures	Arrivals	Departures	Arrivals	
1500–40	18,000	16,140	9,190	8,400	6,950
1540–70	17,370	16,136	11,640	10,146	4,500
1570–1600	24,136	22,134	16,600	13,700	5,534
Total	198,000	180,000	122,000	105,000	58,000

Source: Bentley Duncan, "Navigation between Portugal and Asia," Table I, 22.

estimates by Bentley Duncan, between 1497 and 1600, around 198,000 persons embarked for Asia from Lisbon by the Cape route, of which some 180,000 reached their destination (the rest dying en route). Over the same period, some 122,000 persons left Asia for Portugal by way of the Cape, of whom some 105,000 may be thought to have returned home safely (this figure excludes slaves brought from Asia and East Africa to Europe).[49] Putting these figures together, we may conclude that over this period of just more than a century, some 58,000 persons from among the Portuguese (and their associates who took part in the Portuguese enterprise) who left Europe for Asia, did not return, either because they settled in Asia, or because they died before they could return (Table 8.6).[50]

Given the smallness of this expatriate population, it might be thought a relatively easy task to trace their social and geographical origins in Portugal. In fact, no convincing study exists of this to date, and we are therefore forced to rely on impressionistic evidence. Table 8.7 presents the population profile in Portugal, divided by region, in the late 1520s.[51]

It appears that in the first half of the sixteenth century, emigrants to Asia were drawn more or less indifferently from all of these regions. Thereafter, and especially in the last third of the same century, and after 1600, the northern regions of Entre Douro e Minho and Trás os

[49] Bentley Duncan, "Navigation between Portugal and Asia," 10–11. These figures are calculated on the following assumptions concerning the ratio of persons to tonnage: Outward-bound voyages from Europe to Asia, (i) 1501–60, 0.4 persons per ton, (ii) 1561–1600, 0.5 persons per ton; Return voyage, (a) 1502–60, 0.3 persons per ton, (b) 1561–1600, 0.4 persons per ton.

[50] Duncan, ibid., Table I, 22.

[51] Cf. Maria Beatriz Rocha Trinidade. *Estudos sobre a Emigração Portuguesa* (Lisbon, 1981), 13.

Table 8.7. *Distribution of Population in Portugal*

Region	Households	Percentage
Entre Douro e Minho	55,099	19.6
Trás os Montes	35,616	12.7
Estremadura (w/o Lisbon)	52,402	18.7
Beira	66,800	23.9
Entre Tejo e Guardiana	48,804	17.4
Algarve	8,797	3.1
Lisbon	13,010	4.6
Total	280,582	100.0

Source: Cf. Maria Beatriz Rocha Trinidade, *Estudos Sobre a Emigração Portuguesa*, (Lisbon: 1981), 13.

Montes, which accounted for just under a third of the total population, dominated emigration to Asia, as well as to northern Brazil. Recent work suggests that this fact may be ascribed to the peculiar demographic and ecological regime that obtained there; it should be noted that such a pattern of emigration would have a certain significance, for the natives of the north of Portugal in this period are likely to have been less exposed to Islam than their southern counterparts.[52] Indeed, although Lisbon – which has been described as a too-large head for this small body – exercised a cultural and linguistic influence on the rest of the country in the period, something of a north-south cultural divide may be seen to exist in the Portugal of the period.

Once in Asia, the Portuguese, as well as the mixed-blood offspring they produced, appear in the documentation under various official categories. The first major distinction that was made was between those who resided in the settlements that officially constituted the *Estado da India* (as Portuguese Asia came to be termed from the mid-sixteenth century) and those who did not. Those who resided outside the *Estado* comprised mercenaries and private traders for the most

---

[52] Cf. the useful discussion in V. M. Godinho, "L'émigration portugaise (XVe-XXe siècles)," esp. 19–20. Godinho notes, "Des sondages que j'ai faits concernant les provenances des portugais qui s'en vont aux Indes Orientales pendant la première moitié du XVIe siècle il ressort que les émigrants viennent un peu de partout . . . Mais déjà au cours du dernier tiers du XVIe siècle le Nord-ouest portugais vient se placer au premier rang des provenances d'émigrants." On the north-south linguistic and cultural divide, also see G. Bouchon and L. F. Thomaz, *Voyage dans les Deltas du Gange et de L'Irraouaddy: Relation Portugaise Anonyme* (1521) (Paris, 1988).

part, and were often referred to derisively as *arrenegados* or *chatins*, an exception being naturally made for the ecclesiastics who tended flocks outside the *Estado* proper. But within the *Estado da India* itself, various categories existed. If one takes a settlement such as Goa, the Portuguese and other Europeans and Eurasians resident there fell into the following categories: 1) *ministros* or government officials; 2) *soldados* or soldiers; 3) ecclesiastics; 4) Jews and New Christians; 5) the *casados moradores* or married settlers.[53] These categories, though clearly articulated only fairly late in the sixteenth century, seem to have crystallized already by mid-century. They represent a considerable modification and refinement of the thirteenth and fourteenth century Portuguese division of society into the estates. Of these groups, the single most important is without doubt the *casados moradores*, a juridical category whose roots can be traced to earlier uses in Iberian society such as *cidadãos honrados* or *homens-bons*.[54] It is useful to preface any discussion of the *casados* with the distinctions that existed within the group. One basic divide was between the *casados pretos* and *brancos*, with the former (the so-called "black" *casados*) being converted Asians who had been acculturated to a lesser or greater extent in Portuguese ways. Among the *brancos*, further distinctions were made (though not so much by the administration as by the *casados* themselves) on the basis of blood and place of birth. The major categories were: (1 the *reinois*, born in Portugal of white parents; (2 the *castiços*, born in Asia of white parents, and (3 the *mestiços*, of mixed race, which in the sixteenth century usually meant a Portuguese father and an Asian or Eurasian mother. Resentment existed among these groups, and the *reinois* in particular both considered themselves superior to the others, and were strongly disliked by them.

It is possible to arrive at a geographical distribution of the *casados brancos* in settlements in Asia, but only in the 1630s, for no comprehensive information exists for any earlier date. While doing so, one is conscious that several major *casado* settlements had been lost in the decades before 1630 to various rivals, a good example being Hormuz, which in about 1600 had sheltered roughly two hundred *casados*.[55] Also, other settlements probably suffered a reduction in population

---

[53] On these categories, see T. R. De Souza, *Medieval Goa: A Socio-Economic History* (New Delhi, 1979), 120–2; also the more recent discussion in Geneviève Bouchon, "Premières experiences d'une société coloniale: Goa au XVIe siècle," in *Histoire du Portugal – Histoire Europeénne* (Paris, 1987), 85–96.

[54] Cf. the useful discussion of Portuguese social categories from the fourteenth to the sixteenth centuries in A. H. de Oliveira Marques, *Portugal na Crise dos Séculos XIV E XV* (Lisbon, 1987).

[55] This number is cited in Godinho, "Os Portugueses e o Oriente."

Table 8.8. *"White" Casados in Portuguese Asia, 1635*

Settlement	Number	Settlement	Number
Macao	850	Cranganor	40
Goa	800	Crananur	40
Daman	400	Mangalore	35
Bassen	400	Basrur	35
Colombo	350	Honawar	30
Cochin	300	Caranja	30
Melaka	250	Agashe	30
Chaul	200	Sena	30
Nagappattinam	140	Caliture	< 30
Jaffna	140	Chipangura	25
São Tomé	120	Manora	20
Thana	80	Rachol	20
Galle	70	Trincomali	20
Mannaar	70	Tete	20
Moçambique	70	Mombassa	15–20
Kollam	< 60	Negombo	6
Diu	59	Sofala	5
Mahim	50	Chuambo	4
Tarapur	50	Gangens	4
Total	4,898 – 4,903		

Source: This table is derived from António Bocarro, "Livro das plantas de todas as fortalezas, cidades e povoações do Estado da Índia Oriental," pubished in A. B. de Bragança Pereira, ed., *Arquivo Português Oriental*, (New Series, Tomo IV, Vols. I and II, Goa: 1938–39).

over the first three decades of the seventeenth century. Nevertheless, with all its problems, it is still useful to bear in mind the *casado branco* profile for ca. 1635, which is presented in Table 8.8.[56]

This figure of roughly 4,900 may be contrasted to other statistics on the Portuguese presence in Asia : João Ribeiro's estimate that, in about 1610, there were roughly 5,000 Portuguese in Asia who were employed as renegades and mercenaries between Sri Lanka and Mak-

---

[56] Table 8.8 is derived from António Bocarro, "Livro das plantas de todas as fortalezas, cidades e povoações do Estado da India Oriental," published in A. B. de Bragança Pereira, ed., *Arquivo Português Oriental* (New Series, Tomo IV, Vols. I and II, Goa, 1938–9).

Table 8.9. *Ecclesiastics in Portuguese Asia, 1636*

Order	Number
Jesuits	660
Franciscans	400
Dominicans	250
Augustinians	210
Capuchins	170
Carmelites	40
Total	1,730

Source: Minutes of the Council of State in Goa, dated January 1636, in P. S. S. Pissurlencar, ed., *Assentos do Conselho do Estado (1634–1643),* (Goa: 1953), 32.

assar,[57] as also a report of January 1636, showing the numbers of ecclesiastics of the major orders in Portuguese Asia to be as listed in Table 8.9.[58]

The total arrived at by summing up these three categories, of roughly 12,000, should be adjusted to take account of other Portuguese – soldiers, officials, and private traders – who for whatever reason were not counted. Even so, the number is in marked contrast to what obtains in Brazil, where the Portuguese colonists numbered some 2,000 in around 1550, 25,000 by the early 1580s, and some 30,000 by the end of that century.[59] Thus, if one were to take the Asia-Brazil balance as to where Portuguese overseas emigration went, it would be fair to say that it was in favor of Asia in the first two-thirds of the sixteenth century, and then shifted decisively in favor of Brazil. This fits in with what one knows of the so-called Atlantic turning of the sixteenth century, posited by V. M. Godinho and Frédéric Mauro.

Concerning the other major group besides the *casados,* namely the *arrenegados* (or more generally the *chatins*), information is scattered, and systematic work on the question has only begun very recently. Late sixteenth-century evidence suggests some two thousand in the littoral states of the Bay of Bengal, of whom there were perhaps some

[57] Cited in Disney, *Twilight of the Pepper Empire,* 21–24.
[58] Minutes of the Council of State in Goa, dated January 1636, in P. S. S. Pissurlencar, ed., *Assentos do Conselho do Estado* (1634–43) (Goa, 1953), 32.
[59] These figures derive from Godinho, "Fluctuações económicas e devir estrutural," in *Ensaios,* II, 198–200.

900-odd in Bengal alone, and another 90 in the Burmese port of Mar-taban.[60] This phenomenon – of turning coat, becoming a mercenary, or at the very least a footloose commercial agent – has very early roots in the Portuguese presence in Asia, and can be traced to the decade following the capture of Goa and Melaka (1510–11). By 1520, some 200 to 300 Portuguese are reported on the Coromandel coast of south India, "who have arrived there from Melaka."[61] Some of these prob-ably appear in later years as *casados* settled in São Tomé and Nagap-pattinam, but others may have found their way to Bengal, Arakan, or lower Burma. Accounts such as those of Fernão Mendes Pinto, and later in the sixteenth century Jacques van de Coutere, afford us val-uable glimpses of the world of these "outsiders"; indeed, because they are fanciful and picuresque, instead of straightforward descrip-tions or what the authors saw and experienced, works of this kind are particularly useful in helping us penetrate the mental world of such individuals.[62]

Taking one thing with another then, it becomes quite apparent that Portuguese Asia in the sixteenth century was a segmented and strat-ified society, whose dynamics are only slowly becoming apparent to historians. The work of T. R. De Souza and M. N. Pearson, for ex-ample, underlines the vagaries of existence for the lower-class Por-tuguese who arrived in Goa and Cochin, being as they were dependent on the whims of a patron, who might later employ them on patrol fleets, in fortress garrisons, this after surviving an often arduous passage from Lisbon to the Indian west coast.[63] As the six-teenth century wore on, pressures appear to have mounted in Por-tugal toward making this trip, for all its uncertainties; thus, as Table 8.6 shows, the numbers embarking for Asia increased substantially in the last three decades of the sixteenth century. Godinho writes of

[60] Godinho, "Os Portugueses e o Oriente," in *Ensaios*, II, 209–45. For a more general discussion, see Maria Augusta Lima Cruz, "Exiles and Renegades in Early 16th Century Portuguese India," *The Indian Economic and Social History Review* 23 (1986): 249–62.

[61] Letter from Nuno de Castro at Cochin, dated 31 October 1520, in *Cartas de Afonso de Albuquerque*, VII (Lisbon, 1935), 182.

[62] Cf. Fernão Mendes Pinto, *Peregrinação*, ed. J. de Freitas, (7 vols., Porto, 1930–1); Biblioteca Nacional de Madrid, Mss. 2780, "La Vida de Jaques de Couttre, natural de la ciudad de Bruges, puesto en la forma que esta, por su hijo don Estevan de Couttre"; also see E. Stols, "Coutere, Jacques van de," in *Nationaal Biografisch Woor-denboek*, VI (Brussels, 1974), 151–54.

[63] T. R. De Souza, *Medieval Goa*; M. N. Pearson, "The Crowd in Portuguese India," in Pearson, *Coastal Western India: Studies from the Portuguese Records* (New Delhi, 1981), 41–66. For an example of the sort of peripatetic career this might entail, see for example, *The Travels of Pedro Teixeira*, trans. W. F. Sinclair, introduction D. Ferguson (London, 1902).

how, in the latter half of the sixteenth century, "the condition of the popular masses [in Portugal] frankly deteriorates, with the instability of employment, the indigence, the begging and the wandering – we enter a world of picaroons and vagabonds."[64] To put the matter somewhat differently, the world of Don Quixote was only a short distance away, separated by a porous frontier, which could hardly keep the convulsions of one part of the Iberian peninsula insulated from the other.[65] Not only this, the late sixteenth century is likely to have put pressure on the lower nobility and its incomes, as inflation combined with financial crises, in the face of which both the church and the upper nobility managed to secure their positions, to the detriment of other social groups.

If Asia, like Brazil, was an escape for some then, they may well have thought on arriving there that they had left the frying pan for the fire. In the first half of the sixteenth century, the official structure had still been flexible enough to afford a degree of social mobility to those on the fringes of the nobility, as witness the case of Afonso de Albuquerque. Between 1550 and 1671, on the other hand, five families – the Castros, Coutinhos, Mascarenhas, Meneses, and Noronhas – between them accounted for roughly a half of the governors and viceroys of the *Estado da India*. If one turns to other major posts, be they in Melaka, Hormuz, or the city of Goa itself, these again circulated among a small circle, and even the minor posts were often given out on the basis of patron-client relationships. Relative success stories of the late sixteenth century, like Ferdinand Cron, Duarte Gomes Solis, and even Diogo do Couto (who for all his complaints was a beneficiary of the system), are all linked to major *fidalgo* households; the three persons mentioned above are in fact all associated to a lesser or greater degree with D. Francisco da Gama, twice viceroy of the *Estado da India*.[66]

On arriving in Asia in the latter part of the sixteenth century then, the poorly connected Portuguese could strive for one of two or three situations. Either he could attempt to enter the networks of *casado* trade, which were at their height between roughly 1550 and 1630, or he could explore a poorly paid military career, or finally he could explore possibilities beyond the limits of the *Estado*. If the first, it was

---

[64] Godinho, "1580 e a Restauração," in *Ensaios*, II, 259.
[65] See the evocative description in Pierre Vilar, "The Age of Don Quixote," in Peter Earle, ed., *Essays in European Economic History* (Oxford, 1974).
[66] See, for example, Arquivo Nacional da Torre do Tombo, Lisbon, Manuscritos do Convento da Graça, Tomo II-E, (Caixa 3), 1615–16, fls. 81–89, letters from Ferdinand Cron to D. Francisco da Gama.

very often seen as easier to make one's mark in a relatively new settlement such as Macao (founded ca. 1557), which also had the advantage for *cristãos novos* of being distant from the main center of activities of the Inquisition. If the last, the favored regions seem to have been mainland southeast Asia, the eastern Bay of Bengal littoral, and the Deccan kingdoms. The Deccan option seems particularly to have been favored by those who, for criminal or other reasons, were in relatively desperate straits, for it often involved conversion to Islam. Several celebrated examples exist of this sort, including that of Mansur Khan, who after a career in Ahmadnagar, under Malik Ambar, rose to be a quite substantial Mughal *mansabdar* under Jahangir.[67] On the other hand, mainland southeast Asia was the favored stamping ground of a certain sort of marginal nobility, seeking to be upwardly mobile *within* the *Estado*, but prepared to use external politico-diplomatic leverage to this end. Cases of this sort are found to pro-liferate in the last quarter of the sixteenth century, and are frequently linked – in such areas as Burma and Cambodia – with schemes to set up a territorial Portuguese Empire, in contrast to earlier conceptions of the *Estado da Índia* as a thalassocracy.[68]

There has been some discussion concerning whether or not such schemes should be viewed as purely and simply a result of a His-panicization under Philip II and his successors of the nature of the Portuguese Empire. In favor of this view is the remarkable similarity between some schemes of the 1580s and 1590s – like those of Nuno Velho Pereira in east Africa – and the ventures of Castilian conquis-tadores in Nueva España, like Francisco Vasquéz Coronado or Her-nando de Soto.[69] Also some letters of Philip III in particular bear traces of such a view of things; this monarch was even willing to consider

---

[67] On Mansur Khan, see for instance, W. Ph. Coolhaas, ed., *Pieter van den Broecke in Azië*, 2 vols. (The Hague, 1962–3), 151, 153, 256; on other Portuguese in Mughal dominions, also see Alain Désoulières, "La communauté portugaise d'Agra (1633–1739)," *Arquivos do Centro Cultural Português*, XXII, 1986, 145–73.

[68] Cf. the references cited in note 17 above; for an earlier general discussion of this question, see L. F. Thomaz, "Estrutura política e administrativa do Estado da Índia no século XVI," in Luís de Albuquerque and Inácio Guerreiro, eds., *Actas do II Seminário de História Indo-Portuguesa* (Lisbon : 1985), 515–40. Further, on the Southeast Asian case, see A. Cabaton, 'Le Mémorial de Pedro Sevil à Philippe III sur la conquête de l'Indochine (1603),' *Bulletin de la Commission Archeologique de L'Indochine, 1914–16*, 1–102. We are grateful to Pierre-Yves Manguin for bringing this study to our notice.

[69] W. G. L. Randles, *L'Empire du Monomotapa du XVe au XIXe Siècle* (Paris, 1975), 41–58 ; J. Veríssimo Serrão, *História de Portugal*, IV (Lisbon, 1976), 196–8. Compare these to A. Grove Day, *Coronado's Quest* (Berkeley, 1940), and P. W. Powell, *Soldiers, Indians, and Silver : The Northward Advance of New Spain, 1550–1600* (Berkeley, 1952).

a scheme to create a land-based empire in southeastern India.[70] Against such a view is the absence of direct evidence in the Spanish archives concerning explicit moves to reorganize the *Estado da India* along the lines of Mexico or Peru, and the suggestion implicit in documents like the *Livro das Cidades e Fortalezas* (1582) that the Hapsburgs intended to continue in Asia along "traditional" lines.[71] Still, however little weight we might want to attribute to specifically metropolitan initiatives, there is no gainsaying that the image of the *Estado da Índia* becomes distinctly more territorial in the last quarter of the sixteenth century: To the Monomotapa venture, and those in Pegu and Cambodia, we must add the most important of all, the attempt to take over Sri Lanka. It is possible, of course, that these new directions taken by the *Estado da India* reflected in part the experience of Brazil, and this is still another hypothesis on the vexed question of "territoriality."

In sum then, even if initiatives often came at the outset from agents – both ecclesiatic and lay – at the fringes of power, this tendency appears to fit in well with how the metropolitan ideologues of the late sixteenth century might have seen empire. As a consequence, the instructions given in around 1600 to Antão Vaz Freire, in charge of the administrative reorganization of the Sri Lankan enterprise, advocate the creation of military tenures that are suspiciously like what might be found in the New World and the Philippines.[72] Thus, by a complex process, and perhaps not always as a result of conscious policy decision, the spirit of the Cortes of Tomar came to be subverted.

IV

In this final section, the threads of discussion will be drawn together, using to this end the problem of the profitability of the Portuguese Asian empire in the sixteenth century. This also permits us to return to our point of departure, namely Steensgaard's highly provocative discussion of the contrast between the Portuguese enterprise and that of its Northern European successors. It is argued by him that the

---

[70] Letter from Philip III to the viceroy at Goa, dated 21 February 1610, in R. A. de Bulhão Pato, ed., *Documentos Remettidos da India*, I (Lisbon, 1880), 359.

[71] Cf. "Livro das Cidades e Fortalezas," *Documentos Remettidos da India*. Also J. H. da Cunha Rivara, ed., *Archivo Portuguez-Oriental*, 6 Fascicules in 9 Volumes (Goa, 1855–76), Fascicule III, Part 2, passim.

[72] "Regimento que Sua Magestade deu a Antão Vaz Freire," in Cunha Rivara, ed., *Archivo Portuguez-Oriental*, Fascicole VI, 802–9 ; also see Arquivo Nacional da Torre do Tombo, Lisbon, Manuscritos Miscelâneos, 1109, 25–34.

Dutch, for instance, were truly rational profit-maximizers, whereas the Portuguese were essentially medieval seekers after power: thus, it would seem that the question of the "profitability" of the Portuguese Asian empire is for the most part an irrelevant one. It is evident from this that the ghost of Karl Polanyi in fact presides over Steensgaard's formulation, for what we have here is an early seventeenth century Great Transformation (termed a "structural crisis"), culminating in the triumph over the Portuguese of the Dutch *homo economicus*.[73] Even if we do not enter here into such thorny questions as whether Jan Pieterszoon Coen did his sums before exterminating the Bandanese, this may appear too bald a contrast. For, the Dutch Company – we know – was far from being a profit-maximizer in fact, even bearing in mind that it worked with a fragmented and highly imperfect information set. The VOC maintained factories long after they had lost their utility, because of factional infighting, because the factors themselves found the "lodges" useful to pursue their ostensibly illegal private trade, and for a host of other reasons.[74] Even as modern theorists of the "firm" abandon the simplistic shorthand of the single-minded profit-maximizer, it would be strange if historians were to insist on the appositeness of this axiom in the context of quasi-state entities like the chartered trading companies.

Still, it may be worth our while to ask whether the Portuguese Asian empire was profitable or not, if only because it leads us to ask: profitable for whom? The Portuguese state is one candidate, and the question has already been partially addressed by V. M. Godinho in the context of a discussion of the finances of that state. He shows that, already in 1506, the trade in Asiatic spices accounted for roughly 27 percent of Crown revenues, and that this figure had gone up by 1518–19 to some 39 percent. Equally, he provides us data for the late sixteenth and early seventeenth centuries, some of which is summarized in Table 8.10.[75]

Yet, how meaningful are these figures? In order to treat them as representing any notion of profit, we would have to look at expenditures as well, which would require us to consider *saldo* figures in all the rows. In the case of the *Estado da India*, these stand at 43,102 *mil*

[73] Niels Steensgaard, "The Companies As a Specific Institution in the History of European Expansion," in L. Blussé and F. S. Gaastra, eds., *Companies and Trade : Essays on Overseas Trading Companies during the Ancien Regime* (Leiden, 1981), 245–64. The reference in the text is in particular to Karl Polanyi, *The Great Transformation* (New York, 1943).

[74] Cf. Ashin Das Gupta, "Pieter Phoonsen of Surat, c. 1730–1740," *Modern Asian Studies* 22 (1988): 551–60.

[75] Godinho, "Finanças públicas e estrutura do Estado," in *Ensaios*, II, 27–63.

Table 8.10. *Asia in Portuguese State Revenues (milreis)*

Sources	1588		1607		1619	
Cape route	191,801	(17.3)	234,360	(16.3)	234,360	(15.0)
Estado da India	288,942	(26.0)	355,560	(24.7)	412,500	(26.5)
Atlantic empire	143,920	(13.0)	164,120	(11.4)	173,821	(11.2)
Other	485,482	(43.7)	685,038	(47.6)	735,836	(47.3)
Total	1,110,145		1,439,078		1,556,507	

Source: Godinho, "Finanças públicas e estrutura do Estado," in *Ensaios*, Vol. II, 27–63.

reis, 120,153 *mil reis* and 7,719 *mil reis* respectively for the three years considered above.[76] Seen in these terms, it appears that trade on the Cape route yielded a far greater "neat return" (to borrow a term from the classical economists) than did the *Estado da India*. But it should be noted in turn that the revenue surplus of the *Estado* represents a "return from empire" in far clearer terms than do figures for the Cape route. However, in the 1580s and 1590s, when the Crown contracted out the intercontinental trade, the return on the Cape route *is* a monopoly rent, and hence comparable to the other figure. Later, when Crown capital was invested, the question becomes far more complex, indeed impossible to resolve in the present state of our knowledge.

But, moving away from the state, it is evident that the Asian enterprise also meant a great deal from another point of view – that of the private trader, both on the Cape route and within Asia. In addition to the concession-voyages within Asia, the Cape route too produced returns to private persons of a similar character, on account of the system of liberty-chests. It was calculated in the early 1580s that the captain-major of the *Carreira da India* made some ten to twelve thousand *cruzados* as a result, and each ship's captain found himself the richer by around 4,000 *cruzados*.[77] In addition, it must be noted that in terms of overall value and volume, Portuguese intra-Asian trade was worth a great deal more than trade on the Cape route, though the returns from this trade accrued above all to private persons. A Dutch estimate of 1622, which puts the value of all Portuguese intra-Asian trade at around 50 million *florins*, certainly lends credence to such a view.[78]

Might it be concluded then that as long as it was not seriously set upon by north European rivals, the Portuguese Empire in Asia did "pay," both for the Crown and private Portuguese? The answer would appear to be in the affirmative, though as the sixteenth century wore on the real gainers were it seems the private *casado* traders, and the large commercialized households of the *fidalgos tratantes*, in alliance with their Middle European and *cristão novo* banker associates. This does not mean that the Crown no longer gained, but that the gains of the Crown were far more complex. In a situation of a growing social gulf in the peninsula, the Asian empire (like Brazil or Peru and

---

[76] Derived from Matos, "The Financial Situation of the State of India." Note, however, that Matos has the receipts of the *Estado da India* in 1588 higher than Godinho, namely at 303,051 *mil reis*.

[77] Calculated from the "Livro das Cidades e Fortalezas."

[78] This figure is cited in George B. Souza, "Portuguese Country Trade in the Indian Ocean and the South China Sea, c. 1600," *Moyen Orient et Océan Indien*, I (1984): 117–128.

Spanish America) was an affirmation of the possible, a safety valve, and thus crucial as a social catalyst as much as a source of simple economic return.

To conclude, therefore, future generalizations on the Portuguese enterprise in Asia have to adopt a more complex vision than has so far been the case, one in which metropolitan developments – such as changing imperial ideology, or the influx into Portugal of New Christian capital and ideas – have to be balanced against developments in Asian political and economic structures, and the changing profile of the Portuguese and Lusitanized populations in the latter area. Neither the perspective still preferred by many Portuguese historians – of peering cautiously out of the ramparts of the sixteenth century fortresses of their forbears – nor that fashionable in another branch of the literature – which declares that the Portuguese were by 1550 so Asianized that it is of little analytical value to distinguish them from the Asians themselves – does adequate justice to the processes of subtle modification, which ensured that *Asia Portuguesa* in 1600 was quite different from what it had been in the first quarter of the sixteenth century.

CHAPTER 9

Comparing the Tokagawa Shogunate with Hapsburg Spain: Two silver-based empires in a global setting

DENNIS O. FLYNN

INTRODUCTION

In a recent article, two Japanese scholars point to the need for viewing sixteenth- and seventeenth century Japanese silver production in the context of a global market, concluding that "Japan's silver played an active, if supporting, role in the unfolding Price Revolution which the Western world experienced during the 16th century and the early decades of the 17th."[1] Data problems notwithstanding, there can be no doubt that immense quantities of silver were traded among all continents at that time. Silver (along with gold) must have been the first product in history traded across all oceans, seas, and continents simultaneously; it comprised the first global market in the emergence of a world economy. Spanish America was the largest source of silver in the world; it was the only area to outproduce Japan. American production is estimated by Attman at more than 300 metric tons per year during the seventeenth century, compared with Japanese production of at least 200 metric tons per year early in that century.[2] The final destination of much of both areas' silver output was giant China,

Several people have been kind enough to read and criticize this exploratory essay, though probably none agrees with all (and some may not agree with any) of it. Thanks to Ward Barrett, K. N. Chaudhuri, Akira Hayami, Heita Kawakatsu, Rus Menard, John Munro, Michael North, Frank Perlin, Kaoru Sugihara, James Tracy, Eddy Van Cauwenberghe, Kozo Yamamura, and participants at the 1986 Keio Conference on Monetary History, where an earlier version was presented.
[1] Kozo Yamamura and Tetsuo Kamiki, "Silver Mines and Sung Coins: A Monetary History of Medieval and Modern Japan in International Perspective," in J. F. Richards, ed., *Precious Metals in the Later Medieval and Early Modern Worlds* (Durham, 1983), 356.
[2] Artur Attman, *American Bullion in the European World Trade, 1600–1800* (Goteborg, 1986), 78.

which contained roughly the same proportion of world population then as today. India was also a silver sink.[3]

Spanish American silver took two general routes to China and India, the widely discussed Atlantic route (shipped from Vera Cruz and Puertobelo through Europe) and the largely ignored Pacific route (shipped out of Acapulco through Manila). Estimation of bullion flows out of the New World is difficult, however, because of a massive unreported contraband trade. Morineau and others argue convincingly that the seventeenth-century decline in *official* European receipts of bullion was dwarfed by a huge and growing flow of *unofficial* bullion. Attman, Barrett, Kindleberger, and virtually everybody now accepts this upward revision.[4] Attman's estimates of the overall influx into Europe range from 208 to 325 tons per year during the seventeenth century. A high percentage of the influx flowed to the East; rough interpolation of Attman's "minimum figures" suggests that the drain of specie from Europe to the East may have been around 15,000 or 16,000 metric tons over the seventeenth century.[5]

Caution is required in using Attman's estimates of West-to-East flows of precious metals. Large as his numbers may appear to some, they are presented as minimum estimates. They are based on estimated trade balances via major seaports and do not include overland trade. They also do not include most bullion (as opposed to specie) flows. Attman is very clear about what is included (specie via seaports) and excluded (overland specie and bullion) from his estimates; he deliberately avoids spurius estimates of the unknowable portion, irrespective of how large it may have been. The actual volume of minted and unminted silver flowing eastward, via sea and land, through Europe must have been considerably larger than Attman's 15–16,000 ton figure. Thus, although Ward Barrett's survey article in *The Rise of*

---

[3] See Frank Perlin, "World Economic Integration and the Euro-Asian Monetary Continuum: Their Implications and Problems of Categories, Definitions, and Method"; Om Prakash, "Sarrafs, Financial Intermediation, and Credit Network in Mughal India"; Sanjay Subrahmanyam, "Precious Metal Flows and Prices in Western and Southern Asia, 1500–1750: Some Comparative and Conjunctural Aspects"; and V.B. Gupta, "Imports of Treasure and Surat's Trade in the Seventeenth Century," all in E. Van Cauwenberghe, ed., [Papers from the 1989 Delhi Conference on Monetary History – title unknown] (Leuven, forthcoming). Also see Chapter 10 in Charles P. Kindleberger, *Spenders and Hoarders: The World Distribution of Spanish American Silver, 1550–1750* (Singapore, 1989).

[4] Michel Morineau, *Incroyable gazettes et fabuleux metaux: Les retours des tresors americains d'apres les gazettes hollandaises (XVIe–XVIIIe siecles)* (New York and Paris, 1985); Attman, *American Bullion*, esp. 25, 34; Ward Barrett, "World Bullion Flows, 1450–1800," in J.D. Tracy, ed., *The Rise of Merchant Empires*; Charles P. Kindleberger, *Spenders and Hoarders*, 15.

[5] Attman, *American Bullion*, 78.

Merchant Empires is excellent in other respects, I have difficulty accepting his conclusion that Europe accumulated surpluses amounting to hundreds of tons of New World treasure annually.[6] Certainly Spain retained practically nothing of the silver that passed through its borders. Domestically, Spain was on a copper monetary standard by the early seventeenth century, and paper monies displaced hard currencies throughout Europe in early modern times.[7] Other than church interiors and dinnerware, in what form did Europeans stockpile tens of thousands of tons of silver? The answer perhaps awaits empirical information from historians, but to my knowledge the qualitative evidence indicates that Europeans did not stockpile much of the American silver. Instead, Europeans acted as middlemen in the trade of silver from America to China and (to a lesser extent) India, just as they were middlemen in trading Japanese silver to China. Further, middleman-Europe should not be viewed as the principal agent for the dispersal of American silver into Asia or within Asia.

A parallel scenario was unfolding in the neglected Pacific side of the story: American silver went to China. TePaske estimates the *official* drain of bullion from New Spain to the Philippines at 1,123 metric tons of silver between 1581 and 1800, but he cites Boxer's overall (that is, official plus unofficial) estimate of the Mexico-to-Philippines flow at about 128 metric tons annually early in the seventeenth century and a staggering "reported 12 million pesos (307,000 kilograms) being smuggled out in 1597."[8] Official numbers drop off after 1620, but for tax-evasion purposes there was considerable smuggling of the white metal as time passed, just as there was in the Atlantic trade. The volume of this unreported smuggling activity may never be known. If one were to assume that the early annual flow of silver via the Pacific Ocean remained constant throughout the century – a conservative assumption, given augmented silver production in America, expanding Atlantic exports, and other considerations – the Pacific flow of the white metal might be put at around 13,000 metric tons (that is, roughly 128 tons/year times 100 years).[9] Thus, one of the best

[6] Barrett, "World Bullion Flows, Table 7–8. p. 253.
[7] Dennis O. Flynn, "A New Perspective on the Spanish Price Revolution: The Monetary Approach to the Balance of Payments," *Explorations in Economic History* 15 (1978): 388–406.
[8] John J. TePaske, "New World Silver, Castile, and the Philippines, 1590–1800," in Richards, ed., *Precious Metals*, 436.
[9] According to Woodrow Borah, *Early Colonial Trade and Navigation between Mexico and Peru* (Berkeley, 1954), 116–27, the Peru-Philippines silver trade, which was apparently significant, did not go through official channels in Acapulco. By the beginning of the seventeenth century, according to Kindleberger, *Spenders and Hoarders*, 23, the Manila trade "had grown so large – equal to the shipments across the Atlantic to Spain –

estimates available suggests that at least 15,000 tons of the American silver flowed out of Europe via seaports into the East in the form of specie alone; and my admittedly flimsy guess here suggests that perhaps 13,000 additional tons of silver flowed from Mexico to the East via Manila. By any reckoning, it is clear that the Pacific leg of silver's global journey has not received the attention it deserves. TePaske offers the tentative conclusion that the "Philippines were the major conduit for the flow of American silver westward into the Orient; this westward flow was as significant as the flow of silver from the east, particularly in the late sixteenth and early seventeenth centuries."[10] Historical Eurocentrism might explain the disproportionate attention focused on the Atlantic leg of the trade, and surely some estimates need revision, but both oceans apparently did carry enormous amounts of silver toward a common destination. Because of this common destination, there are good reasons to view the Atlantic and Pacific Silver trades as facets of a coherent global market.

After Spanish America, Japan was the world's most important source of silver in the late sixteenth and early seventeenth centuries. Japanese silver flowed through Nagasaki and later through Korea and on – once again – to China. Yamamura and Kamiki estimate Japanese silver exports to China in the period 1560–1640 at as much as 9,450 metric tons, possibly a realistic figure because Tashiro says that "silver exported abroad reached about 200,000 kg. per year at its peak [in the early seventeenth century]."[11] In round numbers, therefore, it

that the King increased his measures to stop it . . . [but] The trade lasted in all two and a half centuries with the regulations a dead letter." My argument here is that market forces in America and Asia explain the inexorable flow of silver from the West to the East. If the theory of this essay is useful in explaining the growth in silver flows through Europe during the seventeenth century, then the same theory would predict that, if anything, the flow of silver over the Pacific must have grown as well. If the Pacific silver flow failed to grow, or even subsided, simultaneously with growth over the Atlantic route, then some market-blocking explanation must be offered. I know of no such market-blocking argument relating solely to the Pacific Ocean.

[10] TePaske, "New World Silver," 439.

[11] Yamamura and Kamiki, "Silver Mines and Sung Coins," 351; Kazui Tashiro, "Coinage and Exports of Silver during the Tokugawa Era," in Eddy Van Cauwenberghe and Akira Hayami, eds., [Proceedings of 1986 Keio Conference on Monetary History – title unknown] (Brussels, forthcoming). Tashiro estimates that 3,900 metric tons in the form of Keicho silver coin (80% pure silver) was exported via Nagasaki alone in the seventeenth century. Silver exports slowed down after the so-called *sakoku* (i.e., "closure" of the country) in 1638 and certainly after the ban on silver exports from Nagasaki in 1668, but Atsushi Kobata, "The Export of Japanese Copper on Chinese and Dutch Ships during the Seventeenth and Early Eighteenth Centuries," (unpublished manuscript), estimates that 1,050 tons of silver were exported during the two decades from 1648 and 1667 and another 270 tons between 1673 and 1684. Kobata's numbers are supported by Yamamura and Kamiki, "Silver Mines and Sung Coins," 350, and by Tashiro, "Coinage and Exports." Even after the silver embargo,

seems that about 10,000 tons of silver was exported out of Japan and into China during the late sixteenth and seventeenth centuries, perhaps two-thirds as much as that coming eastward out of Europe (in the form of seaborne specie) and possibly almost as much as arrived from America via the Pacific trade. In a very real sense, Japan and Spain were major competitors in the world's first global market; China was the most important customer, followed by India.

The purpose of this chapter is to speculate about the causes of the integration of the world market for silver, as well as some of its effects. I am particularly interested in discovering similarities and differences in the way that Shogunate Japan and Imperial Spain reacted to the powerful forces emanating from an increasingly integrated world silver market. The next section sketches a model of the world silver market. Although not wishing at all to deny the multitude of complicated differences in localized mine characteristics,[12] I will argue that similar forces generated the mining booms in both hemispheres. The model also provides a simple explanation for the global nature of the period's price inflation. Sections three and four expand the basic model into a two-region model to explain why particular geographical regions exported silver while others imported it. Section five attempts, in a very preliminary way, to compare Japanese and Spanish strategies in an emerging, global context. The final section summarizes the central ideas of the paper and speculates about the relative economic success of post-silver Japan and Spain.

Tashiro, "Exports of Japan's Silver to China via Korea and Changes in the Tokugawa Monetary System during the 17th and 18th Centuries," in E. Van Cauwenberghe, ed., *Precious Metals, Coinage and the Changes of Monetary Structures in Latin America, Europe and Asia (Late Middle Ages–Early Modern Times)* (Levven, 1989), 99–116, estimates that 188 tons of silver currency (80% fine) passed via Tsushima and Korea into China between 1684 and 1710. In a previous article, Tashiro, "Foreign Relations during the Edo Period: Sakoku Reexamined," *Journal of Japanese Studies* 8 (1982), 296, provided these numbers: "This 'silver road' began at Kyoto, passed through Tsushima and Korea, and finally ended at Peking. Only recently was it learned that in the 52 years from 1684 to 1735, approximately 80,000 kan (300,000 kg) of silver coins passed along this route from Japan to China."

[12] Adam Szasdi, "Preliminary Estimate of Gold and Silver Production in America, 1501–1610," in Herman Kellenbenz, ed., *Precious Metals in the Age of Expansion: Papers of the XIVth International Congress of the Historical Sciences* (Stuttgart, 1981), 151–224, contains an excellent account of the numerous cost-saving innovations introduced in the American mining industry. Other geographical areas are discussed throughout the Kellenbenz collection. In reality, all of these studies demonstrate that there was enormous diversity from mine to mine and region to region; the theoretical "cost of production" alluded to in the figures of this paper intentionally abstracts from the complexities of individual mining operations and regions. The simplified models offered in this essay should be viewed as vehicles with which to sketch outlines of general market forces at an abstract level. They do not pretend to do anything more.

THE EMERGENCE OF THE FIRST
GLOBAL MARKET

The traditional Western textbook explanation for the West-to-East flow of silver is based on a type of macroeconomic reasoning that views money as a passive balancing item. Westerners liked Asian spices and silks, for example, much more than Easterners appreciated Western products. Because European imports greatly exceeded exports, precious metals flowed eastward in order to balance the books. The "monetary" sector merely responded to an imbalance in the "real" sector. This conventional wisdom is defective. Precious metals were produced for profit just like any other commodity – they were neither more nor less "real" than any other product. Moreover, *silver* flowed to Asia in exchange for various articles, including significant quantities of *gold* that moved in the opposite direction – from Asia into Europe. Macroeconomic reasoning provides no help in explaining why one precious metal flowed eastward while another flowed westward. Disentanglement of the metals requires microeconomic reasoning because the task of microeconomics is to focus on the interaction of *specific* products. Doherty and Flynn created a microeconomic model specifically for application to individual precious metals and I have offered an alternative explanation for the East-West trade – one that emphasizes the *causative* role of silver – based on the Doherty/Flynn model; this alternative explanation, in turn, essentially provides new theoretical support for the Ricardian argument contained in Chaudhuri's classic work.[13] The following discussion outlines those portions of the model pertinent to the issues at hand.

No one disputes the existence of a world market for silver. The issue is how to model it. In conventional terms, microeconimic supply refers to the profit-maximizing rate of production, and microeconomic demand refers to the utility-maximizing rate of consumption. A central problem is that goods like silver are not eaten up like, say, bread;

---

[13] See, respectively, K. W. Doherty and D. O. Flynn, "A Microeconomic Quantity Theory of Money and the Price Revolution," in E. Van Cauwenberghe, ed., *Precious Metals*, 185–208. D. O. Flynn, "The Microeconomics of Silver and East-West Trade in the Early Modern Period," in W. Fischer, R. M. McInnis, and J. Schneider, eds, *The Emergence of a World Economy, 1500–1914*, Vol. I (Stuttgart, 1986), 37–60; K. N. Chaudhuri, *The Trading World of Asia and the English East India Company, 1660–1760* (Cambridge, 1978). Chaudhuri agrees with the great early nineteenth-century economist David Ricardo, who viewed forces within precious metals markets as causes in the metals' migration. My argument follows in their tradition.

rather, they tend to accumulate for years, decades, centuries, and indeed, for millenia. Durable products like silver are therefore not amenable to analysis by conventional "flow" microeconomic supply-and-demand analysis.[14]

The relevant supply concept in this case is a "stock" (that is, an inventory) of all of the silver accumulated throughout history up to the time under consideration. (Stock supply is thus clearly distinct from conventional microeconomic supply, which refers to the optimal contemporary rate of production.) So, at any point in time there is a stock of silver in existence in the world (though its magnitude may be unknowable) – the supply curve is vertical because at a point in time the accumulated stock is unresponsive to price. The difficulty lies in creation of a stock (inventory theoretic) microeconomic demand function for superimposition with the vertical supply function; the Doherty-Flynn model generates such a demand function through application of optimal control theory, a type of dynamic mathematics.

Figure 9.1 depicts the world silver market some time early in the sixteenth century. Suppose that profits in the silver-production industry were initially typical of those in other industries; this would imply that the price of silver (P^*) equalled its average cost of production (COP^*). With important mine discoveries, especially in America and in Japan, coupled with a multitude of cost-reducing technological innovations, the cost of producing the product dropped considerably (say, to COP^{**}).[15] The result was huge economic profit because price now exceeded production costs, which in turn fueled a tremendous boom in the silver-mining industry. Microeconomic reasoning tells us that market price eventually gravitates to the new cost of production (COP^{**}). But how long does it take to re-achieve equilibrium? If the accumulated stock of silver throughout the world were large –

[14] A wine cellar provides a good example of the distinction between stock and flow demand concepts. I drink wine at a certain time rate – the utility-maximizing number of bottles imbibed per week is the time-dimensioned (flow) demand concept found in conventional microtheory. But I also hold a certain inventory of wine at any instant in time – the utility-maximizing number of bottles held in stock is the stock demand concept used in this essay. Obviously, the two demand concepts are related: If I drink a bottle of wine from my cellar, other things being equal, the inventory stock shrinks. A similar distinction holds for conventional flow supply (production) and what we call stock supply (the total quantity in existence); new production, other things being constant, increases the existing stock. The purpose here, therefore, is not to argue against "flow thinking"; the need is to demonstrate how stock and flow concepts interact.

[15] For the purpose of analytical simplicity, Figure 9.1 shows a discrete, one-shot drop in production costs; Szasdi, "Preliminary Estimate," makes it clear that cost-saving innovations were in fact numerous and complex. The reader should also note that the model is not designed to address the issue of which discoveries and innovations were accidental and which were not.

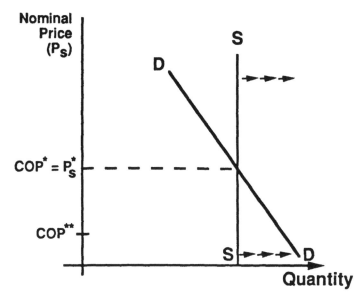

Figure 9.1. The World Silver Market

which it had to have been for so durable a product – it could take a very long time for growth in stock supply to outpace the growth in stock demand sufficiently to lower silver's price all the way down to COP**, despite the fact that rates of silver production were extraordinary high. I argue that it took a century or so for the market value of silver to descend to its new, lower cost of production; the disequilibrium lasted about a hundred years.

The reason for arguing that a century is the correct time interval has to do with the fact that silver served the monetary role of medium of exchange in much of the world at the time. We know that "silver-content prices" generally rose some two and one-half or three times during the price revolution. Research seems to indicate the same general trend in (silver-content) prices all over the world, including China.[16] But to say that it takes three times as much silver to buy a basket of goods is to say that the purchasing power of silver fell to one-third of its previous value vis-à-vis that basket. The fact that silver's purchasing power fell by a similar amount relative to products all over the world (for example, vis-à-vis European and Chinese bas-

[16] Michel Cartier, "Les importations de metaux monetaires en Chine: Essai sur la conjoncture Chinoise," *Annales E.S.C.* 36 (1981): 454–66.

kets of good) suggests that it was a fall in silver's value, rather than a rise in value of the other products, that explains the price revolution.[17]

The mounting evidence of significant silver production in the second half of the seventeenth century, at least in the West, now seems incontrovertible. World silver production was greater in the seventeenth century than in the sixteenth century. This is particularly disturbing news for proponents of the traditional monetary interpretation of the price revolution because silver-content prices stabilized in the seventeenth century. How could the price revolution end when bullion flows were still growing? Significant silver production poses no such contradiction, however, for the Doherty-Flynn microeconomic interpretation outlined above. Silver's value had descended to its cost of production by, say, 1630. The price revolution was over. Substantial subsequent silver production merely offset growing demand in an increasingly international, monetized world economy. Just as high rates of production today are consistent with lower, stabilized prices for, say, wheat or steel, so too was high silver production consistent with a lower, stabilized market value of silver.

A WORLD OF INTERCONNECTED SILVER MARKETS

One often hears the comment today that we now live in a world economy, but what does a "world economy" mean? In a way, it is a nonsense phrase. There is something like a world market for oil, but Stockton, California, is clearly not in the same housing market as San Francisco (eighty miles to the west). There is a world market for diamonds, but only a local market for firewood. People who provide services like haircuts tend to cater to local residents, some important financial instruments are traded worldwide, and so on. The point is that everyday commerce is simultaneously conducted in a set of over-

---

[17] In terms of the Doherty-Flynn model, the silver-content price of any commodity is obtained by dividing the unit-of-account price of the commodity (say, wheat) by the unit-of-account price of silver – the result is the commodity's price in terms of silver. One cannot say *a priori* whether a commodity's higher silver-content price is caused by supply-demand factors in the commodity market itself (the numerator) or supply-demand factors in the silver market (the denominator). The global character of early modern price inflation leads me to believe that silver's reduced cost of production is the underlying cause. This does not preclude supplemental arguments about rising costs in other commodities' markets, however, so I am forced to admit that theoretical portions of my earlier, antipopulation-thesis argument are no longer sustainable [D.O. Flynn, "The 'Population Thesis' View of Inflation versus Economics and History," in E. Van Cauwenberghe and F. Irsigler, *Münzprägung, Geldumlauf und Wechselkurse/ Minting, Monetary Circulation and Exchange Rates* (Trier, 1984): 361–82].

lapping markets. "The market" does not exist, but all of us partake simultaneously in local, regional, international, and global market activity for specific products. One of the main determinants of the geographical limits of a market is the cost of transporting the product to the customer (or the customer to the product). Durability and high value-to-weight, along with worldwide acknowledgment of value, were characteristics that made silver and gold the world's first globally traded goods. And it is best to view the precious metals this way – from a microeconomic perspective that emphasizes interaction among individual products, rather than from the traditional, macroeconomic "national markets" point of view.

At a highly abstract level, therefore, it is proper to view the entire world as silver's market in early modern times. But, even in the case of specific precious metals, the "world market" was really a series of interconnected regional markets dispersed and overlapping around the globe. It took a great deal of time to integrate these interconnected, but partially segmented, markets.

Differences in bimetallic ratios in Western Europe versus China are often (correctly) cited as evidence that there were distinctive markets in these places. Similarly, differential bimetallic ratios between China and Japan indicate that markets in these two places were not perfectly integrated at all times either. Indeed, realization of arbitrage profits because of differential bimetallic ratios is one of the principal mechanisms that acted to integrate these markets.[18] Anytime one can sell a product in one place for more than it costs elsewhere (including all explicit and implicit costs), it will be transported to the favorable market area. But transportation of silver from Amsterdam all the way to Beijing was not the only option. One party might transport the product into Eastern Europe, another into the Middle East or Russia, and finally into China in the umpteenth transaction. The point is that there may have been numerous somewhat distinctive, overlapping markets for a singular product, but these overlapping markets were interconnected at a global level. Thus, there was a single world market and simultaneously there were numerous localized "submarkets." A simplified two-submarket model is presented in Figure 9.2 for purposes of illustration, with the clear understanding that we are really implicitly thinking in terms of an n-submarket model, where "n" is an arbitrarily large number.

Silver is initially undervalued in "Area 1," the exporting submarket (that is, the West or Japan), and overvalued in "Area 2," the importing

---

[18] Chaudhuri, *The Trading World of Asia*.

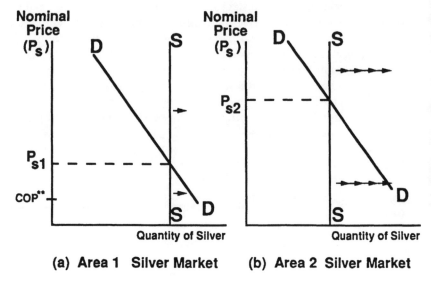

(a) Area 1 Silver Market   (b) Area 2 Silver Market

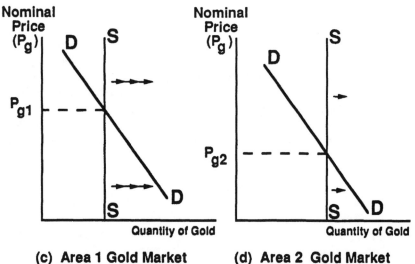

(c) Area 1 Gold Market   (d) Area 2 Gold Market

Figure 9.2. Treasure Flows and Bimetallic Ratios

submarket (that is, China or India). Just the reverse holds for gold for a time; it is overvalued in the West, as well as Japan, and under-valued in China. It would obviously be profitable to export silver to and import gold from China in this situation, which is precisely what happened between the mid-sixteenth and mid-seventeenth centuries.[19] The very act of doing this, however, augments the stock of silver in China (relative to the rest of the world) and augments the stock of gold in the rest of the world (relative to China). This process continues until arbitrage profits are eliminated, which occurs when the price of each metal roughly equilibrates in all submarkets. This model is consistent with evidence of unified global bimetallic ratios sometime around 1640: "As a consequence of this large outflow of silver from Japan during the 1560–1640 period, by 1640 the relative value of gold to silver in Japan had become virtually identical to that in China and in the world market."[20] Silver had been overvalued in China since the fifteenth-century collapse of its paper currency[21] and it took two centuries of imports to equilibrate bimetallic ratios throughout the world.

NONARBITRAGE WORLD TRADE

But how does one explain evidence of substantial flows of silver from the West to China *after* the 1630s? I can think of two answers. First, elimination of arbitrage profits between silver and gold does not imply elimination of arbitrage possibilities between silver and other goods; that is, silver did flow eastward in exchange for items other than gold. Equilibration of silver's price relative to gold does not necessarily imply equilibration of silver's price relative to all goods. Second, gain from arbitrage is not the only motivation for selling a product. Businesses today are often happy to sell their products at the same price in many regions. The price of Pepsi Cola is the same in Seattle and Miami; the fact that one area may receive a greater volume of shipments has to do with more extensive *volume* demanded, not because of price differentials. There is no reason to think that businesses of the past ignored volume demand when price differentials were negligible. Nonarbitrage trade can be illustrated (Figure 9.3) by adding production to the two-submarket model sketched above. For simplicity, assume first that we are dealing with a consumable product (obviously *not* silver this time because it is not "consumed" in our inventory-depleting sense) that is produced in one region that does not consume it, while the consuming area does not produce it. Both

[19] Flynn, "The Microeconomics of Silver and East-West Trade."
[20] Yamamura and Kamiki, "Silver Mines and Sung Coins," 352.
[21] Han-Sheng Chuan, "The Inflow of American Silver into China during the 16th–18th Centuries," in *Proceedings of the Academic Sciences International Conference on Sinology* (Taipei: 1981): 849–53.

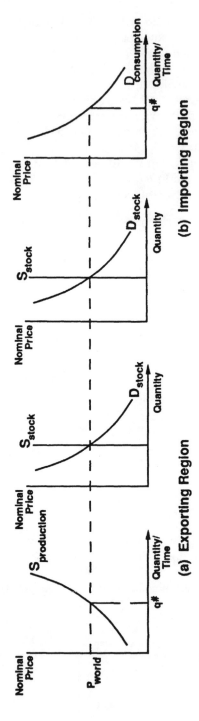

Figure 9.3. Non-Arbitrage Trade of a Consumable

choose to hold stocks of the item. Note that an equilibrium world price has already been established in this scenario; sufficient quantities of the product have already been moved from the exporting region to the importing region such that stock demand and supply intersect at the same world price for the item in all submarkets. Because all markets share the same price, opportunity for arbitrage profit has already been eliminated (assuming other product markets are also in equilibration). Yet export and import activity continues because production in the exporting area is relocated for consumption in the importing region. The point is that equilibration of price – and thus elimination of arbitrage profit – does not eliminate interregional trade; indeed, interregional trade is what guarantees that prices will continue this tendency toward equilibration.

The same type of analysis holds for a nonconsumable commodity like silver (Figure 9.4). World price can obtain in both markets when one region produces it and the other region does not. As long as growth in stock demand in the nonproducing importing region continues, either price will rise in that area (above the level of the exporting region) or stock supply would have to increase enough to maintain price at the world level. The source of growth in stock supply in this second case, of course, would be importation of silver. The point is that a multitude of demand-side forces – whether from population growth, economic prosperity, tax policy, or a host of cultural considerations – can be responsible for importation of silver. These forces can reinforce the arbitrage motive or exist independently. I would argue that both kinds of forces explain the West-to-East flow of silver up to the 1630s, after which time the arbitrage motive was eliminated, but augmented demand continued to attract silver. (Japan is here considered "Western" in this time period.)

The importance of demand-side forces can scarcely be overemphasized. Kindleberger criticized an earlier application of the Doherty-Flynn model: "[Flynn] claims that the precious metals were the cause of the expansion of intercontinental trade, not the response. This leaves unanswered why the East wanted silver and gold more than it wanted luxury consumer goods."[22] Professor Kindleberger has not seen this essay, which is unfortunate, because I agree with him, as well as Perlin, Prakash, and others who insist that demand-side considerations deserve at least as much attention as divergent bimetallic ratios in explaining the movement of treasure.[23] The production-point-

[22] Kindleberger, *Spenders and Hoarders*, 78.
[23] Perlin, "World Economic Integration"; Prakash, "Sarrafs, Financial Intermediation."

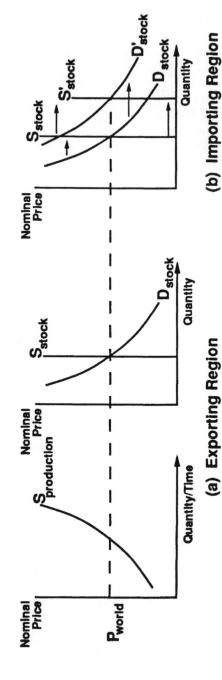

Figure 9.4. Non-Arbitrage Trade of a Non-Consumable (Silver)

of-view model sketched above and described in more detail elsewhere[24] explains why silver left Japan and Spanish America, but why did it gravitate to particular areas like China? One reason is that China did not produce much silver domestically: "[I]t should be noted that the fertility of China's own mines had declined drastically during the late fifteenth and early sixteenth centuries."[25] In addition to this slackening of Chinese silver production, we must acknowledge the overwhelming demand side of the Chinese market. Chuan specifically links a substantial portion of the Chinese demand for silver to the collapse of China's paper-money system. In 1436 the Ming government initiated a five-century switch to silver as legal tender, raising silver's price to record levels: "As there were few good silver mines in China, the output of silver had failed to keep pace with demand. But the fact that large quantities of American silver were imported into China must account for the successful adoption of this monetary unit in China."[26] The implications of the point made by Chuan – that Chinese monetary disruptions were linked to American and Japanese silver – are startling in the context of the model of this chapter. I will return to this point in the concluding section; suffice it to say that Chinese monetary policy may have indirectly supported the financial foundations of both the Spanish Empire and the enemy Shogunate because augmented demand meant a higher price for silver and greater profits for them as silver producers.

THE DISPOSITION OF JAPANESE AND SPANISH SILVER PROFITS

The fact that it took a century to reattain a new equilibrium price in the world silver market had important implications for the centers of its production. Once again, the initial stock of silver was so massive that even a major mining boom in both hemispheres was capable of augmenting the stock by but a few percentage points a year. This is important because it implied that silver's market price would have to have declined very gradually; in point of fact, annual price inflation in silver-content terms never did exceed two percentage points. The market value of silver normally fell (via various market baskets of goods around the world) by around one percentage point per year during the Price Revolution. The difference between market price and

---

[24] Doherty and Flynn, "A Microeconomic Quantity Theory of Money."
[25] William S. Attwell, "Notes on Silver, Foreign Trade, and the Late Ming Economy," *Ch'ing-Shih wen-t'i* 3 (1977): 4.
[26] Chuan, "The Inflow of American Silver into China," 850, 853.

cost of production is economic profit; the slower price declines toward cost of production, the longer it takes to squeeze out excess profits. Thus, the reason that Spanish-American and Japanese mines generated huge profits over an extended period of time is that price, though declining slowly, exceeded cost of production for generations. Chinese demand for silver was instrumental in slowing the fall in the world price of silver, which prolonged the period of mining profits in Japan and Spanish America. Japanese and Spanish mining profits, in turn, supported their respective empires.

Numerous authors, from conservatives (for example, Earl J. Hamilton and J.M. Keynes) to pseudo-Marxists (for example, Immanuel Wallerstein) have utilized various arguments in support of the proposition that New World silver promoted the birth of capitalism in Northwestern Europe in the early modern era.[27] I have argued the reverse, that the Spanish government used its super-profits – derived from control of silver production – to launch a deadly, multifront war against the emerging capitalistic states to the north.[28] The northern powers nearly went bankrupt defending themselves against Iberia's religion-inspired military fanaticism. When relentless market forces eliminated profits from American silver, which was inevitable, the Spanish Empire collapsed and Spain quickly became a second- or third-rate power. Spain squandered its windfall gain of wealth. Rather than investing super-profits in infrastructure or some other sort of long-term productive base, Castile dissipated its New World-based wealth on the first global war.

A brief digression about the decline of Spain may be helpful at this point. Carla Rahn Phillips recently surveyed the literature on early modern Spanish social, economic, and political history. She concludes with a call for systematic investigation of interconnections between

---

[27] Earl J. Hamilton, "American Treasure and the Rise of Capitalism (1500–1700)," *Economica* 9 (1929): 338–57; John M. Keynes, *A Treatise on Money* (New York, 1930), II:161; Immanuel Wallerstein, *The Modern World System: Capitalist Agriculture and the Origins of the European World-Economy in the Sixteenth Century* (New York, 1974). I call Wallerstein's work "psuedo-Marxist" because his theory is most vulnerable to attack from a Marxist perspective. For severe (and correct) criticism of the East European leg of Wallerstein's hypothesis, see Robert Brenner, "The Origins of Capitalist Development: A Critique of Neo-Smithian Marxism," *New Left Review* 104 (1977): 25–92.

[28] D. O. Flynn, "El desarrollo del primer capitalismo a pesar de los metales preciosos del Nuevo Mundo: Una interpretacion anti-Wallerstein de la Espana Imperial," *Revista de Historia Economica* 2 (1984): 29–57. For a version in English, see D. O. Flynn, "Early Capitalism Despite New World Bullion: An Anti-Wallerstein Interpretation of Imperial Spain," *Journal of European Economic History* (forthcoming).

political and economic forces, rather than simply assuming that connections exist:

[W]e should remember that economic power was not necessarily associated with political power. The Dutch enjoyed their brief golden age of commercial dominance with no pretentions to political hegemony; the Spanish enjoyed more than a century of political hegemony and four centuries of empire, despite meager economic resources. To understand the changing fortunes of Spain in the early modern period, we need to understand both political and economic developments, and we must explore the connections between them with an open mind.[29]

Phillips examines conditions in agriculture and industry by region within Spain against the backdrop of important international demographic and economic trends. Price historians are called to task for pushing the timetable for Spain's decline forward as far as 1650 – so that decline coincides better with bullion-flow trends – which "ignores clear signs of earlier difficulties in the economy as a whole."[30] I too have argued that it is inappropriate to focus on the *quantity* of precious metals imports.[31] Profit per ounce of silver declined steadily – due to silver's falling price – so total profit (price times quantity) to the Crown shrank simultaneously with a rise in the quantity of imports in the late sixteenth century. Scholars have become confused because of a subconscious assumption that volume and profits must be positively related. The scenario offered here is thus consistent with the late sixteenth-century crisis described by Phillips and others as opposed to a mid-seventeenth century crisis. Moreover, the argument for a silver-based fiscal crisis in the empire does not exclude arguments based on nonsilver internal and international factors. Discovery of the exact connections between silver and internal markets is left to experts in Spanish history.

Returning to Japanese silver mines, it is possible that similar profit-generating forces were at work there. The shogun did gain control of the major mining regions: "The shogunate policy concerning precious metals was focussed at first upon management and operation of mines. While taking power at the beginning of the 17th century, the Tokugawa controlled all mines directly or indirectly, and seized

[29] Carla Rahn Phillips, "Time and Duration: A Model for the Economy of Early Modern Spain," *American Historical Review* 92 (1987), 562.
[30] Phillips, "Time and Duration," 544.
[31] D. O. Flynn, "Fiscal Crisis and the Decline of Spain (Castile)," *Journal of Economic History* 42 (1982): 139–47.

the gold and silver produced there."[32] Aside from direct profits from control of silver production, there must have been an enormous amount of secondary economic activity generated via multipliers attributable to the silver industry. As was the case within Spain's domestic economy, there must have been opportunities to tax domestic activity linked directly and indirectly to the mining surge.[33] Control of international trade in Nagasaki also generated revenues for the shogun and there were Spanish-style seigniorage profits from forced minting.[34] In short, silver production generated tremendous direct and indirect opportunities for profit. It is possible that the emergence of a shogun capable of forging and enforcing political unification – out of so many competing feudal powers – required some unusual source of finance like silver mines: "The Tokugawa Bakufu, which took an active role in promoting mining and smelting technology, directly controlled all the silver and gold mined in Japan. After 1601, the Bakufu possessed a virtual monopoly over the gold and silver output."[35] It is no coincidence that the particular daimyo achieving dominance happened to be the one in control of the silver mines. So great was the emerging power of the shogun that Hideyoshi even "harbored the outrageous ambition of conquering Ming China."[36] This dream failed, of course, but he did manage to maintain 160,000 troops in Korea in the period 1592–8. To the extent that the campaign contributed toward independence from the Chinese world order,

[32] Kazui Tashiro, "Coinage and Exports of Silver during the Tokugawa Era," in Eddy Van Cauwenberghe, ed., [Proceedings from the 1986 Keio University Conference on Monetary History – title unknown, forthcoming], 3.

[33] J. H. Elliott, "The Decline of Spain," *Past and Present* 20 (November 1961); 70, points out that approximately 70% of Castile's income came from domestic taxation, the implication being that internal sources of finance were more important than external sources. I for one do not see how a backward country could possibly have generated internally the resources needed to finance such an empire. The state of Nevada today generates a significant portion of its tax receipts in the form of sales and other internal taxes, but this does not diminish the overwhelming importance of out-of-state gaming. It is the "export" of casino activity that generates the internal economy – the derivative multiplier effect – that is taxed. Nobody would argue that Nevada's internal taxes are independent of its casino-export activity. Similarly, the Spanish Empire was financed out of New World silver profits. Whether the Crown chose to tax the activity within Spain or outside of Spain is incidental to the contention that the source of imperial surplus was directly and indirectly the silver mines.

[34] So obvious was the motivation to profit from seigniorage that Japanese mints actively solicited – for a fee – the job of melting the very coins they minted. See Tashiro, "Coinage and Exports of Silver," 2. Spanish mints did not attempt to profit from melting their own coins, on the other hand, perhaps because of some bullionist confusion about damage from a smaller stock of silver coins.

[35] Yamamura and Kamiki, "Silver Mines and Sung Coins," 347n.

[36] Akira Hayami, "Chapter 3: The International Environment and *Sakoku*," in Hayami (unpublished manuscript), 17.

however, it was not a complete failure. *Sakoku* was important, not because Japan became isolated economically (which it clearly did not), but because it broke out of the Chinese tributary world order. Hayami argues that the importance of *sakoku* is that it meant establishment of an independent, albeit small, Japanese "world order": "We must not overlook the fact that the current boundaries of Japan were almost entirely determined in this period."[37] He contends elsewhere that Japan's transformation into an essentially decentralized, capitalistic, profit-oriented society dates back to 1600.[38] The argument in favor of market-oriented institutions evolving for centuries from the early Tokugawa period – as opposed to the "recent miracles" explanation for Japan's success today – is bolstered by the research of Hanley and Yamamura (who emphasize demographic considerations) as well as numerous others.[39]

SUMMARY AND FURTHER SPECULATIONS

In the early modern era, new mines and mining technologies created unprecedented silver-mining booms at opposite ends of the earth – Spanish America and Japan – and the controlling governments were quick to procure the lion's share of the resulting profits. The Hapsburg emperor and the shogun behaved in a predictable manner: they gathered profits as long as they could. Super-profits existed as long as silver's price exceeded its cost of production. Because of the immense accumulation of silver throughout prior history, even unprecedented rates of production only slowly increased the world's stock supply; gradual growth in its mass pushed down silver's price by 1 or 2 percent per year for a century. Because silver was used as money, the eventual decline in its purchasing power to one-third of its previous level implies a tripling of a silver-content price level. That is, the worldwide price revolution (in silver-content terms) – caused by discoveries and new mining technologies – ended around 1630 or 1640 because silver's value had finally descended to its new, lower cost of production.

In comparing the silver giants, one is forced to ask why Japanese silver production declined after the 1630s while Spanish production apparently did not. The production point of view offers some clues:

---

[37] Hayami, "Chapter 3," 27–8.

[38] Akira Hayami, "A 'Great Transformation': Social and Economic Change in Sixteenth and Seventeenth-Century Japan," in E. Pauer, ed., *Silkworms, Oil, and Chips: Proceedings of the Economics and Economic History Section of the Fourth International Conference on Japanese Studies, Paris, September 1985* (Bonn; 1986).

[39] Susan B. Hanley and Kozo Yamamura, *Economic and Demographic Change in Preindustrial Japan 1600–1868* (Princeton, 1977).

Spain had lower-cost mines, partly because of convenient access to mercury, an important input in the production process, and partly because the American mines were simply naturally richer. Nef long ago noted that the flood of American silver eventually reduced its price sufficiently to drive the previously profitable Central European silver mines out of business in the sixteenth century.[40] Perhaps the *world* stock of silver had grown sufficiently to depress its price to near its cost of production at the best Japanese mines by the 1630s/1640s and below cost of production at inferior (and hence abandoned) locations. Profits at Spanish mines were also squeezed, but cost advantages at least allowed many of them to survive in a much tougher environment. The shogunate government controlled production much more closely than did the Hapsburgs, perhaps because Spain's production centers were thousands of miles away from the king. American silver production was decentralized in the sense that mining claims were awarded to privileged citizens; the main source of direct government revenue was the famous *quinto,* a 20-percent severance tax on mined silver (though there were many other taxes and the Crown monopoly of mercury production was profitable). A good case can be made that Spain was quite efficient in collecting revenues for the state; taking a share of private production was probably a smart move compared with more bureaucratic alternatives. Yet the ability of Spain to outproduce and outlast its Japanese competitor probably had more to do with access to mercury and to differential characteristics of mines than to administrative efficiency.

Yamamura and Kamiki go to the heart of the matter in emphasizing the fact that Japan was indeed an important player in the emerging world economy:

As the collective efforts of monetary historians of Japan, China, and the West continue, we may soon be able to ask the tantalizing question: what would the course of the relative prices of gold and silver in China and the rest of the world (and the price levels in the rest of the world) have been had Japan not exported the large quantity of silver it did during the 1560–1640 period?[41]

Elimination of Japanese silver mines would have had major ramifications across the global economy. For one thing, the world stock of silver would certainly have grown more slowly than it actually did; thus, the market value of silver would have fallen more slowly. Not only would this have implied a lower rate of (silver-content) price

---

[40] John U. Nef, "Silver Production in Central Europe," *Journal of Political Economy* 49 (1941): 575–91.
[41] Yamamura and Kamiki, "Silver Mines and Sung Coins," 357.

inflation around the world, but it also would have meant a much more deliberate decline in per-unit profits in American (and Central European) silver mines. Microeconomics does tell us that price eventually gravitates to cost of production, but elimination of excess Spanish American profits may have been delayed until late in the seventeenth century in the absence of Japanese production. Rather than a century of disequilibrium in the silver market, attainment of a new equilibrium might have taken a century and a half. Who knows the outcome for Europe if Hapsburg Spain had a significantly enhanced financial base for its religious motivated war machine: Suffice to say that a, say, fifty-year postponement in the decline of the Spanish Empire could have had an impact of mind-jarring proportions. Without Japanese silver, the West-to-East flow of the white metal certainly would have been far greater, which would have affected trade through the Baltic, Russia, the Levant, and virtually every major trade route in the world. And what about an alternative counterfactual assumption: that *Spanish American* mines were not discovered (not implausible considering that Potosi was stranded some 15,000 feet and two and a half months by pack animal in the Andes)? I am convinced that there would have been no Spanish Empire. What would have been the power of the shogun? Would higher and prolonged silver profits have financed a successful attack on China, altering Asian history in some unimaginable way? Would there have been an East-to-West flow of silver in early modern times? Counterfactual imagination can be fun, if kept in perspective, but let's return to an attempt to uncover outlines of a world economy that actually did evolve.

Reference has already been made to arguments which claim that New World treasure financed the birth of Western capitalism, whether via profit inflation (Hamilton and Keynes), transfer of surplus value (Wallerstein), or some other route. I have argued the reverse: that Spain captured the surplus value (or profit, if you prefer, though the terms are not technically interchangeable) and used it in a near-fatal attack on the fledging capitalists in Northwest Europe. The situation was reversed in Asia, where the dominant silver producer was already market-oriented. Japanese silver profits helped finance an escape from the Chinese tributary system. Although Chinese trade routes flourished under the silver trade,[42] I would suggest that the shogun must have captured the bulk of silver's profit. Arguing the converse – that

---

[42] See Ping-Ti Ho, "Economic and Institutional Factors in the Decline of the Chinese Empire," in C. M. Cipolla, ed., *The Economic Decline of Empires* (London, 1970), 264; and Atwell, "Notes on Silver," 5.

China benefited most via accumulation of precious metals – flirts with the bullionist confusion of enhanced welfare accompanying larger bullion holdings. I prefer the view that the shogun's success in capturing silver's surplus value contributed toward what Hayami views as the escape of Japan from China's orbit and indeed financed military attacks against the Chinese. Early capitalism in the West survived despite New World bullion. In the East, early capitalism received a boost from silver because silver profits financed the defection of an independent, market-oriented Japan.

If it is true that the power base of Japanese and Spanish governments were both dependent on silver in the early modern age, then why did Spain alone suffer a precipitous economic decline during the twilight of the silver-profit era? There are numerous partial explanations. I will emphasize three points.

One reason for the decline of Spain relative to Japan was that Japan became a major exporter of copper after the silver years. The biggest customer was, once again, China. Exports were huge, topping out at over 5,000 tons annually around 1697 and 1698.[43] Not only did Spain lack the kind of substitute product enjoyed by Japan, it is also ironic that a huge volume of this copper flowed through Amsterdam to Europe's biggest customer – the Spanish mints – on some of the same ships that carried Spanish American silver to the East. During the peak years 1672–5, Dutch imports of Japanese copper equaled perhaps half of the calculated Swedish exports at that time.[44] In addition, Japan was endowed with important gold mines, though there is no record of the magnitude of total output. It is known that at least twenty-seven new veins were discovered between 1598 and 1696. Some were very rich. At least twenty gold mines were still actively worked in the 1720s and 1730s.[45] In short, Japan was endowed with a variety of rich resources. Spain had only silver (and mercury) in colonies that were distant, difficult to administer, and inevitably less profitable for the Crown over time.

Second, Spain squandered its windfall gains on global warfare[46] and was, in addition, a far less developed country than Japan. Spain may have been the most heavily taxed country in the world, yet very

---

[43] Atushi Kobata, "The Export of Japanese Copper on Chinese and Dutch Ships during the Seventeenth and Early Eighteenth Centuries," in T. Yamamoto, ed., *Proceedings of the Thirty-First International Congress of Human Sciences in Asia and North Africa* (Tokyo; 1984): 437–38.

[44] Kristof Glamann, *Dutch-Asiatic Trade, 1620–1740* (The Hague; 1981), 174.

[45] Hanley and Yamamura, *Economic and Demographic Change*, 127–128.

[46] D. O. Flynn, "Fiscal Crisis and the Decline of Spain (Castile)," *Journal of Economic History* 42 (1982): 139–47; Flynn, "El desarrollo del primer capitalismo" 42

little was spent on domestic infrastructure. In the 1630s, Olivares acknowledged the technological backwardness of Spain: "I am certain that no man who comes from abroad to see Spain can fail to blame us roundly for our barbarism, when he sees us having to provision all the cities of Castile by pack animal – and rightly so, for all Europe is trying out internal navigation with great profit."[47] Elliott describes Castile's economy as "closer in many ways to that of an Eastern European state like Poland, exporting raw materials and importing luxury products, than to economies of Western European states."[48] Carla Rahn Phillips reaches the same conclusion:[49] "Most of the surface area of Spain is not suitable for cultivation... Overall, Spain's natural resources present more challenges than opportunities and make its rise as a world power all the more impressive." When the forced-labor silver industry declined, backward Spain had nothing comparable to fall back on. Compare this with the Japanese situation. There was an agricultural revolution that more than doubled the amount of rice paddy in Japan in the period from 1550–1650, a century that spawned 34 percent of all major reclamation projects during the centuries between 781 and 1864.[50] Land reclamation and improvements in productivity (for example, irrigation projects) were encouraged by daimyo, sometimes in the form of tax exemptions and rebates.[51] In addition, productivity rose because institutional change – sometimes related to extremely low *marginal* tax rates – provided incentives for improvement: "The new class of peasants had every reason not to shirk because they could now share in the gain."[52] Waswo also emphasizes the role of incentives in her survey of the Tokugawa agricultural revolution. Early Tokugawa Japan was simply

---

[47] Quoted in John H. Elliott, "The Decline of Spain," *Past and Present* 20 (1961): 67.

[48] Elliott, "The Decline of Spain," 54.

[49] Phillips, "Time and Duration," 533.

[50] Kozo Yamamura, "Returns on Unification: Economic Growth in Japan, 1550–1650," in J. W. Hall, N. Keiji, and K. Yamamura, eds., *Japan Before Tokugawa: Political Consolidation and Economic Growth, 1500–1650* (Princeton, 1981), 330–4.

[51] Keiji Nagahara, "The Sengoku Daimyo and the Kandaka System," in Hall, Keiji, and Yamamura, eds., *Japan Before Tokugawa*, 45.

[52] Yamamura, "Returns on Unification," 347. As the entire Hall, Keiji, and Yamamura volume points out in detail, there was a multifaceted pre-Tokugawa trend toward a free-market economy. For example, Haruko Watika, "Dimensions of Development: Cities in Fifteenth- and Sixteenth-Century Japan," 325–6, emphasizes the city's role in the transition to a free market: "The castle towns of the Sengoku daimyo were substantially different from medieval cities. When creating the castle towns of the late sixteenth century, the daimyo abolished the rights of self-government that had typified cities of the Kinai. However, in order to attract merchants and artisans to the castle towns, the daimyo had to grant some degree of self government and extend other privileges, such as free markets and exemptions from debt moratoriums and land rent."

Dennis O. Flynn

not feudal in the European sense: "First, political rule was not based
on the possession of specific land . . . The political rule of the *bakufu*
and *daimyo* was limited to taxation of the rural community . . . Villages
were self-regulating units, left alone as long as peace and order were
maintained."[53] Hayami argues that Tokugawa centralization established property rights and other institutions favorable for an essentially free-market economy:[54] "Regardless of one's social class, an
individual possessed the chance to improve his economic status . . .
In Tokugawa Japan, political power did not translate into economic
wealth for the ruling warrior class . . . Eventually, there was no legally
prescribed status of "unfree men" or serfs as in medieval European
history . . . [Urban] residents did not pay land tax or income tax to the
political authorities. Although rich merchants frequently were forced
to donate money to the impoverished warrior class, they could get
certain priviliges in return. Economic development led to the loss of
control over the economy by the warrior class." Hanley and Yamamura likewise find market-oriented Japan to be highly advanced in
terms of infrastructure, education, transportation, agricultural expansion, and living standard.[55] One of the most dynamic regions, the

---

[53] Ann Waswo, "Innovation and Growth in Japanese Agriculture, 1600–1868," in Akira
Hayami, ed., *Pre-Conditions to Industrialization in Japan*, 1–9.
[54] Hayami, "A 'Great Transformation,' " 11–12.
[55] Hanley and Yamamura, *Economic and Demographic Change*. There is, however, plenty
of controversy on these issues. See, for example, Susan B. Hanley, "A High Standard
of Living in Nineteenth-Century Japan: Fact or Fantasy?" *Journal of Economic History*
43 (1983): 183–92; Yasukichi Yasuba, "Standard of Living in Japan Before Industrialization: From What Level Did Japan Begin? A Comment," *Journal of Economic History*
46 (1986): 217–24; Susan B. Hanley, "Standard of Living in Nineteenth-Century Japan:
Reply to Yasuba," *Journal of Economic History* 46 (1986): 225–6. Yasuba, "Standard of
Living," 221–2, estimates that average real income in Japan in the 1870s was only a
little lower ($286) than in England on the eve of its Industrial Revolution during
1765–85 ($298); Hanley, "Standard of Living" and "The Standard of Living, Popu-
lation Patterns," argues that differences in the quality of life were even smaller.
Yasuba, "Standard of Living," 2, 13, says that life expectancy in Japan in 1751–1800
was as high as in Japan in 1923 and as high or higher than in Britain in 1799–1803.
Shunsaku Nishikawa, "The Economy of Choshu on the Eve of Industrialization,"
in Hayami, ed., *Pre-Conditions*, 10, reports that "per capita food consumption was
nearly 2000 calories [per day in Choshu in 1700] . . . only 20% lower than the food
intake in 1960." Yasuba, "Standard of Living," 221, reports a remarkable climb in
U.K. wages to $720 by the 1870s, but he does not provide an estimate of the cor-
responding Japanese wage for the interval 1765–85. By glancing at his Tables 1 and
2, or his Tables 3 through 5, it is not clear that Japanese real wages rose between
the late-eighteenth and the late-nineteenth centuries. If real wages did flatten out
over this time interval, then Japanese wages in the interval 1765–85 may not have
lagged far behind English wages in the 1765–85 period, which bolsters the contention
that the Japanese economy was highly advanced by the middle of the Tokugawa
period. The central question may not be why Japan industrialized so quickly in the
late nineteenth century, but why did this not occur in the late eighteenth century;

Kinai, had a strong merchant class and a weak (and therefore less-meddlesome) bureaucracy.[56]

Although it is no doubt true that Hapsburg silver profits were considerably larger than those of the Tokugawa regime, Spain squandered its wealth on war.[57] With no substitute for the forced-labor profits from America, Castile was forced to face the unsightly reality of its domestic underdevelopment. The Tokugawa Shogunate waged war too, but the battle for political unification had been settled and military activity was in any case not on the century-long, global scale sustained by its competitor, Imperial Spain. As the term *Pax Tokugawa* implies, the island-nation Japan benefited economically by centuries of isolation from the ravages of war. There was a considerable investment in infrastructure in an economy that numerous scholars of Japanese history describe as increasingly capitalistic.

A third point is that Japan had an abundance of navigable waterways, having eliminated major coastal shipping bottlenecks in 1624 and 1672, an "incalculable [advantage] because the services of the ships on these routes cost significantly less than earlier methods of transportation."[58] On the other hand, Spain had (and still has) one of the most hopeless natural river systems in Europe. Access to inexpensive transportation is a prerequisite for commerce. It cannot be coincidence that the early modern Europe's centers of capitalism were on navigable water: England, the Low Countries, and Northern

Eric Pauer, "Traditional Technology and Its Impact on Japan's Industry during the Early Period of the Industrial Revolution," in Hayami, ed., *Pre-Conditions*, argues that industrialization required an understanding of modern science, rather than the trial-and-error approach of Tokugawa craftsmen, and Western science did not catch on until noncraftsmen samarai introduced it in the late nineteenth century.

[56] Hanley and Yamamura, *Economic and Demographic Change*, 91.

[57] After multiple state bankruptcies, by 1623 Castile's debt was still immense, even by today's standards – the equivalent of at least ten years' total Crown revenue, according to Geoffrey Parker, "The Emergence of Modern Finance in Europe, 1500–1730," in C. M. Cipolla, ed., *The Fontana Economic History of Europe* (Glasgow; 1974), II, 188. Even at the apex of Spain's receipts of official treasure in the 1590s, the entire influx of treasure both public and private, was insufficient to pay even the interest on the public debt. Despite ownership of the richest mines in world history, the Spanish Empire was a financial shambles. Spain's incredibly expensive war machine could not be maintained in the face of declining profits from the New World. The contrast with the Tokugawa Shogunate, as reported by A. Hayami, "Introductory Address – International Congress of Economic History," in A. Hayami, ed., *Pre-Conditions to Industrialization in Japan* (Bern, 1986), 5, is stark: "The security of Japan from foreign aggression allowed for a relatively low level of military expenditures and permitted the economic growth of Tokugawa Japan, and this interaction can be said to be one of the major characteristics of the Japanese economy at this time. The people of Japan could enjoy two and a half long centuries of urban life without paying for military defenses and in cities that typically had no defensive barracades."

[58] Hanley and Yamamura, *Economic and Demographic Change*, 93.

France. At issue is not just a matter of getting one's product to market after it has been produced. Transportation is not something that happens after production; *transportation is production*. Production in fishing is almost entirely transportation (from the sea to your plate), as is the harvesting of fruit and other food products. Much of what we call production inside of factories today is transportation – movements on conveyor belts, for example. One reason that capitalists located on navigable water in Northwest Europe was because those were the places with the lowest production (read: transportation) costs. Access to navigable water (in addition to accessible land paths) is a necessary condition for commercial advance, particularly when bulky inputs and outputs are involved. Cheap transportation is clearly not a sufficient condition for development, but it is necessary. A sophisticated transportation network was a precondition for provisioning the one million inhabitants of Edo (Tokyo, the world's largest city) in 1700, in a country of large metropolitan areas (for example, Osaka reached 500,000).[59] Japan apparently had an excellent transportation system, and Spain has always been plagued with geographical disadvantages regarding internal transportation:[60] "Coastal areas are well supplied with good natural ports, but inland transport faces extraordinary obstacles. For all practical purposes, the rivers are not navigable."

The argument that the late sixteenth and early seventeenth cen-

---

[59] Hayami, "A 'Great Transformation'," 5. Twelve percent of seventeenth-century Japan was urban, according to Hanley and Yamamura, *Economic and Demographic Change*," 65. Gilbert Rosnan, "The Tokugawa Urban Network: A Foundation for Modernization," in A. Hayami, ed., *Pre-Conditions to Industrialization*, 6, emphasizes the extent of Japanese urbanization: "It is likely that Japan was the only large-scale premodern society outside of Europe with more than 10 percent of its population in cities of this size [more than 10,000]. Moreover, the sudden increase in Japan's urban population prior to the 1700s may well have had no parallel in world history before industrialization." More recently, Rosnan, "The Tokugawa Urban Network: A Foundation for Modernization," in A. Hayami, ed., *Pre-Conditions to Industrialization*, 6, compares five countries – Japan, England, France, Russia, and China – using five indices of urbanization. He finds that in "all five dimensions Japan stands at or near the top in comparisons with four of the most powerful countries in the world both in the eighteenth and the twentieth century. Only England in the 1680s is clearly ahead of Japan in composite urbanization, and trade with colonies undoubtedly boosted the English figure. The small-scale of England also makes the high figure for vertical coordination (and the low measure of the urban competitive force) of questionable utility." There were as many as 4,500 wholesale merchants in Osaka in 1710, according to Matao Miyamoto, "Emergence of a National Market and Commercial Activities in Tokugawa Japan – With Special Reference to the Development of the Rice Market," in A Hayami, ed., *Pre-Conditions to Industrialization*, 4. In fact, large urban centers thrived more than a century before the Tokugawa period, according to H. Watika, "Dimensions of Development: Cities in Fifteenth- and Sixteenth-Century Japan," in Hall, Keiji, and Yamakura, *Japan Before Tokugawa*, 299.
[60] Phillips, "Time and Duration," 533.

turies constitute the true dawn of modern Japan is intriguing. There was a highly educated population[61] living in the world's largest cities and even "25 to 30% of adult males in rural areas were literate by the late Tokugawa period."[62] One purpose of this chapter has been to speculate about whether a global perspective on silver supports the hypothesis that silver profits helped finance the shogun's consolidation of the country. Acceptance or rejection of the hypothesis is left, of course, to those knowledgeable about the details of Shogunate financial power. The theoretical interpretation of silver's role tentatively offered here is based on microeconomic principles – looking at the white metal from the point of view of cost of production, profitability, and its distribution around the globe – rather than from a traditional, macroeconomic perspective. The microconomic view suggests that perhaps early modern Japan could be seen as a sort of Asian version of England (or Holland) and Spain combined. With financial clout along the lines of Imperial Spain, combined with strong, market-oriented institutions, a unique demographic history, favorable geography/climate, and sound infrastructure, Japan's promising future may have been assured centuries ago.

[61] Yasukichi Yasuba, "The Tokugawa Legacy: A Survey," in Hayami, ed., *Pre-Conditions to Industrialization*, 5.
[62] Waswo, "Innovation and Growth," 5.

CHAPTER 10

Colonies as mercantile investments: The Luso-Brazilian empire, 1500–1808

JOSÉ JOBSON DE ANDRADE ARRUDA

THEMATIC FOCUS

Within the context of the historical formation of commercial empires, our emphasis will focus on the Luso-Brazilian Empire. From this, we hope to be able to establish comparative relations with the other colonial empires at precisely those essential points that could give us an understanding of the global process. Obviously, the first chronological point will be the year 1500 – when Portuguese commercial and maritime expansion reached Brazil. The ending date will be 1808: the date the opening of ports broke the Portuguese monopoly on its Brazilian colony. In more restrictive terms, that is, in terms of a colony as a mercantile investment, the beginning date has to be delayed until the 1530's. This was the start of the first commercial agricultural activity in the colony: the sugar mill in São Vicente. If one considers the topic of commercial empires from the perspective of the colonies, a 1750 date has meaning for the struggle for European hegemony, which England had by now wrested from Holland,[1] and which figures largely in the definition of a new pattern of colonialism. But, for the colonial system in a broad sense, 1776 is a much more important date because it marks the rupture of the colonial compact, with the transformation of a former colony into an independent nation. The year

Translated from the Portuguese by Timothy J. Coates.
[1] See the important summary presented in P. J. Cain and A. G. Hopkins, "Gentlemanly Capitalism and British Expansion Overseas, I, The Old Colonial System, 1668–1850," *Economic History Review* 39 (1986): 501–25. The date 1763 appears as a transition in V. T. Harlow, *The Founding of the Second British Empire, 1763–1793, I, Discovery and Resolution* (2 vols., London and New York, 1952), 10, 64, 166, 592.

1810, when Spanish colonies rose in revolt during French intervention in Spain, has a similar meaning for Spanish America.

CONCEPTUAL FRAMEWORK

Discussing the meaning of the phrase "colonies as mercantile investments" would be a meaningful first question to pose. What is it that we are considering here? A metropolitan perspective of the history of the nature of commercial empires is, fundamentally, a history of colonies. Without fail, the question will emerge of return on capital invested in colonial enterprise. This is summed up in the well-known question "Do colonies pay?" This formulation molded nineteenth-century colonialism and was framed within the limits of a competitive capitalism in transition to becoming monopolistic. Analyzed by Hobson, Lenin, and Rosa Luxemburg[2] and, in the case of France by the work of Henri Brunschwig, this model presents itself in a different guise during the period when mercantile capital dominated the sphere of production.[3] Returns were made on capital invested by the metropole in its colonies. Indirect profits were made on the resale of colonial products, on the supplying of the colony with the means of production in the form of technology and the manpower of slaves, and even on the conspicuous consumption by the colonial elite. However, there were direct repercussions in the process of urbanization and the valuation of properties in the colonizing countries. The increase in population and improvements in the quality of life in the great rural properties known in Portugal as *quintas* is a unique example.[4] Recent studies on the European use of wealth obtained from the colonial world reveals this same process occurring in Seville. Van der Wee demonstrates the trajectory of urban and mercantile capital looking

---

[2] For an overview of the historiography on New Imperialism, see: D. K. Fieldhouse, "Imperialism: An Historiographical Revision," *Economic History Review* 19 (1961): 187–209; N. Etherington, "Reconsidering Theories of Imperialism," *History and Theory* 21 (1982): 1–37; D. R. Headrick, "The Tools of Imperialism: Technology and the Expansion of European Colonies in the Nineteenth Century," *The Journal of Modern History* 51 (1979): 231–62; and D. C. M. Platt, "Economic Factors in British Policy during the 'New Imperialism,' " *Past and Present* 39 (1968): 120–38.

[3] Henry Brunschwig, *Mythes et Réalités de l'Impérialisme Colonial Français, 1871–1914* (Paris, 1960). Brunschwig states that public and private funds invested in the overseas colonies surpassed these colonies' total budget in the period 1890 to 1914 (141–2). On the lucrative mechanisms of colonies, see M. M. Knight, "Do Colonies Pay?" in *War As a Social Institution: The Historian's Perspective*, eds. Jesse D. Clarkson and Thomas C. Cochran (New York, 1941).

[4] See: Anne Stoop, *Quintas Portuguesas* (Porto, 1986).

for a more rational investment and the revitalization of the countryside around Antwerp in the first decades of the fifteenth century.[5] In the sixteenth century, when Antwerp became a dynamic pole of world markets, one sees a "villa rustica" phase, in which an urban middle class, including wealthy financiers and important merchants, replaced the older land-owning nobility.[6] Erasmus Schetz stands out among these newcomers. The profits from his sugar mill in the Captaincy of São Vicente (which was directed by his agent Jan Van Hielst) made it possible for him to buy the Duchy of Ursel in Brabant.[7] When Antwerp experienced a crisis around 1585, many merchants invested their entire fortunes in real estate (houses, land, and rental properties) and left commerce completely. In the seventeenth century, the "villa rustica" reflected a new life-style.[8] How many more examples of this process could be found if research were done! In all likelihood, the long-term economic impact of this investment in real estate, in the improvement of the quality of life, and in the subsequent rise in levels of consumption, was an important factor in economic growth of Europe and of the beginnings of the Industrial Revolution.

The reverse of this perspective in its colonial variation is to consider the action of the metropole in its colonies as a policy of *fomento* (development): "The monopolistic company revealed open, promising horizons in the extreme north of Brazil . . . measured entirely in accordance with a *fomento* program of Pombal's despotism. The huge mercantile organization accomplished an important colonizing mission . . . turning the efforts of the company into real contributions for the economic development of the *Estado do Pará e Maranhão*."[9]

Directly opposing the concept of *fomento* is the idea of colonial exploitation. In this view, the colony is organized for exporting highly profitable goods to support the growth and economic development

---

[5] H. van der Wee, "Conjunctuur en economisch groei in the Zuidelijke Nederlanden tijdens de 14e, 15e, en 16e eeuw," in *Mededelingen van de Koninglijke Academie voor Wetenschap, Letteren en Schone Kunsten van België, Klasse der Letteren* 27 (1965): 9–10. On the quantitative aspects of commerce in Antwerp, see W. Brulez, "Le Commerce International de Pays-Bas au XVIe Siècle: Essai d'Appréciation Quantitative," *Revue Belge de Philologie et d'Histoire* 4 (1968): 1205–21.

[6] Roland Baetens, "La 'Villa Rustica,' Phénomène Italien dans le Paysage Brabançôn au 16ᵉ Siècle," in *Aspetti della Vita Economica Medievale.* Atti del Convegno di Studi nel X Anniversario della morte di Federico Melis (Firenze-Pisa-Prato, 1984), 176.

[7] Ibid., 177. On Schetz's mill (São Jorge) in São Vicente, see C. Laga, "O Engenho de Erasmos em São Vicente: resultado de pesquisas em arquivos belgas," *Estudos Históricos* 1 (1963): 113–43; Eddy Stols, "Um dos primeiros documentos sobre o engenho dos Schetz em São Vicente," *Revista de História* 35 (1968): 407–19.

[8] Baetens, "La 'Villa Rustica,' " 182.

[9] Manuel N. Dias, *Fomento e Mercantilismo. A Companhia Geral do Grão Pará e Maranhão, 1755–1778*, 2 vols. (Universidade Federal de Pará, 1970), 2:256.

of the European metropole. This could be achieved by a latifundist-monoculture-slave system or through mining.[10] In this case, the truth is probably in the middle. It was neither *fomento* nor exploitation; perhaps, more accurately, it was both at the same time. This presumes that the economic exploitation of New World colonies would have been impossible without at least a minimal degree of development in terms of a bureaucracy, an infrastructure that would include ports and roads, and an internal and external defense force. It is obvious that the exploitation of colonial riches cannot occur without developing the colony, without increasing its population, and thereby generating tension, conflict, and resistance.[11] The diversification of production in Luso-Spanish America, escaping the basic order of the colonial project, is an example of this argument. Around 1600 the central areas of Spanish America had become densely populated and had churches, monasteries, and other religious institutions, along with intense commerce, horticulture, and some specialized industry. In the intermediate areas, food and export crops were grown; many facets of industry used local raw materials. In the fringe areas, commerce was more "rustic" and was tied to horse and mule raising.[12] In Brazil, between the years 1750 and 1796, a profound diversification of crop and livestock production has been documented. Beginning with the export of 33 products (sugar and gold dominating), Brazil later exported 126 products among which gold was minimal and sugar only 35 percent of the export profile.[13] This demonstrated a dynamic domestic economic life for the colony with a marked tendency toward a relative internalization of the income flow stimulating the development of small-scale industry associated with the transformation of these crops and livestock products.[14] By all of these indications, the colony had deviated from the rigid scheme of a colonial pact by pre-

---

[10] Important works that present this analysis are: Caio Prado Junior, *Formação do Brasil Contemporâneo* (4th ed., São Paulo, 1953); and Fernando António Novais, *Portugal e Brasil na Crise do Antigo Sistema Colonial, 1777–1808* (São Paulo, 1979).

[11] The contradiction between exploitation and development was clearly discussed by Fernando António Novais, "As Dimensões da Independência," in *1822 Dimensões*, ed. Carlos Guilherme Mota (São Paulo: 1972). See especially 22: "It is not possible to exploit a colony without developing it." On resistance, tension, and conflict, see the classic work by Kenneth R. Maxwell, *Conflicts and Conspiracies: Brazil & Portugal, 1750–1808* (Cambridge, 1973).

[12] B. Slicher van Bath, "Economic Diversification in Spanish America around 1600: Centres, Intermediate Zones, and Peripheries," in *Jahrbuch für Geschichte von Staat, Wirtschaft und Gesellschaft Lateinamerikas* 16 (1979): 78.

[13] José J. de A. Arruda, *O Brasil no Comércio Colonial, 1796–1808* (São Paulo, 1980), 604 ff.

[14] Geraldo Beauclair, "A Pré-Industria Fluminense, 1808–1860," Diss., Universidade de São Paulo, 1987.

senting notable regional variety in the systems of labor, in the nature of economic activity, in the types of property, in per capita income, and in the level of prices.[15]

THE CONCEPT OF A COLONIAL SYSTEM

The understanding of this historical process necessarily involves an operative conception of this universe within which colonies and modern metropoles revolved and which could be called a world capitalist economy,[16] a modern world system,[17] a colonial system,[18] or a mode of colonial production dependent upon slaves.[19]

These first two concepts are of the same nature and come from the same source: Braudel's work *Civilisation Materièlle et Capitalisme*. In an explicit manner, they appeared in the lectures offered at the Johns Hopkins University in 1977 from which the book *La Dynamique du Capitalisme* originated. In this work, Braudel states: "From the Middle Ages and even from Antiquity, the world was divided into economic zones which were more or less centralized and coherent, that is to

---

[15] José J. de A. Arruda, "A Prática Econômica Setecentista no Seu Dimensionamento Regional," *Revista Brasileira de História* 10 (1985): 123–46.

[16] See especially the third volume of Fernand Braudel, *Civilisation Matérielle, Economie et Capitalisme* (Paris, 1979), 3 vols. A type of guide for this work, *Afterthoughts on Material Civilization and Capitalism*, trans. Patricia M. Ranum (Baltimore, 1977), was developed after three conferences held by Braudel at Johns Hopkins University in 1977. The French edition appeared later: *La Dynamique du Capitalisme* (Paris: 1985).

[17] An idea developing as a result of Braudel's concepts, with a masterly unfolding offered by Immanuel Wallerstein, *The Modern World System. Capitalist Agriculture, and the Origins of the European World-Economy in the Sixteenth Century* (New York, 1974); See also Wallerstein and Terence K. Hopkins, "Patterns of Development of the Modern World-System," *Review* 1 (Fall 1977): 111–45; and Wallerstein "A World-System Perspective on Social Science," *British Journal of Sociology* 27 (1976): 343–53.

[18] Concerned with the same all-inclusive view as Wallerstein, Fernando Novais has published and defended his view in articles and books even before the view presented by Wallerstein. Novais's position differs essentially in his strong attachment to the method of Marxist analysis, which, when combined with his great ability as a first-class historian, resulted in the already-mentioned text, *Portugal e Brasil na Crise do Antigo Sistema Colonial (1777–1808)*. See also his "O Brasil nos Quadros do Antigo Sistema Colonial," in *Brasil em Perspectiva*, ed. Carlos Guilherme Mota et al. (São Paulo, 1968), 47–62.

[19] Cf. Jacob Gorender, *O Escravismo Colonial* (São Paulo; 1978); Antônio Barros de Castro, "As Mãos e os Pés do Senhor do Engenho," and "A Economia Politica, o Capitalismo e a Escravidão," in *Trabalho Escravo, Economia e Sociedade*, ed. Paulo Sergio Pinheiro (Rio de Janeiro, 1983); Ciro Flamarion Cardoso, "O Modo de Produção Escravista Colonial na América," in *América Colonial*. ed. Theo Araujo Santiago (Rio de Janeiro, 1975); see also the articles published in *Modos de Produção e Realidade Brasileira*, ed. José Roberto do Amaral Lapa (Petrópolis, 1980).

say there were several world economies which coexisted."[20] For Immanuel Wallerstein, *The Modern World System* is exclusively part of the economic and social history of Europe. From the sixteenth century especially, "this arena of modern social action and modern social change has been and continues to be the modern world system, which emerges in the sixteenth century as a European-centered world-economy."[21] In essence, the system is defined by the movement of centers or cores, peripheries and semiperipheries that are united and reproduced through the accumulation of capital and unequal exchange. It is possible to see Marxist roots in this formulation, which makes the process of accumulation the dynamic element of the system and which considers "cores" and "peripheries" as *opposing pairs*.[22] At the base, that which defines the theoretical position articulated in the concept of a *modern world system* is its absolute heterodoxy and its most complete eclecticism. This involves a meritorious blending that originates in the globalizing history of the *Annales*, which integrates functionalism and idealism, and which adheres to Marxist formulations distinct from Marxist analysis, which manipulates Marxist analysis with theoretical and methodological procedures.[23] From a concrete historical viewpoint, what is really achieved is a functional analysis that looks for specifics within the system. These specifics and their failure to adhere to the model generate additional articulations for the system and are followed by successive layers, omitting an explanation of the forces behind these contradictions and class conflicts in spite of referring to them constantly. What remains is a type of 'naturalizing' capitalistic process that is outlined for eternity. The continual changing of economic precedence among the central poles (cores), the peripheries, and the semi-peripheries reveals, at base, a more selective sophistication of the theory of centers and peripheries, of the successive equilibriums and imbalances that do not and could not involve real transformations.[24] On the other hand, it is incorrect to believe that the transfer of "surpluses" among the accumulating core areas was "the central factor in the growth of cap-

---

[20] "Dès le Moyen Age et dès même l'Antiquité, le monde a été divisé en zones économiques plus ou moins centralisées, plus ou moins cohérentes, c'est-à-dire en plusieurs économies-mondes que coexistent." *La Dynamique du Capitalisme*, 87.

[21] Hopkins and Wallerstein, "Patterns of Development of the Modern World System," 112.

[22] Ibid., 112.

[23] José J. de A. Arruda, "Immanuel Wallerstein e o Moderno Sistema Mundial," *Revista de História* 115 (1983): 174.

[24] Ibid., 167–74.

italism."[25] What one actually finds here is the privileged metropolitan-Eurocentric view of modern history in which the colonies function as submissive elements without any independent identity.

To the historian reared in the world of a former colony, it appears totally aberrant that one could even ask a question like the following: *"Does the history of European expansion in fact exist; should it not instead be incorporated in the national and regional histories of the areas affected?"* The statement "overseas history does indeed exist" to us seems a flagrant platitude. Furthermore, to subsume a *colonial history* in an *overseas history* means that we view the object of study from the perspective of European or metropolitan history.[26] The extreme opposite of this view would be to see the colonial world as a whole, as a world of its own, capable of defining itself in terms of a colonial-slave mode of production.[27] Yet it would not be correct to define

the dominant mode of production in colonial social structure only from the form that basic social relations assumed, as if slavery were the same as a slave mode of production or serfdom the same as feudalism . . . Such a procedure ignores the level and organization of the forces of production and their articulation with the social means of production, and no less importantly, the historical processes which constitute these societies and gave them their meaning.[28]

Fundamentally, it is necessary to understand that colonial modes of production were not self-determined; that is, the cycle of the transfer of capital was completed outside the colony. Only at that stage were goods transformed into money and the money into means of production – especially in acquiring slaves from the external market. There were no means within the colony for a reproduction of the work force to take place. A portion of the surplus taken from production, part of the overall profit, occurred in the exterior and in the hands of the mercantile bourgeoisie. Political decisions, critical for mercantilism, were made in the metropolitan homeland and not in the colony.

It is therefore obvious that the dominant relationship was that es-

---

[25] Ciro Flamarion Cardoso, "As Concepções acerca do 'Sistema Econômico Mundial' e do 'Antigo Sistema Colonial'; a Preocupação obsessiva com a Extração de Excedente,'" in *Modos de Produção e Realidade Brasileira,* ed J. R. Amaral Lapa, 109–32.

[26] This problem is discussed (from our perspective, in a distorted view) in "What is Overseas History? Some Reflections on a Colloquium and a Problem," *Reappraisals in Overseas History,* eds. P. C. Emmer and H. L. Wesseling (Leiden, 1979), 1–17.

[27] We refer to the works of Jacob Gorender, Antonio Barros de Castro, and Ciro Flamarion Cardoso, cited in note 19 above. The reader should not assume that these authors are in complete agreement because they are listed together.

[28] João Manuel Cardoso de Mello, *O Capitalismo Tardio* (São Paulo, 1982), 35.

tablished between the metropole and the colony; it should not be forgotten that this relationship made colonial society unique. In these terms, global understanding of this particular historical process centers on the perception of this dialectical interaction between the status of the colony, determined by the metropole, and the slave-oriented social formation in the colony, an interaction directed from outside because the reproduction of the means of production could not be achieved internally.[29]

All of this constitutes the concept of a colonial system, or perhaps better stated, the old colonial system. This demonstrates the role of the history of colonies in their widest historical framework and shows the privileges of a colonial relationship. In other words, the network existing between the metropole and colony is shown as the central axis on which this system turned and by which an understanding of this global process and its particular structures can be achieved.

THE OLD COLONIAL SYSTEM

The starting point to achieve an overall understanding of colonial economies, in particular to reach an understanding of the colonies as privileged places for the investment of capital, is the concept of a colonial system. This subject deals with one of the most useful theoretical and historical concepts designed by historians. In the case of Brazil, the publications of Caio Prado, Jr., demonstrate an effort toward a definition of the *meaning of colonization*.[30] Above all others, Fernando António Novais took these themes to their ultimate conclusions; by highlighting the role of the colony in the primitive accumulation of capital, he effectively created a new paradigm for the study of colonial history.[31] The primary function of the colony is defined as follows: to produce a commercial surplus sold on the international market to generate great profits for the metropole; to expand the internal market of the colony for products from the European homeland that were produced or purchased for this overseas market;

---

[29] José J. de A. Arruda, "A Produção Económica," in *Nova História da Expansão Portuguesa*, ed. Joel Serrão and A. H. de Olivera Marques (Lisboa, 1986), Vol. VIII: *O Império Luso-Brasileiro*, 90.

[30] The influence of Caio Prado Junior, especially his concept of a "definition of colonization," is clearly acknowledged in Fernando Antonio Novais's concepts of an 'old colonial system' in Novais's essay "Considerações sobre o Sentido da Colonização," *Revista de Estudos Brasileiros* (São Paulo) 6 (1969): 55.

[31] The first formulation of this theme made by Novais appeared in "Colonização e Sistema Colonial: Discussão de Conceitos e Perspectiva Histórica," in *Anais do IV Simpósio ANPUH* (São Paulo, 1967).

and to establish a profitable environment for the mercantile bourgeoisie. In this last example, profit is not by chance but through monopoly: a guaranteed profit based on an exclusivity of the mechanics of colonial commerce.[32]

From the perspective of the metropole, mercantile capital was the historical presupposition for consolidation of the capitalist mode of production, to the extent that it was a necessary condition for the emergence of industrial capital; at the same time, it maintained a dominance over the productive base of the system.

In truth, the era of mercantile capital was the period of the historic formation of capitalism in which fixed capital played a relatively small part in the process of production. Excluding land, a considerable part of this wealth consisted of circulating capital that demanded almost immediate monetary payment. At the same time, this situation created a great availability of funds that were always in search of good investments and were able to function within the demands of the rapid circulation of mercantile investments. This explains why large capitalist entrepreneurs did not specialize – a virtual constant among the members of the lesser-wealthy bourgeoisie (masters, shop owners, et cetera). The wealthy merchants were, depending on the opportunities available, shipowners, financiers, insurance brokers, bankers, and even industrial or agricultural entrepreneurs. A certain intrinsic instability was rooted in the movement of mercantile capital: losses were incurred in the commerce of Malabar pepper, but there were gains in *cochonilha*: losses in finances for the state were recouped from small agricultural lenders; freight lost at sea was compensated by insurance; losses at the warehouse were regained at the shipyards. In this sense, a lost chain of events emerges. We note a certain operative identify between mercantile capital and monopolistic capital with growing tendencies to go beyond its national borders, to dominate – by way of a financial system – the productive structure of the system, and to retain an ability to flee rapidly when threatened by loss of profit or by uncontrollable po-

---

[32] "Without monopoly, there probably would have been no European Empire in the East before 1800"; E. J. Hamilton, "The Role of Monopoly in the Overseas Expansion and Colonial Trade of Europe before 1800," *The American Economic Review* 38 (1948): 53. Monopoly in this case means "the possession of the *sole right* to deal in a certain article or to trade with a certain country; and this sole right might be granted either to individuals or to companies, or indeed might be claimed by a nation." In agreement with the ideas expressed by H. B. Gibbins, Hamilton adds, "imperfect competition resulting from staple ports, convoyed fleets, royal favoritism, and other governmental or institutional restrictions," p. 33.

litical circumstances. Might it not be, then, that mercantile capital was more "modern" than industrial capital – intimately connected with its product and subjected to the same fate as its investments? Braudel has suggested that there was no branch of economic activity that provided satisfactory remuneration, capable of absorbing all the potential from mercantile capital. From this came its tendency to seek out other avenues of activity and to take refuge in the search for investments carrying social prestige. These would include acquiring land, including land for "speculation" (in modern terms), and fixed assets such as mining and industry.

What was the "calling" of mercantile capital, if one could attribute a 'will' to it? Certainly, it was investment done to promote and grease the circulation of capital: raw materials, goods, warehouses, equipment, ships, and coins. It was also credit for clients and agents, exchange services, and banking and insurance operations. A given of mercantile capital was that it sought to obtain a tight grip on monetary circulation. This resulted in exceptional profits that, in turn, were made easier by numerous investment opportunities. In this essential sequence of events, mercantile capital resisted entering production and directly submitting it to its own control; it hid its control in layers, preferring a form of indirect subordination. This was in spite of the fact that the majority of circulating capital represented expenses for labor. These expenses were high because independent producers (craftsmen, masters of manufacturing) did not sell their labor but the product of it – incorporated within the goods sold. In return, however, the two extreme points of capital circulation were brought into close connection, since there were no fixed factors of production (tools, machines, offices) and mercantile capital preserved a certain versatility: the freedom to move quickly to the best opportunities the market offered. For this reason, in the era of mercantile capital, places are assured for the independent work of the European producer integrated or not into the "putting out system" as well as for slave work on tropical plantations. Both represented high costs for circulating capital, but the responsibility for administration and replacement remained with those immediately in charge. The great importance acquired by circulating capital is thus not surprising, especially since the monetary system was dependent upon gaining access to metals, and was determined by the flow of external commerce. Considering the idea of an inelastic market, imperative at the time of mercantilism, the results were an aggressive nationalism in which monetary and commercial policies became vital parts of a power system. These enhanced the role of the state in its economic life.

In this manner, one is not observing mercantile capital in relation to what it would become (industrial capital) but in regard to what it was. A historical equation could be made for that time combining the meaning of a colony and of the entire colonial system in the historical process of the formation of capitalism. Emulating mercantile capital, this colonial system resisted becoming too closely tied to production in spite of its unrestrained tendency to occupy colonial space. If it could have simply joined (from outside) the various forms of preexisting production, its goal would have been achieved – as Mantoux has so authoritatively pointed out in defining the role of manufacturer-merchants. This explains the conservative, non-revolutionary, nature of mercantile capital. It was only when the opportunity for profit, via the rapid mercantile cycle, declined that mercantile capital and production blended. This meant becoming tied down to fixed capital and a substantial loss of one of its main characteristics: versatility. In this critical phase, the colonies played a decisive role because it was exactly there – in this world of the colonies – where fat profits were made with little fixed capital. Be it from the state or from the bourgeois mercantile metropole, the obligation fell upon the colonial people. This was the power and the weakness of mercantile capital: it created the conditions under which the colonies would have to define themselves.

In these terms, the expansion of mercantile capital hastened the development of values of exchange, a decisive element in the transformation of labor power into goods. Within the internal aspects of the colonial world, mercantile capital went beyond the limits of circulation and invaded the arena of production in the process of establishing colonial economies. Thus, it guaranteed for itself the production of goods in the world market. In this manner, a subordination of the process of production to mercantile capital was achieved. This was done by reintroducing the institution of compulsory labor (slaves), transforming the traffic in slaves itself into a propulsive element in the accumulation of wealth. Internal limitations on the reproduction of labor made its replacement from outside a necessity and favored the role of the slave trade at the expense of reproduction within the society.[33] The most critical element is, then, to retain this total subordination to mercantile capital within the history

---

[33] Fernando Antonio Novais, "Brasil nos Quadros de Antigo Sistema Colonial," 62.

of the colonial economy. This subordination was also present in the expansion of the central economies of Europe, where production in the form of crafts and manufacturing was likewise controlled – as was the model and the limits on the process of accumulating private wealth, and the general pace of the colonial economy.[34] Mercantile capital, as it is used here, is understood to mean the global process of the system in which both the area and the forces of agro-industrial production were dominated by the sphere of circulation. Also included would be the forms of appropriating capital dominating the social means of production; to us, this last aspect seems most pertinent at this particular stage in the formation of European capitalism.

Understanding the historical processes involved in the old colonial system assumes an awareness of the particularities of European nations as each passed through different stages in its unique historical development. These differences might appear in the form and pace of accumulation, within social relations, or in the nature of the state itself. This same understanding is required for the world of the colonies. The economic and social factors forming the colonial world were far from being identical. On the contrary, they demonstrated profound differences and varied from ancient, complex civilizations to others that were comparatively simple. The colonies comprising *the old colonial system* differed fundamentally from the numerous, commercial, and highly lucrative outposts the Portuguese maintained along the African and Indian coasts. They also differed from the new form of colonies – developments of the slave trade – that sprouted along the African coasts.[35] Colonies could be divided into two groups; those for settlement and those for exploitation or plantations.[36]

The colonies for settlement. . . . are located in areas with few inhabitants, with a physical environment similar to that of the homeland; settlers with their goods and families come to these colonies, they establish themselves individually and, little by little, they better themselves. They have loose ties with the motherland . . . They do not demand large investments but they do require heavy immigration . . . The production is, by and large, similar to that of the

---

[34] Cardoso de Mello, *O Capitalismo Tardio*, 89.
[35] Basil Davidson, *The African Slave Trade, Precolonial History, 1450–1850* (Boston, 1965), 205–6.
[36] "Portugal has two types of settlements in the two Indies and along the African coast. Those in the East Indies and in Africa have commerce as their objective. Those in America have culture and commerce as joint objectives." "Ensaio Económico sobre o Comércio de Portugal e suas Colônias" (1794), in *Obras Económicas de J. J. da Cunha Azeredo Coutinho* (São Paulo: 1966), 138.

homeland's; development is slow; the general environment is democratic; independence is inevitable.[37]

Those colonies selected for exploitation or plantations were established in places suitable for providing the homelands with "colonial products" such as: sugar, coffee, indigo, tobacco, and cotton. Naturally, the physical environment would be distinct from that of the metropole – the tropics being the desired area. The colonists were, above all else, entrepreneurs who clamored for large investments of capital and new forms of labor organization, especially slavery or indentured servitude. In other words, this outlines the same concept expressed by Wakefield's *systematic colonization*: a rational organization of property; that is, a guarantee of property to the entrepreneurs in order to keep the new colonists from becoming small producers and thereby limiting the supply of manpower. The products of these colonies were exported to the metropole; riches were made quickly; the population grew slowly; the fragile spirit of democracy was slow to develop into a sense of emancipation. Typical examples of such colonies would be those in the Antilles.[38]

The observation that the planting system developed on the Mediterranean and Atlantic islands, where there is very little available land in comparison with America, or that, in the territory forming the United States, it was possible for both small and large property holdings to coexist[39] does not weaken the fundamentals of Novais's argument regarding the large-scale production of "colonial products" bound for market in the metropole. The natural and ecological conditions and the degree of development of pre-colonial societies required that this system develop variations. This can be seen in Spanish America – where slavery was secondary. The exploitation of Indian communities predominated; partially deprived of their lands, the Indians became forced laborers.[40]

"Slavery, the slave trade, and varying forms of servitude were, therefore, the axis on which revolved the economic and social life of the colonial world created for the benefit of European mercantilism."[41] The political direction of this process rested with the absolutist state – the centralizing element in the politics of colonialism, in the

[37] Fernando Antonio Novais, "Considerações sobre o Sentido da Colonização," 57.
[38] *Ibid.*, 57, citing Wakefield. The typology of settlement and development colonies is summarized in Paul Leroy-Beaulieu, *De la colonisation chez les peuples modernes* (2 vols., Paris, 1902), II, 563 ff.
[39] Jacob Gorender, *O Escravismo Colonial*, 146–7.
[40] Ciro Flamarion Cardoso and Héctor Pérez Brignoli, *História Económica da America Latina* (Rio de Janeiro, 1983).
[41] Novais, "O Brasil nos Quadros do Antigo Sistema Colonial," 62.

structure of mercantilism, and in the era of the preponderance of mercantile capital.

SYSTEMATIC COLONIAL DEVELOPMENT

As Carla Phillips has said, the impressive growth of long-distance trade since approximately 1450 was intimately connected with overseas colonial markets, leading to the emergence of a global system that was connected to trade but not necessarily determined by it. If Portugal's empire in the East was characterized by goods of low volume and high prices, the empire of Brazil was, by contrast, characterized by low-priced, high-volume merchandise, creating conditions in which Portugal could reproduce here its own agro-maritime economy, as if having no connection with the indigenous population.[42]

The first thirty years of the Brazilian colony are completely within the framework that Celso Furtado calls the "external flow of payments" of colonial economy.[43] The only natural resource immediately of use to the metropole, brazilwood, was cut and transported to Europe. This did virtually nothing to increase the value of the colonial territory, nor did it establish a stable population or material installations. Rather, it gave the colony the transient feeling of a wood-cutting station. Brazil was nothing more than a secure port of call on the route to India.[44] Without taking into account fraud and contraband,[45] brazilwood composed 90 to 95 percent of the export profile in 1530 and was estimated to have had a value between 80,000 and 100,000 pounds sterling.[46] The specific form of commercial enterprise took varied forms: royal monopoly, liberal enterprise, a regime of contracts, and a return to royal monopoly.[47] In the areas of agricultural activity, colonists mobilized the available work force and animals to cut and transport the wood. Production reached a total amount of 2,000 *quintais* of extracted wood (dye). At 7 or 8 *tostões* per *quintal* this yielded

[42] Carla Rahn Phillips, "The Growth and Composition of Trade in the Iberian Empires, 1450–1750," in *The Rise of Merchant Empires*, 34–101.

[43] Celso Furtado, *Formação Econômica do Brasil* (Rio de Janeiro, 1959).

[44] Pierre Chaunu, *Conquête et Exploration des Nouveaux Mondes (XVIe Siècle)* (Paris, 1969), 240.

[45] Frédéric Mauro, *Le Portugal, Le Brésil, et L'Atlantique au XVIIe Siècle (1570–1670)* (Paris, 1983), 155.

[46] Miercea Buescu, *História Econômica do Brasil, Pesquisas e Análises* (Rio de Janeiro, 1970), 57.

[47] Mauro, *Le Portugal, Le Brésil, et l'Atlantique*, 149.

an excellent profit.[48] During the first thirty years of the sixteenth century, when the purchase and transport were controlled by the king, the profit was the difference between the price of buying the product (in Brazil) and selling it (in Europe). In the first years of the seventeenth century, when the system had returned to royal monopoly, profit was estimated at 76 percent not taking into account the risks of the voyage at state expense. At the time of the contract system, profit for the contract holder was reduced to 15 percent. Profit was certainly much higher for French, English, and Dutch smugglers. Brazilwood had a special financial meaning for the king of Portugal because it represented private resources that could be mobilized by the monarchy for specific goals: to prepare a fleet, to equip troops, or to provide more resources for the queen. It came to act as an instrument of payment at times when money was lacking.[49] In European terms, brazilwood helped the important dye industry – an integral part of the industrial motor of proto-industrialization. In this context, brazilwood represented a mercantile investment that yielded a high profit, that did not tie up financial resources, and that gave an increased return by being a dynamic factor in a productive European system. In terms of a colonial process, the trade with American Indians for brazilwood only represented the continuation of purely predatory methods adapted for Africa and India that did not go beyond the commercialization of natural products.[50]

A stable, growing population and the real occupation of the territory effectively began with sugarcane cultivation. One could even go so far as to state that Brazil's growth was directly related to the multiplication of sugar mills. Benefiting by their previous experience on the islands of Madeira and the Azores, where the Portuguese began their first phase of colonization, systematic investment began in Brazil in 1531 with the construction of the first sugar mill in São Vicente. This was followed in 1540 by four additional mills in Espirito Santo, one in Pernambuco in 1542, and another in Paraiba in 1546.[51] Stuart Schwartz has shown that Brazilian sugar appeared in Europe by 1510, if not earlier.[52] However, it is significant to note that, from 1570, when 60 mills were

---

[48] Chaunu, *Conquête et Exploration des Nouveaux Mondes (XVIe Siècle)*, 314.
[49] Mauro, *Le Portugal, Le Brésil, et l'Atlantique*, 153–60.
[50] On this point, see Alexander Marchant, *From Barter to Slavery: The Economic Relations of Portuguese and Indians in the Settlement of Brazil, 1500–1580* (Baltimore, 1942).
[51] Mauro, *Le Portugal, Le Brésil, et l'Atlantique*, 192.
[52] Stuart B. Schwartz, *Sugar Plantations in the Formation of Brazilian Society, Bahia, 1550–1835* (Cambridge, 1985), 161.

producing around 3,000 *arrobas* valued at 270,000 pounds sterling (corresponding to approximately 71 percent of colonial exports), the 100,000 pound sterling export of brazilwood represented only 26 percent of the total.[53] According to Mauro, between 1570 and 1710, the number of sugar mills was as follows:

Year	South	Center	North	Total
1570	5	31	24	60
1583	13	52	66	131
1610	40	50	140	240
1629	70	84	192	346
1710	136	146	246	526

The outline presented by Roberto Simonsen, in spite of the diverse and unrelated materials on which it is based, is one of the few cumulative quantitative indicators of exports during the colonial period.[54] It allows us to identify general tendencies of the colonial economy. It is important to note that, after 1570, the rise of colonial exports was determined by sugar – indeed it practically accounts for the entire increase, when calculated in pounds sterling. This situation ended in 1690, when the export of precious metals began (Figure 10.1). Using the data presented by Simonsen, as well as additional information on the number of sugar mills, slaves, and free men, Buescu presents the following outline of Brazil in 1600. Total exports at this time were reaching 2.4 million pounds sterling; sugar represented 2.16 million pounds sterling, or 90 percent, of the total.[55]

Number of sugar mills	200
Number of slaves	30,000
Slaves in the export sector	24,000
Slaves at mills	20,000
Annual production of sugar, in *arrobas*	1,200,000
Average price per *arroba*, in pounds	18/10
Value of total exports, in pounds sterling	2,400,000
Value of exported sugar	2,160,000
Average production per mill, in *arrobas*	6,000
Average annual production of a slave	60
Number of slaves per mill	100

From these figures, it is possible to calculate the internal income of the colony – an important indicator to measure its potential for eco-

---

[53] Buescu, *História Económica do Brasil*, 57.
[54] Ibid., 91; Mauro, *Le Portugal, Le Brésil, et l'Atlantique*, 219, citing Simonsen, *Economic History of Brazil*, table on p. 170.
[55] Data from Simonsen, *Economic History of Brazil*, trans, Auriphebo Simões (São Paulo, 1968), discussed by Buescu, *História Económica do Brasil*, 84.

nomic growth. This calculation assumes a total population of 100,000 individuals: 30,000 slaves, 30,000 Indians, and 40,000 whites. Of the total £2.4 million income from exports, 20 percent, or £480,000, went to the government. It is also necessary to deduct an additional £30,000 for the annual cost of slaves and to add to that £48,000 for personal income received by free workers (estimated at the ratio of one per five slaves). The remaining £1,848,000 therefore went to the approximately 2,000 sugar mill owners, other land owners, intermediaries, and capitalists. "It was quite possible that two-thirds (of this figure) remained outside the borders of the colony."[56] Because the metropole extracted an additional 20 percent of this monetary income in the form of import taxes and other charges, £1,478,000 remained for the land owners; the state actually received £849,600. These heavy taxes that were levied on the colonial economy, especially on the sugar industry, were not reinvested for colonial growth; they were not invested in improving the shipping or transport sector, nor were they used to improve the sugar refineries or warehouses, all of which would have increased the economic performance of the colony. They were channeled instead to cover "diplomatic debts and war expenses that produced no direct benefit to Brazil." Because of these excesses in tribute, prices went up and the product stopped being competitive. This opened the way for rivals to break the Portuguese monopoly on sugar production.[57] In addition, much of the profit from sugar commerce went into the hands of Dutch merchants and distributors, who even transported sugar out of Brazil on their own ships.[58]

Constructing the expenses of a theoretical, typical sugar mill, Mauro concluded that they would have been distributed as follows:

Salaries	24.4%
Combustibles	21.3%
Copper	11.0%
Boats	10.4%
Repair work	8.1%
Slaves	10.3%
Diverse expenses	14.5%

Mauro's calculations demonstrate that profit in years with good harvests was 3 percent in relation to capital and 7.8 percent in relation to all business, before taxes. If this was the case, net income on capital never surpassed 2 percent or 2.5 percent. Nevertheless, expenses for

[56] Buescu, *História Econômica do Brasil*, 88.
[57] Schwartz, *Sugar Plantations in the Formation of Brazilian Society, Bahia, 1550–1835*, 187.
[58] Ralph Davies, *The Rise of the Atlantic Economies* (London, 1973), 173.

the sugar mill owner and his family were limited to purchase of luxuries. Most of the needed food and clothing was obtained locally without money being exchanged.[59]

Starting with a gross income in the sugar sector of £1.5 million, estimating 10% spent as payments for salaries, purchasing livestock, firewood, etc., and replacement expenses for imported goods at around £120,000; we can deduce that the net income of this sector was something near £1.2 million. Subtracting £600,000 in expenses for imported consumption goods, £600,000 still remained. This was the potential sum for investment in this sector. Since fixed capital rose to £1.8 million, and at least a third of that sum represented buildings or other installations built by slaves, we can conclude that this capital could have been doubled in two years.[60]

Because investment growth did not occur at this rate nor would market conditions allow it, the obvious conclusion is that a significant part of the capital invested in sugar production belonged to the merchants and thus generated "income to non-residents, remaining outside the colony." Because of this subjugation of production to mercantile capital, coordination between production and consumption bypassed the tendency toward super-production that would have led to lower prices and an unworkable sugar industry.

The reduction in income felt by the sugar mill owners put them in a difficult financial situation under unfavorable conditions. This forced the Portuguese state to guarantee continued colonial business by granting fiscal immunity or a suspension of debt – which then became an important source of remuneration for the slave owners in the sugar economy.[61] In 1612 royal provisions suspended debt; the Lisbon merchants complained and were given relief. Then, in 1663, the state dispensed with the payment of the *dizimo* and made it more difficult for creditors to confiscate slaves or equipment. In 1690 sugar mill owners asked that the decree forbidding foreclosure on mills and sugar cane industries be made permanent. In 1710 the king, ruling against the land owners and in favor of commerce in the kingdom, ordered the collection of taxes on debts. What followed was a succession of restrictions and immunities that at times favored the producers and at other times the merchants. In short:

---

[59] Frédéric Mauro, *L'Expansion Européenne, 1600–1870*. Collection Nouvelle Clio, 3d ed. (Paris, 1988), 146.

[60] Celso Furtado, *Formação Econômica do Brasil*, 60.

[61] Vera L. A. Ferlini, "Terra, Trabalho e Poder, O Mundo dos Engenhos no Nordeste Colonial," Diss., Universidade de São Paulo, 1986, IV–60. In his chapter in this volume, Jacob M. Price shows the continuance of seizing colonial property, in the form of merchandise, as a guarantee for debts contracted with metropolitan merchants.

agricultural activity for the colonist was not a method to accumulate capital, but to acquire wealth in terms of additional land and slaves. The noble sugar business, under the State's direction, received the necessary conditions for continuation and growth. The exploitation of these conditions was a large commitment among the King, the merchants, and the colonial land owners. It was not something foreign, imposed by the *metropole*, but an all-encompassing system which used the land as a basis for super-profit via an external market, and as a foundation for internal power.[62]

As Furtado explains, capital investments made in the colony did not create a flow of monetary income but only increased the amount of assets.[63] Sugar, as Boxer has stated, for the homeland at the end of the sixteenth century, was "more profitable to the Iberian dual Monarchy than all the pepper, spices, jewels, and luxury goods imported in the Indiamen from 'Golden Goa.' "[64]

Vitorino Magalhães Godinho quantifies the assertation. Based on reports by Fernão Cardim, he calculates that in 1583 and 1584 sugar sent from Brazil to Portugal tripled in value, thus from 1 *cruzado* at the point of origin to 3 at the final destination. Between 1550 and 1583, white sugar was worth between 400 and 460 *reis* in Brazil, and raw sugar between 300 and 320. In Lisbon, it sold for between 1,000 and 1,650 *reis* wholesale (per *arroba*), and between 1,600 and 1,920 *reis* retail (by the pound). Madeira sugar was much more expensive, selling for between 2,600 and 3,000 *reis* per *arroba*. Brazilian sugar in whatever form yielded between 2 1/2 and 4 times the original price. Not seldom, Lisbon merchants made gigantic profits by selling Brazilian sugar as it if were from Madeira. Transatlantic trade assured Portugal's mercantile bourgeoisie elevated profits insofar as the control of colonial possessions raised the terms of exchange above the marketing conditions normal for a product.[65]

The pointed competition among the colonizing metropolitan powers, especially wars increasingly conducted for "colonial' reasons,"

---

[62] Ferlini, "Terra, Trabalho e Poder, O Mundo dos Engenhos no Nordeste Colonial," IV–71. A similar situation occurred in Spanish America, where "the costs of tribute and mortgages required a constant expenditure of capital which could only be obtained by profits derived from agricultural sales and returns to the *hacendados* above costs;" for this reason, "it was impossible to hold both Indians and lands without using them productively and profitably." Herbert Klein, "Accumulation and Inheritance among the Landed Elite of Bolivia: The Case of Don Tadeo Diez de Medina," *Jahrbuch für die Geschichte Lateinamerikas* 22 (1985): 219.

[63] Celso Furtado *Formação Econômica do Brasil*, 64.

[64] C. R. Boxer, *The Portuguese Seaborne Empire, 1415–1825* (New York, 1969), 105: "By rewards we do not mean short-run profit, although even here the Americas seem to do better than Asia by about 50%;" Wallerstein, *The Modern World System*, 336.

[65] Maghães, *Os descobrimentos e a economia mondial* (First ed., 2 vols., Lisbon, 1963–1971), II, 472.

demonstrates the importance of colonies as places for mercantile investments. Important aspects of this reality were the creation of specific companies for commerce, the organization of the slave trade, and the continued contraband trade. At the same time, expansion of sugar production in Brazil at the end of the sixteenth century prompted monopolistic legislation aimed at guaranteeing for Portugal the exclusive control of the colony's commerce.[66] "A monopoly on colonial trade was contractually connected with European expansion into the West. The monopoly on trade granted the Dutch, English, and French East India Companies afforded the incentive to commerce and empire in the East."[67] By way of monopolies, it was possible for companies to depress prices of colonial products and inflate the cost of metropolitan goods, or goods that were reexported. The high prices paid in European markets for imported colonial goods became income concentrated in the hands of the commercial intermediaries rather than being directed to the productive sectors of the exporting countries. Because of this situation, it became the profit of monopoly. Those Dutch companies of commerce that were organized under the influence of liberalism had disastrous results during the entire seventeenth century. This shows the dominating character of monopolies as the principal articulation of colonial commerce.[68] The initial success of the Dutch West India Company, organized in 1621, demonstrates the essential need for monopoly. The 1672 merger of the French West India Company, formed in 1664, with the Franco-African Company and its obtaining of the monopoly on supplying slaves to the Antilles in 1679 were critical for the company's continued viability. It would appear that the actions of these colonizing companies were not identical in the East and in the West. In order to maintain its commercial capital in circulation, the Dutch East India Company, formed in 1602, acquired products in areas not controlled by the Company by way of goods from their fleets and operated under the more or less normal pressures of free trade – thus imposing on them monetary expenses in the form of silver coin. At any rate, European impact in the Orient was on a much smaller scale, except in some limited areas.[69]

---

[66] Vicente de Almeida Eça, *Normas Económicas da Colonização Portuguesa até 1808* (Coimbra, 1921), 127.

[67] E. J. Hamilton, "The Role of Monopoly in the Overseas Expansion of Europe," 52.

[68] Novais, *Portugal e Brasil na Crise do Antigo Sistema Colonia*, 76.

[69] B. R. Pearn, *An Introduction to the History of South-East Asia* (Kuala Lumpur, 1963), 80: "The Portuguese colonial regime . . . did not introduce a single new economic element into the commerce of Southern Asia. The Portuguese regime only introduced a non-intensive drain on the existing structure of shipping and trade." In the Congo, by contrast, the Portuguese destroyed a pagan kingdom, introduced Christianity,

On the other hand, in Brazil the Dutch West Indies Company attempted the effective occupation of the territory, concentrating its forces on the sugar-producing northeast. The Portuguese Restoration in 1640 changed the Dutch into allies against Spain – which would explain the concessions given by the Portuguese to the Dutch as well as to the English.[70] The colony became a type of "hard currency" among the European metropoles. The agreements of 1654 and 1661 with England, and in 1641 with Holland, conceded advantages to these countries in the commercial exploitation of Brazil. At the same time, attempts were made to limit the concessions by placing the enterprises under the direction of the *Conselho Ultramarino*[71] and of the *Companhia Geral do Comércio* for Brazil, formed in 1649.[72]

In Spanish America the same regime of exclusive monopoly was adopted within the framework of a colonial system. The Royal Monopoly was directed from the *Casa de Contratación* in Seville, which became the only port allowed to trade with the colonies – facilitating the control over mercantile goods going to the colonies and operating through a system of fleets and galleons. The result was high profits and high prices for goods in America. English, French, and Dutch pressures led to the mounting of competing economies in the Antilles; in this way, contraband was forced into the Spanish Indies.[73] The largest opening in the Spanish system in America was the slave trade. The Portuguese, Dutch, and French disputed control over this traffic. Each of these powers, in succession, controlled the *asiento* – which finally was passed to the English with the Treaty of Utrecht.

The traffic in slaves was an important activity in establishing sugar colonies in the New World – so much so that this traffic became the

---

and built a base to supply manpower to maintain the colonization of South America, according to Alfredo Margarido, "L'ancien royaume du Congo," *Annales, E. S. C.* 25 (1970): 1725. For the impact of the Dutch, see C. Van Leur, *Indonesian Trade and Society* (The Hague, 1955), 118–19.

[70] G.D. Winius, "India or Brazil. Priority for Imperial Survival during the Wars of the Restoration," *The Journal of the American Portuguese Cultural Society* 1 (1967): 34–42. See also the (still) solid study by C. R. Boxer, *Salvador de Sà and the Struggle for Brazil and Angola* (Oxford, 1960).

[71] Novais, *Portugal e Brasil na Crise do Antigo Sistema Colonial*, 82.

[72] Gustavo de Freitas, "A Companhia Geral do Comércio do Brasil (1649–1720)," *Revista de História* (São Paulo) 2 (1951): Parte 1, 307–28; Parte 2, 85–110; Parte 3, 313–44.

[73] On the threat of Dutch sugar production in the Antilles, see M. Edel, "The Brazilian Sugar-Cycle of the 17th Century and the Rise of the West-Indian Competition," *Caribbean Studies* (Puerto Rico) 9 (1969): 22–44. Wallerstein, *The Modern World System* Vol. II; *Mercantilism and the Consolidation of the European World Economy, 1600–1750* (New York, 1980), 166: "Smuggling thereupon became a way of life that linked the merchants of the core countries to the producers of peripherals countries they did not directly control."

single most profitable element in fact determining the movement of accumulation in the colonial system. This is according to Novais, who also believes this trade was the clearest example of the process of accumulation in the hands of the kingdom's mercantile bourgeoisie. This was to the detriment of the colonial sugar mill owners while, at the same time, these merchants transferred profits to the state. As a matter of fact, agricultural expansion in the colonies completely changed the sixteenth-century slave trade. It profoundly influenced African society, populated America, and enriched the Europeans. It also made the process of accumulation more dynamic, linking it to the trade in slaves and to the triangular trade – of which it became an integral part.[74] Very rough estimates suggest 20 million Africans were transported to the New World in three centuries; two-thirds were used in sugar production.[75] Slaves were obtained in Africa by intermediaries (*pombeiros*), Portuguese merchants, mulattos, or free blacks who entered the interior to bring slaves to where they were sold on the coasts.[76] In this system, English goods were exchanged for slaves in Africa, who were then transported across the ocean (the Middle Passage) to colonies in the West Indies or on the continent and were, in turn, exchanged for sugar, tobacco, and other goods.[77] In Brazil, the production of leaf tobacco was directly linked to the slave trade on the so-called "India" route (*Carreira da India*).[78] Around the middle of the eighteenth century, 185,000 *arrobas* of this tobacco were exported to Africa, especially to Angola. Calculating three *arrobas* per roll (*rolo*), this would be 61,700 rolls – for which 20,000 slaves could be exchanged.[79] Taking the high risks involved in this commerce into consideration, it could be calculated that the capital invested in

---

[74] Samir Amin, *L'Accumulation à l'echelle mondiale* (Paris, 1970).

[75] R. B. Sheridan, "The Commercial and Financial Organization of the British Slave Trade, 1750–1807," *The Economic History Review* 11 (1958): 249, citing N. Deerr, *The History of Sugar* (1950), II:284. Solid studies on the traffic in slaves are: Phillip Curtin, *The Atlantic Slave Trade: A Census* (Madison, 1969); Herbert S. Klein, *The Middle Passage: Comparative Studies in the Atlantic Slave Trade* (Princeton, 1978); and Filipe Alencastro, "La traite négrière et les avatars de la colonization portugaise au Brésil et en Angola, 1550–1825," *Cahiers du CRIAR* (Paris) 1 (1981): 1–69.

[76] C. R. Boxer, p. 102. On state formation in Africa before and during the Atlantic slave trade, see A. Norman Klein, "West African Unfree Labor Before and After the Rise of the Atlantic Slave Trade," in *Slavery in the New World*, eds. Laura Foner and Eugene D. Genovese (New York, 1969); 87–95.

[77] R. B. Sheridan, "The Wealth of Jamaica in the Eighteenth Century: A Rejoinder," *The Economic History Review* 21 (1968): 249.

[78] José Roberto do Amaral Lapa, *A Bahia e a Carreira da India* (São Paulo, 1968), 255.

[79] Buenscu, *História Económica do Brasil*, 206. See also Pierre Verger, *Flux et reflux de la traite des nègres entre le golfe de Benin et Bahia de Todos os Santos du dix-septième au dix-neuvième siècle* (Paris, 1968).

the traffic in slaves produced the standard profit enjoyed by other overseas commerce: 15 percent of the sale price.[80] A multiplying effect occurred, however, when the final components of colonial production – goods to be exported to the European market – entered the picture, greatly increasing this profit.

Contraband became a modern form of appropriation of colonial surplus. The countries involved in the practice of smuggling economized their productive investments, avoiding indirect appropriations. Because of this, they depended on the cooperation of the colonists – subjected to high prices by the monopolistic regime, to which they could offer products cheaper. "Licenses, concessions, and smuggling, to us, seem to be phenomena which fall most directly in the area of disputes among the various metropolitan European powers appropriating the advantages of colonial exploitation."[81]

THE NEW SYSTEM OF COLONIZATION

The general crisis of the seventeenth century represented a breathing spell in the evolution of the *modern world system*, as Wallerstein has emphasized.[82] Fundamentally, this crisis was a problem of growth in which two distinct systems collided. One system was predominantly responding to the mercantile market, was directed by mercantile capital, and was centered on urban centers and commercial routes. The other system was essentially agrarian and characterized by a rural self-sufficiency. This perspective of Hobsbawm,[83] contrary to other studies,[84] defines the general framework of dynamic centers of the European economy and suggests a readjustment of the old colonial system to the new conditions of the seventeenth and eighteenth centuries. We confront a new system of mercantile accumulation, different from that which characterized the first part of the modern period from the sixteenth to the middle of the seventeenth century.

[80] R. B. Sheridan, "The Wealth of Jamaica in the Eighteenth Century: A Rejoinder," 54.
[81] Novais, *Portugal e Brasil na Crise do Antigo Sistema Colonial*, 93.
[82] Wallerstein, *The Modern World System*, II, especially his introduction, "Crisis of the Seventeenth Century?" 2–12. For a critique of this explanation, see José J. de A. Arruda, "A crise do século XVII e a consolidação da Economia-Mundo (1600–1750)," *Revista de História* 116 (1984): 183–92.
[83] Eric Hobsbawm, "The Crisis of the Seventeenth Century," in *Crisis in Europe 1560–1660*, ed. Trevor Aston (London, 1965): 5–58.
[84] A variant explanation blames the crisis of the slow development of capitalism in this phase on manufacturing and not on hindrances imposed by the surrounding rural areas, Cf. A. D. Lublinskaya, *French Absolutism: The Crucial Phase, 1620–1629*, tr. Brian Pearle (Cambridge, 1968).

In the first phase, metropolitan monopolies dominated relations with their colonies: in particular, the Portuguese controlled the sugar industry. After the Dutch were expelled from Brazil and established themselves in the Caribbean, the monopoly on sugar production was broken. This started a phase of accelerated competition among the European powers as well as among their colonies. English West Indian sugar mill owners pressured the English Parliament to stop the growing commerce with the French West Indies. This culminated in the 1732 *Molasses Act* – in spite of strong opposition from New England colonists.[85] Two things are demonstrated by this example: the growing importance of the colonies in the definition of metropolitan mercantile policies, and the internationalization of mercantile capital looking for profit – independent of national or imperial borders. The new colonialism of the seventeenth century, according to Hobsbawm, is characterized by the notable expansion of production. This resulted in increased European consumption, caused by lower prices, as well as increased consumption in the colonies – by their transformation into markets for metropolitan production.[86] Clearly, the planters of the Antilles – French or English – opposed the expansion of production into new territories. They initiated an aggressive phase, especially in the Caribbean, aimed at militarily destroying competitive productive structures or severing them from their supply of slaves and provisions if it were not possible to impede the export of their production.[87] The War of Austrian Succession, beginning in 1739 and involving England and Spain, was essentially a commercial war representing the first conflict between great European powers involved in overseas disputes. In this war, the colonies came to be considered as extensions of national territory; in terms of the threat to commerce, they became questions of fundamental security.[88] For the colonies, the result of the crisis would have had to present appreciable differences. We have already demonstrated that (in François Simiand's terminology) phase A of the European economy coincided with phase B for the colonial economy and vice-versa. In this time of depression for phase B, the reduction in profit opportunities for European capital could have forced entrepreneurs to seek a higher return on their investments within the colonial world.[89] The reduction in prices for goods could

[85] Andre Gunder Frank, *Acumulção Mundial, 1492–1789* (Rio de Janeiro, 1977), 142.
[86] Eric Hobsbawm, "The Crisis of the Seventeenth Century," 51.
[87] J. H. Parry and Philip Sherlock, *A Short History of the West Indies* (London, 1971), 113–14.
[88] Williams Glyndwr, *The Expansion of Europe in the Eighteenth Century* (London, 1966), 63.
[89] The overseas world increasingly responded to the tempo from Europe, as Chaunu

have meant an increase in per capita income caused by increases in real salaries paid to free workers and reductions in expenses for sumptuary consumer goods – always high in estimates of colonial costs.[90]

The English revolution of 1640, at the same time a manifestation of and a means of rising above the crisis of the seventeenth century,[91] marks the turning point of English foreign policy toward one characterized by the military and diplomatic conquest of the international market, especially in the colonies. The wars against the Dutch represented a shift from a foreign policy that had been satisfied with the profits of mines and of piracy to the development of manufacturing, agriculture, and naval industries. "The Dutch War of 1664–7, one manifestation of the outburst of imperial enterprise of the 1660's which followed on the capture of Jamaica, is being seen increasingly as a turning point in history."[92] The war did not give the English access to the commerce of West Indian spices, but it did break the Dutch monopoly on commerce in sugar, leaf tobacco, hides, slaves, and fish. Between 1673 and 1697, a structure of mercantile regulation was created in which England desired a monopoly as well as a monopsony (exclusive purchasing rights).[93] This new configuration of the structure of mercantile accumulation, which Cain and Hopkins call *The*

---

states in "Place et rôle du Brésil dans les systèmes de communications et dans le mécanismes de croissance de l'économie du XVIe siècle," *Revue d'Histoire Economique et Sociale* 48 (1970): 470; Frédéric Mauro, *L'expansion européene, 1600–1870*, 303, notes that a period of depression in Europe could correspond to a period of expansion in the colonies, where capital would thus have a higher profit. Using Chile as an example, R. Romano found a lack of concurrence between metropolitan and colonial rhythms, affirming separation of the colonial situation. See his two articles: "Une économie coloniale: Le Chili au XVIIIe siècle," *Annales E. S. C.* 18 (1960):278–9; "Mouvement des prix et developpement économique. L'Amérique du Sud au XVIIIe siècle," *Annales E. S. C.* 18 (1963): 68. For Phase A and B, François Simiand, *Les Fluctuations Economiques à la Longue Periode et la Crise Mondiale* (Paris, 1932), 15–62.

[90] Rationale developed after considering the arguments presented by Douglass C. North and Robert Paul Thomas in "An Economic Theory of the Western World," *The Economic History Review* 23 (1970); 12.

[91] José J. de A. Arruda, *A Revolução Inglesa* (São Paulo, 1984), 65.

[92] D. A. Farnie, "The Commercial Empire of the Atlantic, 1607–1783," *The Economic History Review* 15 (1962): 206. The relationship between political and maritime power was studied by Charles Wilson in *Profit and Power: A Study of England and the Dutch Wars* (London, 1957); G. D. Ramsay, *English Overseas Trade during the Centuries of Emergence* (London, 1957); B. E. Supple, *Commercial Crisis and Change in England, 1600–1642* (Cambridge, 1959); C. G. A. Clay, *Economic Expansion and Social Change: England 1500–1700*, Vol. II, *Industry, Trade, and Government* (Cambridge, 1984); and Kristof Glamann, "European Trade, 1500–1750," in *The Fontana Economic History of Europe*, ed. Carlo M. Cipolla (Vol. 2, Glasgow: 1974), 427–526. For the impact of English pressure on the Dutch, see C. R. Boxer, *The Dutch Seaborne Empire, 1600–1800* (New York, 1970).

[93] Farnie, "The Commercial Empire of the Atlantic."

Old Colonial System, 1688–1850,[94] portrays a new England foretelling the Industrial Revolution. In 1688 some 33 percent of the national income came from industry, including manufacturing, construction, mining, and commerce (inclusive of transportation). In 1770 these same sectors of the economy contributed 37 percent. The significant leap was before 1688,[95] demonstrating that it was closely tied to the 1640 revolution and the transformations their revolution produced in the structure of the state, the society, and the economy.[96]

In the middle of this new colonialism, Brazilian sugar production collapsed – beaten by external competition from the Antilles and internal gold production. The substitution of gold fleets for those carrying sugar is symptomatic of this development.[97] Sugar exportation, which had reached 3,750,000 pounds sterling in 1650, hit its lowest point in 1690, when its value did not exceed £2 million. It was at this time that gold's steep rise began (Figure 10.1). This was to have two initial effects on Portugal: the liquidation of the Count of Ericeira's industrial policies, which were germinating during the height of this crisis,[98] and the signing of the Methuen Treaty, by which important concessions were given to England with correspondingly great advantages for English manufacturing.[99]

The exploitation of Brazilian gold during the eighteenth century represented the tardy realization of the Portuguese plan outlined in the sixteenth century but carried out only by Spain in its American colonies during the entire span of the old colonial system. Therefore, its framework falls within the old colonial system – as can be con-

---

[94] P. J. Cain and A. G. Hopkins, 501. Also their article "The Political Economy of British Expansion Overseas, 1750–1914," *The Economic History Review* 33 (1980): 463–90.

[95] Cf. Phyllis Deane and W. A. Cole, *British Economic Growth, 1688–1959* (Cambridge, 1962), 156.

[96] The definitive interpretation of the English Revolution as bourgeois appears in several publications by Christopher Hill, but especially "A Bourgeois Revolution," in *Three British Revolutions: 1641, 1688, 1776,* ed. J. G. A. Pocock (Princeton, 1980), 109–39.

[97] Vitorino M. Godinho, "Portugal, as Frotas do Açucar a as Frotas do Ouro (1670–1770)," *Revista de História* (São Paulo) 4 (1953): 69–88.

[98] Jorge B. Macedo, "Portugal e a Economia 'Pombalina': Temas e Hipóteses," *Revista de História* (São Paulo) 5 (1954): 81–100. For a general synthesis of this period, see Carl A. Hanson, *Economy and Society in Baroque Portugal, 1668–1703* (Minneapolis, 1981).

[99] A. D. Francis, *The Methuens and Portugal, 1691–1708* (London, 1966). For a more detailed discussion of the economic relations between Portugal and England, cf. H. E. S. Fisher, *The Portugal Trade: A Study of Anglo-Portuguese Commerce, 1700–1770* (London, 1971). Also very significant is Sandro Sideri, *Trade and Power: Informal Colonialism in Anglo-Portuguese Relations* (Rotterdam, 1970). For the Portuguese side, see Jorge B. Macedo's indispensable: *Problemas de História da Industria Portuguesa no Século XVIII* (Lisboa, 1963).

Brazilian Gold Production
in the Eighteenth Century - Quinquennial Means
1700-1750

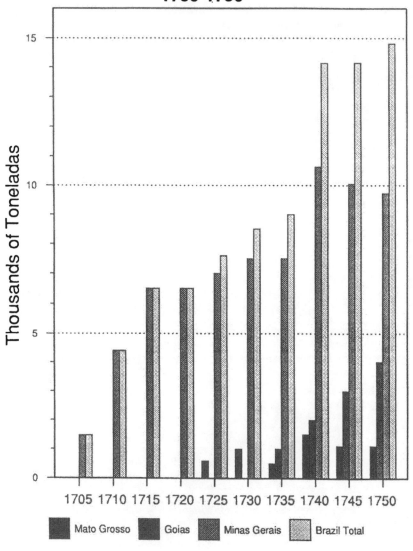

Figure 10.1a.

Brazilian Gold Production
in the Eighteenth Century - Quinquennial Means
1755-1800

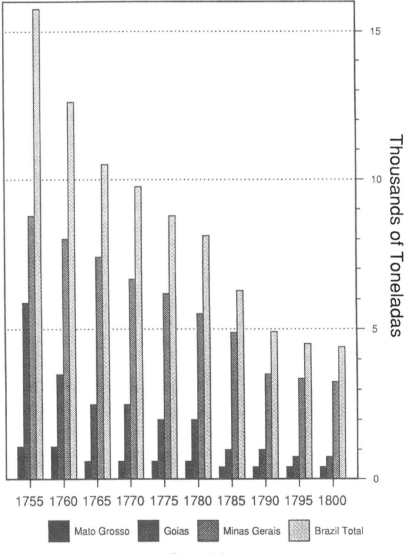

Figure 10.1b.

firmed at the metropolitan level by the continued Portuguese dependence on (shown by its commercial deficit with) England. The amount of gold extracted from Brazilian mines was extremely significant since it equaled the total gold produced in the Spanish American colonies between 1492 and 1800 and also represented half of the gold production in the rest of the world between the sixteenth and the eighteenth centuries.[100] Obtaining an accurate measure of Brazilian gold production is a difficult task considering the vigor of illegal commerce, which Godinho estimated to be around 20 for each 35 *arrobas* exported legally. Boxer concludes that only 10 to 30 percent of royal production went on ships headed for Lisbon.[101] Based on reports from French consuls in Lisbon, Noya Pinto has made a calculation of the total amount of gold extracted from Minas Gerais, Goiás, and Mato Grosso. This estimate excludes the mines in Jacobina, Rio das Contas, and Araçuai (in Bahia); including these could increase the final estimate by hundreds of *arrobas*[102] In Figure 10.1 it can be noted that the peak of production for Minas Gerais was between 1735 and 1740 after which there began an irreversible decline. At the same time, production accelerated in the mines in Goiás while those of Mato Grosso maintained an even keel. The overall result locates peak production in the five-year period 1750–5, when the mines in Minas Gerais were in decline. The totals suggested by Noya Pinto are questioned by Michel Morineau, whose own work is based on consuls' reports as well as on Dutch and Portuguese gazettes. He suggests that the great movements of gold came between 1726 and 1750, with a peak in the years 1726– 30.[103] Only considering registered documents, ignoring embezzlement and contraband, between 1720 and 1742, fleets brought annual cargoes to Portugal that averaged 30 tons of gold. In the lean years when this figure was not reached, with certainty it exceeded twenty tons. Between 1743 and 1755, rare are the fleets which transported less than twelve or more than seventeen tons yearly.

Figure 10.1 shows the strong reduction in the value of exported gold, calculated in pounds sterling, after 1760 when it attained a value

---

[100] Roberto C. Simonsen, *História Econômica do Brasil (1500–1820)* (6th ed., São Paulo, 1969), 258.

[101] Vitorino M. Godinho, *Prix et Monnaies au Portugal (1750–1850)* (Paris, 1955); Boxer, *The Portuguese Seaborne Empire*, 59

[102] Virgilio Noya Pinto, *O Ouro Brasileiro e o Comércio Anglo-Português* (São Paulo, 1979), 115.

[103] Michel Morineau, *Incroyables Gazettes et Fabuleux Metaux. Les retours des trésors américains d'après les gazettes hollandaises (XVIe-XVIIIe siècles)* (London and Paris, 1985), 188–95. For a comparative discussion of the bullion production indices proposed by various authors, see Ward Barrett, "World Bullion Flows," in *The Rise of Merchant Empires*, 224–54.

of £2.2 million. Between 1776 and 1796, exportation hit a plateau at £800 thousand and then virtually disappeared by the first years of the nineteenth century. In addition to gold production, the Portuguese Crown benefited greatly from diamond extraction. They first used a contract system for their mining, until 1771, when this activity came under direct royal administration. This was exactly the same time that gold production had begun its decline. The diamond district became a veritable fort controlled by Portuguese administrators. The large quantity of these precious stones introduced into Europe contributed to their popularity with the resulting increase in consumption – until then they were a characteristic of aristocrats and wealthy merchants. Tables 10.1a–10.1c show the volume and price of these gems extracted from Brazil between 1753 and 1790.

The huge Brazilian gold production multiplied the value of the colonial market by a factor of five during the first half of the eighteenth century. This meant the financing of a demographic push into the interior of Brazil. It caused an increase in the production and subsistence of agrarian essentials, consumer goods, and transportation. These effects were first felt in the most remote regions and afterward, due to high prices, in Minas Gerais itself. In this manner, integrated production on diversified *fazendas* with more than one production sector,[104] the process of urbanization, and the specific characteristics of slave labor in the mining areas were the results. In spite of a common foundation on slavery, the mineral and sugar economies were distinct. In the mining economy, small-and medium-sized capitalists predominated because mining demanded little fixed capital. This industry presented relative mobility, high profit, and a great concentration of resources. The income flow followed a more intense rhythm and circulation was more accelerated. The average income was also less than that in the sugar industry; however, its potential for growth was greater. The concentration of income was also less, with ample importation of consumer goods. Slaves did not constitute the majority of the population; they were given a certain portion of initiatives in production, they had some possibilities of gaining their freedom through work and limited possibilities of a higher style of life.[105] In the colonial economy, gold

---

[104] Maria Arminda N. Arruda, "Mitologia da Mineiridade, O Imaginário Mineiro na Vida Política e Cultural do Brasil," Diss., Universidade de São Paulo, 1986, 234 ff.

[105] The nature of slave-master relations was not exactly the same in all locations and times because it depended on the specific conditions of local production. For examples, see Stefano Fenoaltea, "Slavery and Supervision in Comparative Perspective: A Model," *The Journal of Economic History* 44 (1984): 635–68; and Silvia Hunold Lara, "Campos da Violência. Estudo Sobre a relação senhor-escravo na Capitania do Rio de Janeiro. 1750–1808," Diss., Universidade de São Paulo, 1986

Table 10.1a. *Extraction of Diamonds by Contract, 1755–1771 (values in milreis)*

Contract	Contractor	Carats extracted (annual average)	Value	Average price per carat
4th contract (1755–59)	Bristows, Warde & Co.	390,094 (55,728)	3,625,580	9.294
5th contract (1760–62)	John Gore & Josué Van Neck	106,416 (53,203)	929,476	8.743
6th contract (1762–71)	Daniel Gildeineester	704,209 (70,420)	6,108,579	8.674

Source: Adapted from J. P. Calógeras, *As Minas do Brasil*, no. 7, 307–308, 312, 323.

Table 10.1b. *Sale of Diamonds by Contractor, 1755–1771*
(values in milreis)

Year	Contractors	Carats sold	Value	Average value per carat
1753	Bristows, Warde & Co.	5,000	46,000	9.200
1754		43,000	463,157	10.771
1755		37,814	347,890	9.200
1756		36,000	331,200	9.200
1757	John Gore & Josué Van Neck	25,000		
1758		30,159	227,462	9.200
1759		29,369	270,194	9.200
1760		31,131	286,405	9.200
1761	Daniel Gildeineester	44,200	380,120	8.600
1762		42,239	355,597	8.418
1763		60,463	514,877	8.515
1764		61,665	531,193	8.614
1765		84,862	729,813	8.600
1766		91,380	785,885	8.600
1767		70,942	610,101	8.600
1768		74,450	640,270	8.600
1769		76,639	659,525	8.605
1770		55,414	476,560	8.600
1771		35,369	304,173	8.600

Source: Adapted from J. P. Calógeras, *As Minas do Brasil*, no. 7, 307–308, 312, 323.

had the dynamic and integrating role and accelerated the growth of the colonial economy by internalizing the income flow.

Comparatively speaking, the investments required for gold production were minimal. Given the alluvial nature of Brazilian deposits, deeper exploration of the subsoil was not necessary. The purchasing power of gold reversed the nature of the Brazilian market. It became a seller's market, the reverse of the buyer's market that had dominated the first two centuries of colonial life.[106] In this sense, to the colony,

[106] Frédéric Mauro, "Structure de l'Economie Interne et Marché International dans une Epoque de Transition: Le cas du Brésil, 1750–1850," in *The Emergence of a World Economy 1500–1914*, ed. Wolfram Fischer (Erlangen, 1986), 338.

Table 10.1c. Diamonds Extracted by The Crown and Sold by Contract, 1772–1790 (values in milreis)

Royal Extraction			Sale by Contracts in Europe			
Year	Carats	Carats sold	Value	Average price per carat	Contractor
1772	33,493	39,981	343,936	8.600	Daniel Gildemeester
1773	50,343	41,795	359,127	8.600	
1774	37,083	60,945	524,127	8.600	
1775	36,877	65,547	563,704	8.600	
1776	37,414	65,794	665,828	10.119	
1777	40,517	63,969	569,328	8.900	
1778	39,068	65,753	585,290	8.901	
1779	39,479	40,201	369,849	9.200	
1780	31,947	37,000	340,400	9.200	
1781	38,605	20,000	184,000	9.200	
1782	51,262	20,000	180,000	9.200	
1783	48,117			9.000	
1784	62,038	37,500	345,000	9.200	
1785	37,528	12,500	115,000	9.200	
1786	30,677	40,567	360,216	8.870	
1787	28,404	12,000	79,200	6.600	João Ferreira e
—	—	12,000	123,752	8.839	Paulo Jorge
1788	28,630	43,000	387,800	9.018	Benjamin Cohen e
1789	29,557	36,000	315,000	8.750	Abrahao B. Cohen
1790	31,664	16,000	138,000	8.625	

Source: Adapted from J. P. Calógeras, As Minas do Brasil, no. 7, 307–308, 312, 323.

gold represented a new colonial era. To Portugal, it meant immediately overcoming the crisis of the seventeenth century, the abandonment of the manufacturing policy, and the complete submission to English commercial hegemony. This is evident in Portuguese commercial deficits with England – which grew in equal proportion to the importation of precious metals into Portugal. It is evident that Portugal transferred the advantages of its colonial assets to England. To England, the Luso-Brazilian market represented 610 million pounds in 1701–5 compared with £305 m. for the West Indies, £259 m. for the continental colonies, and £248 m. for Ireland. This primacy continued between 1726 and 1730, when it represented £914 m.; the other figures were £473 m., £507 m., and £506 m., respectively. In the period 1736–40, the totals were £1,164 m., £494 m., £724 m., and £690 m. Finally, between 1741 and 1745, the figures were £1,125 m., £728 m., £738 m., and £790 m.[107] Morineau demonstrates the close relationship among: the arrival of Brazilian gold in Portugal, the English advantage in its commercial balance with Portugal, the arrival of packet-boat cargoes in Falmouth in pounds sterling, and English coinage in pounds sterling. "Upon its arrival in Portugal, and for stronger reasons in Great Britain, the yellow metal was integrated into a more subtle and efficient system. Economic circulation seized it and gave it greater momentum – by promoting it, withholding it, repromoting it, and consequently multiplying its power at the exchange."[108] Commercialization of the Brazilian agricultural food sector as well as its raw materials sustained and strengthened British exports, guaranteed a real increase in income for the English masses – at least in the textile industry – and made buying easier. The benefits of this process were in turn passed on to American and Dutch markets. In short, Brazilian gold stimulated British textile exports, increased British coinage, and permissively infiltrated the British economy – duplicating its efficiency as an instrument of exchange.[109] It should also be remembered that, as Vilar has suggested, the long depression during the seventeenth century reduced the prices of goods and raised the price of metals, stimulating the search for and

[107] Michel Morineau, *Incroyables Gazettes et Fabuleux Métaux*, 171.

[108] Ibid., 184 Boxer, *The Portuguese Seaborne Empire*, 460, makes reference to the mechanisms of transferring Brazilian gold to the English: "In war and peace alike Brazil gold went to England on board Royal Naval vessels and by the weekly Falmouth-Lisbon packet-boat service. Both warships and packet boats were immune from search by Portuguese customs and all other officials. Naturally, the merchants at Lisbon, both British and foreign, preferred to remit their gold to England by this means, since the export of specie and bullion from Portugal had been strictly forbidden since the Middle Ages."

[109] Michel Morineau, *Incroyables Gazettes et Fabuleux Métaux. Les retours des trésors américains d'après les gazettes hollandaises (XVIe–XVIIIe siècles)*, 189.

production of precious metals. Once discovered, they caused a reversal of this situation: the value of metals declined and that of goods, valued in terms of gold and silver, increased.[110]

Of no less importance to England was the transfer of silver, extracted by the Spanish in America – above all from Mexican mines – by means of the trade. Chaunu has estimated that in the sixteenth century, for each 25 tons of American silver received in Spain, three-quarters were exported to other parts of Europe or to Asia. England received from Spain the equivalent (in pounds) of 3 percent of its total imports in the period from 1712 to 1770 – some 14 million pounds. This reserve financed the English commercial deficit in the Baltic, where many important raw materials originated. In the same manner, Brazilian gold paid for delicate cloth imported from the Orient. By reexporting this cloth to a warmer climate (especially to colonies), England accelerated mercantile trade.[111]

The peak of Brazilian gold production represents the crystallization of the new system of colonization in England. This crisis, the decline in production after 1760, created the necessary conditions in Portugal for this new system of colonization to become established. British commerce attained its maximum surplus in relation to Portuguese trade in 1760. In the next five-year period, this surplus was reduced by almost one-half; in the years directly following, this surplus continued to be reduced. In the period 1791–5, England for the first time had a deficit; Portugal had its first surplus in its historic commercial relations with England. As measured in absolute numbers, the Luso-Brazilian market lost its importance to English commerce while the West Indian, North American, and Irish markets all increased. Paradoxically, to Portugal this did not represent a crisis; rather, it was a transformation of its mercantile policy and the adoption of new systems of mercantile accumulation. The mercantile policies of Pombal, systematically applied after 1760 when gold production was declining, were very lucid and well suited to the historical conditions surrounding them.[112] This program envisioned promoting economic develop-

---

[110] Pierre Vilar, *Oro y Moneda en la Historia, 1450–1920* (Barcelona, 1969), 228, 230, 265, 268.

[111] H. E. S. Fisher, *The Portugal Trade*, 138–9.

[112] For the era of Pombal, see the excellent study by Francisco C. Falcon, *A Epoca Pombalina (Politica Económica e Monarquia Ilustrada)* (São Paulo, 1982). Equally excellent is the classic study by Jorge R. de Macedo: *A Situação económica no tempo de Pombal* (Porto, 1951). On a more specific theme, see Susan Schneider, *O Marquês de Pombal e o Vinho do Porto* (Lisboa, 1980). For the relationship among the Pombaline State, the strengthening of the Portuguese mercantile bourgeoisie, and the new outline of the empire, see Kenneth R. Maxwell, *O Marquês de Pombal: Despotismo, Iluminismo e Império* (Lisboa, 1984).

ment within the kingdom by a global integration of the imperial economy, making industrial activities more dynamic, and expanding and
closely integrating agriculture through mercantile trade. In this context, the creation of new commercial companies was of great importance. These companies were governed by a policy of

> expanding and integrating the internal market of the *metropole* as well as
> externally in the colonies . . . By way of the companies, the expansion of
> mercantile activities would be promoted, closely tied to increased production
> and consumption essential for the output of an enormous variety of metro-
> politan industrial goods and, on a smaller scale, of the *metropole's* agriculture,
> all for colonial consumption.[113]

In effect, what was being attempted was to increase national resources
by means of integrating the diverse areas of their colonial world –
putting these companies under the most rigid, royal despotism.[114]
During the reign of Dom José, modern Portuguese companies were
created and organized along the patterns of their most efficient European counterparts. Almost simultaneously, six companies emerged:
the *Companhia do Comércio Oriental* and the *Companhia do Comércio de
Moçambique*, directed toward commerce in the Indian Ocean; the *Companhia da Agricultura das Vinhas do Alto Douro* (Alto Douro Wine Company) and the *Companhia das Pescas do Algarve* (Algarve Fishing
Company) for purposes within the metropole; and the *Companhia Geral
do Grão Pará e Maranhão* and *Companhia de Pernambuco e Paraíba*, both
oriented toward Atlantic commerce in general, and the Brazil market
in particular. The first of these last two companies, at the time of its
conception, played a key role in the colonization of Grão-Pará and
Maranhão. Later, this same role thwarted the development that had
earlier allowed for the company's expansion. This can be seen by the
substantial increase of its exports when the company was dissolved
in 1778.[115] The second (The *Companhia de Pernambuco e Paraíba*) received
the monopoly on produce from the entire Brazilian northeast – traditionally the most developed area in the country because of its sugar

---

[113] Francisco C. Falcon and Fernando A. Novais, "A Extinção da Escravatura Africana
em Portugal no Quadro da Politica Económica Pombalina," in *VI Simpósio da ANPUH*
(Goiâna, 1971), 9. According to A. R. W. Chapman in "The Commercial Relations
of England and Portugal, 1487–1807," *Transactions of the Royal Historical Society* 1
(1907): 175, "The Board of Trade, established in 1756, clashed very directly with
English privileges. It took cognisance of all matters touching on smuggling, retail
trade, recovery of debt, bankruptcy, superintendence of manufactures, the inspection of the Brazil fleet, and so forth."

[114] José Ribeiro, Jr., *Colonização e Monopólio no Nordeste Brasileiro* (São Paulo, 1976), 204.

[115] José J. de A. Arruda, "A Circulação, as Finanças e as Flutuações Económicas," in
O Império Luso-Brasileiro, 1750–1822, 161.

industry. The commercialization of this product gave the metropole profits between 32 percent and 200 percent after it was sold in other European locales. The traffic in slaves, done through the exchange of colonial products – especially *aguardente* (a very strong alcohol made from sugarcane) and tobacco – produced large profits that had been enjoyed by local *colonos* but that were now transferred to the kingdom. This company's profits reached 110 percent during this period, the equivalent of more than 5 percent annually. The majority of these profits were retained in the colony after the extinction of the company in the form of nonliquidated debts.[116]

The new colonization policy, which increasingly considered the colony as an extension of the metropole or as part of a greater national territory, presented several weak spots that were typical of this phase: commercial licenses, intercolonial commerce, and contraband. Licenses tended to increase with the precariousness of the means of transportation and the concession of benefits to English merchants in Portugal, especially during the second half of the eighteenth century.[117] The advantages conceded to England revealed its growing naval hegemony and the basic contradiction of the Portuguese Empire: it was a small kingdom with a vast colonial empire. In 1801 the accountant José Mauricio Teixeira de Moraes complained that English commerce had grown excessively in Brazil because the English had received permission to enter ports with their manufactured goods – to the detriment of products shipped from Portuguese factories.[118] Intercolonial commerce was the object of alternating permissive and restrictive legislation. In 1699 authorization was given for twenty-four ships to leave annually from Rio de Janeiro to look for slaves on the African coast. The number of ships increased until this system was prohibited in 1772. After that date, the system underwent a progressive liberalization until it reached the possible limits on stimulating exchange among the Portuguese colonies. Trade with Africa grew rapidly. Co-

---

[116] Ribeiro, *Colonização e Monopólio no Nordeste Brasileiro*, 208. Cf. Chapman, "The Commercial Relations of England and Portugal," 177: "Thus the Company appears rather to have increased than diminished Anglo-Portuguese trade. How far it really injured the English merchants is uncertain; certainly they themselves attributed the subsequent diminution of their numbers to its influence . . . The English merchants attributed this decline to the fact that the Brazil Companies were directed to prefer Portuguese to English goods, thus narrowing the English market in Brazil, whither the best woollen goods had formerly been sent."

[117] On the role of the British Factory in Portugal, see A. R. Walford, *The British Factory* (Lisbon, 1940); and John de la Force, *The Factory House at Oporto* (London, 1983).

[118] "Balança Geral do Commercio do Reyno de Portugal com seus Dominios no Anno de 1800." (Biblioteca Nacional de Rio de Janeiro, Secção de Manuscritos). Introdução de José Mauricio Teixeira de Moraes, contador e organizador da Balança.

lonial merchants came to be competitors with the Portuguese, but under conditions favorable to the Brazilians. They had the essential product for exchange: tobacco. After establishing themselves in the *Castelo de São Jorge da Mina*, the Dutch demanded 10 percent of the tobacco cargo as a condition for commerce in slaves. Merchants from Bahia took advantage of this, acquiring French or English manufactured goods and selling them at low prices in Brazil.[119] Leaving from Recife, Salvador, and Rio de Janeiro, Brazilian merchants reached Angola, Moçambique, Goa, and Macao. They also developed a triangular trade that included ports in Portugal, Brazil, Asia, Africa, the Islands, and Spanish America. Many products that reached Brazil were reexported to Rio de la Plata, Cochabamba, Chiquitos, Upper Peru, and so forth.[120]

As we have already seen in the previous section, contraband implanted itself within the logic of the colonial system.[121] However, in moments of crisis, the aggressive penetration of foreign commerce into the colony could lead to a disintegration of the system or the loss (independence) of the colony. In 1785 tougher anticontraband legislation was passed. This demonstrated that these pressures had be-

---

[119] José R. do A. Lapa, *A Bahia e a Carreira da Índia*, 254. Cf. Verge, "Flux et Reflux de la Traite des Nègres entre le golfe de Benin et Bahia." The excellent study by Jacob Price, *France and the Chesapeake: A History of the Tobacco Monopoly, 1694–1791, and of Its Relationship to the British and American Tobacco Trade* (Ann Arbor, 1973), 375, establishes links among the tobacco monopoly, the agrarian crisis, overseas expansion, the commercial revolution, and the development of absolutism. "At their peak, tobacco revenues accounted for 7.3% of the total State revenue . . . So precarious were the finances of the French crown all through the eighteenth century that a monopoly which produced seven or even five percent of those revenues ranked as an unassailable interest."

[120] The intense commerce with Africa influenced Brazilian trade with Portugal, as the accountant José M. T. de Moraes stated in the "Balança Geral do Commercio do Reyno de Portugal com seus Dominios no Anno de 1800" (Biblioteca Nacional de Rio de Janeiro): "Our commerce with the trade stations in Africa seems to be advantageous since we are always creditors, as is shown in the trade balance since 1796. However, it should be noted that we are failing to make any real inroads into the interiors of Angola, Bissau, Cachéu, etc. in obtaining their commerce of wax, ivory, and slaves to Rio de Janeiro, Bahia, Maranhao." On the extension of this commerce to the Rio de la Plata, see Alice P. Canabrava, *O Comércio Português no Rio da Prata (1580–1640)* (São Paulo, 1944).

[121] On the cycles of contraband trade in the eighteenth century, see G. D. Ramsey, "The 'Smugglere' Trade: A Neglected Aspect of English Commercial Development," *Transactions of the Royal Historical Society*, 5th per., no. 2 (1952): 131–158; W. A. Cole, "Trends in Eighteenth Century Smuggling," *The Economic History Review* 10 (1958): 395–410; and Lorna H. Mui and Hoh Cheung, "Trends in Eighteenth Century Smuggling Reconsidered," *The Economic History Review* 28 (1975): 28–43. For contraband operations in Brazil, see C. R. Boxer, "Brazilian Gold and British Traders in the First Half of the Eighteenth Century," *Hispanic American Historical Review* 49 (1969): 464.

come intolerable, as can also be shown statistically. Considering that, by the nature of the colonial system all commerce outside its limits can be regarded as having gone astray, we can calculate the rate of contraband. Colonial exports to Portugal grew by 20 percent between 1796 and 1808; colonial imports also grew by this same amount from 1796 to 1800 and then decreased sharply. Assuming that colonial production could not have grown without imported means of production (slaves, tools, consumer goods), it is possible to conclude that the difference between what Portugal actually acquired and the real buying potential – determined by the rate of increase in the movement of commerce – can be attributed to contraband. Estimating the total movement of imports during the period from 1796 to 1808 at 102,929,087$799, contraband would have been 17,893,500$00 in absolute terms, or 17 percent of the total.[122]

In spite of these restrictions, the practical result of the policies undertaken by the Portuguese showed their wisdom. The value of Brazilian exports declined from 4.8 million to 3 million pounds between 1760 and 1776. At that point, they first grew slowly until 1796 and then sharply increased in value until 1808 when they once again were at a level around 4 million pounds sterling (Figure 10.2). The fleets arriving in Portugal did not carry just gold or sugar: from Rio de Janeiro, they brought gold, piasters from Buenos Aires, and hides from Spanish America; from Bahia, came sugar, tobacco, and brazilwood; from Pernambuco, they transferred wood to be used for shipbuilding and for furniture in addition to sugar; from the north – Grão-Pará and Maranhão – they carried cacao, cotton, and other natural products.

What we are seeing here is a diversification process of Brazilian colonial production, which became responsible for increased income from the export sector, while the amount of gold and sugar exported was in steep decline. Brazilian exports in 1760, totaling only 35 products, were dominated by gold and sugar. However, 124 products left the colony in 1796 (Table 10.2). Concentrating exclusively on the 13 principal export products (Tables 10.3a and 10.3b) representing 82.3

---

[122] These figures represent calculations done with a reasonable expectation of accurately reflecting reality, but subject to some limitations: "The value of exported colonial goods could be much greater. [since we are not aware of] smugglers' reactions to colonial goods . . . not all income gained from the export sector was necessarily spent on imports: this surplus was not transported in the form of money, but in credit to be repaid in merchandise in the following years; these profits could have been transferred to the *metropole* by Portuguese merchants, who by guilding their profits in Brazil, had in this system, the origin of their branches in Brazil." José J. de A. Arruda, *O Brasil no Comércio Colonial*, 325.

Brazilian Colonial Exports (1650-1730)
Approximate Value of Exports

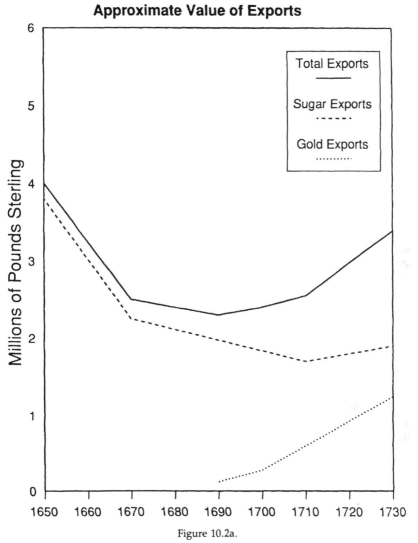

Figure 10.2a.

percent of the overall total from 1796 to 1808, white sugar and *mas-cavado* (brown sugar) totaled only 36 percent – a far cry from the dominance they had in 1650. Cotton exports totalled 24.4 percent – an impressive increase that underlines the relation between its production and the Industrial Revolution. Cacao, rice, and coffee were

Brazilian Colonial Exports (1730-1808)
Approximate Value of Exports

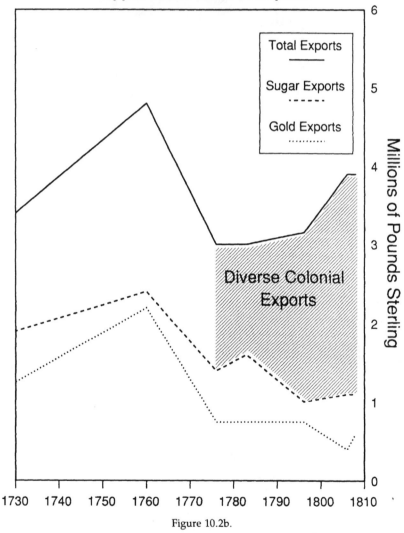

Figure 10.2b.

Table 10.2. *Brazilian Products Exported to Portugal*

Food supplies

1. Sugar cane brandy
2. White sugar
3. Brown sugar
4. Ice
5. Coffee
6. Honey
7. Sweets
8. Bread flour
9. Pork meat
10. Cocoa
11. Tapioca
12. Sesame seeds
13. Molasses
14. Pork fat
15. Fine clove
16. Walnuts
17. Flour

31. Salted leather
32. Soft sole leather
33. Sole
34. Half soles
35. Panther skin
36. Wolf skin
37. Tiger skin
38. Bear skin
39. Bull hair
40. Leather with hair
41. Deer hair
42. Sea wolf
43. Goat skin
44. Ermine
45. Veal skin
46. Sheep skin
47. Wild pig

61. Parsley
62. Poyaya
63. Tamarind branches
64. Balsam of Capivi
65. Ourucu
66. Liana roots
67. Contrayerva root
68. Sarsparilla
69. Cochineal
70. Rosin
71. Bula root
72. Balsam
73. Quine
74. Nutmeg
75. Vine
76. Copal glue
77. Arabian glue

91. Stick wax
92. Embisa Tow
93. Tow
94. Turtle
95. Yellow wax
96. Tobacco leafs
97. Ivory
98. Sunuruma (?)
99. Linen
100. Small seed
101. Cocoanuts
102. Candles
103. Rolled tobacco
104. Silvery sand
105. White wax
106. Palmtree wool
107. Nerve Rubber

Table 10.2 (cont.)

18. Bacon	48. Coati skin	78. Saltpetre	108. Vegunia wool
19. Coarse clove	49. Swan skin	79. Fish glue	109. Copper
20. Meat	50. Fox skin	80. Yellow wood	110. Tin
21. Carima	51. Horse leather	81. Holy seed	111. Maranhão Walnut
22. Beans	52. Tapir skin	82. Violet wood	112. Starch stick
23. Pork Butter			113. Topazes
24. Corn	Drugs	Miscellaneous	114. Elastic glue
25. Legumes			115. Amethyst
26. Maranhão clove	53. Indigo	83. Fish oil	116. Feathers
27. Lime	54. Epecacuanha	84. Whale	117. Basin
28. Gerofa clove	55. Glue	85. Starch	118. Plumes
	56. Brazilwood	86. Abbada	119. Wool
Leathers	57. Cashew resin	87. Tallow suck	120. Cat skin
	58. Glue	88. Cattle pieces	121. Mineral crystal
29. Tanned leather	59. Ginger	89. Black rush	122. Cotton
30. Dry leather	60. Salpa	90. Little cocoanut	123. Cotton thread
			124. Woods

Source: Compiled by the author.

Table 10.3a. Total Amount and Percentage of the 13 Main Colonial Export Products (in milreis)

Year	White sugar	Cotton	Brown sugar	Dry leather	Rice	Tobacco	Cocoa
1796	4,344,332	2,201,150	986,384	325,840	248,619	572,712	333,995
1797	1,747,005	801,876	410,349	102,062	250,689	437,531	156,124
1798	4,684,490	1,583,730	925,105	178,647	349,691	531,748	209,091
1799	3,124,742	2,180,781	1,240,254	3,890	241,568	1,139,112	273,542
1800	2,174,812	3,342,010	668,745	807,116	368,323	339,347	381,081
1801	3,744,474	3,618,202	1,108,524	1,274,378	259,588	5,226	129,946
1802	2,560,053	3,158,685	496,151	247,933	389,721	498,673	167,877
1803	2,749,133	3,650,240	617,751	485,564	619,829	418,563	294,880
1804	4,266,820	3,263,442	872,035	675,262	660,628	416,387	189,131
1805	3,668,166	4,041,916	1,166,856	1,407,506	590,953	559,265	352,460
1806	3,820,572	3,532,110	1,156,360	1,834,699	624,714	387,790	517,860
1807	3,108,229	4,524,605	984,478	1,029,745	577,409	397,889	335,912
1808	184,647	57,389	44,251	7,804	32,392	54,005	49,395
1809	1,036,015	1,222,146	255,857	337,186	291,687	293,618	539,359
1810	869,151	544,478	152,206	526,567	361,771	—	191,183
1811	361,880	12,680	55,301	217,861	240,578	313,819	97,899
Total	42,444,529	37,555,446	11,140,613	9,411,068	6,108,170	5,917,453	4,219,747
	27.5%	24.4%	7.2%	6.1%	4.0%	3.8%	2.7%

Source: Compiled by the author.

Table 10.3b. *Total Amount and Percentage of the 13 Main Colonial Export Products (in milreis)*

Year	Coffee	Soft sole leather	Sugar cane brandy	Salted leather	Half soles	Tanned leather	Total exports
1796	124,162	141,624	18,682	124,622	99,232	110,874	11,474,863
1797	19,913	48,911	12,866	62,849	33,043	21,976	4,258,823
1798	289,841	93,894	41,251	68,995	92,179	66,598	10,816,561
1799	101,620	138,572	57,452	32,998	70,152	33,415	12,584,505
1800	204,876	149,047	70,354	91,933	75,313	54,772	12,528,091
1801	118,162	139,028	93,430	77,084	89,480	32,243	14,776,706
1802	78,545	218,177	117,372	96,119	82,884	66,816	10,353,244
1803	93,805	190,206	123,078	133,159	149,767	55,213	11,332,290
1804	162,035	249,582	65,048	127,905	79,780	50,193	11,199,922
1805	210,811	188,855	147,116	146,600	75,676	29,883	13,948,658
1806	316,732	131,290	57,856	188,769	41,284	45,281	14,153,761
1807	446,384	85,180	157,321	183,484	79,772	54,659	13,927,799
1808	20,238	2,394	5,972	10,490	6,720	1,225	546,930
1809	121,397	129,127	30,565	130,978	103,996	135,912	4,819,373
1810	129,607	10,508	259,335	40,224	75,458	19,109	3,683,385
1811	367,157	183,855	693,478	70,077	90,442	26,424	3,633,586
Total	2,775,791	2,100,257	1,951,182	1,586,293	1,245,135	804,601	154,038,451
	1.8%	1.4%	1.3%	1.0%	0.8%	0.5%	82.5%

Source: Compiled by the author

exports of minor importance, but their cultivation demonstrated an expanding world market for these specific food products.[123] The wide variety of leather products reveals additional expansion in the European market for these industrial raw materials. Of the 124 products cited, 69 were exclusively for the Portuguese market. The nature of these products, as can noted in Table 10.4, demonstrates the intimate connection between the stimulating policies of colonial agriculture and encouraging an expanding industry in Portugal. The 55 remaining products were reexported by Portugal. Thus, they guaranteed the metropole a favorable balance of trade with other European nations, even with England, after 1790 (Table 10.5). Products originating in Brazil represented 83.7 percent of all Portuguese imports from its empire and provided 60 percent of value of Portuguese exports. Portugal's own internal production accounted for an additional 30 percent (Tables 10.6a and 10.6b).

If the Brazilian colony had become a market providing the strategic products capable of supporting an industrialization process in Portugal by way of food products and raw materials, it had also become a market consuming Portugal's industrial products.[124] Using the port of Rio de Janeiro and its 38.1 percent of Brazilian imports as an example, we can see that the variety of imports included 450 items. Of this group, 92 came from Portuguese industries. Between 1796 and 1811, the commercial balance showed 32.2 percent of imported industrial products originating in Portugal and 38.9 percent from foreign industries now being reexported from Portugal (woolen goods 13.4 percent, linens 11.6 percent, metals 8.1 percent, silks 2.3 percent).[125] In one isolated year – 1798 – products from industry reached 42.2 percent of total imports. Therefore, there was a process of industrial growth underway in Portugal that was abruptly cut short with the loss of the colony in 1808 due to the opening of Brazilian ports and the breaking of the mo-

---

[123] Richard Pares, "The London Sugar Market (1740–1769)," *The Economic History Review* 9 (1956): 254–70; Alfred Rive, "The Consumption of Tobacco Since 1600," *The Economic Journal* (Supplement) 1 (1926): 57–75.

[124] José J. de A. Arruda, *O Brasil no Comércio Colonial*, 642, and "O Brasil e a Crise Económica de Portugal na Primeira Década do Século XIX," *Ler História* 8 (1986): 61–74.

[125] Valentim Alexandre, "Um momento crucial do subdesenvolvimento português: efeitos da perda do Império Brasileiro," *Ler História* 7 (1986): 7, makes the interesting suggestion that "if 'industrial products from the Kingdom' did not include a complete range of goods manufactured by the Portuguese for export, excluding – at least in principle – handicrafts, one has to investigate their possible presence in other forms on these same tables (of commercial balance), which until now have been reserved for re-exports (woolen goods, linens, silks, metals, and other varied items)."

Table 10.4. *Brazilian Products Consumed Only in Portugal*

Food Supplies

1. Honey
2. Sweets
3. Pork meat
4. Pork fat
5. Sesame seeds
6. Walnuts
7. Flour
8. Bacon
9. Meat
10. Manioc flour cake
11. Beans
12. Pork butter
13. Corn
14. Legumes
15. Gerofa clove
16. Cayana

Leathers

17. Panther skin
18. Wolf skin
19. Tiger skin
20. Bull hair
21. Bear skin
22. Sea wolf
23. Goat skin
24. Ermine
25. Sheep
26. Wild pig
27. Coati skin
28. Tapir skin
29. Swan skin
30. Fox skin
31. Veal
32. Deer skin

Drugs

33. Glue
34. Cashew resin
35. Tamarind Branches
36. Cochineal
37. Resin
38. Buta root
39. Quine
40. Balsam
41. Nutmeg
42. Vine
43. Saltpetre
44. Arabian glue
45. Fish glue

Miscellaneous

46. Abbada
47. Cattle pieces
48. Black rush
49. Tow
50. Turtle
51. Yellow wax
52. Tobacco leafs
53. Ivory
54. Sumauma
55. Linen
56. Small seed
57. Wax
58. Silvery sand
59. White wax
60. Palmtree wool
61. Vegunia wool
62. Copper
63. Tin
64. Basin
65. Feathers
66. Plumes
67. Wool
68. Cat skin
69. Mineral crystal

Source: Compiled by the author.

Table 10.5. *Brazilian Products Reexported by Portugal*

Food Supplies	Leather		Miscellaneous
1. White sugar	13. Dried leather	23. Ourucu	33. Nerve rubber
2. Brown sugar	14. Salted leather	24. Brazilwood	34. Cocoa skin
3. Rice	15. Half soles	25. Yellow wood	35. Rolled tobacco
4. Coffee	16. Leather with hair	26. Sarsparilla	36. Capivi balsam
5. Cocoa	17. Horse leather	27. Poyaya	37. Whale
6. Molasses	18. Soft sole leather	28. Peixerim	38. Rubbers
7. Tapioca		29. Lians root	39. Starch
8. Sugarcane brandy	Drugs	30. Holy seed	40. Fish oil
9. Bread flour		31. Violet wood	41. Small cocoanut
10. Fine clove	19. Contrayerva root	32. Parsley	42. Cocoanuts
11. Coarse clove	20. Indigo		43. Maranhão
12. Maranhão clove	21. Ginger		walnut
	22. Epecauanha		44. Copal glue

Source: Compiled by the author.

Table 10.6a. *Trade Between Selected Foreign Nations and Portugal 1776–1807*

Imports of European Primary and Secondary Products
from Selected Foreign Nations to Portugal
(in millions of milreis)

	England	Holland	France	Hamburg	Castile	Russia	Sweden	Denmark	Italy
Primary Product	24.4	3.9	3.7	2.2	2.6	3.4	1.0	0.5	3.2
Secondary Product	7.6	2.5	3.4	8.0	2.5	8.2	3.5	0.1	5.0

Total Portuguese Imports
195,855,570 milreis

Reexports of Colonial Primary Products
from Portugal to Selected Foreign Nations
(in millions of milreis)

	England	Holland	France	Hamburg	Castile	Russia	Sweden	Denmark	Italy
Primary Product	24.0	3.7	16.0	29.1	3.5	0.4	0.4	0.8	20.2

Total Portuguese Reexports
144,395,051 milreis

Source: Compiled by the author.

Table 10.6b. *Trade Between Portugal and Brazilian Provinces 1776–1807*

Exports of European Primary Products
from Portugal to Brazilian Provinces
(in millions of milreis)

	Rio de Janeiro	Bahia	Pernambuco	Maranhão	Pará	Paráiba	Santos	Ceará
Primary product	5.8	4.8	3.1	2.0	1.2	0.1	0.2	0.02
Secondary product	32.7	22.7	16.9	6.7	3.4	0.2	0.1	0.1

Total Brazilian Imports
117,025,030 milreis

Reexports of Colonial Primary Products
from Brazilian Provinces to Portugal
(in millions of milreis)

	Rio de Janeiro	Bahia	Pernambuco	Maranhão	Pará	Paráiba	Santos	Ceará
Primary product	34.4	26.6	22.8	11.1	4.3	0.3	0.3	0.2

Total Brazilian Exports
140,397,500 milreis

Source: Compiled by the author.

nopoly. The colonial market was ideal for a young Portuguese industry; Brazil had to buy from this monopoly and it demanded little so long as its rustic rural population (much of it slaves) consumed products appropriate for beginning industries.[126] The loss of this monopolized Brazilian market did not occur by chance. It was the result of the English imperial expansion policy, formed in the framework of the English Revolution of the seventeenth century. It was also not by chance that in 1785 a decree issued by Dona Maria I attempted to stop manufacturing industries from beginning in the colony – in order to prevent any competition with Portuguese factories.[127] These were empty measures, however, because in 1800 there was still a large population of some 600,000 people in the vast interior of Minas Gerais, centered on gold mining, integrated into an economy of "accommodation."[128] Spinning and weaving were integral parts of daily life on mixed-economy *fazendas*. As a result of this combination, a peculiar form of regression occurred in the mining areas: a mercantile subsistence economy that remained resistant throughout the nineteenth century; it was characterized by slow, quiet growth; molded by a vast slave work force; and located in nonexport sectors of the economy.[129]

This illustration of Portuguese mercantilism reveals its contradictory nature. The economic recomposition of the empire required the mobilization of a critical spirit. The efforts put into effect achieved their desired results by increasing colonial enterprise and accelerating the accumulation of capital in the metropole and its European partners. In order to continue this enterprise, above all else, more long-lasting investments were required in the colony. This accelerated its growth and caused it to collide with the limits imposed by its colonial status. The Portuguese advanced to the limits of reform. However, with the transfer of the court to Brazil, they sacrificed the European homeland in order to try to save the colony. At this point, the colony ended its status by assimilating the metropole.[130]

---

[126] The relationship between the loss of the colonial Brazilian market and the blocking of industrialization in Portugal was explicitly demonstrated by way of quantitative studies on the balance of trade in the author's dissertation at the Universidade de São Paulo in 1973 (see note 149). See also the unpublished article "O Comércio entre Portugal e a Itália (1796–1811) (from 1978). More recently, this argument has been aired, albeit without real proof, by Sandro Sideri, *Trade and Power: Informal Colonialism in Anglo-Portuguese Relations*, 171, and by Valentim Alexandre, "Um momento de subdesenvolvimento Portugues."

[127] Novais, *Portugal e Brasil na Crise do Antigo Sistema Colonial*, 277.

[128] Douglas Cole Libby, "População e Mão-de-Obra Industrial na Provincia de Minas Gerais (1830–1889)," Diss. Universidade de São Paulo, 1987.

[129] Roberto Borges Martins, *Growing in Silence: The Slave Economy of Nineteenth-Century Minas Gerais, Brazil* (Nashville, 1981).

[130] Novais, *Portugal e Brasil*, 298–302.

DO COLONIES PAY?

The polemic surrounding the theme of profit (or lack thereof) from colonies is quite old, having been raised by Adam Smith. More recently, this theme reappeared with force in the works by R. B. Sheridan on the English West Indies, especially his works on Jamaica.[131] In spite of the strong restrictions interposed by R. P. Thomas,[132] to our way of understanding the essence of Sheridan's conclusions retains its validity – not only from a methodological point of view but also in content. The hypothesis put forward by Thomas, that investments made in the colonies retarded the economic development of England, clashes with reality. It is sufficient to observe the rapid growth of England during the eighteenth century, its primacy along the road to the Industrial Revolution, and the indisputable statement that this growth was indelibly linked to the colonial world – which it directly or indirectly exploited. That is, direct exploitation was achieved by integrating colonies into the "Formal Empire" (which are exemplified by the Navigation Acts); indirect exploitation was accomplished through the use of an "Informal Empire" – unequal relationships such as England enjoyed with Portugal.[133] The question restated by Phillip Coelho,[134] going in the same direction as Thomas, starts

---

[131] Richard B. Sheridan, *The Development of the Plantation to 1750: An Era of West Indian Prosperity, 1750–1775* (Barbados and London 1970); "The Plantation Revolution and the Industrial Revolution," *Caribbean Studies* 9 (1969); "The Wealth of Jamaica in the Eighteenth Century: A Rejoinder," *The Economic History Review* 21 (1968): 46–61; "The Wealth of Jamaica in the Eighteenth Century," *The Economic History Review* 28 (1965): 292–311.

[132] R. P. Thomas, "The Sugar Colonies of the Old Empire: Profit or Loss for Great Britain?" *The Economic History Review* 21 (1968): 30–45, affirms that "Adam Smith was correct, at least with respect to the sugar colonies–they were 'mere loss instead of profit.' " This position is diametrically opposed to that of Richard Pares in "Merchants and Planters," *The Economic History Review* Supplement 4 (Cambridge, 1960), 50: "In this sense, Adam Smith was wrong: the wealth of the British West Indies did not all proceed from the mother country; after some initial loans in the earliest period which merely primed the pump, the wealth of the West Indies was created out of the profits of the West Indies themselves, and, with some assistance from the British tax-payer, much of it found a permanent home in Great Britain."

[133] J. Gallagher and R. Robinson, "The Imperialism of Free Trade," *The Economic History Review* 6 (1953): 1–55. See also Bernard Semmel, *The Rise of Free Trade Imperialism* (Cambridge, 1970).

[134] Phillip R. P. Coelho, "The Profitability of Imperialism: The British Experience in the West Indies, 1768–1772," *Explorations in Economic History* 10 (1973): 253–280, especially p. 256 and ff.: "Britain could have benefited from the possession of these colonies only if the colonial arrangement it imposed upon the British West Indies allowed the British to import colonial goods at a lower price than the same goods were sold for on the world market... British West Indies plantation owners were the main beneficiaries of British colonialism. Their benefits consisted of a higher price for sugar than they received on the world market, and the protection provided by the British military."

from an absurd premise of an England without colonies and reaches a somewhat tautological conclusion, considering the nature of capitalism. So many mathematical calculations are not necessary to conclude that, in the economic exploitation of Jamaica, profits went to individuals and costs were socialized. This was the essence of the system. The process of accumulation involved social losses, but also represented the possibility of constant advance for capitalism. This is in the sense that accumulation achieved in the previous period opened the way for the plateau following it.

Sheridan calculates that £1.5 million in profit was extracted from Jamaica in the single year 1773.[135] Thirteen years earlier, in the year 1760, English profit on the Luso-Brazilian Empire reached £1,308,909.[136] It is obvious that this profit was very significant because it involved small investments in the productive colonial apparatus. However, it is no less true that the lion's share of capital invested by the British in sugar colonies came from the Dutch. This same capital was generated by profits obtained from Portuguese colonies, Brazil above all others. Even after being dislocated by wars or the Navigation Acts, a significant portion of Dutch capital continued to flow toward the English colonies by way of the Anglo-Dutch companies.[137] More than anything else, this process cannot be considered in isolation. The importance of the triangular trade for the development of New England should not be underestimated, in particular the critical role played by the sugar colonies of the West Indies. Indirectly, these islands contributed to the growth of the continental colonies. The market in New England consumed English manufactured goods and had no small part in the sudden start of English industry.[138] If the East and West Indies were most important in regard to English imports, North America was critical to English exports, especially for domestic manufacturing. Even though North America's participation in English imports was not greater than 14.7 percent in 1772, its role in English exports was 19 percent – absorbing 26 percent of exports from domestic manufacturing.[139] Even the colonies of the South (of North America), where large plantations dominated and whose internal markets were more restrictive toward

[135] Richard B. Sheridan, "The Wealth of Jamaica in the Eighteenth Century," 292–311.
[136] Michael Morineau, *Incroyables Gazettes et Fabuleux Métaux*. 182
[137] Richard B. Sheridan, "The Wealth of Jamaica in the Eighteenth Century: A Rejoinder," 61.
[138] Ralph Davis, "English Foreign Trade, 1700–1774," *The Economic History Review* 15 (1962): 295.
[139] Jacob M. Price, "Colonial Trade and British Economic Development, 1600–1775," in *La Révolution Américaine et l'Europe* (Colloques Internationaux du CNRS, Paris-Toulouse, 1978), 225.

English manufactured goods, became net exporters of capital because "the accumulation of money and credit in agriculture . . . in effect permitted investment where credit was more expansible."[140]

The rise and nature of these investments could be discussed because, in a general manner, a work force, capital, markets, manufacturing, and naval protection were required.[141] Strictly speaking, the essential contribution from the colonizing metropoles for their colonies was in providing people and materials: "Skills and habits of organization have migrated with capital equipment, and the two have worked together overseas to produce a joint result. It is questionable whether either type of migration has cost the mother countries anything, net."[142]

What was the level of profit generated by the commercialization of Brazilian products by the Portuguese metropole?

The lucrativity of Portuguese trade in reselling or reexporting Brazilian products can be evaluated by the data below, corresponding to the average lucrativity reached during the period from 1796 to 1811, considering twenty-four of the main colonial products (Table 10.7).

We denominate x as the export price and y as the price of reexport. For each product, a series of n pairs can be determined, corresponding to a period of approximately twelve years, because some products have gaps in the data on reexportation. The gain, here called the monopoly profit, is defined by the following equation:

$$g = (\frac{y}{x} - 1) \times 100$$

The determination of the average gains made by monopoly for diverse products was made by the statistical method of linear regression by which we attempted to find coefficient a in the equation:

$$y = a x$$

---

[140] William N. Parker, "The Slave Plantation in American Agriculture," *First International Conference of Economic History* (Stockholm, 1960), 327–8: In the nineteenth century, "The revenue from capital invested overseas played an important role in the equilibrium of balance of payments . . . To these revenues should be added the balance and renumeration paid by the colonies, the growing importance of pensions . . . The positive trade balance was accompanied by invisible exports because of services which remained for the monopoly from the *metropole*, freight in particular." Cf. Jean-Louis Miège, *Expansion Européenne et Décolonisation de 1870 à nos jours*, Collection Nouvelle Clio (Paris, 1973), 240–1.

[141] D. A. Farnie, "The Commercial Empire of the Atlantic, 1607–1783," *The Economic History Review* 15 (1962): 206.

[142] M. M. Knight, "Do Colonies Pay?" in *War as a Social Institution: The Historian's Perspective*, eds. Jesse D. Clarkson and Thomas C. Cochran (New York, 1941), 50.

Table 10.7. *Profitability in Percent of Brazilian Goods Sold or Reexported From Portugal, 1796–1811*

Ipecacuanha (a medicinal plant)	39.45	Coarse clove	74.44
White sugar	41.70	Ourucu	75.47
Dry leather	43.27	Coffee	84.68
Fine clove	52.63	Tapioca	98.28
Sugar cane brandy	51.00	Starch	98.32
Indigo	53.80	Cocoa	99.70
Soft sole leather	54.75	Rice	101.29
Sole	57.32	Tobacco	103.74
Salted leather	57.95	Balsam Capivi	144.08
Tanned leather	58.71	Ginger	216.07
Cotton	64.58	Brazilwood	778.71
Sarsaparilla	69.22		

Source: See note 143.

Therefore, considering the n pairs (x_i, y_i), and calculating their deviations ∂_1, given in:

$$\bar{o}_1 = y_1 - ax_i$$

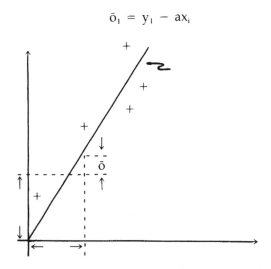

[143] José J. de A. Arruda, "Commercial Trends Within the Luso-Brazilian Empire: Brazil's Integration in the World Market," in *The Emergence of a World Economy, 1500–1914*, vol. I., Wolfram Fischer (Erlangen, 1986), 320–2.

In using the method of linear regression, the sum of the squared deviations (Δ) can be calculated and the value of a is given by the sum that is a minimum. This is done considering the derivative of Δ in relation to the parameters of a and making that derivative equal to zero:

$$\Delta = \sum_{i=i}^{n} (\sigma_1): = \sum_{i=i}^{n} (y_1 - ax_i):$$

and

$$\frac{d\,\Delta}{d\,a} = \sum_{i=i}^{n} 2(y_1 - ax_i)\,(-x_i) = 0$$

or finally:

$$a = \frac{\sum\limits_{i=i}^{n} y_i\,x_i}{\sum\limits_{i=i}^{n} x^2}$$

from which we can get:

$$\frac{y}{x} = a$$

By using a computer program, the values of a were calculated for the various products. The gains, in percent, of the monopoly were obtained from this expression:

$$g = (a - 1) \times 100$$

These values refer to the prices paid for Brazilian products, in relation to prices paid as exports to foreign countries, as quoted in Lisbon. Even by taking into consideration the added costs of freight and insurance, profits were significant within the averages – around 15 percent – of the system during this period. Sugar, cotton, and the various leather products, which totalled 68.4 percent of all colonial exports, offered profits between 40 percent and 60 percent. Profits derived from coffee, rice, cacao, and tobacco were between 85 percent and 104 percent. This does not even mention the highly profitable products providing 778 percent profit, such as brazilwood. In order to provide a more precise outline, we have calculated the profits on the thirteen principal products listed in Tables 10.3a and 10.3b which accounted for 82.5 percent of the profile. Excluding the shipments of gold registered in the trade balance (10.5 percent) during the period

Table 10.8 *Export Value/Profits on Brazilian Goods Shipped From Lisbon, 1796–1811 (in milreis)*

Product	Export Value 1796–1811	Profit Achieved
Sugar	53,585,148[1]	22,505,595
Cotton	17,555,446	24,411,039
Dry leather	9,411,068	4,140,869
Rice	6,108,170	6,230,333
Tobacco	5,917,453	4,388,533
Coffee	2,775,791	2,359,422
Leather strips	2,100,257	1,134,138
Sugar cane brandy	1,951,182	995,102
Salted leather	1,586,293	920,049
Half soles	1,245,135	684,824
Tanned leather	804,601	474,724
Total	127,260,690[2]	68,244,782

[1]White and brown sugar were totalled together for this calculation, using the figures from the lower, white sugar.
[2]Total exports were actually 154,038,451 milreis.
Source: See note 143.

1796 to 1811, Table 10.8 can be considered as a real indicator of the measure of profit attained by Portuguese commerce in Brazil:

One can conclude, therefore, that imports received from merchants in Brazilian ports totaled 127,260,690 *milreis* and gave a profit of 68,244,782, or more than 50 percent. Equal sums were not obtained on products introduced into the colony by Portuguese merchants:

Product	Profit
Copper	12.30%
Olive oil	17.23%
Butter	20.22%
Iron	41.00%
Maize	42.01%
Codfish	50.98%
Breton linen	74.82%

All the evidence would indicate that the Portuguese did not seek greater profits in goods sold to the colony. This could happen with a few foodstuffs (codfish) or special cloth (Breton linen), but the indispensable items for the continuation of colonial production (iron and copper) had reduced profits. Fundamentally, it was the profit from the resale of colonial products that was important.

It is quite true that the measurement of colonial profit has limited significance by itself. In agreement with the statement by Sheridan, we believe that "a more fruitful question is whether or not Great Britain would have had a sufficient base for her Industrial Revolution in the absence of tropical colonies."[144] Brazil found itself in a dialectical relationship with the industrial takeoff of England and with the blockage of Portuguese industrialization in the eighteenth century. It was one of the necessities for the realization of the first and, at the same time, a condition of the starting and closing of the second. Exports of food and colonial reexports composed more than 50 percent of French exports in 1787.[145] "Plantation colonies and trade played a vital role in French economic growth in the half-century or more prior to the revolution."[146] However, the parity that France had maintained with England in terms of industrial development[147] was broken after 1780, when English dominance was achieved in all seas and in all world markets – where cotton cloth and Albion's trinkets arrived.[148]

On this issue, that is, on the role of external commerce in determining the takeoff of industry in England, there is no agreement. Ralph Davis, M. W. Flinn, and Paul Bairoch[149] downplay or negate preemptorily the importance of the external market in this process. Hartwell says that this direct contribution to the Industrial Revolution

---

[144] Sheridan, "The Wealth of Jamaica in the Eighteenth Century: A Rejoinder," 61.

[145] According to Ruggiero Romano, "Documenti e Prime Considerazioni intorno alla 'Balance du Commerce' della Francia dal 1716 al 1780," in *Studi in Onore di Armando Sapori* (Milano-Varese, 1957), 1278, colonial commerce represented 18 percent of French exterior commerce: "Tuttavia, bisognera osservare che il ruolo del commercio coloniale é molto piu importante di questo 18 per cento . . . Importazione di prodotti coloniali su grande scale; arresto di parte di questo prodotti in Francia per il consumo nazionale e riesportazione del rimanente, insieme ai maufatti nazionali verso i paesi europei, da cui si importavano pochi manufatti, materie prime a prodoti di consumo, che venivano di nuovo, parzialmente, riesportati verso le 'colonie.' "

[146] François Crouzet, "Wars, Blockade, and Economic Change in Europe, 1792–1815," *Journal of Economic History* 24 (1964): 568–9. The conclusions of Paul Butel, "France, the Antilles, and Europe in the Seventeenth and Eighteenth Centuries," in *The Rise of Merchant Empires*, 153–73, point in the same direction.

[147] François Crouzet, "Croissances comparés de l'Angleterre et de la France au XVIII siècle," *Annales, E.S.C.* 21 (1966): 254–91, and *De la Superiorité de l'Angleterre sur la France* (Paris, 1985).

[148] Pierre Leon, "Structure du Commerce extérieur et évolution industrielle de la France à la fin du XVIIIe siècle," in *Conjoncture Economique Structures Sociales. Hommage à Ernest Labrousse* (Paris, 1974), 421.

[149] These positions are discussed in depth in José J. de A. Arruda, "Raizes do Industrialismo Moderno, Estudo Historico sobre as Origens da Revolução Industrial na Inglatera" (Tese de Livre Docencia, USP), 204.

was small at the beginning and only acquired importance in the later stages of industrial expansion.[150] Flinn points out the importance of small industries: metal, linen, silk, glass, cotton, and naval construction.[151] Bairoch gives external commerce a marginal role, insisting that profits from external commerce invested in production never surpassed 10 percent to 20 percent and were more probably between 6 percent and 8 percent. Nevertheless, he does refer to the external market as an explananatory factor[152] By contrast, Peter Mathais, W. E. Minchinton, P. Deane, and W. A. Cole highlight the external market's role, in particular the colonial market. "In the period between 1600 and 1775 foreign trade played a more important role in stimulating economic development than at any other period in the history of this country."[153] For Deane and Cole, the existence of external markets consuming English manufactured goods, supported by raw materials and foodstuffs, were strategic conditions for all stages of industrialization. External commerce increased the savings and this capital became critical in economic development during the last decades of the century. It became concentrated in industries with declining costs and more elastic markets.[154] The export sector was, without question, the most dynamic sector of the English economy during the eighteenth century. Real income increased 44 percent between 1700 and 1770. Products from export industries grew by 156 percent while goods produced for the internal market and the agricultural sector grew by 14 percent and 17 percent respectively.[155] The English export profile changed substantially in the eighteenth century. Exports to Europe went from 85 percent to 30 percent; to North

---

[150] R. M. Hartwell, "The Cause of the Industrial Revolution: An Essay in Methodology," *The Economic History Review* 18(1965): 164–82.

[151] M. W. Flinn, *Origins of Industrial Revolution* (London, 1966), 60.

[152] Paul Bairoch, "Le rôle du grand commerce dans la Reévolution Industrielle Anglaise," *Annales E. S. C.* 2 (1973): 543. The rationale presented by Bairoch has a certain circular definition as can be noted in the following:" Si incontestablement, il y a eu des relations assez étroites entre l'évolution du commerce extérieur et celle de la croissance économique, il apparait que l'élément moteur de cette évolution a été, en règle générale, la croissance économique," Cf. Paul Bairoch, *Commerce extérieur et développement économique de l'Europe au XIXe siècle* (Paris, 1976), 309.

[153] W. E. Minchinton, "Introduction," in *The Growth of the English Overseas Trade*, ed. W. E. Minchinton (London, 1969), 52.

[154] Deane and Cole, *British Economic Growth, 1688–1959*, 28, 32, 35, 68.

[155] Ibid., 156. According to Christian Palloix in *Problèmes de la croissance en economie ouvert* (Paris, 1969), 183, products for export had a notable increase, particularly textiles – with 14.1 percent between 1780 and 1800, iron and tin amalgam 5.1 percent, other finished metals averaged five percent. Considering the modest rate of increase in the agricultural sector, consumption in the internal market had to have serious limitations, not allowing the accelerated development of the productive forces that could have assimilated domestic production.

America, 6 percent to 32 percent; to the West Indies, 5 percent to 25 percent; and to the East Indies and Africa, 4 percent to 13 percent.[156] This shows that the colonial world scattered among the continents of America, Africa, and Asia only consumed 15 percent of the English products at the beginning of the eighteenth century but increased that figure to 70 percent by the end of that period. It is not possible, therefore, to negate the importance of the global market, especially a colonial market, in the transformation of the technical structure of English industrial production. Until then, it had been based on manufacturing via the two factors of tools and human energy. A structural change, demanded by the accelerated world market, made the old methods of crafts and manufacturing impractical.[157]

There are, however, several senses in which external demand, particularly colonial demand, may have had a disproportionate effect on British economic development before 1775. Insofar as external demand results in the employment of factors of production, particularly labor, that otherwise would have been unemployed, or underemployed, there should be a multiplier effect operative in the economy.[158]

This means that the colonial world fulfilled its role. It fulfilled its chief function as a link providing growth for the early accumulation of capital. It promoted a transfer of colonial riches to the metropoles, which then fought for the appropriation of colonial surplus. This surplus, in the form of net transfers or credits in the trade balance, sustained the national treasuries of the colonizing states and filled the private coffers of the mercantilist bourgeoisie. Here is an answer to the enigma that elucidates the role of the colonies: the specific

[156] P. Deane, *The First Industrial Revolution* (Cambridge, 1965), 56:

Distribution in Percent of English Domestic Exports				
Regions	1700–1	1750–1	1772–3	1797–8
Europe	85%	77%	49%	30%
North America	6%	11%	25%	32%
West Indies	5%	5%	12%	25%
East Indies and Africa	4%	7%	14%	13%

[157] José J. de A. Arruda, *Revolução Industrial e Capitalismo* (São Paulo, 1984), 241. Using the same rationale, Price, "Colonial Trade and British Economic Development," 241, argues that "with domestic demand more than fully utilizing existing local supplies of bar iron and linen and cotton yarn, the extra or marginal demand coming from overseas (particularly the colonies) should have exerted a marked upward pressure on prices and thus significantly have increased the incentives to experiment with new cost-reducing technologies. In this sense, colonial demand was particularly strategic." In other words, "overseas demand put pressure on specific resources . . . the force that pushed the cork (of innovation) through the (technological) bottleneck."

[158] Price, "Colonial Trade and British Economic Development," 241.

nature of mercantile capital, or of commercial capitalism (if we want to revive that disparaged phrase).

In short, commercial investments made in the colonies, integrated into the circuit of mercantile capital and tied to the bonds of mercantile policies, substantially and strategically contributed to the economic growth of Western Europe. They opened new areas for investments – areas essential for the growth and mobility of the circulation of capital; consequently, this combination of conditions allowed the assertion of capitalism as a dominant system. THESE COLONIES DID PAY.

CHAPTER 11

Reflections on the organizing principle of premodern trade

K. N. CHAUDHURI

THE RATIONALE OF PREMODERN TRADE

In the history of human civilization, there are a number of recurrent events and activities that have played a profound and fundamental role. Warfare and trade, so different from one another in their psychological origins, nevertheless are the two indivisible symbols of man's basic desire to look beyond his inner self and of the urge to master the constraints of his immediate natural environment. The demarcation of state frontiers through military and political means breaks up the unity of economic space that long-distance trade subsequently attempts to restore. As a result, the function of trade in social institutions and in the rhythm of economic life is possessed of a dynamic complexity, a variegated richness, that is more easily sensed than it is capable of a single unified analysis. Like the perennial glaciers that sometimes come forward into the valleys and at other times retreat up the mountain sides in long slow movements, the spatial and qualitative dimensions of trade have also expanded and shrunk in response to a wider climate of social, political, and economic frontiers. The sources of energy vitalizing the exchange of objects and movements of long-distance trade can be easily traced to an aggregate composed of many different strands of motivations. The differential rate of technological progress obviously created uneven gradients of material civilizations in which the very inequality of production itself was an incentive to trade. Similarly, division of labor, urbanization, artistic expressions, and acquisitive urges can be listed as some of the organizing principles of commercial exchange. The aesthetic sensibilities in man and the need for magical defenses obviously made certain substances such as incense, amber, coral, or rare sea shells highly prized, and even indispensable. The fact that the supply of these natural products was strictly localized introduced the dimensions of space explicitly into the process of exchange. The wide dif-

421

fusion of luxury objects and jewelry made from amber, coral, and cowries must be seen as an indication that prehistoric communities throughout Asia and Africa knew and practiced economic exchange among different, widely separated geographical regions.

Other signs of early trade may also come from the distribution of artifacts fashioned out of natural volcanic glass known as obsidian, which was extensively used for making tools with sharp cutting edges and for the manufacture of fine objets d'art. Obsidian is a relatively rare substance, though not actually precious. Recent scientific studies using optical spectroscopy have confirmed conclusively that the raw material for the obsidian tools discovered in Italy, the Aegean, and the Near East came from identifiable volcanic quarries. At the great neolithic site of Catal Huyuk in Anatolia, which was only 200 kilometers or so from the volcanic deposits, obsidian finds, polished mirrors, and fine pressure-flaked daggers are so abundant that the suggestion of the place serving as a center of trade or distribution seems inherently plausible. There is little doubt that the material was transported to Catal Huyuk and other semiurbanized sites over considerable distances.[1] Whether such a traffic was conducted on the backs of animals or through human porterage or in organized caravans or in individual journeys and whether it was part of a known universe of information, economic activities, and geographical locations are problems to which archaeology alone at present cannot provide definitive solutions.

Although it can be taken as axiomatic that the systematic organization of the multifaceted forms of long-distance trade was aimed at reducing transaction costs, it is extemely difficult to analyze theoretically the nature of these costs and practically impossible to measure them precisely. However, there is no difficulty in agreeing with Adam Smith's ex cathedra pronouncement that man's propensity to barter, truck, and exchange one thing for another created the basic conditions for the division of labor and the emergence of markets, both of which extended beyond the technical boundaries of actual economic production and subsumed the entire society and the state. Adam Smith was not the first economic historian to emphasize the role of the division of labor. Four centuries earlier, in sonorous Arabic prose the greatest historian of his time, who was also a practical statesman and

---

[1] Colin Renfrew, "Trade and Culture Process in European Prehistory", *Current Anthropology* 10 (1969): 151–9; "Obsidian in the Aegean," *Annual of the British School of Archaeology at Athens* 60 (1965): 225–47; "Further Analysis of Near Eastern Obsidian," *Proceedings of the Prehistoric Society* 34 (1968): 319–31.

political economist, outlined some of the essential economic facts underlying urban life.

> With regard to the amount of prosperity and business activity in them, cities and towns differ in accordance with the different size of their civilization [population]. The reason for this is that, as is known and well established, the individual human being cannot by himself obtain all the necessities of life. All human beings must co-operate to that end in their civilization. But what is obtained through the co-operation of a group of human beings satisfies the need of a number many times greater than themselves. For instance, no one, by himself, can obtain the share of the wheat he needs for food. But when six or ten persons, including a smith and a carpenter to make the tools, and others who are in charge of the oxen, the ploughing of the soil, the harvesting of the ripe grain, and all the other agricultural activities, undertake to obtain their food and work toward that purpose either separately or collectively and thus obtain through their labour a certain amount of food, that amount will be food for a number of people many times their own. The combined labour produces more than the needs and necessities of the workers.

Ibn Khaldūn's comments immediately following the above analysis were even more revealing. The basic economic needs of towns, he argued, tended to leave the urban population underemployed. It was the "conditions and customs of luxury" that created the super-structure of society and laid the foundations for trade. "They import the things they need from people who have a surplus through exchange or purchase. Thus the people who have a surplus get a good deal of wealth."[2]

THEORETICAL EXPLANATIONS OF LONG-DISTANCE TRADE: RICARDO, BRAUDEL, WALLERSTEIN, AND POLANYI

The great Moroccan historian had sensed correctly that economic specialization possessed the property of increasing return to both labor and capital and that it was in some way related historically to the appearance of towns. Furthermore, socially determined demand was as important to trade as differential costs of production. The question that has emerged in the forefront of academic debate on the organization of long-distance trade, whether conducted by sea or land, is of course that of social reciprocity, as opposed to redistributive

---

[2] Ibn Khaldūn, *The Muqaddimah*, ed. Franz Rosenthal, (Princeton, 1967), II, 271–2.

exchange operating through values established by prices, money, and integrated markets. It is interesting to note that the whole body of theoretical analysis on international trade derived from David Ricardo's original and famous theorem on comparative costs is seldom, if ever, applied to the early modern period as an explanatory tool. Indeed, Fernand Braudel categorically dismisses the "pseudo-theorem" of Ricardo as unhistorical. International trade, admittedly, might add to welfare; more often it created conditions of profound economic inequalities. The division of labor on a world scale, Braudel believes, did not take place as a result of mutual agreement between equal parties, nor was it open to constant review. Premodern trade always operated through a chain of greater or lesser subordination, and the gains were distributed unevenly.[3] The perspective adopted by Braudel in this particular instance is to relate the organization of trade to the concept of the balance of power and the extraction of wealth through a combination of the state functions and those of the merchant. Immanuel Wallerstein's model of a world system was at the forefront of Braudel's own analysis, but it differed from that of Wallerstein in being less deterministic. However, it will be wrong to dismiss the theory of comparative costs altogether as an irrelevant argument. Although the theory as developed by David Ricardo was primarily the result of the emerging world industrial economy, its basic premises are not entirely irrelevant to the operation of premodern trade. International differences in prices as measured by factor costs did fix the pattern of trade among competing regions, and examples can be cited from the history of Indian textiles trade in the seventeenth and eighteenth centuries to show that areas with lower cost levels easily displaced those with higher costs. What the Ricardian theory obviously cannot explain is the persistence of inelastic demand for certain products that were essential for the functioning of social life.

In contrast to the model developed by Wallerstein and Braudel, the concept of reciprocity and redistribution, which owes so much to the work of Karl Polanyi, is not dependent on a theory of subordination or unequal exchange; the theory is much more concerned with the mechanism of trade and its actual organization. Polanyi defined trade as an activity that takes place in two separate dimensions. The first is the institutional organization of trade. Local communities seek to acquire objects or goods that are external to their society, and the

[3] Fernand Braudel, *Civilization and Capitalism, the Perspective of the World*, (London, 1984), III, 48. Braudel's viewpoint was considerably influenced by the work of I. Wallerstein. See also Braudel, *Une leçon d'histoire de Fernand Braudel, Chateauvallon/Octobre 1985*, (Paris, 1986).

transaction is essentially a peaceful one. It is not an extension of piracy or raiding expeditions, though John Hicks in his *Theory of Economic History* has hinted that this might have been the way that merchants at first accumulated capital. Polanyi himself thought that hunting, expeditions, and raids were different forms of "pretrade." The initial part of the theoretical scheme is seen in the movement of goods from a distance as a reciprocal or bilateral exchange between two parties that are equally motivated to trade. The second dimension is the distribution of commodities through the market embodying a supply-demand-price mechanism. The immediate factor in the market-oriented trading is not the social acquisitiveness of the commercial partners but the distributive function of relative prices. Merchants and traders are able to take advantage of price differences that exist in different consuming regions, and the profit motive is the main instrument of movement. The notion of market trading also involves the concept of redistribution because a market-place is used by people from separate localities.

The most elaborate theoretical extension of Polanyi's ideas on premodern trade can be found in Colin Renfrew's essay in which he categorized no less than ten separate forms of trading.[4] The most important of these are trade between two parties with direct access, trade down-the-line, with goods passing from hand to hand in a single direction, central-place market-exchange, emissary trading, and the port of trade. Each typology is associated with a whole range of social and economic institutions, and trade can take place between societies at divergent stages of development. To take a single example, the presence of coastal trading cities in east Africa in the early medieval period clearly betrays the existence of a redistributive market that included China, India, and the Middle East. Towns such as Mogadishu and Kilwa were ports of trade where merchants could come and go free from direct political control of the local rulers. But the distribution of goods from the coastal city-states to the interior tribal areas of Black Africa was almost certainly a case of trade down-the-line. Imported commodities such as cowries, damascened-steel, cotton textiles, and porcelain passed successively from one community to another. We do not know if the tribal exchanges included any notions

---

[4] Colin Renfrew, "Trade As Action at a Distance: Questions of Integration and Communication," in J. A. Sabloff and C.C. Lamberg-Karlovsky, eds., *Ancient Civilization and Trade*, (Albuquerque, 1975), 149; Polanyi, "Evolution of the Market Pattern," in his *The Great Transformation*, (Boston, 1957); Polanyi, "Traders and Trade," and Dalton, "Karl Polanyi's Analysis of Long-Distance Trade and His Wider Paradigm," in Sabloff and Lamberg-Karlovsky, eds., *Ancient Civilization and Trade* (1975). Sir John Hicks, *A Theory of Economic History* (Oxford, 1969).

of relative prices as opposed to those of social gifts; in ports of trade the economic transactions were conducted on well-understood principles of value. When Ibn Battuta visited the east African trading towns in the fourteenth century, he was clearly surprised by the high status accorded locally to visiting merchants from the Arab world.[5]

THE TYPOLOGY OF TRADE, ATTITUDE TOWARDS MERCHANTS, AND THE CONCEPT OF ECONOMIC VALUE

Polanyi continued to believe that the trade of the ancient Middle and Near East was organized on the basis of "market-less" trading and that merchants whose existence is so clearly revealed in the records were merely agents of powerful temple or secular authorities. The redistribution of economic products, according to this theoretical point of view, was a political and not a strictly economic process. From such ideas about the fundamental nature of premodern long-distance trade have come an equally emphatic model of merchants and traders that would see them as being completely dependent on the political will of the great territorial rulers.[6] There was of course plenty of historical evidence available to show that the expropriation of merchants and their personal wealth was a common practice among premodern governments. Ibn Khaldūn, himself, stressed the point with the obvious example of merchants in mind: "[A merchant is] a sedentary person who has a great deal of capital and has acquired a great number of estates and farms and become one of the wealthiest inhabitants of a particular city, who is looked upon as such and lives in great luxury and is accustomed to luxury, competes in this respect with amirs and rulers. The latter become jealous of him." The political elite watch such people with the intention of catching them unaware. It was no use for the wealthy would-be victims to rely on abstract justice, for "pure justice is found only in the legal caliphate that lasted only a short while." The only remedy for the merchants was to create favorable political interests by a judicious distribution of presents.[7] The grey area of "legal capitalism" continued well into the modern period. For example, in the 1690s, when the English East India Com-

---

[5] Ibn Battuta, *The Travels of Ibn Battuta*, trans. H. A. R. Gibb, (London, 1929), 110–13.
[6] For a documented and general discussion of the political weakness of Indian merchants in the seventeenth and eighteenth centuries, see Ashin Das Gupta, *Indian Merchants and the Decline of Surat c. 1700–1750*, (Wiesbaden, 1979); M. N. Pearson, *Merchants and Rulers in Gujarat* (Berkeley, 1976).
[7] Ibn Khaldūn, *The Muqaddimah*, ed. Rosenthal, II, 285.

pany was under pressure from Parliament to wind up its share capital every twenty-five years or so and give legal guarantees of assured valuations, the directorate replied that the proposal was not only ridiculous for the commercial operation of the company but also unjust in law: no man was obliged under English law to give security for his possessions.[8] The distinction between the personal wealth of merchants and the legally protected capital of impersonal business organization took a long time to emerge and the principle was not introduced to Asia before the colonial period.

However, there is little doubt that trade across national and cultural frontiers can hardly take place unless two sides in the transactions derive some mutual satisfaction. To see this, we have only to read a letter written in about 1800 B.C. by a princely merchant of Qatna in the Orontes valley of western Syria to Ishme Dagan, the eldest son of the king of Assyria. In this, the Syrian complained that he had sent to the king two fine thoroughbred horses valued at 600 shekels of silver and received only 40 pounds of tin in return. The unjust bargain was a reflection on the royal house of Assyria.[9] This was an example of what Renfrew calls emissary trading. The abstract notion of value and the practical device of indexing its scale in prices made it possible for two parties separated by long distances to exchange high-quality horses against an essential commodity such as tin. In the commercial history of the world during the centuries from about A.D. 1000 to about 1750, the public attitudes to trade and its economic importance fluctuated between two opposing poles. Some states owed their existence and survival unambiguously to trade. It gave them the basis of a material wealth impossible to achieve otherwise with the technology of a premachine age. Others despised the merchants and their humble calling. Braudel has drawn a distinction between the commercially oriented city-states and the national territorial states in Europe to highlight the difference. But, even in those political empires that sought to control and curb commercial transactions beyond their national boundaries – and the example of imperial China immediately comes to mind – internal trade and economic exchange acted as an invisible bond cementing and holding together the component parts of a large, centralized, and bureaucratically directed structure.

---

[8] "The humble Answer...of the East India Company," India Office Tracts, vol. 268; K.N. Chaudhuri, *The Trading World of Asia and the English East India Company, 1660–1760,* (Cambridge, 1978), 431.
[9] M. E. L. Mallowan, "The Mechanics of Ancient Trade in Western Asia: Reflections on the Location of Magan and Meluha," *Iran* 3 (1965): 1–7.

THE TRADING CITY-STATES AND
THE TERRITORIAL EMPIRES:
TWO DIFFERING MODELS

The historical illustrations of these two opposing types are not difficult to find. The maritime grandeur of Venice is inconceivable without trade. Its political empire combined a conservative, patrician social tradition with an amazing capacity for quick commercial resolution and collective artistic expression. Throughout the fifteenth century as the Ottoman Turks relentlessly pursued their counter-offensive against the great tide of Christian *reconquista* in the eastern and western Mediterranean, Venice and her rulers, the Signoria, remained secure in the knowledge that the republic's great *galeria da mercato* could not be rivaled as a system of commercial distribution stretching from Flanders to the islands of the Aegean. The economic decline of Venice in two subsequent centuries did not destroy the vital qualitative functions performed by trade in Europe's expanding economies, though it pointed clearly to a shift of direction away from the eastern Mediterranean to the western and to the countries of Atlantic Europe. How did Venice and its merchants achieve this position of supremacy? The specific question conceals a general one concerning the rise and fall of commercial emporia as state and economic systems. From the civic and architectural splendors of Venice to the bourgeois comforts of Amsterdam was a long step in history. The northern city was a newcomer in the distinguished league of seafaring trading towns. The common ground between Venice and Amsterdam was an astonishing skill in merchandising that no other contemporary European nation was able to imitate. Even in the mid-eighteenth century, when France and Britain had both become formidable economic powers in Europe, the Dutch model remained in the minds of theorists and writers on trade as the greatest example of the fusion of statesmanship, economic policy, and commercial success. In the words of one observer (Postlethwayt): "The Dutch, by their large stock in trade, by their interests of money being lower than ours, and by their having little or no duties upon the goods imported into Holland, are, by such policy, enabled to make their country a general magazine of merchandise, and therewith to carry on a general traffic throughout the world."[10] Similar views were uttered even in France. Deputies to the French Council of Trade in 1700–01 identified French weakness in relation to the Dutch and English maritime strength by pointing to

[10] M. Postlethwayt, *Great Britain's True System*, (London, 1757), xxi.

the complexity of Colbert's regulations and control of overseas trade. Commerce was too constrained both internally and externally when more than anything else it needed to be free. It was this lack of freedom rather than a shortage of capable merchants that crippled French overseas trade. With an eye on Holland, the deputy from Lille observed that the art of trade was better practiced in republican states than in monarchies, where princes and royal ministers devoted too much time to military matters and paid too little attention to trade.[11] There was general agreement among seventeenth-century observers that the two essential conditions of national and political strength, the capital accumulation and the control of vital transport routes, were won for the Dutch republic by her merchants and sailors.

The spectacular achievements of Venice and Amsterdam weigh heavily in the scale of values in the historian's mind. It is worth remembering that the economic contributions of the Venetian *Terraferma* or the Dutch rural areas were neither negligible nor unimportant. Indeed, even in the mid-seventeenth century, an official of the English East India Company could make disparaging remarks about the insolence of the Dutch "butterboxes." In the case of England, the social hierarchy remained permanently hinged on an alliance of interest between a dominant landowning aristocracy and an elite merchant community able to command large cash resources. It is a truism that, without a secure source of food supply or the alternative of an agricultural hinterland, no place of trade could long survive. The surplus generated by a productive and innovative agrarian economy may act as a stimulant to trade. It may also reduce the dependence of powerful territorial empires on merchants and traders. It is certainly true that for Ming China, Tokugawa Japan, and perhaps even for Mughal India we are faced with a different typology. The reason for Chinese imperial indifference to trade is far from clear. The first Ming emperor himself was the son of a peasant family and hostile to the acquisitive urges of Chinese merchants. The neo-Confucian Mandarin tradition adopted by the scholar-bureaucrats answerable to an authoritative emperor, their conviction of the superiority of rural activities over any others, the treatment of external trade as a system of political tribute rather than as one of economic exchange – are all candidates in an explanation for China's official withdrawal from the Indian Ocean trade just when powerful forces were coming together for an expansion of world trade. The ideological hostility to trade in

[11] W. C. Scoville, "The French economy in 1700–1701: An Appraisal by the Deputies of Trade," *Journal of Economic History* 22 (1962): 231–52.

Japan under the Tokugawa rule was equally marked. Although one Japanese writer in the eighteenth century expressed the view that the merchants deserved little sympathy if they ruined themselves, another actually suggested that their power should be crushed and their privileges of trade taken away and made the possession of rulers. The reason for these extreme views was that the apparent wealth of the merchants had become so great that the samurai and the ruling classes had to bow their heads before them. In spite of the social hostility or official indifference, neither China nor Japan could live without some form of trade; and the traffic in commodities was so vast that it not only drew the attention of foreign travelers but was also used by them as one of the explanations for China's evident economic self-sufficiency. This belief was well expressed in Father Du Halde's famous eighteenth-century work on China in which he claimed:

The particular riches of every province, and the facility of transporting merchandise by means of the rivers and canals, have rendered the empire always very flourishing. As for foreign trade it scarcely deserves to be mentioned, for the Chinese, finding among themselves proper supplies for the necessaries and pleasures of life, seldom trade to any place far distant from their own country . . . The trade carried on within China is so great, that that of all Europe is not be compared therewith; the provinces are like so many kingdoms, which communicate to each other what they have peculiar to themselves, and this tends to the preservation of union, and makes plenty reign in all places.[12]

The creative powers of China's remarkable economy gave an opportunity to western Sinologists for a certain degree of exaggeration. At the same time, the records of the European East India Companies trading with the Celestial Empire for the same period tend to confirm rather than contradict Du Halde's testimony.

According to a much earlier Chinese work, the great city of Hangchow with more than 100,000 families lived on the supply of rice that came to its markets from Suchow, Huchou, Ch'ang-chou, Hsiu-chou, the Huai River region, and Canton. The merchants and the rice guilds of Hangchow sold innumerable varieties of rice: early rice, late rice, medium-quality white rice, lotus pink rice, yellow-eared rice, rice on the stalk, ordinary rice, glutinous rice, and old rice. This lyrical enumeration of the different kinds of rice supplied to Hangchow's grain markets was more than just a flight of poetic fancy. It is a pointer to an important social and cultural duality. Ruling elites and patricians unconnected with trade may have traditionally looked

[12] J. B. du Halde, *Description Geographique, Chronologique, Politique, et Physique de la Chine et de la Tartarie Chinoise* (The Hague, 1736).

down on the merchants. They demanded paradoxically a wide choice for the table that only the merchants could have supplied. From Egypt to China, all the way across Asia, food habits demanded rice as an indispensable accompaniment to special social occasions. The rice economies of Asian countries as a result became commercialized quite early in their history, and the rice trade was just as important in the maritime commerce of Asia as it was in the purely inland trade.

The contrast between the functional importance of trade and social attitudes that regarded trade as beneath the occupations of state officials and aristocratic military men was at its strongest in the Confucian-dominated ideology of the Far East. In the Islamic countries, similar examples could no doubt also be found, but it was diluted by a more favorable treatment of merchants and an awareness that even the great territorial empires drawing huge revenues from a productive agriculture could not turn that revenue into disposable state income without the intermediary of merchants and their role as bankers. If these empires were ruled by princes and warriors, they were also financed in reality by merchants. It was difficult for an agrarian economy growing forty to fifty different kinds of subsistence and cash crops within two separate harvest cycles (the summer and winter growing seasons) to standardize revenue payments in kind or even develop the concept of a "grain-money" as was done in the case of China and Japan. Islamic and Indian states invariably associated political sovereignty with the right and privilege of issuing metallic money. The practice was not an empty gesture. Without the concept of a universal value established by money, the finances of Islamic states would have collapsed into chaos. The official mints, of course, could not operate without the assistance of merchants and bankers who were responsible for obtaining and redistributing the three monetary metals – copper, gold, and silver – through international trade. The most explicit and spectacular instances of the state's encouragement and tolerance of merchants were, of course, the decrees issued by the Mamluk government in Egypt. Here is a fifteenth-century document that outlines the duties of the official responsible for overseas trade:

He will welcome the Karim merchants coming from the Yemen, seeking their good-will, showing them courtesy, dealing with justly, so that they may find a felicity which they have not found in Arabia Felix [Yemen]; likewise the merchants who came from the West . . . both Muslim and Frankish. Let him receive them kindly, and treat with them justly, for the profits . . . accruing from them . . . are very great.[13]

---

[13] Ibn al-Furat, *Ta'rikh*, ed. Zurayk and Izzedin (Beirut, 1939), 65ff, quoted in P. Holt, A. Lambton, and B. Lewis, eds., *The Cambridge History of Islam* (Cambridge, 1970), IA, 224.

The regulation was based on an acute awareness that the customs revenue from Egypt's Mediterranean and the Red Sea trade provided a vital supplement to the agrarian tax revenue that had been hit hard by the depopulation of the countryside following the Black Death. In his history of Mamluk Eygpt, Ibn Taghri Birdi referred to the interest taken by Sultan Barsbai in the report sent by the Amir of Mecca and the Controller of Jedda in 1432 that a number of Chinese junks had arrived in Aden from the seaports of India. The interior regions of the Yemen were disturbed in these years by political events, and the captain of the Chinese vessels had either not found good markets or was afraid to land his goods, which included porcelain, silk, musk, and other valuable items. He requested permission from the Controller of Jedda to allow the junks to sail into the Red Sea. The sultan granted the request and asked his officials to treat the visitors with honor.[14]

UNFAVORABLE IMAGE OF MERCHANTS

In general, even the urban-based territorial magnates, who had direct access to food supplies, could not provide their families and retainers with all the necessities of life. The functional complexity of trade and its intensity in differing civilizations sprang from a continual interaction between social attitudes and the economic reality. The contemporary moralists, the public, and their political representatives retained a profound distrust of merchants and their commercial organizations. Commerce, Ibn Khaldūn remarked, is a natural way of making profits. But most of its practices and methods, he thought, were composed of tricks and designed to obtain a profit through the difference between the cost price and the selling price. The law permitted cunning in commerce because commerce contained an element of gambling. It did not, however, mean taking away the property of others without giving anything in return.[15] The Islamic prohibition against usury, reflected in medieval Christian laws also, pointed in a direction opposite to the honorable position occupied by merchants among Muslim society, the Prophet himself having been a merchant in his early life. The apparent paradox was analyzed by Adam Smith in some detail:

In years of scarcity the inferior ranks of people impute their distress to the avarice of the corn merchants, who become the object of their hatred and

---

[14] Ibn Taghri Birdi, *Abul Mahasin Ibn Taghri Birdi [History of Egypt, 1382–1469]*, English translation (W. Popper, Berkeley and Los Angeles, 1957–8), IV, 86.
[15] Ibn Khaldūn, *The Muqaddimah*, ed. Rosenthal, II, 317.

indignation... The popular odium, however, which attends it in years of scarcity, the only years in which it can be very profitable, renders people of character and fortune averse to enter it. It is abandoned to an inferior set of dealers; and millers, bakers, mealmen, and meal factors, together with a number of wretched hucksters are almost the only middle people that in the home market come between the grower and the consumer. The ancient policy of Europe, instead of discountenancing this popular odium against a trade so beneficial to the public, seems, on the contrary, to have authorised and encouraged it.[16]

European merchants in Asia were certainly aware of the prevailing feeling about the grain trade long before Adam Smith drew attention to it. In 1695 Samuel Baron, one of the East India Company's officials in Madras, wrote a memorandum on the coastal trade of southern India and in a reference to the famine that had occurred during the year, he remarked, "The scarcity of grain hath increased the Trade to Bengal. But the plentiful season of rain will, it is hoped, put a stop thereto. For surely there can be no advantage more uncomfortable than that which arises from the poverty and misery of the poor, though it may be as well charity as interest to deal therein at sometimes."[17]

The image of bankers and merchants in premodern social order remained tarnished. So persistent was this reflection that even those actually dependent on trade were unable to discard it. When John Fryer, a physician in the service of the East India Company, landed in 1672 at the great Mughal port of Surat, he thought the place had two sorts of vermin: real fleas and the Hindu banyan traders. Neither Fryer nor his corporate masters in London could have made their living without the help of the Surat merchants. A century or so later, another English traveler in India, John Henry Grose, reversed the viewpoint and described the Gujarati merchants as among the most fair and open dealers in the world.[18] Fryer's strictures stemmed from a preconceived image of Asian social and political practices, and he had no time or inclination to examine the fundamental basis of such behavior among merchants of different national origins. Even the judicious and practical Gerald Aungier, the chief of the English trading house in Surat, could not help commenting in 1672 that, as long as his masters in London failed to send a sufficiency of funds to carry

---

[16] Adam Smith, *The Wealth of Nations*, 1776, vol. II, Book IV, Chapter V, "Of Bounties."
[17] British Library, Add. Mss. 34123, p. 41; K. N. Chaudhuri, *The Trading World of Asia*, 207.
[18] John Fryer, *A New Account of East India and Persia* (London, 1909–14); John Henry Grose, *A Voyage to the East Indies* (London, 1757); K. N. Chaudhuri, *The Trading World of Asia*, 62.

on trade, the company's account books would continue to be "laden with an unpleasant catalogue of heathen creditors."[19] The current rate of interest in Surat – at 9 percent compounded monthly – was invariably equated by these European merchants with usury. They must have been well aware that money was lent on similar terms in London and Amsterdam and that the price of capital was determined by commercial forces. What was perhaps unacceptable to them was the vexatious obligation to have to rely on loans made by foreign and non-Christian bankers. For the relationship between borrowers and lenders in that age was more than just an economic one. It was a social process as well. The East India Company's directorate pointed this out in 1740, when they dismissed John Stackhouse, the president of Calcutta and Bengal factories, from their service. He was accused of serious financial malpractices. He had also borrowed large sums of money from Indian merchants, the very people who supplied the company's textile investments. A borrower, in the opinion of the directors, was a servant of the lender. Stackhouse had automatically dismissed himself from the president's chair in Calcutta.[20]

In premodern communities, the social attitude to trade was largely determined by a moving continuum between the fear or the distaste of foreigners and the desire for economic gain. By definition, trade involved transactions among different groups of people. Where a society was completely homogenous without barriers of class or other forms of differentiation, the foreigner was simply the man beyond the national frontiers. In a divided society, as for example in India, he could well be the member of another caste or religious community. The feeling of insecurity engendered by unfamiliar and unanticipated social behavior was tempered only by the knowledge that commercial dealings were an unfailing path to material profits, and trading with enemy countries under flags of convenience was of course a time-honored practice. The inevitable result of this tension was the recognition that well-defined laws protecting the claims and rights of individuals were an absolutely necessary condition of successful cross-cultural and interregional regional trade. Philip Curtin has analyzed in detail (*Cross-cultural Trade in World Trade*, Cambridge, 1984) the different methods used to overcome the problem of assimilating merchants into the general social structure. The extent to which political rulers were prepared to fulfil their obligation to preserve law and order, enforce the claims of one class of citizens against those of

[19] K. N. Chaudhuri, *The Trading World of Asia*, 62–3.
[20] India Office Records, East India Company, Despatch Book, Court of Directors to Fort William Council, 21 March 1740, vol. 108.

another, and extend toleration and welcome to strangers determined also the extent of their commerce. The necessity for legal or political protection was the first sign, and a formal recognition, that trading connections were no longer part of an earlier, prehistoric economic exchange such as the mysterious silent trade of the gold-producing regions of western Africa. Even in Africa, by our period transregional trade had become highly institutionalized in terms of social usage. It was said that the first Muslim king of the African commercial town of Jenne in the inner delta of the river Niger asked the worshippers at the Friday mosque to offer three prayers: that those who come to settle in the town be given wealth by God, that the number of foreigners in town be greater than its local population, and finally that the merchants who come to trade there would tire of its attraction and sell their goods quickly and cheaply so that they could return to their own countries. It is significant that, in a social climate dominated by intense military and warlike traditions, such as prevailed among the medieval Arabs, Tuaregs, and the African people of the Sahel, no threats could conceivably be uttered against traveling merchants.

THE LEGAL AND INSTITUTIONAL FOUNDATIONS OF PREMODERN TRADE: FROM TRAVELING MERCHANTS TO JOINT-STOCK COMPANIES

In medieval Europe, as is well known, merchants took few chances and seldom traveled abroad unless they were protected by safe-conduct passes issued by princes within whose jurisdiction they were to go. The *hajj* journey of Ibn Jubayr (1183–4 A.D.), the secretary to the Amir of Granada in Andalusia, took him through many countries both Muslim and Christian. The Spanish pilgrim often complained bitterly of the rapacity of the customs and excise officials in Egypt, which Saladin was trying at the time to curb. But he also noted that, even in the prevailing state of war between the Ayyubids and the Crusaders, merchants could freely travel through enemy-held territory on the payment of a small fee.

Likewise, in Muslim territory, none of the Christian merchants is forbidden entrance or is molested. The Christians impose a tax on the Muslims in their land, which gives them utmost security, while the Christian merchants also pay customs for their goods in the land of the Muslims. Reciprocity prevails and equal treatment in all respects. The warriors are engaged in their wars, while the people are at ease.

Ibn Jubayr embarked for Europe from a Latin-controlled port in Palestine.[21] The appearance of permanent colonies of merchants in Syria, Byzantium, north Africa, and Western Europe in the early Middle Ages was an expression of both a greater velocity of international trade and a political willingness to accept the presence of foreign merchants.

The principle of an international convention toward merchants and external trade admittedly came about gradually, and there were many violations by financially pressed rulers. As a double insurance, merchants preferred to live in self-contained buildings where the safety of numbers was reinforced by the government's capacity to provide protection and supervision. In the Islamic world, various terms were used to describe the residential and commercial quarters used by merchants: *khans, caravansarai, wakelas* (Eygpt), *samsara* and *funduq* (the Yemen and Syria). The Italian term *fondaco* was clearly derived from the Arab *funduq*, and later by association the financial expression "fond" and "fund" described the banking and exchange operations of the *fondacos*. The *kontors* founded by the Hanseatic League in Bruges, Antwerp, and London were a variant of the Mediterranean type of settlements and a particular form of extraterritorial trading. Although the security of person and property both in one's native land and abroad was long regarded as a sign of civilized behavior, the actual political implications in terms of the law of nations did not come about until much later. The principle of extraterritorial jurisdiction rights of foreign merchants in particular was the instrument most favored in Asia for overcoming the defects in international law. For example, there is an interesting case of this practice (1110 A.D.) in the magnificent collection of merchants' papers discovered in the Cairo Geniza attached to the synagogue. When a Muslim judge of Alexandria intervened in the financial inheritance of a deceased Jewish merchant at the request of a fellow Jewish claimant, the entire community reminded the governor in a petition that a decree from the sultan himself was in force to effect that no one was permitted to interfere in the affairs of a dead person belonging to the community and that these matters were to be settled by the official Jewish authorities. It was also mentioned that all the Christian European merchants had similar privileges granted to them.[22]

With the rise of territorial and nation-states in Europe and with the development of commercial "firms" handling goods on the principle

[21] Ibn Jubayr, *The Travels* (London, 1952); S.D. Goitein, *A Mediterranean Society* (Berkeley, 1967), I, 70.
[22] See S. D. Goitein, *A Mediterranean Society*, I, 62–66.

of consignment, the extraterritorial trading station was in decline in the West. Merchants no longer needed to accompany their goods in person. In many parts of the Middle East and in the countries of the Indian Ocean, however, the trading station continued and even gathered a stronger momentum with Europe's eastward expansion. Consignment trade, operating through informal association of merchants, of course existed in Asia alongside the extraterritorial trade.[23] The long-term historical movements may be simplified in the following model. The existing sources give a clear impression that between A.D. 1000 and 1400, if not earlier, in spite of many wars between Islam and Christendom, a status of legality had returned in the conduct of long-distance trade between the Indian Ocean and the Mediterranean. This relative peace and accepted international conventions were greatly weakened in the sixteenth century by two new developments. The first was the Ottoman bid for maritime supremacy in the Red Sea and in the Mediterranean. The second factor was the decision of the Portuguese Crown to wage wars on the Muslim seafarers of the Indian Ocean. Acts of violence on both sides bred a profound feeling of insecurity; and the fear of possible retaliation led to the demand, when the Dutch and the English went to trade in Asia, that their person and property should enjoy the protection of a fortified settlement independent of the political control of local rulers and rival Europeans.

The claim was such a radical departure from the normal commercial practices followed in contemporary Europe that it provided a running theme for many comments and legal justification. The historical background to the long anti-Islamic sentiments in Europe was outlined in a remarkable English legal document dated 1728. The issue at question was whether the testimony of non-Christians should be admitted to the newly created law-courts in Madras. The opinion of the counsel whose advice the East India Company had sought was as follows:

As the laws of England were expounded in former ages both Turkes and other Infidels were not only excluded from being witnesses against Christians but were deemed also to be perpetual Enemys and capable of no property at all and not entitled even to the Protection of the Laws. And this furious zeal so far prevailed that so late as in the Reign of Henry 8 a Turk being beat and wounded in London, the Judges resolved that an Indictment for an assault not would lye for him against the Person who beat him, because the Turk was not entitled to the protection or benefit of the Law. But by degrees

---

[23] For an interesting analysis of the consignment trade during the Ayyubid period, see A. L. Udovitch, "Formalism and Informalism in the Social and Economic Institutions of the Medieval Islamic World," in A. Banani and S. Vryonis, eds., *Individualism and Conformity in Classical Islam*, (Wiesbaden, 1977).

this Savage Temper of the Laws and of the Exposition of them began to alter into more humanity and the great extent of our commerce with respect both to persons and things did necessitate the Courts of Justice to admit persons for witnesses who in elder times would not be admitted ... And for this reason I am of opinion that the Evidence of any Turk or any heathen or Idolator is to be admitted in any Court of Justice.[24]

It is significant that international trade is mentioned as one of the reasons for secularizing the law. The next step was an explicit demand that merchants should make financial payments to political authorities in order to secure protection and an uninterrupted movement of goods. The theoretical aspects of the problem have attracted considerable attention from many trade historians. Frederic Lane, Polanyi, Niels Steensgaard, and Curtin have discussed in some detail the role of protection costs in the institutional framework and organization of long-distance trade in the premodern age.

The economic institution concerned with the selling of protection to merchants is described by Steensgaard, following the theoretical ideas of Lane and Polanyi, as a redistributive enterprise because it diverted income away from a primary agency. The task of distributing commercial goods, however, remained the preserve of professional merchants, and they were permitted to enjoy a considerable part of the economic gains. The authorities claimed the right to redistribute some of the financial benefits of trade not only as a way of enriching their own income, but also in order to benefit other members of society as well. The merchant was essential to the politically powerful as an economic agent, who understood the business of turning commodities into disposal income. Without the intervention of the market, no centralized government in Europe and Asia could have functioned for any length of time. Of course, the dividing line in history between organized banditry and piracy and the redistributive enterprise of legitimate and respectable governments was always very thin. The tribute exacted from the spice trade by the Egyptian rulers always remained in the eyes of the Mediterranean merchants as an example par excellence of the connection between trade and politics. The Portuguese were quick to see in the first decade of the sixteenth century that their naval superiority over land-based Asian empires gave them a means of sharing in the profits of the existing redistributive powers. They not only refused to pay protection costs to the Asian rulers, but, by forcing some of the Indian Ocean traders to pay customs duty at

[24] India Office Records, "Mr Hungerford's opinion upon the 33rd paragraph in the Governour and councel's Letter dated Fort St George January 20th 1727/8," Memorandum of the Committee of Correspondence, vol. 101.

the Portuguese ports and by compelling them to take out naval passes, the *Estado da India* became a redistributive enterprise in its own right. When the Dutch and the English East India companies set up their own trading organization in Asia, the Portuguese example provided a powerful model. To a considerable extent, all European traders in Asia internalized their protection costs by building fortified settlements and arming their ships as fighting machines. The usefulness of the theory of protection costs in premodern commercial history lies in the fact that it enables us to break out of a conventional polarity between European merchants and Asian. With the rise of the trading republics in Italy, the professional skills of their merchants gradually became an integral part of Western social self-awareness and acceptance. By the sixteenth and seventeenth centuries, the personal standing of the merchant and the need to preserve his economic interests had become universally acknowledged in European political life. In contrast, the Asian merchants remained vulnerable to external pressures and were often victims of actual physical violence from the ruling elites, though, as it has already been emphasised, the Asian political order could not do without the banking function of the merchant. How do we explain this contrast and the apparent paradox? A possible answer may be that in Europe the process of extracting protection costs from merchants became strongly institutionalized and therefore was anticipated and discounted in advance, but in Asia it remained subject to individual decisions even in cases where centralized empires had established clear administrative rules for taxing the merchants.

The rise of the European joint-stock companies trading with the different parts of the Indian Ocean represented not only a new development to the principle of the law of nations but also a strengthening of the capitalistic organization of international trade. The principle of armed trading introduced by the Portuguese conquistadores in the Indian Ocean was taken over by the Dutch and English East India companies without any attempt to find an explicit justification for the practice. That merchants with peaceful intentions toward trade should nevertheless heavily arm their ships and constantly threaten the weaker territorial rulers was a phenomenon without a precedent in the history of Asia. The situation was brought about by the quasi-political role given to the chartered companies by their respective national governments. The fact that the policy of armed trading could be successfully implemented and even made to pay in the case of the VOC was due to the collective financial strength of the East India companies. Both the Dutch and the English corporate organizations represented at the height of their commercial careers a concentration of capital and economic power that was as unprecedented as their naval and political might. Both the companies had become important banking and financial institutions comparable to the national central banks, and the bonds issued by them enjoyed a measure of confidence from the investing public that was in many ways superior to the status given to the state bonds. The principle that the institutionalized debts could also become institutional or private assets, of course, introduced one of the essential conditions of capitalism: the separation between permanent income-streams, the ownership of capital, and its professional management. The European East India companies, as joint-stock institutions, were the ancestors of the modern multinational companies operating in many different geographical environments and dealing with a large number of products. This was a characteristic they shared with the large and successful private merchants who also diversified their business and areas of operation. The East India companies did not set the general institutional norm of long-distance trade in the seventeenth and eighteenth centuries, which was firmly based on private partnerships and individual family-owned business houses both in Asia and Europe. Their historical role found its symbolic importance when the industrial capitalism of the nineteenth century adopted the same principle of capitalistic control and management.

THE STRUCTURING PRINCIPLE OF LONG-DISTANCE TRADE AND THE UNITY OF DISCOURSE

Premodern long-distance trade received its organizing principles from a wider environment that incorporated the entire social structure. In turn, it also structured society. In a world starved of exact and reliable information, disbelief and incredulity at physical manifestations not seen, heard, or experienced could be partially overcome by first-hand geographical descriptions provided by merchants, objects of trade, and transcontinental travelers. Ibn Khaldūn with his usual perceptiveness outlined the role of trade and merchants in the fourteenth-century Eurasian world:

At this time, we can observe the condition of the merchants of the Christian nations who come to the Muslims in the Maghreb. Their propserity and affluence cannot be fully described because it is so great. The same applies to the merchants from the East and what we hear about their conditions, and even more so to the Far Eastern merchants from the countries of the non-Arab Iraq, India, and China. We hear remarkable stories reported by travellers about their wealth and prosperity. These stories are usually received with skepticism."[25]

Perhaps the most powerful impact of trade was to be found in its ability to conceptualize space. Even the sober and practical Chinese, who were apt to think that the Middle Kingdom occupied the center of the earth, adopted a prudent attitude when confronted with Master Ma Tsung-tao's (Ma Huan's) account of the Indian Ocean countries, which the Arabic-speaking linguist had visited (1413–33) in the course of the famous Ming maritime voyages organized by the Grand Eunuch Cheng Ho. The much-traveled author of the *Ying-yai sheng-lan* admitted that in his youth, when he had looked at a book describing the seasons, climate, topography, and the people of distant oceans, he had asked himself in some surprise: "How can there be such dissimilarities in the world?" His own travels however convinced him that the reality was even more wonderful.[26]

Lack of knowledge only partially explains the disbelief and the feeling of marvels. It was heightened by an acute sensitivity toward the scheme of physical differences, which seemed to lie in waiting just beyond the known limits of the familiar world. Distances appeared unduly magnified, given the pace of human mobility as measured on a space-time scale. The memory of a long journey by land and sea reverberated against the outer shell of collective knowledge, eventually adding to its growth after the initial resistence to the assimilation of new information had been overcome. The sea stories told by Buzurg Ibn Shahriyar in his "Incredible Book of the Indian Ocean" mirrored the transcontinental world of the Sirafi metropolis in the tenth century, a period when the Muslim ship captains and merchants were already sailing on regular though hazardous voyages to India, Southeast Asia, and China. The mixture of fantasy, daydreams, and sober narratives in the "Incredible Book" might have come from the remembrances of Ulysses himself. In the historical works of al-Mas'udi and al-Muqaddasi on the other hand, written at about the same time, the imaginative elements of space, the need for popular entertainment, were kept strictly within bounds,: and the text of al-Idrisi (ca. 1099/110–62), composed as a commentary on his planisphere known as the *Book of Rogers*, epitomized contemporaneous scientific geography. However, travelers' tales that claimed to represent the real world were another matter. Even Ibn Battuta was suspected of having invented his experiences in the Indian Ocean.

[25] Ibn Khaldūn, *The Muqaddimah*, ed. Rosenthal, II, 281.
[26] Ma Huan, *Ying-yai sheng-lan,* ed. J. V. G. Mills (Cambridge, 1970), 69, 179.

During the reign of the Medinat Sultan Abu Inan, a *shaykh* from Tangier went on a long journey to India, Ibn Khaldun tells us, and lived in the court of the sultan of Delhi as a Malakite judge. His stories were so fantastic that whispers went round questioning his veracity. Ibn Khaldun's own scepticism was dismissed by the celebrated Wazir Faris b. Wadrar with the argument that limited and confined knowledge should not be a test of the truth. The wazir humorously compared the aspiring statesman, as Ibn Khaldūn then was, with the young son of a distinguished political prisoner, who was entirely brought up in the prison and who asked his father one day at mealtime what kind of meat they were eating. On being told that it was mutton and having a sheep described to him, the boy said in some perplexity, "Father, you mean it looks like a rat."[27]

In the landscape of daydreams where the public opinion of the day located them, the transcontinental journey of a Hsuan-tsang, Marco Polo, the "Rihla" of the Malakite jurist of Tangier, and the peregrinations of the Portuguese adventurer Fernão Mendes Pinto created two kinds of unities.[28] One was the unity of discourse, the other the unity of abstract topological space. Within a single discourse, the dispersion of objects, people, social systems, and individual responses to images of space were all brought together by an ongoing epistemology in the first place, which led to the appearance later of a new order in knowledge. The discourse suggested the unity of space in the manner of a line drawn on an empty background. The geographical contours of Ibn Battuta's "Rihla" would trace an implicit unity of possibilities in states of affairs, of which the ancient linkages between the Mediterranean and the Indian Ocean was not the least important. People in the Maghreb, in the Spice Islands of the Eastern Archipelago, and in the rice plains of greater China, could discover for themselves in the discourse, assuming literacy, not only the existence of sea-lanes and caravan routes that held together the commercial unity of the Old World but also how exogenous societies organized and derived their civilizational identies under another sky. Of course, traders and merchants living inside their own communal shells, like colonies of hermit crabs, had long profited from the transoceanic highways. But they refrained, as if by mutual agreement, from any explicit intellectual diffusion of the specialized knowledge available readily at their command. The idea that knowledge must be capable of being shared and verified is a very recent one.

[27] Ibn Khaldūn, *The Muqaddimah*, ed. Rosenthal, I, 369–71.
[28] Mendes Pinto, *Peregrincam de Fernam Mendez Pinto*, 1614; for a discussion of the fact and fiction in the geography of Mendes, see Gentil, *Fernão Mendes Pinto* (Paris, 1947).

Select bibliography of secondary works

I. EUROPEAN BACKGROUND

Anderson, Perry. *Passages from Antiquity to Feudalism*. London, 1974.
First in a planned four-part series. Examines the problems of human development created by the fall of the ancient and the rise of the medieval world. Charts the "slave mode of production" during the barbarian invasions and how its collapse made feudalism possible. The second half of the volume discusses the types of feudalism that arose in Eastern and Western Europe. Marxist/historical materialist interpretation.

————. *Lineages of the Absolutist State*. London, 1974.
Second book in the series. Argues that absolutist monarchy in Western Europe did not come at the expense of the feudal nobles, but functioned rather as a "carapace of a threatened nobility"; hence, the state became a machine for making war.

Andreades, A. *A History of the Bank of England, 1640–1903*. 2 vols. 4th ed. Reprint. New York, 1967 (1st English ed., 1909).
Narrative history of the institution. Volume I deals with the bank's development from 1640 to the Napoleonic Wars and Industrial Revolution.

Aston, T. H., and C. H. E. Philpin, eds. *The Brenner Debate: Agrarian Class Structure and Economic Development in Pre-Industrial Europe*. Cambridge, 1985.
Reprint of Robert Brenner's original article advancing the primacy of class relationships in European economic development during the early modern period (thereby rejecting demographic and commercialization explanations), along with rejoinders from leading European scholars, published between 1976 and 1982 in *Past and Present*.

Berman, Harold J. *Law and Revolution: The Formation of the Western Legal Tradition*. Cambridge, Mass., 1983.
Treats law as a separate "causative" force in European history, therefore consciously anti-Marxian. Argues that the papacy was the first state and from its example the others followed. The process of the papacy becoming a state he dubs "the papal revolution." By the thirteenth century, most of the important legal concepts, such as universality and reciprocity of rights, were in place.

443

Black, Anthony. *Guilds and Civil Society in European Political Thought from the Twelfth Century to the Present*. Ithaca, 1984.

A study of guilds and corporations, and the social values that accompanied them, in an attempt to demonstrate that guild and corporate notions of politics were more influential in the European political tradition than liberal and Marxist historians have previously believed.

Blickle, Peter. *The Revolution of 1525: The German Peasants' War from a New Perspective*. Translated by Thomas Brady, Jr., and H. C. Erik Midelfort. Baltimore, 1981.

A reinterpretation of the Peasants' War as the participation of the "Common Man" in the politics of the sixteenth century. Argues that, though the revolt was repressed, it was not completely a failure. Peasants in many parts of the empire won an ameliorization of their condition and a voice in local political-administrative bodies.

Bossy, John. *Christianity in the West, 1400–1700*. Oxford, 1985.

Advances the thesis that Christianity was transformed in the sixteenth and seventeenth centuries from a traditional to a doctrinal religion. Traditional Christianity was sacramental and ritualistic and served to strengthen and extend kinship bonds. Doctrinal Christianity was more ethical and therefore more individualistic and less social.

Brady, Thomas A., Jr. *Turning Swiss: Cities and Empire, 1450–1550*. Cambridge, 1985.

A study of the political options open to south German cities in their attempt to keep themselves free from the domination of local princes: join the Swiss Confederation (turn Swiss) or ally themselves with the House of Hapsburg. The cities found the former option too revolutionary, and the second impossible as the result of the Reformation. This left south Germany politically stunted, a condition not fully "remedied" until Bismarck (particularism).

Braudel, Fernand. *La Mediterrannée et le monde Mediterranéen à l'epoque de Philippe II*. 2 vols. Paris, 1966. English version: *The Mediterranean and the Mediterranean World in the Age of Philip II*. Translated by Sian Reynolds. London, 1972–3.

Volume I discusses the influence of environment on the culture and political development of the peoples of the European Mediterranean and the slow long-term and periodic short-term trends of the environment. The argument is that there is an interrelationship, between natural conjuncture and human structure. Volume II examines the human Mediterranean (events, people, and politics) from 1550 to 1600.

Checkland, S. G. *Scottish Banking: A History, 1695–1973*. London, 1975.

Detailed, comprehensive, scholarly account of the development of Scottish banking industry. Author sees systems as very flexible and innovative.

Cipolla, Carlo M., ed. *The Fontana Economic History of Europe*. Vols. I-III. London, 1972–4.

Covers the early modern period.

——. *Before the Industrial Revolution: European Society and Economy, 1000–1700*. New York, 1980; originally published in 1976.

An economic appraisal of the economic and social system of medieval and early modern Europe. The first half of the work treats a static system characterized by high consumption and low government spending and investment. The second half examines the dynamics in the system (population growth, technology and business innovation, and geo-political shifts of power) that made the Industrial Revolution possible.

Dickson, P[eter] G. M. *The Financial Revolution in England: A Study in the Development of Public Credit, 1688–1756*. New York, 1967.

Concerned with the development of government borrowing in England in the six decades preceding the Seven Years' War, which saw the creation of the national debt, the South Sea Bubble, the rise of the Bank of England, and the financial policies of a series of powerful ministers.

Duby, Georges. *The Three Orders: Feudal Society Imagined*. Translated by Arthur Goldhammer. Chicago, 1980.

A history of the conception of medieval society as orders of those who worked, fought, and prayed, from its formulation in 1025–30 through its general diffusion as a political ideology by the 1220s.

Faure, Edgar. *Le Banqueroute de Law, 17 Juillet 1720*. Paris, 1977.

A sober discussion of the system of monopolies set up by John Law, including its institutional structure, political context, economic benefits in rural areas, debt-reduction success, and its general stimulus to the French economy. Meant to counter the judgment that the system failed and that Law was a swindler.

Gellner, Ernest. *Nations and Nationalism*. London, 1983.

"Gellner argues that nationalism is characteristic of industrial society, not solely because of economics, but also owing to the interactions of education, power, and culture." *Choice*.

Gerhard, Dietrich. *Old Europe: A Study of Continuity, 1000–1800*. New York, 1981.

Survey of preindustrial Europe which argues that the entire era saw a single economic and social system that was closed and self-regulating. Histories that deal with political and intellectual development mask the underlying continuity of the age.

Goldthwaite, R. A. *The Building of Renaissance Florence: An Economic and Social History*. Baltimore, 1982.

A discussion of the organization, production, and procurement of building supplies, the structure of the guilds, and architecture of Florentine building industry. Argues that profits earned abroad were invested in the city through the building industry, generating a ripple of prosperity through the city's economy, and providing in part the economic vitality on which the Renaissance was based.

Guenée, Bernard. *States and Rulers in Later Medieval Europe.* Translated by Juliet Vale. Oxford, 1985.
A comparative study of the structure of European states from 1300 to 1500. Considering ideas of political authority, the functions and resources of the state, and its relationship to society at large and estates, Guenée rejects the notion that the fourteenth and fifteenth centuries marked the transition from a medieval to a modern form of state.

Heers, Jacques. *Gênes au XVe siècle:* Activité économique et problemes sociaux. Paris, 1961.
Based on Genoese notarial registers from 1447 to 1466, a Braudelian analysis of the city with respect to its geography, population, monetary system (flow of precious metals), capital investment, trade (both local and regional), manufacture (shipbuilding), and society (politics and government).

———. *L'Occident aux XIVe et XVe siècles:* Aspects économiques et sociaux. Paris, 1963.
The work begins with an overview of the countryside, where the author argues that agriculture in the fourteenth century was hampered by a series of natural disasters and that only in the fifteenth century was there expansion and specialization as well as a relaxation of seignorial oversight. The next section deals with cities and covers topics from urban life to trade, industry, and merchant organization. Charts the beginnings of capitalism. The third section deals with current areas of research and historiographical problems.

Hellmann, M. *Grundzüge der Geschichte Venedigs.* Darmstadt, 1976.
Illustrates the importance of political and institutional factors in the making of Venice as a commercial crossroads of the East and West.

Holton, R. J. *The Transition from Feudalism to Capitalism.* New York, 1985.
This book is divided into two parts. The first is a critical review of the dominant theories advanced to explain the rise of capitalism in the West (Adam Smith and his followers, Marx and his, and Max Weber). The second explores the usefulness of explaining capitalism's appearance via the rise of the postfeudal state, the attitudes and activities of landowners, and regional and global factors on a nation-by-nation basis.

Kriedte, Peter. *Peasants, Landlords, and Merchant Capitalists: Europe and the World Economy, 1500–1800.* Cambridge, 1983. Original German title: *Spätfeudalismus und Handelskapital* (1980). Marxist analysis of European economic and social development in the early modern period. Provocative but uneven survey that suffers from obscure prose and sweeping generalizations.

Lane, F. C. *Venice,: a Maritime Republic*. Baltimore, 1973.
A survey primarily of medieval and early modern Venice in which maritime matters predominate because Lane believes "they were important in determining Venetian social structure and the city's fortunes." Secondary are political, intellectual, economic and financial, and social issues.

Mackenney, Richard. *Tradesmen and Traders: The World of the Guild in Venice and Europe, 1250–1650*. Beckenham, 1987.
A study of Venetian guilds in the late Middle Ages and the Renaissance which argues that the guilds did not inhibit innovation nor keep wages artificially high; rather the guilds adapted as times changed. It was the Counter Reformation church that successfully attacked "commercial culture" and brought on the city's economic decline.

Neal, Larry. "The Integration and Efficiency of the London and Amsterdam Stock Markets in the Eighteenth Century." *Journal of Economic History* 4 (1987):97–115.

———. "Integration of International Capital Markets: Quantitative Evidence from the Eighteenth to the Twentieth Centuries." *Journal of Economic History* 45 (1985): 219–26.

Oakley, Francis W. *The Western Church in the Later Middle Ages*. Ithaca, 1979.
Argues that the Reformation was the successful culmination of the period's impulse toward reform. As such it is an attempt to rehabilitate the late Middle Ages; the era between scholasticism and Reformation was not a period of decadence, but a period of religious vitality and rising spiritual sensitivity.

Phillips, Carla Rahn. "Time and Duration: A Model for the Economy of Early Modern Spain." *American Historical Review* 93 (1987): 531–62.
A major revision of traditional views, arguing that Spain's economic decline was not due to the absence of a bourgeoisie oriented to trade.

Poggi, Gianfranco. *The Development of the Modern State: A Sociological Introduction*. Stanford, 1978.
A history of the institutional evolution of the modern state from the late medieval *Ständestaat* to trends in the modern Western state. Addresses in particular three questions: the nature of secular changes in state's internal arrangements, the shifting balance of power among classes and social groups, and the trend toward the separation of state and society in the West.

Prodi, Paolo. *The Papal Prince, One Body and Two Souls: The Papal Monarchy in Early Modern Europe*. Translated by Susan Haskins. New York, 1987. (Italian edition: Il *sovrano Pontefice: Un Corpo e Due Anime: la Monarchia Papale nella Prima Eta Moderna* [1982])
A study of the modern papacy with respect to the general political devel-

opment of early modern Europe. Argues that the papacy was the archetype of the absolutist state, the first effectively to claim a monopoly of political and religious authority.

Scoville, Warren C. *The Persecution of the Huguenots and French Economic Development, 1680–1920.* Berkeley, 1960.
Challenges the belief that the revocation of the Edict of Nantes led to France's economic decline. Argues that the flight of the Huguenots was no more debilitating than periodic war and famine, administrative confusion, and counter-productive state regulation.

Tierney, Brian. *Origins of Papal Infallibility, 1150–1350: A Study on the Concepts of Infallibility, Sovereignty, and Tradition in the Middle Ages.* Studies in the History of Christian Thought, vol. 6. Leiden, 1972.
Argues that radical Franciscans were the first public proponents of papal infallibility.

Tilly, Charles. "Reflections on the History of European State-Making." In (Charles Tilly, ed. *The Formation of National States in Western Europe.* Princeton, 1975.
Rejects the notion that modern theories of political development have significant explanatory value for European nation-states in the early modern period. Concludes that political development was expensive and largely bound up in the conduct of and preparation for war.

Tracy, James D. *A Financial Revolution in the Hapsburg Netherlands: Renten and Renteniers in the County of Holland, 1515–1565.* Berkeley, 1985.
A study of how the method the Hapsburgs used to finance their wars with France revolutionized government finance. By inducing provincial parliaments to issue debt instruments that were sold publicly at half the bankers' rates for government loans, the government capitalized future revenues, thereby creating a funded public debt.

II. EUROPE FROM EXPANSION TO HEGEMONY

Baechler, Jean, John A. Hall, and Michael Mann, eds. *Europe and the Rise of Capitalism.* Oxford, 1988.
This collection is consciously comparative and global. Many of the essays discuss connections between political power and economic change, or seek to explain why capitalism did not evolve in Asia.

Braudel, Fernand. *Civilisation matérielle, économie et capitalisme XVᵉ-XVIIIᵉ siècle.* 3 vols. Paris, 1967–79. English translations of this work appeared under the following titles: *Civilization and Capitalism, 15th–18th Century,* Vol. 1: *The Structures of Everyday Life: The Limits of the Possible* (1981): Vol. 2: *The Wheels of Commerce* (1982); Vol. 3: *The Perspective of the World* (1984).

A survey of the world demographic, social, and economic system of the early modern period and the rise of capitalism. Volume I discusses the limits and dynamism of demographic and social structures. Volume II examines the background of capitalism or the preindustrial competitive market economy. Volume III illustrates how Europeans created a Eurocentric world economy, or world as a single operating unit.

————. *After-thoughts on Material Civilization and Capitalism*. Translated by Patricia Ranum Baltimore, 1977. French version: *La dynamique du capitalisme*. Paris, 1985.

A reconsideration of issues raised in the three-volume work cited immediately above, following conferences at the Johns Hopkins University in 1977.

Chaunu, Pierre. *L'expansion Européenne du XIIIe au XVe siècle*. Paris, 1969.

" . . . an effective narrative of the emergence of medieval Europe along the shores of Africa and into the Atlantic, up to the discovery of the New World islands by Columbus, with a close structuralist analysis in the *Annales* style of the technical developments which made this expansion possible and the economic and social changes in Europe itself which caused and were caused by the overseas movement." D. B. Quinn, *English Historical Review*.

Diffie, Bailey W., and G. D. Winius. *Foundations of the Portuguese Empire, 1415–1580*. Minneapolis, 1977.

Argues that Portuguese expansion was the result of long-term economic and maritime developments, not solely the work of Henry the Navigator. First half of the book examines the fifteenth-century voyages of exploration to Da Gama's voyage to India. Second half sketches the formation of the empire in Asia.

Hall, John A. *Powers and Liberties: The Causes and Consequences of the Rise of the West*. Berkeley, 1985.

The author contends that the economic dynamism (that is, the rise of capitalism) of the West is the consequence of the West's conception of liberty, which is unique to it. The second half of the book is an examination of Western capitalism's interrelationships with (that is, exploitation of) the Third World.

Jones, Eric L. *The European Miracle*. 2d ed. Cambridge, 1987.

Seminal and influential, emphasizing the importance of plurality and competition among the European states; see the comments in the chapters by Michael Pearson and Thomas Brady in this volume.

North, Douglass C., and Robert Paul Thomas. *The Rise of the Western World*. Cambridge, 1973.

Establishes a theoretical framework for European success (the rise of nation-states and the expansion of European power). From premises taken from classical economics, the authors deduce the reasons for the decline of feudalism and the rise of a new economic and political regime that stimulated economic growth.

Parry, J. H. *Trade and Dominion: European Overseas Empires in the Eighteenth Century*. London, 1974.

Companion to Parry's *Age of Reconnaissance*, which explains the "second stage" of Europe's overseas expansion. This stage is characterized by large informal empires, the predominance of trade (exports from the colonies to the home country), a "second age of discovery" (the systematic exploration of the globe, especially the Pacific), and the beginning of British maritime and imperial dominance. The second stage ends when the colonies become markets for industrial Europe.

Pearson, M. N. *Before Colonialism: Theories on Asian-European Relations 1500–1750*. New Delhi, 1988.

Focuses especially on Wallerstein, of whose views the author offers a pointed but sympathetic critique.

Phillips, J.R.S. *The Medieval Expansion of Europe*. Oxford, 1988.

Three purposes of book: to determine 1) what Europeans knew about Asia, Africa, and America between 1000 and 1500; 2) the extent to which that knowledge was integrated into scholarly knowledge and popular conceptions; and 3) to discuss the relationship between the medieval expansion of Europe and current ideas about the world outside Western Europe. The expansion of Europe in the Middle Ages made the big push in the fifteenth century possible.

Reinhard, Wolfgang. *Geschichte der Europäischen Expansion*. 3 vols. Stuttgart, 1983–8).

The major German-language survey of the topic.

Scammell, G. V. *The World Encompassed: The First European Maritime Empires, C. 800–1650*. London, 1981.

A survey of European expansions from the Norsemen to English and French attempts to establish exclusive trade empires. Central to these attempts are advances in shipbuilding and seafaring that allow further probes into the unknown.

———. *The First Imperial Age: European Overseas Expansion, C. 1400– 1715*. London, 1989.

The best one-volume survey of the topic; written from a European perspective, as such a book perhaps must be, but fully conversant with recent scholarship.

Wallerstein, Immanuel. *The Modern World System*. 2 vols. (4 vols. projected). New York, 1974–80.

Broadly a neo-Marxist perspective. In Volume I, Wallerstein sketches the capitalist system as a world economy centered in "the Core," the Northwestern European seaboard, and which exploits the semiperiphery, broadly Western Europe, and the periphery, Eastern Europe, the East, and America, via coerced labor of varying severity. Volume II moves from the origins of the world-system in the transition of feudalism to capitalism to its intensification in the seventeenth and first half of the eighteenth centuries. Like Weber, Wallerstein is attempting to formulate a sociology of development.

Wolf, Eric R. *Europe and the People without History*. Berkeley, 1982.
Broadly, an analysis of the development of Western Europe since 1400 from "a marginal frontier of the Old World" into the center of power and wealth and its consequences for the rest of the world. The volume is an attempt to throw off Eurocentrism and view the process as a worldwide one in which Europeans and non-Europeans make significant contributions (Wolf is an anthropologist). Proceeds from the Marxist premise that capitalism is inherently exploitative.

III. EUROPEAN TRADE; EUROPE AND THE MEDITERRANEAN

Ashtor, Eliyahu. *Levant Trade in the Later Middle Ages*. Princeton, 1983.
Investigates the significance for the Levantine trade of Southern European nations' reexport trade and its changing composition. The author also summarizes the work of other scholars concerning the development of commerce and transportation in the period.

The Cambridge Economic History of Europe. Edited by M. M. Postan, H. S. Habakkuk, et al. Vols. 1–4. Cambridge, 1963–77).
—Robert Lopez. "The Trade of Medieval Europe: The South." In M. Postan, E. E. Rich, eds. *The Cambridge Economic History of Europe*, vol. 2: *Trade and Industry in the Middle Ages*. Cambridge, 1952. Chapter 5, 257–354.
—M. M. Postan. "The Trade of Medieval Europe: The North." In M. M. Postan, E. E. Rich, eds. *The Cambridge Economic History of Europe*, vol. 2: *Trade and Industry in the Middle Ages*. Cambridge, 1952. Chapter 4, 119–256.
—Charles H. Wilson. "Trade, Society, and the State." In M. Postan, et al. *Cambridge Economic History of Europe*, vol 4: The Economy of Expanding Europe in the Sixteenth and Seventeenth Centuries. Cambridge, 1975). Chapter 7, 487–575.

Carrera Pujal, Jaime. *La Lonja de mar y los cuerpos de comercio de Barcelona*. Barcelona, 1963.

Carrière, Charles. *Negotiants Marseillais au XVIIIe siècle*: Contribution à l'ètude des économies maritimes. Marseilles, 1973.
A 1,100-page study of the "setting," "conditions," and "means" of trade in the city. The city's trading network was worldwide and growth of trade

was faster than in Bordeaux, which made Marseilles much more important to the national economy. Also studies the merchants as a separate social class connected by intermarriage yet very diverse.

Childs, Wendy R. *Anglo-Castilian Trade in the Later Middle Ages.* Manchester, 1978.

Surveys commercial activities between England and Castile, 1254–1485: what was traded; shipping and mercantile organization; those who were involved in the trade; differences in weights, measures, and ship types; and patterns of investment, insurance, credit, and shipping routes.

Christensen, A. E. *Dutch Trade to the Baltic about 1600.* Copenhagen, 1941.

Focuses on seafarers, but treats generally Dutch European merchant shipping. An attempt to determine the accuracy of Sound Toll records and to analyze the composition, volume, and significance of Dutch trade in the Baltic. Concludes Toll records are indispensable for the quantity of Dutch trade and that Baltic trade grew well into the seventeenth century.

Coornaert, E. *Les Français et le commerce international à anvers, fin du XVe–XVIe siècle.* 2 vols. Paris, 1961.

Monograph on French and north German merchants. The author "builds . . . a picture of the revival of the French economy in the second half of the fifteenth until the second half of the sixteenth century, stimulated chiefly by growing participation in the world trade of Antwerp." Herman van der Wee, *Economic History Review.*

Dardel, Pierre. *Navires et marchandise dans les ports de Rouen et du Havre au XVIIIe siècle.* Paris, 1963.

A sizable compilation of trading and shipping statistics for two big and eleven small ports included in the customs *direction* of Rouen, with an extensive commentary that explains, anatomizes, compares, and first infers terms of import and export values, then of shipping of French, European, and overseas origin.

de Roover, Raymond. *L'evolution de la lettre de change, XIVe au XVIIIe siècle.* Paris, 1953.

A comprehensive study of negotiable instruments of every sort over the period. Traces the lineage of these documents, their role in the overall development of banking, and the widespread acceptance and discounting of such instruments in the sixteenth and seventeenth centuries.

de Smedt, Oskar. *De Engelse natie te Antwerpen in de 16^e eeuw (1496–1582).* 2 vols. Antwerp, 1950–54.

Deals primarily with Antwerp as the destination of English continental trade. Devotes considerable attention to complicated business transactions involving the hiring of ships, tonnage, organization of fleets, freight rates, insurance, storage, and so forth.

Dollinger, Philippe. *La Hanse, XIIe-XVIIe sieècles.* Paris, 1964.

One of those foundational works that synthesizes the scholarship of previous historians of the Hanseatic League, which covers the entire life of the league, but which offers no overarching generalization about it. Scammell called it "a lucid, coherent, and comprehensive handbook to the Hane" *EHR.*

Gascon, Richard. *Grand commerce et vie urbaine au XVIe siècle: Lyon et ses marchands (env. de 1520–env. de 1580).* 2 vols. Paris, 1971.
Analysis of Lyon's trade network, commercial and financial techniques, the social impact of trade in prosperity and depression, and the changing mentality of the commercial class that contributed to the decline of the city's trade. Model *Annaliste* economic and social history, which works to place the city in a global perspective.

Goris, Jan-Albert. *Etude sur les colonies marchandes méridionales à Anvers de 1488 à 1567.* Louvain, 1925.
A description of Antwerp's commercial relations (especially with Portugal, Spain, and Italy) and practices during the years of its greatest prosperity. Includes a look at the minutiae of business practices, statistics on imports and exports, and financial matters and practices including business ethics.

Heyd, Wilhelm. *Histoire du commerce du Levant au moyen age.* Translated by F. Reynaud, 2 vols. Leipzig, 1885.
Examines the political background as well as the early commercial conditions of the late medieval Levant trade and includes areas other than just Syria and Egypt. A "classic" study according to Herman van der Wee.

James, Margery Kirkbridge. *Studies in the Medieval Wine Trade.* Oxford, 1971.
Collection of articles and other extracts concerning the decline of the Anglo-Gascon trade after the war of 1294–1303.
The trade was significant not only economically, but politically because it provided a large part of royal-ducal revenues in Gascony and a source of revenue against which the king of England could borrow.

Kellenbenz, Hermann. "Venedig als internationales Zentrum und die Expansion des Handels im 15. und 16. Jahrhundert." In *Venezia centro di mediazione tra Oriente e Occidente (secoli XV–XVI), aspetti e problemi,* vol. 1. Florence, 1977.
Deals with commercial and financial relations.

———. *Unternehmerkrfte im Hamburger Portugal- und Spanienhandel, 1590–1625.* Hamburg, 1954.
A study of the "human network" of Hanseatic [Hamburg]-Iberian trade. Deals with the merchant families and business connections of native Hamburgers, Low and High Germans, Dutch, Portuguese Jewish, and Italians on the Iberian Peninsula.

Lopez, Robert S. *The Commercial Revolution of the Middle Ages, 950–1350.* Cambridge, 1976 (1st ed., 1971).

Moral and material conditions were right to touch off economic expansion. There was an agricultural surplus, a middle-class active in producing and importing, a growing diversification of commodities, and financial innovation. Most of these developments are connected with the rise of the cities.

Lopez, Robert S., and Irving W. Raymond, eds. *Medieval Trade in the Mediterranean World*, New York, 1955.
A argues that there was a commercial revolution in the medieval Mediterranean equally as momentous as the Industrial Revolution. Mostly, however, an anthology of translated commercial documents of the later Middle Ages.

Mitchell, William. *An Essay on the Early History of the Law Merchant*. Reprint. New York, 1969 (1st ed., 1904).
A sketch of the growth of "private international law in the Middle Ages," of courts that enforced it, and its fundamental principles.

Mollat, Michel. *Le commerce maritime Normand à la fin du moyen age: Étude de'histoire économique et sociale*. Paris, 1952.
A study of Anglo-Norman trade from ca. 1450 to 1540. Part I deals with the economic dislocation and depression during the twenty-five years after the English withdrawal from Normandy. Part II deals with Normandy's economic revival after 1475 to 1530. The broadening of commerce had a beneficial effect on agriculture and industry. Part III, dealing with the commercial revolution in Normandy, concludes that individual enterprise contributed the most.

Morineau, Michel. "Le balance du commerce franco-néerlandais et le reserrement économique des Provinces Unies au XVIIIᵉ siècle." *Economisch-Historisch* Jaarboek 30 (1964): 170–235.
Analyzes Amsterdam statistics for 1753.

Posthumus, N. W. *Nederlandsche Prijsgeschiedenis, deel i: Goederenprijzen of De Beurs van Amsterdam, 1585–1914; Wisselkoersen te Amsterdam, 1609–1914*. Leiden, 1943.
A survey of the sparse comprehensive information about Dutch trade that exists, including price series from the Amsterdam Commodity Exchange and foreign exchange rates of the Bank of Amsterdam. Concludes prices rose slightly until ca. 1650, fell to ca. 1680, advanced to ca. 1690, languished for the next sixty years, and then rose sharply in 1775–9, and peaked at three times the base rate in 1810–14.

Ramsay, G. D. *The City of London in International Politics at the Accession of Elizabeth Tudor*. Manchester, 1975.

———. *The Queen's Merchants and the Revolt of the Netherlands*. Dover, N.H., 1986.
A study of the manner in which London merchants shaped Elizabethan

foreign policy toward the Netherlands. Argues that the merchants played a critical role in the decline of Antwerp as an international market.

Renfrew, Colin. "Trade and Culture Process in European Prehistory." *Current Anthropology* 10 (1969): 151–9.
A survey of theories of trade.

Rosch, G. *Venedig und das reich: Handels- und Verkehrs-Politische Beziehungen in der Deutschen Kaiserzeit.* Bibliotheck des Deutschen Historischen Instituts in Rome, vol. 53 Tübingen, 1982.
Sketches the important economic relationships between Venice and the German hinterland from the ninth to the thirteenth centuries.

van Royen, P. C. *Zeevarenden op de koopvaardijvloot omstreeks 1700.* Amsterdam, 1987.
Focuses on seafarers, but treats generally Dutch European merchant shipping.

Svoronos, Nicolas. *Le commerce de Salonique au XVIIIe siècle.* Paris, 1956.
A study of the rise of the Greek commercial middle class, who created a network throughout the Balkans, the eastern Mediterranean, Russia, southern Italy and France, and Central Europe. Motivated by enlightenment rationality and fierce Greek nationalism.

Watt, R., and J. Zimmerman. "Agency Problems, Auditing, and the Theory of the Firm: Some Evidence." *The Journal of Law and Economics* 26 (1983): 613 34.

van der Wee, Herman. *The Growth of the Antwerp Market and the European Economy in the Fourteenth to the Sixteenth Centuries.* 3 vols. The Hague, 1963.
A survey of the economic growth of and social impact of it on Antwerp. Volumes I and III are statistical compilations of economic, demographic, and meteorological data. Volume II is a narrative of Antwerp's growth (economic strength and expanding commercial network that linked Italy, Germany, and the low Countries) and decline. Argues that the city's growth was slow and steady from the fifteenth century to mid-sixteenth century; expansion was in two phases: 1500–20 and 1537–57. Recession hit in 1567 and Antwerp ceased to be an international market in 1585 when it surrendered to Farnese.

———. "Un modèle dynamique de croissance interseculaire du commerce mondial, XIe-XVIIIe siècles." *Annales, économies, sociétes, civilisations* 25 (1970): 100–26.
Surveys the relationship between Italian reexports and the structural changes in the long-distance trade of Europe.

Willan, T. S. *The Muscovy Merchants of 1555.* Manchester, 1953.
A sociological study of the 200 plus members of the Muscovy Company drawn from the merchant class of Tudor England. Argues that there was a tight grouping of merchants linked both by marriage and generationally,

and that many members of this company were also members of the Staplers and Merchant Adventurers. "What we have before our eyes, however, is not a book but a gigantic footnote . . ." Robert Lopez, *Speculum.*

Wilson, Charles H. *Profit and Power: A Study of England and the Dutch Wars.* London, 1957.

" . . . a brief, provocative analysis of the interplay of theories, competing interests, and personalities which in the third quarter of the seventeenth century precipitated three wars between England and the Dutch Republic." *American Historical Review* 63 (1958/1959): 469.

Wilson, Robert Gerald. *Gentlemen Merchants: The Merchant Community in Leeds, 1700–1830.* New York, 1971.

Examines the economic, social, and political activities of the close group of families that dominated the West Riding woolen trade in the eighteenth and early nineteenth centuries. Concludes they had a definite political outlook and valued social advancement over economic efficiency.

Wolff, Phillipe. *Commerces et marchands de Toulouse, vers 1350–vers 1450.* Paris, 1954.

A description of the lackluster provincial trading town of Toulouse. Argues that Toulouse was only of regional importance, that it produced no great or wealthy enterpreneurs, its business organizations were simple, it lacked specialization, was starved for money and credit, and did not extensively use bills of exchange.

IV. EUROPEAN OVERSEAS TRADE: GENERAL

Aymard, Maurice, ed. *Dutch Capitalism and World Capitalism.* Cambridge, 1982.
Papers delivered at a conference of Dutch and French historians on the Golden Age of the Netherlands. Includes papers by Jean-Claude Boyer on social structure; Immanuel Wallerstein on Dutch world hegemony (1625–75); J. R. Bruijn, F. S. Gaastra, and I. Schöffer on Dutch-Asiatic trade and bullion flows; and Niels Steensgaard on the innovative structure of the VOC.

Boxer, C. R. *The Dutch Seaborne Empire, 1600–1800.* London, 1965.
The best overview of Dutch society and empire over the period of its advance and stagnation.

———. *The Portuguese Seaborne Empire, 1415–1825.* London, 1969.
An overview of the Portuguese Empire from its beginning to the breakaway of Brazil. Argues that the empire survived not as the result of any enlightened racial policies, but due to narrow Portuguese nationalism that kept the shaky empire together despite the home country's increasing economic and technological poverty.

Brugman, H. "Statistiek van den In- en Uitvoer van Amsterdam, 1. October

1667–30. September 1668." In *Bijdragen en Mededelingen van het Historisch Genootschap* (1898).

The only complete year of registration of trade in Amsterdam in the seventeenth century, 1667–8, is presented in this article.

Cain, P. J., and A. G. Hopkins. "Gentlemanly Capitalism and British Expansion Overseas. I: The Old Colonial System, 1668–1850." *Economic History Review* 39 (1986): 501–25.

Curtin, Philip D. *Cross-Cultural Trade in World History*. Cambridge, 1984.

Advances the thesis that before ca. 1800 long-distance commerce was stimulated by the migration of people to regions where they hoped to sell or buy particular commodities. Comparative study from ancient to modern times of such "trade diasporas."

Dias, Manuel Nuñes. *O capitalismo monarquico Portugues, 1415–1549*. 2 vols. Coimbra, 1963.

Argues that "Portuguese mercantile capitalism assumed a unique feature" as the result of this small kingdom's "precocious centralization: a capitalistic Portuguese monarchy . . . Organized along military lines, the system guaranteed exclusive rights and the profits . . . " Jose Jobson de Andrade Arruda.

Godinho, Vitorino Magalhães. *L'economie de l'empire Portugais aux XVe et XVIe siècles*. Paris, 1969. Portuguese version: *Os descobrimentos e a economia mundial*, 2d ed. 4 vols. Lisbon, 1981–85.

The major survey of Portugal's overseas empire during the period of its expansion, making use of qualitative evidence as well as quantitative data.

———. *Ensaios*. Vol. II: *Sobre historia de Portugal*. Lisbon, 1968.

The author's interpretative views are more readily accessible here than in the monumental work cited immediately above.

Israel, Jonathan. *Dutch Primacy in World Trade, 1585–1740*. Oxford, 1989.

Supplants Boxer (see above) in regard to the topics covered; will henceforth be the standard account.

Kling, Blair B., and M. N. Pearson, eds. *The Age of Partnership*. Honolulu, 1979.

—Pearson examines Portuguese activities in sixteenth-century western India and warns of the dangers of being beguiled by twentieth-century prejudices or European terminology.

—On Prakash demonstrates how the arrival of Europeans in the Indian Ocean limited Indian freedom in the seventeenth century and poses fascinating questions about the decline of the Mughal Empire.

—Joseph Brennig examines the limited success of attempts to impose the joint-stock principle on south Indian traders.

—"Ashin Das Gupta demonstrates the small impact Europeans had on Gujarati trade with the Red Sea in the early eighteenth century."

—"Sinappah Ayasaratnam describes the limited success of the Dutch in rehabilitating Malacca against local competition." *English Historical Review* 96 (1981): 446.

Lane, F. C. *Profits from Power: Readings in Protection Rent and Violence-Controlling Enterprises*. Albany, 1979.
Government is treated as an enterprise whose product, protection, is a fundamental factor in capitalist production. Lane shows how comparative costs of protection in the early modern period were a principal determinant of where capitalism flourished. Essays include an important explanation of the author's concept of "protection rent."

Morineau, Michel. "Hommage aux historiens hollandais et contribution à l'histoire èconomique des Provinces Unies." In Maurice Aymard, ed. *Dutch Capitalism and World Capitalism*. Cambridge, 1982.
Analyzes and discusses problems concerning overall Dutch trade statistics that have been published for the year 1667–8 (see H. Brugman).

Musgrave, Peter. "The Economics of Uncertainty: The Structural Revolution in the Spice Trade, 1480–1640." In P. L. Cottrell and D. H. Aldcroft, eds. *Shipping, Trade, and Commerce: Essays in Memory of Ralph Davis*. Leicester, 1981.
A summary of reasons why the Cape route became dominant after 1600.

O'Brien, Patrick. "European Economic Development: The Contribution of the Periphery." *Economic History Review*, 2d ser., 35 (1982): 1–18.
Influential statement of the view that Europe's colonies contributed little to the surge of development culiminating in the Industrial Revolution.

Reesse, J. J. *De suikerhandel van Amsterdam*. Amsterdam, 1908.
Enough reliable data covering the imports of sugar from both Brazil and the West Indies exists for the period 1637–44 to form a reliable research basis for this book.

Schumpeter, Elizabeth Boody. *English Overseas Trade Statistics, 1697–1808*. Oxford, 1960.
A basic collection of English commercial statistics.

V. EUROPEAN OVERSEAS TRADE: THE ATLANTIC WORLD

Andrews, K. R. *Trade, Plunder, and Settlement: Maritime Enterprise and the Genesis of the British Empire, 1480–1630*. London, 1984.
Andrews argues that the British Empire was not built on the explorations in the sixteenth and seventeenth centuries, but driven by the commercial force of trade and plunder. These promised the Crown the quickest return. Colonization was an afterthought.

Anstey, Roger. *The Atlantic Slave Trade and British Abolition*. London, 1975.
Surveys the profitability from 1761–1810 and the trade's impact on Atlantic

African societies. The second part of the work is an overview of the antislavery intellectual tradition, including religious strains. The final part deals with the political process of abolition. Concludes that the slave trade was not enormously profitable, that the main antislavery impulse was religious, and therefore is contra-Williams (q.v.).

Butel, Paul. *Les négociants Bordelais, l'Europe et les iles au XVIII*^e *siècle*. Paris, 1974.

Studies the role of these merchants in the distribution of goods in Northern Europe, especially those from the Caribbean. Also examines the finance and trade methods of the city's merchants as well as the life of the merchants as a distinct social group.

Chaunu, Pierre and Huguette. *Seville et l'Amerique aux XVI*^e *et XVII*^e *siècles*. Paris, 1977.

Monumental study of the volume of trade between the Indies and Spain. Relies on ship tonnage and fleet sizes to estimate the volume in the early years when more precise trade figures are lacking. Estimates that the value of the Indies trade was two or three times that of the largest European commerce, on the basis of taxes levied on the trade.

Clark, John G. *La Rochelle and the Atlantic Economy during the Eighteenth Century*. Baltimore, 1981.

A quantitative study of the merchant class, a group of ninety families of La Rochelle, in which the author examines the kinship and commercial relationships among them as well as the careers of leading merchants during a period of decline in overseas commerce.

Coughtry, Jay. *The Notorious Triangle: Rhode Island and the African Slave Trade, 1700–1807*. Philadelphia, 1981.

Revisionist; seeks to undermine the traditional notion of a triangular slave trade between Africa, the Indies, and North America. Studies the social and economic impact of the trade on Rhode Island.

Curtin, Philip D. *The Atlantic Slave Trade: A Census*. Madison, 1969.

Fundamental work, widely cited. A quantitative analysis of the Atlantic slave trade that includes such topics as estimates of slaves shipped from various African points, fluctuations in supply, and demand, and the ethnic and geographical origins of slaves. Points out the sources of previous errors, and avoids drawing conclusions.

Davies, K. G. *The North Atlantic World in the Seventeenth Century*. Minneapolis, 1974.

An economic, demographic, and social (including slavery) overview of major colonial empires that synthesizes the scholarship of the last fifty years. Strong on British Empire, but relatively weak on French Empire.

———. *The Rise of the Atlantic Economies*. Ithaca, 1973.

Surveys the economic history of the countries on the western fringe of

Europe and of the colonies they established or dealt with in North and South America. Author seeks to explain why the economic leadership passed from the Mediterranean and German states to those bordering the Atlantic. Gives detailed consideration to the interplay of economic growth, population, and politics in the cases of Spain, Netherlands, and England.

Delafosse, M., ed. *Histoire de la Rochelle*. Toulouse, 1985.
Series of essays surveying the history of the city from the thirteenth to the nineteenth centuries. Argues that the city reached its economic height in the eighteenth century on the strength of colonial trade. Not exclusively an economic history, but includes political and religious topics of the city's history.

Fisher, H. E. S. *The Portugal Trade: A Study of Anglo-Portuguese Commerce, 1700–1770*. London, 1971.
Standard work that analyzes the four commodity trades that dominated trade between the countries (textiles, grain and fish, wine, and Brazilian gold). Includes an analysis of this trading relation to the development of the English economy in the eighteenth century.

Garcia-Fuentes, Lutgardo. *El comercio Espanol con America, 1650–1700*. Seville, 1980.
Quantified analysis of the volume and value of Spanish-American trade, including silver and merchandise. Relies on ship manifests as primary sources, and therefore says nothing about illegal trade and fraud. Argues against a decline in Atlantic trade over the period, including a marked rise in silver imports.

Girard, Albert. *Le commerce Français à Seville et Cadix au temps des Habsbourgs: Contribution à l'étude du commerce étranger en Espagne aux XVIe et XVIIIe siècles.* Paris, 1932.
A study of the nature, volume, and organization of French commerce in Spain. Before the seventeenth century, Franco-Spanish trade was mostly the exchange of goods between Brittany and Normandy and northwest Spain. With the discovery of America, the most important axis of this trade was the Indies via Andalusia. With the Treaty of the Pyrenees of 1659, France gained most-favored-nation status.

Gonzalez, Antonio Garcia-Baquero. *Cadiz y el Atlantico (1717–1778)*. 2 vols. Cadiz, 1976.
Choosing a structurally homogeneous period (1717–79), dominated by the Cadiz monopoly and providing a homogeneous data series, the author inquires whether the evolution of the colonial trade may have been partly responsible for Spain's slow economic development in the eighteenth century.

Hamilton, E. J. *American Treasure and the Price Revolution in Spain* Cambridge, Mass., 1934 (reprint, New York, 1964).

The work most often associated with the idea that bullion exercised the single most important pressure on European prices.

Klein, Hebert S. *The Middle Passage: Comparative Studies in the Atlantic Slave Trade.* Princeton, 1978.

A quantitative study of the transoceanic crossings of slave ships that includes data on origin of slaves, age, sex, landings of shipments, ship types, tonnage, slaves per ton, frequency of crossings, and so forth. Argues that mortality rates among the slaves on the middle passage declined over the period (1700–ca. 1850) as conditions and preventive measures aboard improved.

Knight, F., and P. Liss, eds. *Atlantic Port Cities: Economy, Culture, and Society in the Atlantic World.* Baltimore, 1988.

Papers from a conference at Johns Hopkins.

Lorenzo-Sanz, Eufemio. *Comercio de Espana con America en la epoca de Felipe II.* 2 vols. Valladalid, 1980.

Analysis of the volume and value of American commerce and Spanish government policies (1555–1600). Quantified. Also examines important merchants, their families, and their associations.

MacLeod, M. "Spain and America: The Atlantic Trade, 1492–1720." In The *Cambridge History of Latin America*, vol. 1. Cambridge, 1984.

Overview of the maritime dimension of Spanish trade in both directions, cargoes (especially gold and silver), changing composition over time, and piracy. Concludes that the Atlantic link was a major result of the expansion of Europe and a powerful stimulation to it.

Malamud Rikles, Carlos Daniel. *Cadiz y Saint Malo en el comercio colonial Peruano (1698–1725).* Jerez de la Frontera, 1986.

Author views the "official" trade of French firms based in Cadiz and the "contraband" or "direct" trade between Brittany and Peru as part of a single trading system, noting how the same firms were sometimes involved in both.

Mauro, Frédéric. *Le Portugal, Le Brésil et L'Atlantique au XVIIᵉ siècle, 1570–1670: Étude Économique.* Paris, 1983; expanded version of *Le Portugal et L'Atlantique*, 1960).

A survey of Portuguese economic activity in the Atlantic giving primary importance to Brazil as the keystone of the Portuguese imperial economy. In that economy, sugar production was most significant. "He also provides data and analyses on the commerce of dyewood, grains, wine, and other products, and, by doing so, integrates the history of Brazil, the Atlantic Islands, Portugal, and . . . North and West Africa," Stuart Schwartz, *HAHR*.

Mettas, Jean. *Repertoire des expeditions negrières françaises au XVIIIᵉ siècle.* 2 vols. Edited by Serge and Michele Daget. Paris, 1978–84.

A recent large-scale study that includes new archival evidence on the French slave trade. Annotated lists of ships involved in the voyage from French ports to Africa, on to America, and back to France.

Meyer, Jean. *L'armement Nantais dans la deuxieme moitié du XVIIIe siècle*. Paris, 1969.
Economic history of organization of the trading companies of Nantes in order to assess their profitability. Shows that direct trade with the Indies was more profitable than the triangular trade, and that trade in general was not significantly more profitable than other sorts of investment. One reviewer has noted that these conclusions fly in the face of what historical actors believed.

Minchinton, W. E., ed. *The Growth of Overseas Trade*. London, 1969.
Includes Ralph Davis, "English Foreign Trade, 1600–1700," and "English Trade, 1700–1774."
Davis analyzes selected triennial periods of English trade in America.

Palmer, Colin. *Human Cargoes: The British Slave Trade to Spanish America, 1700–1739*. Urbana, 1981.
First study of South Sea Company's slave deliveries under Treaty of Utrecht. Topics include the Middle Passage, distribution of slaves in South America, and the sociology, demography, and profitability of the trade. Augments existing knowledge by exploring documents previously unused in Great Britain and Spain.

Johannes Postma, *The Dutch in the Atlantic Slave Trade, 1600–1815*. Cambridge and New York, 1990.
Fine study of a hitherto neglected segment of the slave trade.

Preciado, Jorge Palacios. *La trata de Negros por Cartagena de Indias*. Colombia, 1973.
Quantitative study of slave trade to Cartagena (Colombia) from the sixteenth to the eighteenth centuries.

Price, Jacob M. *France and the Chesapeake: A History of the French Tobacco Monopoly, 1674–1791, and of Its Relationship to the British and American Tobacco Trade*. Ann Arbor, 1973.
A reconstruction of the political, commercial, and financial aspects of the French tobacco monopoly. Illustrates how the monopoly was created, how it affected ordinary people in France and overseas, and how the monopoly is a case study of the function of finance, commerce, statecraft, and society in the ancient regime.

———. "The Transatlantic Economy." In Jack P. Greene and J. R. Pole, eds. *Colonial British America: Essays in the New History of the Early Modern Era*. Baltimore, 1984.

Steele, Ian K. *The English Atlantic, 1675–1740: An Exploration of Communication and Community*. New York, 1986.
Examines the evolution of and improvements in the seaborne lines of com-

munication between England and its American colonies. Steele rejects the notion that the ocean was viewed as a barrier that isolated England's colonies and allowed them to develop separate societies and identities. Steele sees the communication lines as ties that created and maintained an Atlantic empire.

Stein, Robert Louis. *The French Slave Trade in the Eighteenth Century: An Old Regime Business.* Madison, 1979.

Comprehensive overview that describes such aspects as the size of the trade, its legal and political background, the effects on the slave trade of the struggles to maintain a colonial empire, its organization, and its financing. Studies communities of slave traders in French ports through the nineteenth century.

Verger, Pierre. *Bahia and the West African Trade, 1549–1851.* Ibadan, 1970.

(Translation of *Flux et reflux de la traite des Negres entre le Golfe de Benin et Bahia de Todos os Santos du dix-septième au dix-neuvième siècle* [Paris 1968]

Definitive work including masses of information taken from archives in Europe, South America, and Africa. Gives a detailed picture of the mechanisms of the slave trade on both sides of the Atlantic.

VI. EUROPEAN OVERSEAS TRADE: ASIA

Anderson, Gary, Robert McCormick, and Robert Tollison. "Economic Organization of the English East India Company." *Journal of Economic Behavior and Organization* 4 (1983): 221–38.

Arasaratnam, Sinnappah. *Merchants, Companies, and Commerce on the Coromandel Coast, 1650–1740.* Delhi, 1986.

An overview of the interaction of European and native merchants in the area. Argues that the Coromandel merchants successfully competed with Europeans in the Asian markets. From 1700 to 1740 Coromandel trade shifted eastward, while connections with west Asia and Surat declined.

Blussé, L., and F. S. Gaastra, eds. *Companies and Trade: Essays on Overseas Trading Companies during the Ancien Regime.* The Hague, 1981.

Collection of essays dealing with the general questions of how companies functioned in linking metropolitan Europe with the periphery and how or whether they produced wealth or were the conduit through which capital moved to Europe.

Bouchon, Geneviève. *L'Asie du sud à l'epoque des grandes decouvertes.* London, 1988.

Collected essays of a distinguished student of conflicts between the *Estado da India* of the sixteenth century and merchant communities of the Malabar ports.

464   *Select bibliography of secondary works*

Bouchon, Geneviève, and Pierre-Yves Manguin, eds. *Asian Trade and Civilization: Essays in Honor of Professor Charles Boxer*. Cambridge, 1989.

Boxer, C. R. *From Lisbon to Goa, 1500–1750: Studies in Portuguese Maritime History*. London, 1984.

———. *Portuguese Conquest and Commerce in Southern Asia*. London, 1985.

Collected works on a variety of topics dealing with the Portuguese in South and Southeast Asia, including essays published since his *Portuguese Seaborne Empire*.

Bruijn, J. R., F. S. Gaastra, I. Schöffer, and A. C. J. Vermeulen. *Dutch-Asiatic Shipping in the Seventeenth and Eighteenth Centuries*. Grote Serie, Rijks Geschiedkundige Publicatiën, vols. 165–167. The Hague, 1979–87.

Volume I sketches the movement of goods and bullion in both directions as well as the organization and management of the VOC, shipbuilding and ship types, routes and lengths of voyages, maritime technology, navigation, and organization and social life of the voyages. There is also some comparison of the VOC with other European East Indies companies. Volumes II and III tabulate the basic information of the voyages (to and from Asia), including ship name, type, personnel, tonnage, and captain.

Chaudhuri, K. N. *The English East India Company: The Study of an Early Joint-Stock Company, 1600–1640*. London, 1965.

Surpasses older studies of the quantitative aspects of the company's history. Study of the problems facing the company in the period.

———. *The Trading World of Asia and the English East India Company, 1660–1760*. Cambridge, 1978.

A monumental work. The fullest and richest study of any of the great trading and companies, with an important argument about the economic rationality of such enterprises.

———. *Trade and Civilization in the Indian Ocean: An Economic History from the Rise of Islam to 1750*. Cambridge, 1985.

Magisterial overview, in the tradition of Braudel's *Mediterranean*, of the material and human structures of the Indian Ocean civilizations. The author surveys the rise and decline of successive trading empires, and also examines commodities, markets, shipping problems, shipbuilding, the rise of commercial capitalism, and bullion flows.

Das Gupta, Ashin. *Indian Merchants and the Decline of Surat, C. 1700–1750*. Beiträge zur Sudasien Forschung, Sudasien-Institut, Universitat Heidelberg, no. 40. Wiesbaden, 1979.

A fundamental work, arguing that Surat's trading economy, still strong ca. 1700, declined less because of European competition than because of political instability in the Moghul Empire, which cut Surat's links to the Indian hinterland and its products.

Das Gupta, Ashin, and M. N. Pearson, eds. *India and the Indian Ocean, 1500–1800.* Calcutta/Oxford, 1987.

—Joint paper by Geneviève Bouchon and Denys Lombard deals with Indian Ocean trade prior to the Portuguese.

—Pearson's article restates his view that Portuguese impact on the area's patterns of trade was minimal.

—Das Gupta's essay is on the fall of Indian trade in the seventeenth and eighteenth centuries. Part of the crystallization of India as a land-based colony.

—P. J. Marshall traces the steady rise of private European (especially British) trade and shipping.

Disney, A. R. *Twilight of the Pepper Empire.* Cambridge, Mass., 1978.

Study of the Portuguese commercial empire in India under the Hapsburgs, from the raising of pepper to its delivery in Lisbon. Contains an explanation for why the Portuguese could neither modernize nor meet challenges to their trading system.

Van Eyck van Heslinga, E. S. *Van compagnie naar koopvaardij. de scheepvaartverbinding van de Bataafse Republiek met de koloniën in Azie 1795–1806.* Amsterdam, 1988.

A study of how shipping and trade with Asia continued after the Dutch East India Company had been dissolved.

Foster, W. *English Factories in India, 1668–1669.* Oxford, 1927.

An edition of papers and dispatches concerning English commercial activity in India. Illustrates the tension between the company and the Crown over direction of affairs in India.

Furber, Holden. *Rival Empires of Trade in the Orient, 1600–1800.* Minneapolis, 1976.

The best survey of the conflict between the Dutch and English East India companies.

Gaastra, F. S. *De Geschiedenis van de voc.* Bussum, 1982.

"The best modern survey of the history of the Dutch East Indian Company." J. R. Bruijn.

———. "De verenigde Oost-Indische Compagnie in de zeventiende en achtiende eeuw: de groei van een bedrijf." In *Bijdragen en medelingen betreffende de geschiendenis der Nederlanden.* Deel 91. 1976.

Glamann, Kristof. *Dutch Asiatic Trade, 1620–1740.* Copenhagen, 1958 (reprint, 'S-Gravenhage, 1981).

Seeks to demonstrate that the company was not such an effective monopoly as previously thought, neither in trade of spices nor in the fixing of their price. Also examines the changing composition of the company's trade.

Godinho, Vitorino Magalhães. *Les finances de l'etat Portugais des Indes Orientales (1517–1635).* Paris, 1982.

A collection of documents with a substantial introduction.

de Korte, J. P. *De jaarlijkse financiele verantwoording in de voc.* Leiden, 1984.
Retired accountant J. P. de Korte has assiduously checked and described the financial administration of the company and also provides many tables.

Lombard, Denys, and Jean Aubin. *Marchands et hommes d'affaires Asiatique dans l'ocean Indien et la mer de Chine, 13ᵉ–20ᵉ siècles.* Paris, 1988.
Papers from a conference in Paris (1985); the emphasis is on indigenous reaction to European efforts to establish trading monopolies.

Meilink-Roelofsz, M. A. P. *Asian Trade and European Influence in the Indonesian Archipelago between 1500 and About 1630.* The Hague, 1962.
A fundamental work, comparing Asian trade in Malaya and Indonesia before and after the arrival of Europeans. See the review article entitled "European Influence in South-East Asia, c. 1500–1630," by D. K. Bassett, in *Journal of South East Asian History* 4 (1963): 175–209.

Murphey, Rhoads. *The Outsiders: The Western Experience in India and China.* Ann Arbor, 1977.
The author argues that European presence had little impact on the great land empires of Asia prior to the era of industrialization, and that, for a variety of reasons, China proved significantly more resistant to European influence than India.

Pearson, M. N. *Merchants and Rulers in Gujerat: The Response to the Portuguese in the Sixteenth Century.* Los Angeles, 1976.
Argues that the indifference of the Moghul state to seaborne trade, together with the fact that indigenous merchants lacked political influence, provided a crucial opening to the Portuguese.

—— *The Portuguese in India.* The Cambridge History of India. Cambridge, 1987.
Unable to make headway on land, the Portuguese constructed a seaborne empire built around maritime taxes and coastal strongholds. Even at that, the Portuguese were only able to manipulate, but not significantly change the existing Indian Ocean trading system.

Prakash, Om. *The Dutch East India Company and the Economy of Bengal, 1630–1720.* Princeton, 1985.
Examines the early growth of the Bengal export industry, one of the greatest examples of preindustrial growth related to the European world economy that did not produce disastrous effects on the exporting society. The Bengalese silk trade with Japan was replaced by an equally profitable one with Europe after the fall of the Japanese market.

de Reus, Klerck. *Geschichtlicher Überblick der Administrativen, Rechtlichen und Finanziellen Entwicklung der Niederländish-Ostindischen Compagnie* (Batavia/ The Hague, 1894.
Still useful.

Rothermund, Dietmar. *Asian Trade and European Expansion in the Age of Mer-cantilism*. New Delhi, 1981.

Argues that European trading practices had profoundly bad effects on the Eastern world from the time of Vasco da Gama. Mercantilism was a justifica-tion for political takeover and imposition of monopolies. "Modern theories of international trade are not adequate to explain 'what happened to Europe and Asia in the age of mercantilism to the present.' " *Choice* 19 (1982): 298.

Souza, George Bryan. *The Survival of Empire: Portuguese Trade and Society in China and the South China Sea, 1630–1754*. (Cambridge, Mass., 1986.

A political and economic study of an otherwise little known period of Portuguese history in the East. Argues that Portuguese settlers on Macao sustained themselves by pragmatically adapting to new political and eco-nomic conditions.

de Souza, T. R. *Indo-Portuguese History: Old Issues, New Questions*. New Delhi, 1985.

Articles by K. S. Mathew, "Indian Merchants and the Portuguese Trade on the Malabar Coast during the Sixteenth Century"; Niels Steensgaard, "Return Cargoes of the Correira in the Sixteenth and Early Seventeenth Century"; Geneviève Bouchon, "Glimpses of the Beginnings of the *Carreira da India* (1500–1518)"; Leonard Blussé and George Winius, "The Origin and Rhythm of Dutch Aggression against the Estado da India, 1601–1661"; A. R. Kolkarni, "Portuguese in the Deccan Politics: A Study of New Marathi Documents From Lisbon," and Steensgaard, "Asian Trade and World Econ-omy from Fifteenth to Eighteenth Centuries."

Steensgaard, Niels. *The Asia Trade Revolution of the Seventeenth Century* Chi-cago, 1974.

"This book examines the 'shift of balance' in the European-Asian trade in the decades following 1600 as a significant structural change [the inter-nalization of protection costs] from the peddling trade of the trans-Asia caravans and the Portuguese *Estado da India* to the new role of the Dutch and English companies." Part of the general shift of economic power from the Mediterranean to northwestern Europe. Quote from *Book Review Index*.

———. "Asian Trade and World Market: Orders of Magnitude in 'The Long Seventeenth Century.' " In *L'histoire à Nice, actes du colloque Franco-Polonais d'histoire*, T.III. Université de Nice, 1983.

An attempt to compare the value of the Asian trade and the value of the American trade before 1730 as seen from Europe.

Steur, J. J. *Herstel of ondergang, de voorstellen tot redres van de VOC*. Utrecht, 1984.

A counter-argument to common views on the decline of the VOC.

Subrahmanyam Sanjay. *The Political Economy of Commerce: Southern India, 1500–1650*. Cambridge, 1990.

An "outstanding book" That makes a "strong case for the existence of an important connection" between regional politics and maritime trade. M. N. Pearson.

Sutherland, Lucy S. *The East India Company in Eighteenth-Century Politics.* Oxford, 1952.
"The purpose of this book," in the words of the author, "is to elucidate 'the part played by the East India Company in the politics of [the] time.' " Concludes that the company was caught in personal rivalries and shifting alliances so that there was no consistent policy guiding its administration. A. H. Basye, *AHR.*

Wills, John E., Jr. *Embassies and Illusions: Dutch and Portuguese Envoys to K'ang-Hsi, 1666–1687.* Cambridge, Mass., 1984.
Examines two Dutch and two Portuguese embassies to the Chinese emperor. Studies their failure and examines such details as the speed of travel, cost, how they were received and behaved, and how each side perceived the other. Uses both Western and Eastern documents.

VII. MONEY, BULLION FLOWS

Attman, Artur. *The American Bullion Flow in the European World Trade, 1600–1800.* Goteborg, 1986.
Synthesis of works on the integration of American bullion into the early modern world economy. Argues that New World gold and silver flowed from Europe to the East in order to offset Europe's importation of goods from the East.

———. *The Bullion Flow between Europe and the East, 1000–1750.* Translated by Eva and Allan Green. Goteborg, 1981.
Overview of bullion flows from Carolingian times to the eve of the Industrial Revolution. Argues that the general West-to-East bullion flow was continual, but the reverse was true from 750 to 950. The West was starved for bullion between 1500 and 1650 and continually exported bullion to the Baltic region and Russia throughout the period.

———. *Dutch Enterprise in World Bullion Trade, 1550–1800.* Acta Regiae Societatis Scientiarum et Litterarum Gothoburgensis. *Humaniora,* 26. Goteborg, 1983.
Argues that the Dutch free trade in goods and bullion policy made the United Provinces a clearing house for the flow of bullion worldwide. The Dutch were thus critically important in maintaining a balance of payments between Europe and the rest of the world. The Dutch were able to accumulate enough New World bullion to cover their own needs, but also for other nations, such as Great Britain.

Bakewell, P. J. "Registered Silver Production in the Potosi District, 1550–

1735." *Jahrbuch für Geschichte von Staat, Wirtschaft und Gesellschaft Latein-amerikas* 12 (1975): 67–103.

A survey of the problems of unregistered silver production for estimating silver production.

————. "Mining in Colonial Spanish America." In Leslie Bethell, ed. *The Cambridge History of Latin America*. Cambridge, 1984.

Overview of the technical, economic, and social aspects of Spanish mining (mostly silver) in South America. Includes estimates of silver and gold production

Bovill, E. W. *The Golden Trade of the Moors*. London, 1968.

Survey of the trans-Saharan gold trade with the Maghreb.

Brading, D. A. *Miners and Merchants in Bourbon Mexico*. Cambridge, 1971.

Examines the terms of labor, the structure of commerce, and silver production in Guanajuato, Mexico, the nation's leading mining center.

Cross, Harry E. "South American Bullion Production and Export, 1550–1750." In J. F. Richards, ed. *Precious Metals in the Later Medieval and Early Modern Worlds*. Durham, 1983.

Curtin, Philip D. "Africa and the Wider Monetary World, 1250–1850." In J. F. Richards, ed. *Precious Metals in the Later Medieval and Early Modern Worlds*. Durham, 1983.

Doherty, Kerry W., and D. O. Flynn. "A Microeconomic Quantity Theory of Money and the Price Revolution." In E. Van Cauwenberghe and D. O. Flynn, eds. *Production and Transfer of Precious Metals, Coinage, and the Changes of Monetary Structures in Latin America, Europe, and Asia, 1500–1800*. Brussels, 1987.

Gaastra, F. S. "The Exports of Precious Metal from Europe to Asia by the East India Company, 1602–1795." In J. F. Richards, ed. *Precious Metals in the Later Medieval and Early Modern Worlds*. Durham, 1983.

von Humboldt, Alexander. *Political Essay on the Kingdom of New Spain*. 4 vols. Translated by John Black. London, 1811.

Remains the finest account of eighteenth-century New Spain. Fundamental work on bullion production and flow.

McCusker, John J. *Money and Exchange in Europe and America, 1600–1775: A Handbook*. Chapel Hill, 1978.

A rare and useful handbook designed to aid the historian make accurate conversions from one currency to another.

Morineau, Michel. *Incroyables gazettes et fabuleux metaux: Lex retours des tresors Americains d'après les gazettes Hollandaises (XVIᵉ–XVIIIᵉ siècles)*. London, 1985.

An examination of bullion imports from America to Spain from reports in Dutch newspapers. Morineau's conclusions question E. J. Hamilton's thesis that after 1660 there was a downturn in bullion imports. Argues that the annual imports in the second half of the seventeenth century were significantly larger than previously estimated, or reported in scattered state papers.

Noya Pinto, Virgilio. *Ouro Brasiliero e o commercio Anglo-Portugues*. São Paulo, 1979.

The author seeks to relate the curve of Brazilian gold production to Brazil's trade with Portugal, to Portugal's trade with England, and to the nascent capitalist economy of the eighteenth century.

Richards, J. F. *Precious Metals in the Later Medieval and Early Modern worlds*. Durham, 1983.

Papers from an international conference on precious metal movement.

Yamamura, Kozo, and Tetsuo Kamiki. "Silver Mines and Sung Coins: A Monetary History of Medieval and Modern Japan in International Perspective." In J. F. Richards, ed. *Precious Metals in the Later Medieval and Early Modern Worlds*. Durham, 1983.

VIII. SHIPS, GUNS, AND PIRATES

Asaert, G., Ph. M. Bosscher, J. R. Bruijn, W. J. van Hoboken, eds. *Maritieme Geschiedenis der Nederlanden*. 4 vols. Bussum, 1976–8. Basic information on a wide range of subjects in the maritime history of the Netherlands and Belgium. Chapters are written by experts in such areas as shipbuilding, shipowning, and merchant shipping. At the end of each chapter is a bibliographic survey.

Bernard, Jacques. *Navires et gens de mer à Bordeaux vers 1400–vers 1500*. 3 vols. Paris, 1968.

Volume I deals with ships and the various maritime industries; Volume II treats seamen; and Volume III is a compilation of ships leaving the port of Bordeaux between 1445 and 1520.

van Beylen, J. *Shepen van de Nederlanden van de late Middeleeuwen tot het Einde van de 17ᵉ Eeuw*. Amsterdam, 1970.

Discusses the great variety of ship types and the structure of shipbuilding process in detail.

Burwash, Dorothy. *English Merchant Shipping, 1460–1540*. Toronto, 1947.

Overview of English shipping industry including seamanship, ship types and size, and shipbuilding, but excluding trade and commerce. Surveys the rise of English shipping capacity and rising ability to undertake long-distance voyages.

Cipolla, Carlo M. *Guns and Sails in the Early Phase of European Expansion, 1400–1700*. London, 1965.

Argues that the West developed armaments and naval technology so advanced the East could not resist European expansion.

Davis, Ralph. *The Rise of the English Shipping Industry in the Seventeenth and Eighteenth Centuries.* Reprint, Newton Abbot, 1972 (originally published London, 1962).

"Rightly famous for its wide scope and depth of treatment" (Bruijn). Begins with the rise of tonnage between 1560 and 1775, the result of rapid growth in the seventeenth century followed by stagnation in the early eighteenth century. Argues that Britain was not a major maritime power in the later sixteenth century (time of the Armada). Weak on ships and shipbuilding. Best sections are on trade and seamanship.

Harley, Knick. "Ocean Freight Rates and Productivity, 1740–1913: The Primacy of Mechanical Invention Confirmed." *Journal of Economic History* 48 (1988): 851–76.

Lewis, Archibald R., and Timothy J. Runyon. *European Naval and Maritime History, 300–1500.* Bloomington, 1985.

An overview of trading communities, the shipbuilding industry, the rising sophistication of financial institutions, and government policy relating to the development of maritime power in the Middle Ages. Relying on recent scholarship, authors compare the successive maritime fortunes of Rome to those of the Spanish maritime expansionists.

McNeill, W. H. *The Pursuit of Power: Technology, Armed Force, and Society Since A.D. 1000.* Oxford, 1982.

An analysis of the relationships between military technology and armies and politics and society. McNeill argues that military know-how determines the structures of society; however, population growth is also a significant contributor to war. This book also explores the relations between a command economy, based on national security requirements, and a market economy.

North, Douglass C. "Sources of Productivity Change in Ocean Shipping, 1600–1850." *Journal of Political Economy* 76 (1968): 953–70.

The conclusion which emerges from this study is that a decline in piracy and an improvement in economic organization (not an advance in the technological state of the art) account for most of the productivity change observed.

Parker, Geoffrey. *The Military Revolution: Military Innovation and the Rise of the West, 1500–1800.* Cambridge, 1988.

Parker argues that the transition to firearms as the main battle weapon in the sixteenth century had a ripple effect on the political development of Western Europe. The changeover to this technology and counter-measures against it were so expensive that governments had to centralize and bureaucratize to use it.

Parry, J. H. *The Discovery of the Sea.* New York, 1974.

"This book describes the evolution of shipbuilding, navigation, geographical knowledge (including Arabic and Chinese) and trade and politics that made possible the voyages by European seafarers at the end of the fifteenth century and the beginning of the sixteenth which established beyond dispute that the earth's seas were connected." *Book Review Index.*

――――. *The Age of Reconnaissance.* London, 1963.
An outline of European geographical exploration in the early modern period, the reasons that stimulated such endeavor, and the consequences of European contact.

Pérotin-Dumon, Anne. "The Informal Sector of Atlantic Trade: Sabotage and Contraband in the Port of Guadalupe, 1650–1800." In F. Knight and P. Liss, eds. *Atlantic Port Cities.* Baltimore, 1988.

Shepherd, James F., and Gary M. Walton. *Shipping, Maritime Trade, and the Economic Development of Colonial North America.* Cambridge, 1972.
Addresses the contribution of transportation costs to the growth of commerce. An attempt to measure productivity gains in transportation despite inherent conceptual difficulties and a paucity of evidence.

So, Kwan-wai. *Japanese Piracy in Ming China during the Sixteenth Century.* Ann Arbor, 1975.
"Japanese piracy" was neither Japanese nor piracy. It was more like an unofficial trade or smuggling carried on by Chinese along the southern coast. The work is an attempt to place this trade in the context of Ming state and politics, to explain its heyday and ultimate suppression by more effective military means.

Tenenti, Alberto. *Piracy and the Decline of Venice, 1580–1615.* Berkeley, 1967.
Study of the impact of British and Dutch piracy on the Venetian republic and its inability to resist the influence. Concludes that Venice could not successfully meet the piracy threat because its shipping organization, equipment, and discipline in the navy could not adapt.

Unger, Richard W. *Dutch Shipbuilding Before 1800.* Assen, 1978.
Discusses at length the great variety of ship types and the structure of the shipbuilding process in detail.

――――. *The Ship in the Medieval Economy, 600–1600.* London, 1980.
A description of how design changes reduced construction and operating costs, and how technological changes relate to economic changes in the Middle Ages. The volume also discusses changes in tools, use of dockyards, and the impact of changes in units of cargo.

IX. EAST ASIAN HISTORY

Chan, Wellington. *Merchants, Mandarins, and Modern Enterprise in Late Ch'ing China.* Cambridge, Mass., 1977.
A comprehensive survey of the structures and bureaucracies, including the

merchant class of late Ch'ing dynasty. Argues that, though the central government had a close relationship with merchants, its efforts to modernize China were too small and disorganized to significantly break with the past.

Eberhard, W. *Conquerors and Rulers: Social Forces in Medieval China.* 2d ed. Leiden, 1965 (1st ed., 1952).

Eberhard tries to show that during the longer part of its history (from 200 B.C. to the eleventh or thirteenth centuries) China's society was dominated by a class of landlords-officials-scholars: the *gentry*. Attacks the notion of "oriental society," in which great land-reclamation projects gave all Eastern society a common, bureaucratic character.

Elvin, Mark. *The Pattern of the Chinese Past.* London, 1973.

Seeks to answer such questions as why China created and preserved such a huge empire for so much of its history. Concludes that China was economically and technologically superior to its rivals. To the question as to why China was not able to compete with the West, the author responds that the old technology had solved old problems so completely that there was no stimulus for further innovation.

Fairbank, John K., ed. *The Chinese World Order.* Cambridge, Mass., 1968.

The work puts forward the general theme that "the Chinese empire consistently sought by coercion or appeasement to subjugate or make friends of its non-Chinese neighbors within and without the empire". Romeyn Taylor, *JAS*.

———. *Trade and Diplomacy on the China Coast.* 2 vols. Cambridge, Mass., 1958.

Argues that "the Western and Chinese traditions merged to produce the treaty-port arrangements finally completed ca. 1860." "The conclusion seeks to depict in general the Chinese view of the treaty system. Fairbank suggests that for China it "supplanted the tribute system as a device for incorporating the foreigner into the universal [Chinese] state". *AHR.*

Fletcher, Joseph F. "China and Central Asia, 1368–1884." In John K. Fairbank, ed. *The Chinese World Order.* Cambridge, Mass., 1968.

A discussion of late Ming and early Ch'ing between the Manchus and Islamic central Asia.

Foust, Clifford M. *Muscovite and Mandarin: Russia's Trade with China and Its Setting, 1727–1805.* Chapel Hill, 1969.

A study of trade as a goal of foreign policy and how other political factors affected it. Surveys the rising trade relations between the two countries that survived into the nineteenth century.

Hall, John W., Nagahara Keiji, and K. Yamamura, eds. *Japan Before Tokugawa: Political Consolidation and Economic Growth, 1500–1650.* Princeton, 1981.

Collection of papers that illustrates how "the creation of a national military

hegemony was accompanied by a series of legal and administrative changes
... transformed society" (Introduction, p. 8). Those changes include agricultural, commercial, and urban development.

Hanley, Susan B., and K. Yamamura. *Economic and Demographic Change in Pre-
Industrial Japan, 1600–1868.* Princeton, 1977.

Argues for the evolution of market-oriented institutions (products of demographic and economic forces) over centuries from the early Tokugawa
period. This book thus takes issue with "recent miracles" theories of Japan's
current success.

Needham, J., Ho Ping-Yu, Lu Gwei-Djen, and Wang Ling. *Science and Civilization in China.* Vol. 5, Pt. vii: *Military Technology: The Gunpowder Epic.*
Cambridge, 1986.

Needham argues that the Chinese were knowledgable of and possessed a
written tradition about the use of firearms before their introduction into
the West in the fourteenth century. The new standard work on the "Gunpowder Age" in China.

Ng Chin-keong. *Trade and Society: The Amoy Network on the China Coast, 1683–
1735.* Singapore, 1983.

Perrin, N. *Giving Up the Gun: Japan's Reversion to the Sword, 1543–1879.* (New
York, 1979).

A study of how military customs are reflective of cultural values. Argues
that the firearm was rejected due to the samurai's code of honor, for aesthetic reasons, and because of Japan's unique geography.

Rawski, Evelyn S. *Agricultural Change and the Peasant Economy of South China.*
Cambridge, Mass., 1972.

A regional/comparative study of agriculture in sixteenth-century Fukien
and eighteenth-century Hunan. "Two themes principally concern the author: that market expansion in both the areas surveyed, principally through
the influence of growing long-distance trade gave a stimulus to agriculture;
and that the creation and diffusion of better farming methods occurred on
a significant scale in Ming Fukien and Ch'ing Hunan." Mark Elvin, *JAS.*

Rossabi, M. *Khubilai Khan: His Life and Times.* Berkeley, 1988.

Not merely a biography, but also a treatment of politics and culture in
thirteenth-century China and central Asia. An attempt to fill a gap in the
"interior history" of the Mongols. Strong on military and bureaucratic
developments.

Spence, Jonathan D., and John E. Wills, Jr., eds. *From Ming to Ch'ing.* New
Haven, 1979.

As a whole, this book of nine essays discusses the transition to the Ch'ing
dynasty from military, political, and socioeconomic points of view as well
as its effects. Morris Rossabi, "Muslim and Central Asian Revolts," argues

against the traditional notion that Muslim-central Asia played an insignif-
icant role in the Ming rebellions.

Toby, Ronald P. *State and Diplomacy in Early Modern Japan*. Princeton, 1984.
An examination of Japanese foreign relations and domestic politics, 1600–
1868. Rejects the notion that Japan was isolated from the world, arguing
for the continued importance of foreign relations with Korea, Ch'ing, and
the kingdom of the Ryukyus.

Yoshinobu, Shiba. *Commerce and Society in Sung China*. 2 vols. Translated by
Mark Elvin. (Ann Arbor, 1970.
A collection of (uneven) essays on the economy of China under the Sung
dynasty. Among the more original essays are those concerning shipbuilding
and the shipbuilding industry, the development of cities and markets, and
the development of commercial organization. No notes.

X. SOUTH AND SOUTHEAST ASIAN HISTORY

Abeyasekere, Susan. *Jakarta: A History*. Singapore, 1987.
An urban history from its time as a Dutch East India Company town to
the present. The author traces its development from a city of many separate
ethnic enclaves to one integrated city of the present.

Blair, E. H., and J. A. Robertson. *The Philippine Island, 1493–1898*. 55 vols.
Cleveland, 1903–07.
Rich in translated sources, in fact appears to be primarily a documentary
history.

De Souza, T. R. *Medieval Goa: A Socio-Economic History*. New Delhi, 1979.
An important work, though strident in tone and somewhat weak in its
approach to economic problems.

Gupta, Satya Prakash. *The Agrarian System of Eastern Rajasthan, C. 1650–C.
1750*. Delhi, 1986.
Regional study of agricultural production, prices, trade as well as the social
structure (including land rights, taxation, administration, and the upper
class) in the Mogul empire. Concludes that this region differed little from
the overall picture of the Mughal empire's agrarian system as a whole.

Habib, Irfan. *Agrarian System of Mughal India*. London, 1963.
Discusses the extent of farming, the trade of agricultural products, the
organization of rural villages, and the standard of life. Also examines the
relationship of Mogul government to farmers and farming, which he char-
acterizes as military colonization over against the preexisting rural
aristocracy.

Moosvi, Shireen. *The Economy of the Mughal Empire, C. 1595*. Delhi, 1987.
An analysis of the late sixteenth-century economy compared with similar

data from the nineteenth century. Concludes that 50 percent of the land under cultivation in 1910 was worked in 1595, that agricultural yields in both periods were nearly the same, that taxes consumed 60 percent of peasant produce, and that rural consumption was roughly the same per capita though urban wage-earner consumption was three times as high in 1601 as in the late nineteenth century.

Reid, Anthony. *Southeast Asia in the Age of Commerce, 1450–1680.* Vol. 1; *The Lands Below the Winds.* New Haven, 1988.
Deservedly acclaimed overview of the mores and culture of the region. Volume II will deal with trade.

———. *Europe and Southeast Asia: The Military Balance.* Southeast Asian Studies Committee Occasional Paper XVI. James Cook University of North Queensland, 1982.

Tripathi, Dwijendra, ed. *Business Communities of India: An Historical Perspective.* New Delhi, 1984.
Collection of essays by Indian scholars on topics pertaining to merchants and merchant organization from the medieval to the modern period.

XI. HISTORY OF THE MIDDLE EAST

Arjomand, Said Amir. *The Shadow of God and the Hidden Iman: Religion, Political Order, and Societal Change in Shi'ite Iran from the Beginning to 1890.* Chicago, 1984.
Sociological analysis attempting "to establish the historical roots of Ayatollah Khomeini's theocracy. The author analyzes the relationship between the Shi'i Muslim belief system and the political organization of premodern Iran and addresses the broader issue of the role of religion in social change." *Choice.*

Ayalon, D. *Gunpowder and Firearms in the Mamluk Kingdom: A Challenge to Medieval Society.* London, 1956.
A sociological study of the impact of the introduction of firearms on the Mamluks of Egypt. Argues that the structure of Mamluk society (based on race) and outlook (chivalric) contributed to their inadequate response to the challenge of firearms. This led to their defeat by the Ottomans, who had successfully adopted firearms.

Hodgson, Marshall. *The Venture of Islam: Conscience and History in a World Civilization.* Vol. 3: *The Gunpowder Empires and Modern Times.* Chicago, 1974.
The central theme of this superb overview is the gradual Islamization of the ancient Irano-Semitic tradition and its alterations or accommodations

to the technical age. Analyzes religious, cultural, political, economic, and social factors.

Holt, P. M., Ann K. S. Lambton, and Bernard Lewis, eds. *The Cambridge History of Islam.* 2 vols. Cambridge, 1970.

Inalcik, Halil. *The Ottoman Empire: The Classical Age, 1300–1600* London, 1973.

Overview of the political history of the Ottoman Empire from its beginnings as small nomadic bands to its rise as conqueror of Asia Minor to its classical age: 1301 (first holy war against Christians) to 1606 (death of Mehmed III).

Islamoglu-Inan, Huri, ed. *The Ottoman Empire and the World Economy.* Cambridge, 1987.

"This collection marks a qualitative improvement in the literature available in English on the Ottomans. It is also important in terms of theory, for it is consciously oriented to Wallerstein's world-systems theories, and makes clear the very great value of his work." M. N. Pearson.

McGowan, B. *Economic Life in Ottoman Turkey: Taxation, Trade, and the Struggle for Land, 1600–1800.* Cambridge, 1980.

A study of exports to Europe, land, taxation, and population in the province of Manastir (now Bitalia) from 1620 to 1830. Supports the Braudelian-Wallerstein position that the empire was linked to the Western European economy, and that wealth created in the empire flowed to Western Europe.

Masters, Bruce. *The Origins of Western Economic Dominance in the Middle East: Mercantilism and the Islamic Economy in Aleppo, 1600–1780.* New York, 1988.

Analysis of the structure of trade at this important terminus of the caravan route, from its high point through the period of decline.

Parry, V. J., and M. E. Yapp, eds. *War, Technology and Society in the Middle East.* New York, 1975.

A study of how war changed society in the Middle East. Essays argue that the process of military modernization was the driving force in social change, from the seventh to the twentieth century.

Shaw, Stanford. *History of the Ottoman Empire and Modern Turkey.* Vol. 1: *Empire of the Gazis: The Rise and Decline of the Ottoman Empire.* Cambridge, 1976.

Standard survey of the subject over the period. Treats the traditional military, political, and economic topics as well as administration of the state, society, art, and culture.

Udovitch, A. L. *Partnership and Profit in Medieval Islam.* Princeton, 1970.

A study of Islamic juridical texts and legal formulae for the purpose of sketching the outlines of commercial institutions and the actual practice of merchants in the Near East.

XII. AFRICAN HISTORY

Austen, Ralph A. *African Economic History*. London, 1987.

Argues that unlike Europe, where the efficiency of production was always far ahead of efficiency of transportation, Africa was a place where, with the introduction of camels, transportation was always more efficient than production. Production was retarded by many other nontransportation factors. One such factor was a lack of technological innovation.

———. "The Trans-Saharan Slave Trade: A Tentative Census." In H. Gemery and J. Hogendorn, eds. *The Uncommon Market: Essays in the Economic History of the Atlantic Slave Trade*. New York, 1979.

"Ralph Austen offers quantitative conjectures on the magnitude of the trans-Saharan slave trade and the East African-Red Sea slave trade between 600–1900. According to Austen, as many enslaved Africans were exported in these trades as in the Atlantic trade." Roger L. Ransom, *AHR*.

Bulliet, Richard. *The Camel and the Wheel*. Cambridge, Mass., 1975.

A study in medieval technology. An examination of why the camel and not the wheel became the basis of transportation in some societies. Concludes that it displaced the wheel from Morocco to Afghanistan in the Middle Ages for obvious economic reasons.

Curtin, Philip D. *Economic Change in Precolonial Africa: Senegambia in the Era of the Slave Trade*, 2 vols. Madison, 1975.

An economic study of a society on the fringe of the Western world before its colonization. Studies not only European trade in west Africa but trade and trade networks within the region, and proves the internal economy was a money economy, not a barter one.

Hogendorn, Jan, and Marion Johnson. *The Shell Money of the Slave Trade*. Cambridge, 1986.

The study of the manufacture, trade, and use of cowries to purchase slaves on the west African coast. Authors trace its introduction by Arab traders from the Maldives via the Mediterranean; intrusion of the Portuguese, and later the Dutch and British when millions were shipped in the seventeenth and eighteenth centuries; and the decline of the trade and the use of cowries as a currency. After the slave trade, was still used in the nineteenth century as a medium of exchange for palm oil.

Lovejoy, Paul E. *Transformation in Slavery: A History of Slavery in Africa*. Cambridge, 1983.

After defining slavery and explaining the reasons for its spread, the author examines the medieval Islamic slave trade and the origins of the Atlantic slave trade. He goes on to examine the process of enslavement, the marketing of slaves, Muslim commercial networks, the administered trade in west-central Africa, and the rivalry between the state and private traders. Conclusion looks at the impact of abolition on African history.

————. "The Trans-Saharan Trade and the Salt Trade of the Central Sudan." In W. E. El-Hesnawl, ed. *The Trans-Saharan Trade Routes*. Tripoli, forthcoming.

Gives an approximate value of trans-Saharan trade before 1500 and argues that "the development of internal merchant networks in the Sudan depended more on the distribution of goods traded between the desert, forest, and savannah than upon trans-Saharan commerce." Ralph Austen.

Ogunremi, Gabriel Ogundeji. *Counting the Camels: The Economics of Transportation in Precolonial Nigeria*. New York, 1982.

A comparative analysis on the relative costs and advantages of porterage, pack animals, and riverboats. Includes information on the speed of travel and volume of goods as well as currencies in use in the Nigerian region.

XIII. BRITISH AMERICA AND THE CARIBBEAN

Andrews, Kenneth A. *The Spanish Caribbean: Trade and Plunder, 1530–1630*. New Haven, 1978.

A maritime history of Caribbean and English piracy in the area from the sixteenth century. Argues that Spanish control of the area was not uniform, but an interlocking web of interests and local adaptations, permutations. Argues that English interests were primarily predatory.

Debien, Gabriel. *Etudes Antillaises (XVIIIe Siècle)*. Paris, 1956.

Volume includes two studies. The first is a case study of a pioneering coffee plantation in west-central Santo Domingo. The second is of the first repercussions of the revolution on the Breda lands in the Cape district.

————. *Les esclaves aux Antilles françaises (XVIIe-XVIIIe siècles)*. Basse-Terre, 1974.

A study of slavery primarily on the island of Santo Domingo that includes observations on the importation, demographics, economics, and avenues to freedom of the slaves. Argues that after 1770 there was a marked decline in the quality of life among French slaves that corresponded to the intensification of capitalism. Yet, at the same time, there was an increase in legal and voluntary attempts to ameliorate the hardships of slavery.

Deerr, Noel. *The History of Sugar*. 2 vols. London, 1949–50.

" . . . still useful and unique for its ambition to provide statistics for sugar production from all areas" (Steensgaard). Volume I deals with the expansion of sugarcane cultivation over the world. Disproportionate interest is given to English West Indies. Volume II treats the political and economic developments related to the cultivation of sugar.

Dunn, Richard S. *Sugar and Slaves: The Rise of the Planter Class in the English West Indies, 1624–1713*. Chapel Hill, 1972.
Social history of sugar plantations in the Caribbean from its origins. Includes sugar production techniques, the characteristics of the slave system, the problems of English adaptation to tropics, and high mortality. Also seeks to explain why the planter class was not uniformly rich and powerful when compared to other British colonies.

Eltis, David. *Economic Growth and the Ending of the Transatlantic Slave Trade*. New York, 1987.
The most complete reanalysis of the abolition of slavery that rejects the loss of economic motivation for slaves in British West Indian plantations bringing abolition and the simple view of abolition as a great moral crusade. British West Indies continued to thrive after abolition and remained competitive on world market.

Galenson, David W. *Traders, Planters, and Slaves: Market Behavior in Early English America*. Cambridge, 1986.
Analysis of Royal African Company's operation of the slave industry in the late seventeenth and early eighteenth centuries. A study of market behavior of the company and its customers, the sugar planters in the Caribbean. Issues discussed include shipping and mortality of slaves, their sale, demographic composition of slave population, and economic structure of early Atlantic slave trade. *Choice*.

Kulikoff, Allan. *Tobacco and Slaves: The Development of Southern Culture in the Chesapeake, 1680–1800*. Chapel Hill, 1986.
A survey of "tobacco culture, white society, and slavery" relying heavily on quantified data. First third of the book traces the development of the tobacco economy in eastern Maryland and Virginia. The second third discusses the major trends in family structure and class relations of whites. The final third treats the evolution of black society.

McCusker, John J., and Russell R. Menard. *Economy of British America, 1607–1789*. Chapel Hill, 1985.
Universally praised. The first section argues that the export-led growth model more adequately describes the American economy of the period than the Malthusian explanation of economic growth. The second is a region-by-region analysis of Canadian-Atlantic and West Indian economies. Final chapter explains the growth in the nineteenth century as the consequence of the American Revolution.

Menard, Russell R. "The Tobacco Industry in the Chesapeake Colonies, 1617–1730: An Interpretation." *Research in Economic History* 5 (1980): 109–77.
Menard argues that the growth of the tobacco industry prior to 1680 was the result of efficiencies that lowered the cost of production and shipping.

After 1680 growth was spurred by rising demand. Within this grand scheme was a cyclical pattern of boom and bust.

Ragatz, L. J. *The Fall of the Planter Class in the British Caribbean, 1763–1833.* New York, 1928.

Argues that the peak of prosperity came in 1763 and this prosperity was based on trade monopoly with Great Britain and American mainland. Decline was produced by new British holdings won from the French in 1763 that could produce products more cheaply and without tariff. After 1799 these planters found themselves in a losing battle with Brazil and Oriental sugar producers. War's beginnings in 1776 also disrupted trade to the disadvantage of the planters.

Sheridan, Richard B. *Sugar and Slavery: An Economic History of the British West Indies, 1623–1775.* Baltimore, 1974.

"Sheridan argues for an important role for the sugar plantation area in stimulating economic growth in the mother country. He concludes that slavery and plantations were profitable to the planters and the profits meant that, after some initial losses early in the settlements, the colonies became a source of capital . . . Moreover, he links the development of the sugar plantation to the Industrial Revolution." Stanley Engerman, *BHR.*

Solow, Barbara L., and Stanley L. Engerman, eds. *British Capitalism and Caribbean Slavery.* Cambridge, 1987.

Essays provide a good point of entry into the debate concerning the relations between the British West Indies depression and the abolition of slavery.

Van de Voort, J. P. *De westindische plantages van 1720 tot 1795.* Ph.D. dissertation. Nijmegen, 1973.

After 1700 there exists fairly reliable information concerning imports from Surinam, the most important sugar producer among the Dutch colonies. It is published and discussed in this dissertation.

Williams, Eric. *Capitalism and Slavery.* Chapel Hill, 1944.

Classic statement of the argument that the British West Indies were in decline and that it was economic motivation that explained the wellspring of the British abolition campaign against foreign slave traders because the British West Indian plantations could not compete with the French, Spanish, and Brazilian ones.

XIV. LATIN AMERICA

Borah, Woodrow. *Early Colonial Trade and Navigation between Mexico and Peru.* Berkeley, 1954.

Based upon manuscript materials from Seville and Mexico, with adequate printed materials for Peru. A thorough coverage to 1585; and the last chapter, which discusses the end of the early trade and the start of the era affected by the Philippine trade, carries the story more sketchily to 1631.

Boxer, C. R. *The Dutch in Brazil, 1624–1654*. Oxford, 1957.

An explanation of how the Dutch were able to make inroads at the expense of the Portuguese and how the Portuguese were able to again expel the Dutch after they had for a time established themselves in Pernambuco and Angola.

Brading, D. A. "Bourbon Spain and Its American Empire." In Leslie Bethell, ed. *The Cambridge* History of Latin America, vol. 1. Cambridge, 1984.

Buescu, Miercea. *Historia economica do Brasil, pesquisas e analises*. Rio de Janeiro, 1970.

Series of essays on the Portuguese colony's economy and Portuguese exploitation of its resources, from the sixteenth to the nineteenth centuries. Author is a neo-classical economist who treats traditional historical problems from an economic point of view.

Furtado, Celso. *Formação economica do Brasil*. Rio de Janeiro, 1959.

An interpretative account of Brazilian economic history largely in terms of the effects of the income structure on Brazilian economic development. A significant contribution to the literature on economic development in all countries.

Jobson de Arruda, José. *O Brasil no comercio colonial, 1796–1808*. São Paulo, 1980.

Quantitative study of the *balanas do comercio*, annual trade statistics of the Portuguese government. Analysis of imports and exports by region.

Klein, Herbert S. *African Slavery in Latin America and the Caribbean*. New York, 1986.

Contains a bibliography on the non-economic aspects of the slave trade. First six chapters are an overview of southern American slavery from the sixteenth through the nineteenth century. The last five chapters are topical and deal with such noneconomic aspects of slavery as the family, slave communities, resistance, and the transition to freedom. The purpose of these chapters is to rebut the "Tannenbaum" thesis that South American slavery was less brutal than slavery in the North, and the view that sugar production was such a great killer of slaves that new imports were constantly needed to replenish their numbers.

Maxwell, Kenneth R. *Conflicts and Conspiracies: Brazil and Portugal, 1750–1808*. Cambridge, 1973.

The foundational work on "resistance, tension, and conflict" between Brazil and Portugal. Interprets the 1789 revolution against Portuguese rule as motivated by social and economic goals, not the ideals of the Enlightenment.

McAlister, Lyle N. *Spain and Portugal in the New World, 1492–1700*. Oxford, 1984.

Wide-ranging survey of the first two centuries of Spanish rule in America. Includes discussions of race, religion, government, the economy and society, and points out issues that remain under scholarly debate.

Novais, Fernando Antonio. *Portugal e Brasil na crise do antigo sistema colonial, 1777–1808*. São Paulo, 1979.

Contends that the economy constitutes a historic, privileged reserve exporting highly profitable goods to support the growth and economic development of the European metropole. However, colonies cannot produce unless first developed.

Schwartz, Stuart B. *Sugar Plantations in the Formation of Brazilian Society, Bahia, 1550–1835*. Cambridge, 1986.

Comprehensive reappraisal of economic roles and relative power wielded by slaves, wage earners, planters, and millers. Argues that, as a microcosm of the development of Brazilian society and economy, the sugar plantations manifest a high degree of cooperation among their constituents. This tended to soften conflicts among the groups and the harshness of slavery. Schwartz argues that slavery in this context cannot be viewed as outright exploitation or the antithesis of freedom.

Index

Abbas I, Shah of Persia, 100
absentee estate owners, 282–3
Abu Inan, Medinat Sultan, 442
accounting methods, development of, 30
Aceh, 12, 18, 70, 168, 169; rise of trade from, 316; and use of slave soldiers, 172
Aden, 6, 70
administrators, mandarin class of, 66
Adyar River, Battle of, 181, 181n46
Africa: Europeans in, 166; and growth of trade with Brazil, 396; and piracy, 211; Portuguese coastal fortress network, 300; and use of guns, 167–8; wars fought for slaves, 167
agazalhados ("liberty-chests"), 312
agents, control of, 28
Agra, 111, 178
agrarian system, 382
aguardente, profits from, 396
Akbar, Emperor: army of, 176–7n36
Albuquerque, Afonso de, 5, 5n13, 10, 298, 300, 304, 325
Albuquerque, Bras de: *Commentaries*, 10, 169
Alcacér-Ceguer, abandonment of, 302
Alexander the Great, 205
Alexander VI, Pope, 130
Alexandria: and overland routes, 70; spices through Mamluk territory, 65
Algiers, conquest of, 200n5
Algonquin Indians: and warfare, 164
Almeida, Francisco de, 300
Amazon river, 224
amber, 421–2
Amboina, 2, 8, 11; citadel at, 170; conquest of Portuguese fort on, 3; massacre of (1623), 9, 9n25, 91
Ambonese, in Indonesia, 181
America: discovery of, 118; labor

shortage in, 277; rule of Spanish colonies in, 81
American Revolution, 254, 287; and sugar freight costs, 264
Americas, and ecological exchange, 118
Amsterdam: and bills of exchange, 283–4; and trade, 428
anarchy, 36
Anatolia, 63
Anderson, Perry, 81, 122
Andrews, Kenneth R., 88, 89, 153, 200
Anglo-Dutch wars, 86, 94
Anglocentrism, 122
l'Anglois, Jean, 206
Annales, 365
Antilles, 379, 380, 380n73
antimonopoly movement, in Germany, 151
Antonino of Florence, Saint, 151
António, prior of Crato, 303
Antwerp: as a "free" port, 75; Hanseatic League quarters in, 436; revitalization of, 362; and spices from Portugal, 78
Arabian Sea: and pirates, 112
Araçuai (in Bahia), gold production in, 388
Aragão, Ximenes d' (firm), 311
Arakan, 316
Arasaratnam, Sinnappah, 108
Arcot, nawab of, 71, 99
Arles, Archives of, 210
armed trading, 19, 439
Armenia, 73; merchants from, 111
arrenegados: number in Portuguese Asia, 323–4
artillery, 183; quality of, 175, 175n33, 176
Arzila, abandonment of, 302
Asia: and local country trade, 80; models of empire in, 304; and tributary mode of production, 61

18082867R00298

Made in the USA
Lexington, KY
21 October 2012